THE ENCYCLOPEDIA OF
WARFARE

THE ENCYCLOPEDIA OF
WARFARE

FROM EARLIEST TIMES TO THE PRESENT DAY
Adrian Gilbert

FITZROY DEARBORN PUBLISHERS
LONDON • CHICAGO

For information, write to
Fitzroy Dearborn Publishers
310 Regent Street
London W1B 3AX
UK

or

Fitzroy Dearborn Publishers
919 North Michigan Avenue
Chicago, Illinois 60611
USA

British Library Cataloguing in Publication Data.
A catalogue record for this book is available
from the British Library

A Cataloging-in-Publication record for this book
is available from the Library of Congress

ISBN 1-57958-216-8

For Brown Partworks Limited

Editors: Pete Darman, Chris Westhorp
Designer: Matthew Greenfield
Cartographer: Bill LeBihan
Picture research: Susannah Jayes
Managing editor: Lindsey Lowe
Production manager: Matt Weyland

This edition first published by
Fitzroy Dearborn Publishers 2000

Printed in Singapore by C.S. Graphics, PTE

Contents

Introduction

Warfare has played a key role in human progress, profoundly influencing political, economic, and social change. Indeed, the history of mankind and the history of warfare are inextricably linked, with both the rise and fall of civilizations often depending on the application of military force. This volume charts the development of warfare over several millennia, from its earliest origins in prehistory to the present day.

As far as can be ascertained from documentary and archeological records, organized warfare between warriors, rather than skirmishes between groups of individuals, probably dates back to at least the sixth or seventh millennium BC. But our knowledge of such warfare is necessarily limited, and it is only with the advent of the Egyptians and Summerians – who left pictorial and written records – that we have any clear idea of how our distant ancestors fought. From this period (approximately 3000 BC) onward, we can trace the history of warfare with reasonable certainty.

The first great army was that of the Assyrians, whose knowledge of strategy and tactics, including such complex matters as siegecraft, set the pattern that other, later classical armies would follow. The latter included the armies of the ancient Greeks, most notably those of Philip of Macedonia and his son, Alexander the Great, and the Romans. The foot soldier held the key to victory, be he the Greek hoplite or the Roman legionnaire. However, after the collapse of Rome in the fifth century AD, warfare in Europe degenerated, the highly trained legions replaced by marauding and ill-disciplined mounted war bands. In the East, however, the armies of Islam, and later those of the Mongols, proved highly effective in harnessing the power of the horse, carving out huge empires in the Middle East and Eurasia by using large cavalry armies.

Notwithstanding the introduction of the stirrup, which made the control of horses and hence cavalry formations easier and so increased their effectiveness on the battlefield, the weapons of warfare had changed little since ancient times: men were still slaughtered by swords, lances, axes, spears, and bows. Toward the end of the 15th century, though, gunpowder technology made its appearance on Western battlefields, and marked the first beginnings of European military ascendancy. The success of what has become known as the Western way of warfare depended on technological advance, allowing small, highly trained European armies to destroy far larger forces virtually anywhere in the world. Central to this ascendancy was ocean-going sea power, which provided economic riches from international trade, as well as enabling European armies to strike at will around the globe.

By the end of the 19th century, most of the world had been colonized or was in thrall to Europeans and their descendants. During the 20th century, however, following two world wars, the balance of power swung inexorably away from the states of Europe to the two superpowers of the United States and the Soviet Union, although by the end of the century the latter state had been broken up following the collapse of Communism. Today, the United States occupies a unique position as the only genuine global superpower.

Despite the many changes that have taken place in the history of warfare, certain constants remain. Success in war goes to those who are best prepared for it, and the training, equipping, and organization of armies are the key factors in this preparation. Armies as chronologically distant as the legions of Julius Caesar and the German Army in World War II displayed similar characteristics, benefiting from tight discipline, flexible and imaginative leadership, sound logistical support, and an effective tactical doctrine.

Alongside adequate preparation, the general and his political masters must have agreed aims: that armed conflict is the best option to secure an objective, and that once war has been chosen the general has the means to secure the objective. When the combination of aims and means are mismatched even the most powerful nations can falter, as was the case with the United States in Vietnam.

Leadership is another of the constants in warfare, ranging from the commanding general to the most junior NCO. If leadership is poor, then it follows that an army will perform poorly. The general must have a sound knowledge of strategy and tactics, and all other technical aspects of his profession. He must also be confident in his own plan of action, to be able to seize the strategic initiative and impose his will on his opponent. Lastly, he must be able to empathize with and inspire his troops: to know what they are capable of, and to encourage them in the execution of the most difficult of tasks. The great captains of history – Alexander the Great, Hannibal, Julius Caesar, Frederick the Great, and Napoleon Bonaparte – all had the above qualities in abundance.

Field officers must direct their troops competently on the battlefield, while junior officers and NCOs require the ultimate courage to advance into utmost danger so that their men will follow.

The five thousand years of recorded warfare provide a fascinating and instructive overview of the history of mankind. War seems innate to the human condition, but now that military technology has provided us with the means to bring about our annihilation, war must necessarily be limited. And the more that we know of war, the greater our ability to restrain its worst consequences.

Warfare in the Ancient World

Warfare has dominated human activity since the earliest times. In prehistory, wars were localized and short-lived tribal conflicts, engagements between men on foot, armed with wooden or stone weapons. But by the time of the classical age – approximately 500 BC onward – wars had become more complex, fought between nations and even empires. Conflicts became longer in duration and distances increased. Battlefield tactics developed to the highest levels, and several generals, notably Alexander the Great and Hannibal, were truly outstanding leaders against whom all other generals have come to be compared.

Our knowledge of warfare in the prehistorical period is sparse, derived from patchy archaeological findings or comparative evidence gleaned from more recent stone-age societies in the Pacific islands and New Guinea.

Anthropological research suggests that prehistorical warfare was limited in nature and bound by ritual. Once a dispute could not be resolved without recourse to violence, then "battle sites" were prearranged by the combatants and the fighting confined to a number of rapid, one-on-one engagements without any higher direction. The action might be preceded by displays of martial prowess intended to overawe the enemy. The weapons were those used when hunting: stone axes, knives, and flint-tipped spears and arrows. Deaths were few and were confined to young males – biologically and economically the tribe's most dispensable members.

The reasons why stone-age tribes went to war remain conjectural, although plunder and the enhancement of warrior prestige seem likely. The stone-age pattern of life suggests that warfare became more organized when competition increased for scarce resources, such as access to water or good grazing land. And as societies became more numerous and widespread across the globe, so the possibility for competitive conflict increased.

Right: The Persian emperor Darius (center, mounted on chariot) tries to rally his fleeing troops at the Battle of Gaugamela (also known as Arbela) in 331 BC.

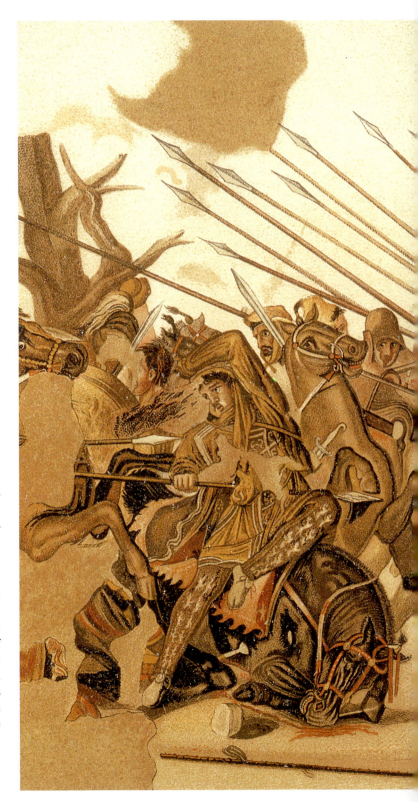

Ancient Egypt

The first battle of which we have any sort of knowledge took place at Megiddo in 1469 BC between a force of Palestinians and an Egyptian army of 20,000 men. Surprise and mobility both played their part in the victory secured by Pharaoh Thutmosis III, but while the exact tactics remain unknown, the compositional elements that were to last centuries were already in place: chariots, cavalry, and infantry units.

The first evidence of a systematic approach to conflict was discovered through the archaeological excavations of sites in the Middle East, which have dated fortified structures at Çatal Hüyük in Anatolia (7000 BC) and Jericho (6000 BC). But apart from the fact that these early cities were protected by walls, little more is known until the advent of writing, and our knowledge is therefore very scanty until about 500 BC. Even then, our knowledge is concentrated in the Mediterranean and Middle East, with some detail from China and India. For warfare over most of the globe, we must simply guess at causes and methods.

Warfare in the ancient world was about fighting at close quarters. Most missile weapons would give at best a striking distance of tens of feet rather than hundreds. There were important technological advances (such as the use of iron rather than bronze) that gave one state or another an advantage; there were also significant tactical developments like the Macedonian phalanx; generalship, as shown brilliantly by Hannibal, was important; and logistics, as in the superb organization underpinning the triumphs of the Roman legions, were often critical. However, in the end battles were won or lost by the courage and confidence of the troops doing the fighting and killing. Confidence that their comrades and leaders would not let them down, and that their fighting formation or weapons were capable of victory, was crucial to success. Thus relatively small forces often defeated much larger ones, and some military forces – such as those of the Assyrians, the Macedonians, or the Romans – enjoyed centuries of success in battle as a result.

Sumeria, in southern Mesopotamia, and Egypt were the first two areas of human settlement to develop an urban civilization with its own written records, sometime between 3500 and 3000 BC. They had the agricultural surplus to create complex societies, and warfare became part of their culture. At much the same time they began to use metals to make objects, including weapons. The first metal weapons were made from copper, but this element was so weak that such weapons were more commonly used for ceremonial purposes than combat. The real breakthrough came at some time in the third millennium BC, when early metallurgists began to combine tin with copper to make bronze, a fairly hard alloy that enabled weapons to take an edge.

Sumerian records tell of Sargon of Akkad, a bronze-age king who reigned from 2371 to 2316 BC and fought 34 battles to create an empire that controlled

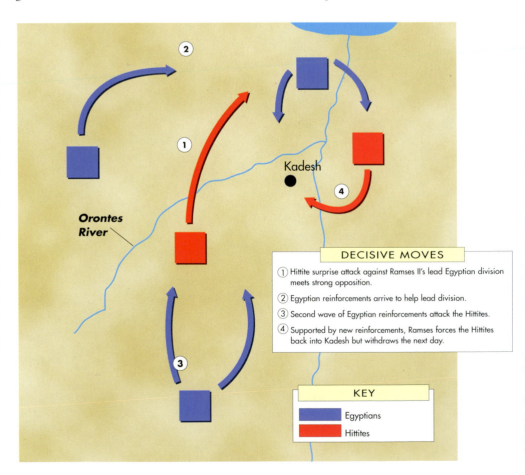

Right: At the Battle of Kadesh, Ramses II's superior leadership was offset by his enemies' use of iron weapons, while his own men had bronze swords and spears.

DECISIVE MOVES

1. Hittite surprise attack against Ramses II's lead Egyptian division meets strong opposition.
2. Egyptian reinforcements arrive to help lead division.
3. Second wave of Egyptian reinforcements attack the Hittites.
4. Supported by new reinforcements, Ramses forces the Hittites back into Kadesh but withdraws the next day.

KEY

- Egyptians
- Hittites

Left: A carving of Sumerian troops advancing in battle wearing helmets and carrying large wicker shields.

Mesopotamia. Although nothing is known about his campaigns, like most rulers of the time it would seem that Sargon led his armies personally and was expected to fight the enemy himself to win personal glory.

The first battle that can be reconstructed in any detail took place in 1469 BC at Megiddo, in the north of what is now Israel, between Pharaoh Thutmosis III of Egypt and an alliance of Palestinian cities. The Palestinians expected the 20,000-strong Egyptian Army to conduct a frontal attack, and had deployed their forces in a strong defensive position facing the Egyptians. Thutmosis, however, advanced from an unexpected direction, catching his opponents by complete surprise.

Despite the information relating to the Battle of Megiddo, such knowledge is rare. And until around 750 BC the paucity of written records prevents any certain knowledge of how military operations were conducted. In the second millennium BC, it is thought the armies of the Middle East were largely made up of cavalry and chariots, and semi-trained foot soldiers who might be armed with bows, slings, clubs, or spears. Bronze was used to make weapons, and armor, if worn at all, was made from leather, wicker, wood, or quilted cloth.

The infantry was recruited from the poorer classes of society, and their function was to provide a stable mass of men around whom the more mobile elements – cavalry and chariots – would maneuvre. What distinguished the major civilizations like the Sumerians and Egyptians from smaller states, was not only their greater natural and human resources, but the organizational sophistication in which they employed these resources. Sumer and Egypt formed the first armies, which contained soldiers who were uniformly armed and equipped and who fought in units rather than as individuals.

For a period, horse-drawn chariots dominated the battlefield. The stirrup, which gives a horseman stability in the saddle and enables him to wear heavy armor, swing heavy weapons, or put his body weight firmly behind a lance thrust, was not in general use until around AD 700. In a chariot, with a driver to control the horses, a warrior could fire a bow or wield a heavy hand weapon from a secure platform. Chariots may also have reflected the social hierarchy, in that the upper classes may have monopolized them.

Chariots were probably introduced to the Middle East by invading tribes from the north, most notably the

Hyksos who conquered and dominated Egypt between 1800 and 1600 BC. The most famous battle between two armies of chariots occurred at the Hittite-held city of Kadesh, Syria, in 1294 BC between Ramses II of Egypt and the forces at the disposal of the Hittite Empire.

In 1294 BC Ramses invaded Hittite territory to capture Kadesh on the Orontes River. His army consisted of four divisions: the Amurru, the Amun, the Re, and the Ptah. While the Egyptians were crossing the Orontes, supposedly "defecting" Hittite spies informed Ramses that the Hittite Army was at Aleppo, farther to the north.

In fact the Hittite king, Muwatallis, and his army were concealed at Kadesh. Ramses believed the Hittite deception plan and marched ahead with the Amun division. The Amurru was deployed to guard the crossing for the Re and the Ptah. Muwatallis now sent 2,500 chariots across the Orontes, and attacked the Re as it crossed the river. The Hittite strike force routed the Re, but was in turn attacked by the Egyptian Amurru division. The Amurru broke through the Hittites and joined Ramses and the Amun.

Muwatallis then released another 1,000 chariots from his reserve. These were defeated by the combined attack of the Amurru and the Amun. The next day Ramses, his forces somewhat the worse for their experiences, withdrew across the Orontes because Muwatallis still had 30,000 fresh infantry.

Although something of a hard-fought draw, Kadesh was particularly noteworthy for the Hittites' use of iron weapons, while the Egyptians relied on bronze. Iron was harder than bronze and, most importantly, could be worked into a much sharper cutting edge. Gradually iron replaced bronze as the medium for edged weapons (and for spear and arrow heads), although the wearing of bronze armor continued until Roman times.

The Hittites lived in central Asia Minor and for two centuries they fought Egypt for control of what is now Lebanon, Israel, Palestine, and Syria. The action at Kadesh enabled Hittite influence to extend to Damascus and halted the Egyptian resurgence in Syria. The Hittites also fought several wars in Syria against the Mitanni from northern Mesopotamia. These conflicts were fought to gain tribute from smaller states.

Right: The Middle East at the height of the Egyptian Empire. The Battle of Kish was an Assyrian victory.

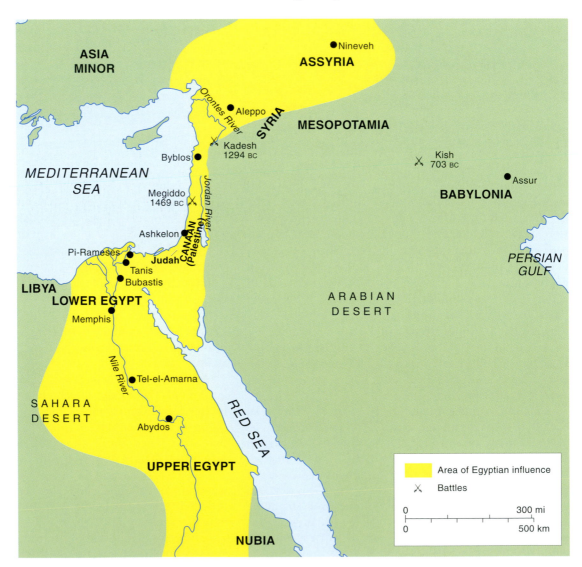

CHARIOT WARFARE

The horse-drawn chariot relied on speed in combat. Lines of chariots would race toward the enemy, the bow-armed crew rapidly shooting arrows at the foe. This kind of attack could cause heavy casualties among tight-packed masses of infantry who wore no armor, as they could not run fast enough to catch the chariots or to escape them.

Prior to a charge, the chariots were spaced far enough apart to allow them to turn at the end of their run. This also allowed two lines of chariots charging one another to pass through the other's formation, and as they passed each other, the crews would throw spears or shoot arrows. Because horses were very valuable if captured, both sides tended to aim at the smaller targets of the crew instead. But the shaking of the chariot as it bounced along over rough ground did not allow very accurate missile fire.

Chariots were very fragile vehicles, and the long pole to which the horses were harnessed was easily damaged and was difficult to replace. For chariots to be effective, both crews and horses had to be trained to a high degree.

Egyptian rule over Palestine illustrates some of the aims and methods of warfare at that time. The Egyptians established their authority over Palestine during the reign of Amenhotep III (1390–1353 BC). In each city in the region the Egyptians placed a small garrison, which was fed and paid for by the city's inhabitants. The cities also sent an annual sum of money or amount of produce – a tribute – to the Egyptian pharaoh. In return, the cities could appeal to the pharaoh to help them settle disputes. The pharaoh would sometimes allow the Egyptian garrison to join a city's army during a dispute with a neighbor.

In 1200 BC, about 500 years after the Hyksos swept through the ancient Middle East, another similar migration shook the region. The Egyptians called these enemies the Sea Peoples. The Sea Peoples at first attacked the Hittites, and it is possible that they destroyed their empire. They subsequently moved south against the Egyptians. The contest between the Sea Peoples and the Egyptian Empire was decided by a naval battle fought off the coast of Egypt in 1189 BC. The Egyptian fleet was victorious and the Sea Peoples scattered throughout the Mediterranean. Some of them settled in Palestine, where they became known in the Bible as the Philistines.

Toward the end of the second millennium BC, a ferocious new aggressor, Assyria, brought new perspectives to warfare. The Assyrians – or people of Assur – had established a presence in northern Mesopotamia as early as the third millennium BC, based around the three city states of Ashur, Nineveh, and Arbela. Constantly at war with their neighbors – including the Hittites – they became a major military power in the 12th century BC.

The first Assyrian army reached the Mediterranean coast during the reign of Tiglath-Pileser I (1120–1093 BC). The Assyrian state was organized around war, and Assyrian rulers left many detailed carvings glorifying their various campaigns. Attacks by Aramean nomads from Babylonia in southern Mesopotamia halted Assyrian expansion around 1050 BC. Assyrian power then went through cycles of decline followed by military expansion. The Assyrians invaded Babylonia, Iran, and eastern Asia Minor. But after the death of Shalmaneser III (824 BC), civil war in Assyria enabled many cities to rebel against their masters.

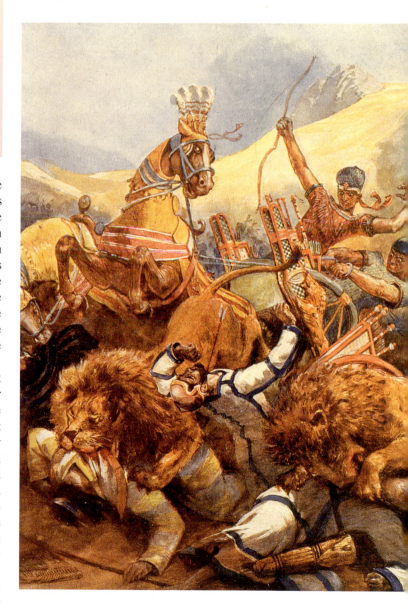

Above: A fanciful depiction of the Battle of Kadesh, in which a total of 6,000 chariots are estimated to have taken part. There are no records of lions being present!

The Assyrians and Persians

Both the Assyrian and Persian empires were notable for the massive, well-organized armies they could put into the field. Of particular interest was the fact that their forces were composed to a significant degree of subject peoples of the empire, rather than of manpower from the imperial homeland itself; the Persian Army that invaded Greece in 480 BC, for example, contained men from 20 provinces of the Persian Empire.

Like the Egyptians, the Assyrians did not establish direct political control over the lands that they conquered. The imperial power demanded tribute from its subjects, and any rebellion was subject to savage reprisals. The era of weakness that followed the death of Shalmaneser III only ended in 745 BC, and in that year an Assyrian general called Pulu became king and took the name Tiglath-Pileser III. He reorganized the governmental system and army. Particular attention was paid to training, weaponry, siege warfare, and logistics.

Before Tiglath-Pileser III, the Assyrian Army was probably a part-time militia composed of soldiers who served the king for a certain number of days each year and then returned to civilian life. To enhance army effectiveness, Tiglath-Pileser III created four different categories of soldiers. First there were the royal guards. Most of these were units of cavalry and chariots, although there was an infantry unit known as the "Heroes." The second category was the King's Standing Army, which included cavalry, chariots, and infantry. These soldiers wore uniforms and were recruited from all the different peoples of the empire; in peacetime, these men garrisoned towns and cities throughout the empire. Third there were the King's Men, a semi-trained militia, possibly similar to the army before Tiglath-Pileser's reforms. The fourth group, consisting of all other able-bodied men in the empire, made up the General Levy, to be used only in times of national emergency.

It has been estimated that the Assyrians could put about 100,000 men in the field, a huge figure by the standards of the day, and, more to the point, they could keep them supplied for long periods. By Tiglath-Pileser III's death in 727 BC, Assyria's frontiers were safe thanks to the strength of his new army and his annual campaigns against neighboring kingdoms.

Right: Tiglath-Pileser III (second from left), emperor of Assyria and military innovator, takes part in a procession.

The Assyrian ruler Sennacherib (705–681 BC) left descriptions of his campaigns, which archaeologists discovered at his palace at Nineveh, the Assyrian capital. The first battle of his reign took place in 703 BC against the Babylonians at Kish in Mesopotamia. Sennacherib used his chariots to attack the enemy's front and his cavalry to assault the flanks. Such combined tactics enabled the Assyrians to achieve decisive results.

In 702 BC the Assyrians campaigned in the north. In this mountainous, forested countryside their chariots could not operate effectively, unlike on the flat plains of Babylonia. However, Sennacherib combined infantry and cavalry to achieve success. The following year he attacked an alliance of Palestinian rulers, supported by Egyptians. The alliance fell apart and Sidqa, the Philistine king of Ashkelon, was deported to Assyria.

During one campaign Sennacherib besieged a fortress controlled by Judah. The techniques and machines the Assyrians developed formed the bases for siegecraft until the advent of gunpowder. In fact, one of the reasons for Assyrian military dominance lay in their ability to master various disciplines of warfare, whether

Right: A relief from the time of Ashurbanipal (688–625 BC) showing Assyrian archers during a siege.

in the combined chariot–cavalry attacks on the plains of the Middle East, or in mountain operations, or in siege warfare.

The Assyrian Empire reached its height during the reign of Ashurbanipal (688–625 BC), when it controlled the entire ancient Middle East, including Egypt. However, the use of terror eventually backfired, as widespread revolts broke out. In 626 BC the Babylonians rebelled, and were joined by the Medes of northwestern Iran and Scythian tribesmen. Quite why the empire collapsed so quickly is not known, but in 612 BC Nineveh itself was captured and destroyed. The Assyrian defeat was total as former subject peoples took their revenge, destroyed their cities, and enslaved the people.

The Medes became the leading power in the region, but were conquered in their turn by a related people, the Persians, in 559 BC. During the late sixth century BC, Persian influence in Mesopotamia grew steadily, and during the reign of King Cyrus I (559–529 BC) the Persians supplanted the Medes and Babylonians as the major power in the region. The Persians subsequently conquered Egypt and Asia Minor; and by 500 BC they had forced Thrace and Macedonia, to the north of Greece, to accept the overlordship of the Persian king.

On the Aegean shores of Asia Minor there was a bustling Greek presence. Known to the Greeks as Ionia, this region had an uneasy relationship with the Persians, and when in 499 BC the Persians demanded greater control, the Ionian Greeks rebelled and appealed to the other Greek states for military assistance. The ancient Greeks thought of themselves as one community, even though they lived in many separate city states scattered across the region. But the Greek response to the request for help was muted, and only Athens and Eretria, a city on the Aegean island of Euboea, agreed to contribute.

Despite the imbalance of forces, the Greeks took the initiative. The Ionians attacked Sardis, the capital of the Persian satrapy (province) of Lydia in 498 BC, and burned it down. The Persian king, Darius, mobilized his forces and by 494 BC he had crushed the revolt and reimposed Persian rule. Darius also prepared to invade mainland Greece, his ire chiefly directed against Athens.

In 492 BC he sent a large army and navy to the north of the Aegean Sea, but before the invasion could go ahead a storm forced a withdrawal. Darius saw this only as a temporary setback and began to plan another assault against Greece. In 490 BC a large fleet carrying 20,000 Persian soldiers left Ionia and attacked the island of Naxos and then Eretria. The Persians captured Eretria and destroyed it, then sailed for Athenian territory, landing near the town of Marathon. Here, the well-organized Persian Army met a foe it was to find impossible to beat: the Greek phalanx.

THE PERSIAN MILITARY SYSTEM

The Persians' control of a huge empire enabled them to field exceptionally large armies by the standards of the ancient world. Herodotus, a Greek historian who wrote about the Persian Wars, claimed that over a million soldiers took part in the invasion of Greece in 480 BC. This was an exaggeration, but the Persians could easily bring together an army of more than 100,000 men, recruited from the 20 provinces of their empire.

The best troops were those raised in Persia itself, and those from the warlike Scythian tribes to the north of the empire. The Persian infantry relied on their powerful composite bows made from layers of animal horn and wood. They also carried spears and light shields. The shield could be rested against the spear to create a miniature "barricade."

As preparation for an attack, the archers fired their arrows at the enemy formations. At the same time, horse-archers from Scythia rode around the flanks and rear of the enemy. When the enemy had been sufficiently disorganized by the Persian archery, the infantry picked up their spears and shields and joined Persian cavalry armed with short spears in a final charge against the enemy.

The Ancient Greeks

The Greeks were responsible for the creation of the dominant infantry unit of its time, the phalanx. The type of warfare that was inextricably linked with it was the single, decisive encounter between two slow-moving, highly disciplined bodies of men advancing upon one another in tight, well-protected formations until they engaged in an exhausting shoving-and-stabbing encounter that ended when one side yielded.

From about 700 BC, the city states – the most common form of political organization in the Greek world – had established armies composed of farmers and relatively wealthy citizens, who were prepared to fight for short periods and provide their own equipment. Their equipment consisted of a heavy, round wooden shield just under 3.2 feet (1 m) in diameter, covered in bronze; a bronze helmet and body armor, and greaves to protect the legs. Offensive armament consisted of a stabbing spear 9.8 feet (3 m) long and a short sword. These well-protected infantrymen – hoplites – had a social cohesion in that they were usually fighting for their own city state to protect territory or to seize it from another city state, and they came from a similar social background.

The hoplites fought in close ranks, with the shield of one man protecting the body of his neighbor to his left. The formation was known as a phalanx, from the Greek word for "roller" or "stack." The hoplites advanced relatively slowly, in blocks sometimes 16 men deep, toward the enemy, and as long as they maintained their formation, their shields and armor provided good protection against an enemy shooting arrows or thrusting spears. Conflicts between city states were decided by a single encounter on level ground. The two sides would advance against one another, shields forming a wall with spears protruding to the front. Then, after a bloody, tiring pushing-and-stabbing match, one side would eventually give way.

The hoplite phalanx was relatively unmaneuverable, but warfare between Greeks before the middle of the fifth century BC rarely involved the use of missile weapons or sophisticated tactics; indeed, the city states seem to have tacitly agreed to keep warfare simple. What it did require was the bravery to undergo intense hand-to-hand fighting and the discipline to keep in formation under the strain of battle.

At Marathon the Athenians gathered together about 9,000 hoplites to fight the Persian invaders. But when the Athenian Army reached Marathon it refused to engage in direct combat with the Persians, and carefully waited to assess the situation. The Persians then unwisely decided to divide their forces, embarking a part of their army to sail to Athens while the rest advanced by land. But before the Persians could put their plan into

Right: Greek soldiers during the era of the Persian Wars. The central figure is a hoplite. In battle the front row of hoplites would point their spears toward the enemy, while those in the rear ranks would rest their spears on the shoulders of the men in front.

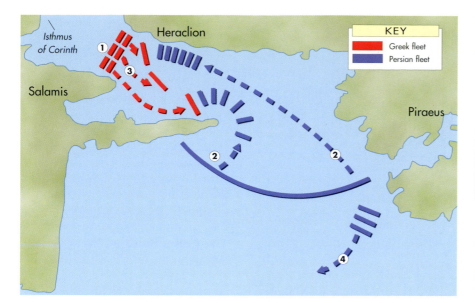

KEY
- Greek fleet
- Persian fleet

Left: The Battle of Salamis cost the Persians half their fleet – around 350 vessels. The Greeks lost only 40 ships during the course of their naval victory.

DECISIVE MOVES

1. Outnumbered Greek fleet forms its battle line in narrow section of channel.
2. Larger Persian fleet advances into narrow part of channel and its warships become jammed together.
3. Greek fleet advances and overwhelms the Persians who cannot maneuver.
4. Remnants of Persian fleet retire.

operation, the Athenians attacked. They thinned their centre in order to match the width of the frontage of the larger Persian force, but their wings crashed through the Persian forces, whose arrows could not slow the charge of this heavy infantry. The Greek force carried out a brilliant encircling maneuvre that caught their enemy off-balance, killed about a third of the Persian Army, and burned many ships. The remaining Persian forces retreated across the Aegean to Ionia. Athens was saved.

Marathon was one of the key moments in the wars between the Greeks and the Persians, which have been described by several Greek writers. Greek, and later Roman, historians have given us much more information about the history of the period from 500 BC in the Mediterranean and the Middle East than exists for earlier periods. Although there are still many gaps, we can be more certain about the information that we have because archeological finds and these written records can be used in conjunction with each other.

The Wars Between Greece and Persia

After the defeat at Marathon, Darius decided that he would have to conquer Greece by an overland route, but he died before the invasion could get under way. Darius's successor, Xerxes, was similarly determined to destroy the Greek nuisance, and in 480 BC he assembled a huge army, perhaps 100,000 strong, and used a bridge of boats to cross the Hellespont (Dardanelles), the narrow stretch of water separating Europe from Asia Minor. This was the next great phase of the Greco-Persian Wars.

Although some Greek city states allied themselves with the Persians, others, led by Athens and Sparta, formed a league of opposition. The Greeks, commanded by the Spartan king Leonidas, chose to place a force at a natural choke-point called Thermopylae. This narrow pass, with mountains on one side and the sea on the other, would hopefully prevent the Persians from outflanking the smaller Greek Army.

The Persian Army was unable to overcome the small force guarding Thermopylae, until a Greek deserter informed Xerxes of a narrow trail that led over the mountains, which allowed his troops to outflank the Greek position. He sent 1,000 of his best soldiers – the famed "Immortals" – to follow this path while others attacked from the front. Realizing the hopelessness of his position, Leonidas despatched the bulk of his forces to safety, while he and his royal guard (along with some Greek allies) held their ground. In the ensuing battle, the Persians gained the pass but at a cost of heavy casualties; all of the Spartans died rather than surrender. After the Battle of Thermopylae, the Persians advanced into central Greece. They captured and burned Athens, but the entire population had been evacuated. Meanwhile, the Athenian fleet held its position just offshore by the island of Salamis.

To conquer Greece it was necessary for the Persians to cross the narrow Isthmus of Corinth. The Greeks held a strong defensive position on the isthmus, and the Persians decided to outflank them by landing troops in their rear in an amphibious operation. But before this move could be carried out, the defending Greek fleet would have to be eliminated. Although outnumbered by the Persians, the Athenian admiral, Themistocles (524–459 BC), lured the Persian fleet into the narrow waters between the mainland and the island of Salamis, which would prevent the Persians from exploiting their numerical advantage. The Greeks relied on superior fighting qualities, and in a desperate and confused battle they inflicted heavy casualties on the Persians.

After the setback at Salamis, Xerxes returned to Persia with some of his army, although powerful forces remained in Greece ready to resume the campaign. In 479 BC the Persians and Greeks met at the decisive Battle of Plataea, northwest of Athens. Mardonius, the Persian commander, attempted to force the Greeks to fight on a flat plain, where the Persian cavalry would be most effective. When the Greeks tried to change their position, Mardonius believed they were fleeing. He attacked but the Greeks again proved superior at close-quarter fighting. Persia lost and Mardonius was killed.

world. The ferocious discipline that ran like a thread through all Spartan life ensured its battlefield supremacy. But while Sparta depended on agriculture, the Athenian state had become rich through trade and could afford a powerful navy, which it used to develop an economic empire around the Aegean Sea.

The Peloponnesian Wars

Antagonism between Athens and Sparta broke out into open conflict in what became known as the First Peloponnesian War. This began as a war between Athens and Sparta's ally Corinth in 460 BC. (Corinth blocked the main route into the southern Greek area of the Peloponnese, hence the name of the war.) Sparta joined in three years later, defeated Athens at the Battle of Tanagra, and then withdrew to its southern Peloponnese heartland. The war concluded in a deadlock in 445 BC, heralding the period of the Thirty Years Peace, although hostilities resumed 14 years later.

A few weeks after the Battle of Plataea, a Greek fleet sailed across the Aegean Sea to Mycale in Ionia and defeated the Persian Army and fleet stationed there. The Ionian Greeks, who had been absorbed into the Persian imperial armed forces, switched sides as the battle began and helped tip the balance in the Greeks' favor. After the Greek victories of 479 BC, Ionia became part of the anti-Persian Delian League, led by Athens. This alliance continued a sporadic war against Persia until 448 BC. Its strategy was to liberate all the Greek cities around the Aegean, and bring them within the Athenian economic and naval orbit. In 466 BC a Delian League fleet defeated the Persians at the Eurymedon River on the coast of Asia Minor. In 448 BC the Athenians and Persians came to an agreement called the Peace of Callias (after the chief Athenian negotiator). The conflict between Persia and Greece petered out, although both continued to interfere in one another's affairs.

Although the Greeks were successful in resisting the Persian Empire, Greek politics and warfare were changed profoundly. Athens emerged from the wars as the leading Greek state and established a large maritime empire – the Delian League – based upon sea power. There was tension with other Greek states, notably Sparta, whose hoplite phalanx was the best in the Greek

During the war the Athenians had built a walled corridor that linked Athens with its port on the coast, Piraeus. This ensured that Athens could withstand a long siege, as supplies brought by ship could be carried into the city along the road between the walls. At this time, siegecraft in the Greek world was in its infancy, and a walled city could hold out for long periods with only the threat of starvation as a serious cause for concern.

Traditionally, commanders planned invasions to take place at around harvest time. The grain in the fields would burn easily and the work of a year could be lost, with a winter famine being the likely result. Consequently, it was important to defeat an invader in battle before he could rampage through the countryside. But Athens, with its "long walls" to Piraeus and powerful navy, could rely upon food supplies from its Aegean allies and avoid taking on Sparta in open battle.

The Thirty Years Peace ended in 431 BC Athens and Corinth fought a naval battle near Corfu and a land battle at Potidaea, a town in the northeast of Greece. These provided Sparta with sufficient pretext to go to war against Athens. The conflict lasted until 404 BC, with a brief period of peace between 421 and 414 BC. A notable change in the conduct of the second and major Peloponnesian War related to strategy. The Athenians knew they faced a long struggle. Pericles, Athens's chief political leader, convinced his citizens that they had to send expeditions of ships and hoplites to attack Sparta's allies from the sea, and slowly grind down their resolve. This "indirect" approach to warfare marked a dramatic shift away from the simple strategy of a war being won or lost through the result of a single, decisive battle between hoplite forces. Sparta attempted to counter the strategy by taking the war directly to Athens and the surrounding area, building a fortress on Athenian territory at Decelea in 413 BC. Instead of being confined to seasonal raids at harvest time, the Spartans could now attack Athenian farms all year round, forcing Athens to be dangerously dependent on food imports.

The war also witnessed significant changes in naval operations. The Athenians had developed their skill with the trireme galley to a high level. They no longer needed to board enemy vessels and fight hand-to-hand; they were able to use their galleys as weapons in their own right, rather than just as fighting platforms for soldiers turned marines. The Athenians sailed in a formation known as the "line ahead." Squadrons of 10 or 20 triremes followed the changes of heading of the lead galley in the line. This allowed the squadron to carry out more complicated, coordinated maneuvers than were possible with the traditional line abreast formation.

Athenian tactics concentrated on the use of the bronze ram, placed at the bow of a galley just below the waterline and capable of smashing through the thin hulls of opposing war galleys. However, despite the Athenians' mastery at sea, the Peloponnesian War eventually went the way of Sparta and her allies. The turning point came in the Athenian expedition to Sicily (415–413 BC). In 415 BC a large fleet was sent to capture Syracuse. Divided leadership and poor tactics gave the people time to prepare their defenses. The Athenians failed to make headway in two years. Then a large Spartan and Corinthian force came to the city's aid and destroyed the Athenian forces. A further defeat at Aegospotami in 405 BC sealed the fate of Athens, whose citizens were now

being starved into submission. The next year Athens was forced to surrender and accept Spartan peace terms, which included demolition of the "long walls" to Piraeus.

The greatest change to the nature of Greek warfare in the latter part of the fifth century BC took place on land, and undermined the former dominance of the phalanx. As a fighting formation, it worked well on flat ground but was slow and cumbersome, and could be disordered by rough terrain. In 426 BC an Athenian army fighting in the rugged terrain of western Greece faced Aetolian soldiers who carried light shields and javelins. The Athenian general Demosthenes attempted to give chase but the enemy easily outran the phalanx, kept its distance, and then threw javelins until the tired hoplites could no longer keep formation. The Aetolians then charged and ripped the phalanx to shreds. Demosthenes survived, and during a subsequent battle he skillfully combined a mixed force of hoplites and light infantry called peltasts. It proved highly maneuverable, and was able to take a larger but slower hoplite force in the flank to secure victory. Peltasts originated in Thrace, the name deriving from the curved shield (pelta) carried by these skirmishing infantry.

Demosthenes used peltasts at the battles of Idomene and Sphacteria in 425 BC. Another Athenian, Iphicrates (415–353 BC), became an expert in light infantry tactics during great victories in Sparta at Lechaion in 393 BC and Abydus in 388 BC, in a series of wars fought between 400 and 362 BC as Athens and other city states challenged Sparta's supremacy. During the conflict, Epaminondas, a general from the city of Thebes to the northwest of Athens, made another important tactical contribution to ancient Greek warfare.

At Leuctra in 371 BC, he conducted the first recorded use of an oblique order of attack. Hoplite armies traditionally formed their phalanx by placing the best troops on the far right of the line. Epaminondas, instead, placed his best troops – including the elite Theban Sacred Band – on his left. He then advanced in a staggered or oblique line, which ensured that his best met the enemy first. In addition, he more than doubled the normal depth of the phalanx on his left wing, which may have been up to 50 ranks deep. This gave his troops a momentum that allowed them to crash through the ranks of their opponents. The phalanx surged forward and wiped out the best Spartan troops, including their king. The Spartan Army wavered and then fell back. Within a few minutes, Epaminondas had ended Spartan military supremacy.

Left: Greece's civil wars were fought mainly around the coast of the eastern Mediterranean and the Greek mainland.

Macedonia and Alexander the Great

While the Greek states had learned much about the conduct of war during the long years of internecine struggle between the blocs that coalesced around Athens and Sparta, the lessons had also been absorbed and developed upon by others – most notably the Macedonian Army of Philip II (382–336 BC) and his genius son, Alexander the Great (356–323 BC).

Macedonia was a state in the north of the Greek peninsula, whose people were not considered properly Greek. The constitutional monarch, Philip, was ambitious and a profound military thinker; his reforms of the Macedonian Army began a process of fundamental change in the warfare of Greece and the Middle East. When Philip commenced his reign, Macedonia already had some of the best and most numerous cavalry of all the armies in the Greek sphere of influence, so the new king concentrated his efforts on reforming the infantry. He gave them a new weapon, a pike – the sarissa – some 16 feet (4.9 m) long, more than double the length of the normal spear. It was a difficult weapon to use, because it was heavy and required well-drilled soldiers to wield it effectively. But the new pike-armed infantry – called phalangites – proved formidable against the old hoplite phalanxes of Greece. Philip put more emphasis on training than did the part-time militia armies of the city states; this training would pay off handsomely in the many campaigns that followed.

As part of a grand plan to bring Greece under his control, Philip exploited a dispute over the control of the religious shrine at Delphi on the slopes of Mount Parnassus, which eventually left him master of northern Greece. When the next major round of hostilities opened in 339 BC, Thebes and Athens, who feared Philip's territorial ambitions, allied themselves against Macedonia. The rival forces met at Chaeronea in central Greece in 338 BC. The Athenian and Theban force totalled 35,000 men. The Macedonians deployed 30,000 infantry and 2,000 cavalry. The battle was as much a triumph for Philip's son, Alexander, as for Philip himself. Alexander led the Companion cavalry, which like Philip's infantry was armed with long spears, or lances. Alexander's decisive cavalry charge wiped out the elite hoplites of the Theban Sacred Band, and Philip's infantry killed or captured 3,000 Athenians.

The victory made Philip master of Greece. He used his mastery to create a new political organization, the Confederacy of Corinth, which he intended to use to wage war against Persia (Sparta was a notable absentee from these proposals). Philip was elected the

Above: Alexander the Great was one of the great captains of history. His military, intellectual, and administrative achievements have never been equaled by any one individual. He was the greatest military commander of the ancient world.

Left: The army of Philip of Macedonia defeats the Athenians at the Battle of Chaeronea in 338 BC, and in the process makes Philip the master of Greece.

confederacy's general in 337 BC, and began assembling an army and navy with which to attack Persia. However, he was assassinated in 336 BC, leaving his son Alexander, only 19 years old, to be crowned king.

The young Alexander first had to establish his personal authority over Greece. He was a popular and brave military leader but when drunk he was prone to violent bouts of rage, even against his closest friends. Alexander led the Macedonian Army into Greece to force the Confederacy of Corinth to elect him general in his father's place. Then, in 335 BC, he was forced to counter a barbarian attack against Thrace and Illyria, which he did brilliantly. While Alexander's attention was focused elsewhere, a rumor spread of his death and Thebes rebelled against Macedonian power. Alexander offered negotiation but was rebutted. His reaction was swift and merciless: he besieged Thebes and, bolstered by loyal Greek allies, he relieved the Macedonian garrison and captured the city and its 30,000 population. A Greek form of reprisal, known as *andrapodismos*, was decided upon, by which the buildings were razed to the ground, the inhabitants were enslaved, and the territory was redistributed among the victors. The other city states were cowed by the severity of the sentence.

Alexander was now ready to commence his great adventure: the conquest of the Persian Empire. He was the fortunate beneficiary of his father's superbly trained Macedonian Army, and while there was no doubting Alexander's own military genius or personal charisma, the army that marched into Asia Minor and destroyed Persian hegemony over the Middle East remained the creation of Philip.

The central core of Alexander's army was provided by the Companions, the elite cavalry led in person by the king, consisting largely of Macedonian landowners who also acted as the monarch's bodyguard. Originally there were 1,800 Companions divided into eight squadrons or *ilae*, each man being responsible for his own weapons and equipment.

Companion armor was relatively light – a helmet, leather or metal breastplate, and sometimes greaves – while armament consisted of a round shield and a thrusting spear. As with all other cavalry in the ancient world, the Companions did not have stirrups, and so were unable to use their spear as a lance, couched under the arm, but instead used a thrusting technique against opponents. Capable of swift yet highly disciplined movement, the Companion cavalry were the most feared horsemen of their day. A large contingent of heavy cavalry was supplied from Thessaly, and the mounted arm was completed by light cavalry armed with javelins.

The bulk of the phalangite infantry – armed with the long sarissa – were called pezetaeri, and were raised from among the Macedonian peasantry. As a self-conscious attempt to increase their *esprit de corps*, they were given the title of Foot Companions. A more genuinely prestigious arm were the hypaspists ("shield bearers"), who were more lightly armored and equipped with a shorter pike around 10 feet (3 m) in length. Their role was to move swiftly on the battlefield, providing tactical continuity between the cavalry and the main pezetaeri phalanx. Light infantry – peltasts and psiloi armed with javelins and swords – were deployed as skirmishers in front of the main body of the army, or could be used to prevent the enemy attempting to outflank the phalanx.

Apart from their discipline and well-honed battlefield drill, what made the Macedonian Army most effective was the way in which the various units managed to work in close cooperation with one another. The centerpiece of the Macedonian tactical system was the audacious employment of cavalry (with Alexander at the head), which pivoted around the phalanx. While the infantry engaged and pinned down the mass of the enemy army, the cavalry smashed into the flank or exploited any disorganization in the enemy line. It was Alexander's genius that he could "read" the battlefield astutely and swiftly, and discover where the enemy was weakest. Alexander was criticized at the time for, and all observers since have always remarked upon it, his near suicidal bravery, often leading his troops from the front and risking death or serious injury. However, his personal courage was part of his identification with his troops, whom he required to face death unflinchingly. The cavalry, without stirrups, had to be prepared to risk being pulled off their horses in hand-to-hand combat, while the phalangites needed steady nerves as they pressed forward toward enemies who would be unleashing volleys of arrows at the near-unmissable target of the large phalanx. To modern commentators, the most noteworthy part of the Macedonian Army has often seemed the phalanx. However, to contemporaries, Alexander's use of cavalry as a shock weapon and his mastery of siege warfare seemed more astonishing.

The Defeat of Persia

Alexander crossed the Hellespont in 334 BC and marched into Asia Minor with an army of 40,000 soldiers. The Persian governors of the provinces of Asia Minor attempted to stop him at the Granicus River, but Alexander swiftly took the initiative. Leading his Companion cavalry, he forded the river and overwhelmed the Persian left flank. The main Macedonian phalanx then locked horns with the Persian force (the infantry of which included a large contingent of Greek mercenaries) and defeated it comprehensively.

Despite this promising victory, Alexander was in a potentially dangerous situation. He was a long way from home, the Persians would be able to build a new army thanks to their huge reserves of manpower, and they still had a powerful navy in the Mediterranean. Alexander, however, displaying the strategic vision that was one of his greatest traits, chose to deal with the navy first. Alexander's plan was simple but not without risk. He decided to capture the main Persian ports along the Mediterranean coast, depriving the Persian fleet of the

Left: Alexander at the siege of Tyre in 332 BC. It took him eight months to capture the city, after which he razed it to the ground and sold the inhabitants into slavery.

bases necessary to operate against Alexander's lines of communication to Greece. Alexander had few naval resources, so he planned to lay siege to the Persian ports one-by-one. The Macedonians spent the next year capturing the coastal cities, and only Helicarnassus put up any real resistance to Alexander.

In 333 BC the Persian emperor, Darius III, gathered an army of 100,000 soldiers and advanced through Syria with the intention of cutting Alexander's line of communication back through Asia Minor to Greece. This forced Alexander to temporarily abandon his march along the coast, and to turn back and face the Persian threat along the Pinarus River.

At the Battle of Issus, Alexander inflicted a massive reverse on Darius's army, and almost killed the Persian emperor himself. Some 50,000 Persians may have been slaughtered, while Macedonian losses were estimated to have been as little as 450 men. Alexander, as usual, led his cavalry in a decisive charge that opened up the Persian line while his infantry took advantage of the disorder. Darius fled the battlefield, leaving his wife and family to be captured by Alexander.

During the next two years Alexander marched south into Syria and Phoenicia and conquered the Mediterranean coast of the Middle East and Egypt. His most difficult task was capturing Tyre. Alexander placed the great port under siege in January 332 BC, but the defenders proved surprisingly resolute in their city's defense. They held out for eight months before the Macedonians finally breached the city walls. Tyre was destroyed and those that survived the ensuing massacre were sold as slaves. Alexander's use of terror was a deliberate and successful ploy; he met little further resistance as his army marched down the Levantine coast to take Egypt, where at Gaza he sustained a shoulder wound in some bitter fighting. The people of Egypt, however, welcomed him as a liberator from the Persian satrap, who wisely chose to surrender.

The Decisive Encounter

Now that Alexander's lines of communication were secure, he returned to Tyre and in 331 BC he advanced into the heartland of Persia, heading toward the Tigris. Darius assembled another large army recruited from the central and eastern provinces of his empire and gathered his forces around Babylon in Mesopotamia. This final encounter between Darius and Alexander took place at Arbela (Guagamela), about 300 miles (480 km) north of Babylon on the plain between Nineveh and Arbela (it lies today near Irbil in northern Iraq) – a battle that decided the fate of the Middle East for hundreds of years to come.

Alexander managed to assemble a joint Macedonian–Greek army of around 47,000 men, which although the largest force he ever deployed in battle, was still vastly outnumbered by the Persian Army, which may have been 200,000 strong. Both Persian wings outflanked the Macedonian Army, and Darius hoped to use them to encircle his enemy while punching through the center with his best troops. He even levelled some of

Right: The Battle of Gaugamela was a crushing defeat for the Persians, who lost an estimated 50,000 dead. Alexander, on the other hand, lost only 500 slain.

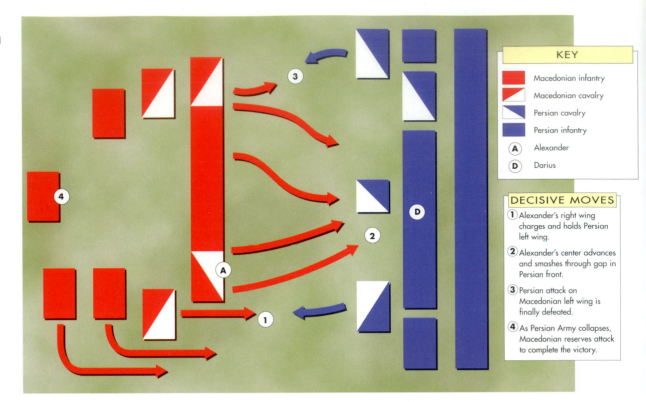

KEY

- ▮ Macedonian infantry
- ◩ Macedonian cavalry
- ◪ Persian cavalry
- ▮ Persian infantry
- Ⓐ Alexander
- Ⓓ Darius

DECISIVE MOVES

① Alexander's right wing charges and holds Persian left wing.

② Alexander's center advances and smashes through gap in Persian front.

③ Persian attack on Macedonian left wing is finally defeated.

④ As Persian Army collapses, Macedonian reserves attack to complete the victory.

the terrain so as to enhance the potential effectiveness of his chariot forces (his best infantry, the Greek mercenaries, had been largely destroyed at Issus).

Alexander's plan was for his left wing to hold its ground, while he delivered the main blow on the Macedonian right wing. As the battle commenced, the bowed shape of the Macedonian line, advancing at varying speeds, drew in Darius's cavalry and caused gaps to open up in the central Persian infantry lines – which the Macedonians were quick to exploit.

As usual, Alexander's personal actions in the battle were decisive. Leading his elite Companion cavalry, he smashed through a gap in the Persian left-center, into which poured the best Macedonian infantry. As the Persian left wing began to buckle, Alexander transferred his Companion cavalry over to his own hard-pressed left wing, where he helped his troops hold their ground against superior odds.

The turning point of the battle came when the panic-stricken Darius suddenly fled from the field. The initiative now passed over entirely to the Macedonians. Alexander's victory was total and his forces pursued the fleeing Darius, with his Bactrian cavalry and a few Greek mercenaries, as far as Arbela, but he escaped into Medea where he was subsequently killed by his own troops, and the Persian Empire collapsed.

Alexander now occupied Babylon and shortly afterwards he conquered Susa, the great Elamite city and Persian capital which yielded massive amounts of treasure. Pressing on into Persia proper, the former capitals and magnificent cities of Persepolis and Pasargadae both fell. Persepolis was the capital

THE ELEPHANT AT WAR

Indian armies used elephants in war from at least the sixth century BC. Their widespread military use in Europe and the Middle East only occurred after Alexander's campaigns in 327 and 326 BC. The army of the Seleucid Empire that succeeded Alexander made the greatest use of elephants, but they were also used by many of the states of the Mediterranean during the second and third centuries BC. In 275 BC, Anthiochus, the successor to Seleucus, for example, made particular use of elephants to defeat an army of Celts that invaded Asia Minor.

Elephants were usually placed in the first line of an army. They might open the battle with a charge that would crash into enemy troops. They might also be used against enemy cavalry in an army without elephants, as horses were usually unsettled by the elephants' smell.

An elephant carried a crew of two to four soldiers armed with bows, javelins, or spears. A small "tower" was sometimes attached to the back of an elephant to give the crew greater protection.

The most successful tactic against elephants was to use light infantry fighting in open order and armed with javelins. They could swarm around the elephant, stabbing at its sensitive trunk or hind quarters; wounded and maddened elephants would often crash into their own supporting troops.

established by Xerxes and Alexander burned the palace there to the ground in revenge for the Persian actions in Greece. In 330 BC he headed north to Medea, still in pursuit of Darius who had retreated to Bactria, where the usurper Bessus had deposed him and incited his murder. When Alexander retrieved the corpse of Darius he sent it to Persepolis for burial.

Alexander was undoubtedly a great general and certainly more than a match for his Persian enemies. However, Alexander had several advantages, not least was the fact that his army was united under him. By contrast, the Persian Army was made up of men of many different nationalities, few of whom had much desire to die in battle for their Persian masters.

A master of battlefield tactics, Alexander also proved himself brilliant at military improvisation. In a subsequent campaign against tribesmen to the north of Persia, Alexander found his way blocked by the Jaxartes River, the far bank of which was defended by the enemy. Alexander ordered his soldiers to fill their tents with hay and sew them up, turning them into crude rafts, which allowed his men to float across the river. As they crossed the Jaxartes, they were given protection by their own archers. Once Alexander's men were on dry land, the tribesmen were overwhelmed and killed.

The Invasion of India

Alexander's ambitions extended beyond the already vast Persian Empire, so that in 327 BC he marched his army into India. In May of the following year, Alexander defeated an Indian army at the Battle of the Hydaspes River. Only a mutiny by his own troops, weary of the excessive demands made upon them, prevented Alexander from continuing to campaign farther east. In 324 BC Alexander returned to his new capital in Babylon. He was faced with the immense task of ruling over an empire that stretched from Greece in the west

to the Indus River in the east, and from the Jaxartes River in central Asia to Egypt. He began to plan fresh conquests in Europe, but in 323 BC he suddenly fell ill with a fever and died. He was only 33 years of age.

Alexander's death was unexpected, and the choice of his successor fell to the commanders of his army. Alexander's wife and son were murdered as the generals fought each other for power. Known as the Diadochi — or successors – the squabbling generals finally carved out three separate kingdoms from Alexander's empire. Antigonas ruled in Greece, Seleucus (the origin of the Seleucid Empire) in Persia and much of Asia Minor, and Ptolemy in Egypt, the latter establishing a dynasty that was to last until Cleopatra was overthrown by the Romans in 30 BC.

The wars between these successor kingdoms, which had all inherited troops and techniques from Alexander's army, saw further technical developments. There were attempts to make the phalanx more destructive by lengthening the pike; elephants were often employed, particularly as a way of frightening cavalry horses. In 275 BC, Anthiochus, Seleucus's successor, made particular use of elephants to defeat an army of Celts that had invaded Asia Minor. Great ingenuity went into creating weapons for siege warfare, and there were many naval innovations, both in the construction of larger ships and smaller, more maneuverable vessels.

The successor kingdoms looked west, as well as east; in 280 BC, Pyrrhus, king of Epirus in what is now northern Greece, led a force of 20,000 men into Italy, to help Greek cities such as Tarentum, which were under threat from the rising power of Rome. This was a portent of what was to come: in a further 250 years, the Romans had defeated the successor kingdoms and the Roman Legion had become the decisive fighting force in Europe, North Africa, and the Middle East.

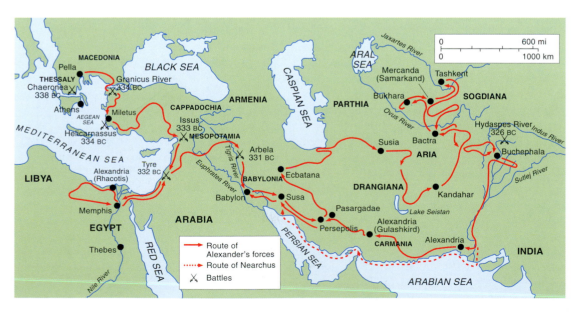

Left: Alexander's empire stretched from the Mediterranean to the Arabian Sea, but following his death it collapsed as his successors fought among themselves.

Republican Rome

The city of Rome went within a century from being a small, provincial city to the mightiest in Italy and with ambitions beyond, which alarmed neighboring Greece. Rome's military prowess was principally due to the organization of its soldiers into legions and centuries, providing battlefield flexibility and an efficient method of waging war somewhere between the packed phalanx and the overspaced Celtic warrior ranks.

In 396 BC the small city of Rome, founded in 753 BC, finally secured its independence from Etruscan overlordship by winning a war against the city of Veii to the north. There followed over 100 years of war, during which the Romans established their rule over the Italian peninsula. Just six years after the overthrow of Etruscan rule, a large war band of Gauls invaded central Italy and crushed the Romans at the Battle of Allia River in 390 BC. The Gauls captured and sacked Rome, only leaving after the Romans agreed ransom terms. But not for the last time in their history, the Romans demonstrated an extraordinary ability to recover from disaster. Within a few years, they had created a Latin Confederacy that increased their power and extended their dominions.

The Greek cities of southern Italy watched Roman expansion with increasing alarm. So, in 281 BC, they invited Pyrrhus (319–272 BC), the king of Epirus in western Greece, to help them fight Rome. Pyrrhus brought an army of 20,000 troops across the Adriatic Sea; it included 20 elephants – the first time the Romans met these animals in war. Pyrrhus fought two battles, at Heraclea in 280 BC and at Asculum in 279 BC. Although

Right: The early expansion of the Roman Empire saw the Romans winning a number of victories in Italy, Spain, and North Africa.

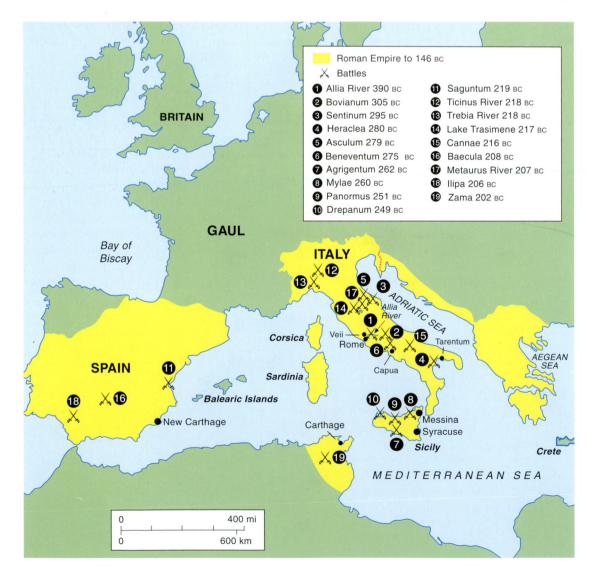

Roman Empire to 146 BC

✗ Battles

❶ Allia River 390 BC
❷ Bovianum 305 BC
❸ Sentinum 295 BC
❹ Heraclea 280 BC
❺ Asculum 279 BC
❻ Beneventum 275 BC
❼ Agrigentum 262 BC
❽ Mylae 260 BC
❾ Panormus 251 BC
❿ Drepanum 249 BC
⓫ Saguntum 219 BC
⓬ Ticinus River 218 BC
⓭ Trebia River 218 BC
⓮ Lake Trasimene 217 BC
⓯ Cannae 216 BC
⓰ Baecula 208 BC
⓱ Metaurus River 207 BC
⓲ Ilipa 206 BC
⓳ Zama 202 BC

BRITAIN

GAUL

Bay of Biscay

ITALY

ADRIATIC SEA

Allia River

Corsica

Veii
Rome

Tarentum

AEGEAN SEA

SPAIN

Sardinia

Balearic Islands

New Carthage

Capua

Carthage

Messina
Syracuse

Sicily

Crete

MEDITERRANEAN SEA

0   400 mi

0   600 km

Pyrrhus won both, his losses were heavy, giving us the expression "Pyrrhic" victory. In 275 BC, however, the Romans defeated him at the Battle of Beneventum and forced him to retreat to Greece.

A New, Flexible Form of Organization

The basis of Roman military success lay in the organization of its soldiers into legions. Originally, Romans had fought in solid phalanxes, like the Greek hoplites, but gradually Roman tactical organization had become much more fluid. A legion of about 4,200 men was divided up into units called centuries of about 70 men. These fought in pairs, in the key tactical unit, the maniple (literally "handful"). The infantry of the legion were grouped in three lines: the first two were armed with throwing spears and short stabbing and slashing swords, while the third had stabbing spears. The main defensive equipment was a rectangular shield, but leather or metal armor and a helmet were also worn.

The organization of the legion, its equipment, and the precise tactics used varied greatly over the 800 years or so in which the Roman legionary dominated battlefields. However, the main tactical elements were constant. Relatively small units (100–500 men) could be combined in a very flexible manner on the battlefield, giving the legion an advantage over the cumbersome Macedonian phalanx, especially where the terrain was not flat and open. (This flexibility also meant that the Romans, at least in the republican period, needed relatively few light infantry. The legionary fulfilled all infantry roles.) Secondly, the Roman soldier carried his own missile weapon in his throwing spear, which when thrown in numbers could break up or weaken many enemy formations. Finally, the short sword that was the legionary's principal weapon imposed its own disciplines. The Roman soldier knew that to kill his foe he had to close with him, and that he needed space to use his sword and shield as he engaged an enemy in close combat. Romans thus fought in a relatively open formation, not packed together, but not requiring the space that Celtic warriors, for example, needed to wield their axes or slashing swords. For the legionary there was no romance about fighting; his sword was designed to inflict maximum damage and he needed to look pitilessly into the eyes of the man he was killing as he stabbed him to death.

The legion needed great internal cohesion if it was to operate effectively. The man closing with an enemy had to be absolutely confident that those on either side of him would not give way. This cohesion came partly through social bonds: initially, legionnaires were all of the same farming stock, fighting for their republic and often serving for a limited time. As Rome acquired overseas possessions this changed, although the notion of being Roman remained very important. Such general factors were reinforced by a strong organization surrounding the legion, in terms, say, of how encampments were built, in terms of medical and other support, but above all in

THE REPUBLICAN LEGION

The Roman republican legion consisted of four types of infantry. The velites were young men taught to fight as light infantry. The hastati were slightly older and more experienced. The principes were veterans of around 30 years of age. The triarii were the oldest soldiers.

These groups were organized into maniples, or subdivisions, of between 120 and 160 men, except for the triarii, who were organized in groups of 60 to 80. Above the maniple was the cohort. This larger unit consisted of maniples of velites, hastati, principes, and triarii, and a cavalry turma (unit) of 30 men. A standard Roman legion, with a strength of around 4,500 to 5,000 troops, consisted of 10 such cohorts.

The legion proved a flexible, fast-moving unit. The maniples were placed in a checkerboard formation and this allowed them to maneuver over rough ground.

Legionaries carried a variety of weapons. The hastati and principes carried seven-foot (2.1-m) javelins, which were thrown at close range. The javelin, known as a pilum, had a head of soft metal with a slender neck, which tended to bend or break when it struck a target and so could not be reused by an enemy. The triarii carried a 12-foot (3.6-m) thrusting spear. All of these troops also used a short sword — the gladius — which was thrust rather than used as a slashing weapon. The velites carried javelins and darts. Extra firepower was provided by slingers and bowmen.

terms of constant training and drill. Throughout Rome's expansion and for most of the empire, the legionary was surrounded by a tight organization, and he knew it. Everything he did had a pattern – and his confidence on the battlefield sprang from the fact that he and all his comrades were aware of how they fitted into it. Success was not inevitable, however, and Rome had rivals. From the mid-third century, a series of wars was fought against the Carthaginians, in which Rome suffered great defeats.

The First Punic War

The first area of Roman–Carthaginian competition was Sicily. Since the beginning of the fifth century BC, Sicily had been a cause of conflict between the North African state of Carthage and the Greek city state of Syracuse, a dispute the Romans entered in 264 BC – beginning the First Punic (Carthaginian) War. A Roman army landed on the island and in 262 BC besieged the Carthaginian stronghold of Agrigentum. An army sent to the assistance of the besieged city was defeated, allowing the Romans to gain control of most of Sicily.

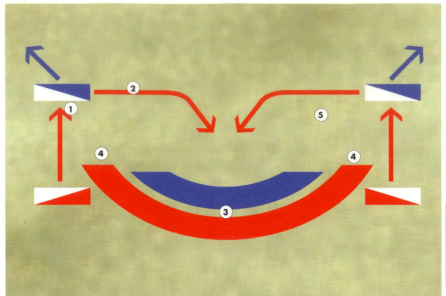

Left: The Battle of Cannae in 216 BC was a crushing defeat for Rome, and Hannibal's greatest victory.

DECISIVE MOVES

① Carthaginian cavalry charges and sends Roman right wing fleeing.

② Victorious Carthaginian cavalry charges around behind advancing Roman center.

③ The Carthaginian center halts Roman attack.

④ Carthaginian infantry advances against both flanks of stalled Roman attack.

⑤ After driving off enemy cavalry, the Carthaginian right flank swings around to complete the destruction of the Roman Army. The Roman legions are surrounded and slaughtered.

KEY

- Roman cavalry
- Roman infantry
- Carthaginian cavalry
- Carthaginian infantry

The war now shifted to the sea. The Carthaginians had an excellent navy while the Romans had no such tradition, but they recognized their shortcomings and developed new tactics to minimize their weakness as sailors and maximize their superiority in hand-to-hand fighting. The Romans invented a device called the corvus (crow), which consisted of a plank with a spike at the top, positioned at the front of a warship. When an enemy ship came close, the plank was dropped onto it; the spike prevented escape and allowed Roman soldiers to board and take the vessel. At Mylae in 260 BC the corvus enabled the Romans to win a significant victory.

In 256 BC the Roman Senate decided to strike against Carthage. The two fleets met off the south coast of Sicily, with the Romans again defeating the Carthaginians. The Romans followed this up by landing a large force in North Africa, commanded by Marcus Atilius Regulus, who defeated the first army sent against him, encouraging some Carthaginians to sue for peace terms. But in 255 BC a Spartan mercenary general named Xanthippus arrived in Carthage, reorganizing its forces and destroying Regulus's army at the Battle of Tunes. The Roman fleet also lost more than 280 ships in a storm. These events encouraged Carthage to renew its war effort and the focus returned to Sicily, with both sides experiencing victories and reverses. The tide eventually turned in favor of the Romans in 242 BC when they seized the Carthaginian bases at Drepanum and Lilybaeum, defeating the Carthaginian fleet the following year. The Carthaginians accepted defeat and surrendered all of Sicily to Rome.

Between 241 and 219 BC the Romans seized Sardinia, while the Carthaginians created a new empire in Spain – to the alarm of the Romans who allied themselves with the northeastern city of Saguntum in an attempt to halt this expansion. In 219 BC the young general in command of the Carthaginians in Spain, Hannibal Barca (247–183

BC), captured Saguntum. Hostilities against Carthage resumed in the Second Punic War.

Hannibal was a man of resolute bravery, tactical skill, and strategic vision who inspired great loyalty in his army – one of the great captains of history. He recognized that Rome's great strength lay in its control of Italy and he decided on an audacious plan to invade

FORTIFICATIONS AND SIEGE WARFARE

The ordinary Roman soldier carried a huge weight of equipment on a forked stick over his shoulder. Part of this heavy load included tools for digging earthworks for sieges, and for the fortified camps the soldiers constructed each night while marching in the vicinity of the enemy.

Sieges featured frequently in Roman warfare, although the basic principles were little different from those laid down by the Assyrians several centuries before. The first step was to dig trenches/palisades around the place under siege. At Alesia, during Julius Caesar's wars in Gaul, two sets of trenches/palisades were built, one facing the town and the other facing outward to defend against a relieving force. A prime objective was to prevent supplies from reaching the besieged army. At the siege of Athens in 86 BC, for example, the defending Greek Army was reduced to boiling leather for food.

For the assault, a huge ramp might be built to allow siege towers to be trundled forward to the walls. If the Roman attack succeeded, civilians would be slaughtered or sold into slavery, and any treasure discovered would be looted and carried back to Rome.

by leading his army overland from Spain, through southern France, and across the Alps.

The march began early in 218 BC, and arrived in Italy that fall. Before winter put a stop to the fighting, Hannibal had won two battles in Italy: at the Ticinus River and at the Trebia River. In the spring of 217 BC Hannibal ambushed the next Roman army sent against him as it marched along Lake Trasimene in central Italy. He now marched into southern Italy, where he hoped to encourage cities to break their alliance with Rome.

The Genius of Hannibal

Under the command of Fabius the Romans shadowed the Carthaginians, but avoided battle, while another, even larger army of 75,000 soldiers was organized. However, Fabius's strategy was overruled, and new commanders led the Romans into battle at Cannae in 216 BC. Hannibal encircled and then destroyed the Roman Army. It was a masterly display of tactical genius in which 60,000 Romans were killed for the loss of just 6,000. A weakness of the Roman system – the quality of a high command that often changed – had been exposed. Ironically, having exposed its weakness, the Roman system's strengths now reasserted themselves. The Romans refused to give in, conscripting virtually the entire male population in an attempt to defeat Carthage.

The Romans went back to Fabius's strategy, avoiding open battle with Hannibal in the hope of wearing him out with small-scale actions. Hannibal was disappointed that few of the non-Roman cities in Italy joined his cause. Worse still, he failed to swiftly gain control of a port, enabling supplies and reinforcements to reach him from North Africa. It was not until 212 BC that Tarentum fell, but by this time the advantages gained at Cannae had been lost. In 215 BC a Roman army won a victory in Spain over Hannibal's brother, Hasdrubal, and instead of reinforcing Hannibal the Carthaginian Council chose to send troops to Spain. Elsewhere, in Syracuse a pro-Carthaginian faction had gained power but the Romans had besieged the city. The Carthaginians did not have the military strength to support Hannibal as well as Syracuse and Hasdrubal.

In 211 BC Hannibal marched as far as the outskirts of Rome. Symbolically, it was intended to demonstrate that the Romans could do nothing to stop him. In fact it was an indication that, while he was winning battles, he was losing the war. The Romans still refused open battle. Instead, they attacked those few cities that had joined his alliance. Hannibal had hoped the Romans would abandon the siege of Capua, his most important ally, if he advanced on Rome. But the Romans left enough troops to maintain the siege and captured Capua later that year. They also captured Syracuse.

In 210 BC the Senate sent Publius Cornelius Scipio (237–183 BC) to command Roman forces in Spain. He captured New Carthage on the coast of eastern Spain in 209 BC, before defeating Hasdrubal's army at Baecula.

Hasdrubal knew that Hannibal's army in Italy could not survive for long without reinforcements. He decided after the battle to take what was left of his army to Italy. He arrived in 207 BC and marched south to meet Hannibal. The Romans, however, learned of Hasdrubal's plans and defeated him at Metaurus River, where some 10,000 Carthaginians were slaughtered (including Hasdrubal himself).

In 206 BC Scipio destroyed the Carthaginians in Spain at Ilipa. Spain was now in Roman hands. The Romans took the war directly to the Carthaginians when, in 204 BC, Scipio invaded North Africa. Hannibal rushed back to defend Carthage, and met Scipio at Zama in 202 BC. Scipio's superiority in cavalry proved too much for the Carthaginians, who were decisively beaten. Hannibal managed to flee, but was pursued by the Romans for the rest of his life. The treaty ending the war reduced Carthage to a small, emasculated city state.

Carthage and Rome went to war again in 149 BC. The city of Carthage was captured in 146 BC and razed, and of the inhabitants who had not died through hunger, disease, or battle, the survivors were sold as slaves.

Above: A Roman soldier on campaign with his heavy load. On the wooden poles he carries pots, pans, tools, spare clothing, and canvas to make a tent.

Shortly after Scipio's victory at Zama, Rome won another decisive victory on the west coast of Greece, helping the states of Rhodes and Pergamum. An army of two legions had been sent to take on the forces of Philip V of Macedonia. Philip stopped the Romans in Illyria, but under a new commander, Titus Quinctius Flamininus, Philip's army was routed at the Battle of Cynoscephalae in 197 BC. The battle revealed to the world the superiority of the tactically flexible Roman legion over the cumbersome and brittle Macedonian phalanx. Rome now declared Greece to be under its sphere of influence.

Roman attention then shifted to the west coast of Asia Minor and the Seleucid emperor Antiochus III. The Roman fleet – supported by its Rhodian ally – defeated Antiochus's navy twice during 190 BC. (At the first of these battles, one of Antiochus's squadrons had been commanded by Hannibal, who had found asylum with the emperor after fleeing Carthage.) The Romans had elected Lucius Cornelius Scipio, whose brother Publius had won at Zama in 202 BC, to command the army against Antiochus. Lucius (along with his brother) crossed into Asia Minor and fought Antiochus's army at Magnesia. While conducting a flank attack with his cavalry, Antiochus left his phalanx unsupported. The Romans were able to push the phalanx into a hollow square, while at the same time forcing Antiochus's elephants to panic and run back into the phalanx. The Roman legionnaires charged and won a complete victory. Asia Minor was at their mercy.

Antiochus lost all his empire in western Asia Minor. He was also required to surrender Hannibal, although he managed to slip away to Bithynia, on the north coast of Asia Minor. In 183 BC Rome mediated an end to a war between Bithynia and Rome's main ally in the eastern Mediterranean, Pergamum; Rome demanded the surrender of Hannibal, but he committed suicide instead.

In 172 BC the Roman Senate declared war on King Perseus of Macedonia. The Macedonians had some initial success, but at Pydna in 168 BC the Romans routed them. It was now clear that the legion was a superior form of military organization to the phalanx: some 30,000 Macedonian soldiers were killed or captured and the kingdom became a province of the Roman Empire. However, those Romans who fought at Pydna described graphically the dangers of taking on the phalanx from its front, where each legionary seemed to be confronted with 10 spear points.

Meanwhile, a lengthy guerrilla war in Spain came to a close. After the Carthaginians had been defeated in Spain in 206 BC, the Roman Senate placed a permanent garrison of two legions in the country. But the tribal states of the Iberian peninsula had no wish to exchange Carthaginian rule for Roman subjugation. For over 50 years war dragged on and few Roman soldiers wanted to fight in Spain, as there were few chances for plunder – an important incentive for the Roman soldier fighting away from Italy. In 149 BC, the Lusitanians and the Celtiberians from the west of Spain rebelled after the Romans had killed their chiefs. A Lusitanian named Virathus, who had previously commanded troops in the Roman Army, led the revolt. For 10 years he defended Lusitania against the Romans until killed by a traitor,

Left: At the Battle of Ticinus in 218 BC, the Roman general Publius Cornelius Scipio was defeated by Hannibal and barely escaped with his life. Contrary to the depiction here, Ticinus was mostly a cavalry affair.

which led the revolt to collapse. Two years later the Celtiberians rebelled again. They established a capital at Numantia in northeastern Spain, but in 133 BC a besieging Roman army captured and destroyed the city.

Roman expansion continued unabated, as it imposed direct rule over every single state or tribal area that had access to the Mediterranean. After Spain, the success of the guerrilla tactics of the Numidian king, Jugurtha, in North Africa led to reforms within the Roman Army. Roman soldiers normally paid for their own equipment, attracted by the prospect of enrichment, but these campaigns had afforded few attractions for the ordinary soldier. Thus in order to acquire sufficient volunteers, the Senate agreed to pay for the equipment. Rome's poorest citizens could now join the army, with the prospect of a grant of land at the end of the war as an added incentive. Sufficient volunteers came forward; the Roman Army had become a fully professional fighting machine, paid for and maintained by the empire's vast wealth.

The Reforms of Marius

An imaginative commander, Gaius Marius (157–86 BC), won the Numidian War in 106 BC. He placed garrisons throughout Numidia, denying the North Africans bases for their guerrillas. Marius's most lasting claim to fame lay in his reorganization of the legion. The troops armed with stabbing spears (the triarii) were henceforth equipped with the throwing spear and the short sword, while on the organizational level the maniple was replaced by the larger cohort (of up to 500 men) as the basic tactical unit. In the new Maurian or imperial legion, it still lined up for battle in three lines. The first line would consist of four cohorts, with wide spaces behind them. The second line of three cohorts could move forward into the spaces in the first line, if required, and form a long cohesive front to the enemy. The third line (three cohorts) was employed as a reserve, either to reinforce an attack or cover a retreat. Another consequence of the homogenization of the legionary infantry was that it lost some of its flexibility, so that the Romans were required to make greater use of auxiliary troops to perform light infantry and cavalry roles.

A young officer in Marius's army named Lucius Cornelius Sulla returned to Italy, then took part in a war to restore Roman rule over a number of rebellious allies. Afterward, he took an army to the Black Sea coast where Mithridates, king of Pontus, had invaded Greece. Sulla defeated his army at Athens in 86 BC and soon found himself the most powerful general in Rome. Sulla became increasingly active in political life. Disputes between rival factions in the Senate had escalated into civil war, and Sulla acted as a mediator while increasing his influence. This outbreak of violence was the first in a series of wars that would transform Rome from republican to imperial rule. Sulla defeated his rival generals in 82 BC and established a dictatorship; he also murdered all the losing side's political leaders. Sulla surrendered his dictatorship in 79 BC, but his example of

the successful military leader who intervened in politics now became the model all Roman politicians copied. It was renewed war against Mithridates between 75 and 65 BC that helped establish the reputation of another ambitious Roman officer, Gnaeus Pompeius.

In 59 BC, three successful generals, Pompeius, Marcus Licinius Crassus, and Gaius Julius Caesar (100–44 BC), effectively took control of the Senate. The Senate gave each of them control of the military forces in a part of the Roman Empire. Crassus in the Middle East and Caesar in Gaul instigated wars to expand the empire and their military prestige. While Crassus's expedition against the Parthian kingdom of Mesopotamia ended in defeat (and his death) at Carrhae in 53 BC, Caesar's campaigns in Gaul were a triumphant success. Caesar even mounted two expeditions to Britain in 55 and 54 BC, although he did not stay for long on either occasion.

Civil War

The death of Crassus left Pompeius and Julius Caesar rivals for supreme power in Rome, which turned into civil war in 49 BC. Pompeius withdrew from Italy (with most of the members of the Senate) to assemble an army in Greece. Julius Caesar first invaded Spain, where a large army loyal to Pompeius had to be defeated. He then returned to Italy and crossed the Adriatic to land at Dyrrachium in western Greece. After capturing this port, he advanced into Thessaly and defeated Pompeius at the Battle of Pharsalus in 48 BC. Pompeius fled to Egypt, where he was murdered. Julius Caesar followed, and found Egypt close to civil war between Ptolemy XII and Cleopatra, the two sibling but rival monarchs of Egypt. Julius Caesar backed Cleopatra, eliminated Ptolemy, and effectively added Egypt to the Roman Empire. In 45 BC, after victories in North Africa and Spain over the remaining armies of Pompeius's supporters, Caesar returned to Rome. Having destroyed his rivals, Caesar seemed invincible, but in 44 BC he was assassinated by nobles fearful of his growing power.

Another civil war ensued. Caesar's assassins fled to Greece, where they raised an army. They were followed by an army led by Marcus Antonius (Marc Anthony), Caesar's former second-in-command, and Caesar's nephew, Octavian (63 BC–AD 14). At Philippi in 42 BC the army of the assassins were defeated. Octavian and Antonius split the empire between them, Octavian taking the west and Antonius the east, where he made an alliance with Cleopatra.

For 10 years Octavian and Antonius uneasily shared power, until in 32 BC Octavian persuaded the Senate to declare war on Egypt. Antonius stood by Cleopatra and despatched a fleet to the west coast of Greece to meet the threat from Rome. Octavian's fleet defeated Antonius and Cleopatra at Actium in 31 BC. Cleopatra and Antonius committed suicide, and Octavian became sole ruler of the Roman world, taking the title Augustus. Rome had its first emperor.

Imperial Rome

As Rome expanded her frontiers further and further beyond her Italian heartland, the army gradually found itself defending the empire's gains, not least due to the intractability of the barbarian tribes who opposed her. While logistical and recruitment problems were handled well, an ominous sign was the increasingly political nature of generalship and the fractious repercussions it had for Rome's internal stability.

During the imperial period, there were four major developments with consequences for the army and for warfare. Up to the second century, while there were some attempts to expand frontiers, in general there was a quest for stability and the construction of viable frontiers. The second major development was the involvement of the army in politics, and particularly in the choice of emperor. A third constant factor was the instability of the eastern frontier, leading to long-running conflict with the Parthian and then the Sassanid empires. Finally, the Roman Empire became the object of attack from barbarian tribes. Even as the empire was breaking up, however, and the army was changing radically, Roman military skill remained at a high level.

Whereas Caesar had invaded Gaul to gain personal wealth and glory, Augustus conquered territory to give his empire stable frontiers that would be easy to defend from attack. These frontiers often coincided with rivers or mountain ranges. Augustus first visited Gaul and set up a number of military camps along the Rhine River and near important passes through the Alps. He then went to Spain to impose Roman rule on the warlike tribes of the country's northwest region.

After the Spanish wars had been concluded in 19 BC, Augustus embarked on a new phase of expansion. He aimed to create a river frontier from the North Sea to the Black Sea, at first following the courses of the Rhine and Danube rivers. Between 29 and 27 BC, a Roman army occupied the land north of Macedonia and pushed northward into modern-day Serbia. Ten years later Augustus sent his adopted son, Tiberius Caesar Augustus, and Tiberius's brother, Nero Claudius Drusus, to conquer what is now Austria. An invasion of Gaul in 16 BC by the Germanic Sagambri tribe made Augustus alter his plans. Instead of the Rhine, he considered it prudent to push farther east to the Weser River.

Roman troops now advanced deep into Germany. Some legionnaires in the north even reached the Elbe, well beyond the Weser. In the south the army crossed the Danube into Bohemia. By AD 5 the Romans felt confident enough to send a fleet to the mouth of the Elbe to meet the advancing legions. But a revolt by Germanic tribes in AD 6 showed how fragile the gains were. It took three years of hard fighting in central Europe to restore Roman authority. Augustus had to deploy the largest field army seen since the civil wars.

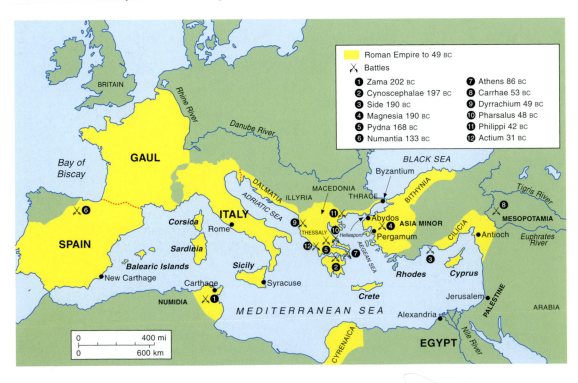

Left: The final years of the republic saw the consolidation of Roman power in the Mediterranean through a series of successful wars and alliances.

Roman Empire to 49 BC
✗ Battles
❶ Zama 202 BC
❷ Cynoscephalae 197 BC
❸ Side 190 BC
❹ Magnesia 190 BC
❺ Pydna 168 BC
❻ Numantia 133 BC
❼ Athens 86 BC
❽ Carrhae 53 BC
❾ Dyrrachium 49 BC
❿ Pharsalus 48 BC
⓫ Philippi 42 BC
⓬ Actium 31 BC

Left: The Roman Empire at the height of its power in the second century AD.

No sooner was Bohemia reconquered than a major disaster struck Augustus's plans. The massacre of three legions marching through the dense Teutoberg Forest in northern Germany in AD 9 shattered the dream of a Weser River frontier. Those Romans who were captured became human sacrifices to the Germanic gods; six years later the army found the bones of 15,000 comrades. For the rest of his life Augustus was often reduced to tears by the memory of the catastrophe. The hard fighting in Bohemia and the disaster in the forest contributed to a mutiny in the army after Augustus died in AD 14. Tiberius, his successor, used this unrest and the difficulty of finding recruits to halt further Roman advances in northern Europe. The last act of expansion was an invasion of Britain in AD 43 by the Emperor Claudius.

The defeat of a Roman army by Parthia at the Battle of Carrhae, Mesopotamia, in 53 BC had been a factor in turning Augustus away from conflict in the eastern reaches of the empire. A negotiated settlement between Rome and Parthia in 20 BC was drawn up to set the boundaries between the two protagonists. Tiberius continued the policy by refusing to take advantage of a Parthian civil war to expand eastward. Tiberius made a new agreement in AD 18 with the victor of the civil war that confirmed the treaty. Parthia then broke it in AD 35, launching the first of two wars against Armenia, an ally of Rome, but was defeated both times.

The new emperor, Nero, was envious of the popularity of the victorious general in the second of these wars, Gnaeus Domitius Corbulo. Nero charged him with treason and ordered him to commit suicide. Besides depriving Rome of a successful military leader, this act also led the empire into civil war. Partly because of this, the Senate declared Nero a public enemy.

Nero took his own life, but there was no acceptable candidate to replace him. During AD 69 no fewer than four men claimed the title. Different sections of the army supported rival candidates, and it was only after sustained military conflict in northern Italy that Vespasian emerged as the winner. During Vespasian's reign, two rebellions, one by the Jews in Palestine and the other in northeastern Gaul and Germany, were suppressed with typical Roman ruthlessness.

In Europe, on the edges of the empire, new kingdoms emerged that were not, in Roman terms, quite barbarian but not fully civilized either. One of these – the Dacians in what is now Romania – was sufficiently powerful locally to repel a Roman invasion in AD 85. But a second attempt between AD 101 and 107, led by the Emperor Trajan, conquered them. Trajan also extended the territories eastward. He added Mesopotamia to the empire after a successful war with Parthia.

The empire reached its greatest extent under Trajan, and afterwards the Roman Army increasingly began to act as a force to defend the frontiers from outside incursion. When a legion was serving along the frontier it was unusual for the whole formation to march out as a whole; more commonly operations would be carried out by smaller units – such as cohorts – acting in a semi-independent capacity. Legionary equipment became lighter to reflect the needs for fighting in small-unit actions. A lighter, oval shield was introduced and armor was reduced; mail was replaced by overlapping metal strips (lorica segmentata), which were easier and cheaper to produce and lighter to wear.

During garrison duty on the frontier, it was often necessary for the Romans to deal with cross-border raids launched by relatively small but highly mobile

THE SASSANID WAR MACHINE

Heavily armored horsemen formed the elite of the Sassanid Army. Their armor covered them from head to foot, and sometimes their horses wore armor as well. The Romans called them clibanarii, a word meaning "in an oven" and describing the effect such equipment might have in the hot Middle Eastern summer. They were armed with 12-foot (3.7-m) spears, and if the enemy were disorganized, a charge by them usually delivered the decisive blow.

On the flanks were swarms of horse-archers. These men would ride up to the enemy, firing arrows when they were in range, and then fall back. The archers were intended to make the enemy formation lose cohesion before the heavy cavalry charged.

Behind the mounted archers, the Sassanids placed elephants imported from India. These were used mostly because their smell upset horses that had never encountered an elephant. In the rear of the army was a mass of poor-quality infantry armed with spears and shields; they were more useful for digging trenches and building camps than for direct combat.

bands of barbarians. As a result, the role of cavalry became more important, being able to react to such attacks speedily. Most of the cavalry was recruited from indigenous people in the frontier regions, although the Romans mounted some of their own infantry on horses who fought on foot once they reached the battlefield.

Despite the success of Trajan's campaigns, the latter part of the second century AD gave indications of the Roman Empire's eventual fate. Most alarmingly in AD 168 an alliance of German tribes – the Marcomanni, the Langobardi, and the Quadi – crossed the Danube River. Some of the invaders even reached Aquileia in northern Italy. Emperor Marcus Aurelius personally took the field to drive them back across the Danube by AD 179. This major attack by a confederation of German tribes was a powerful portent of things to come.

Equally disturbing was the erosion of what remained of the Roman imperial tradition. In AD 193 a new civil war broke out. The ruling emperor, Commodus, had been assassinated in AD 192 because of his unpopularity with the Senate. There was no obvious candidate to succeed him, and the imperial bodyguard – the Praetorian Guard – cynically sold the rights to the throne to the highest bidder. Different armies put forward their own candidates for the position of emperor. This inability to maintain a legitimate line of succession fatally undermined the military and economic power of the Roman Empire.

Right: Roman troops under Galerius launch a successful surprise attack on a Persian camp near the Tigris River in AD 297. Rome found it increasingly difficult to combat growing Persian power in the Middle East.

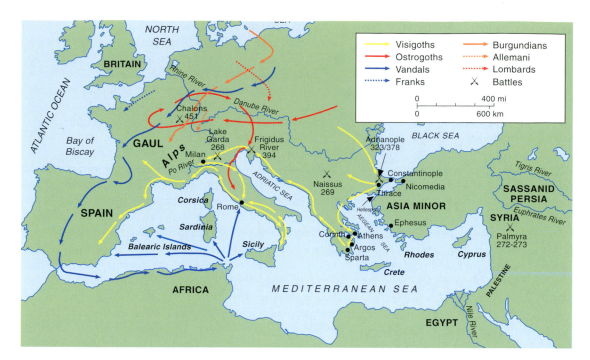

In AD 193 Lucius Septimus Severus, the commander of the Danube frontier, emerged victorious from the war between three rival claimants for the position of emperor. Severus set about regaining the loyalty of the legions that had supported his opponents during the civil war. The new emperor advised his sons: "Work together, enrich the soldiers, and scorn everyone else." Severus knew where the true power in the empire lay. The future of the empire was now entirely in the hands of its legions, and the men they promoted to lead it. Rome was no longer run for the benefit of the empire as a whole but for the army and its generals.

Throughout the second century, there had been conflict between Rome and the Parthian Empire: Marcus Aurelius had invaded Mesopotamia in 165; Septimius Severus sacked the Parthian capital in 197, and the emperor Caracalla was assassinated in 221 while leading another invasion. In 226, the Parthians were overthrown by a new dynasty, of indigenous Persian origin. Claiming to be a descendant of the Persian emperors Darius and Xerxes, the new ruler, Ardashir, demanded that Rome surrender the eastern provinces of its empire, formerly a part of the old Persian Empire. In AD 230, to make his claim good, Ardashir invaded the Roman province of Mesopotamia, and initiated a long-running series of wars.

The first response from Rome was slow: three years were required before a Roman army took to the field. Although there are few known facts about the war that followed, it would seem that Ardashir at first retreated to Persia but in 241 renewed hostilities. Ardashir died during this campaign, probably of old age, to be succeeded by his son, Shapur I. Shapur I captured several important cities before being brought to battle by a Roman army at Resaena in 243. While historians

know a battle was fought there at that date, the result of it is not clear. Shapur claimed victory and that the Romans paid him a large sum of money to release their leader from captivity. No information from the Roman side survives, although it seems certain that they suffered some sort of reverse. This war marked the first Roman setback in the Middle East since the reign of Augustus.

Roman rule in the Middle East began to look somewhat fragile in the face of growing Persian assertiveness, but between 282 and 283 the Romans did reconquer much of the territory they had given up 40

THE LIMES

The limes – from a Latin word used for roads marking boundaries between farms or orchards – provided a barrier that kept barbarians out of the Roman Empire. They also gave a Roman army crossing the frontier a protected base for its supplies and a refuge in case it had to retreat after a defeat. The structure of the limes varied depending on the type of frontier being defended.

In Britain, it took the permanent form of Hadrian's impressive stone wall dividing north and south. Along the Rhine River a wall of upright logs and an earthen rampart connected legionary and auxiliary camps. Here the barbarians lacked the technology to undertake a siege.

In arid North Africa and the Middle East, where the Parthians and Sassanid Persians challenged Rome, the Romans preferred a network of legionary forts and fortified towns.

years before. Narses, a son of Shapur, succeeded to the Persian throne in 294, bringing much-needed stability to the Persian cause. In 296 he won a major victory over the Roman Army at the Battle of Callinicum, very close to Carrhae where the Romans had been defeated by the Parthians in 53 BC. In 297, however, a Roman army led by Galerius avenged Callinicum, despite the 25,000-strong Roman force being outnumbered four-to-one. The Persians were soundly defeated and Narses's family and harem captured. Narses asked for peace talks, which culminated in the Treaty of Nisibis that established a frontier that lasted for 40 years.

Narses died in 302 and his successor, Hormizd II, ruled for only seven years. Shapur II (310–379), the heir to Hormizd, was only a child when the Arab king, Thair, exploited Persia's weakness by raiding Iran in 320. Eight years later Shapur took his revenge in the first campaign of his reign by invading Arabia and defeating Thair.

Shapur II instigated a new war with Rome in 337. The years since the Treaty of Nisibis seem to have been used by the Persians to construct a system of fortresses along their border with Rome. Before this war Romans had entered Persian territory with little difficulty but histories of the 337 war are full of accounts of sieges in Persian territory. The Persians had also built siege engines of their own, an innovation not previously encountered in Sassanid warfare. This phase of the Roman–Persian conflict came to a temporary end in 350, when both Rome and Persia agreed to a truce.

The Rising Importance of Cavalry

The wars in the east underlined to the Romans the growing impact cavalry was having in military affairs. The highly mobile and exclusively mounted armies of the Asian steppe people had influenced first the Parthians and then the Sassanids. Both heavy and light cavalry were used in conjunction with each other to great effect, and as the quality of the famed Roman infantry gradually began to decline, so barbarian and Sassanid cavalry became ever-more threatening.

The key factor in the cavalry renaissance was the development of stirrups and a hard leather saddle. This made the cavalryman more secure on his steed and made shock action possible: the spear now became a lance that combined the kinetic energy of both rider and galloping horse. Against all but the best infantry, a mass cavalry charge was now a terrifying phenomenon. Shapur renewed the war in 358 with an attack on the Roman fortress of Amida. His advance was unexpected and he could have reached the Mediterranean coast had it not been for the siege of Amida, where a gallant Roman garrison held out for 73 days. When Amida was finally captured, winter was approaching and Shapur was forced to halt campaigning until the spring.

During the winter, the Romans rushed forces to the area and Shapur faced a series of difficult sieges during the following year. By this time, a powerful Roman army

of 65,000 men had been assembled at Antioch in Syria under the command of the Roman emperor, Julian (332–363). In 363 Julian advanced into Mesopotamia, and from his writings, historians have concluded that he aimed to eliminate the Persian threat for good.

Shapur, however, shrewdly avoided combat with the Romans. Julian's plan was to march down the Euphrates River to capture the Persian capital, Ctesiphon. But with a Persian army in the area, he could not besiege Ctesiphon without leaving his own forces vulnerable to attack. Julian then chose to bring the Persian Army to battle and marched back northward up the Tigris River. During one of the many Persian ambushes that took place during the march, Julian was mortally wounded while leading a counterattack at night.

The new Roman emperor, Jovian, negotiated a peace treaty that left several major fortresses in Persian hands. The Romans agreed to abandon Armenia in the Caucasus, into which Shapur placed his own candidate for the Armenian throne. The Romans did nothing for 10 years but then supported a rival candidate to the throne. Shapur declared war.

The Romans had recovered their previous strength along the Syrian–Mesopotamian frontier. They defeated Sassanid armies twice but could not break Persian control over Armenia. The stalemate was brought to an end by an invasion of the Roman Empire by barbarian Goths across the Danube River. The Romans made a peace with Shapur in order to assemble an army to confront the Goths. In 390 Rome and Persia agreed to partition Armenia, which finally brought an end to this series of wars that had cost both sides much but settled little. For the next century, Rome and Persia found their attentions now fixed on barbarian invaders from the steppes to the north.

The Barbarian Threat

The wars on the eastern frontier of the empire were a constant drain on Roman resources that were urgently needed elsewhere. For from the early years of the third century, an evolving threat from barbarian peoples moving against the empire in Europe gradually led to its collapse. The German tribes that Marcus Aurelius had defeated in Dacia in the second century were just the first arrivals in a long movement of peoples that eventually wore out the empire in the west. These peoples were pushed into each other by the movement of nomads (notably the Huns) from the steppes of Eurasia. The period we are talking about is a long one: from the early third century to the late fifth century: 250 years during which the Roman Army had to take on a variety of enemies.

It is to the great credit of the Roman military system that the empire lasted so long under such great pressure. The Romans proved able to come up with answers to an evolving range of military problems, and the successor state, the Byzantine Empire, continued to do so until it eventually fell to Ottoman attack in 1453. However, the period when Rome could decisively defeat external military challenges ended with the invasions of the third century. The Romans were not fighting states that they could defeat or overawe: they were coping with movements of whole populations and the effort eventually wore out the military apparatus.

Between 217 and 268, the northern borders of the Roman Empire gave way in three places and barbarian tribes moved across the Rhine and Danube, and into northern Italy. The Franks, a Germanic people, poured across the Rhine in 236. They crossed the Alps every year for three decades to savagely raid the fertile valley of the Po River, until they were defeated by the Roman emperor Claudius II (214–270) at the Battle of Lake Garda in 268.

When Claudius II came to power in 268, Rome looked on the verge of collapse. But he reversed the tide of events. After his defeat of the Alemanni, he crushed the Goths at the Battle of Naissus in 269, earning himself the nickname "Gothicus." While preparing to campaign in the east, however, he died suddenly of the plague.

Fortunately for the survival of the empire, an equally capable ruler was found in his place, the Emperor Aurelian, who defeated the Goths in 270, then the Alemanni in 271. Between 272 and 273 he successfully waged war on Palmyra in the Middle East. The last of Rome's great emperors, Diocletian, reorganized the empire in 286. It was divided in two – east and west – with two rulers, although Diocletian retained overall authority over both. Diocletian retired in 305, and civil war broke out between his successors. Constantine bought this conflict to a temporary halt in 323 when he defeated his last rival at the First Battle of Adrianople. Constantine (280–337) founded a great new city – Constantinople (Byzantium) – to replace Rome as the capital of the whole empire, although he kept Diocletian's east–west division.

Diocletian and Constantine changed the Roman military system to meet the barbarian threat. Numbers were increased, and by the early fourth century the overall strength of the Roman Army had expanded to approximately 500,000 men – a massive increase. But one consequence of this increase was to incorporate increasing numbers of barbarian peoples into the army. Although the barbarians often fought loyally for Rome, the old Roman military system was fatally diluted, and by the middle of the century the distinctions between barbarian and Roman soldiers had decreased dramatically. Constantine divided his army into two separate elements. Roughly two-thirds of the army acted as frontier troops, holding the frontline against invaders. Behind them were the mobile units, which had greater numbers of cavalry and acted as a reserve to stem any breakthrough beyond the frontier regions.

The pressure from the Goths increased in intensity, and following on behind was an even greater threat: Attila the Hun. The Huns originated in central Asia and destroyed all in their path. In 451 Attila turned west and crossed the Rhine River at the head of 100,000 troops. His plundering was only halted by his defeat at Battle of Chalons by a combined Roman and Gothic force that had come together to face the common threat posed by the Huns. Attila changed tack by invading Italy the following year. However, an outbreak of plague caused him to withdraw, and in 453 he suffered a nosebleed and drowned in his own blood while asleep.

The defeat of Attila by Aetius, the last great Roman commander in the west, was also the last great victory of Roman arms in the region. By then, the Roman world, and the army, had changed utterly from that of the great days of the empire. Large communities of barbarians settled in the empire, obeying their own rather then Roman laws, and as the century progressed still more barbarians, from north and central Europe, crossed over the Rhine and Danube into Roman territory.

Left: The Emperor Octavian, who began an era that witnessed the growth of the Roman Empire. Some 500 years later, however, his successors proved incapable of preventing the empire being split in two, and the subsequent collapse of the western half.

Chinese Warfare

The development of armies and tactics in China owed much to the fighting that erupted frequently between the ethnic majority communities and the northern barbarian tribes who frequently invaded and ransacked their rich neighbor. An interesting evolution, mainly through the work of Sun Tzu, is that of a philosophy associated with warfare and an acknowledgment of broader politics and strategy.

By 600 BC the warfare waged in China had become characterized by highly ritualistic codes of behavior. The conduct of this warfare was controlled by warlords; dominant individuals who drove into battle on board their distinctive chariots, making Chinese war similar in many ways to the accounts drawn from Homer's description of the siege of Troy: the Chinese charioteers fought duels with a chosen enemy, invariably another noble of similar rank.

One story illustrates the ritual nature of Chinese warfare and tells of how two warriors exchanged bowfire. One fired an arrow and missed, but as he prepared to fire a second arrow his opponent objected that he had not had a chance to fire, and that this was unfair. The first warrior put down his bow and allowed his opponent to fire; the first warrior was killed. Armies also did not usually engage in surprise attacks, ambushes, or even wage war on a state whose ruler had recently died. Indeed, rival forces are known to have exchanged messengers to arrange the time and place of battle, and before combat took place the ground would be smoothed over so that the movement of chariots would not be impeded.

As the use of chariots became more widespread in China, a tactical system began to emerge based on the cheng, a sub-unit consisting of a chariot, which might contain three to five soldiers (two of them archers), and about 20 spear-armed foot soldiers. The chariot would act as the cutting edge of the unit, while the infantrymen would protect the occupants of the chariot when surrounded by enemy troops.

The old military rituals that had previously defined warfare in China declined in the seventh century BC as a result of barbarian invasions from the north. Barbarian tribes attacked China during the eighth century BC and destroyed the imperial capital, Hao, in 771 BC. The ruling dynasty, the Chou, was forced to move the capital to Loyang. The lord of Ch'in, a state in northwest China, then fought off the barbarians, giving the emperor the protection he needed to get to Loyang. The emperor, in turn, granted part of his lands to the lord of Ch'in, and so reduced his own power in the face of powerful emerging Chinese warlords.

The Warring States

By 500 BC three important states had evolved in China: Ch'in, north of the Yellow River; Ch'u, an area between the Yangtze and the Yellow rivers; and Wu, controlling the coast between the mouth of the Yangtze and the Shantung peninsula. Between 519 and 506 BC Wu and Ch'u were engaged in a war that ended in Ch'u's destruction. Part of the reason for the success of Wu lay in organizational changes instigated by the Wu king, He Lu, which involved the full-scale recruitment of peasants to his forces – a new innovation.

He Lu's peasant army marked the beginning of a transformation in Chinese warfare. Peasant infantry replaced the aristocrats in their chariots as the troops who would decide the course of a battle. These foot soldiers were armed with long spears or crossbows – the first time such weapons had been used in warfare. Hu Lu's reforms instigated an era of incessant conflict, known as the Warring States Period.

There were seven main kingdoms involved: Wei, Ch'i, Ch'u, Yen, Ch'ao, Han, and Ch'in. Wei was the strongest but suffered major defeats in the middle of the

THE CH'IN ARMY

In 1974, archaeologists digging in Sian in west-central China discovered the tomb of the Ch'in emperor Shih Huang Ti. Inside the tomb was an entire life-size army made out of terra-cotta figures, presumably based on the soldiers of the emperor.

Unlike their counterparts in Europe and the Middle East, the Chinese gathered together archers and soldiers armed with spears in the same unit. They did not carry shields but wore armor made up of small bronze plates sewn to a quilted jacket. The Ch'in Army also had much better cavalry than most Chinese armies. Some may have been equipped with the crossbow, the preferred cavalry weapon (although the cavalry of the terra-cotta army were mostly equipped with spears).

The emperor filled the ranks of his army from among the peasant farmers of his realm. Any man between the ages of 17 and 60 owed service either as a soldier or a laborer. The soldiers received pay and were fed from stocks of rice kept in fortresses across the empire.

Left: Reconstruction of a Chinese chariot dating from around 220 BC. They were larger than those used in the Middle East, and were pulled by four rather than two horses. The Chinese continued to use chariots long after they had been abandoned elsewhere.

fourth century BC at Ma Ling (353 BC) and Guai Ling (341 BC). These pitched battles witnessed the demise of the old rituals of warfare in that in both encounters the Wei forces were ambushed by their enemies.

Wei's defeats allowed two other states to expand. Ch'u advanced along the Yangtze River to the coast; Ch'in similarly gained greater control over the Yellow River. Between 315 and 223 BC these two states began a long conflict to settle the question of who would dominate China. In the wars of this period, infantry made up the most important part of any army. Most infantrymen wore armor, but the best troops were lightly equipped, and were used to attack the flanks of an enemy army or were placed in reserve until committed to the key stage of the battle.

Chinese generals remained behind the frontline in a place where they could observe and direct the battle. From their position in the rear they signalled to their troops by means of drums or gongs. A drumbeat told an army to advance, while beating a gong was a signal to withdraw. Flags were also used to signal in which direction troops were to move.

The Art of War

Chinese tactical and strategic doctrines were strongly influenced by the writings of Sun Tzu, whose famous treatise on military theory, *The Art of War*, was probably produced as early as 500 BC. Sun Tzu's book – a series of maxims or precepts – dealt with the fundamentals of strategy, especially the art of command. It discussed the interrelation of politics with war, and taught that the true object of strategy was the fulfillment of the political objective and a secure peace, rather than the destruction of an enemy. Victory, believed Sun Tzu, must be achieved with the minimum cost in lives and material destruction.

During the Warring States Period cavalry also began to make an impact, while chariots were eventually relegated to the role of mobile command posts. Chinese cavalry fought in the manner of the nomads of central Asia they had encountered north of the Yellow River. Armed with composite bows, they did not engage directly with the enemy, but repeatedly closed and retreated from the enemy while firing their bows. Only when their archery had caused enough casualties to seriously weaken the enemy was any attempt made to engage in hand-to-hand combat.

By the middle of the third century BC Ch'in had become the dominant power in China. In 249 BC its king overthrew the Chou emperor, who by this time was little more than a figurehead. In 247 BC Ying Cheng, aged 13, became king of Ch'in. In 228 BC he launched a war to conquer China and took the name Shih Huang Ti – "First Autocratic Emperor." In 214 BC he colonized the area around Canton, the first time Chinese rule had reached that far south. He also began construction of earth fortifications along the empire's northern border. His successors would replace these with the stone wall known today as the Great Wall of China. When Shih Huang Ti died, his generals began fighting for the prize of inheriting this great empire. By 207 BC only two main contestants were left, Hsiang Yu and Liu Pang. Liu Pang triumphed at the Battle of Kai-hia in 202 BC, and founded the powerful Han dynasty.

Medieval Warfare
500–1500

Spanning some 1,000 years of conflict, from the fifth to the 15th century, the Middle Ages was a period in which the mounted warrior, armored or otherwise, dominated the battlefield. This was particularly true of the nomadic warrior societies from the Eurasian steppes and central Asia, who had a massive impact on settled societies as far apart as China, South Asia, the Middle East, and central Europe.

So far as the methods of warfare were concerned, there were differences but the constant was the importance of cavalry. In Europe, there was a great emphasis on the importance of fortifications, with siege warfare the key to many campaigns. In terms of technology, there were many innovations: the universal adoption of the stirrup, which gave horsemen much greater battlefield impact; in Europe at least the development of bigger breeds of horse; better missile weapons in the form of the crossbow and the longbow; better protective armor; and, toward the end of the period, the use of gunpowder weapons, both cannons and handguns.

Perhaps the most important military aspect of this era was the nature of the fighting men. In many areas, there was little or no distinction between civil and military society. This was most obvious in the armies of people such as the Mongols, but it was also true of much of the Middle East, Europe, south Asia (where warrior castes were of great importance), and Japan. The exception was China, except when it was under Mongol rule.

In Europe, for example, the feudal system was based around the ownership of land and the obligation of individuals to provide military service for the monarch. The king was the chief landowner, and would assign land to his nobles in return for their fealty, and so on down through the social order. Feudal societies were thus warrior societies, and this structure naturally led to almost institutionalized violence: near constant conflict, whether between monarchs, among nobles, or between ambitious nobles and their king.

Right: The Battle of Agincourt on October 25, 1415, was a triumph for English arms, and demonstrated the lethality of the longbow in the hands of skilled archers against both mounted and dismounted medieval knights advancing in dense formation.

The Byzantine Empire

The forces of Byzantium, or the Eastern Roman Empire, found themselves defending the remnants of Rome's territorial conquests from the assorted forces of the barbarian hordes in both east and west. The army and its leadership performed the task reasonably well for a number of centuries, but eventually the pressure from the fierce Turkic peoples proved too much and Constantinople and Asia Minor fell.

The Roman tradition did, however, carry on in the Byzantine, or Eastern, Empire, with its capital at Constantinople. While the western half of Rome's empire collapsed in the face of the barbarian invasions, the Eastern Empire reasserted itself as a military force in the eastern Mediterranean and Asia Minor, using combinations of infantry, cavalry, and bowmen to defeat less-sophisticated foes. In the fifth century the Byzantine Empire stretched from the Balkans in the west, across Asia Minor, and into the Middle East. It also included Egypt and parts of Libya. At its eastern edge lay the border with Byzantium's great rival, Persia.

Conflict between Rome and Persia had a long history, and Byzantium would continue it. In 502 the two states clashed in a series of wars that lasted intermittently for the next century. The fundamental reason was continuous Persian encroachment, although lesser causes included the religious differences between the Orthodox Christian Byzantines and the non-Christian Persians – and the quarrel over who was to pay for their joint defense against the incursions of the Huns to the north.

The First Persian War (524–532) was fought during the reign of Emperor Justinian I (483–565). Justinian launched the career of Belisarius (505–565), one of the most brilliant of Byzantine generals. In 530, heavily outnumbered, Belisarius defeated the Persians at the Battle of Dara. He tricked the 40,000-strong Persian Army into assaulting his foot soldiers, whom he deployed in trenches. As the Persians advanced toward the infantry, the Byzantine heavy cavalry advanced on both flanks,

before encircling and destroying the Persians. At the conclusion of the First Persian War, Justinian ambitiously decided to attempt to regain the old Western Empire from the barbarians, and chose Belisarius to lead the campaign.

The two men had an uneasy relationship, with Justinian being constantly jealous of the success of Belisarius and fearful that he might usurp him from the throne. But despite the fact that Justinian had him imprisoned for a time, Belisarius remained resolutely loyal to his master. The general struck first in North Africa, then ruled by the Vandals. They were a Germanic

Right: Constantinople – the heart of the Byzantine Empire. Its capture by the Ottoman Turks in 1453 marked the end of the 1,000-year-old empire.

FRANKISH KINGDOM
Danube River
Verona
Ravenna ✗ 538-539 ✗ Taginae 552
Viminacium ✗ 601
BLACK SEA
Rome ✗ Casilinum 536-538 554
Constantinople
Neapolis ✗ Monte Lacteria 536 553
Dara ✗ 530
Cordoba
VANDAL KINGDOM
Carthage ✗ 533
Sicily
Athens
Antioch
Tricameron ✗ 533 Ad Decimum 533
MEDITERRANEAN SEA
Alexandria
ARABIA

Early Byzantine Empire 526
✗ Battles
0 — 500 mi
0 — 800 km

Left: The strength of the Byzantine Empire lay in its disciplined heavy cavalry – the cataphracts. Both men and horses were trained to a high degree, and were capable of carrying out complex drills on the battlefield. As well as proficiency in the lance, cataphracts were adept in the use of their bows.

barbarian tribe that had migrated through northern Europe into France and then Spain, before crossing over to North Africa in the fifth century AD. A Byzantine fleet landed in Tunisia in September 533. Some 15,000 men then marched on the site of the ancient city of Carthage, now the Vandals' capital.

They met no resistance until they neared the city. At this point three forces commanded by the Vandal king, Gelimer, attacked the Byzantine invaders as they moved into a valley 10 miles (16 km) from Carthage, in what became known as the Battle of Ad Decimum. The timing was poor: instead of concentrating their forces, the Vandals struck in three separate waves, allowing Belisarius and his troops time to deal with each in turn. The Byzantine Army had Hun mercenary cavalry, much feared for their lightning attacks and devastating archery skills. After the engagement the Byzantines marched unopposed into the capital.

The Vandals made another attempt to expel the Byzantines but were soundly defeated at Tricameron in December. The Vandal kingdom in North Africa was crushed, but it was to take until 548 for the Byzantines to complete their conquest. Justinian recalled Belisarius almost immediately after Tricameron and sent him to invade Italy, then ruled by the Ostrogoths, another Germanic barbarian tribe. Belisarius began by invading Sicily in 535. He conquered the island easily, and then besieged the city of Neapolis (Naples) on the mainland.

After weeks of blockade, a soldier discovered a disused waterway leading into the city, which allowed Belisarius to smuggle a force under the city walls. A simultaneous attack by these troops and the besiegers outside ended in a Byzantine victory. Belisarius's forces then rampaged through the city, looting and killing.

Rome was Belisarius's next target. He arrived there in December 536 to find the city undefended; the

Ostrogoths had withdrawn to Ravenna, a port on the east coast, to rebuild their forces. The following March, the Ostrogoths returned and surrounded Rome. They cut off its water supply and instigated a siege of the city. The Ostrogoths lacked the necessary equipment to break down Rome's walls, but neither were the Byzantines strong enough to break out. The stalemate was eventually resolved when Byzantine reinforcements arrived and the Ostrogoths withdrew in 538.

Belisarius chased the Ostrogoths back to Ravenna, where he put the city under siege. Sensing imminent defeat, the Ostrogoths offered to make Belisarius their king if he turned against Constantinople. When he seemed to agree, the Ostrogoths opened the gates of

CATAPHRACT CAVALRY

The Byzantine cataphract – from the Greek word for "covered" – was equipped with full metal-scale armor, which extended to the horse as well as the rider. The Parthians had been the first army to make use of cataphracts, and their Roman opponents were sufficiently impressed to create heavy cavalry units of their own. The Byzantines later made the cataphracts the major strike force within their army. Mounted on a powerful warhorse, the Byzantine cataphract bristled with weapons, which included a bow, lance, sword, and even a dagger. Besides body armor he wore an iron helmet and carried a shield, the latter strapped to the arm so he could use both hands to control his horse. The main cataphract tactic depended on shock action – a ferocious charge that could crash through virtually any enemy.

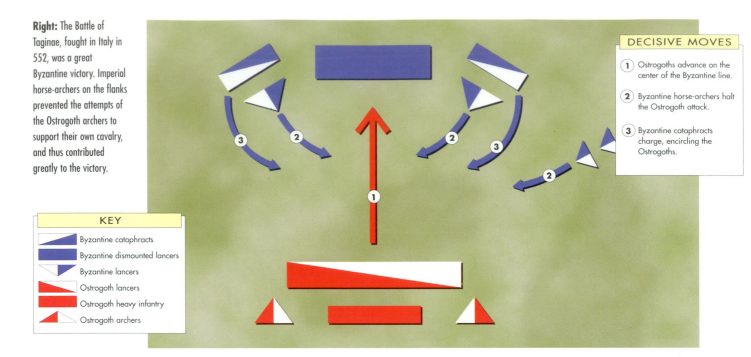

Right: The Battle of Taginae, fought in Italy in 552, was a great Byzantine victory. Imperial horse-archers on the flanks prevented the attempts of the Ostrogoth archers to support their own cavalry, and thus contributed greatly to the victory.

DECISIVE MOVES

1 Ostrogoths advance on the center of the Byzantine line.

2 Byzantine horse-archers halt the Ostrogoth attack.

3 Byzantine cataphracts charge, encircling the Ostrogoths.

KEY

Byzantine cataphracts
Byzantine dismounted lancers
Byzantine lancers
Ostrogoth lancers
Ostrogoth heavy infantry
Ostrogoth archers

Ravenna. Once inside, however, Belisarius captured the Ostrogoth leaders and led them back to Constantinople as his prisoners. Ever the man of the hour, Belisarius was allowed no rest and was ordered eastward to thwart another invasion by the Persians. The Ostrogoths, however, were not finished in Italy. As soon as Belisarius had left, they broke out of their remaining strongholds and took back most of the territory the Byzantines had captured; Belisarius returned in 544 but lacked the resources to dislodge them. Justinian sent another general, Narses, with a larger force, up to 35,000 men-strong. Narses was not a trained soldier; his background was that of an official at the Byzantine court (he was a eunuch), and yet he proved to be a fine general.

In June 552, the Byzantine Army in Italy came face to face with an Ostrogoth force in a narrow valley at Taginae. Narses arranged his men in a semicircle. In the center he placed foot soldiers armed with short spears and shields. To each flank he positioned cataphract armored cavalry and foot archers. Narses also deployed a group of archers high up on one side of the valley. As the 15,000 Ostrogoths came into range, his archers on the ridge opened fire. Then the cataphracts and foot archers on the valley floor joined in the slaughter, bringing the barbarian advance to a standstill. Narses then moved in for the kill. While the foot archers kept the Ostrogoths pinned down, the cataphracts charged the disorganized enemy. More than 6,000 Ostrogoths were killed – including their leader Totila. Narses then continued south and recaptured Rome. The Ostrogoths headed to Naples. Narses followed and inflicted a complete defeat at the Battle of Monte Lacteria in 553.

The commander's task was not over, however, as he faced a new threat in the form of a force of Franks driving south over the Alps. In the spring of 554 the Frankish and Byzantine forces met at Casilinum. Narses, outnumbered nearly two-to-one, took up a defensive position and, as he had done at Taginae, prepared to weather the storm before counterattacking. The plan

Left: The Byzantine commander Belisarius as an old man. He was a truly outstanding general of the early medieval period. Constantly mistreated by the Emperor Justinian, who was jealous of him, he proved a consistently loyal and effective commander.

Right: Monte Lacteria was a crushing victory over the Ostrogoths by the Byzantine commander Narses in 553. This one-sided affair resulted in the death of thousands of Ostrogoths and their leader, King Teias.

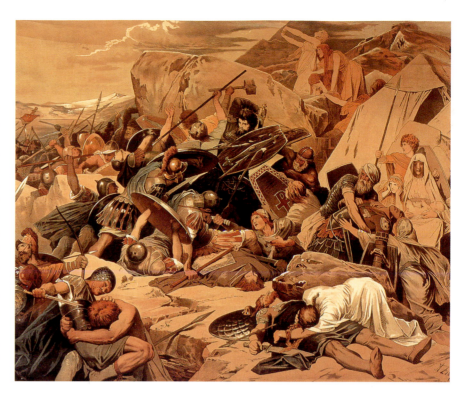

worked to order and the Franks were routed; Italy was once again part of the Byzantine Empire.

While Belisarius and Narses were securing Italy, other peoples were threatening the empire's borders elsewhere. Nomadic tribes were pouring out of Asia into Europe, forcing all in their path to move or be destroyed. The Bulgars and the Slavs found themselves in the way of these Asian nomads in about 530, and in order to escape them both peoples sought safety in the Balkan area of the Byzantine Empire. To halt these incursions, the Byzantines hired another group of barbarians, the Avars. However, the Avars, who were skilled horse-mounted archers, began to create a power-base of their own in the region. In 568 they drove the Lombard people out of their homelands along the Danube River, forcing them into Italy. The Lombards, in turn, conquered all the Byzantine territory in Italy except for a few areas in the south. Then the Avars began to strike at the Byzantine Empire in the Balkans. Finally, the Byzantine emperor Maurice took up arms and defeated the Avars at the Battle of Viminacium in 601.

Maurice was a skilled general: besides his success in halting the Avars in the Balkans, he had also brought the war with Persia to a successful conclusion in 591. But the discipline that he exerted over his forces led to mutiny in 602 – and his murder. Maurice and his successors established a durable military system that would last until the end of the 11th century. From the seventh century the empire was on the defensive, mainly because Arab armies, exporting the new religion of Islam by force, conquered much of the Middle East (except for Asia Minor, which remained under Byzantine control) and North Africa in a series of whirlwind campaigns that the Byzantines never managed to reverse, while there was constant pressure from peoples such as the Bulgars from the north. Constantinople itself was besieged by Arab forces in 717, but a great military leader, the emperor Leo III, "the Isaurian," beat back the invaders.

The skill of the Byzantine Army was the single most important factor in the continued survival of the empire, protecting its boundaries in the Balkans and Asia Minor from attack. The cornerstone of Byzantine military success was the close analysis of their own army and that of their enemy. Military manuals were published and distributed to senior commanders instructing them how best to conduct military operations. These included the *Strategicon of the Emperor Maurice* (written circa 590) and the *Tactica of Leo the Wise* (circa 900). These laid down the foundations of Byzantine strategy and tactics, which emphasized the minimum use of force to achieve the objective. Unlike the warriors of the barbarian west or Islam, the Byzantine commander did not crave glory, merely military efficiency.

The Byzantine military system was based on the *theme* or army-corps district, of which there were 46 throughout the empire. The *themes*, which in some ways were analogous to the feudal organization of western Europe, were combined military and civil organizations and came under the command of a *strategos* or general. Each *theme* was responsible for raising troops, who were given grants of land on completion of their service. The heavily armored cataphract was the mainstay of the army, although infantry played an important auxiliary role. There were two main types of foot soldier: light infantry armed with bows, and heavy infantry equipped with a thrusting spear and large shield.

At the Battle of Manzikert in 1071 in Asia Minor, Alp Arslan led an army of Seljuk Turks that defeated a Byzantine Army weakened by internal political squabbles. Manzikert was a body blow from which the empire never recovered, because the Turks occupied the prosperous lands of central Asia Minor where the major *themes* were located. Western crusading forces sacked and occupied Constantinople itself in 1204, and although a new Byzantine dynasty asserted itself, the empire was a shrunken enclave bypassed by Ottoman Turkish armies that moved into southeast Europe, until Sultan Mohammed II took the city in 1453.

The Islamic Empire

The role of cavalry – and the status of the horse and its rider – was of paramount importance in the religiously inspired territorial expansion of the Arab tribes, fuelled by a desire for booty combined with the new faith of Islam, and the tenet of *jihad* or holy war. And, as with preceding wars, mercenary forces were to the fore, in this instance the Turkic horsemen from farther north known as the Mamelukes.

It was not only Byzantium that felt the force of Islam. The founder of the new religion, Mohammed, died in 632, and almost immediately his converts began to conquer and convert. In 633, Muslim forces struck blows against both the Byzantine and Persian empires. Islamic armies swept east into Persian Mesopotamia and west into Byzantine Syria. The two empires were exhausted after years of war against each other, and the dynamic, religiously inspired Islamic armies were in a perfect position to exploit their weaknesses.

In Syria, the Muslims defeated the Byzantines at the Battle of the Yarmuk River (636). The Muslim victory was aided by a mutiny in the Byzantine Army before the battle. The Muslim forces went on to capture the region's major cities, including Jerusalem. They also attacked Egypt, capturing Alexandria in 642. In Mesopotamia, the Persians were defeated at the battles of the Qadasiya River and Jalula (637). By 650 Arab rule had been established over Persia.

The Muslims also extended their empire westward. They advanced into North Africa in 642, immediately after their invasion of Egypt, and soon made further gains that included the conquest of Libya. But when the Muslims then tried to push farther west along the North African coast they met fierce resistance from the Berber tribesmen.

It took until 705 for the Muslims to conquer the large area of North Africa that now consists of Tunisia,

Algeria, and Morocco. Six years later they invaded the Iberian peninsula, conquering much of Spain and bringing Islam to western Europe. By 715 the Muslim Empire extended from Spain in the west and eastward into central Asia. In 727 the Muslims went to war with the Khazars, a kingdom to the north of Persia, and succeeded in pushing the Khazar frontier back to the Caucasus region. While this struggle was taking place, Muslim armies in central Asia were fighting the Chinese and Turks. In 751 the Muslims defeated the Chinese at the Battle of the Talas River. This victory extended their empire to the borders of China itself.

The Power of the Arabs

The Arabs carried out this extraordinary sequence of conquests by the application of appropriate tactics to suit the geographical situation; initially this was of camelry in the deserts of Arabia, and then it was the use of cavalry elsewhere.

In terms of combining infantry and cavalry, the early Arabs were never the equal of the armies of Byzantium, but they learned from their enemies and during the seventh and eighth centuries they developed into the most successful soldiers in the Middle East. The fighting qualities of the Islamic armies lay not so much in equipment and organization as in superior morale: the product of religion, mobility, and the exceptional powers of endurance gained from hard living in the desert.

Right: The Islamic Empire at its height at the end of the eighth century. As well as possessing religious fanaticism, Muslim forces were aided in their conquests by the exhaustion and internal political and religious unrest within both the Persian and Byzantine empires.

Left: The prophet Mohammed (center) was the founder of the Islamic religion. His teachings promised a place in heaven for all those who died in holy wars against the infidel. In battle this meant Islamic forces displayed a complete disregard for death and personal danger. The result was a string of victories, though often achieved at an appalling cost in lives.

Their weapons were the bow, the scimitar sword, and the spear, and their chief tactic was the use of the mobility of light cavalry to strike at weak areas of an enemy, and to disorganize more ponderous forces with the arrow fire unleashed by light cavalrymen.

Despite their early successes, the forces of Islam also met setbacks: the Byzantines withstood a Muslim siege of Constantinople in 717–718, and at the Battle of Tours (or Poitiers) in 732, an army from the Frankish kingdoms under Charles Martel repelled a Muslim invasion of southwest France led by Abd-al-Rahman. The Muslim forces had already defeated the Duke of Aquitaine, but Martel formed his army into a human wall several men deep. The Franks traditionally fought on foot, with light battle axes and spears as their major weapons. As the infantry waited, the Muslim cavalry charged, only to be hurled back by the defenders. Hour

after hour the charges continued but the cavalry could find no way through. The turning point of the battle came with Abd-al-Rahman's death; the Arabs fell back in disarray and retired. The Frankish victory ended the threat to Christian Europe and marked the Pyrenees as the main frontier between the two groups of territories.

What accounted for this termination of activity above all else was a major dynastic split within the Muslim world that undermined the unity of Islam. In 750 a rebellion overthrew the Umayyad ruling house, which withdrew from the Syrian city of Damascus, the capital of the empire, to rule from Cordoba in southern Spain. A new dynasty – the Abbasids – established an opulent caliphate in Baghdad and took control of the majority of the empire. Although relatively minor conquests were still to be made, the great phase of Arab military expansion was over.

The Carolingian Empire

Charlemagne was the greatest ruler of the age. He broke the petty, warring kingdoms and brought a measure of peace to the region that had not existed since the time of the Romans. Despite the extent of their conquests, his Frankish forces fought few pitched battles. The secret of success lay in their mastery of siege warfare, the devastation of enemy lands, and the use of garrisons to control conquered peoples.

Throughout most of western Europe, the years from 500 to 700 are poorly chronicled. It was a period when the barbarian tribes settled in various areas – Franks in France, Visigoths in Spain, Angles and Saxons in England – mingling with, or dispossessing, local populations. Political and military organization was slight, and tactical or technological skill rudimentary. Courage more than intellect defined military success. Gradually, however, coherent political units developed. One of the first was in France, named after the Franks, where the Merovingian dynasty established some unity. During the seventh century, the rulers gradually lost their authority and power passed to independent lords who effectively ended up controlling the Frankish kingdom. One of the most important was Charles Martel, who assumed power in 714 at a time of civil war. The kingdom's regions – Austrasia, Neustria, Burgundy, and Aquitaine – were divided, although by 719 Martel had successfully brought all but the latter under his control.

Aquitaine was threatened by the expansion of Islam, with Muslims raiding over the Pyrenees from Spain. In 719 the capture of Narbonne provided the Muslims with a foothold in Frankish terrain. Military operations intensified until it seemed Aquitaine would fall. In 732, the Duke of Aquitaine turned for help to Charles Martel, who immediately rushed his army west to stem the Muslim advance. As Martel's army approached, the Muslims tried to retreat into Spain, but were slowed down by the quantities of plunder they had ransacked. The Franks caught up with them near the city of Tours, the Muslim force accepted battle, but once its leader had been killed it withdrew, plunderless, across the Pyrenees. Martel followed up his victory by driving the Muslims back into their forts along the Mediterranean coast.

Charles was succeeded as the Franks' most powerful lord by his son Pepin. In 751 Pepin overthrew the last Merovingian king, Childeric III, and had himself crowned in his place, thereby founding the dynasty of the Carolingians. Pepin brought Aquitaine back under his control, and recaptured the coast around Narbonne from the Arabs, who retreated back into Spain. When Pepin died in 768, his sons Carloman and Charles succeeded him as joint rulers. Carloman died soon after, but his brother, who became known as Charles the Great, or Charlemagne (747–814), continued to exercise power. He established an empire in which warfare and religion (he was a devout Christian) were both held in high regard. Much of his reign was taken up with warfare: he pursued a long-running series of campaigns against the mostly nomadic, pagan Saxons in what is now northern Germany, for example. The Saxons were old enemies of the Franks, and Charlemagne was determined to eliminate their presence and convert them. In 772 he launched the first of a series of campaigns to bring them to heel. The Saxons could not defeat Charlemagne's forces in open battle, but they refused to accept his authority and waged a form of guerrilla warfare. The fighting was prolonged and bitter, and it was not until 804 that Saxon resistance finally broke.

CHARLEMAGNE AND FEUDALISM

Charlemagne needed large armies to fight his campaigns, and he raised them with the help of his nobles. Each noble was responsible for providing a certain number of men when the king demanded military service. They were to be armed and equipped according to Charlemagne's commands, and they were also to bring enough food to keep them supplied on campaign for up to three months.

Initially, the nobles could call on any free man to fight for the king, where they served as infantry. But as Frankish armies turned into predominantly cavalry forces, the situation began to change. Cavalry equipment and warhorses were expensive, and only the richer people and their servants now went on campaign. Foot soldiers were used to garrison towns, and were sent to war only in times of great emergency. When the Vikings began to raid the empire after Charlemagne's death in 814, the nobles used these cavalry units to defend their lands. The units gradually turned into small semipermanent armies of knights and their personal followers. Weaker neighbors swore loyalty and paid taxes to these nobles in return for their protection. This system developed into feudalism, where the strong protected the weak in exchange for loyalty and services – a system that would underpin social, political, economic, and military life throughout the Middle Ages.

Left: Charles Martel leads his Franks to victory over the Muslims at the Battle of Tours in 732. This engagement was one of the decisive battles in history, as it halted the advance of the Islamic Empire north of the Pyrenees and ensured that Europe would remain Christian.

able to capture Barcelona from the Muslims. When the Muslims sued for peace in 811, the "march" extended as far as the Ebro River. Besides his successes against the Saxons, the Lombards, and the Muslims of Spain, Charlemagne subdued the Avars on the eastern borders of the Frankish kingdom and the Slavs in the Balkans. He also extended the kingdom deeper into southern Germany, and confronted the Byzantine Empire.

Charlemagne was a remarkable figure. His successful campaigns brought a measure of peace and security to the region that had not existed since the time of the Romans. Alongside a mastery of siege warfare and the setting up of garrisons to control conquered peoples, Charlemagne also introduced military reforms. These included defining the military obligations of his nobles, the organization of units, and the weapons and equipment to be carried by individual soldiers. He raised his armies by commanding people to serve in his forces for a set number of days, and also by requiring landowners to supply men and horses.

Whereas the army of Charles Martel had relied on its infantry to defeat the Muslims, Charlemagne's army employed cavalry to decide the battle. The growing prosperity of the Frankish kingdom had allowed it to raise a substantial number of mounted warriors, or knights, who became the backbone of the army. Although these troops were not particularly numerous, they were of high quality, equipped with a chain-mail shirt, helmet, shield, lance, sword, and axe. Little is known of Carolingian tactics on the battlefield, but they would seem to have been fairly elementary, relying on the formidable shock action of the charging cavalry arm.

Despite being at war with the Saxons for most of his reign, Charlemagne also managed to expand the Frankish Empire in other directions. In 772, the pope appealed for help against the Lombards who were threatening his territories around Rome and elsewhere in Italy. Charlemagne's father had once made a promise of military support to the pope in time of crisis, and that pledge was honored in 773 by Charlemagne marching his forces over the Alps. He besieged the Lombard capital of Pavia. In June 774 the Lombard king, Desiderius, surrendered his kingdom.

Four years later Charlemagne launched a long-running campaign against Muslim Spain. Although allied with Muslim rebels, Charlemagne's first expedition failed to make any headway. During the campaign of 778, Charlemagne's nephew Roland was killed in an ambush at the Pass of Roncesvalles by Basques. His heroic death became the stuff of legend, the basis for the medieval poem, *The Song of Roland*.

Conflict with the Muslims continued throughout the rest of the century. The Franks captured a number of towns south of the Pyrenees, and in 795 Charlemagne decided to turn the area into a buffer zone, or "march," between his kingdom and the Muslims – castles were built and towns fortified. In 801 Charlemagne was also

Right: The extent of Charlemagne's empire in the eighth century, which brought a degree of peace and stability to the region unknown since Roman times.

The Vikings

During the ninth and 10th centuries Europe was ravaged by organized raiders. In central and eastern Europe the threat came from the Magyars on horseback, in the Mediterranean from the Saracens, and in northern Europe from the Norsemen. Of all these mobile groups, motivated by their desire for plunder and love of violence, the pagan warrior-seamen of Scandinavia are the best known.

Charlemagne's empire virtually collapsed in the late ninth century, partly as a result of infighting between his descendants, but also because of new military threats. The first of these came from the Norsemen, or Vikings, from Scandinavia whose first raids began in the 790s, initially directed against coastal monasteries in the British Isles and mainland Europe. The pagan Norsemen were looking for valuables, and the rich, undefended monasteries were ideal targets. The raids continued into the ninth century and became more frequent.

The military advantage possessed by the Norsemen lay in their skilled seamanship and their hardiness as warriors. The longship was a supreme technical achievement; it could have as many as 30 pairs of oars, which were used for speed over short distances, or when there was insufficient wind to operate the simple square sail. Their ships gave them strategic mobility – they could strike where and when they liked, invariably catching their opponents by surprise.

Besides attacking coastal targets, the Vikings also raided inland on foot or on horseback. They took their longships up rivers deep into the interior, and even crossed over river systems by rolling their vessels overland on logs. In 834 they attacked the important port of Dorstadt, 50 miles (80 km) from the sea, along the Rhine River, returning for more plunder in each of the three following years. Vikings even traveled up the Seine River as far as Paris in 845, where they were bought off by the fearful inhabitants. Six years later a Viking band sailed up the Elbe River and plundered the rich trading city of Hamburg.

The suddenness with which the Vikings appeared added to a fearsome reputation built on their ferocity and their liking for torturing adversaries. Man for man, the hardened Viking was invariably superior to the levies recruited to oppose them. Only the best infantry could hope to defeat them in battle.

Raiding expeditions normally only took place in summer, but to save themselves from having to return home for the winter, the Vikings began to set up bases near the areas they raided. When the opposition became too strong in one area, or the local ruler paid "protection money," the Vikings would simply move on. In some instances, nobles hired groups of Viking warriors to help them fight off other marauding Viking bands.

In 865 raiding activity concentrated on England. That year a huge Viking force – called the Great Army – attacked eastern England from Denmark. The Vikings captured one fortified town after another, using them as bases from which to plunder the surrounding areas. By about 870 the Danes controlled much of the north and east of the country. They then invaded the southern

Left: The Vikings were essentially raiders who were interested in plunder. They were also skilled warriors whose discipline — based on loyalty to their immediate chieftain — made them very effective in combat and feared throughout much of Europe.

kingdom of Wessex, but here they came up against King Alfred the Great (849–899), who after initial disasters defeated the Vikings at the Battle of Edington in 878.

The Great Army returned to England in 892 and attacked Wessex again, but Alfred was ready. He had built an effective navy to challenge the Vikings at sea, and he had strengthened town defenses. Four years later the Great Army broke up. One group repeatedly raided northern France, but in 911 the Frankish monarch, Charles the Simple, gave a grant of land to the Viking leader, Rollo, in return for his loyalty. Rollo and his followers settled on a permanent basis, founding the Duchy of Normandy. The remainder of the Viking Great Army moved into northern and eastern England, then still under Danish rule, and continued to attack Wessex.

Early in the 10th century, King Edward, Alfred's son, campaigned to reconquer the Danelaw areas. By 954 the Anglo-Saxons had succeeded in uniting the country under the leadership of the royal house of Wessex. In the 980s, however, Viking raids resumed. A large force of 93 ships and perhaps 7,000 men landed in the east of the country and defeated an Anglo-Saxon army at the Battle of Maldon in 991. Three years later this force tried to take London; it accepted payment to leave, but kept returning for more plunder. In 1013 King Swein of Denmark invaded and added England to his North Sea kingdom, although his successor Canute would establish England's independence. By then, however, the Viking menace had receded to manageable proportions.

VIKING ARMIES

Viking raiders, armed with spears, swords, and axes, crossed the seas from Scandinavia in longships powered by sail or oars. Those from Norway attacked targets mainly in Ireland and Scotland; the Danish Vikings struck at England and northwestern Europe; and the Swedish Vikings raided Russia and the Ukraine, reaching as far as the Byzantine Empire. Early raiders traveled and fought on foot once they were ashore. However, faced with cavalry, the Vikings were quick to adapt, and to maintain speed and surprise they began to ride to their targets on horseback, although they preferred to fight dismounted.

The size of Viking armies remains conjectural. The early raids were probably by small forces, perhaps one or two ships carrying 60 men each. Over time, raiding forces banded together, and by the 850s thousands may have been taking part in raids along the coastline of Europe.

The Great Army that marauded through England and western Europe was a substantial force. However, it is likely that it consisted of only a few thousand men; it certainly never reached the staggering 40,000 Vikings reported by an eyewitness to the siege of Paris in 885.

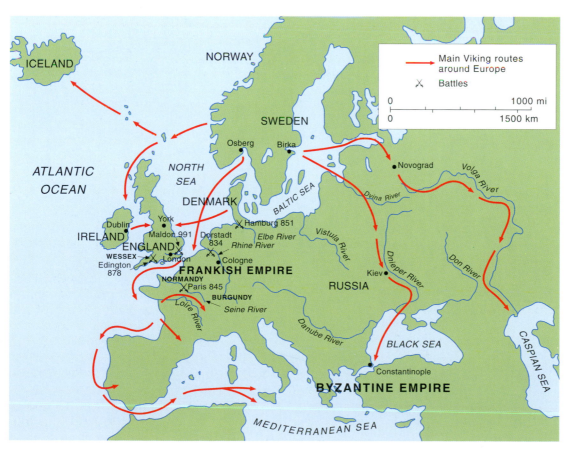

Left: Viking seamanship meant that their longships traveled far from Scandinavia in the ninth century. During the course of the century their longships increased in size, some being capable of carrying up to 200 men each.

Cavalry and Fortifications

The notion of defense was paramount in the development of armor and fortifications. Both things have done much to shape our image of medieval warfare, dominated as it is by the protectively armored feudal knight issuing forth from his moated castle, carried on horseback into the fray. And to carry the weight of such a knight, as well as its own armor, required a special breed of horse.

Given the weakness of European states early in the 10th century, it was a great achievement for western European armies to defeat outside invaders, and then go on to undertake a period of centuries of military expansion in Spain, eastern Europe, the Mediterranean, and the Middle East.

The key to this success lay in a combination of three elements. The first was the feudal organization of society discussed on page 40, which was not only able to provide sufficient troops to fight the invaders, but also provided a motive, later on, for expansion: the aristocracy of France and Germany led wars of conquest and crusades largely to take over new lands, and the men who followed them wanted to take and hold their own share of this land. The second element was the importance of the castle as a fortification in which a relatively small force could hold out against a larger one, or could dominate an unruly peasantry. (This is dealt with below.)

The third element was the development of the heavy cavalry that had become an important part of Charlemagne's army.

Among the raiding peoples, the Magyars were defeated first. These nomadic horsemen had moved west in the latter half of the ninth century, raiding then eventually settling in the Hungarian plain. Strategic mobility had enabled these warrior people, fighting as light cavalry armed with bows and spears, and moving rapidly before local forces could assemble against them, to attack relatively unhindered for long periods. But they owed their defeat to the superior fighting power of the mailed knights of Otto I, emperor of Germany. The armor of his knights enabled them to charge through the first volley of arrows from the Magyar horsemen at the Battle of the Lechfeld in 955, and once at close quarters these knights, mounted on big horses, using lances and swinging heavy swords, proved irresistible.

Right: The Crusader castle at Krak des Chevaliers. The lessons learned from the Byzantines completely changed western European concepts concerning fortifications. Not only did the Europeans copy Byzantine style, they also sited their castles in the most inaccessible places, making it extremely difficult for an attacker to reach and assault them.

There has been, and still is, considerable debate about the precise impact and importance of armored cavalrymen. There is no doubt that a charge by knights and men-at-arms could be very effective; there is equally no doubt that in a number of battles, from the ninth century onward, armored horsemen were thoroughly worsted by infantry carrying pikes or using efficient missile weapons such as the longbow. It is important to realize that for much of the period under discussion, the heavily armored horseman was at the center of a way of waging war, and of a way of organizing society. He would come to war attended by a larger or smaller group of retainers, and he himself would often require the use of a number of horses: three per cavalryman was typical in the 12th century.

Then again, much of the warfare of the medieval period was not on a large scale; big battles were relatively few. Mobile, well armored individuals were disproportionately effective against lightly armored inhabitants on the borders of Christendom. The kings of Scotland, for example, seem to have realized the importance of knights, in that from the early 12th century they began creating feudal lords in Scotland, offering knights grants of land in return for military service: the Bruces were one family invited in, and it was a Bruce who led the Scots forces that defeated the English knights of Edward II at Bannockburn in 1314.

The Attributes of the Medieval Knight

European medieval heavy cavalry had several advantages over similar troops of previous ages. The first, and most important, was the stirrup, which enabled an armored man to stay balanced in his saddle and to absorb the impact of hitting an adversary with his lance couched under his arm, or to stay on horseback while putting all his weight into slashing at an enemy with a sword or axe. During the medieval period there were other cavalry forces that enjoyed these technical advantages – the Byzantine cataphracts, for example – but there were few that also displayed the sometimes reckless courage of the medieval knight. This courage could be disastrous; but it could also bring victory against a foe that had not confronted it before.

A second advantage lay in the size and weight of their warhorses, the "destriers" that carried these horsemen, and which were sometimes armored themselves. These were large animals, deliberately created by selective breeding derived from a more sophisticated understanding of inherited characteristics that was a feature of the agricultural expansion of Europe during the period from 900 onward. This process was greatly accelerated by the development and spread of monasteries, in which such knowledge was carefully stored as the monks created their own prosperous farms. These big, heavy horses gave armored European soldiers an edge over more lightly mounted foes in any close-quarter combat.

If there is debate about the effectiveness of knights in warfare, there is general agreement about the other military dimension that coincided with the military expansion of western Europe during the early Middle Ages: the creation of the castle.

The Development of Castles

From late Roman times, fortifications had become more important, principally as a way of defending towns and cities from attacks by barbarian forces. However, from the ninth century a new set of fortifications began to become prevalent: castles. At first, most were little more than wooden towers that housed the local nobleman, who had been given a grant of land by his king. In order to ensure a good defensive position, the nobleman would often construct a huge mound (motte) of earth and erect the fortress on top of it. To make the castle more difficult to attack, a ditch would be dug around the base of the mound.

These castles were not designed to protect the local population directly; they were designed to shelter a relatively small group of fighting men. These fighting men could come out to threaten the rear or the communications of a larger army; they could also, in different circumstances, retreat into the castle if there was a rising of a conquered but unsubdued peasantry. Thus, castles were the physical base within which the

SIEGE WEAPONS

Siege weapons, first used by the Assyrians, were one of the standard methods of destroying a castle's defenses. The ballista was a huge arrow-firing crossbow, while the mangonel was a torsion-powered catapult with a vertical throwing arm. Soldiers wound back the mangonel's throwing arm and placed a stone ball in a cup at its end. The arm was released, it flew forward and launched the missile at the enemy. The trebuchet was a third kind of siege weapon. Like the mangonel it had a vertical throwing arm, but it worked by counterweight propulsion. The end of the trebuchet's throwing arm carried a sling that contained the missile; at the other end a huge weight acted as the balancing force. When the throwing arm was released, the weight dropped suddenly making the throwing arm fly forward, releasing the missile toward its target.

Although siege weapons usually threw stones to smash castle walls, they sometimes lobbed dead horses and bodies into besieged castles to spread disease among the defenders and lower their morale. They also lobbed burning bundles of cloth or wood in an attempt to set fire to a castle's wooden buildings or rafters.

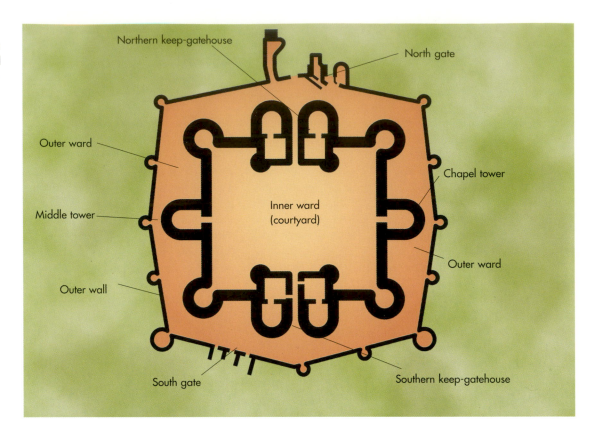

Right: The concentric design of Harlech castle in Wales. It has an outer and inner wall, with the keep-gatehouse built into the inner wall. It was also constructed on top of a high peak to create even more problems for an attacker.

Northern keep-gatehouse

North gate

Outer ward

Chapel tower

Middle tower

Inner ward (courtyard)

Outer ward

Outer wall

South gate

Southern keep-gatehouse

armored cavalrymen, the knights, and men-at-arms could feel secure, either from invasion or from the inhabitants of a land they had recently conquered.

As the castles slowly developed in size and complexity, nobles began to enclose land at the base of the mound by building fences and ditches. Between the mound and the fence was a safe area, or bailey, where the castle-dwellers lived. Motte and bailey castles became the standard pattern for fortifications throughout much of western Europe. These castles were quick and cheap to build; the Normans in England could construct one in a week. However, a noble needed a large supply of wood to build a timber castle, and his fortress could be destroyed by fire.

During the 12th century, nobles began to replace their wooden structures and build stone castles. For greater protection the castle builders often filled the ditch around the castle with water to create a moat. They also placed a drawbridge across the moat leading to the castle entrance. When the castle came under attack, the drawbridge was raised, forcing the enemy to find another way across the moat. The entrance to the castle itself was guarded by a well-protected gatehouse, or barbican. The gatehouse was often fitted with a portcullis: a heavy wooden or iron gate that could be lowered to block the doorway.

The main fortified element of the stone castle was a square (later round) tower, or keep, usually built on the motte. This building was the strongest and best-protected part of the entire system of fortification; the noble and his family and followers retreated to the keep

if the enemy captured the rest of the castle. Castles steadily became stronger during the course of the Middle Ages, although the greatest area of development came as a consequence of the Crusades. While they were in the Middle East, the Crusaders were profoundly influenced by Byzantine and Arab castle-building methods. The keeps of their castles in the Middle East were generally protected by two or three concentric rings of stone walls, which made them far stronger – if one wall was lost to the attackers, then the defenders simply retired to the next wall.

On their return to Europe, the Crusaders built concentric castles in their home countries. Typically perched on rocky crags, or surrounded by a wide defensive moat, these were among the most complex castles ever built. One of the most outstanding is Harlech castle, constructed in northern Wales during the 1280s by King Edward I, soon after he had conquered Wales. Harlech was built with an outer wall, behind which was an inner wall with four large, round towers situated at each corner, enabling defenders to fire down on anyone between the two walls. The castle's strong, well-defended keep-gatehouse was built into this inner wall. A particular feature of Harlech was the small garrison needed to man the castle walls, an important consideration for the English overlords who did not want to tie down large numbers of their troops in garrison duties.

To capture a well-built stone castle, the attackers had first of all to decide how to get into the fortification. One choice was to construct siege towers, which could be

ARMOR

During the period from 900 to 1450, there was a great technical development of armored protection in European armies. Early in the period, the main defensive equipment was a long leather garment on which were sewn iron rings (chain mail) or iron scales. The most common helmet covered the skull and had a nosepiece. In the 12th century, chain mail that was linked together rather than sewn onto a leather backing became common, and being more flexible could be worked into coverings for arms and legs, while a helmet that covered the entire head, and had eye slits and breathing holes, was developed. The next development was for solid plates of armor to be used, initially as breast and backplates but later over much of the body as segmented, jointed plates were developed.

By the mid-15th century, many high-ranking warriors wore entire coats of plate armor, and helmets had been given moveable visors. Armor had got stronger partly to deal with better missile weapons such as the crossbow and longbow, but although plate armor for battlefield use was not as heavy as is sometimes imagined, a man in his suit of armor could weigh up to 200 lbs (90 kilos) and there was undoubted restriction of mobility, especially when such men tried to fight dismounted.

In the Far East, in contrast, the development of armor took a different route, with chain mail or plates being attached to soft, padded garments that were light and helped absorb blows.

would have to rely on starvation through blockade. But a determined and well-stocked castle could hold out against even a well-equipped army for a long period, and this was a method that could take months if not years to come to fruition.

Attacking armies also had to be on their guard during a siege. The defenders could sally out to strike at the besiegers and burn their siege weapons. Because of such a danger, attacking armies sometimes built fences or simple walls between them and the castle as protection against the defenders. The Romans had been aware of such problems centuries in the past, and had developed elaborate techniques to deal with virtually any eventuality. The soldiers of the medieval period were simply following in their footsteps.

The arrival of effective gunpowder firearms in the 15th century transformed siege warfare. Large cannon, such as bombards, could smash through the strongest walls. High stone walls simply could not stand up to these weapons – the siege gun marked the end of the great medieval castle.

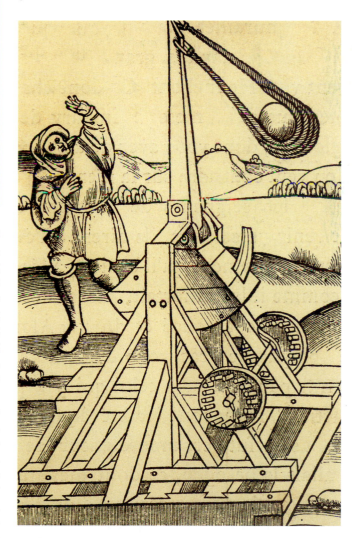

Above: A medieval wooden catapult in action. The rock in the sling (top right) was flung forward against an enemy wall by releasing a heavy counterweight.

pushed up to the walls, allowing a small force to cross over the battlements and overwhelm the defenders. Attackers could try to bring down a castle's walls using a variety of different techniques that had altered little since classical times. Rock-throwing weapons were employed to smash holes in the walls, while battering rams were used punch a way through. As the battering ram was very vulnerable to fire from defenders manning the castle walls, it was usually necessary to build a kind of armored shed over the ram that protected both the ram and its operators.

A particularly effective way of destroying castle walls was by mining, carried out by specially trained tunnelers called sappers. They dug beneath the castle walls and propped up the roofs of their tunnels with wooden supports. Once the tunnel was beneath the foundations, the supports were set on fire, and as they burned the roof of the tunnels caved in, bringing down the walls above and opening a gap in the castle's defenses. Moats and castles built on rocky outcrops obviously made any mining operation exceptionally difficult. If all other methods failed, then the attackers

The Normans

The rivalry over who should accede to the throne of England led to an invasion by the forces of William, Duke of Normandy, to confront his Anglo-Saxon rival, Harold Godwineson. The confrontation between their two forces would demonstrate the superiority of the mounted Norman knight – in combination with the archer – over the Anglo-Saxon infantry arrayed in a defensive shield wall.

If the armored horseman and castle were the physical signs of the expansion of western Christendom during the period from the mid-10th century onward, then there were other, less obvious aspects that were just as important: greed, ruthless ambition, and a willingness to take risks where the rewards were high enough. Those people who best embodied these were the Normans, descendants of the Vikings granted land in France.

The Normans were most successful in Italy and England. From the early 11th century onward, Norman knights undertook mercenary expeditions to southern Italy. Gradually, however, they began to acquire lands of their own and their growing power caused friction with Pope Leo IX, whose territories lay to the north. In 1053 the pope's forces confronted the Normans at Civitella in southern Italy. The Norman Army was composed of mounted knights and lined up in the standard medieval practice of three formations or "battles": center, left, and right. The right flank charged the pope's cavalry and scattered them. A body of Norman knights then headed for the rear of the pope's infantry, while the two remaining cavalry formations attacked the front. The pope's forces were trapped and defeated.

From their base in southern Italy, the Normans struck next at Sicily, then under Muslim Arab rule. In May 1061 Roger de Hauteville captured Messina. He

succeeded in transporting the cavalry's horses by boat and then began the long task of conquering all of Sicily. Meanwhile, his elder brother Robert Guiscard expelled the Byzantines from the rest of southern Italy. By 1068 only Bari on the Adriatic Sea remained under Byzantine control. Guiscard laid siege to it, but the defense stood resolute for almost three years before it eventually fell. In 1081 he crossed the Adriatic and besieged the coastal city of Durazzo (Durris in modern Albania). A Byzantine army was sent to relieve it, and in the ensuing battle the crack Byzantine infantry, the Varangian Guard (themselves of Viking origin), drove the Norman cavalry back into the sea. Then, with his army at the point of defeat, Guiscard rallied his wavering knights for one last effort that scattered the Byzantine forces.

One of the reasons for Norman success lay in their ability to use cavalry and archers in a well-coordinated manner. At Durazzo the archers played a vital role by pinning down the Varangian axemen, disorganizing their ranks with arrow fire, and giving the knights a chance to break through them. The Byzantines won back Durazzo in 1083, and two years later Guiscard died. But in Sicily Roger was victorious; by 1093 he had conquered the island, leaving it and southern Italy in Norman hands. Over the next century, Norman naval forces diminished the threat from Saracen pirates who had plagued the western Mediterranean for two centuries.

This success was matched in England. In January 1066 Edward the Confessor, king of England, died

Below: A scene from the Bayeux tapestry, which tells the story of the Norman invasion of England in 1066, and William's victory at the Battle of Hastings.

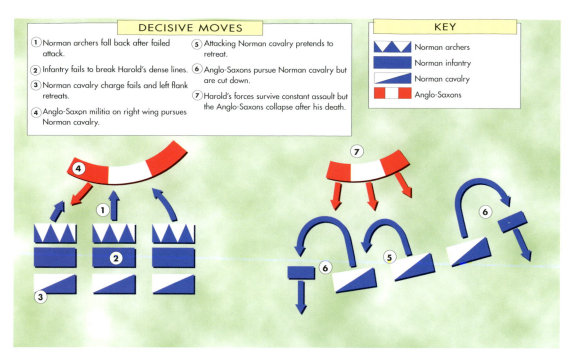

DECISIVE MOVES

① Norman archers fall back after failed attack.

② Infantry fails to break Harold's dense lines.

③ Norman cavalry charge fails and left flank retreats.

④ Anglo-Saxon militia on right wing pursues Norman cavalry.

⑤ Attacking Norman cavalry pretends to retreat.

⑥ Anglo-Saxons pursue Norman cavalry but are cut down.

⑦ Harold's forces survive constant assault but the Anglo-Saxons collapse after his death.

KEY

Norman archers

Norman infantry

Norman cavalry

Anglo-Saxons

Left: The Battle of Hastings was a hard-fought affair that lasted all day. By the evening, with King Harold dead, the Normans held the crest of Senlac Hill and were the victors. However, William was almost killed in the pursuit into the woods behind the ridge when he came up against a rearguard of Harold's housecarls (bodyguards).

childless and was succeeded by Harold Godwineson, an Anglo-Saxon nobleman. But Duke William of Normandy insisted that he was the rightful choice to be king. To enforce his claim, he prepared an army to invade and seize the crown.

William's main attacking force consisted of cavalry, made up of armored knights mounted on heavy warhorses. Small groups of Norman knights trained in tournaments; later they fought side-by-side on the battlefield. A knight's armor consisted of a coat of chain mail, helmet, and a long, kite-shaped shield. His weapons were a lance about eight feet (2.6 m) long and a flat sword used for slashing rather than stabbing. The main heavy cavalry tactic was the massed charge in which the knights rode directly at the enemy, their lances tucked in under their arms.

Fighting on horseback gave the knight his great advantage, enabling him to wear the armor protection and carry a shield impossibly heavy for an infantryman. When engaged in combat, the knight stood in his stirrups rather than being seated in his saddle, giving himself greater height and leverage. The war between William and Harold would show the superiority of the mounted Norman knight over the Anglo-Saxon infantry arrayed in a shield wall.

William landed on England's south coast on September 28, setting up base at Hastings. Meanwhile, Harold's army had been in the north dealing with an invasion from Norway. On October 13, William was told that Harold had marched from London with his army and was close-by. The following day the two forces met near Hastings. The Anglo-Saxon infantry took up position on Senlac Hill, and awaited the onslaught. Initially, William's archers, infantry, and cavalry made little impression against the Anglo-Saxon line. Harold's foot soldiers fought with determination. At one stage, a precipitate retreat by a body of Normans led some of the Anglo-Saxon Army to pursue them, and make themselves vulnerable to a cavalry charge. William then simulated a retreat by his cavalry, in the hope that further defenders would give chase down the hill. They did so, and the horsemen turned back and slaughtered them. In the meantime, Norman archers continued their attack. As evening approached, an arrow is supposed to have struck Harold in the face. Norman knights then broke through the Anglo-Saxon line and killed Harold. Resistance crumbled, and the remainder of Harold's army fled.

The Anglo-Saxons only surrendered London after William had raided and terrorized the people outside the city. On Christmas Day, 1066, William of Normandy was crowned King William I of England. Norman rule began.

Left: Robert Guiscard, who tried to carve out a Norman kingdom in southern Italy but died before he had done so.

The Crusades

The most well-known crusades were those in the eastern Mediterranean, where European forces set themselves to conquer the lands that are now Israel, Syria, and Lebanon, and to make Jerusalem a Christian city, but there were also Christian crusades in Spain and along the Baltic. And in the Middle East, the Crusaders often had to learn the hard way from their adversaries.

England and Sicily were not the only areas where the success of the armored knight and the castle were the physical aspects of the expansion of western Christendom. German knights steadily extended their influence eastwards along the Baltic littoral and into Poland and Bohemia; in Spain, there were centuries of warfare as the Christian kingdoms gradually conquered the Muslim states that had been set up in the seventh and eighth centuries. The wars in Spain were proclaimed

a holy crusade, and in 1212 an international crusading army gained a decisive victory over the Muslim Almohad dynasty at Las Navas de Tolosa.

The First Crusade was proclaimed by Pope Urban II in 1095. The aims of the First Crusade, as outlined by Urban, were to make it safe for pilgrims to visit Jerusalem, and to help the Byzantine Empire in its struggle against the forces of the Seljuk Turks, who had become dominant in the Middle East from the mid-11th

Right: The Christian states in the Middle East and the major battles and sieges of the Crusades from the 11th to the 13th centuries.

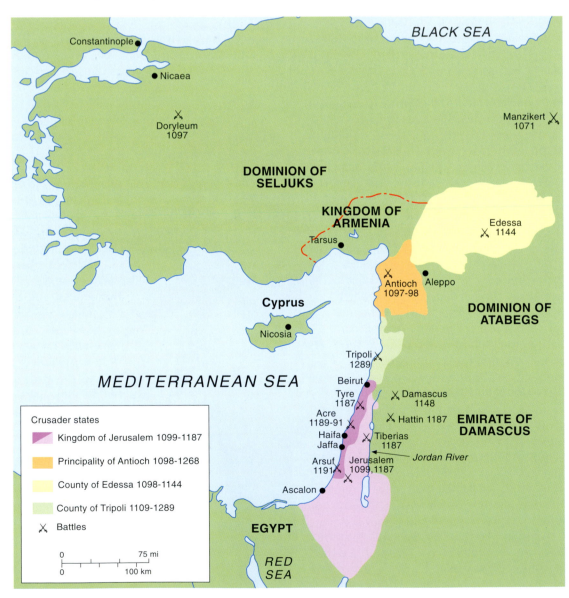

BLACK SEA

Constantinople

Nicaea

Doryleum
1097

Manzikert
1071

DOMINION OF
SELJUKS

KINGDOM OF
ARMENIA

Edessa
1144

Tarsus

Antioch
1097-98 Aleppo

DOMINION OF
ATABEGS

Cyprus

Nicosia

MEDITERRANEAN SEA

Tripoli
1289

Beirut

Tyre
1187

Damascus
1148

Acre
1189-91

Hattin 1187

EMIRATE OF
DAMASCUS

Haifa
Jaffa

Tiberias
1187

Arsuf
1191

Jerusalem
1099,1187

Jordan River

Ascalon

EGYPT

RED
SEA

Crusader states

- Kingdom of Jerusalem 1099-1187
- Principality of Antioch 1098-1268
- County of Edessa 1098-1144
- County of Tripoli 1109-1289
- ✗ Battles

0 ———— 75 mi
0 ———— 100 km

century. In fact, the enterprise became a war of conquest, and the crusades became a series of wars between two different religious and political systems, with very different ways of waging war. In tactical terms alone, the Seljuks relied on lightly armed cavalry, while the Crusading armies were dependent on armored heavy cavalry. In discussing the Crusades, it is important to bear in mind that although each side demonized the other as a monolith of evil, in fact both Christian and Muslim forces were never fully united.

During 1096, several separate Crusader armies from western Europe began to advance toward Constantinople. There, the Crusaders combined together under their chief leaders, Raymond of Toulouse, Godfrey of Bouillon, and Bohemond, the son of the Norman leader Robert Guiscard. They crossed into Seljuk territory in the spring of 1097. The Crusaders' first operation was against the city of Nicaea (Iznik in modern Turkey). Assisted by the Byzantine Army, the Crusaders captured the city, before marching south toward Syria.

On July 1 a Seljuk cavalry force attacked the Crusaders near Doryleum (Eskisehir). The Seljuks, armed with bows, refused to close with the slower but more powerful Crusader cavalry. The Seljuk archers inflicted heavy casualties amongst the Crusader horde – anything up to a 100,000 – many of whom were civilian pilgrims. To prevent their forces suffering further casualties, the Crusaders formed a defensive camp. A section of Crusader cavalry then attacked the Seljuks in the rear as the main force of knights charged from the front. The result was an expensive Crusader victory; they lost about 4,000 men compared with Seljuk losses of about 3,000, but the power of the Crusader cavalry charge had been demonstrated to the Seljuks. Almost four months after the Battle of Doryleum, the Crusaders' long march finally brought them to the gates of the city of Antioch, which was in Seljuk hands. Besides its sentimental value as one of the earliest Christian communities, Antioch was strategically important, situated astride the main trading routes from Asia Minor into Syria.

The Crusaders besieged Antioch for seven months until one of Bohemond's spies persuaded a Seljuk officer to let Crusader soldiers in through one of the city's towers. On June 3, 1098, the Crusaders poured into Antioch. Once inside the city, the Crusaders massacred the inhabitants, both Christian and Muslim.

No sooner had the Crusaders taken Antioch than a Seljuk army arrived outside the city and began to besiege them in turn. After the long Crusader siege there was no food left in Antioch, leaving the Crusaders weak with starvation. On June 28, inspired by the discovery of a holy relic in Antioch's cathedral, the Crusaders took a gamble and marched out of the city to do battle with the Seljuks. The Muslims attacked but were pushed back, and a Crusader counterattack drove off the Muslim force. In January 1099 the Crusaders pushed on toward Jerusalem. They followed the coast

most of the way, enabling an Italian and English fleet to keep them supplied. By June 7 the Crusaders had arrived outside the Holy City.

The Crusader force was far too small to surround Jerusalem and starve it into surrender, and the defenders had made sure that it was well stocked with supplies. The Crusader leaders decided to take the city by force, and built huge siege towers outside the northern and southern walls. On July 14 the Crusaders pushed their towers up against the walls as the defenders rained down rocks, arrows, and Greek fire (believed to have been a mixture of sulfur, naptha, and quicklime) that exploded and burst into flames when ignited. The troops on top of the towers were able to lower drawbridges onto the walls and fight their way into the city. Once inside, the Crusaders went on the rampage as they had at Antioch, slaughtering the city's Muslim and Jewish inhabitants.

The following month the Crusaders defeated an Egyptian army outside the city of Ascalon. With the help of European fleets, the Crusaders then besieged and captured the remaining coastal cities of the region, among them Beirut, Haifa, Tripoli, and Tyre. By 1124 the Crusaders controlled the seaboard of the eastern Mediterranean, with the exception of Ascalon, which remained under Egyptian control.

The Crusaders divided their conquests in the Middle East into four states, consisting of a major city and its

THE CROSSBOW

The crossbow was one of the more important Crusader infantry weapons, consisting of a short bow mounted crossways on a wooden stock. The high velocity of the crossbow enabled it to send a bolt (arrow) through virtually any armor of the time. The crossbow was, in fact, considered such a vicious weapon that in 1139 the papacy decreed that it must not be used against Christians, although they permitted its use against Muslims. Despite the papal injunction, crossbows were extensively used in all parts of Christendom.

Loading a crossbow was a slow operation, however, and even experienced soldiers could rarely exceed one or two bolts per minute. To load, the archer required the aid of a hook carried on his belt. Pointing the weapon toward the ground and anchoring it there with his foot, he crouched down and slipped the hook over the bowstring. The archer then slowly stood up, hauling the string with him as he rose until he could pull it over a catch known as a nut. To operate the weapon, the archer pressed a trigger on the underside of the stock, releasing the string and sending the bolt toward its target.

surrounding area. The states comprised Jerusalem, Antioch, Tripoli, and Edessa (which lay to the northeast of the main Crusader strongholds). In theory, Jerusalem exercised control over the other three states, but in practice Antioch, Tripoli, and Edessa jealously preserved their independence from any central authority. To defend their states against the constant Islamic threat, the Crusader rulers had the added benefit of being able to draw upon the newly appointed Military Orders of the Templars and the Hospitalers: religious orders composed of warrior-monks who pledged their lives to defend the Holy Land against the infidel. These orders were mirrored in other orders that were later formed in Europe – such as the Teutonic Knights in Prussia. These orders maintained a powerful morale and were efficiently run. However, within a feudal military world they held disadvantages: the dominance of celibate monks within the forces of the kingdom of Jerusalem contributed to the difficulties of keeping up the birth rate.

In 1127 a new Seljuk leader, Zengi, moved against the Latin kingdoms, and in 1144 he recaptured the city of Edessa. When this news reached Europe, religious leaders called for a new Crusade to retake the city. King Louis VII of France and Emperor Conrad III of Germany led this new force, which arrived in the Middle East in 1148. Eager for plunder, Louis and Conrad persuaded King Baldwin III of Jerusalem to attack the city of Damascus, an ally of the Crusaders. The operation was a disaster for the Christians and ended the Second Crusade almost as soon as it had begun.

Saladin's Wars against the Crusaders

The Seljuks, now commanded by Zengi's son, Nur el-Din, continued to attack the Crusader states. In 1163, the focus of attention in the Middle East turned to unrest in Egypt with both Seljuks and Crusaders becoming involved in attempts to take over the country. A Seljuk general called Shirkuh eventually became chief minister of Egypt but died soon after. He was replaced by his nephew, Saladin (1137–93), who was to prove an outstanding leader of the Seljuks. Saladin had taken complete control in Egypt by 1171. When Nur el-Din died in 1174 Saladin seized power in the Seljuk Empire, sweeping aside all who challenged him and building up a power-base for future operations against the Christians. By 1187 Saladin felt sufficiently strong to declare a holy war against the Christians.

On July 1, Saladin's army – 30,000 strong – crossed the Jordan River and laid siege to Tiberias, a city in the kingdom of Jerusalem under the command of Count Raymond. On July 2, 1187, Saladin captured Tiberias; Raymond was absent at the time, but his wife was captured and honor demanded that the Crusaders go to her aid. The following day King Guy of Jerusalem led a Crusader army of about 20,000 men, including 1,200 knights, on a rescue mission. Saladin's army was waiting and repeatedly attacked the marching force during the day. That evening, tired and thirsty, the Crusaders camped near a well, only to find that it was dry. During the night Saladin's troops gave the Crusaders no respite. On the morning of the 4th, as Guy and his army tried to reach the springs at Hattin, the Muslims attacked in force. In the blistering heat Saladin succeeded in separating the Crusader cavalry from their infantry. Without one another's support the two Crusader arms were helpless. Saladin destroyed them both, winning a great victory which denuded the overall fighting strength of the Crusader kingdoms. Saladin's army consisted of both professional soldiers and forces drafted in for the campaign. Among the former were the elite units of Saladin's mounted bodyguard, who, like Saladin himself, were Kurds – rather than Seljuks or Arabs who formed the bulk of the Islamic Army. Another elite mounted group were the Mamelukes, Egyptian slaves who had been trained as soldiers since childhood. Besides these crack troops, thousands more horsemen were provided by local Muslim rulers. Saladin also employed infantry, chiefly spearmen and archers, of varying quality.

The Loss of Jerusalem

Saladin moved over to the offensive, and many of the coastal cities fell to his troops. At the beginning of October Saladin captured the great prize of Jerusalem. Tyre managed to hold out against Saladin, aided by reinforcements recently arrived from Europe by sea. In the summer of 1189 the Crusaders struck back against the Muslims, laying siege to the great and strategic port of Acre.

The loss of Jerusalem came as a profound shock to the Christian world and led to the Third Crusade, led by King Richard I (the Lionheart) of England and King Philip II of France. Philip's forces arrived near Acre in the spring of 1191. Richard landed in June, having conquered the island of Cyprus to act as a base for Crusader operations in the Middle East. Richard took command of the Crusader Army, although his leadership was challenged by Philip. Disputes between the two kings hampered the effectiveness of the whole enterprise, with Philip eventually withdrawing from the Crusade. Meanwhile, Richard fought off an army that Saladin had sent to the aid of Acre and he used the Crusader fleet to cut off supply lines to the city from the sea. A little more than a month later, on July 12, Acre surrendered to the Crusaders.

Richard was a highly capable soldier, and as his title "Lionheart" suggested, a brave fighter too. Having heard that Saladin had captured Jaffa in 1192, he personally led a small fleet of boats to the city, jumped into the surf and waded ashore, fighting as he went. But he could also be ruthless. After the capture of Acre in the summer of 1191, for example, Richard massacred an estimated 3,000 Muslim prisoners, including a large number of women and children.

Richard's objective was to retake Jerusalem, and he led his forces on a long march down the Mediterranean coast, accompanied by a Crusader fleet. Saladin's troops attacked the Crusaders as they advanced south; they tried to provoke the knights into giving chase so that the Muslims could cut them off from the main force and destroy them when the knights' warhorses tired. Under strict orders from Richard, however, the otherwise headstrong Crusader knights did not respond. Realizing that his tactics were not working, Saladin launched a full-scale assault against the Crusaders.

On the morning of September 7, 1191, the Crusaders were marching toward Arsuf, when a Muslim force of perhaps 20,000 cavalry and infantry struck at the Hospitalers, who were bringing up the rear of Richard's army. The warrior-monks beat the Muslims off as best they could, but Richard insisted that his forces remain intact and not launch precipitate counterattacks. But unable to hold themselves back from the promise of eternal glory by killing the infidel, the Hospitalers charged. Richard swiftly changed his plans, and immediately ordered his knights to charge in support of the Hospitalers. A wall of cavalry bore down on the Muslims and forced them to withdraw. Saladin eventually pulled back all the way to Jerusalem. Although Richard got within sight of the holy city in 1192, he was unable to lay siege. The Muslim Army was too strong, and Saladin had destroyed all the crops in the area and poisoned the wells. In September, Richard reached an agreement with Saladin that allowed the Crusaders to remain on the coast of the Middle East and gave Christians the right to visit Jerusalem. Richard then sailed home; Saladin, already ill, died the following year.

The forces of the Fourth Crusade (1204) allowed themselves to be sidetracked by the lure of plunder and sacked the city of Constantinople. After thoroughly looting the city, the Crusaders carved out a "Latin empire" in the region, although this only lasted until 1261 when the Byzantine Empire re-established itself and ejected the Crusaders. Despite the cynical sack of Constantinople, the crusading impulse was still not dead. The Fifth Crusade (1217–22) attacked Muslim strongholds in Egypt, but achieved little. More successful was the Sixth Crusade (1228–29), which, under the leadership of the Holy Roman Emperor Frederick II, concluded a treaty with the sultan of Egypt to return Jerusalem to Christian control. In 1244, Jerusalem was again taken by Muslim forces, provoking the Seventh Crusade (1248–50), led by Louis IX of France. Captured in Egypt, Louis managed to escape and carry on the war in Palestine, although he was unable to capture Jerusalem. A final Eighth Crusade, again led by Louis IX, tried unsuccessfully to capture Tunis in 1270.

In 1250, a warrior caste, the Mamelukes, took over Egypt. They had learnt much from Mongol methods, and were very effective, flexible cavalrymen who used a variety of weapons with great skill. Under their first great leader, Baibars, they defeated the Mongols (somewhat fortunately) at Ain Jalut in Syria in 1260, and then gradually took over the remaining Crusader strongholds. The final Crusader citadel, Acre, was captured by them in 1291.

The Mongols and Warfare in the East

The rise of the Mongol Empire – affecting South Asia, China, the Middle East, and Europe – owed most to the ruthless leadership of Genghis Khan and the superbly disciplined and fast-riding horsemen available to him. He was a military leader of genius, in terms of tactics, strategy, logistics, training, and organization, but above all he understood how to get the best out of the men under his command.

The defeat of the Magyars had temporarily ended the pressure on Europe from the steppe peoples, but in the 13th century a new and potent threat emerged from the Mongol Empire of Genghis Khan (1167–1227), at its height the largest land empire in history.

Named Temujin, in 1206 he was accepted as Genghis Khan ("Great Leader") of the people of the Asian steppes. He was proud of his violent ambitions: "Happiness lies in conquering one's enemies, in driving them in front of oneself, in taking their property, in savoring their despair." He opened his great offensive by invading China, but disputes with the Islamic Khwarizm in 1217 forced Genghis to temporarily halt his campaign. Genghis responded by sacking several major Khwarizm

cities, including the fabled Samarkand. Mongol armies then raided across an enormous area: north India, the Middle East, and southern Russia. By 1224 the Mongols were able to turn their attention back to China, but in 1227 Genghis died and the invasion of China was put on hold. Genghis's son, Ogatai, was chosen to succeed him.

Ogatai had ambitious plans for expansion. However, he looked not to China but westward toward Europe. In the winter of 1237, armies commanded by his nephews Batu and Mangu and the great general Subotai advanced west into Russia and the Ukraine. By early 1241 they had overrun the whole of Russia and the Ukraine. The Mongols then moved into Poland and Hungary.

The European reaction was slow and piecemeal.

Right: The extent of the Mongol Empire was staggering, and is testimony to both their prowess on the battlefield and their expertise in the fields of logistics and administration.

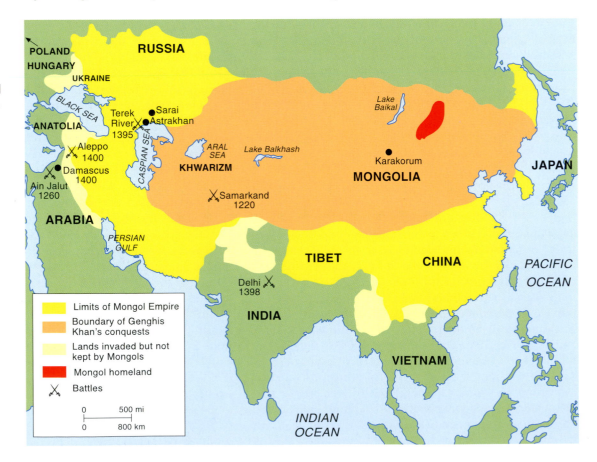

WARRIOR SOCIETIES

A feature of the Middle Ages was the importance of social groups totally dedicated to war. Sometimes, this could be an entire society, like the Mongols. But sometimes it could be a group within a society. This occurred worldwide: from the Samurai in Japan to the Mamelukes who ruled Egypt from 1250. In Europe, the armored cavalryman became an exclusive social institution also. In the mid-11th century (at the time of the Battle of Hastings, for example) the Roman word *miles* merely described a cavalryman protected by a mail coat. These cavalrymen needed land to support themselves: in England, a knight's fief – the land that he controlled – was six to seven square miles (1,550–1,800 hectares) in size, while in Normandy in 1172 it was about five square miles (1,300 hectares). However, by this time, the need for the mounted cavalryman to control this amount of land had turned him into more than just a soldier: he was a knight, with a social status and was supposed to live his life according to the code of chivalry. One of the problems that historians of the medieval period have to deal with is how the description of armored cavalry means different things at different times, especially when rather vague Latin terms like *miles* are used. The distinction between a knight and a sergeant or a man-at-arms is often hard to follow – especially when payments for military service as well as feudal obligations are involved.

Ogatai's grandson, Kaidu, defeated Henry of Silesia at Liegnitz in Poland, while Subotai smashed a Hungarian force at the Sajo River. The Europeans seemed at the Mongols' mercy, but the sudden death of Ogatai came to their rescue. In keeping with Mongol custom, Ogatai's family and his armies returned to Mongolia to choose a successor. The campaign in Europe was suspended.

Despite the withdrawal from Europe, the Mongol Empire continued to expand under Ogatai's successors. In 1243 the Mongols defeated the Seljuks, and pushed deep into Asia Minor. During the reign of Mangu (Ogatai's successor), they initiated campaigns against Vietnam. One of the consequences of the expansion of the empire, however, had been the loss of central unity. It came to be divided into four smaller sub-empires or khanates. The Khanate of the Golden Horde included northwestern Asia and Russia. The Jagatai Khanate consisted of much of central Asia. Persia and southwest Asia were known as the Il-Khanate. The region around the capital, Karakorum, remained the empire of the great khan, who nominally controlled the other three khanates.

One last wave of conquest was initiated toward the end of the 14th century. It was the work of one of the most ruthless Mongol leaders, Tamerlane, or Timur the Lame (1336–1405; actually probably a Tartar rather than a Mongol). Tamerlane's base was Samarkand in the Jagatai Khanate, and in 1369 he overthrew the Jagatain khan and then conquered the Il-Khanate. He set his sights on the Golden Horde and defeated its khan, Toktamish, at the Battle of the Terek River in 1395, before destroying the cities of Astrakhan and Sarai. His next target was India. He attacked in 1398 and took Delhi. He then turned westward and led his army into Syria and Anatolia, again inflicting terror on all who opposed him. Tamerlane died in 1405, and after his death the steppe tribesmen never posed as great a threat.

The Mongol armies consisted of fast-riding mounted troops. The individual horsemen were superbly trained and disciplined; but, unlike other armies of the time, they were tightly organized, in units of 10, then 100, then 1,000 and finally 10,000 men. The latter formation, known as the *touman*, was the basis of Mongol warfare, the equivalent of the modern division, able to fight on its own or to combine with other *toumans*. In an advance toward an enemy or through hostile country, for example, *toumans* would advance in parallel along a broad front, and the individual commanders would use their judgement to pull back or to attack when they came into contact with enemy forces.

Mongol commanders were able to control these dispersed, fast-moving formations with a series of mounted messengers and a code of visual signals from flags (in daylight) and flaming arrows at night. The Mongols understood the importance of rapid, controlled movement to confuse their enemies by attacking on the flanks or from the rear; their commanders usually aimed to surround their enemies and then overwhelm them with volleys of arrows and cavalry charges. The unarmored light cavalry, about 60 percent of the army, carried out reconnaissance and patrol work. They also bombarded the enemy with arrows and javelins before units of heavy cavalry, armed with lances, were sent in to finish off the disorganized enemy.

On both the strategic and tactical fronts, the Mongols showed an appreciation of the principles of speed, dispersion, and concentration such as no army had yet demonstrated. Equally impressive was their command of logistics. There were always spare horses, the vast majority mares, and horses' milk was a staple of the cavalrymen in many campaigns. It is also notable that Genghis Khan had a sound appreciation of when he risked overextending his forces: in 1222 after victory in the Punjab, for example, he pulled back to consolidate. Finally, in spite of their successes, the Mongols were prepared to learn from their enemies; from the Chin campaign they learned the techniques of siegecraft. At another level, they made use of foreign experts, such as Chinese doctors. And they also used engineers who had been captured from the enemy.

The Hundred Years War

In European warfare during the late Middle Ages, infantry became more important and gunpowder weapons were introduced. This change coincided with the development of more professional armies, some of which were effectively international mercenary forces. The growth of more powerful states, notably England and France, meant more money could be spent on creating armies, which meant long-term wars.

For 200 years after the Battle of Hastings, infantry had played a subordinate role on Europe's battlefields. At numerous engagements cavalry charges had proved decisive, but at Courtrai in 1302 Flemish pikemen defeated French knights, and at Bannockburn in 1314 Scottish pikemen worsted English cavalry. The pike was also to become a deadly weapon in the hands of Swiss infantry (see below). Two events, however, did not signal a decisive change in western European warfare. What did make a change was the development of potent missile weapons, and, importantly, their integration with mounted and dismounted armored men.

The crossbow had been the most potent missile weapon in Europe from the late 11th through the 12th and 13th centuries. King John of England selected the crossbowmen for execution when the garrison of Rochester surrendered to him in 1215. However, in the

13th century the English armies of Edward I began using the longbow, which they had discovered during their wars in Wales. It was made from a length of tapering wood – usually yew – about six feet (1.8 m) in length. A fearsome weapon, it had a greater range (sufficient to kill a man at 750 feet/230 m) than the crossbow and a more rapid rate of fire (between six and 12 arrows a minute as opposed to three for a crossbow). Special longbow arrow heads were developed to punch through armor or attack horses. The longbow was drawn back to the ear, and required not only physical strength but long training. For this reason, it did not spread quickly. At Falkirk in 1298, Scottish pikemen formations were destroyed by English longbow fire before mounted knights finished them off; again, at Halidon Hill in 1333 a Scots army was defeated by an English combination of archers and men-at-arms. At Bannockburn in 1314,

Right: At first the English had the better of the fighting during the Hundred Years War, but the French achieved ultimate victory in the 1450s, by which time they were making effective use of artillery against English strongholds.

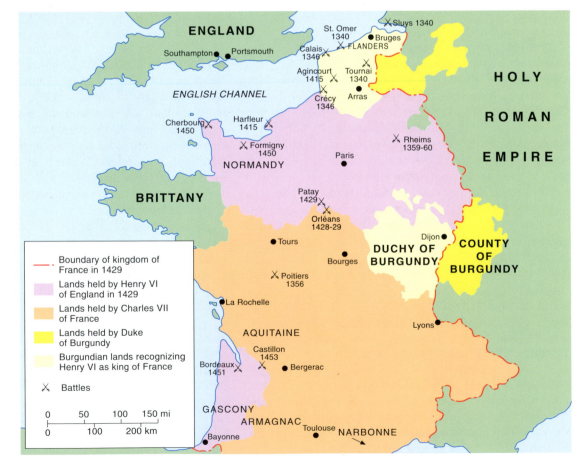

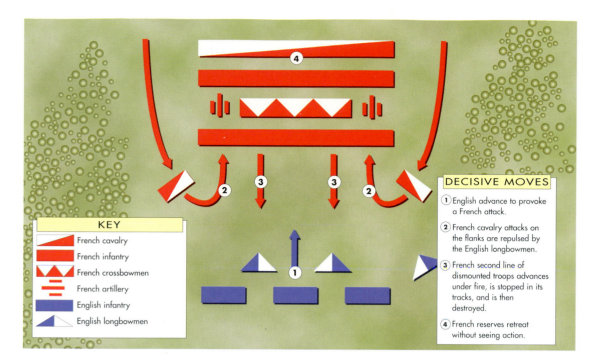

KEY

French cavalry	
French infantry	
French crossbowmen	
French artillery	
English infantry	
English longbowmen	

DECISIVE MOVES

1. English advance to provoke a French attack.
2. French cavalry attacks on the flanks are repulsed by the English longbowmen.
3. French second line of dismounted troops advances under fire, is stopped in its tracks, and is then destroyed.
4. French reserves retreat without seeing action.

Left: The English victory at Agincourt in 1415 once again demonstrated the vulnerability of densely packed armored cavalry formations to missile firepower. For the French, the defeat was especially galling because it was inflicted on them by soldiers drawn from the lower social classes.

incompetent leadership meant that longbowmen were not properly utilized by the English.

The most important series of wars in western Europe in the late Middle Ages was the Hundred Years War, ostensibly a dynastic quarrel between the crowns of England and France, but which developed its own momentum and drew in other disputes, such as that for the succession of the Duchy of Brittany and the allegiance of the rich cities of Flanders.

King Philip VI of France sparked the conflict by attempting to confiscate English lands in Gascony, an area of Aquitaine. Edward III of England could not afford to lose these wealthy possessions (which provided England with wine) and prepared for war. Edward escalated the dispute when he declared that according to the laws of inheritance it was he – via his mother – and not Philip who had the right to the French crown. In 1339 Edward led a raiding force across the English Channel, which plundered much of the northeast of France. When Philip arrived with the French Army, Edward, whose force was too small to give battle, withdrew and sailed home. It was an inconclusive end to the first campaign of the war, but it led to a hardening of attitudes between the two countries.

Edward planned to return to France, but first he had to eliminate the French fleet, which had raided the southern English coast in 1338 and 1339, and represented a threat to any future cross-Channel operations. In the summer of 1340, Edward discovered that Philip was gathering his fleet off the coast of Flanders. Edward seized his chance and sailed the English fleet across the Channel. The English took the French by surprise, and smashed their 200-ship force at Sluys on June 24. Edward then laid siege to St. Omer and Tournai. Unable to force either of the towns to

surrender, however, he made peace with Philip and sailed for England once again.

The peace did not last: in 1345 Edward sent a force of 2,500 troops to Gascony, following a French invasion of English-controlled territory. But this was only a stopgap measure, and in the following year Edward landed in Normandy with an army of about 20,000 men. Edward believed the presence of his troops in Normandy would force the French to send troops away from Gascony to oppose him in the north. Edward immediately began a campaign of devastation to provoke the French into attacking his forces. His men rode through the countryside looting and burning, and although the French remained in Gascony, Philip gathered troops from in and around Paris and prepared to march on the English. Outnumbered, Edward headed away from Normandy for Flanders, whose rebellious subjects had allied themselves with England. With Philip snapping at his heels, Edward's way northeast was slowed when he tried to find crossings over the Seine and Somme rivers. Realizing he could not outrun his pursuers, Edward turned to face the approaching French forces.

The English knew that they would be outnumbered in any major battle with the French, but they relied upon their superior battlefield tactics to offset the French numerical advantage. During August 26, the English army prepared for battle, setting up defensive positions on a ridge near the village of Crécy. Edward split his force into three divisions, each made up of knights, men-at-arms on foot, and archers. Edward protected his troops from cavalry attack by placing rows of sharpened wooden stakes in front of his infantry.

The French Army of about 60,000 caught up with Edward on the evening of 26th. The next morning, Philip sent his crossbowmen ahead to soften up the English line. These skilled soldiers were mercenaries from the Italian city of Genoa, but they came under such a torrent of English arrows that they were forced to retreat. As the crossbowmen turned back, the French cavalry, following up behind, rode over the top of them, trampling many underfoot. As a consequence, the French attack turned to chaos. As arrows continued to rain down on the French, wave after wave of their cavalry rushed headlong at the English defenses. Some French horsemen managed to reach the English lines, only to be stopped by Edward's dismounted knights and men-at-arms. Then the Englishmen came out from behind the sharpened stakes and killed the exhausted and confused French knights.

When the fighting ended, thousands of French troops, including 1,500 knights and nobles, lay dead on the battlefield. Crécy signaled the beginning of the end of the armored knight as the dominant medieval soldier. The battle won, Edward marched north and laid siege to the coastal town of Calais. He wanted a port on the French coast directly opposite England so that he could move troops in and out of France with minimum delay. After a year's blockade by land and sea, Calais surrendered.

The Black Prince

The Black Death, the bubonic plague that swept through western Europe in the 1340s, called a temporary halt to hostilities. Fighting resumed in 1355 when Edward organized a series of raids in northern and southwestern France. His son, Edward the Black Prince, directed operations in the southwest. Toward the end of the year the prince led a three-month expedition across much of southern France, campaigning from Bordeaux to Narbonne. Almost unopposed by French forces, his army stormed and burned a number of towns before returning to base with their plunder. The next summer the Black Prince set out on another raid, this time into central France. The French responded and caught up with the English forces near the town of Poitiers.

The Black Prince placed his 12,000-man army in a solid defensive position with a vineyard to the front, a small wood to the rear, and swampy ground on the left. His main defensive line consisted of dismounted knights and men-at-arms; archers lay hidden behind vines and hedges. The French attacked on the morning of September 19, 1356. First came a cavalry charge, which was promptly halted by the Black Prince's archers, who aimed at the enemy horses. The second French cavalry division then advanced on foot, but without their horses these armored troops were clumsy and slow. Even so, some reached the English lines and engaged the Black Prince's forces. After a fierce hand-to-hand struggle the English drove the French back, but not before both sides had suffered heavy losses.

The third French wave, seeing the bloody destruction ahead of them, withdrew from the battlefield, but the fourth division, commanded by the French king, John II, marched into the attack. Instead of waiting for the French to arrive, the Black Prince ordered his troops to charge. At the same time he sent a cavalry force around the outside of the advancing French to strike them in the flank and rear. The French were caught between the frontal assault and the flank attack and soundly defeated. About 3,000 French troops died at Poitiers, and many others were taken prisoner, among them King John.

Edward III still had ambitions to be crowned king of France, but when his winter campaign of 1359–60 failed to take the important French city of Rheims he renounced his claim to the French throne. In the peace talks that followed, the French agreed to grant Edward large areas of southwest France, not as a subject of the king of France but as its sole overlord. The French also agreed to hand over a large ransom in return for their captive king, although John died before he could be released by the English.

Nature of the War

England and France were now officially at peace, but the French continued to suffer from mercenaries and other brigands who roamed the countryside, terrorizing and robbing the population at will. The great set-piece battles, such as Crécy and Poitiers, were not, in fact, typical of the war as a whole; small skirmishes and raiding parties were more characteristic, attracting soldiers and adventurers from much of Europe, adding to the misery and devastation caused by the Black Death.

In 1368, the nobles of Gascony rebelled against their English overlords and the heavy taxes they exacted from them. When the French king, Charles V, sided with the rebels, Edward III claimed the throne of France once again and the English invaded northern France. They tried their old tactic of looting the countryside in an attempt to provoke the French into a battle, but the French adopted a new approach to foil the English plans. Under the orders of Bertrand du Guesclin, Charles V's new and capable commander, the French shut themselves in castles and fortified towns. The English were left to roam an increasingly devastated countryside, with few opportunities for plunder. Meanwhile, French troops shadowed the English wherever they went, harassing them in small actions but refusing to engage in full-scale battles.

The English were also losing their hold on their territories in southwest France, as French troops besieged and captured a succession of key positions and towns. By the time of Edward's death in 1377, the English possessed little more than they had at the beginning of the war in 1337. In 1396, France and England signed a 30-year truce that they hoped would bring the war to a permanent conclusion.

The peace lasted until 1415, when Henry V, the newly crowned king of England, broke the terms of the treaty

Left: Joan of Arc leads the French to victory over the English during the relief of Orléans in 1429. Even after her execution in 1431, her name continued to inspire the French, while English morale fell due to the fear that they had killed a saint.

and invaded France. Henry, a dynamic and vigorous monarch, was determined to regain England's former possessions. He struck while the French were engaged in hostilities against the Duke of Burgundy, with whom Henry had made an alliance. Henry landed in Normandy in August, and laid siege to the town of Harfleur, which surrendered the following month. The English then set off on a 120-mile (192-km) march across northern France to the English possession of Calais. In order to reach Calais, Henry had to cross the Somme River but he struggled to find a crossing. The English eventually succeeded in getting across the river, but only to run into the French Army near Agincourt.

On October 25, a short distance from the French, Henry stopped and took up a defensive position. He placed dismounted knights and men-at-arms in the center and his archers on the left and right. Sharpened wooden stakes were placed in front of his line to prevent mounted French knights from getting to close quarters.

The French launched a cavalry charge, and the English archers shot the French horsemen down. The next wave of French knights came forward on foot, through a confined, ploughed field. The slow-moving French were so tightly packed together they could hardly move their arms. Eventually they clashed with the English defensive line. But as they did so, unarmored English archers began swarming around the clumsy, metal-clad knights, striking at them with axes, knives, and swords. The second dismounted French wave also suffered badly, and the third wave came to a standstill, before Henry scattered the remaining French forces with a cavalry charge. His 6,000-strong army had beaten a French force five times its size. Some 5,000 French were killed, while the English lost little more than 100.

Agincourt confirmed once again the importance of a combination of arms: infantry on their own were not enough. Agincourt was won by the skillful coordination of infantry and cavalry – the infantry, on the defensive, blunted the French attacks, leaving the cavalry to take the offensive and mop up the remainder of the French Army.

By 1419 Henry controlled the whole of Normandy, and had set his sights on conquering northern France. In August 1422, however, Henry died, ending English hopes of a speedy end to the war with France. He was succeeded by his young son, Henry VI.

Just weeks after Henry V's death, the French king, Charles VI, also died. The Duke of Burgundy, an ally of the English and enemy of France, was eager to exploit the situation, and immediately declared Henry VI of England to be the new French king. Burgundy's enemies, meanwhile, supported Charles VI's son, who was crowned King Charles VII of France. The English resumed the offensive: by 1428 they had conquered all of northern France and planned to invade the south, Charles VII's stronghold. In October the English attacked the city of Orléans. The siege wore on until April 1429, when a French relief finally arrived.

The French force included Joan of Arc, a peasant girl who believed God had sent her to drive the English from France. Inspired by Joan, the French won. The following month the English were defeated again at Patay. Joan, however, was captured by England's Burgundian allies in 1430, and she was burned at the stake the next year. But England's hold on France was weakening, especially when the Anglo-Burgundian alliance collapsed in 1435.

Following a five-year truce (1444–49), the French attacked English-held territory in Normandy. The English strongholds in Normandy fell one by one. When Cherbourg surrendered in August 1450, English rule in northern France was finished. The English defeat at Castillon in July 1453 ended the Hundred Years War.

The Rise of the Ottoman Turks

In only a century or so the Ottoman Turks overthrew the Byzantine Empire, renamed its capital Istanbul, and proceeded to bring almost the whole of Greece and much of the Balkans firmly under their control. Possessing a swathe of Asia Minor, Anatolia, and points farther south, the Ottomans retained their hold on them with the most powerful naval and land forces in Europe and the Middle East.

After the defeat of the Seljuk Turks by the Mongols, another Turkish power had arisen in Asia Minor: the Ottomans. With Mameluke and Mongol power still dominant to the east of them, they looked west, and were able to take advantage of the enfeebled Byzantine Empire. By the mid-14th century they had conquered much of Asia Minor and held onto territories in Europe against a Hungarian army. In about 1370 they created a unique military institution – the Janissaries – a corps comprised of captured Christian children brought up to be soldiers. In 1389 at Kossovo they crushed a combined Christian–Balkan army, and by 1400 controlled much of the Balkan peninsula.

The final flourish of the Mongols under Tamerlane affected the Ottomans, but his victory at Ankara in Anatolia in 1402 brought only a temporary halt to their ambitions. From 1413 onward, Sultan Mehmed I began the process of bringing Anatolia and the Balkans back under Ottoman control. From 1421, Sultan Murad II continued his father's work. His first campaign was against the Venetians, who had extensive commercial and military interests in the eastern Mediterranean. In 1423 the tottering Byzantine Empire granted Venice control of the Greek city of Thessalonika. Murad considered this a challenge to his power, and in 1425 he initiated a five-year naval war. In the end Thessalonika fell to Murad's forces.

Murad turned his attention to Hungary. For years the Hungarians had fought Ottoman expansion into the Balkans, and in 1441 Murad crossed the Danube River and invaded Hungary. The Ottomans came up against the gifted Hungarian general John Hunyadi (1387–1456), who expelled them. In January 1443, as part of an attempt to stem the Muslim Ottoman tide sweeping into southeast Europe, Pope Eugenius IV called on all Christians to go to war to save the Balkans and Constantinople from the Ottoman threat. Hunyadi led his "crusaders" into Ottoman territory and that summer the Christians captured several Ottoman cities, while at the same time Murad's enemies in the east attacked his territories in Anatolia. Facing a war on two fronts, the sultan felt it prudent to make peace with his enemies.

The next year the Christians planned an invasion by a Hungarian land army supported by a Venetian fleet, which would link up with it at Varna on the Black Sea coast. The fleet failed to rendezvous, leaving the way clear for an Ottoman counterattack. On November 10, the Ottomans reached Varna and overwhelmed the Christians. Hunyadi escaped the slaughter, but there was no disguising the severity of the defeat. Although the Battle of Varna marked the end of the "Crusade," Hunyadi continued his mission and in 1448 he again invaded Ottoman lands. Murad marched 100,000 men to meet the 25,000-strong Hungarians. The Second Battle

Right: The extent of the Ottoman Empire in the latter part of the 15th century. The pinnacle of Ottoman success came in 1453, when Mehmed II captured Constantinople.

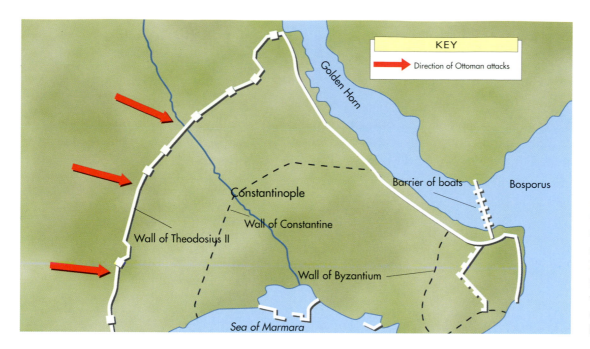

KEY

Direction of Ottoman attacks

Golden Horn

Barrier of boats

Bosporus

Constantinople

Wall of Constantine

Wall of Theodosius II

Wall of Byzantium

Sea of Marmara

Left: The city of Constantinople fell to the Ottoman Turks at the end of May 1453. They used 70 heavy cannon to batter their way through the walls, and plundered the city for three days after it had fallen.

of Kossovo was an Ottoman victory. The Turks were most impressed by the firearms used by the German infantry holding the center of the Christian line, and their interest in the potential army use of firearms grew.

GUNPOWDER WEAPONS

The first time guns were fired in a European battle occurred when Edward III's English Army used three small cannon against the French at the Battle of Crécy in 1346. They did not play much of a part in Edward's victory, but their use was a portent of things to come. Until the early 16th century armies rarely used gunpowder weapons in open warfare, as they were better suited to the conditions encountered in siege warfare. These siege weapons were usually heavy, difficult to move, inaccurate, and prone to explode – but they could break through castle walls.

By the beginning of the 15th century there were many different types of gun. Among them were culverins, which were fairly small, relatively light cannon, and bombards – big guns used for smashing city walls. At the siege of Constantinople in 1453, the Turks had a cannon that could hurl a large stone ball more than a mile (1.6 km).

Handguns also existed in the 1450s, although they did not become widely used until the next century. These primitive weapons consisted of a metal tube fitted to a wooden handhold. They were fired by applying a lighted match made from cord or rag, which was covered in saltpeter. They were difficult to load and slow to operate, and their inaccuracy was compounded by their unreliability.

Turkish armies were often larger than those of their opponents, their best troops consisting of cavalry. The majority were light, unarmored horsemen equipped with bows, lances, and swords, and while they could not stand up to Europe's heavy cavalry they were far more mobile and maneuverable. The elite of the Ottoman cavalry – the *spahis* – acted as the sultan's bodyguard and as shock troops when in battle. The *spahis* were also a recruiting nucleus for other cavalry, as each man was expected to raise and train from two to six other horsemen who would accompany him on campaign.

The Janissaries were the elite of the infantry, recruited mainly from the Balkans. They were sent to special training camps where they converted to the Muslim faith and underwent rigorous military training. The remainder of the infantry was a poorly trained, lightly equipped militia, and of limited use except for chasing a defeated enemy. But the vast numbers of infantry that the Turks were able to deploy on the battlefield was seen as an aid in weakening the morale of the enemy.

In 1451, Murad II died and was succeeded by his highly capable son Mohammed II. Before advancing further into the Balkans, Mohammed II decided to capture Constantinople, the last bastion of the now exhausted Byzantine Empire. The siege began in early April 1453. The 10,000 troops defending Constantinople fought off the first attacks and the Ottomans suffered severe losses. On May 29, Mohammed's cannon finally broke down sections of the outer city walls. A hand-to-hand battle followed, but the defenders had so few troops they had to leave parts of the inner walls unmanned. The Ottomans found one of these points and charged into the city. The defenders were slaughtered almost to a man, including Constantine. It marked the end of the Byzantine Empire.

Toward a Professional Army

In the wake of the Hundred Years War, one of Europe's best armies was to be found in the service of Charles of Burgundy. Containing many mercenary veterans, the force was highly trained and had good equipment. It met its match on the battlefield, however, in the form of the Swiss infantry, whose speed and power canceled out the Burgundian Army's advantage of being an all-arms force.

Although the English had been ejected from France at the close of the Hundred Years War, some nobles continued to reject the authority of the monarch and mercenary bands roamed the country. The French king restored order by forming *compagnies d'ordonnance*, which, commanded by loyal and reliable officers, would form the basis of a standing army in France.

In 1461 Charles VII died. His son, Louis XI, shared this desire to limit the nobles' power. Chief among the king's opponents was Charles the Bold (or Rash), Duke of Burgundy, who sought to establish a kingdom equal to that of France. He built up a professional army, many of them veterans of the Hundred Years War, including a proportion recruited from his former English ally.

By the early 1470s Burgundy had 8,000 troops. Armored horsemen and mounted bowmen accounted for half; the rest were infantry – a combination of

archers, handgunners, and pikemen. Charles divided his troops into self-contained companies, consisting of the various types of cavalry and infantry, who trained closely together to ensure cooperation on the battlefield.

The army of Burgundy was widely feared. In 1474, for example, Charles intervened in a dispute over the control of the German city of Neuss, whose inhabitants had rebelled against the archbishop of Cologne. Charles supported the archbishop and marched an army to Neuss and laid siege. Charles's artillery pounded the walls, but his troops could not break into the city.

The next year the German emperor, Frederick II, stepped into the quarrel and led an army to the city's rescue. Charles turned his army on Frederick's forces and opened fire with his artillery. Frederick withdrew and opened peace talks. Charles agreed to end the siege of Neuss in return for Frederick's help in the future.

Charles's interventions outside Burgundy alarmed the south German cities and the Austrian Hapsburgs, who allied themselves with the Swiss, whose infantry were the foremost soldiery of the day. Armed with pikes, halberds, and crossbows, they had asserted Swiss autonomy from the Austrian Hapsburgs during the 14th century, notably at the Battle of Sempach in 1386.

The Swiss carried a reputation as ferocious foes. In 1444 a French army slaughtered a small Swiss force of 1,500 men; but while being annihilated themselves the Swiss killed double that number of French. So, in November 1474, it came as no surprise when the Swiss repulsed a Burgundian incursion and advanced into Burgundian border lands. Charles responded in February in 1476, marching with an army of 15,000 men into the Swiss town of Granson and hanging all the Swiss troops he could find. By March 2, a Swiss force had arrived seeking revenge. Charles had archers, heavy cavalry, handgunners, and artillery, and he formed up outside Grandson, with Lake Neuchatel on his right. The Swiss infantry force of 18,000 men was divided into three tightly-packed columns equipped with pikes.

The speed of the Swiss advance caught the Burgundians by surprise, the complex enveloping action ordered by Charles became disorganized, and his center fell back in disarray. Charles's army then started to

Left: Three soldiers from the Burgundian Army of Charles the Bold, circa 1470. They were among the finest soldiers in Europe, but were bettered on numerous occasions by the Swiss.

THE HUSSITES

One of the most interesting military developments in the Middle Ages was in Bohemia, roughly what is now the Czech Republic. Here, political and religious conflict gave rise to a form of warfare based on using wagons equipped with gunpowder weapons. John Ziska developed this way of fighting as part of the Hussite religious reform movement during the period from 1419 to 1436. The wagons were able to move relatively quickly toward the battlefield, and presented a formidable defensive obstacle (especially when linked by chains) when on it. However, the defeat of the Hussites, developments in field artillery, and combinations of infantry and cavalry meant that Ziska's methods gained little following outside Bohemia.

retreat, but the Swiss marched on and cut down his men wherever they caught up with them. About 1,000 Burgundian troops were killed at Grandson, along with 200 Swiss. Charles refused to be deflected from his ambition to drive the Swiss from his lands, however.

In June 1476 he laid siege to the fortified position of Morat with an army of 20,000 men. Expecting the Swiss to send an army to its rescue, Charles had his men dig field fortifications, and he then placed his archers and artillery behind them and waited for the enemy. The Swiss army of 25,000 reached Morat on June 22. Due to bad weather and inadequate sentries, the Burgundians were unaware of the Swiss advance and the Swiss came upon the Burgundian lines while most of Charles's army was resting. The pikemen and halberdiers ploughed through the half-empty defenses, slaughtering all in their way. A substantial Burgundian force of 7,000 men were trapped and killed to a man.

The Swiss and their allies then took the offensive, entering Burgundian territory. Charles reorganized his forces and, on January 5, 1477, he met the Swiss outside Nancy. The Burgundians were caught between two Swiss forces and thrown back. Charles was killed as he tried to rally his troops, and his defeat and death put an end to any pretensions that Burgundy might develop into an state independent from France. Louis XI adroitly took most of the duke's lands for France.

Charles had possessed one of the most modern armies of the day, well trained and with good equipment, but he had not used it effectively on the battlefield. He had underestimated the speed and power of the Swiss infantry, who canceled out the Burgundian Army's advantage of being an all-arms force. The war with Burgundy established the Swiss as the most fearsome soldiers in Europe. Machiavelli wrote of them: "No troops were ever more expeditious on the march or in forming themselves for battle, because they were not

overloaded with armor." Their mobility allowed them to outmaneuver their opponents and force battle on them when they were unprepared. Some pikemen wore limited armor – steel cap and breastplate – but many preferred to fight with a leather jerkin or buff coat.

The Swiss fought in deep columns with long pikes and halberds, a bristling hedgehog similar to the phalanx of classical times. The halberd was not as long as the pike, but had a heavy steel head tapering to a point, to which was attached an axe blade and a secondary spike or hook used to catch the reins and pull down charging horses. At Nancy, it was a halberd that brought down Charles the Bold with a single blow that split his skull open. The pikemen and halberdiers were preceded into battle by light infantry who carried crossbows (and subsequently handguns), their role being to unsettle the enemy and draw fire away from the pike columns.

Despite the success of the Swiss in defending their homeland, they did not represent the future of warfare. They were conservative in their military thinking and did not absorb the changes that were taking place as the 16th century dawned. Above all, they failed to take into account the new role of firearms, especially artillery, although their reputation ensured that they would have a career as effective mercenaries. The future of military operations fell to those armies that had the support of an economically powerful state prepared to harness the resources of the nation. To be successful in warfare, an army had to combine the latest gunpowder technology with large and disciplined bodies of infantry and cavalry. Of these, the armies of the Ottoman Empire, France, and Spain would be in the forefront.

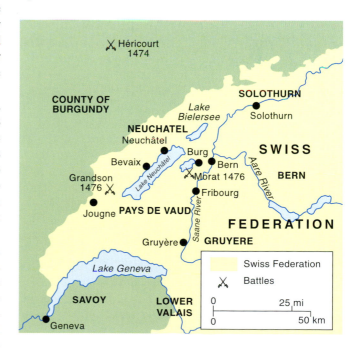

Above: The wars conducted by Charles the Bold were a disaster for the Burgundian Army. On numerous occasions it was defeated by more mobile and aggressive Swiss forces, and at Nancy in 1477 Charles was killed trying to rally his forces against the enemy.

Warfare in the Renaissance World
1494–1700

This period witnessed the rising importance of firearm-equipped infantry on the battlefield at the expense of cavalry. In general, armies began to develop into more professional, larger organizations, though logistics remained a fragile art. Developments in artillery were matched by improvements in fortification design, while at sea technological advances signaled the move away from hand-to-hand combat to long-range broadside engagements between fleets.

Warfare in the 16th and 17th centuries – sometimes called the Renaissance period – underwent a transformation so fundamental that it has justifiably been described as a military revolution. In Europe, this was an intensely bellicose period in which wars became an integral part of political life; over the two centuries in question, for example, Europe experienced only 10 years of peace, and Germany suffered an estimated population reduction of 30 percent due to conflict.

Technology was the guiding force behind this transformation. The development and diffusion of gunpowder weapons – both artillery and hand-held firearms – was a key factor, followed by a revolution in fortification design, which, in turn, moderated the influence of gunpowder weapons. Equally important too was the introduction of ocean-going vessels — armed with heavy cannon — which gave those states possessing modern navies a decisive advantage, both economically and militarily. The galleon, and later ship-of-the-line, provided genuine strategic mobility on a global scale, the first stage in Western domination of the world.

Apart from technological advance, the other great changes to the conduct of war were economic and political, and gave rise to the standing or permanent army, organized and led by professional soldiers in the service of the state.

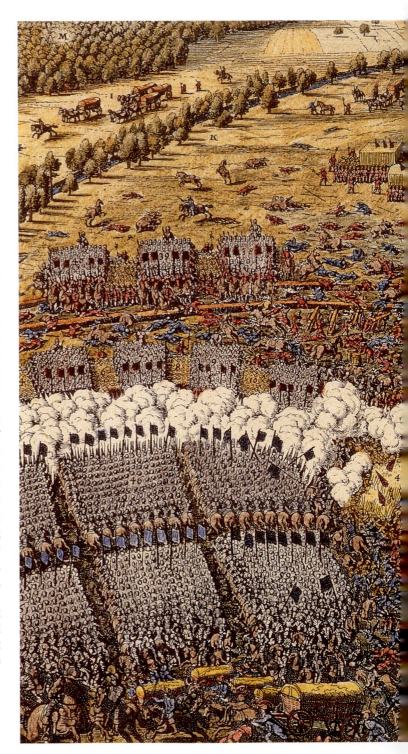

Right: The Battle of Lützen, November 16, 1632, was a victory for the Swedes over the Imperial Army. Triumph was bought at a heavy cost, however, as the Swedish king, Gustavus Adolphus, was killed, along with 12,000 Imperialists and 10,000 Swedes.

The Wars between France and Spain in Italy

In 1494 Charles VIII of France invaded Italy. His army was probably the finest and most professional in the world at that date. Gone were the days of mass feudal levies; instead, the French monarch marched with well-trained crossbowmen and professional Swiss mercenaries. But his well-served bronze cannon signaled the real change that warfare was undergoing at the end of the 15th century.

The first signs of the military revolution occurred in Italy, as part of a dynastic struggle for Italian territory and influence between France and Spain. At the end of the 15th century Italy was the richest region of Europe, its prosperity derived through agriculture, manufacture, finance, and trade. But Italy did not owe its wealth to political unity, being divided into many states usually ruled over by the government of a single city. Some of these states, like Milan or Naples, were large and relatively powerful. Others, like Venice and Florence, were merely rich.

Many of the Italian states, both large and small, sought the support of more powerful kingdoms outside Italy for help against their neighbors. And the prospect of rich economic reward only encouraged these kingdoms to interfere in Italian political affairs.

King Charles VIII of France (1470–98) claimed the throne of Naples, through a distant family connection, and in 1494 prepared to invade Italy to secure the Neapolitan kingdom. Leading an army of 25,000 men, including 8,000 Swiss mercenaries, Charles marched down through the "boot" of Italy and captured Naples. His force included large numbers of French crossbowmen, and its bronze cannon were mounted on wheeled carriages to give them sufficient speed to keep up with the army's march, and they were served by well-trained crews.

The family who had been ruling Naples in 1494 was related to the Spanish royal family, and when Charles took Naples, the Spanish helped form an anti-French alliance. Other European states – the Holy Roman Empire, the Papal States, Venice, and Milan – were fearful of French domination in Italy and joined the Spanish in the alliance called the Holy League. Faced with such a powerful force, Charles decided to march the bulk of his troops back to France in 1495. On his return journey, Charles encountered an alliance army of the Holy League at Fornovo in July.

The alliance army, led by Giovanni Gonzaga, was largely made up of *condottieri*: Italian

Left: Italy at the end of the 15th century was divided into a number of kingdoms, and was the site for a series of wars between France and Spain and their Italian allies.

mercenary bands that had dominated warfare in Italy for the previous two centuries. The *condottieri* were hired by a city or state for fixed periods, and when their term of service ended they might easily sign up with their former employer's enemy. The *condottieri* soldier did not fight to fulfil feudal obligations or for the honor of the state; he was a true mercenary who was prepared to sell his services to the highest bidder.

In Italy, the constant fighting between different *condottieri* bands had led to a reduction in the violence of warfare, so that rather than suffer heavy losses, the *condottieri* preferred to fight elaborate battles of maneuver. But the mercenaries of Switzerland and Germany worked to a different code, relying on their ferocity in battle to ensure regular and remunerative employment. And at Fornovo, the *condottieri* would come up against Swiss mercenaries and a French Army well supplied with artillery.

The Holy League alliance attempted to ambush the French in a narrow defile on July 6, but the French were ready for action. French artillery repulsed an alliance cavalry attack, before a general counterattack swept the *condottieri* from the battlefield. Rain had turned the ground into a slippery morass, which hampered the Italian cavalry – mounted knights – who had their throats slit or their heads split open as they lay helpless in their armor on the battlefield. The French had brutally exposed the military weakness of the Italian city states, and would continue to do so over the coming decades.

The invasion by Charles VIII was the first in a series of wars between France and Spain in Italy. In 1500, hostilities over the control of Naples resumed when the two nations proved unable to agree to divide the Neapolitan state between themselves.

In March 1502, a fleet of Spanish galleys landed an army at Taranto commanded by Gonzalo Fernandez de Cordoba (1453–1515), one of the finest generals of the age. He led a brilliant campaign that drove the French out of Naples. At the Battle of Cerignola on April 28, 1503, he deployed his firearm-equipped infantry behind a palisade, and their steady fire repulsed the attacking French and their Swiss mercenaries. It was the first battle in European history won solely by gunpowder weapons, and confirmed Spain as a major power in Europe.

On December 29, 1503, Cordoba planned a surprise crossing of the Garigliano River. His engineers used the cover of bad weather to secretly build a bridge across the swollen river. Spanish forces then swarmed across the bridge and stormed the enemy camp, throwing the French back in confusion and causing heavy casualties. In 1505 the new French king, Louis XII, duly gave up the French claim to Naples.

During the latter part of the 15th century, Spain had united under the dual monarchy of Ferdinand and Isabella and gained a vast empire in the New World – one that would generate great riches to finance military

GERMAN *LANDSKNECHTS*

The infantrymen of the permanent army built up by the Holy Roman Emperor Maximilian in the late 15th century were known as *landsknechts*, a name meaning "land knights" that came to be applied to all German mercenaries who copied the colorful uniforms of these troops.

The *landsknechts* considered themselves a special society of soldiers, and organized elaborate initiation ceremonies that emphasized loyalty to the *landsknecht* company. Their armament comprised halberds and pikes (shorter than those of the Swiss), and a short stabbing sword called a *Katzbalger*.

The *landsknechts* were usually excellent soldiers, certainly better than the poorly trained troops they typically faced on the field of battle. Only the Swiss and the Spanish fielded infantry units equal to those of the *landsknechts*. Indeed, battles between Swiss and *landsknechts* were particularly bitterly contested, as each side sought to prove their superiority over the other.

operations in Europe. The Spanish Army was one of the first in Europe to be organized by the state, although it was never quite a national army as chronic manpower shortages forced the Spanish to rely extensively on foreign contingents.

One of the reasons behind the organized character of the Spanish Army was that a large part of its manpower was raised by conscription. The 1494 Ordinance of Valladolid decreed that one in 12 men between the ages of 20 and 45 were liable for paid military service at home or abroad. The French had also tried this scheme, but it was the Spanish who made it work, creating a solid core of professional soldiers.

The Spanish infantry formed the backbone of the army, and were tough and well disciplined, but flexible enough to seize upon the opportunities offered by firearms and artillery. And in contrast to the practice current in most other armies, the infantry attracted men of noble birth. As the Duke of Alva wrote: "In our nation nothing is more important than to introduce gentlemen and men of substance into the infantry so that all is not left in the hands of laborers and lackeys."

The company of around 200 men, recruited and commanded by a captain, was the smallest unit within the army. Five companies would make up a *colunela* (column), which combined all the various infantry arms: pikemen, halberdiers, arquebusiers, and sword-and-buckler men. The *colunela* was commanded by a *cabo de colunela* (colonel), and was the prototype of the regiment or battalion. The Spanish military system was codified by King Ferdinand in 1505, and represented the

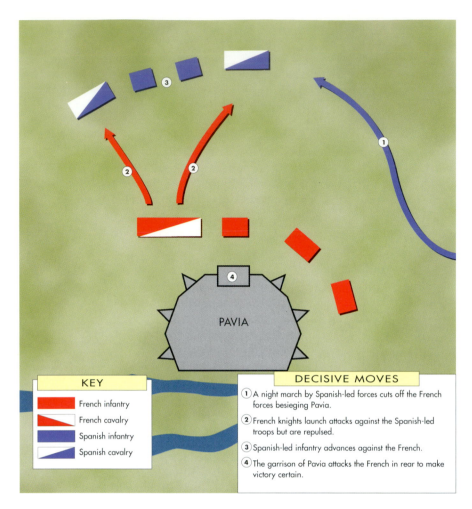

Left: The Battle of Pavia on February 24, 1525, witnessed the triumph of musket-armed infantry over mounted nobility. Ironically, the French cavalry charge prevented their own artillery from firing at the Spanish infantry.

KEY

■ (red)	French infantry
■ (red/white)	French cavalry
■ (blue)	Spanish infantry
■ (blue/white)	Spanish cavalry

DECISIVE MOVES

① A night march by Spanish-led forces cuts off the French forces besieging Pavia.

② French knights launch attacks against the Spanish-led troops but are repulsed.

③ Spanish-led infantry advances against the French.

④ The garrison of Pavia attacks the French in rear to make victory certain.

loading musket – its slow rate of fire – as infantry deployed in a series of ranks, the first firing together and then retreating to reload, while the next rank took their place, and so on. The result was a continuous hail of fire.

The introduction of volley fire resulted in several developments. Firstly, armies spread out into more linear deployments to maximize the effects of fire, and in the process maximized the size of the target for incoming missiles. Secondly, linear formations exposed more men to the rigors of face-to-face combat, thus requiring greater courage, proficiency, and discipline. Thirdly, there was a greater emphasis on the ability of tactical units to perform motions necessary for volley fire at speed and in unison. Therefore, troops had to practice more, and commanders were forced to divide their armies into smaller formations that were easier to handle and instruct. Thus, in Holland, companies were reduced from 250 men and 11 officers to 120 men with 12 officers, with the latter making extensive use of drill books. The Dutch model was to spread throughout Europe, though the irony was that this military reformation was unrealized in the Netherlands itself, as the Dutch Army rarely exposed itself to battles.

France and Spain went to war again in Italy in 1510, when Pope Julius II formed another Holy League alliance to thwart French designs on Italy. The battleground now shifted to northern Italy, where the armies of Louis XII had taken over Milan in 1499. In 1512 a French army invaded the Papal States and won a victory over a Spanish–Papal force at Ravenna on April 11. Much of the disciplined Spanish infantry made good their retreat, fending off the French cavalry by maintaining tight formations. This illustrated the ineffectiveness of cavalry against disciplined blocks of infantry. French success was short-lived, however, when at the Battle of Novarra on June 6, 1513, they were resoundingly defeated by a Swiss–Italian army, and forced to withdraw from Italy once again. Nevertheless, the battle did show the increasing lethality of artillery against dense infantry formations. Before it was overrun, the French artillery inflicted 700 casualties on the Swiss infantry in a three-minute period.

first serious attempt since Roman times to develop a coherent and regular military organization that would utilize all the various infantry arms.

By the 1530s, battlefield experience encouraged the Spanish to brigade a number of *colunelas* (usually three) into a larger formation known as the *tercio*, or "Spanish Square." These *tercios* – slightly over 3,000 men strong – would dominate infantry warfare for over a century.

At the start of the 16th century there were about 200 pikemen and halberdiers and 20 arquebusiers in a typical company. As a consequence of encountering Swiss infantry in the Italian wars, de Cordoba replaced the sword-and-buckler men with arquebusiers, emphasizing the growing importance of firepower. The proportion of shot to other arms increased steadily, so that by the beginning of the 17th century there was a roughly equal ratio of firearms to pikemen. Toward the end of the 16th century, the matchlock arquebus began to be replaced by the musket, which was more powerful but heavier and more cumbersome – sufficiently so to require a forked rest to fire the weapon. However, it was a Dutch military leader, Maurice of Nassau, who in the 1590s introduced measures that maximized infantry firepower. He drilled his troops in the manner advocated by Roman writers. By using rotating ranks of musketeers, he overcame the weakness of the muzzle-

In June 1515 the new French king, Francis I, forged an alliance with the Italian city state of Venice, and attacked other Italian city states, focusing his attentions on Milan, which was then under Swiss control. The French and Swiss forces met at Marignano, and after two days of fighting the Swiss withdrew. In December 1516, French control over Milan was reluctantly recognized throughout western Europe.

Peace might have lasted had not the ruler of Spain and the Netherlands, Charles I (1500–58), been elected Holy Roman Emperor in 1519, becoming Charles V. He now controlled almost all the territory running along France's borders and was determined to curb French territorial ambitions. As a consequence, Charles and Francis I of France were to fight four wars, largely in Italy, over the next 25 years.

The pendulum of advantage swung from one side to the other, but the net result of these wars was to establish Spanish/Imperial influence over Italy at the expense of France. And while the French lost out in Italy, they made gains in the north and west of France, notably along the borders with the Spanish Netherlands (modern Belgium).

The French artillery victory at Bicocca on April 27, 1522, dealt a body blow to the Swiss, whose reliance on infantry alone made them fatally vulnerable to a well-led all-arms force. At the Battle of Pavia – February 24, 1525 – the flower of French chivalry was cut to ribbons by Spanish arquebusiers, confirming the decline of armored cavalry as the determining factor on the battlefield. Towards the end of the battle, Francis's own horse was shot dead; he was wounded and captured. Most of the 8,000 French losses were due to gunfire in this humiliating defeat.

Pavia came to be seen as a pivotal battle in history of warfare, emphasizing the importance of infantry firearms, but other new trends were also becoming apparent. As a consequence of the gunpowder revolution, new low-walled earthwork forts replaced the old, high stone walls of the medieval castle.

The new forts utilized a number of features that made them largely proof against artillery. The low but very thick main wall was surrounded by a wide ditch, and the earth from the ditch was used to build a glacis that gently sloped away from the ditch counterscarp. The combination of glacis and low main wall was a highly effective method of absorbing the energy of the besiegers' cannon balls. The old towers of the medieval castle were replaced by low bastions: triangular-shaped stone-dressed earthworks that jutted out from the main wall and provided the defenders with interlocking fields of fire. This so-called *trace italienne* system of artillery fortresses spread rapidly from Italy. By 1610, for example, there were 50 such fortresses along France's 600-mile (960-km) frontier between Calais and Toulon.

The balance of power moved away from attack to defense, and besiegers were forced to dig complex entrenchments to avoid the artillery of the defenders, securely mounted on the main walls and bastions. As a result of these developments, set-piece battles became less common, and the new science of fortifications and siegecraft became ever more significant. The new forts required longer sieges and a large besieging army. On the other hand, multiple fortresses could tie down a large percentage of a state's forces for garrisons to man those fortresses. For its 1640 campaign, for example, the Spanish Army of Flanders planned to man 208 separate places in the south Netherlands – which would tie down 33,399 soldiers out of a total strength of 77,000 men. In addition, the proliferation of artillery fortresses increased the overall cost of warfare, firstly by increasing the longevity of military operations; secondly, by increasing the number of troops and amount of equipment needed to fight wars.

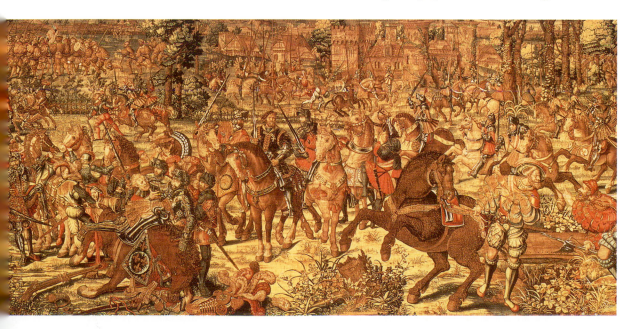

Left: French cavalry in retreat following their mauling at Pavia. The battle proved that cavalry alone could not break disciplined, unbroken infantry, notwithstanding social superiority.

French Wars of Religion

The French Wars of Religion were noted for their brutality between French Protestants and Catholics. From a military point of view, neither side was able to achieve ultimate victory, despite foreign powers adding their weight to each belligerent. Even the generalship of Henry of Navarre, though outstanding, was not enough to bring the wars to an end on the battlefield.

The 10-year-old Charles IX of France came to the throne as a result of the death of his brother, Francis II. Because of his youth, real power resided in his mother, Catherine de Medici and an eminent noble, Francis, Duke of Guise. Their fervent anti-Protestantism convinced many Protestant nobles, such as Louis, Prince of Condé, that they should seize the reins of power to safeguard the followers of their faith from persecution. Thus began the slide toward civil war.

Protestants attempted to assassinate Guise early in 1562. In response, on March 1, enraged Catholics in Vassy, a town in eastern France, massacred its Protestant inhabitants. In April, Condé and the Lord High Admiral, Gaspard de Coligny, another Protestant noble, called for a national uprising of French Protestants (Huguenots). They seized the city of Orléans and fighting broke out across the country. Atrocities and massacres were committed by both sides, and became widespread.

Protestant strength was concentrated in the outer regions of France. Catholic France's strength lay around Paris, northern France, and in Burgundy. Protestants were generally stronger in the provincial towns and Catholics in the countryside. The Huguenots also received help from England's Protestant monarch, Queen Elizabeth I. Foreign interference became a common occurrence in the French Wars of Religion, as both Protestant and Catholic kingdoms attempted to influence the outcome of the conflict to favor their own national and religious interests.

The English sent an expedition to capture the Catholic-held Channel port of Le Havre. The Huguenots also sent an army to besiege Le Havre. While marching from Orléans to Le Havre, the Huguenots fought a Catholic army at the Battle of Dreux on December 19, 1562. Both of the rival commanders – the Protestant Condé and the Catholic Duke Anne of Montmorency –were captured. The Catholic Army, now with Francis Guise in command, was able to continue to Orléans and lay siege to the city. When Guise was assassinated, Catherine de Medici encouraged both sides to negotiate a peace settlement.

The uneasy peace lasted five years, until Huguenot nobles, led by the released Condé and Coligny, attempted to kidnap the French royal family. A Huguenot attempt to seize Paris failed and the coup faltered. Fighting in the Wars of Religion tended to be inconclusive, with a victory by one side countered by a success for the other.

Condé was murdered in March 1569, after capture at the Battle of Jarnac. Coligny, however, kept the war

Right: The Battle of Dreux, December 19, 1562. This engagement resulted in a narrow Catholic vicotry. Of interest in this engraving are cavalry making no impression on a square of pikemen and musketeers (top left), and cavalry using pistols to halt an enemy cavalry charge (center, left).

CAVALRY *CARACOLE*

The French Huguenots received aid from fellow Protestants in Germany, who included mercenary heavy cavalry known as *reiters* (German for "rider"). These troops used wheellock pistols that had been developed in Germany in the early 16th century.

The wheellock pistol utilized a mechanism consisting of a spring connected to a small wheel, wound tightly using a key. Pulling the trigger caused the spring to lose its tension, and the wheel to spin against a flint. The sparks generated by this action lit the powder in the pan, which in turn ignited the main charge in the pistol barrel.

The *reiter* employed a tactic called a *caracole*, which combined firepower with shock action, and which demanded high standards of discipline and drill. A unit of cavalry, several ranks deep, would trot up towards the enemy and the front rank would discharge its pistols (anything from two to four per rider), and then retire back along the files to become the rear rank, allowing the second rank to fire its pistols. This sequence would continue until all the ranks had fired their pistols. The enemy would then be sufficiently weakened to allow the *reiters* to charge home with the sword.

going by laying siege to Poitiers. A Catholic army raised the siege and then defeated Coligny and his army at Moncontour on October 3. Both sides were evenly matched and made use of mercenaries. The Swiss, employed by the Catholics, took considerable delight in slaughtering the German *landsknecht* mercenaries fighting for the Protestants. Some 8,000 Huguenots perished, while Catholic losses were around 1,000. The way was open for the Catholic Army to take La Rochelle, a port vital to the Huguenot cause. Instead, the army laid siege to nearby Saint-Jean d'Angely, giving time for the Huguenots to create a new army in the southwest of the country.

In 1570, Coligny despatched his army across central France toward Paris. As he approached the capital, Catherine de Medici convinced Charles IX to negotiate a peace settlement. With Coligny was Henry of Navarre (1553–1610), a Protestant relative of the French royal family. The Huguenots arranged his marriage to Margaret, a sister of Charles IX. Thousands of Protestants gathered in Paris to celebrate the marriage in 1572. This was convenient for Catherine de Medici, who was in fact still plotting against the Protestants. On the night of August 23/24, Catholic soldiers butchered thousands of unarmed Protestants in the streets in an orgy of violence. Among the victims was Coligny himself. Medici appeared to have scored a major success. However, the treacherous St. Bartholomew's Eve

massacre outraged Protestants throughout Europe, and also caused disquiet among many French Catholics.

A new group emerged in French politics: Catholics who opposed the Guise family's fanatical hatred of Protestantism. After the death of Charles IX in 1574, the leader of this group (the son of Henry II and Catherine de Medici) was crowned King Henry III. In 1576 he negotiated the Peace of Beaulieu with the Huguenots.

Henry, Duke of Guise, son of Duke Francis, rejected the peace, however. With support from Catholic Spain, which was ever ready to launch a war against "heretics," he prepared to instigate a new war against the Huguenots. He organized the Holy League to defend Catholic interests. Under its influence Henry III found it prudent to decree an end to religious tolerance in 1585. All Huguenot France now rebelled under the leadership of Henry of Navarre, now one of the leading Huguenots.

The Generalship of Henry of Navarre

Henry of Navarre proved to be an able general. He defeated a Holy League army at Coutras in southwest France in October 1587. His musketeers struck down the Catholic cavalry and his own mounted troops swept them from the field. The Huguenot infantry and cavalry then combined to overwhelm the Catholic infantry.

The following year, Henry, Duke of Guise, ordered soldiers of the Holy League to seize Paris. King Henry III briefly became a puppet of the League, but secretly plotted against its leadership. Henry Guise and his brother Louis were murdered in December 1588. In retaliation, in August 1589, Henry III was assassinated by a renegade monk.

The path of succession now passed to Henry of Navarre, who was crowned Henry IV. The Holy League refused to accept the legitimacy of the new king, though, and the war continued. Henry defeated the Holy League's forces in two battles in northern France, at Arques in 1589 and Ivry in 1590. At the latter battle he was forced to agree surrender terms with the enemy's Swiss mercenaries, who remained unbroken despite the rout of the rest of the army – again demonstrating the relative invulnerability of disciplined foot. Henry next laid siege to Paris, still in Catholic hands.

King Philip II of Spain, determined to support the League, ordered his commander in the Netherlands, Alessandro Farnese, Duke of Parma, to invade France. Parma advanced on Paris, forcing Henry to raise the siege. The next two years saw Henry and Parma engage in a war of maneuver, during which neither gained any permanent advantage.

In an adroit political move that resolved the religious impasse, Henry renounced his Protestant faith and converted to Catholicism in July 1593. He entered Paris in March 1594 to properly assume the French throne. The Edict of Nantes, issued by Henry in 1598, guaranteed religious freedom in France and brought the wars to an end.

The Ottoman Turks

Ottoman expansion had temporarily halted in 1503 with the end of a war against Venice. The sultan, Bayazid II, viewed expansionist wars as too expensive and risky. It was not a view shared by his sons, one of whom, Selim I, after emerging victorious from a civil war, looked toward the Middle East and Christian Europe for new lands to add to the Ottoman Empire.

Selim I (1467–1520) first turned against Persia, which had supported one of his brothers during the civil war. Victory at the Battle of Chaldiran in August 1515 enabled his army to capture the Persian capital, Tabriz, in September. The Ottomans did not press their advantage, though, and following a Janissary (infantry elite) mutiny Selim withdrew his forces, allowing the Persian ruler, Shah Ismail, to recover his capital.

Selim gathered his army together in 1516, only to learn that both Persia and Mameluke Egypt had formed an alliance against him. Selim moved his army south to Syria, where the Egyptian forces were gathering. The two armies clashed at Merj-Dabik. The Mameluke cavalry charged Selim's positions, but the disciplined Turkish artillery and arquebusiers brought the cavalry to a disorganized halt, and the death of the Mameluke commander signaled a general retreat by the Egyptians.

The victory at Merj-Dabik enabled the Turks to occupy Syria. They continued their advance south to threaten Egypt itself. In January 1517, at the Battle of Ridanieh, the Egyptians deployed a sizeable contingent of artillery, but the superior range of the Turkish guns was decisive. The Mameluke cavalry was unable to endure the bombardment and impetuously charged toward the Turkish lines. Their desperate charge broke through part of the Turkish line, but a counterattack repulsed the Mamelukes who were driven from the field of battle. Selim then conquered Egypt.

The Ottomans now dominated the Middle East and the eastern Mediterranean. Other Muslim rulers turned to Selim for assistance. The Christians of Spain threatened the religious Islamic ruler of Algiers, Khair-ed-Din. He sent word to Selim that he would acknowledge the sultan as his overlord if, in turn, Selim would protect Algiers from the Spaniards. Since the Algerians had a powerful fleet that would be of great use to the Ottomans in later campaigns in the Mediterranean, Selim readily accepted the offer.

Right: By the end of the 16th century, the Ottoman Empire had spread throughout the Middle East, North Africa, and deep into eastern Europe.

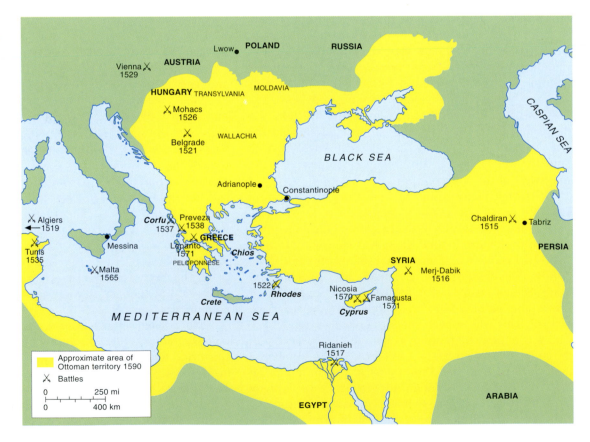

Selim's successor, Suleiman the Magnificent (1494–1566), resumed the siege and spent most of his reign waging war against Christian Europe.

After an offensive in the Balkans in 1521 that captured Belgrade, Suleiman turned his attentions to Rhodes. In June 1522, he landed forces on the island, which was controlled by the Order of the Knights of St. John of Jerusalem. After surviving an earlier Turkish siege in 1480, the knights had greatly strengthened the fortifications of the city of Rhodes. The original high curtain walls had been replaced by walls 30 feet (9.1 m) high and 40 feet (12 m) thick, complete with bastions in which were mounted artillery. Integrated with wide and deep ditches, the new defenses were exceptionally strong.

Suleiman mobilized an army of 100,000 to send against the 700 knights and their 6,000 Rhodian soldiers. The defenders fought with the utmost determination and caused the Turks enormous casualties. In order to minimize further bloodshed, Suleiman entered into negotiations with the exhausted defenders, who were allowed to evacuate Rhodes. Only 180 knights and 1,500 other soldiers were left alive, many of them wounded. They settled on Malta in 1530, a gift to them from the Holy Roman Emperor Charles V.

The Campaign in Hungary and Austria

Suleiman now turned north again, and attacked Hungary in 1526. He destroyed the Hungarian Army at the Battle of Mohacs in that year, and overran the country. In 1529 the Turks attacked Austria and laid siege to Vienna, but the Austrians had constructed powerful defenses and withstood the Ottoman onslaught. As a result, Suleiman decided to withdraw rather than continue the siege through the winter. This setback was followed by another Turkish offensive against Austria in 1532, but this assault also ended in failure.

Turkey now faced enemies in all directions. The Persians invaded the east of the empire, while Charles V dispatched the Spanish fleet to raid the Peloponnese in Greece. Suleiman's alliance with Khair-ed-Din provided the naval forces he required to counter the Christians in the Mediterranean, allowing him to turn east against the Persians. Success in the east, however, was balanced by defeats in the Mediterranean. Charles V captured Tunis in 1535, defeating Khair-ed-Din's fleet during the campaign. A Turkish attempt to capture the island of Corfu, then held by the Venetians, failed in 1537 due to the timely arrival of a Christian fleet.

The tide only began to turn in favor of the Turks in 1538, when Khair-ed-Din outmaneuvered the Christian fleet, commanded by Andrea Doria, off Preveza on the west coast of Greece. Andrea Doria retreated rather than fight on unfavorable terms. Three years later the Spanish tried to capture Algiers, but a storm destroyed their fleet. Khair-ed-Din was able to deploy a fleet in the western Mediterranean, and over the next 20 years terrorize the coasts of Spain, France, and Italy.

The first major Turkish setback occurred in 1565, when Suleiman sent another expedition against the Knights of St. John, who had constructed a new fortress on Malta. Suleiman's expeditionary force, however, was defeated by the brave defense of the island by the knights. The 60,000 Turks, backed by heavy artillery, pounded the fortress and tried to storm its walls. The defenders, about 600 knights and 9,000 soldiers, resisted every attack, and when a Christian relief force arrived, the Turks withdrew, leaving behind 24,000 dead.

Suleiman died the following year. During his reign the Ottoman Empire reached the peak of its power. His son, Selim II, decided to consolidate Turkish power in the eastern Mediterranean, and in 1570 he attacked the Venetian-ruled island of Cyprus. The Turks stormed the walls of Nicosia on September 9, 1570, while Famagusta surrendered on August 3, 1571. At Famagusta, the garrison were executed by the Turks after surrendering.

The pope, Pius V, in response to the outbreak of war between Venice and Turkey, formed a Holy League to conduct a "crusade" against the Turks. The League assembled a fleet at Messina, Sicily, commanded by Don Juan of Austria (1547–78). The combined Christian fleet of mainly Venetian and Spanish ships consisted of 200 galleys and six galleasses – a total force of just over 80,000 men (20,000 were soldiers; most of the remainder rowers). In October 1571, the Christian force advanced toward the Gulf of Corinth, where a large Turkish fleet lay at harbor in Lepanto.

The Battle of Lepanto

The Ottoman fleet, commanded by Ali Pasher, accepted the challenge of battle and sailed out to meet the Christian fleet. The Turks had slightly more ships – 270 galleys – but considerably less firepower. On October 7, 1571, the two fleets faced each other, each in three divisions. As the Turks approached they were raked by galleass fire and suffered considerable damage and disorganization. The collapse of their center and right forced them to withdraw. The Christians captured 117 galleys and 274 guns. Lepanto was the first major sea battle to be decided by firepower.

In 1574 Selim II died, and a weak ruler, Murad III, became sultan. A Turkish advance toward Vienna in 1593 failed, and in 1595 Christian subjects in the provinces of Transylvania, Wallachia, and Moldavia rebelled against their Islamic overlords. Murad died in 1595 and his successor, Mohammed III, scored a number of successes in his campaign in Hungary, undertaken the following year. The Hapsburg Army attempted to halt the Turkish advance at the Battle of Kerestes in October 1596. The Turks emerged victorious after a three-day fight, and the crisis of the Ottoman Empire in Europe passed for the time being. The war dragged on for another 10 years, the fighting mainly confined to the border regions of Transylvania. But conflict between the two sides would resume in due course.

The Spanish Armada

The aid of Protestant Queen Elizabeth I of England to Protestants in the Spanish-controlled Netherlands prompted King Philip II of Spain to organize a large fleet to invade England. This would both sever the aid to the rebellious Dutch and bring England back into the Catholic fold. However, new tactics at sea would dash his hopes and lead to the ruin of his grand Armada.

In 1588, King Philip ordered his Armada of 130 ships to leave their ports in Spain, sail up the English Channel and link up with the Spanish Army in the Netherlands. Once there, the Armada would lead a Spanish invasion force to conquer England. From Philip's perspective, besides supporting the Dutch rebels, the English had also plundered Spanish possessions and ships in the Caribbean – and punishment was long overdue.

Whereas the Battle of Lepanto had marked the high point (and almost immediate demise) of galley warfare, the English fight against the Armada represented the emergence of a new type of naval warfare. Two factors were paramount. Firstly, the battle was fought by ocean-going ships that no longer needed to hug the coasts but were capable of traveling to any point on the globe. Secondly, the battle represented the victory of firepower over shock action, and from 1588 onward, naval engagements would follow the general pattern set by the victorious English.

The Spanish ships mounted over 2,400 guns, of which 1,100 were heavy, short-range weapons intended to smash wooden hulls, demast ships, or destroy enemy cannon. The remainder were chiefly small antipersonnel weapons, to be employed against enemy crews and soldiers. Spanish tactics consisted of closing with the enemy ships so that their heavy armament could do terrible damage to them at short range. The Spanish ships would then come alongside and grapple the enemy, allowing boarding parties to seize the ship in hand-to-hand combat.

The English employed a similar number of ships to the Spanish, but had the advantage in gunnery and seamanship. The fleet carried 1,800 guns, mostly light-shotted, long-range culverins. The English played to their strengths and planned to stay at long range, avoid boarding actions, and slowly pound the Spanish into submission. Most of the English vessels were lighter and more maneuverable than their Spanish counterparts, and their captains, men such as Sir Francis Drake (1540–1596), knew the English Channel's tides and currents extremely well.

The Armada's first sighting of England was made on July 29, 1588. The following day the English fleet, commanded by Admiral Lord Howard of Effingham (1536–1624), put to sea from Plymouth. The Armada moved into its battle formation, adopting a large crescent shape. Fighting between the two fleets began during the midmorning of July 31.

Howard attacked the rear of the Spanish formation, and his ships kept their distance. English long-range gunfire damaged several Spanish ships but only one was sunk, a consequence of the lightweight shot fired by the English. The Spanish commander, the Duke of Medina Sidonia (1550–1619), realized that the English had no intention of slugging it out at close range. He therefore ordered his captains to sail in a defensive circle, believing that this formation would offer a greater degree of protection.

There was no fighting on August 1. The next day, however, the easterly winds favored the Armada and Medina Sidonia turned to attack. Two separate battles

Left: Ships of the Spanish Armada set sail for the English Channel. The campaign became a series of running battles with the smaller, nimbler English ships, which dashed any hopes of the ships landing Spanish troops on mainland England.

Right: Francis Drake was one of the ablest English naval commanders to battle the Armada. Hated in Spain, his exploits included destroying 20 Spanish warships in Cadiz harbor.

were joined between the Spanish and English. The two fleets' flagships traded gunfire as other English vessels joined the attack on Medina Sidonia's *San Martin*. An officer on the *San Martin* estimated that for 80 shots fired by the Spaniards the English fired 500. The English gunfire again had limited impact, and as their ammunition ran low they were obliged to break off the action.

With calm winds on August 3, the Spanish fleet was again ready to fight. Howard knew that the conditions favored the Spaniards so he avoided combat, although heavy fighting broke out on the 4th. Howard divided his fleet into four squadrons for the battle, an early example of fleet tactics. The action began early in the morning with an attack by Howard's squadron on the left of the Armada. Later in the morning, two more English squadrons attacked the Spanish center. The battle ended with an attack on the Spanish right by Sir Francis Drake. Once again, the battle petered out when English ammunition ran low.

First Ship Attack

Both sides avoided combat during the next two days. The Armada reached the port of Calais and dropped anchor. Medina Sidonia learned that the Spanish Army in the Netherlands would not be ready for embarkation for at least another week. This failure of coordination between military and navy left the Armada open to attack while anchored off Calais. To add to Medina Sidonia's problems, a Dutch fleet had blockaded ports in the Spanish Netherlands, preventing the resupply of the Armada, which was now very low on ammunition.

On the morning of August 7, the English commanders decided to send fire ships – old vessels packed with combustible materials – against the Spaniards. English sailors prepared eight vessels from their fleet, and as night fell the fire ships floated toward the Armada. Medina Sidonia had expected this stratagem, and he positioned a number of small boats to tow away any that came near his fleet. In the event, however, only two fire ships were successfully turned away, and to avoid the flames the Spanish ships hurriedly cut their anchors and put to sea. In the confusion that followed this difficult night-time maneuver, much of the Armada became scattered.

On the morning of August 8, Medina Sidonia found his flagship under attack by the whole English fleet. Only five other Spanish ships were able to help at first but others joined during the day, and the Armada slowly regrouped. The battle lasted nine hours and though no ships was sunk, the Spanish suffered heavy casualties.

Medina Sidonia wanted to return to Calais but the winds were blowing from the wrong direction. The Armada was now perilously low on supplies of all kinds, and a decision had to be made without delay. Although a desperate plan, Media Sidonia decided to sail north around Britain and Ireland to return to Spain. The Armada encountered very bad weather. Charts were few and inaccurate, and the Spanish sailors were ignorant of local conditions; dozens of ships were sunk, swamped by mountainous seas or wrecked on rocks. Some 11,000 Spaniards lost their lives, most in the voyage around the British Isles. Over 60 Spanish ships were lost: the English captured or sank 15; while 19 were lost off the Scottish and Irish coasts. The fate of the remainder is not clear, but most were probably wrecked.

The Armada and Warfare at Sea

The defeat of the Armada was much celebrated by the English, who saw the battle as a form of national deliverance from Spanish Catholic tyranny. On a purely military level, the battle was rather less decisive; within a short space of time the Spanish had largely made good their losses. And while the Spanish refrained from attempting another invasion of England, the war against the Dutch continued, and English naval fortunes went into a slow decline.

The events of 1588 pointed the way with regard to naval warfare, though. The more maneuverable English ships avoided Spanish efforts to close and use their boarding tactics and the shock action of their large numbers of excellent infantry. Though the English did little damage due to their remaining at long ranges to avoid the heavy Spanish cannon (the latter included heavy cannon firing 50 lb [22.7 kilo] metal balls), they nevertheless scored far more hits. The success of English shipborne artillery signaled the emergence of a new type of naval warfare: broadside combats conducted by broad, deep sailing ships. In addition, the latter, having a greater cargo-carrying capacity than galleys, increased the overall scope of naval operations.

The Thirty Years War

A semicomical episode in Prague in May 1618 sparked one of Europe's most savage wars, which was to have a profound effect on the development of land warfare, both on the tactics used on the battlefield itself, and on the way armies were supplied during campaigns. The war was also to produce one of the most innovative generals of the early modern period: Gustavus Adolphus of Sweden.

The Thirty Years War was partly an internal struggle for the succession to power within the unwieldy Holy Roman Empire, partly an ideological struggle between Protestantism and Catholicism, and partly a dynastic struggle between the royal houses of Hapsburg, Vasa, and Bourbon.

Germany at this time was not a united country, but a collection of 300 states that, nominally at least, acknowledged the overlordship of the Catholic Holy Roman Emperor. Conflict between the emperor and the various German states had been endemic throughout the Middle Ages, but the Reformation transformed these disputes, dividing Protestant and Catholic states into two competing power blocks. The Protestant Evangelical Union was opposed by the Catholic League, and the combination of religious fervor and political ambition formed a powder keg – ignited by the so-called Prague defenestration crisis of May 1618. On the 22nd of that month, a group of Protestants threw two of the Holy Roman Emperor's advisors and an official out of a window as an expression of their outrage at Emperor Mathias's decree that ended the toleration of the Protestant religion in the empire. The victims were unhurt by their falls, as they landed on a large, fresh pile of dung!

Emperor Matthias died in March 1619 and was succeeded by the Jesuit-educated Ferdinand II, a religious enthusiast who was determined to punish the Protestant outrages in Prague. For their part, the Bohemian Protestants chose a German nobleman, Frederick, as their king and invaded Austria. The Imperial Catholic League launched a counterattack, appointing the able and experienced Johan Tserclaes, Count of Tilly (1559–1632), as their commander. Tilly crushed the main Bohemian army under Prince Christian of Anhalt-Bernberg at the Battle of the White Mountain on November 8, 1620, a victory which brought Prague and Bohemia back under Imperial control.

Left: Gustavus Adolphus, king of Sweden, was a military innovator who made the Swedish Army the elite fighting force of the mid-17th century. He was also a fine general.

Left: Most of the fighting during The Thirty Years War took place in central Europe, especially Germany. As the conflict progressed the land was slowly stripped of food and shelter, resulting in widespread plague and famine. To add to the population's woes, the armies engaged in wholesale looting and committed many atrocities.

Frederick's own lands in both western and central Germany were now open to attack, and by the summer of 1622 he was living as a refugee in France. What remained of the combined Bohemian–Evangelical Union Army, commanded by Count Ernst von Mansfeld, ineffectually roamed northern Germany and the Netherlands, supplying its needs through plunder.

By the summer of 1623, it looked as if the "Bohemian War" was at an end. The Catholic Holy Roman Empire had defeated the main Protestant challenge. But it had received help from Spain, which at the time was at war with France. Cardinal Richelieu (1585–1642), the French king's chief minister, feared Spanish–Austrian influence in Germany and made an alliance with several Protestant states, including Denmark and Sweden. In 1625, conflict resumed.

Encouraged by the French, the Danish king, Christian IV, led an army into Germany. The Holy Roman Emperor Ferdinand II had meanwhile hired a mercenary general, Charles Albert von Wallenstein (1583–1634), to command the Imperial Army. Wallenstein and Tilly fought effectively against the Protestants. Mansfeld's army was defeated while besieging Dessau, as a result of a surprise attack by Wallenstein on April 25, 1626. Tilly inflicted a severe defeat on King Christian at the Battle of Lutter on August 27, 1626; the remnants of Christian's beaten army fled northward.

Once again the war looked to be at an end: Richelieu made peace with Spain and withdrew from the alliance. Ferdinand II appointed Wallenstein supreme commander of the Baltic Sea. The ambitious mercenary now began attacking the ports on the Baltic, but these measures alarmed the king of Sweden, Gustavus Adolphus (1594–1632). Richelieu, ever keen to meddle in German affairs, encouraged the Swedes to intervene in Germany on behalf of the Protestant cause.

Genuinely fearful of Imperial expansion into the Baltic region, Gustavus Adolphus decided to invade northern Germany and help his fellow Protestants. On July 10, 1630, he entered the city of Stettin on the Baltic Sea and spent the fall capturing fortresses nearby to secure his long line of supply with Sweden.

Gustavus Adolphus was the leading soldier of his age. While possessing a sound grasp of strategy and a keen tactical eye, his great strength lay in military administration and organization. Unable to afford mercenaries, the Swedes introduced a system of conscription, which created the first national army to be raised, equipped, provisioned, and paid for by the state.

Gustavus had been influenced by the theories of Maurice of Nassau, who stressed the importance of firepower and mobility, in place of the contemporary reliance upon shock action. In the Swedish Army the musket was made lighter (making a rest unnecessary)

SWEDISH ARTILLERY

Gustavus Adolphus, assisted by his artillery commander Torstensson, completely overhauled his artillery, making it a separate arm with the same standing as the infantry and cavalry. Mobility was the key point, and field guns were made lighter with smaller calbers. An early form of horse artillery was also introduced: lightweight four-pounder guns capable of firing cartridge rounds of grapeshot. These "regimental" guns operated with infantry units to provide them with immediate, extra firepower.

Gustavus also made important organizational changes. Previously, gunners had been civilian contract workers who were not subject to military command and control. Gustavus, instead, drafted his gunners into the army, so that he could train and discipline them like the rest of his forces.

and its caliber and production standardized in Swedish state workshops. Muskets now became the chief weapon of the infantry, with pikemen largely relegated to the role of protecting musketeers from cavalry attack (although pikemen were still expected to take rapid offensive action where necessary).

The Swedish Army developed the tactical and organizational ideas introduced by the Spanish in the 16th century to a higher level. Four infantry companies (each of 72 musketeers and 54 pikemen) constituted a battalion; up to eight battalions formed a regiment, and two to four regiments a brigade. Thus, Gustavus laid down the basic organizational principles that were adopted by all European armies in the late 17th and 18th centuries.

Drill and strict military discipline were the hallmarks of the Swedish system, and to encourage mobility small units were expected to be able to move in close conjunction with each other and with larger units. Not since Roman times were the various elements of a military formation able to move and fight so effectively.

For his cavalry, Gustavus dispensed with the *caracole* system and deployed his troopers three or four ranks deep, with the emphasis given to shock action with the sword, so that the pistol became a supplementary weapon to be used in the confusion of the melee once the enemy had been broken.

These reforms had a transforming effect on the Swedish Army's tactics. The old system of massed formations, based on the *tercio*, were replaced by a linear approach, which emphasized firepower for the infantry and shock action for the cavalry. One of the consequences of linear tactics was to make the flanks more vulnerable to attack. In turn, this encouraged commanders to conduct flank attacks and, at that same time, make them more aware of the need to protect their own vulnerable flanks.

Bolstered by the arrival of the Swedish Army, the Protestant princes in Germany issued a set of demands in March 1631 to the emperor for religious tolerance. Ferdinand rejected their demands and the war resumed.

At this critical moment, Ferdinand dismissed Wallenstein from his service, afraid that the wealthy general intended to establish an independent power-base. The main Catholic forces came under the command of Tilly. Since November 1630 the Imperial Army had been besieging Magdeburg, which held large stocks of food that Tilly wanted for his own forces. When the city fell on May 20, 1631, the besiegers sacked it pitilessly; 30,000 people died at the hands of Tilly's men and in the flames that consumed the city.

The sack of Magdeburg stirred the resolve of the German Protestants, who now believed they could expect no mercy at the hands of the Catholics. In search of provisions, Tilly withdrew south into Thuringia. He was pursued by Gustavus and his army. The two sides maneuvered for advantage in July and August 1631, before meeting in battle at Breitenfeld on September 17. The Swedes had more and better artillery than the Imperial Army, although the effectiveness of the two armies was largely balanced out by the inclusion of uncertain Saxon forces within Gustavus's army.

The Battle of Breitenfeld

The battle began with an artillery cannonade. Galled by accurate Swedish cannon fire, the cavalry on the Imperial left flank advanced and attempted to outflank the Swedish right, but they were outmaneuvered and thrown back in a counterattack. Tilly next attacked the Saxon forces on the left of Gustavus's army. The Saxons were routed, and Tilly ordered his troops to advance and outflank the Swedish left. Gustavus, however, was able to wheel his army to face Tilly's troops and offset any Imperial advantage.

The battle raged in the center but superior Swedish firepower won through. When Gustavus ordered a general attack, the Imperial infantry broke and then fled under the weight of Swedish artillery fire. Tilly, who was wounded, lost 7,000 killed and 6,000 prisoners out of his total of 36,000 troops. Gustavus had a little over 6,000 men killed and wounded from his army of 42,000 men. Breitenfeld had been a hard-fought battle, with the advantage going to the better-trained troops. It was also a triumph of the new military system over the old. The Imperial Army deployed in squares 30 deep and 50 wide, supported by 27 field guns. The Swedes and their allies had 51 heavy guns, while every Swedish regiment included a battery of four light field pieces, and they deployed in six ranks. The battle was decided by infantry, discipline, and firepower, with the Swedish musketeers being the decisive element, firing devastating salvos into the enemy.

Breitenfeld was of immense tactical and strategic importance, as other armies rushed to copy the triumphant Swedish system.

After his victory, Gustavus declined to advance on Vienna, believing this would make his supply lines to the Baltic too vulnerable to Imperial attack. He spent the winter securing a logistical base for the next year's campaigns: on September 22, 1631, he occupied Erfurt, an important road junction, and then captured the city of Mainz on December 11.

The following April, Gustavus Adolphus recommenced his march deep into southern Germany. During the summer of 1632, Gustavus planned to invade both Bavaria and Austria from the west, marching along the Danube River. His first move was to seize the fortress of Donauwörth on March 27. Faced by this new threat, Ferdinand recalled Wallenstein to fight alongside the aged Tilly.

Tilly moved his army to the east bank of the Lech River in southern Bavaria, where he built a strong fortified camp. On April 10, Gustavus reached the Lech at the city of Augsburg. He had his engineers build a pontoon bridge and put his army across the river. On April 16 the Swedes stormed the Imperial camp; Tilly was killed and his army forced to retreat.

The Swedish king advanced up the Danube, only to find his way barred by the Imperial fortress of Ingolstadt. Gustavus could see no way of taking Ingolstadt without incurring prohibitive casualties deep within enemy territory. His plan to seize Vienna was abandoned, and he advanced north toward Nuremberg. Meanwhile, the remnants of Tilly's army had joined up with Wallenstein's forces at Fürth on July 11. They

constructed a large fortified camp and prepared for the arrival of Gustavus.

Gustavus himself was waiting for reinforcements. His Imperial enemies had around 50,000 soldiers, and outnumbered his own forces. He delayed his attack until August, when his own strength finally reached 45,000. He launched his first attack on August 31, and on each day thereafter until September 4. But Wallenstein had chosen his position well. Gustavus's artillery could not get into a position to bombard the Catholic trenches effectively; his infantry attacks were beaten off with heavy loss.

Since he could not fight on his own terms, Gustavus Adolphus broke camp and marched northwestward from Fürth, unsure of his next move. Wallenstein, however, divided his forces, and when Gustavus learned of this, he swiftly attacked the Imperial Army at Lützen. Gustavus led a charge of cavalry supported by infantry against Wallenstein's right. He pushed back the Imperial cavalry, but Wallenstein attacked in the center and Gustavus turned to reinforce the fighting there. The Swedish center held and the Imperial Army was forced to retreat. Both sides suffered heavy casualties, the most important of these being Gustavus himself, killed in a confused melee between cavalry and infantry. Although the death of the king was a disaster for the Protestant cause, the Swedish Army continued the war.

Wallenstein recovered from the defeat at Lützen, and beat the Swedes at Steinau in 1633. Ferdinand, still afraid of his over-mighty commander, had Wallenstein assassinated on February 23, 1634. Despite the removal of their commander, the Imperial troops again defeated the Swedes at the Battle of Nördlingen on September 6.

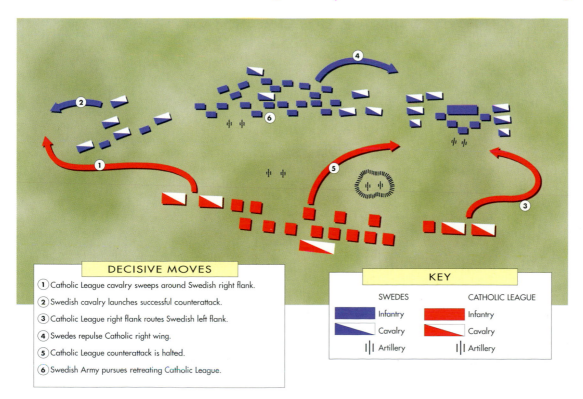

Left: The Battle of Breitenfeld was a triumph for Swedish tactics, which combined mobility with firepower to defeat a more experienced opponent.

DECISIVE MOVES

1. Catholic League cavalry sweeps around Swedish right flank.
2. Swedish cavalry launches successful counterattack.
3. Catholic League right flank routes Swedish left flank.
4. Swedes repulse Catholic right wing.
5. Catholic League counterattack is halted.
6. Swedish Army pursues retreating Catholic League.

KEY

SWEDES		CATHOLIC LEAGUE	
Infantry		Infantry	
Cavalry		Cavalry	
Artillery		Artillery	

Right: A rather idealized view of soldiers from the era of the Thirty Years War. In reality, the hardships of campaign would reduce clothing to rags and give the soldiers of all armies a similar appearance: threadbare.

The following year the elector of Saxony sued for peace on behalf of the Protestant states. This resulted in the Peace of Prague, signed in May 1635, in which the German Catholic and Protestant rulers, their states devastated by war, agreed to end the conflict among themselves – and work to drive the Swedes and other foreign elements out of Germany.

Richelieu, whose policy had been to use the armies of other states to control the Hapsburgs in Germany, entered the war openly in 1635 on the side of Sweden. Richelieu's intention was simply to gain territory for France along the northern and eastern borders of the country at the expense of Spain and the Holy Roman Empire. The campaigns of the following years – the final phase of the Thirty Years War – were particularly destructive.

The first gain for France came on December 17, 1638, when a French army captured Breisach on the east bank of the Rhine. They were also engaged in fighting in the Spanish Netherlands, northwestern Italy, and in Spain itself.

In eastern Germany, the Swedish Army continued its campaign against the Holy Roman Emperor. The Swedes, commanded by Johan Banér (1596–1641), who became a field marshal, and Torstensson, repeatedly defeated larger armies, although the devastation caused through living off the land earned them the deep enmity of all German peoples, regardless of religion.

In 1643, a Spanish army led by Francisco de Melo advanced from the Netherlands in a march on Paris, and on May 13 it laid siege to the fortress of Rocroi. The French commander, Duke Louis d'Enghien, subsequently the Prince of Condé (1621–86), learned of the Spanish advance and chose to attack. At the Battle of Rocroi, fought on May 19, d'Enghien overran the enemy cavalry through spirited shock action, which isolated the Spanish infantry who were subsequently mown down by

French artillery fire. Spanish losses were 8,000 dead and 7,000 captured out of 25,000; d'Enghien's casualties were 4,000 from an army of 23,000 men. It was an illustration of the power of firepower against dense infantry units.

The battle illustrated the decisive role cavalry could have at this time, though only against broken or disorganized foot. Condé led his cavalry around the Spanish infantry to the left of his line to attack the victorious enemy horsemen, driving them from the field. He then turned his cavalry against the enemy infantry. However, they had formed into a dense formation to resist him, so he had to use his artillery and musketeers to create gaps in the Spanish ranks that his horsemen subsequently exploited.

The next year the French captured the Rhine town of Philippsburg. This enabled them to move into Bavaria, but once there they found the devastated countryside could not support an army. The war in Germany ended after a Swedish invasion of Bavaria in 1648. On October 24, France, the Holy Roman Empire, the German Protestants, and Sweden agreed to peace under the terms of the Treaty of Westphalia. France and Sweden gained territory, and the Holy Roman Emperor – whose power was greatly reduced – agreed to tolerate Protestantism in Germany.

The Thirty Years War underlined the importance of supply, and the terrible social consequences of a breakdown in the logistical process. The prevailing doctrine of the period assumed that the local countryside would support an army, but the constant movement of ever-larger forces over the same area completely denuded the countryside of food, provisions, and ultimately people. Famine became commonplace and, exacerbated by the cruelty of a religious conflict, perhaps as many as eight million people died during the war. It is estimated that a third of the population of Germany was wiped out.

Gustavus Adolphus tried to implement a sound logistical system of supply bases stretching back to Sweden, but over the course of time this broke down and the Swedish Army became as rapacious as any other. Wallenstein was arguably more successful in this sphere, applying his business mind to the supply of his forces. Certainly, after the Thirty Years War, commanders became more aware of the need to supply their armies in the field without devastating the lands around them.

Yet it was the Swedish model that stood above all others. Because of its relatively efficient treasury, tax system, and administration, Gustavus Adolphus was able to build a navy to protect his coastline from the Poles and Danes, and also ensure the safe passage of Swedish troops across the Baltic. But the demands of mid-17th century warfare proved beyond even Sweden's resources, and thus the Swedes had to exact payment from the areas they occupied. Thus, friendly principalities in Germany contributed to the cause, while hostile princes and cities were forced to pay ransoms to prevent them being plundered. In addition, the Swedish Army exacted quarter, food, and fodder from the areas it controlled. But in the end, the Swedish Army became a huge parasitic body (it numbered 70,000 men in 1650), having to plunder in order to survive. Ironically, Sweden's success had given her a variety of Baltic lands – Estonia, Livonia, Bremen, and most of Pomerania – which had to be maintained in peacetime and defended in wartime. This cost, combined with the heavy toll of human life suffered by the Swedes during their participation in the Thirty Years War, was to prove a heavy financial burden for the Swedish state. As the French were to discover later in the 17th century, the cost of maintaining large forces could be prohibitive.

With regard to numbers in the field, the problem of subsistence largely determined the size of armies. Availability of fodder for horses and food for troops channeled armies into the more fertile areas of Europe. Armies could live off the land, but this tended to alienate the local population and affected military discipline, which happened with a sad regularity during the Thirty Years War. The alternative was to be supplied from prestocked depots, or via slow-moving convoys and riverboats. However, this required an administrative system that was beyond most states in the early 17th century.

The need to convoy thousands of wagons and their cannon over poor roads also affected the speed and scale of warfare, and the passability of mud roads and major waterways largely restricted campaigning to the months between April and October. The average middle-sized field gun weighed three tons and required 8–10 horses or oxen to pull it. This meant few armies moved more than five miles (8 km) a day. Attendants also slowed movement. In 1610, for example, it is estimated that at least 4,000 women, boys, and wagons accompanied every 3,000-strong *tercio* in central Europe, while Turkish armies often trebled their fighting strength with slaves and attendants.

Left: The superb general Duke Louis d'Enghien leads his French troops to victory over the Spanish at the Battle of Rocroi in 1643. It took a combination of artillery and cavalry to finally break the disciplined Spanish infantry.

The English Civil War

A Scottish rebellion forced Charles I of England (1600–49) to recall Parliament in 1640. Parliament granted him the necessary money to suppress the uprising, but at a price. Charles had to agree to various political and religious reforms in return. However, after Irish Catholics rebelled in 1641, relations between Charles and Parliament became even worse. England began to drift toward civil war.

Members of Parliament, fearful that Charles had sparked the Irish rebellion in order to raise a force that he would use against them, tried to gain control over the small English Army. Puritans and other radical Protestants came to dominate Parliament. More moderate politicians, wanting reform not revolution, rallied to the king's camp. The two sides were unable to compromise and England moved toward civil war.

Charles's chief support lay mainly in northern and western England, while Parliament drew its support from the east and south, including the wealthy City of London with its trained bands (militia). Most of England's major ports, such as Bristol, and the navy were also in Puritan hands, factors that hindered the amount of foreign aid Charles could receive from wealthy supporters in Europe.

England had no standing army and few professional soldiers at the outset of the war. The opening campaigns of the war reflected this general amateurish approach, but over time and through experience, trained soldiers and able commanders began to emerge.

At the first major battle, fought at Edgehill in October 1642, Parliament tried to stop Charles from reaching London. The engagement was indecisive, although the Parliamentarians had the worst of the fighting. The road to London was left open but Charles failed to seize the opportunity. The king established his headquarters in Oxford, which remained the center of Royalist operations for the rest of the war.

Royalist successes in battle predominated in the campaigns of 1643. They benefited from aggressive leadership and the presence of spirited cavalry under the command of Prince Rupert (1619–82), the king's nephew. The Parliamentarians adopted a more defensive strategy, partly through military inexperience, and also because of a general unease felt by many at fighting their sovereign.

In 1643, the Royalist northern army won a victory in Yorkshire at Adwalton Moor in June and at Lansdown in the southwest in July, while Rupert took the great port of Bristol the same month. London now seemed open to Royalist advances from the north, southwest, and Oxford, but Charles wanted to capture the inland port of Gloucester in the west, which gave time for London to be saved for Parliament by a relief force under the Earl of Essex. On its way back to London, Essex's army faced the Royalists at the First Battle of Newbury. The battle was drawn, and Charles fell back to Oxford.

In September the wider strategic picture changed when the Scottish Covenanters joined the Parliamentary cause. By the spring of 1644 the Royalists found themselves under growing pressure. In May, the Earl of Leven led a Scottish force of 21,000 men into England to

Map

Parliamentarian areas
Royalist areas
✕ Battles

0 — 100 mi
0 — 150 km

Tippermuir 1644 ✕

SCOTLAND

Philiphaugh 1645 ✕

Marston Moor 1644 ✕ ✕ York 1644

NORTH SEA

IRISH SEA

Preston 1648 ✕

Adwalton Moor 1643 ✕

Naseby 1645 ✕

WALES

Edgehill 1642 ✕

ENGLAND

Gloucester 1643 ✕

Oxford ●

London ●

Bristol 1643 ✕ Lansdown 1643 ✕

Newbury 1643/44 ✕

Langport 1645 ✕

Lostwithiel 1644 ✕

ENGLISH CHANNEL

Left: Parliamentary possession of London and the richest parts of England meant that Royalist hopes of victory in the war diminished as time went on, especially as Scotland joined the struggle against the king in 1644.

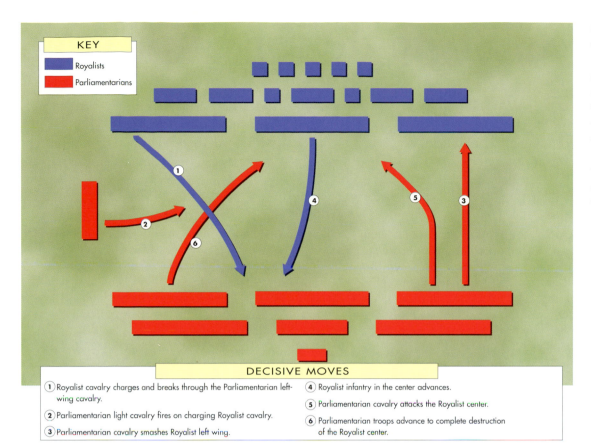

KEY
- ■ Royalists
- ■ Parliamentarians

Left: The Battle of Naseby was fought on June 14, 1645. It effectively ended any hopes King Charles may have had to win the war. The decisive factor was the disciplined and well-trained cavalry of the New Model Army, which first defeated the Royalist cavalry and then forced the surrender of the Royalist infantry.

DECISIVE MOVES

1. Royalist cavalry charges and breaks through the Parliamentarian left-wing cavalry.
2. Parliamentarian light cavalry fires on charging Royalist cavalry.
3. Parliamentarian cavalry smashes Royalist left wing.
4. Royalist infantry in the center advances.
5. Parliamentarian cavalry attacks the Royalist center.
6. Parliamentarian troops advance to complete destruction of the Royalist center.

join Sir Thomas Fairfax's northern army and the Earl of Manchester's Eastern Association Army in Yorkshire. They besieged the Royalist city of York, which drew an army under Prince Rupert northward in an attempt to relieve the city. The two armies met at Marston Moor on July 2, 1644. Rupert's forces, outnumbered by the Parliamentarians, were beaten by well-trained cavalry led by Oliver Cromwell (1599–1658) and superior Parliamentarian infantry. This decisive victory gave Parliament control of the north.

In the south, Parliament lost the chance to capture Charles in Oxford and end the war. And at the Second Battle of Newbury (October 27), the outnumbered Royalists were able to escape from the Parliamentarians. Such events demonstrated to the main Parliamentary leaders that a review of their forces was required.

The Parliamentarian debate over the course of the war ended in victory for the radical wing of the movement, which pressed for total military victory over the king. Cromwell, one of the radical Parliamentarians, gained political support for the creation of a "New Model Army," a professional force of infantry, cavalry, and artillery to be led by experienced commanders.

Under the overall command of Fairfax, the New Model Army embodied many of the lessons learned from the Thirty Years War, owing much to Gustavus Adolphus's principles of firepower and mobility combined with sound organization and strict discipline.

In June 1645, Fairfax, commander-in-chief of the New Model Army, and Cromwell, commander of its cavalry, brought Rupert to battle at Naseby. The Parliamentarians deployed an army of 14,000 against the Royalist force of 7,500. Rupert was reluctant to fight but was overruled by the other Royalist commanders. The battle opened with a Royalist cavalry charge breaking the left wing of the Parliamentarian line, while Cromwell's cavalry, on the Parliamentarian right, delivered repeated charges against the Royalist left, which began to collapse. In the center, the infantry of the New Model Army began to push back the Royalists. Despite Charles's efforts to rally his men, the Royalist lines broke. Many of the surviving Royalist troops fled the battlefield, but 3,500 were captured.

Rupert surrendered Bristol in September. After the collapse of his remaining Royalist forces and the loss of Oxford, Charles surrendered to the Scots in July hoping to secure good terms, but after long debate the Scots eventually handed him over to Parliament in 1647.

Cromwell's negotiations with Charles failed, and in December the Scots, fearful of what the changes might mean for Scotland, agreed to fight for Charles and another civil war erupted. A Scottish army invaded England in 1648 but was soundly defeated at the Battle of Preston by Cromwell's forces.

Charles was executed in January 1649, and the Parliamentarians crushed two uprisings in Ireland and Scotland between 1649 and 1652.

France's Struggle for Supremacy

The end of the Thirty Years War did not bring hostilities between France and Spain to an end. However, the prohibitive cost of the conflict sparked off a series of civil wars in France known as the Wars of the Fronde. In January 1650, Cardinal Giulio Mazarin, the chief minister of France, imprisoned one of his leading opponents, Louis, Prince of Condé. The war started again in February, the rebels aided by Spain.

In July 1652 the leading royalist general, Henri, Viscount of Turenne (1611–75), defeated Condé (recently released from prison) outside Paris. Condé retreated to northeastern France, where, supported by his Spanish allies, he continued to pose a threat to the French crown. The strategic picture changed in 1657, however, when the French received support from England, which had come to blows with Spain following the English seizure of the Spanish possession of Jamaica two years previously. A small English force arrived in France and the combined Anglo-French army laid siege to the Spanish-held port of Dunkirk. A Spanish force marched to relieve the siege but was defeated by Turenne at the Battle of the Dunes on June 14, 1658.

The victory at the Dunes allowed the French to take most of the fortresses along their border with the Spanish Netherlands. The Spanish sued for peace, and the resulting Peace of the Pyrenees, signed in November 1659, ended the war between Spain and France. The treaty confirmed the decline of Spain as a major European power. The latter part of the 17th century also developed into a struggle between France and the rest of western Europe for military and political power, and between the Netherlands and England for economic power in overseas trade.

The Anglo-Dutch Wars

Commercial rivalry between England and the Netherlands escalated into a series of three naval conflicts that began in 1652 and lasted until 1673. The wars were a consequence of the struggle between the two nations over global trading rights and North Sea fishing. In May 1652, an English fleet commanded by Robert Blake exchanged gunfire with a Dutch squadron led by Marten Tromp.

In September, Blake defeated a Dutch fleet off the north coast of Kent, but the following November Tromp defeated Blake's heavily outnumbered fleet off Dungeness. In February 1653, a Dutch convoy passing through the English Channel was successfully attacked by the English, who scored two further victories at the Gabbard Bank in June and Scheveningen in July (in which Tromp was killed). The Dutch agreed to peace terms in April 1654.

Economic rivalries led to the Second Anglo-Dutch War (1664–67), where the tables were turned against the English in favor of the Dutch. The English were defeated in the Four Days Battle (1666) and suffered the humiliation of Dutch ships sailing up the Medway to destroy Chatham docks. The resulting Treaty of Breda confirmed Dutch superiority.

The Third Anglo-Dutch War (1672–73) involved the French, who on this occasion were allied with the English in a general conflict with the Netherlands. A bitterly fought engagement at Sole Bay on May 28, 1672, in which the Dutch were forced to withdraw, was followed by Dutch victories at the Schooneveldt Channel and Texel. Although the Dutch had the tactical edge, the war had exhausted the Netherlands's resources, and its navy no longer dominated the English Channel and North Sea.

The Anglo-Dutch Wars confirmed the importance of naval firepower, first suggested in the English victory over the Armada. Warships were now built solely to deliver broadsides of heavy guns. Small antipersonnel guns were almost completely abandoned in favor of rows of guns mounted on several decks, whose function was to sink or disable enemy ships.

The Control of Fleets

Fleets increased in size, which made handling in the smoke and confusion of battle very difficult. Signaling flags were used but were always of limited use, especially when a fleet of 30 or more ships was sailing in line. In the English Royal Navy, a system of "Fighting Instructions" was introduced that established a fixed tactical doctrine to, hopefully, meet all eventualities. Although the "Fighting Instructions" were useful in coordinating ship movements, they stifled initiative.

During the Third Anglo-Dutch War, King Louis XIV of France pressed a claim against the Spanish Netherlands, which was opposed by the United (Dutch) Netherlands, who feared French territorial ambitions. In May 1672 the French Army invaded the Netherlands, to which the outnumbered Dutch responded by opening the dikes that kept the North Sea from flooding their county. It was a desperate measure that caused great economic damage, but it halted the French Army.

The Dutch convinced the Holy Roman Emperor Leopold I, Charles II of Spain, and the ruler of the German state of Brandenburg to join them against the French. One of Louis's major ambitions was to extend

French territory along the west bank of the Rhine, and the resumption of hostilities in 1674 focused attention on the Rhine. Turenne's campaign in the Rhineland from 1674 to 1675 saw him repeatedly outmaneuver his enemies. Their rigid defensive tactics, in spite of their greater numbers, allowed Turenne to triumph on many occasions. Turenne, however, was killed by a stray cannon ball at the Battle of Sassbach, near Strasbourg, on July 27, 1675, while preparing his forces for an attack.

The war continued for a further three years, until Louis's finance minister convinced him that the cost would bankrupt France. The peace treaties ending the conflict were signed between 1678 and 1679, and gave Louis territory in both the north and east of France.

The other European states now began to combine against Louis, fearing that he was determined to conquer even more of Europe. An anti-French alliance, the League of Augsburg, was agreed on in July 1686. Louis could have chosen to avoid war but instead took the initiative and invaded Germany in September 1688. His one ally, Catholic James II of England, lost his throne in December 1688, when a Protestant, later King William III, was invited by leading English Protestants to take the English crown. James II crossed to Ireland in 1689.

War between France and a combination of states comprising Spain, England, the Netherlands, and the Holy Roman Empire was declared in 1689. In 1690, Louis's forces gained victories over an Anglo-Dutch fleet at the Battle of Beachy Head, and against an allied army in Italy. But the defeat of James II at the Battle of the Boyne – in Ireland that July – lost Louis any chance of victory against England.

The course of the maritime war came to favor the allies. In 1692 an Anglo-Dutch naval victory at La Hougue, off the northern coast of France, saw the French lose 15 warships. The losses became decisive because the French could not afford to replace these expensive vessels, forcing Louis to abandon plans to invade England. The French armies in the Spanish Netherlands, northwestern Italy, and northeastern Spain absorbed most of the government's finances, leaving little money for new warships.

On land, the French were more successful, profiting from the arguments that bedevilled the decision-making of the allied commanders, especially in Italy. In the Netherlands, the French Army won victories at Steenkerke in 1692 and Neerwinden the following year. In Spain, Barcelona was besieged by the French in 1694, which, due to the intervention of an English fleet, held out until 1697. By this time, however, the cost of the war was weighing heavily on all the combatants, and most were looking to end the conflict. In the fall of 1697 the

Right: The Battle of the Boyne was a limited victory for Protestant King William III over the Catholic King James II. William had 34,000 men, while James could muster only 23,000 troops of variable quality.

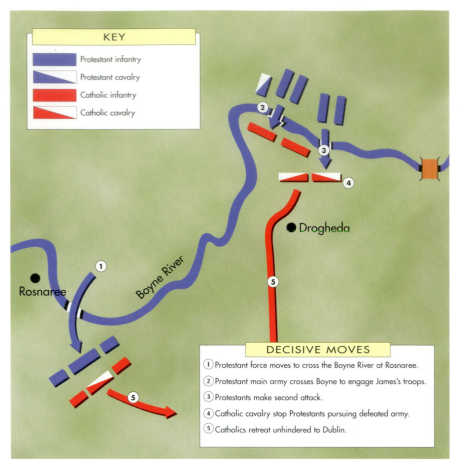

KEY

- Protestant infantry
- Protestant cavalry
- Catholic infantry
- Catholic cavalry

● Drogheda

Boyne River

● Rosnaree

DECISIVE MOVES

1. Protestant force moves to cross the Boyne River at Rosnaree.
2. Protestant main army crosses Boyne to engage James's troops.
3. Protestants make second attack.
4. Catholic cavalry stop Protestants pursuing defeated army.
5. Catholics retreat unhindered to Dublin.

Treaty of Ryswick was signed, bringing the war to a close. France was forced to return much of the territory it had captured in the war, although it retained the city of Strasbourg.

The French Army

The French Army at this time was arguably the best in Europe. Numbering some 400,000 men in 1693, it was superbly led by a series of great captains: Turenne, Condé, Luxembourg, and Villars. The French adopted the Swedish system of organization, the basic infantry formation being the battalion of between 600 and 800 men. In battle this unit was usually organized in one line six deep, with the pikes in the center and the muskets on the flank. The army formed several lines in battle, with battalions arrayed in checkerboard fashion. Two-thirds of the men were musketeers, from which a detachment was detailed to support the cavalry. The interval between battalions was supposed to be equal to their front, allowing the second line – usually 300 to 400 paces behind – to pass through. A reserve was kept twice that distance behind the second line.

The French cavalry consisted of heavy cavalry, carabiniers, light cavalry, and dragoons. The carabiniers numbered around 3,000 men, and were armed with rifled carbines and swords, while the dragoons were armed with muskets and the newly developed bayonet. Thus they combined the advantages of both infantry and cavalry, and their numbers grew: one regiment in 1650 to 43 regiments in the French Army by 1690.

One of the most distinctive features of late 17th-century warfare in western Europe was the growing importance of fortresses and siegecraft. Chains of fortified towns with their magazines (fortified supply bases) were built along an army's likely route of advance and along a country's frontiers. The French, for example, possessed a chain of fortresses, each one fully equipped with all the supplies needed by the army. Thus an army on the march could use any one as a base, confident of finding everything it needed, including heavy artillery. The presence of these forts made rapid movement exceptionally difficult for an enemy, however, and warfare tended to become a matter of sieges punctuated by the occasional battle. Consequently, the construction

and taking of fortresses became two of the main objectives in warfare.

Marshal Sébastien le Prestre de Vauban (1633–1707) dominated fortification and siege warfare during the reign of King Louis XIV. Vauban developed the techniques that had first emerged in the early 16th century, and took them to a higher level through his skill in geometry and his practical eye for the lie of the land.

His fortifications used a design that surrounded the main body of a fortress with a series of ditches, low walls, and earthworks (during his lifetime he built 33 new fortresses and remodeled 3,000 others). Vauban made excellent use of bastions: small triangular forts constructed just beyond the main fortress walls that were arranged in such a way as to ensure that any attack on the main wall faced enfilade fire from three directions. Vauban improved the forts along the French frontiers, a defensive line that remained highly effective well into the 18th century.

Siege warfare also advanced under the Vauban, who personally directed some 50 operations. Vauban integrated the use of artillery at all stages of the siege, whereas before artillery tended to fire from places of safety at long ranges. The ultimate aim was to permit the attacking siege artillery to breach the walls. Siege engineers, or sappers, approached the walls along zigzag trenches (saps), preventing the defenders from firing directly down the length of the trenches. Once the saps

got closer to the fort, a line of trenches running parallel to the fortress walls were dug.

Long-range artillery covered the digging of saps and a second parallel trench line. More artillery and mortars then came forward to give covering fire for a third parallel trench, before a final bombardment to breach the walls was ordered. These parallel lines enabled more fire to be directed against the defenders, gave greater protection to the sappers, and increased the opportunity for simultaneous attacks from different points. Fascines

(bundles of twigs or brushwood) were often used to fill up ditches and the moat (if there was one) before an assault. It usually took one or two days of pounding from the third parallel to make a breach in the enemy wall. The assault then followed.

Vauban's technical writings became a key element in military studies, and although published after his death, his treatise *On Siege and Fortification* both reflected and influenced the science of fortress-taking and -building for nearly a century.

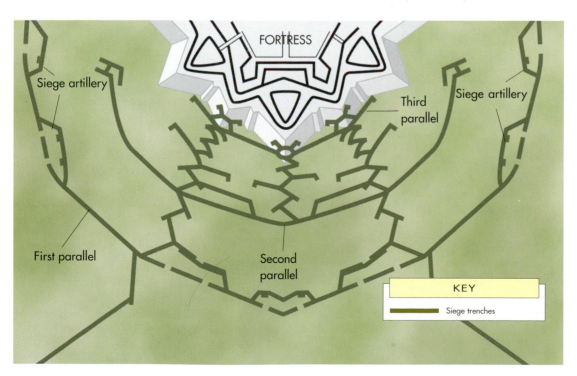

FORTRESS

Siege artillery

Siege artillery

Third parallel

First parallel

Second parallel

KEY

Siege trenches

Left: Representation of a typical system of siege lines around a Vauban-style fortress. Artillery batteries covered the zigzag saps that advanced to the walls of the fortress.

The Ottomans in Decline

The checks at Malta in 1565 and Lepanto in 1571 marked the high tide of the Ottoman Empire. Afterwards the empire was forced to conduct a series of defensive wars to protect its territories from increasingly expansionist Christian European states during the course of the 17th century. Though it was still powerful, the Ottoman Empire had entered a period of slow decline.

The Ottoman sultans, whose empire included the border lands north of the Black Sea, came into conflict with the Polish-controlled Ukraine during the early 17th century. Cossack bands operating from the Ukraine raided Turkish lands along the Black Sea, precipitating the Polish–Turkish War of 1620–21. Neither side gained an advantage from the conflict, and in 1621 Poland and the Turkish sultan, Osman II, agreed to a truce that halted the war. Cossack raids continued, however, a continuing remainder to the Turkish authorities of the need for vigilance to ensure the integrity of the Ottoman Empire.

Turkey faced increasing difficulties controlling its subject peoples and defending its borders. Osman attempted to tighten his control over the country by removing some of the privileges held by the Janissaries, the elite corps of Turkish infantry. The Janissaries objected and overthrew Osman, replacing him with his more malleable brother in 1622. The Janissaries effectively dominated the Turkish government until the arrival of Murad I in 1638, a sultan strong enough to bring the Janissaries to heel. They adopted much the same role as the Praetorian Guard in ancient Rome, and their behavior was equally detrimental to the fortunes of the state they were supposed to be serving.

Conflict with Venice

Throughout much of the 17th century, Turkey found itself embroiled in conflict with the Venetians for control of the eastern Mediterranean. Christian privateers – many of them Venetian ships – had a long history of preying on Turkish shipping. In 1645, ships sailing from the Venetian-controlled island of Crete captured a Turkish vessel carrying the wives of the Turkish sultan, Ibrahim I.

This outrage provoked the Turks to take prompt action, and an army estimated at between 50,000 and 75,000 men was transported to Crete. Aided by local Greeks, who had a long antipathy toward the Venetians, the Turks captured two of the three major fortresses on the island: Canea fell in 1645 and Retino in 1646. The Turks looked set to capture the entire island. However, the fortress of Candia endured a siege lasting 21 years (1648–69), the Venetian Navy sending in supplies in a determined effort to maintain a foothold on Crete.

In 1656, a new grand vizier (chief minister) took control of the Turkish government. Mohammed Koprulu tried to reverse the slow decline of the empire. He reorganized the Turkish fleet, so that by the late 1650s it was a match for the

Left: Two members of the elite arm of the Ottoman armed forces: a Janissary (right) and an artilleryman (left). These two groups were highly trained, but large numbers of Ottoman armies were untrained levies.

Left: Relief forces under the Pole Jan Sobieski attack Turkish troops besieging Vienna in September 1683. The Ottomans suffered a crushing defeat, which marked the end of Turkish hopes of ever taking the major city.

Venetian Navy and was able to capture several Venetian-held islands in the Aegean Sea.

Koprulu also intervened in Transylvania. The ruler of this semi-independent region of the Ottoman Empire, George Rakoczy, with the support of the Holy Roman Emperor, ignored Turkish claims to sovereignty over his realm. The Turks dispatched an army to remove Rakoczy, but he defeated it at the Battle of Lippa in Transylvania in May 1658. But after Crimean Tartars arrived to reinforce the Turks, Rakoczy was forced to flee to Hapsburg Hungary. He returned the next year and drove out his Turkish-backed replacement, only to suffer defeat and death in 1660 at the Battle of Fenes in Transylvania. His successor, Janos Kemeny, was killed at the Battle of Nagyszollos, also in Transylvania, in January 1662.

Conflict with the Holy Roman Empire

The Turks took direct control of Transylvania and then invaded the Holy Roman Empire. At the Battle of the Raab River in Hungary in August 1664, an Imperial army halted the Turks. Mohammed Koprulu's successor, Fazil Ahmed Koprulu, continued his policies of vigorously opposing Transylvanian autonomy. The treaty that concluded this war in 1664 ensured that Transylvania remained part of the Ottoman Empire.

A war against Poland between 1671 and 1677 added territory in the Ukraine to the empire, although this was lost at the end of a war with Russia in 1681. The Polish war had led to the election of the great general Jan Sobieski (1624–96) as the king of Poland. He knew that Turkey would sooner or later attack Poland again. Sobieski signed a treaty with the Holy Roman Empire in March 1683, believing that the alliance offered the best chance of defeating the Turks and solving the problem once and for all.

However, popular unrest in Hungary alarmed Sobieski. The part of Hungary ruled by the Hapsburgs had rebelled against its rulers in 1678, and the rebels turned to the Turks for support. In 1682, Kara Mustafa Koprulu demanded that the Holy Roman Empire grant independence to Hungary. When the emperor refused, a huge Turkish invasion force of anything up to 200,000 men laid siege to Vienna in 1683.

The small Austrian garrison of 15,000 troops lacked heavy artillery but managed to hold out against the besiegers, while awaiting help from outside. In late August, Sobieski left Warsaw and marched south toward Vienna, his 30,000-strong army covering 220 miles (252 km) in just 15 days. Outside Vienna Sobieski was reinforced with German and Austrian troops, bringing his total forces up to 75,000 men. On 12 September the allied army attacked the Turks, supported by the Viennese garrison. The fighting was indecisive at first, until a cavalry charge led by Sobieski turned the tide of battle and forced the Turks to retreat – and permanently abandon the siege of Vienna. The Turkish Army would never return.

The Battle of Vienna marked the end of the Turkish threat to central Europe. The last years of the 17th century saw the Holy League, made up of the Holy Roman Empire, Venice, and Poland, make territorial gains at Turkish expense. Although the Turks recovered some territory, their defeat at the Battle of Zenta in Hungary in 1697 handed Hungary and Transylvania to the Holy Roman Emperor. Turkish ambitions of having a controlling influence in eastern and central Europe were dashed for good.

Warfare in the 18th Century
1700–99

The transformation of warfare during this period from combat that was "merely continental" in scale to that which was truly global frequently necessitated an understanding of international politics and diplomacy, and combined military applications of naval and land arms. While there were new developments, in organizations and logistics, for example, other aspects of change were more limited, and battle was even often avoided unless the odds were sufficiently favorable.

In the 18th century, Europe was beginning to exert its military power and political influence across the globe. There were three important geographical arenas where this warfare took place. The first was in Europe itself, where struggles between various dynasties led to gradual changes in the balance of power. The second area lay in and around the overseas colonies belonging to the European powers – mainly in the Americas and India. The third broad area lay along Christian Europe's frontier with the Muslim Ottoman Empire. From the 14th century onward, Ottoman armies and fleets had continually threatened Europe. All the countries of the Balkan peninsula, up to and including present-day Hungary and Romania, were part of the Ottoman Empire. In 1683, Vienna was actually besieged by Ottoman armies. During the 18th century, however, a decisive shift took place: Ottoman forces were defeated in a number of wars and the long process of dismantling this great empire began.

The wars between the biggest European states assumed a major role in the eyes of contemporary observers, even though in the long term events outside of central Europe had more importance. There were several recurrent themes in this warfare. The first was the continuing importance of France and the Austrian Hapsburgs as the major powers on the continent; the second was the decline of two western European powers: Spain and the Netherlands; the third was the rise of Prussia as a major military power; the fourth was

Right: One of the great captains of history, Frederick the Great of Prussia (mounted on the white horse) salutes his troops following their victory over the Austrians and Saxons at the Battle of Hohenfriedberg in 1745. The engagement cost the Austrians 16,000 casualties.

the decline of Sweden, which had been dominant in the Baltic since the mid-17th century; and the fifth was the rise of Russia, largely at the expense of Sweden.

The nature of these dynastic wars was that they were limited in scope. They were not the fights to the death between rival religious or political systems that had characterized much of the warfare of the previous century. Thankfully for the population of Europe, therefore, the savagery against civilians that had marked great parts of conflicts such as the Thirty Years War (1620–48) was usually, though not inevitably, absent. Nevertheless, there were notable atrocities and wars where civil society was a target, such as the attempt by the British authorities, after the Jacobite Rebellion and Battle of Culloden (see box on page opposite) in 1745–46, to put an end to the Scottish Highland clan system.

The Face of Battle

On the strategic level, warfare in the "age of reason" tended to favor complex maneuvering over the decisive battle that became the centerpiece of strategic thought from the Napoleonic Wars onward. Generals were even encouraged to avoid battle unless the odds were greatly to their advantage.

Military innovation during this period was similarly limited. Weapons, tactics, and levels of generalship evolved slowly. Infantry continued to move in rigid columns, and then deploy in lines that were reduced from the six ranks of the late 17th century to half that number. The pike, for so long the best means for infantry to stop cavalry, finally disappeared at the end of 17th century, and in its stead the bayonet provided the musket-armed infantry with the ability to protect themselves against cavalry. Artillery was standardized and became increasingly mobile, allowing guns a more important role on the battlefield. Cavalry, in general, played a less important part on the battlefield itself, although the Prussian Army did have a great cavalry leader in von Seydlitz.

Infantry soldiers were expected to perform basic maneuvers and fight in close order. Their tactics and drills were practiced frequently in peacetime so that every soldier and officer knew what was expected of him: obedience and discipline, and the ability to follow orders in the heat of battle. As the effective range of muskets was short, firefights were conducted at close range, with victory going to the side that could best carry out the complex drills necessary for loading and reloading a muzzle-loading musket under fire.

Artillery and musket fire wreathed battlefields in clouds of smoke, making it difficult to distinguish friend from foe. Partly as a consequence of this, soldiers wore standardized (and usually brightly colored) uniforms, making identification easier through the "fog of war." The one true military innovation in western European warfare that occurred during the 18th century was the introduction of light troops from the 1740s onward. This was a slow process, as most generals distrusted all forms of military activity that could not be directly controlled. But as the century wore on, so light troops (especially infantry) came to take on a greater role in military operations, fighting in looser formations, in which flexibility and individual initiative were critical.

The origins of light troops lay in two contemporaneous but geographically separate areas. The Austrians were the first to introduce light troops

Right: Soldiers of Frederick the Great's Prussian Army. Through harsh discipline and endless drill the Prussians achieved a high state of military efficiency. A Prussian battalion, for example, could fire five rounds per minute, with each of the battalion's eight platoons constituting a separate fire unit.

Left: British troops try to storm the French defenses outside Fort Ticonderoga in North America on July 8, 1758. The attack proved the futility of mounting frontal attacks against regular infantry placed behind fortified positions. The British suffered 1,500 casualties.

from their border regions in the east: hussar light cavalry from Hungary and *pandour*, or *grenzer*, light infantry from Croatia. These irregular troops had a long history of skirmishing with the Turks, and came to perform a similar function fighting the Prussians and French. Once their worth had been proved while on campaign, they were introduced into other European armies. The other source of light infantry tactics lay across the Atlantic, where Native Americans and colonial backwoodsmen demonstrated their military skill in the rough, wooded terrain of North America.

A major reason for the distrust of light infantry lay in the fear of desertion if individuals were allowed to operate on their own. The ranks of most armies were in principle filled by professionals who had chosen a military career. In practice, however, most men were press-ganged into service and brutally disciplined to make them maneuver effectively, and to stand in line and fire while under fire themselves directed by the enemy. In some cases, men were even kidnapped: Frederick William I of Prussia, Frederick the Great's father, built up his famous guards regiment by abducting tall soldiers from other armies or even from civilian professions.

These 18th-century armies also reflected the social stratification of their societies. Their officers were overwhelmingly composed of landed gentry and aristocrats, with those of superior status serving in the cavalry rather than in the infantry regiments.

RIVAL TACTICS

The Jacobite Highlanders were Scottish clan warriors and not professional soldiers. Their principal "tactic" consisted of a wild charge against the enemy, but if the charge did not make the enemy break then the Highlanders faced almost certain defeat, especially if faced by a well-trained infantry force.

At the Battle of Culloden in 1746, the Duke of Cumberland used his artillery to kill and maim the Highlanders and provoke the rest into making a charge. As the Highlanders' assault was slowed crossing the boggy moor at Culloden, many more were cut down by musket fire.

The duke had also introduced a new tactic for hand-to-hand fighting. In such a situation a soldier would normally use his bayonet to attack the man to his immediate front. A Highland clansman was often able to deflect the bayonet thrust with his shield (held on the left arm), and then cut his opponent down with the sword held in his right hand. At Culloden, each government soldier attacked the Highlander to his right, thrusting his bayonet into the man's unprotected right side. This tactic called for cool nerves and confidence in one's fellow soldiers, but it proved highly effective.

The Great Northern War

When the Baltic powers of Denmark, Poland, and Russia decided to attack the region's chief power, Sweden, in 1700 they underestimated the new, young king, Charles XII. He was to demonstrate how boldness and tactical brilliance could transform the battlefield in favor of even the most outnumbered force, although his actions were also to prove that a truly great commander is one that knows when to stop.

Limited warfare did produce many commanders of note. The two greatest generals of the age were England's Duke of Marlborough (1650–1722) and Prussia's Frederick the Great (1712–86), men who could stand comparison with all but a few in history. They showed strategic imagination of the highest order, combined with a masterly command of tactical detail. There were also several of lesser rank, who included Charles XII of Sweden (1682–1718), Prince Eugene (1683–1736), and two French generals, the Duke of Villars (1653–1734) and Maurice de Saxe (1696–1750).

Of these, undoubtedly the strangest was Charles XII, a tactician of near genius who blindly refused to accept any obstacle in his path – a trait that led to the near destruction of his country. At the end of the 17th century, Sweden's dominance in the Baltic region was contested by Denmark, Poland, and Russia. Charles had become king of Sweden in 1697, and because of his youth and inexperience the other powers initiated the Great Northern War. In April 1700 the Danes invaded the Duchy of Schleswig, an ally of Sweden. The Poles placed the Swedish-ruled city of Riga (now the capital of Latvia) under siege, while the Russians, led by Peter the Great (1672–1725), besieged the port of Narva. Charles made the decision to deal with Denmark first.

Against the advice of experienced officers, Charles boldly transported his forces across some supposedly unnavigable waters and threatened Copenhagen. The Danes almost immediately agreed to end hostilities.

Charles next planned to attack the Poles. However, he changed his mind and advanced against the Russians. His small army (8,000 men) brushed aside a Russian force outside Narva on November 18, 1700, and two days later took on the bulk of the Russian Army. The Battle of Narva was short and bloody. Charles's well-disciplined force, outnumbered five-to-one, cut the Russians to pieces. Riga was relieved by Charles in June 1701; the Russians and Poles retreated in confusion.

Charles now moved against Poland. On July 9 at the Battle of Dunamunde, the Swedes defeated a Russian army that stood in their way. Fighting halted during the winter, but Charles advanced again in the new year and occupied Warsaw on May 14, 1702. Despite the city's capture, campaigning carried on until September 1706, when the Polish monarch, Augustus II, was forced to accept Swedish terms, which included renouncing his claim to the Polish throne and repudiating his alliance with Russia. Peter the Great, having now lost his two allies, offered to sign a peace treaty. Charles, however, was bent on revenge and refused the Russian terms.

Left: The Battle of Narva, fought in November 1700, illustrated how successful bold initiative could be in battle. In a snowstorm the outnumbered Swedes defeated the Russian Army in only two hours of fighting.

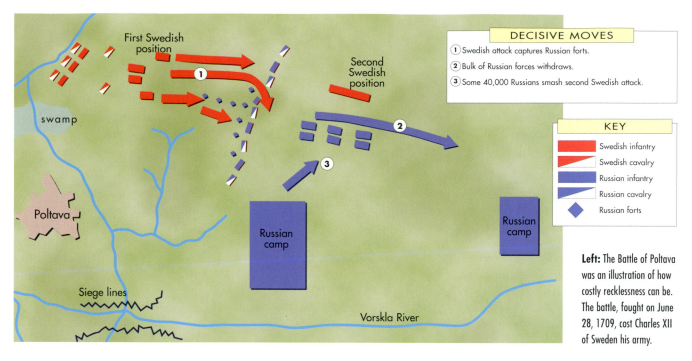

First Swedish position

Second Swedish position

swamp

Poltava

Siege lines

Russian camp

Russian camp

Vorskla River

① Swedish attack captures Russian forts.
② Bulk of Russian forces withdraws.
③ Some 40,000 Russians smash second Swedish attack.

KEY
■ Swedish infantry
◢ Swedish cavalry
■ Russian infantry
◢ Russian cavalry
◆ Russian forts

Left: The Battle of Poltava was an illustration of how costly recklessness can be. The battle, fought on June 28, 1709, cost Charles XII of Sweden his army.

In retrospect, Charles's decision to concentrate his efforts against Poland can be seen as a mistake. Despite its defeat at Narva, Russia could draw on huge reserves of manpower, and while Charles campaigned in Poland Russia was able to raise a new army. This enabled it to recapture Narva in August 1704.

On January 1, 1708, Charles led his army of 45,000 men into Russian territory. At first the invasion went well. Charles inflicted a defeat on Russia at Holowczyn in eastern Poland on July 4, but he was unable to bring its main army to battle. The Russians knew that they could not match the Swedes in open battle for the moment. Peter the Great waited, ordering the main army to avoid battle by retreating deep into the Russian heartland behind a "scorched earth" policy. As Charles advanced deeper into Russia, his forces crossed a land in which crops and fodder had been destroyed, and as he moved farther from his bases so his army began to run short of supplies. Hunger, intense cold, and disease began to thin the Swedish ranks. By October 1708 Charles and his dwindling army were in real difficulty.

Rather than retiring to Swedish territory or even waiting for resupply, Charles, instead, swung southward and headed for the Ukraine. He intended to forge an alliance with the Cossacks; meanwhile, he ordered one of his generals, Adam Loewenhaupt, to gather a supply train in the Baltic and join him in the Ukraine.

Peter ordered an army into the Ukraine and the Cossack capital of Baturin was burned. A Russian force attacked Loewenhaupt's supply column and, although he still linked up with Charles, all the supplies were lost.

Charles's fortunes did not improve. The winter was the coldest in memory, and by the spring Charles's force had been reduced to 25,000 men. Charles needed a victory, and hoped that he could draw the Russians into a battle by besieging Poltava in southern Russia. Charles advanced *en masse*, but such was the Russian material superiority that it was the Swedes who were trapped. On June 28, Charles, though vastly outnumbered, decided to attack. The Russians, however, absorbed the attacks and then unleashed such firepower that the Swedish force disintegrated. The Swedes suffered close to 10,000 men killed and had over 15,000 captured. The Russians lost less than 5,000 troops in total.

Charles fled into Turkish-controlled territory to the south of Poltava. The Russians moved to liberate Poland and put Augustus II back on the throne. The three former allies also set about capturing Swedish territories around the Baltic. Meanwhile, Charles persuaded the Turks to declare war on the Russians in October 1710.

A Turkish army of 200,000 troops gathered along the border with Russia. Peter the Great moved to deal with it, but, perhaps overconfident, he was defeated along the Pruth River. The Turks offered generous peace terms – much to Charles's disgust. Charles continued to propose war and the Turks put him under house arrest. Charles, however, escaped to Sweden in November 1714.

Charles's arrival in Sweden seemed to give new life to his beleaguered forces. He quickly raised an army of 20,000 men, and in 1716 was able to block a Danish–Norwegian invasion. He then invaded Norway in 1717. However, on December 11, 1718, he was killed while besieging the city of Fredriksten. The war continued until the signing of the Treaty of Nystad in August 1721. The peace confirmed Russia as the major power in the Baltic. Charles XII had proved himself a fine leader of men in battle, but in the long run he proved a poor strategist. For the results of this long conflict, known as the Great Northern War, confirmed the final eclipse of Sweden as a great power.

War of the Spanish Succession

The 18th century opened in Europe with a major dynastic war. When King Charles II of Spain died childless in 1700, he left his throne to the grandson of Louis XIV of France. The Austrian Hapsburgs also had a claimant, and so in 1701 war broke out between Austria and France, instigated by the French invasion of the Spanish Netherlands, and soon two major blocks emerged as other states joined the fray.

The French also advanced into northern Italy, then controlled by Austria, but were defeated at the Battle of Chiari on September 1, 1701, by an Austrian army under Prince Eugene.

Other European powers, notably Britain, Prussia and other German states, the Netherlands, Prussia, and later Portugal joined the Austrians to form a Grand Alliance aimed at stopping what they feared would be an overwhelmingly strong union of France and Spain. France forged links with the Italian states of Savoy and Mantua, and the German state of Bavaria. A general war broke out in 1702, and lasted until 1713.

Britain declared war on France on May 15, 1702, and immediately sent General John Churchill, Earl of Marlborough, to assume command of the British and Dutch forces in the Netherlands. Although he had no direct authority over the Dutch troops, Marlborough did his best to improve overall standards. During the winter break in campaigning, for example, he paid full attention to infantry drill and marksmanship, training his men in volley firing by 50-man platoons and the formation of hollow infantry squares to repel cavalry.

The linear formations that dominated the battlefield required high standards of drill if infantry firepower was to be exploited fully. The bulk of the fighting rested with the infantry battalions, who now comprised men armed with flintlock muskets and bayonets. Within the battalion was a company of grenadiers, selected for their size and strength, who were armed with simple grenades (along with their muskets), which were used to dislodge defenders from field fortifications. Over time, these men became an elite with the duties of shock troops.

Marlborough's early operations were hampered by the Dutch authorities' unwillingness to grant him control over their forces. Nevertheless, while Eugene continued to battle against the French in Italy, Churchill launched an operation to secure the lower parts of the Rhine and Meuse rivers where they flowed into the North Sea. Between September and October various cities fell to Churchill, and as a result he was given the title of Duke of Marlborough. The only setback for the Grand Alliance was the defeat by the French, under the

capable Claude de Villars, of an army from the German state of Baden at the Battle of Friedlingen in October.

For the 1703 campaign, Marlborough planned to lead his army down the Rhine to establish links with the Austrians and then retake the French-held forts in the Spanish Netherlands, before securing the key port of Antwerp. The French, meanwhile, were planning to march on Vienna, the Austrian capital. Marlborough succeeded in gaining a route thanks to the capture of Bonn in May 1703, but he failed against Antwerp's strong defenses. The French advance began well. Marshal de Villars defeated two Grand Alliance forces at Munderkingen and Hochstadt. However, France's ally Bavaria was unwilling to cooperate further, and after a quarrel with the elector of Bavaria, Villars resigned. Despite this failure, the French maintained their pressure in 1703. Marshal Camille de Tallard attacked across the Rhine, taking a frontier fortress in September and threatening Austria from southern Germany.

Winter gave both sides time to reconsider their strategies. In 1704 the French decided to focus on seizing Vienna, leaving only a holding force to occupy Marlborough in the Netherlands. Marlborough planned a diversionary attack on Spain and also ordered a naval force to attack Toulon. The bulk of his forces, operating

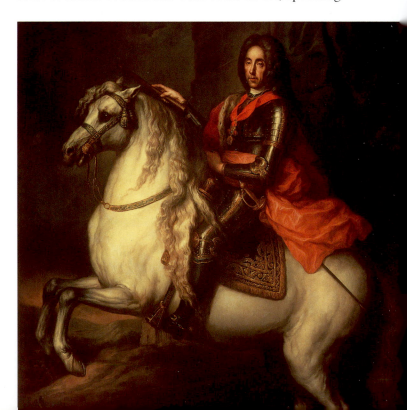

Right: Prince Eugene of Austria was one of the premier soldiers of the age. A master of strategy and tactics, in battle he displayed a reckless courage and expected the same of his men. He became a close friend of Marlborough, and the two worked harmoniously together.

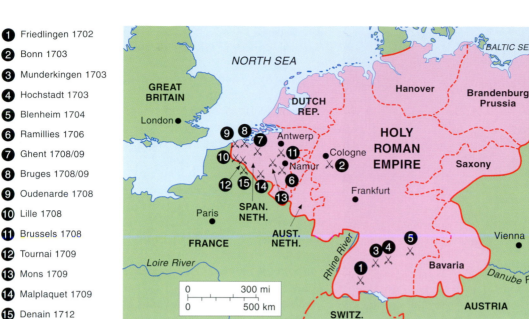

1 Friedlingen 1702
2 Bonn 1703
3 Munderkingen 1703
4 Hochstadt 1703
5 Blenheim 1704
6 Ramillies 1706
7 Ghent 1708/09
8 Bruges 1708/09
9 Oudenarde 1708
10 Lille 1708
11 Brussels 1708
12 Tournai 1709
13 Mons 1709
14 Malplaquet 1709
15 Denain 1712

Left: The War of the Spanish Succession was fought chiefly in the Low Countries (modern Belgium, Luxembourg, and the Netherlands), along the line of the Rhine River, and in the south.

from the Netherlands, had three difficult objectives: to save Vienna, to drive the French out of Germany, and to force Bavaria to end its alliance with France.

By April 1704 France and its allies had over 80,000 troops in Bavaria, while the Austrians could muster about 70,000 men. However, Marlborough moved down the Rhine with some 35,000 men. It was the Grand Alliance's intention to unite its forces, while the French hoped to defeat them before they could link up. By a series of marches that completely outwitted the French, Prince Eugene and Marlborough met at Blenheim, a small village just to the north of the Danube, on August 12.

The two forces were evenly matched. Marlborough and Eugene led 56,000 troops; while the French and their Bavarian allies numbered about 60,000. By midday the Grand Alliance forces were drawn up in their battle lines. The fighting began on August 13 with Eugene attacking the French left wing and a British column attacking the French in Blenheim village. These moves were designed to force Marshal Tallard to draw in his reserves. Rattled by the two attacks, Tallard did, in fact, commit his reserves, with most drawn into Blenheim. The fighting around the village was bitter and the British suffered heavily, but Marlborough's first objective was achieved.

Marlborough then unleashed his cavalry against the French center in the afternoon. The French fought back for an hour, but eventually gave way under the onslaught. Tallard was captured and his men fled. A total catastrophe was avoided only because a portion of Tallard's army managed to escape before Marlborough was able to complete an encircling maneuver.

The French and Bavarians nevertheless suffered terrible casualties: nearly 40,000 killed, wounded, and captured. Marlborough lost about 12,000 men killed and wounded. Blenheim was a shattering defeat for France; any hope of securing Vienna was dashed and Bavaria came under Austrian control.

The following year, 1705, was inconclusive, but in 1706 Marlborough, back in the Netherlands, won another great victory over the French. The battle, at Ramillies, was a consequence of the French belief that Marlborough was intent on capturing Namur and sent some 60,000 troops under Marshal Francois de Villeroi to protect the city. Villeroi, no match for Marlborough, was stopped on his march to Namur and he drew his 60,000 men up in a long, partly fortified line that ran across high ground. He had no intention of attacking, leaving it to Marlborough to take the initiative. Marlborough's tactics were a masterpiece of coordination, and were broadly similar to those used so successfully at Blenheim. He deployed some of his 60,000 troops to suggest that he intended to crush the French left wing, hoping that Villeroi would move his reserves from the center and right of the French line to reinforce the left wing. The ruse worked.

Marlborough then launched his main attack against the weakened French right. The French fought determinedly but were overwhelmed. Seeing the decisive moment had arrived, Marlborough ordered an advance of his whole army and the French were swept from the battlefield.

Ramillies had important results. Firstly, it led to the dismissal of Villeroi, who was replaced in August 1706 by the more able Louis Josef, Duke of Vendome. Secondly, Marlborough's victory led to the capture of some key fortresses, along with thousands of enemy troops. Thirdly, Vendome had been fighting in Italy against Prince Eugene, and his departure to take on Marlborough had disastrous consequences for the French campaign there.

Eugene was outnumbered by the French, and faced a fortified enemy attempting to capture Turin. Even so, he decided to attack an isolated section of the French line on September 7, 1707. The fighting was bitter, but a sudden attack by the Turin garrison decided the day. The

Left: John Churchill, Duke of Marlborough, was one of the great captains of history, and his charm and courtesy made him excel in the diplomacy necessary in a coalition war.

Alliance army had arrived to take his place. For his part, Vendome decided to strike first. That summer he tried to outmaneuver Marlborough, and had some success, capturing Ghent and Bruges in July, although he knew that time was running out. If he did not bring Marlborough to battle soon, Eugene would arrive from central Germany, making his task all the more difficult.

Marlborough was also eager for battle, despite Eugene's army not having arrived. Two matters concerned him. Firstly, he recognized that Vendome held the initiative. Secondly, the morale of the Dutch forces under his command was shaky. He needed a swift victory to steady his allies. Eugene, who had raced ahead of his army to be with Marlborough, agreed.

Marlborough's army covered an astonishing 28 miles (45 km) in less than a day. By July 11 his men were within sight of the French. One of Vendome's generals suggested withdrawal, but Vendome realized that a retreat might imperil his communications with France, so he deployed his forces along the high ground to the north of Oudenarde. The resultant battle lacked the great skill of Blenheim or Ramillies. What counted was firmness of command, cool nerves under fire, and troop discipline. Again, Marlborough and Eugene proved the more able and their forces gained the upper hand.

Marlborough's victory at Oudenarde and the arrival of Eugene's army gave him a numerical advantage over the French. He had some 120,000 men to oppose the 96,000-strong French Army. Marlborough planned to invade France itself but was prevented from doing so by the wary Dutch. Instead, Marlborough sidestepped Vendome and laid siege to Lille in August. Vendome attempted to counter this by making his own advance

French were hit from two directions and broke. They fled back to France, and their remaining garrisons in northern Italy surrendered as the year wore on.

Both sides maneuvered for advantage through 1707, although with little result. In 1708 both sides attempted to gain the upper hand. Marlborough, with 70,000 men, planned to link up with Eugene's 35,000 troops, who would march north from central Germany once a Grand

Right: The Battle of Blenheim was fought on August 13, 1704, and was Marlborough's greatest victory. The French lost over 38,000 men killed, wounded, or taken prisoner.

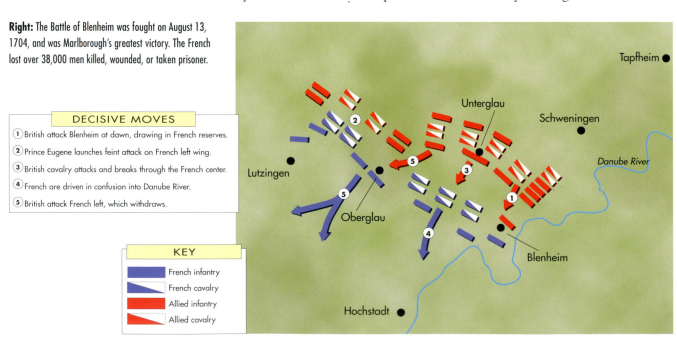

DECISIVE MOVES

① British attack Blenheim at dawn, drawing in French reserves.

② Prince Eugene launches feint attack on French left wing.

③ British cavalry attacks and breaks through the French center.

④ French are driven in confusion into Danube River.

⑤ British attack French left, which withdraws.

KEY

French infantry
French cavalry
Allied infantry
Allied cavalry

against Brussels, but was forced back by Marlborough, who left Eugene to continue the siege of Lille. The fortress city fell to Eugene on December 11.

With the onset of winter, Marlborough chose to abandon accepted military logic. He decided to push the French, who probably expected winter would give them a degree of respite, out of some key cities in the Spanish Netherlands. Ghent and Bruges fell in January 1709. Satisfied, Marlborough decided to stop until the spring and his army went into winter quarters.

Marlborough now believed he had two options: either to avoid battle and bypass the French, or force them to leave their forts. He reckoned that he could draw the French out by besieging key French-held towns and cities. Tournai fell to his troops on July 29 and he then moved against Mons. The French feared such a loss, and Villars was ordered to march against Marlborough.

The Battle of Malplaquet

Villars led some 90,000 men to take up position at Malplaquet, where they hastily built a line of field fortifications. Marlborough left 20,000 men to keep the pressure on Mons, and led 90,000 of his and Eugene's troops to confront the French. The two armies met on September 11, 1709, and the plan reflected the success enjoyed earlier. Eugene was to attack the French right, while Marlborough was to attack the left. However, these feints were intended to force Villars to use his reserves, thereby weakening his center. When Marlborough launched what he hoped would be the deciding attack, the French buckled but were able to reform their line. Marlborough committed the last of his reserves to the battle and eventually forced the French to retreat, although they did so in good order. Malplaquet was close run, decided by the fighting spirit of the ordinary soldier, and the determination of the allied commanders to carry on attacking in spite of losing over 20,000 men killed and wounded, while the French suffered 14,000 casualties. Mons surrendered on October 26.

By 1710 the Grand Alliance was falling apart. It had proposed an Austrian prince to become king of Spain rather than Louis XIV's grandson. This prince, styling himself Charles III of Spain, had headed an army that exploited discontent among Catalans in northern Spain, and used British naval power to undertake a successful campaign in Spain itself. In 1710 Charles's forces took Madrid, although they were defeated later that year at Villa Viciosa and forced to relinquish the capital. However, in April 1711 the ruling Hapsburg, Emperor Joseph, died in Vienna, and Charles III of Spain became Charles VI of Austria as well. The other Grand Alliance members, who had gone to war to prevent a monarch ruling over two major powers in the first place, certainly did not want such a ruler to emerge from their own ranks, especially one that revived fears of the earlier great Hapsburg Empire. And so the campaign in Spain collapsed amid allied mistrust.

The Grand Alliance also lost its best commander. Marlborough, accused of corruption, was recalled at the end of 1711. Eugene was left with insufficient troops to mount a meaningful offensive or even hold onto the gains already won. The French sensed this weakness and were eager to negotiate from a position of strength. The war ended in April 1713 with the Treaty of Utrecht, signed by all the combatant nations, except Austria. Britain recognized the right of French-born Philip V to the throne of Spain, while France guaranteed that the Spanish and French thrones would remain separate. The Spanish were forced to give up their possessions in the Netherlands and most of those in Italy to Austria.

QUEEN ANNE'S WAR

Although the decisive theater of the War of the Spanish Succession was in Europe, there was considerable fighting in the New World, chiefly in the Caribbean and North America. In these areas the conflict was known as Queen Anne's War (after the English monarch of the period). The war in North America was fought by the French and Spanish against the English. All three had colonies in the area, and used their own colonists and Native Americans during their campaigns.

Between 1702 and 1704, fighting was concentrated in the south of North America. In 1702, Native Americans and English colonists from the Carolinas attacked the Spanish town of St. Augustine. The town fell but the Spanish garrison retreated to a fort and held off the attackers, who withdrew when Spanish warships arrived on the scene. Between 1703 and 1704 both sides carried out hit-and-run raids against isolated settlements and missions. In the north, the French raided English colonial settlements from Maine to Connecticut, and twice launched major operations against Newfoundland (1704 and 1708).

English colonial forces twice tried to capture Port Royal in French-controlled Nova Scotia in 1704 and 1707, but failed. Port Royal was eventually taken by 4,000 British troops backed by warships on October 16, 1710, and renamed Annapolis Royal after the queen. In July 1711, colonists and British troops attempted to take Montreal and Quebec, but the campaign was abandoned after several transport ships sank after hitting rocks in the St. Lawrence River.

Queen Anne's War ended with the signing of the Treaty of Utrecht in 1713. The British gained the most from the treaty: France surrendered control of Nova Scotia and Newfoundland to Britain, and the British won the right to supply African slaves to the Spanish colonies in North America.

War of the Austrian Succession

After the Treaty of Utrecht, Europe was relatively peaceful for 26 years. From 1740, however, the "states-system" was upset by a series of wars caused by the ambitions of Frederick II of Prussia. Although arts and philosophy interested him, he was even more attracted by war and politics, and the well-trained, highly maneuverable army he had inherited from his father provided him with the means of achieving his aims.

In October 1745 the Holy Roman Emperor and Hapsburg ruler of Austria, Charles VI, died. He was succeeded by his daughter Maria Theresa, but her rights were still uncertain and Charles Albert, the elector of Bavaria, asserted his right to become Holy Roman Emperor. Frederick II then invaded the Hapsburg province of Silesia, initiating a series of wars that ended with Prussia established as a major European power.

The young king's success in Silesia surprised Europe. Prussia was a small, relatively backward German state with a population of only 2.5 million. The secret lay in its army – for its population size, Prussia's army was very large: 80,000 men, compared to Austria's 100,000-strong army (from her empire's population of over 20 million).

That Prussia was able to field such an army was due to a militaristic society in which officers were normally raised from the landowning Junker class, while the rank and file were conscripted from the peasantry. For serving as officers, the nobles received special privileges in Prussian society. If manpower levels were insufficient, mercenary troops were used from other German states.

Frederick the Great's victories were masterpieces of 18th-century tactics, in which the superior drill and maneuverability of his army enabled him to develop certain methods of attack, notably the oblique order, in which the army concentrated its efforts against one flank of the enemy while refusing contact on the other.

The Prussian conquest of Silesia earned Frederick the undying hatred of Maria Theresa, who spent the rest of her life trying to regain it. During the winter of 1740–41, an Austrian army came over the Sudeten Mountains into Silesia. Frederick gathered his scattered army and confronted the Austrians at Mollwitz in southern Prussia on April 10, 1741. The battle began badly for Frederick at the hands of the Austrian cavalry, but once the ever-reliable Prussian infantry advanced the Austrian Army collapsed.

After Mollwitz, the war sucked in other European countries in 1741. Charles Albert of Bavaria invaded Austria. Saxony and the Italian state of Savoy sided with him and his French allies moved into southern Germany. Britain and the Netherlands backed Austria, although they were in no position to provide direct help.

Right: The War of the Austrian Succession was fought in two main areas. In the east, most of the battles occurred between the Oder and Elbe; in the west, around the Rhine.

Bavaria and France were hoping for the support of Frederick, but the Prussian had signed a secret truce with the Austrians. He was assigned Silesia, and the truce then allowed the Austrians to concentrate forces against the Bavarians and French. Maria Theresa ambitiously believed that her army could defeat the latter two, which would allow her to then recover Silesia from Frederick.

Austrian forces invaded Bavaria on December 27 and captured Munich. The Bavarian and French armies proved ineffective, and so the Prussians intervened to tackle the Austrians. Frederick's hard-fought victory at Chotusitz on May 17, 1742, forced Maria Theresa to sign a treaty that confirmed Frederick's hold over Silesia.

While the war in Bohemia and southern Germany rumbled on, the focus switched to northwest Europe, where King George II gathered a multinational force of 40,000 men and advanced down the Rhine River. The French moved a force of 30,000 to block it. The two armies met at Dettingen on June 27, 1743. George, although brave, was no military genius. A French cavalry charge almost smashed the British left wing. George, whose horse had bolted, drew his sword and personally led his infantry into the attack on foot. The maneuver worked and the French withdrew after hard fighting. Remarkably, the two countries had not yet declared war.

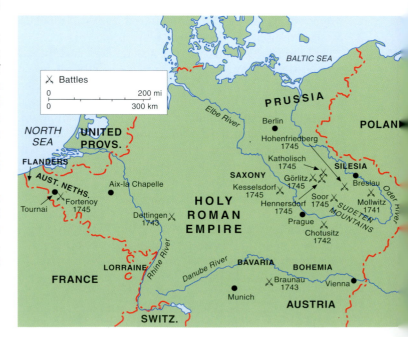

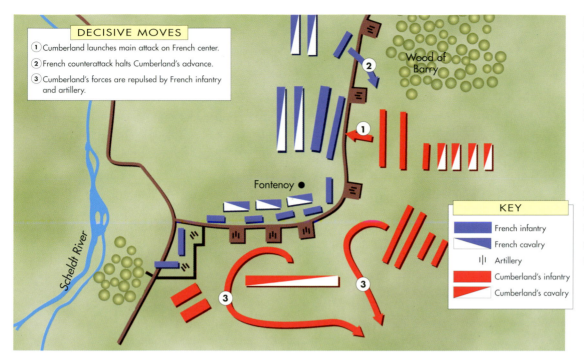

DECISIVE MOVES

① Cumberland launches main attack on French center.

② French counterattack halts Cumberland's advance.

③ Cumberland's forces are repulsed by French infantry and artillery.

Wood of Barry

Fontenoy ●

Scheldt River

KEY

	French infantry
	French cavalry
ı|ı	Artillery
	Cumberland's infantry
	Cumberland's cavalry

Left: The Battle of Fontenoy was an unsophisticated slugging match, in which the Duke of Cumberland tried to batter through the French line with a huge column of 15,000 men. Though Saxe's first line gave way, the sick general was able to organize a second line that halted, and then threw back, Cumberland's men. The battle of attrition cost both sides 7,500 casualties.

France and Britain did declare war in April 1744. Three French armies were made ready; one prepared to invade the Netherlands, another, later commanded by Marshal Maurice de Saxe, was positioned along the middle portions of the Rhine to oppose the Austrians, while the third was ordered to support Spanish attacks against Austrian-held northern Italy. The Austrians struck first, however, advancing across the Rhine.

The Prussians were alarmed by Austrian successes, and in August 1744 allied with the French against the Austrians. Frederick advanced into Bohemia and captured Prague. He then moved to threaten Vienna. The Austrians rushed to block the Prussian advance. Recognizing that he was isolated and facing the might of the combined Austrian armies, Frederick fell back into Silesia. Encouraged, the Austrians invaded Bavaria and had taken most of it by March.

In January 1745, Austria, Britain, the Netherlands, and Saxony formed an alliance to oppose France, Bavaria, and Prussia. On April 22, Prussia lost an important ally when Austria and Bavaria signed a peace treaty: Bavaria gave up all claims to the Austrian throne, while Austria returned the captured Bavarian lands.

In May the French renewed their war in northwest Europe. Marshal de Saxe hoped to lure the enemy into open battle by besieging Tournai in Flanders. The plan worked, and at Fontenoy on May 10 the rivals met: a 52,000-strong French force and a multinational army of 50,000 men led by Britain's Duke of Cumberland.

Saxe positioned his men behind trenches and earthworks protected by artillery. Cumberland launched a massive column of 15,000 men against the French center and, despite a hail of fire, it crashed through the first French line. Saxe, however, organized a second line of defense, and musket and artillery fire at close range

finally halted the huge column, while cavalry charges forced its survivors to fall back, although in good order. Cumberland withdrew and the French were left in possession of the battlefield. Both sides suffered about 7,500 casualties. Taking advantage of their victory, the French were able to conquer Flanders by September.

The 1745 Jacobite Rebellion briefly distracted the British, but had only a limited influence on the main conflict between Prussia and Austria. Frederick allowed the Austrians to advance on Breslau, then made a rapid night march and by dawn on June 4 he was ready to fight. The one-sided Battle of Hohenfriedberg was over by early morning. Caught by surprise, the Austrians suffered 16,000 casualties; Frederick had barely 1,000.

Frederick next advanced into Bohemia, but the Austrians were unwilling to offer battle after the mauling at Hohenfriedberg. Frederick, seeing his army diminishing through disease, fell back into Silesia. In October the Austrians invaded Prussia, but Frederick was undaunted and forced them back to Bohemia after battles at Katholisch, Hennersdorf, and Görlitz. By 1746 Maria Theresa's will to continue the war had been dented by Prussia's victories (and by the withdrawal of British forces from northwest Europe), and she agreed to a peace treaty. Once again, she was forced to recognize Prussia's sovereignty over Silesia.

The war dragged on into 1748 when the Treaty of Aix-la-Chapelle was signed on October 18. Most of the conquered territories were returned to their original owners, although Prussia kept Silesia. The right of Maria Theresa to rule in Austria was agreed. The prewar situation was retained – with one important difference: Frederick was the head of a Prussian state more powerful than ever before. It was a power that he was destined to wield against his rivals in the next few years.

The Seven Years War

The Treaty of Aix-la-Chapelle was merely a truce, for Maria Theresa's determination to regain Silesia was undimmed – and in 1756 a "Diplomatic Revolution" altered the balance against Prussia. Britain, ruled by the Hanoverian dynasty, had guaranteed Prussia's security of Silesia in return for guarantees on Hanover. This prompted France to align with the Hapsburgs, the French throne's greatest rival for the past 250 years.

With the addition of Russia and minor states such as Saxony to the Franco-Austrian alliance, there was now a formidable weight of numbers arrayed against Prussia. Supreme strategist that he was, Frederick the Great knew that although the forces he faced were numerically strong they would find it difficult to combine. He believed that he could defeat each in turn, and so he took the initiative and attacked first.

Saxony was the target. On August 29, 1756, Frederick invaded at the head of 70,000 men, entering Dresden on September 10 before marching against an Austrian force coming to Saxony's aid. The two armies met at Lobositz on October 1. The Austrians were defeated and Saxony's army was incorporated into the Prussian armed forces.

Frederick now moved against Austria, invading Bohemia in April 1757. Frederick led 65,000 men against the Austrian Army near Prague on May 6. The beaten Austrians retreated into Prague and were promptly besieged. Frederick then took half his army to block the approach of a relief force. He fought the 60,000-man Austrian force at Kolin on June 18, and came off worst. Frederick suffered 13,500 casualties, abandoned the siege of Prague, and retreated from Bohemia.

Frederick now had to deal with threats from all directions. One French army, 100,000 strong, invaded the state of Hanover, while a joint Franco-Austrian army pushed across the central Rhine River. A third army, 100,000 strong, was moving from Bohemia into southern Prussia. Some 100,000 Russians were attacking eastern Prussia, and a Swedish army of 16,000 was driving south from the Baltic. On July 26, 1757, Frederick's British allies were defeated at Hastenbeck in Hanover by the French, while the Russians defeated a Prussian force at Gross-Jägersdorf on July 30. Austrian forces also attacked toward Berlin, in October.

Frederick's situation was dire, but he kept a cool head. He was aided by the fact that his enemies were slow in following up their successes. Frederick finally decided to attack the Franco-Austrian forces in the west. The two sides met at Rossbach on November 5, 1757. The battle opened with the vastly superior Austrians and French sending a huge column, some 40,000 men, to get behind Frederick's left flank. Frederick responded

immediately. He moved his entire army, just 21,000 men, south and turned it through 90 degrees. When the slower-moving enemy was able to launch a flank attack, Frederick met them head on. Prussian fire mowed down the advancing enemy. This was followed by a Prussian cavalry charge. Frederick then finished off the enemy with an attack by his disciplined infantry. Less than 90 minutes after the battle started it was over: for the loss of less than 600 men, the Prussians had inflicted 10,000 casualties on the French and Austrians.

Frederick did not rest on his laurels after Rossbach – his chief concern was Silesia, now part of southern Prussia. A large Austrian force had already defeated the Prussians on November 22 at Breslau. Frederick marched his men hard, covering 170 miles (272 km) in just 12 days to link up with the survivors from Breslau. He had 30,000 men to take on 65,000 Austrians.

Right: Frederick the Great of Prussia was the greatest commander of his age. As well as possessing a genius for waging war, he inspired great loyalty among his subjects.

BALTIC SEA

SWEDISH POMERANIA

Kolberg 1761

Gross-Jägersdorf 1757

Danzig

POMERANIA

Lübeck

Hamburg

HANOVER

Elbe River

PRUSSIA

Vistula River

POLAND

Minden 1759

Hanover 1757

Berlin 1757/60

Zorndorf 1758

Kustrin

Kunersdorf 1759

Hastenbeck 1757

Magdeburg

Oder River

Weser River

Torgau 1760

Rossbach 1757

SAXONY

SILESIA

Liegnitz 1760

Rhine River

Wilhelmstal 1762

Dresden

Maxen 1759

Hochkirch 1758

Leuthen 1757

Breslau 1757

Burkersdorf 1762

Freiberg 1762

Lobositz 1756

Frankfurt-am-Main 1759

Prague 1757

Kolin 1757

BAVARIA

BOHEMIA

Olmütz 1758

AUSTRIA

Approximate area of Prussia and its dominions

Boundary of Holy Roman Empire

Battles

0   200 mi
0   300 km

Left: The Seven Years War was fought across much of central Europe. Though the Prussians were outnumbered by a coalition of countries, Frederick moved his disciplined army to defeat enemies before they had a chance to unite.

Frederick next had to move against a large Austrian army that was menacing smaller Prussian forces in Saxony. His army covered over 20 miles (32 km) per day. The Prussians caught the Austrians at Hochkirch on October 14. Frederick came close to disaster: 80,000 Austrians surrounded the 30,000 Prussians overnight and their dawn attack almost succeeded in smashing Frederick's army.

Frederick did manage to regain his initiative over the Austrians by the end of the year, but he had suffered enormous casualties. While his army was still the finest in all Europe, it was slowly but surely declining in quality and quantity. When the spring of 1759 arrived he would have to fight hard to protect Prussia once again.

The two forces met at Leuthen on December 6. The Austrian Army was deployed over a distance of five miles (8 km), with cavalry on both flanks and the bulk of their reserves on the left. A marsh protected their right. Frederick totally outmaneuvered the Austrians by launching a feint attack against the Austrian right and then marching the bulk of his army to overwhelm the Austrian left flank. Leuthen was a brilliant example of Frederick's oblique order attack: the Austrians lost 7,000 troops killed and wounded, while 12,000 men and over 100 cannon were captured.

The Prussians pressed their advantage by advancing into Austrian territory in May 1758. However, he was forced to turn to face the Russians, who were menacing eastern Prussia. By mid-August, hard marching had brought the Prussians close to Kustrin, which was under siege from 45,000 Russian troops. Frederick undertook a dangerous crossing of the Oder River at night and got behind the Russians.

The Russians had no option but to fight. The Battle of Zorndorf on the 25th saw 45,000 Russians pitted against Frederick's 36,000 men. Frederick tried to turn the Russian right flank and then the left, but the Russians proved stubborn in defense. It was only the charges of Frederick's cavalry under General Frederick Wilhelm von Seydlitz that decided the day, forcing the Russians to retreat. About 19,000 Russians fell, while Frederick lost some 12,000 troops. One of the most bloody battles of the war, Zorndorf stopped the Russian advance into eastern Prussia.

The 1759 campaign began with an Anglo-Prussian offensive against the French around Frankfurt-am-Main. The Battle of Minden, fought on August 1, should have been a crushing victory for the 45,000-strong Anglo-Prussian Army over a larger force of 60,000 French troops. An advance by British and Prussian infantry smashed through the center of the French line, but the British cavalry, or rather their commander, Lord Sackville, failed to deliver the decisive charge. The French, who were facing disaster, were allowed to escape, although they suffered some 10,000 casualties and left over 100 cannon on the battlefield. The Allied commander, Duke Ferdinand of Brunswick, did pursue the French but his troops were recalled by Frederick.

Prussia again faced serious problems in the east. Russian forces had defeated a small Prussian army on July 23 and then linked up with the Austrians. These two armies, totalling about 80,000 men, were poised to advance deeper into eastern Prussia. Frederick led his 50,000 men across the Oder River near Kunersdorf and planned a daring twin-pronged attack on August 12.

The battle was a disaster for the Prussians. Their two attacks were thrown back with heavy losses. Frederick stubbornly continued to attack, thereby adding to an already desperate situation. When Frederick finally saw that he could not defeat the Austro-Russian Army, some 19,000 of his best troops had been frittered away.

Frederick was in despair: he had lost the cream of his army; he even considered abdication. He was lucky to escape pursuit by the Austro-Russian forces, which were

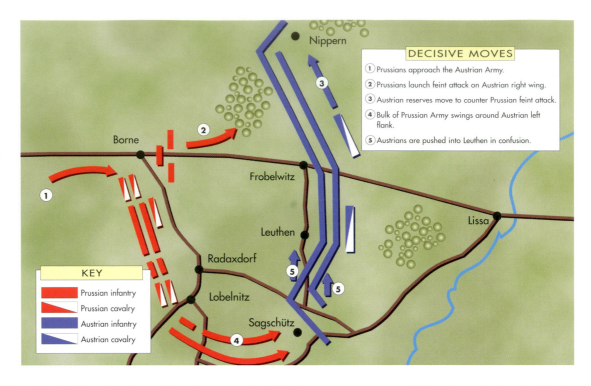

Right: The Battle of Leuthen, 1757, was Frederick's greatest victory. His wide flanking march deceived the Austrian commander, Prince Charles, who tried to respond by rushing troops from his right to his left, but they piled up in helpless masses.

DECISIVE MOVES

1. Prussians approach the Austrian Army.
2. Prussians launch feint attack on Austrian right wing.
3. Austrian reserves move to counter Prussian feint attack.
4. Bulk of Prussian Army swings around Austrian left flank.
5. Austrians are pushed into Leuthen in confusion.

KEY

- Prussian infantry
- Prussian cavalry
- Austrian infantry
- Austrian cavalry

Nippern · Borne · Frobelwitz · Leuthen · Radaxdorf · Lobelnitz · Sagschütz · Lissa

equally shattered by the fighting, having suffered over 15,000 casualties. Frederick, though, did recover from his black mood and regained some of his previous vigor. In the late summer of 1758 and early winter of 1759, he rebuilt his main army, gathering new recruits and drawing off some units from those of his other commanders. He also had a little luck – as so often happened in his career – when the Russians were forced to abandon their positions in eastern Prussia due to supply shortages.

With the Russians out of the way and with a new army at his back, Frederick moved against the Austrians once again. His target was the army of Marshal Leopold von Daun, which had captured Dresden in September. Frederick did not lead the attack on the Austrians in person. He sent one of his generals, Frederick von Finck,

but his forces were too small for the task. At the Battle of Maxen, fought on November 21, 1759, the Prussians were soundly beaten. It was fortunate for Frederick that Maxen had been fought so late in the season; with winter setting in, both sides brought their operations to a close.

By the spring of 1760 an Austrian army of 100,000 men under von Daun was in Saxony, another 50,000 under General Gideon von Loudon were in Silesia, and Swedish and Russian forces were poised to sweep through Pomerania. The plan was correctly based on the knowledge that Frederick was not powerful enough to take on all of these forces at once. If he concentrated on one, then the others would be free to march on Berlin.

Frederick faced von Daun with about 40,000 men under his command. There were about 35,000 Prussian troops protecting Silesia and another 15,000 located in the north to protect Pomerania. The Duke of Brunswick had 70,000 men but faced over 120,000 French troops in the west. Brunswick was able to push the French back to the Rhine, but a defeat at Kloster-Kamp on October 16 brought his offensive to a halt. Frederick meanwhile campaigned in the east, and from June to late July he rushed from one threat to another.

Frederick was desperate to improve his strategic position. Choosing attack as the best form of

Left: Prussians in the attack. The Prussian Army was based around the premise, common in most armies of the time, that the common soldier could be trained but not trusted.

defense, he plunged into Silesia. Driving his army hard, Frederick was able to confront the Austrians at Liegnitz on August 15. The Austrians could muster 60,000 men and were expecting the arrival of 30,000 Russians. Frederick discovered that the Austrians were divided into two unequal halves, and he chose to attack the weaker. At night he marched against the 24,000 Austrians led by Loudon, who, while realizing he had been outmaneuvered, chose to attack the Prussians.

Loudon's attack was repulsed and Frederick badly mauled his forces. The Prussians then retired, aware that Daun was advancing in their direction. Frederick tried a little trickery to outwit the Russians, sending a bogus message to the Russian commander that suggested the entire Austrian Army had been defeated at Liegnitz. The ruse worked and the Russians retreated.

Frederick planned to take on Daun's Austrians but discovered that Berlin, the Prussian capital, had been captured on October 9 and partly destroyed. He hurried north and forced the Austro-Russian force to withdraw, but this allowed the Austrians to concentrate forces at Torgau, which Frederick decided to assault on November 3. The two sides were of roughly equal size, about 50,000 men each. Frederick planned an ambitious attack. He would lead one half of his army around the right wing of the Austrian position and strike from the rear. The other half was ordered to make a frontal assault at the same time as Frederick attacked the rear.

The opening of the Prussian frontal attack was seen by Austrian troops and fire was exchanged. Frederick mistakenly thought that the noise indicated that the main attack was underway. He chose to attack himself, but the fighting was inconclusive and he was repulsed. The Prussian frontal attack finally got to grips with the Austrians at dusk and Frederick renewed his efforts. The

Austrians broke and were forced to retreat, but Frederick had 17,000 men killed, wounded, or taken prisoner. The exhausted Prussians were unable to follow up their victory as both sides entered winter quarters.

Hostilities recommenced in 1761. Frederick could muster about 100,000 men, but was opposed by 300,000 Austrians and Russians in Silesia. Frederick, fighting on the defensive, managed to hold them off and they abandoned their campaign as winter set in. Frederick, however, lost some of the support of his British ally in December; a new king, George III, called most of his army home and reduced his subsidies to Prussia.

In 1762 the Russian ruler, the Empress Elizabeth, died and was succeeded by Peter III, who was an admirer of Frederick and agreed to a peace treaty on May 15. Sweden also withdrew from the war, leaving Frederick free to concentrate on Austria and France. The Duke of Brunswick's Anglo-Prussian Army beat the French at Wilhelmstal on June 24. Frederick matched this by defeating the Austrians at Burkersdorf on July 21. At Freiberg on October 29 the Austrians lost again.

These victories could not hide the fact that all of the warring nations were exhausted. An armistice was agreed upon and the Treaty of Hubertusburg was signed on February 16, 1763, in which Austria accepted Prussian sovereignty over Silesia. Despite the death and destruction to Prussia, Frederick had made his state a dominant power in central Europe and a key player in European affairs. Until the French Revolutionary wars in the 1790s, continental Europe was mainly at peace.

During the period 1740–63, the Prussian Army had proved itself the best in Europe, and the other powers began to adopt the Prussian model. By the end of Frederick's reign, most other armies were emulating the constant drill upon which he had insisted.

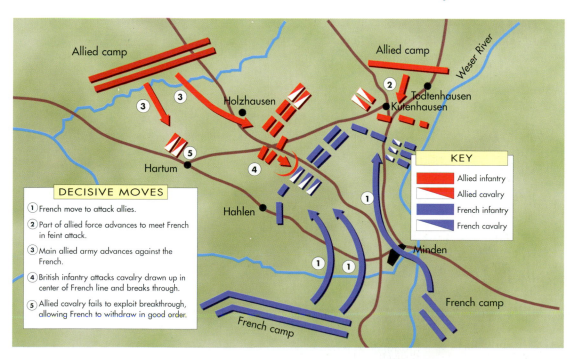

DECISIVE MOVES

① French move to attack allies.

② Part of allied force advances to meet French in feint attack.

③ Main allied army advances against the French.

④ British infantry attacks cavalry drawn up in center of French line and breaks through.

⑤ Allied cavalry fails to exploit breakthrough, allowing French to withdraw in good order.

KEY

▬	Allied infantry
▰	Allied cavalry
▬	French infantry
▰	French cavalry

Left: The Battle of Minden, fought on August 1, 1759, was a triumph for British infantry, but the Anglo-Prussian Army was denied an overwhelming victory by the refusal of the British cavalry to attack. Though the French suffered a defeat, they inflicted 25 percent casualties on the opponent's infantry.

Naval Warfare

The size and skill of Britain's Royal Navy provided the backbone of British imperial expansion worldwide. Even acting in unison, Britain's rivals found it difficult to mount a sustained challenge to her prowess at sea. Ships and maritime technology were broadly similar, but when combat was joined the crucial factors were the quality and audacity of the commanders and the capabilities of the ordinary sailors.

Naval warfare assumed great importance in 18th-century European warfare, partly because of the importance of campaigns outside the continental landmass. During the century, the British Royal Navy steadily asserted its superiority over the naval forces of all other countries (its most important rivals being the Spanish and French navies), and laid the basis for the expansion of the British Empire in the first half of the 19th century.

For much of the 18th century, navies followed a standard battle plan based on the line-ahead approach, with each ship sailing directly behind the other. A fleet in battle would attempt to get to the windward, thereby allowing it to withdraw or close with the enemy at will. Once battle was joined, the two opposing lines would slowly draw near until, at close range, they would attempt to bombard each other into submission. Whichever ship could survive the exchange of gunfire the longer was usually the victor. In the Royal Navy, these tactics were strictly formalized in the so-called "Fighting Orders" that defined how naval engagements must take place.

The warships of all navies were broadly similar. They were square-rigged with three masts, and each carried a variable number of cannon in several decks. The bigger the ship, the greater the number of decks and cannon. The largest ships had a maximum weight of 2,500 tons (2,540 tonnes), a crew of around 1,000 men, and mounted 100 guns on three decks. They were known as "first-rates," the largest of six classifications of warship. The first- and the slightly smaller second- and third-rates were termed ships-of-the-line, in that they were powerful enough to take up their position in the main battle line.

During the course of the 18th century it was found that the two-decked, 74-gun third-rate was the most effective warship, able to hold its own in battle, yet far more seaworthy and versatile than the sluggish second- and first-rates. The French pioneered the third-rate ship and the frigate, the latter a light, fast vessel with around 20 to 40 cannon on a single deck. Frigates – technically fifth- or sixth-rates – did not fight in the line but acted as independent cruisers for scouting and commerce-destruction duties.

Overall ship design did not change much during the century, although two new developments greatly improved a ship's seaworthiness. Firstly, there was the introduction of copper bottoms to the underwater section of the wooden hull. The oak hull was frequently eaten away by a ship's worm (the teredo), and copper sheeting offered an ideal solution to what was a costly problem. Secondly, the tiller, which had been used to steer a ship's rudder, was replaced by a series of cables and pulleys attaching the rudder to a wheel. This new system made steering less tiring and made the vessel more maneuverable.

The two most powerful navies of the age were the British and French. Britain's Royal Navy had the greater number of ships and possessed, in general, the better sailors. The French had the superior ships, although they did not handle them as well, and the British tended to be the more aggressive in action. For example, at the Battle of Quiberon Bay, fought off the west coast of France in 1759, the French believed that the British admiral, Hawke, would not risk sailing his ships through reef-strewn waters in rough seas to attack them. But Hawke did just that and sank seven French warships as a result of his audacious action.

Right: One of only two vessels lost defeating the French at the Battle of Quiberon Bay in 1759 founders on a reef. The battle demonstrated the audacity of Royal Navy admirals.

Left: The British admiral Sir John Byng is executed after being found guilty of "neglect of duty in battle" following his failure to save the island of Minorca from the French. His death also illustrated the obsession in the Royal Navy at the time with maintaining line-ahead formations in battle.

The French did, however, have one outstanding naval officer in the 18th century. Admiral Pierre Andre de Suffren (1729–88) fought in the War of the Austrian Succession, the Seven Years War, and the American Revolutionary War. He was a bold commander who also had a fine tactical and strategic mind that allowed him to outfox and defeat his often more numerous opponents.

While the French captains were usually expected to husband their relatively scarce resources, the captains of the Royal Navy were expected to close with the enemy at every opportunity; any lack of aggression could be severely punished. The fate of Admiral Sir John Byng (1704–57) provided a good example of the harsh attitude adopted by the Royal Navy toward commanders thought lacking in fighting spirit.

Byng was attempting to break the French siege of Port Mahon, the capital of the Mediterranean island of Minorca. He faced a French fleet of equal strength on May 20, 1756, but had difficulty in bringing his warships into the required line-ahead formation. The French took advantage of this and severely damaged a number of Byng's ships before escaping from the fray. Byng believed that he now had no hope of relieving the besieged garrison of Port Mahon and returned to the British base at Gibraltar in southern Spain. The unfortunate Byng was subsequently court-martialed, found guilty, and executed.

During the second half of the 18th century, a group of younger British naval officers began increasingly to dispense with the old "Fighting Orders" and adopted a more open and flexible approach to naval tactics. They recognized that the old line-ahead system left much to be desired in achieving a decisive victory. They argued that a British fleet, divided into separate squadrons, would do better to approach the enemy at right angles and then break through and disorder the enemy battle line. The British ships would then maneuver in small groups, concentrating their firepower against one or two enemy vessels at a time. These tactics demanded high standards of seamanship and gunnery, and required that the commander of the lead ship possess a cool nerve.

The first time such tactics were used in combat occurred at the Battle of the Saintes, fought on April 12, 1782, in the West Indies during the American Revolution, when a British fleet under the command of Admiral George Rodney defeated a French fleet. The French line was successfully broken in two places and although Rodney did not follow up his advantage with the necessary vigor, it demonstrated the efficacy of the new tactics, which were to be further developed during the coming struggle with Revolutionary and Napoleonic France.

RED-HOT SHOT FROM THE ROCK

In September 1782 the British defenders of Gibraltar, who had been under siege by French and Spanish forces for three years, found that their cannon balls were having little or no effect on the enemy ships' massive wooden timbers. One solution to this problem was to use red-hot cannon balls to set the vessels on fire.

The heated cannon balls were carried to the gun muzzles using tongs, and then rammed home; the gunpowder in the barrels did not explode because damp wads were placed between the powder and the red-hot shot.

More than 8,000 of the special cannon balls were fired on September 12. By the following day all of the enemy's warships had exploded or been burned to the waterline. The danger had passed, and the British garrison, although exhausted and close to starvation, survived until fresh supplies arrived in October.

Early Native American Wars

Naval warfare had become important during the 18th century because of European colonization of the world. The rivalries at sea, however, were merely an extra dimension to the bitter struggles taking place on land throughout the Americas and the Caribbean. Spain and Portugal had colonized South America between them as early as the 16th century, while farther north all of Europe's major powers had interests.

In the Caribbean and in North America, Spain, France, and Britain each had important colonies; while in India, there were trading establishments run by the Netherlands, Portugal, France, and Britain, with the latter two countries being the most important.

Spain and the Netherlands had both been major contenders in the colonial struggles of the 17th century, but both were less powerful in the 18th century than Britain and France – and the century was marked by a constant struggle between these two powers, particularly in North America, the Caribbean, and India. In all three areas, Britain ended the century in a dominant position, partly because of the strength of the Royal Navy. The reward for success was wealth, acquired by dominating the lucrative trade in valuable materials, from tobacco, furs, and cotton to cloth, tea, or even slaves.

Thus the War of the Spanish Succession (1702–13) in Europe was paralleled in North America by what is called "Queen Anne's War," during which British attempts to take French Canada were repulsed. The 1740–63 period saw renewed fighting in North America (usually called the French and Indian Wars), as well as conflict in the Caribbean and India (indeed, Britain had gone to war with Spain in 1739, the year before the War of the Austrian Succession began, over trade disputes – a war known to the British as the "War of Jenkins's Ear"). Warfare in India continued throughout the century as Britain consolidated its position; and the French intervened in the American Revolutionary War (1776–83) against the British.

It was not just between European powers that there was fighting: indigenous tribal rulers played an important part in these wars alongside the colonial powers, while there were also conflicts between colonists and the native peoples. In North America, for example, many British settlers saw the Native Americans as nothing more than obstacles to be brushed aside. As the colonists along the eastern seaboard grew, settlers headed west eager to exploit and develop new territory. Native Americans, however, understandably resisted the loss of their lands.

The 17th century saw many small-scale wars between the Native Americans and the great European powers and their respective settler communities. On paper at least the Native Americans had many advantages – overall they possessed superiority in numbers and they were skilled fighters with a profound knowledge of their lands. The colonists lived in small, widely scattered homesteads or small settlements, and the leading European powers were generally unwilling to send anything more than token regular forces to protect their distant colonies in North America.

By and large, the colonies had to provide for their own defense. They relied on militias raised from able-bodied men of military age, although these were civilians in arms and not trained soldiers. Most would fight to protect their own farms or those of their neighbors, but they were unwilling to travel far or to campaign against the Native Americans for long, especially when they had to return home to bring in the harvest. Colonial governments were also often reluctant to go to the aid of another, neighboring colony.

The colonists, at first glance, seemed ill-prepared to take on the Native Americans, but they did have the advantage of superior technology, which included firearms and artillery, and superior military organization. And the Native Americans were far from united in their dealings with the colonists.

Left: Pontiac's warriors keep watch on Fort Detroit during his uprising against the British. The chief was forced to break off the siege after his defeat at Bushy Run.

KING PHILIP'S WAR

In June 1675, the leader of the Wampanoag, Philip (his tribal name was Metacomet), launched a series of attacks against European colonial settlements in southern New England. Philip objected to the steady movement of the European colonists into his tribal homelands, and the conversion of many of his tribespeople to the Christian faith.

A dozen English settlements in Massachusetts were destroyed before the New England Confederation declared war on the Native Americans. Philip, however, was betrayed and suffered a major defeat at the Great Swamp Fight in Rhode Island. Philip was killed at Mount Hope in August 1676, after the position of his hideaway had been revealed to the colonists by one of the chief's own people.

After Philip's death his head was cut off by the colonists and displayed on a pole at Plymouth, a warning to any Native Americans contemplating rising up against the colonists. The war ended in southern New England in 1676, but dragged on in northern New England until 1678. The colonists lost 500 settlers killed or captured, and between 12 and 20 colonial settlements were either abandoned or destroyed.

Tribes often sided with the colonists if the colonists were fighting one of the natives' traditional enemies.

Native Americans found it difficult to form a united front against the colonizers. When a battle or skirmish was won, they failed to take advantage; in Native warfare a single victory often decided the outcome of the whole war but this was not the case with the colonists, who responded to a defeat by calling for reinforcements to go on the offensive against the enemy.

One of the more important threats to British control of North America occurred toward the end of the Seven Years' War (1756–63) in a campaign waged by Pontiac, the pro-French chief of the Ottawa people. Following the departure of many French settlers from Canada toward the end of the war, the British authorities allowed new settlers to move into areas previously occupied by the French. In the process these settlers took over Native American land, and the British did little to stop them.

Pontiac was outraged by this turn of events and was able to unite many of the Native American tribes against the British in 1762. These recruits from other tribes gave Pontiac about 900 warriors with which to take on the British and North American colonists. When the fighting began in earnest the following year, Pontiac decided to attack as many British forts as possible. He saw that the British forces in North America were spread thinly; if he attacked at several points, the scattered British garrisons would not be able to unite against him.

On May 7, 1763, Pontiac led a surprise assault on Detroit, a fort held by the British. Pontiac's plans were, in fact, known to the British, who repelled the attack. Rather than retreat, however, Pontiac decided to besiege the fort. When the defenders of Detroit charged out from their fort to attack his forces in late July, the British troops were defeated at the Battle of Bloody Ridge and forced to retreat to the safety of Fort Detroit.

In the first week of August, a British relief column led by Colonel Henry Bouquet was ambushed by Pontiac's men. Bouquet, however, placed his supply wagons in a circle to protect his men. The Native Americans continued their attack and were defeated by the British troops' superior firepower.

This fight, the Battle of Bushy Run, was decisive. Bouquet was able to relieve Fort Pitt (also under siege), leaving Pontiac no choice but to relinquish the siege of Detroit. The Native American alliance fell apart after Bushy Run. Although Pontiac and a handful of his diehard supporters tried to forge a new anti-British alliance, it failed to materialize and he was forced to agree to a truce in 1765 and a permanent peace treaty on July 25, 1766. Pontiac was then killed by another Native American in 1769.

Native Americans continued to fight against European settlers until the end of the 19th century, but the pattern of territorial loss had already been firmly established in the 17th and 18th centuries.

Left: The major engagements of King Philip's War in the 1670s and Pontiac's uprising in the 1760s. The defeat of the Native Americans in both conflicts allowed European colonists to move farther west into North America.

North America's Anglo-French Wars

For the rival European powers, the fighting against the Native Americans was less important than the struggle against one another. Britain and France fought each other in North America in the late 17th century and this conflict continued in the early 18th century, with the decisive period occurring after 1752, when the French began to move into the Ohio Valley, regarded by the British as their area of settlement.

The French controlled an area of North America stretching from the far northeast coast down the St. Lawrence River to the area around the Great Lakes, as well as a huge territory, known then as Louisiana, that stretched westward from the Great Lakes to the Rockies and south to the coast of the Gulf of Mexico. The British held most of the eastern seaboard, where a growing population, boosted by immigration, was trying to prevent itself being hemmed in.

In July 1752, French troops overran a British trading post in the Ohio Valley, an area the British and their colonists saw as rightfully theirs. Early in 1754 Governor Robert Dinwiddie ordered a young officer, Colonel George Washington (1732–99), and a band of Virginia militia to build a fort where the Allegheny and Monongahela rivers met (now the site of Pittsburgh).

Washington's plans were spoiled by the French, who had already built a stockade – Fort Duquesne – at the junction. Washington therefore built Fort Necessity at nearby Great Meadows, but it was only partly finished when the French attacked. Washington and his militia resisted but were eventually forced to surrender.

Both the French and British began to send fresh troops to North America. First to arrive, in the spring of 1755, was General Edward Braddock with two British infantry regiments. It was agreed that four separate attacks should be made against the French. Braddock was to lead a force of 1,500 British troops and 450 colonial militiamen against Fort Duquesne. It was a difficult journey through dense, dark forest along little more than tracks. The column, burdened down as if going to war in Europe, made slow progress.

A New Kind of War

If Braddock was expecting to meet the French in an open, European-style battle, with his regulars exchanging close-range musket volleys with the enemy, he was much mistaken. The French and their Native American allies, no more than 900 men in total, repeatedly ambushed the British as they were marching through the dense forest. Firing from the cover of trees, bushes, and fallen branches, they destroyed a large part of the front and flanks of the column, as the British attempted to carry out parade-ground maneuvers in the tangled undergrowth.

Panic set in. Some of the British soldiers fled, leaving small groups of their comrades to hold off the French closing in for the kill. Braddock was shot and half his men killed, while Washington, a volunteer with the column, managed to organize a rearguard and lead the remnants of the column to safety.

There was, however, no disguising the seriousness of the defeat. The only sizeable British force in the region had been destroyed. The French and their Native American allies were free to

Left: Geography largely determined the course of campaigns during the Anglo-French Wars, with waterways being the main routes used by the forces of each side.

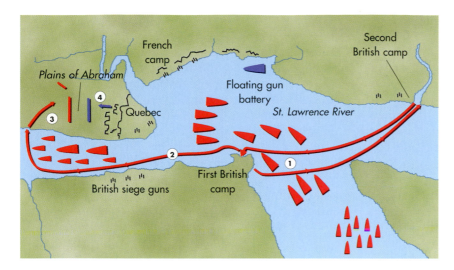

Left: The French defenses around Quebec were extensive, making it difficult for the British to establish siege lines and almost forcing them to abandon the investment.

KEY		
British infantry		French infantry
British ships	Artillery	
		French ships

DECISIVE MOVES

1 British move to new camp on June 9.

2 Wolfe moves troops by flat-bottomed boats on September 12.

3 British troops scale cliffs during the night of September 12.

4 French attack defeated on the Plains of Abraham on morning of September 13.

roam along the Ohio River, attacking isolated farmsteads and settlements at will.

The next expedition to attempt to halt French expansion south from Canada was a local affair. General William Johnson was sent from Albany toward Crown Point at the head of 3,500 colonial militiamen and a few hundred Native Americans. A French force of 2,000 regulars, French-Canadian militiamen, and Native Americans advanced to block Johnson's column.

The two forces blundered into each other at the head of Lake George and the battle, fought on September 8, 1755, was a decisive victory for Johnson. The French

IRREGULAR WARFARE

The regular European troops deployed in the war were not trained to think or fight as individuals. Their role was to stand in tightly packed ranks and exchange close-range volley fire with the enemy. Traditional battles therefore required flat, open terrain where such tactics could be used to effect. However, such places were rare in the dense forests and rugged uplands of North America.

Both sides, the French initially more so, used local forces, colonial militias, volunteers, and Native Americans to wage a guerrilla-type war of swift marches, ambushes from cover, and attacks on the enemy's weak and isolated garrisons.

These troops were tough frontiersmen, men with the skills needed to live off the land and move stealthily through the forest. Most, being hunters, were excellent shots. The British did not make the best use of such men, at least at first, believing their colonial troops were too wild and poorly disciplined to be of much use. But when they recognized their value, various regiments and corps were raised from the backwoodsmen, including the famous Rogers' Rangers.

commander, Ludwig Dieskau, was captured, but Johnson was unable to exploit his advantage, as his militiamen used their right not to advance farther up the Hudson Valley. Accordingly, Johnson decided to build a stockade, Fort William Henry, and station a few troops there as a holding force. The French, meanwhile, fell back to Ticonderoga.

The war began to slow to a stalemate – that is until 1756 when the outbreak of the Seven Years War in Europe transformed the strategic situation in North America. Both Britain and France sent reinforcements to North America in an effort to make territorial gains. Two rival generals crossed the Atlantic: France's Marquis Louis Joseph de Montcalm (1712–59) in May and Britain's Lord Loudoun in July. Montcalm was a charming man, popular with his troops. However, his position in Canada was delicate and difficult. When he arrived, Montcalm discovered that he had no control over the local militias and colonial troops. These valuable additions to his meager supply of regulars were handled by the governor, the Marquis de Vaudreuil. Relations between the two men were always strained, even after Montcalm was given authority over him.

Despite these problems, Montcalm was determined to make his mark, and in August he crossed Lake Ontario. He made a lightning attack against Oswego and then settled down at Ticonderoga. The British response was sluggish, and Loudoun did not intervene before both sides settled into winter quarters.

When spring 1758 brought better weather, Loudoun was ordered to take part in an amphibious operation against Louisbourg, a vital French fort in Nova Scotia. The French had, however, reinforced their garrison in the fort and sailed a fleet into the harbor. When the British fleet was scattered by a storm, the expedition was canceled and Loudoun returned to New York.

With the bulk of the British forces in North America involved in the abortive Louisbourg expedition, the frontier was desperately short of troops to counter any French attack. Montcalm took advantage of this and laid siege to Fort William Henry. Heavily outnumbered by Montcalm's 5,000 regulars, militia, and Native Americans, the British garrison put up a brave defense but the fort could not withstand the pounding of the French artillery. Montcalm, a gracious commander, was impressed by the British defense and granted the commander terms. The garrison would be allowed to leave with its weapons and flags on condition that its members agreed not to take part in further fighting. The terms were agreed.

The events that followed remain controversial. The British garrison marched out of Fort William Henry on August 9, 1757, to make its way back to Albany. Once outside the fort, however, the column was ambushed by Montcalm's Native American allies. Many were massacred, including most of the women and children. What is known is that Montcalm was horrified by the massacre, as he had always made great efforts to prevent the slaughter of prisoners and helpless civilians. Montcalm then destroyed Fort William Henry and took his army into winter quarters. One unfortunate consequence of the massacre was to increase the awe and horror with which he was beginning to be regarded by British and Americans alike.

Stung by the massacre at Fort William Henry, the British prepared to redouble their efforts against the French in the spring of 1758. Under the dynamic leadership of a new prime minister, William Pitt, a two-pronged strategy was devised. Loudoun was replaced by General James Abercrombie, who was ordered to strike at Ticonderoga and Duquesne. General Jeffrey Amherst was given the task of attacking Louisbourg. Montcalm, it was hoped, would not be able to deal with both threats simultaneously.

Amherst's expedition was launched in May 1758. The fortress was surrounded by 9,000 British regulars and 500 colonial militiamen. It was a tough nut to crack and both sides displayed great resourcefulness in the siege. But British material superiority told in the end, and the fortress was forced to surrender on July 27, with one of the British officers, General James Wolfe (1732–59), being singled out for praise. The capture of Louisbourg, the main French base in Canada, was a major British success – but one balanced by a disaster.

While Amherst attacked Louisbourg, Abercrombie was attempting to fulfil his role in the strategy, but with little success. He foolishly launched an all-out frontal assault on July 8 against the French position guarding the main route to Ticonderoga. Abercrombie had 12,000 men under his command; Montcalm just 3,000, making up for his scarcity in soldiers by placing his men behind a ditch protected by felled, sharpened branches and a wooden fence. Safe behind these barriers, his troops shot the British attack to pieces. Abercrombie lost 1,500 casualties – and subsequently his command – at Ticonderoga.

The French, however, suffered two setbacks in the second half of 1758. They were forced to abandon Fort Duquesne (which was retitled Fort Pitt in British hands) in November when confronted by a column led by General John Forbes. A force of colonial militia under Colonel John Bradstreet also captured Fort Frontenac on Lake Ontario in the fall. At both battles American colonial forces played a major role in deciding the outcome of the fighting. They displayed the flexibility and specialist fighting skills often found lacking in the regular British Army regiments. These backwoodsmen, top marksmen and skilled in fieldcraft, could take on the

Left: Wolfe's victory at Quebec on September 13, 1759, confirmed Britain as the major power in colonial North America. During the battle Wolfe's men poured volley after volley into the advancing French ranks. The disciplined British fire broke the enemy, who fled back to the city. Wolfe and his men followed, but the British commander was hit three times during the pursuit, the last shot killing him.

Left: Louis Joseph, Marquis de Montcalm, was a soldier trained in the formal disciplines of 18th-century warfare, who in North America utilized local geography to maximum effect. He entered the French Army in 1724 at the age of 12, and in 1756 was promoted to major-general and sent to Canada with a limited commission. His death following the Battle of Quebec was a grievous loss to France.

French-Canadian militias and Native Americans on their own terms.

In 1759, the decisive year of the war, the British launched a three-pronged offensive against the French. The targets were Fort Niagara, Fort Ticonderoga, and Quebec. Some 2,000 British troops under General John Prideaux captured Fort Niagara on July 25. A large mixed force of colonial and British troops under Amherst took Ticonderoga the next day and then captured Crown Point. The decisive battle, however, was for Quebec. The British, led by General Wolfe, landed just below the city on June 26. They faced a large French force under Montcalm that was amply supplied with artillery and within massive protecting walls sited high above the St. Lawrence River.

Wolfe spent two fruitless months trying to get his men into a position from where they could attack Quebec. Winter was approaching and Wolfe's naval support was preparing to leave the St. Lawrence to avoid being frozen in, when a narrow track was discovered that led up the steep cliffs to the west of Quebec. The track led to a flat area of ground, the Plains of Abraham, just outside the city walls – ideal for a conventional battle.

On the night of September 12, Wolfe and his men landed and, led by Colonel William Howe, scaled the steep cliffs without being spotted. When morning dawned, the mixed British and colonial force of about 5,000 men were deployed for battle on the plains. Montcalm realized that he had no option but to leave the protection of the city and offer battle to the British, otherwise his supply lines would be cut and his forces eventually starved into surrender.

The French, some 4,500 men, marched across to meet the British. Unfortunately for Montcalm, the colonial governor, the Marquis de Vaudreuil, refused him the use of the garrison's artillery and militias – forces that might have influenced the outcome in France's favor.

When the French had advanced close to the British, a single, disciplined volley rang out from the ranks of the British troops. When the smoke cleared, the French attack was over, hundreds of Montcalm's soldiers had been killed or wounded; the survivors retreated back into Quebec. Wolfe never enjoyed his victory, however. Both he and Montcalm died from battle wounds. Wolfe died the same day, while Montcalm lingered on until the following day.

The loss of Montcalm was a particularly heavy blow for the French, for they lost a commander with an open mind who displayed great tactical skill and a real understanding of how to use the geography of North America to his country's advantage. He viewed the vast forests as aids to achieving total surprise over the enemy, rather than as barriers that impeded the "proper exercise of war."

The French made one unsuccessful attempt to recapture Quebec in the spring of 1760. But after losing their main commander and field army at Quebec, and then faced with three British columns marching against Montreal, defeat was inevitable. On September 8, 1760, de Vaudreuil surrendered to the British, ending his country's control of Canada. Britain's domination of Canada was confirmed by the terms of the Treaty of Paris in February 1763. The single volley fired by Wolfe's troops outside Quebec on September 13, 1759, had settled the fate of Canada.

Europe's Struggle for India

India in the early 18th century was the site of one of the world's major empires, that of the Mughal rulers. However, it was no longer the powerful force it had been in the 16th and early 17th centuries. Defeats by Afghans to the northwest, the rise of a powerful military confederacy, the Marathas, in central India's Deccan, and gradual ossification of the institutions of state power had all greatly reduced Mughal power.

For much of the first half of the century Britain and France established coastal bases, from where they traded with local rulers. Both countries created semi-independent organizations to oversee this trade with the subcontinent: the British East India Company and the French East India Company. These two bodies, which also acted as their countries' political representatives, were bitter rivals. Both exploited divisions between local Indian warlords and princes, and both had private armies, although they also received support from their countries' regular armed forces in times of all-out war.

The first clashes between France and Britain in India occurred as a result of events in Europe with the War of the Austrian Succession. The French, led by Marquis

Joseph Dupleix (1697–1763), captured the main British base of Madras in 1746 and then tried to capture Fort St. George. St. George was only saved by the timely arrival of reinforcements under Admiral Edward Boscawen. The British then tried unsuccessfully to capture the main French base at Pondicherry in 1748.

The two companies, although supposedly at peace, used local conflicts to further their ambitions. French troops sided with warlords rebelling against legitimate rulers, while the British aided established powers. The tide of events moved with the French, whose influence rose as their rebels gained influence. The British seemed powerless to prevent the French extending their control over the subcontinent. Dupleix, with local support, ruled over a great swathe of southern India. In the second half of 1751, however, British fortunes underwent a revival.

The Success of Robert Clive

Much of this was due to Robert Clive (1725–74), who had been a junior and not very successful clerk with the British East India Company in Madras. His military career began when he volunteered and was made a junior officer in 1748. His chance came when an Indian army allied to the French laid siege to Trichinopoly in 1751. Clive gathered 500 soldiers and three cannon at Madras, but rather than march directly to Trichinopoly, he captured Arcot, the capital of the Indian ruler besieging the town. The ruler's son, Raja Sahib, was immediately sent to retake Arcot with 10,000 men, and, in turn, laid siege to Clive's force. The siege dragged on and Clive's tiny force was reduced to only 120 European soldiers and 250 sepoys (native troops fighting for the British).

Sensing that the British were close to collapse, the Indians launched an all-or-nothing assault. A herd of elephants charged the city gates. Clive had his men fire on the elephants to wound them and induce them to panic, which they did, trampling many of the besiegers underfoot. A second assault was beaten back at bayonet point and the battle was won.

Clive's successful defense of Arcot was more than just a determined feat of arms. It also had an important impact on the future of India, as France's Indian allies

Left: Robert Clive at the Battle of Plassey in 1757, where he defeated a 50,000-strong Indian army under French command with only 3,000 men. Hie success, which cost him 23 men killed, gave him control of Bengal, and considerable fame and fortune.

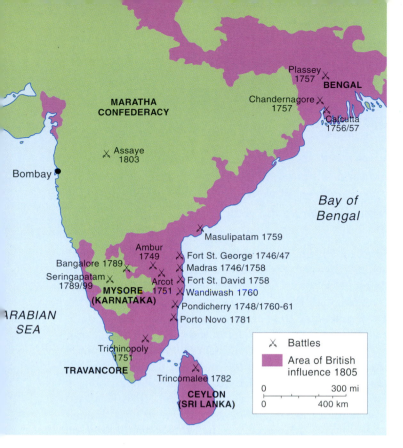

MARATHA
CONFEDERACY

Plassey
1757 **BENGAL**

Chandernagore
1757

Calcutta
1756/57

Assaye
1803

Bombay

Bay of
Bengal

Masulipatam 1759

Ambur
1749

Bangalore 1789   Fort St. George 1746/47

Seringapatam   Madras 1746/1758
1789/99   Arcot   Fort St. David 1758
MYSORE   1751   Wandiwash 1760
(KARNATAKA)
Pondicherry 1748/1760-61

ARABIAN
SEA   Porto Novo 1781

Trichinopoly
1751

TRAVANCORE   Trincomalee 1782

**CEYLON
(SRI LANKA)**

✗ Battles

Area of British
influence 1805

0   300 mi
0   400 km

French then retreated to their base at Pondicherry, which the British besieged for months, but events at sea eventually forced Lally's surrender. On September 10, a French fleet of 11 warships under Commodore Anne Antoine d'Ache had been battered into defeat by a British squadron led by Admiral George Pocock. This naval reverse effectively ended France's hopes of holding on in India. It was only a matter of time before Lally would have to surrender, and on January 15, 1761, he did. The French East India Company was closed down in 1769, giving the British a virtual monopoly in the commercial exploitation of the Indian subcontinent.

Consolidation of Power

The British now moved to extend their influence by taking advantage of the rivalries between various Indian rulers. It was a risky game, as the Indians expected something in return. When the British failed to support Haidar Ali, the ruler of Mysore (Karnataka), against the Marathas, he turned on his supposed allies. In September 1780 Ali defeated a small British force and advanced on Madras. But his success was short-lived; on June 1, 1781, Ali's troops were crushed at Porto Novo.

Some limited French support, particularly the capture of the British base of Trincomalee in Ceylon (Sri Lanka) in August 1782, sustained the war for a time. Much of France's efforts rested on the shoulders of Admiral de Suffren. But the death of Haidar Ali, the ending of French support, and the crowning of a new Mysore ruler, Tippoo Sahib, who favored peace, brought the conflict to an end in 1783.

Sahib, however, sought revenge for Mysore's earlier humiliation. In 1789 he attacked Travancore. The British commander, Lord Cornwallis, captured Bangalore and then laid siege to Seringapatam, where Tippoo Sahib had sought refuge. The war ended in 1792, and the victorious British gained half of Mysore.

In 1799 the British moved to eliminate France's remaining possessions in India. The British governor, Richard Wellesley, ordered Tippoo Sahib to disband the French units under his command. This was done, but the Mysore ruler continued to work closely with the French, thus the British invaded in 1799 and laid siege to Seringapatam. Tippoo Sahib died defending the city. Richard Wellesley's younger brother, Arthur, had fought with distinction and became governor of Seringapatam. He then laid the foundations of a brilliant military career by extending British control across India. His victory at Assaye in 1803, when his 5,000 troops defeated a 50,000-strong French-Indian army, confirmed his promise. His greatest test would come a few years later, when, as the Duke of Wellington, he was destined to take on the might of Napoleonic France in Europe.

began to loose faith in the French. Dupleix, although in no way responsible for Arcot, was dismissed in 1754.

With the French in temporary disorder, the British position seemed more secure. But powerful Indians had ambitions too, and in June 1756 the ruler of Bengal, Suraja Dowla, attacked Calcutta. After a four-day siege the city fell and Dowla's brutal treatment of his 146 European captives only spurred the British to exact revenge. Clive recaptured Calcutta on January 2, 1757. His next task was to seize Chandernagore, held by the French, then he could hunt down Suraja Dowla.

Clive caught up with the Bengalis in June. On the 23rd, Clive's diminutive force of just 3,000 took on the 50,000-strong Bengali Army at Plassey. In one of the most remarkably one-sided battles in history, Clive took the fight to the enemy. All generals need luck, and Clive was fortunate that a rainstorm dampened the enemy gunpowder, while his own men kept their own dry. The dramatic British victory virtually ended Bengali resistance. It also further undermined French prestige in India, as they had never won such a great battle. Dowla was assassinated a few days later, while his replacement, Mir Jafar, became a British ally. Bengal now came firmly within the British sphere of influence in India.

The French sent reinforcements to India in 1758 under General Lally, an Irishman. Lally left Pondicherry and marched against Fort St. David. This fell on June 2 and Lally turned his attention to Madras, which was able to withstand the siege chiefly due to shipped supplies. The tide of war then turned when the British inflicted a reverse on Lally at Masulipatam on January 25, 1759.

The British kept up the pressure on the French. Lally was defeated at Wandiwash on January 22, 1760. The

Catherine the Great's Wars

While the successes of Europe's powers around the world provided indicators of the strength of Europe's military organization and technology, most Europeans were more impressed by victories closer to home – such as the defeat of the long-time enemy power of the Ottoman Empire. In 1683 Ottoman forces had laid siege to Vienna, but it was to be the last serious threat posed by them in the region.

The institutions of the Ottoman Empire had been becoming less effective – long wars against Persia in the 17th century had run down its resources, and the innovation which had characterized elite corps such as the Janissaries was steadily eroding. There was little appetite for reform from within and many provinces had become virtually independent, failing to contribute to the strength of the empire overall. So, after the relief of Vienna, the Hapsburgs led an offensive by armies of the Holy League (Polish and Venetian troops played a major part) to conquer Hungary. Then, from 1714 to 1718, Hapsburg forces under Prince Eugene enjoyed a series of successful campaigns against the Turks, consolidating in Hungary and taking Belgrade. In the 1730s, though, the Ottomans retook Belgrade and defeated Russian encroachments in the Crimea.

Having stalled the Hapsburgs, the Ottomans were to gain a new foe in Russia, which had developed into a major power under Peter the Great and then, under Empress Elizabeth, had played an important part in the Seven Years War. Six months after Elizabeth's death, her daughter-in-law, Catherine, took power in a coup. Catherine set Russia on an expansionist course, using the resources of the vast state to create a large army.

Catherine the Great's (as she became) first major military adventure was conducted against a group of rebellious Polish nobles known as the Confederation of the Bar. They opposed Russia's growing involvement in Poland and objected to their own (pro-Russian) government. The rebellion, which began in 1768, was put down by the Russians, but the rebels had called on Turkey to aid them. The Turks had, in fact, ignored the calls for assistance, but Russian troops chased some of the rebels into Turkish territory and destroyed a town in the process, provoking Turkey to declare war. The Russian Army redeployed southward, defeating the Turks in the Caucasus and then invading the Balkans in 1769. The Russian commander, Count Peter Rumiantsev, smashed a Turkish army on the Dniester River, took the town of Jassy, and then conquered the Turkish-held provinces of Moldavia and Wallachia.

Russian Gains

The Russians then backed revolts in Turkish-controlled Egypt and Greece. These did not succeed, but the Russians were victorious elsewhere. At the naval Battle of Chesme, fought off the Mediterranean coast of Turkey on July 6, 1770, a Russian force led by Admiral Aleksei Orlov overwhelmed a Turkish fleet. And in August, Rumiantsev, taking advantage of his victory on the Dniester, defeated a Turkish force that had been mustered to eject him from Moldavia.

In 1771 Catherine's forces continued to make further inroads into Turkish territory. Prince Vasily Dolgoruky advanced into the Crimea, conquering the peninsula. The Turks opened peace negotiations in 1772. However, this conciliatory move was simply a ploy to allow them to rebuild their forces. War broke out again in 1773, but the Turks only met with further disasters.

Rumiantsev advanced south from his position along the Danube River against the main Turkish field army, which fell back on Shulma. General Alexander Suvarov then tackled the Turks at Shulma in June 1774 and won a famous victory. Weariness began to set in and the Treaty of Kuchuk Kainarji was signed on July 16: Russia

WARFARE IN EASTERN EUROPE

The geography of eastern Europe – vast spaces, broad plains, large areas of forest, wide rivers, and (in the Balkans) mountainous terrain – meant that the style of warfare was often quite different from that in western Europe. A typical example of this was the importance of light cavalry, able to cover long distances quickly and frequently armed with firearms so that they could fight on foot if need be. Cavalry forces, such as Polish lancers or hussars, Cossacks from the steppes of southern Russia, or the *spahis* of the Ottomans, were often crucial during campaigns, whereas they played a more peripheral role in western Europe. Light infantry forces were also able to operate in wooded or mountainous terrain, and were far more important than in the west, where "line" infantry (that is, infantry trained to fight in a solid line) ruled the battlefield. And, given the relative sparsity of major fortified towns or cities, the sieges of such places often became crucial. Belgrade, for example, was the focus of warfare between the Habsburgs and the Ottomans throughout the century.

Key:
- ✕ Battles
- Russian Empire 1762
- Lands conquered by Catherine the Great 1762-96

0 — 500 mi
0 — 800 km

St. Petersburg

Moscow

RUSSIA

LITHUANIA

PRUSSIA

Warsaw
P O L A N D
Maciejowice
1794

Kiev

Dnieper River

Dniester River

HAPSBURG
DOMINIONS

Jassy

Moldavia

Focsani
1789

Kinburn
1788

Liman
1788

Crimea

CAUCASUS

CASPIAN SEA

Wallachia
Ismail
1790

Georgia

Danube River

Shulma ✕
1774

BLACK SEA

Left: Catherine the Great concentrated on expanding the Russian Empire westward, specifically at the expense of two weaker powers: Poland and the Ottoman Empire.

peace agreement with Ottoman Turkey. This was a consequence of renewed problems in Poland, where the Prussians were trying to increase their political influence. The Treaty of Jassy was signed on January 9, 1792: the Russians returned Moldavia and Bessarabia to the Turks but kept hold of the territories to the east of the Dniester. Thus, a century after the siege of Vienna in 1683, the Ottoman Empire was in retreat, grimly hanging on to its possessions in Europe against stronger powers. It was a significant change in the balance of power.

Catherine the Great also had the large but weakly ruled state of Poland in her sights. In 1772 she came to an agreement with Austria and Prussia by which they all occupied some Polish land. There was a further partition agreed between Russia and Prussia in 1792. In 1794 Polish nationalists, commanded by Thaddeus Kosciusko, began to rebel against the dismemberment of their country. Kosciusko's poorly armed forces were soon forced back to Warsaw, which was besieged in late August. The heavily outnumbered Poles, some 35,000 soldiers with 200 guns, defended their capital with great valor, repulsing two major assaults by the Russo-Prussian armies, whose combined strength totalled 100,000 soldiers and 250 guns.

Incredibly, at the beginning of September, the siege was broken by the Poles. The victory was short-lived, however. On October 10 at the Battle of Maciejowice, Kosciusko, with just 7,000 men, was decisively defeated. He was wounded and captured and the rebellion quickly collapsed. Poland disappeared as an independent country in 1795.

Between 1788 and 1790 Catherine the Great had also fought a war against Sweden. Despite two early defeats, the Swedes recovered sufficiently to take on the Russian Navy in July 1790. The battle left the Russian fleet in tatters as 53 ships were sunk by the Swedes. Peace between the two countries followed, on August 15, 1790.

By 1790, Europe was a continent in which there was great expertise in the conduct of warfare, and whose technology and organization for war was superior to those of any other societies in the world. Over the period from 1792 to 1815, this expertise was to be heightened even further, as the conduct of war took a very new turn under one of the greatest commanders in history: Napoleon Bonaparte.

returned some of the territories it had captured but, significantly, gained access to the Black Sea, a stretch of water whose coastline had previously been the sole preserve of the Turks. The Ottoman Empire never recovered from this change in the balance of power.

The peace lasted for 14 years. The Russians intrigued with local tribes to gain control of Georgia, ruled by the Turks, while the latter encouraged the Crimean tribes to rebel against their new overlords. However, in 1788 Suvarov defeated the Turks at Kinburn, thereby preventing them from reconquering the Crimea. The Russians were also successful at sea. John Paul Jones, the naval hero of the American Revolutionary War, led the Russian fleet into action at the two Battles of Liman in June 1788.

The focus of the war switched to Moldavia in 1789. The Austrians invaded from the west, while the Russians advanced from the north. A united Russian and Austrian army was then resoundingly successful at the Battle of Foscani on August 1, forcing the Turks to fall back to the Danube River. With other attacks in the Balkans and the loss of Belgrade, the Turks became alarmed and sought to negotiate a treaty with Austria. The peace deal in 1791 let Turkey regain Belgrade but cede control of other parts of the Balkans.

The Turks had to deal with a revolt in Greece in 1790 that undermined their ability to focus on holding back the Russians. Then, on December 22, General Suvarov captured the important fortress of Ismail at the mouth of the Danube. When it fell, he ordered the massacre of all its Turkish defenders, after which he was promoted. Despite these victories, Russia was eager to reach a

Revolutionary and Napoleonic Wars
1775–1815

The period from the start of the American Revolution in the 1770s to the end of the Napoleonic Wars in 1815 was a time of immense social, political, economic, and military change. The republican armies of the era opened up opportunities for those with talent, and one dominant theme was that of liberty and people's right to self-government as free citizens of a new nation-state in arms.

Military changes occurred primarily in the fields of tactics and organization. The old linear mode of warfare, which emphasized infantry firepower, was challenged by a new tactical system that favored battlefield mobility. Originating in a debate among French military writers after the Seven Years War, theory became a reality in the wars of the French Revolution from 1792 onward.

The new French tactics involved skirmishers advancing in attack columns ahead of the main force. This mobility proved highly effective, and was copied widely. The exception was Britain, whose small army still relied on high-quality infantry delivering massed firepower in increasingly thin lines (the British alone reduced their line formation from three to two ranks).

Dominating this period was, of course, Napoleon Bonaparte (1769–1821). His genius lay in his strategic vision, which enabled him to maneuver his troops to a battlefield of his choosing, in which the enemy was generally at a disadvantage. Often outnumbered, he was usually able to deploy superior forces at the decisive point. He fought and won more battles than any other great general. Napoleon was fortunate in being able to harness the energies of the nation and its army. Armies had been organized as distinct institutions that fought at the monarch's behest. As a result of the revolution – and presaged by events in North America – a sense of pride in the nation's army took hold, in which the citizen had both a right and a duty to bear arms.

Right: The Battle of Borodino, fought on September 7, 1812, was Napoleon's attempt to destroy the Russian Army during his campaign in Russia. His failure to do so ultimately condemned the campaign to failure, notwithstanding his occupation of Moscow.

The American Revolution

The American Revolution saw the transformation of 13 colonies on the eastern seaboard of North America into a new state based upon the rights of the individual, in which men were citizens of the state and not subjects of the crown. As with the later revolution in France, the American Revolution was a violent uprising that witnessed the emergence of a new state through the crucible of war.

The causes of the war do not concern this study. The America colonies were some 3,000 miles (4,800 km) from Britain and this distance was the colonists' greatest advantage. Although the colonial armies had problems retaining their soldiers for more than a few months at a time before they returned home, they could usually be replaced by other local recruits. Replacements for any British soldier had to come across the Atlantic. This simple fact made the British generals unduly cautious.

British leaders proved to be poor at developing plans and coordinating their scattered forces to overcome these disadvantages. American leaders, by comparison, made better use of their resources. George Washington (1732–99) developed into an exceptional and inspiring military leader, and many Americans were accustomed to using firearms for hunting and possessed sufficient skill and fieldcraft to be able to join in an attack on an outpost or supply column. Fighting in a formal battle was a different matter, but with good leadership and training the techniques could be acquired.

After reverses in 1775, the main British forces in America were more successful in the latter part of 1776. Under the command of two brothers, General Sir William Howe and Admiral Lord Richard Howe, the British strategy was to take New York. The British began landing a force of some 32,000 men on Staten Island in July, including 9,000 German Hessian mercenaries.

Washington was based on Manhattan Island but also deployed troops on Long Island. General Howe attacked and defeated Washington's men in the Battle of Long Island on August 27. Washington then had to evacuate New York after defeats at Harlem Heights (September 16) and White Plains (October 28). He and the army fell back to

X Battles

1 Bunker Hill 1775
2 Ticonderoga 1775/77
3 Quebec 1775
4 Valcour Island 1776
5 Trenton 1776
6 Long Island 1776
7 Harlem Heights 1776
8 White Plains 1776
9 Saratoga 1777
10 Brandywine 1777
11 Germantown 1777
12 Princeton 1777
13 Bennington 1777
14 Monmouth 1778
15 Savannah 1778-79
16 Charleston 1780
17 King's Mountain 1780
18 Camden 1780
19 Cowpens 1781
20 Guilford Courthouse 1781
21 Hobkirk's Hill 1781
22 Eutaw Springs 1781
23 Battle of the Capes 1781
24 Yorktown 1781

Left: The American Revolution was at first fought predominantly in the north, but then the focus shifted to the south, with the decisive battle being fought at Yorktown in 1781.

Pennsylvania. Meanwhile, Congress had issued the Declaration of Independence on July 4, 1776, but following these British victories it seemed America's revolution was in trouble. In addition, the British government developed new plans. Lord George Germain, the British colonial secretary based in London, was in charge of British operations. He devised a strategy for General John Burgoyne to attack south from Canada toward Albany, New York, while Howe moved part of his army north from New York to link up with Burgoyne. If all went well, the British would divide the American colonies in two. The idea looked good on paper but to succeed it required the close cooperation of the two commanders and, partly as a result of Germain's unsure direction from London, they failed to coordinate their plans.

General Burgoyne led his army south from Canada and captured Fort Ticonderoga in July 1777, as part of the plan to link up with British forces in New York. In August, he learned that Howe would not be moving up from New York to support him, but Burgoyne decided to carry on with the original strategy and continue his advance. In September his army crossed the Hudson River and advanced on the main American forces near Saratoga. At both the Battle of Freeman's Farm on September 19 and the Battle of Bemis Heights on October 7, the British attacked well-prepared American positions and were repulsed with heavy losses. After the defeat at Bemis Heights the British found themselves outnumbered and increasingly isolated, and on October 17, Burgoyne and his 6,000 troops surrendered to the American commander, General Horatio Gates.

While Burgoyne was advancing to disaster, Howe moved his army south by sea to Chesapeake Bay in order to strike at Philadelphia, the capital city. Washington's defending forces were defeated at the Battle of the Brandywine on September 11, 1777. Howe captured the city on September 26. Washington's force was at a particularly low ebb by this time.

However, a turning point had been reached. A German adviser, Baron Friedrich von Steuben, arrived in the Continental Army camp at Valley Forge, Pennsylvania, and his training helped turn the American militiamen and volunteers into an army. Even more important, when news reached Europe of the victory at Saratoga, France opened discussions for an alliance with American representatives. The alliance was agreed in February 1778, and war between Britain and France followed in June.

A year later, in June 1779, Spain declared war on Britain, and at the end of 1780 Britain and the Netherlands were also at war. Having new defensive commitments, the overstretched British Navy and Army would now have less chance to take the initiative.

The French alliance produced a change in British plans. General Henry Clinton took over as the British commander-in-chief and was ordered to pull out of Philadelphia and withdraw his main force to New York.

The Battle of Monmouth in New Jersey on June 28 was the one major engagement of 1778. Neither side won a clear victory, but from this point onward the British abandoned their attempts to bring the middle colonies and New England back under their control. They, instead, pinned their hopes on making gains in the south.

British successes followed in 1780, as Charleston, South Carolina, was captured and an important battle won at Camden in August. But the British, now led by General Charles Cornwallis (1738–1805), discovered that any detachments from their main army were liable to be caught and defeated.

The new American commander in the south, General Nathanael Greene, fought a battle with Cornwallis at Guilford Courthouse, North Carolina, in March 1781. The battle was sufficient to persuade Cornwallis that he had to abandon his efforts to hold Georgia and the Carolinas. He marched north into Virginia, and in August 1781 established a base at Yorktown. Supported and reinforced by his French allies, Washington decided to attack Yorktown. The British had about 8,000 men to defend the town; Washington had 9,500 Americans and 7,800 French troops. On October 19, 1781, Cornwallis surrendered.

To all intents and purposes the war was over. The Treaty of Paris was agreed in November 1782 and finally signed on November 30, 1783. The United States was recognized as an independent nation.

France's Revolutionary Wars

France's support for the 13 colonies may have aided Britain's defeat, but it is also bankrupted her. Attempts to solve this problem led to revolution in 1789 and the overthrow of the institutions that had underpinned absolute monarchy. Governments elsewhere found the new political ideas a threat and tried to prevent the "contagion" from spreading, while France prepared to export a new type of warfare.

Tension grew, and in April 1792 the new, belligerent French government declared war on Austria and Prussia. At the outset the army of the revolutionary government was disorganized and its soldiers badly trained. Prussian troops captured towns and fortresses in northeast France, but they moved with caution and gave the French time to assemble the army. The two sides met at Valmy, France, on September 20, 1792. A fierce cannonade persuaded the Prussians to withdraw. A few weeks later the French defeated the Austrians at Jemappes. France had a breathing space.

Two days after Valmy, the revolutionaries declared France a republic. King Louis XVI was executed in January 1793, and new, radical leaders took control. The regicide alarmed Europe's monarchs, and Britain, Spain, and the Netherlands joined Austria and Prussia in an anti-French alliance known as the First Coalition.

REVOLUTIONARY WARFARE

The French Revolution brought about a radical change to the recruitment of soldiers. Conscription of all young and able-bodied males became a standard practice in France, and later in most parts of Europe. National governments increasingly tried to give military training to all young men in time of peace, and mobilize as many of them as possible in time of war.

In the early stages of the French Revolution many of the French soldiers were enthusiastic volunteers, and while not professional soldiers, they were determined to fight against the trained soldiers of other European countries to preserve what they saw as their new freedoms.

France's first national army was raised under a law of 1793, which summed up this new trend for all-out war: "Young men shall fight; married men shall make weapons and transport supplies; women will make tents and clothes and will serve in the hospitals; children will convert old linen into bandages; old men will have themselves carried into the public squares to make speeches to inspire the soldiers, to preach hatred against kings, and proclaim the unity of the republic."

In the first half of 1793 it gained the upper hand. France's government, the Committee of Public Safety, declared a *levée en masse* (mass conscription). Many were enthusiastic about defending the nation, and over time raw recruits developed into veterans. These men were not prepared to accept the strict discipline that was necessary for the rigid formations of, for example, the Prussian Army; nor was there the time to train them.

The old armies of the 18th century had adopted close-order formations not only to maximize firepower but to force unwilling soldiers to stay in the ranks – they did not use troops in loose formations for fear of desertion. With the enthusiastic French Revolutionary Army, such considerations were redundant and the army became more flexible.

Large numbers of troops were now used as skirmishers, firing from cover at the well-ordered enemy lines and opposition officers. The French Army could adapt itself to difficult ground far better than its opponents, as was demonstrated by their victories at Arcola (marshes) and Rivoli (hilly terrain). As time went on, such loose formations did not mean a lack of discipline; rather, they were demonstrations of flexible discipline. During the Revolutionary Wars, the *ordre mixte* became increasingly common, in which a brigade of infantry would advance with alternate battalions in line and column formation – a compromise between mobility and firepower.

In this new army anyone – not just a noble – could become an officer, and many of France's most illustrious commanders were of humble origins. Napoleon joked that every one of his soldiers carried a marshal's baton in his napsack. The French command system had opened up a career to talent.

As a consequence of the *levée en masse*, France's army grew massively and the numbers threatened to overwhelm the system, so over the next two years numbers were reduced and quality improved. Much of the credit goes to Lazare Nicolas Carnot (1753–1823), who provided the structure and discipline to channel the enthusiasm of the revolution into an effective army.

During late 1793, the new army came into its own as it defeated attempts to invade northern and eastern France. More victories followed in 1794, and in the first months of 1795 the Netherlands was overrun by French troops. In the face of repeated defeats, Prussia, the Netherlands, Spain, and some German states lost their

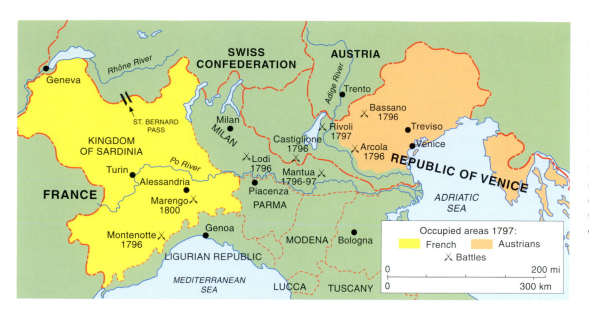

Left: Napoleon's campaigns in northern Italy in 1797–1800 showed the potent mix of a commander of tactical and strategic genius (Bonaparte) and troops filled with revolutionary fervor, which inspired them to feats of valor and energy that their stolid opponents, trained in the tenets of 18th-century warfare, could not match.

appetite for the fight and made peace with France, leaving only Britain and Austria to continue the war.

In mid-1795 a more moderate government, known as the Directory, took power in France and suppressed an uprising of *sansculottes* in Paris later in the year. During this revolt the government forces were led by a young artillery officer called Napoleon Bonaparte, who had distinguished himself by using shore-based artillery to beat off an Anglo-Spanish fleet supporting the royalist-held port of Toulon. In early 1796 Bonaparte was given command of the army in Italy. Just one of many rising stars, within months he had become a national hero.

During 1796 Bonaparte made rapid progress. The French soldiers were dispirited, but Bonaparte inspired them to cross the Alps. During the spring of 1797, the French went over to the strategic offensive in northern Italy, and began to advance up the passes. Vienna itself quickly came under threat, and in October 1797 the Treaty of Campo Formio confirmed French control of Belgium and northern Italy. Bonaparte had won a dozen or more battles as a result of timely forced marches, flexibility in maneuver, and the ability to concentrate his forces at the enemy's most vulnerable point. The display made him France's foremost commander.

The war with Britain continued, with the French masters on land and the British dominant at sea. In July 1798 the French invaded Egypt, but were cut off when their fleet was destroyed by the Royal Navy at the Battle of the Nile (August 1). Bonaparte escaped in October 1798, leaving his army to its fate. The 26,000 survivors eventually surrendered to the British in 1801.

In the meantime Russia, Britain, and Austria had formed the Second Coalition. During 1799, a series of battles in Italy reversed many of the gains Napoleon had made previously, but in Switzerland the skill of General André Masséna forced Russia out of the Coalition.

Upon his return to France, Bonaparte organized a *coup d'état* and made himself First Consul. He took the Army of the Reserve over the St. Bernard Pass into Italy in May 1800 and defeated the Austrians at Marengo on June 14. General Moreau's defeat of the Austrians at Hohenlinden (December 3, 1801) made Vienna sue for peace, leaving Britain alone in the Second Coalition. Maritime Britain and landlocked France could do little to harm one another, and, faced with stalemate, the states signed the Treaty of Amiens in 1802. Europe was at peace for the first time in 10 years, but with Bonaparte's ambitions the treaty was merely a temporary truce.

Right: The Battle of Valmy, September 20, 1792, was not really a battle at all. The 50,000 French troops and 35,000 Prussian regulars never got to engage: the fire from 54 French cannon prompted the Prussian commander, the Duke of Brunswick, to withdraw. Losses were fewer than 300 for each army.

The Emperor's First Campaigns

France's army was an excellent tool for an ambitious Napoleon determined to dominate Europe. France's population was as large as Britain's, Prussia's, and Austria's put together – and had the military manpower to match. Many of the soldiers were now veteran fighters, and they were led by a host of talented young commanders, all made loyal to their emperor through lavish gifts of titles and money.

Napoleon concentrated all authority in his own person. He became obsessed with his own glory and destiny, convinced that his autocratic desires were as one with the wishes of France, and even Europe.

The Napoleonic Wars were hugely expensive. It was part of the secret of Napoleon's success that in his years of triumph France's wars were fought on foreign soil. By living off the land, the French armies not only enhanced their mobility but ensured that the financial burden of supplying them was borne by the indigenous people. Napoleon was also quick to impose stiff reparations on those he had defeated – another means of supplying the hard cash to finance his campaigns of conquest.

Following the collapse of the Treaty of Amiens in May 1803, Britain imposed a naval blockade on France. Napoleon then devised various plans to invade Britain, but these were undermined by Britain's naval triumph at Trafalgar in 1805. Up until 1805 Britain stood alone, then Austria and Russia joined the Third Coalition (a dithering Prussia decided to remain neutral).

Napoleon decided to strike while his enemies were disorganized, and at the end of August the *Grande Armée* marched on Germany. The French surrounded the Austrians at Ulm and forced a surrender. Napoleon then urged his men on and in November Vienna fell. The remainder of the Austrian Army and a large Russian force, under the shrewd leadership of Marshal Mikhail Kutuzov (1745–1813), assembled near Olmütz about 100 miles (160 km) to the north of Vienna. Moving in Kutuzov's direction as winter drew on, Napoleon's army would only get weaker and allied reinforcements were also on the way. Czar Alexander I, however, overruled Kutuzov's patient approach and ordered an assault. The result was the Battle of Austerlitz on December 2, 1805 – Napoleon's greatest victory. Two days later the Austrians surrendered, while the Russians retreated.

Austria ceded control of its former areas of influence in Germany and Italy. Napoleon spent the first half of 1806 organizing these into French-controlled puppet states ready to serve his interests and supply him with troops. Prussia's leaders then decided to oppose Napoleon, and, supported by Britain and in conjunction with Saxony, began to prepare for war.

Napoleon's forces were now routinely divided up into army corps. Each of these, usually commanded by one of his trusted marshals, had infantry, cavalry, and artillery, and was thus capable of independent operations or fighting as part of a larger battle plan. On October 8, 1806, Napoleon invaded Saxony and six days later was ready for the Prussians, but not all went according to plan. Napoleon concentrated 90,000 men at Jena in eastern Germany on October 14 and defeated what he thought was the main Prussian Army, but in fact it was only less than half. At the same time about 15 miles (24 km) away at Auerstadt, the 27,000 men of III Corps, commanded by Marshal Louis

Left: *Napoleon Bonaparte was a military genius who indelibly stamped his personality on an era. His theories about waging war, his conduct of campaigns, and battlefield tactics all became benchmarks for military commanders throughout the 19th century.*

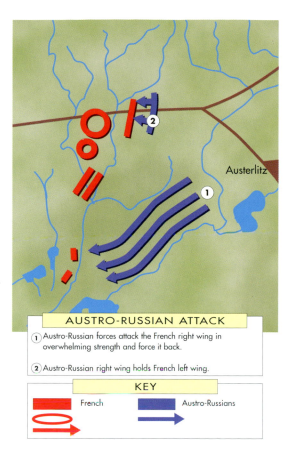

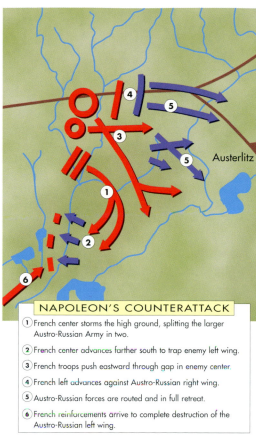

AUSTRO-RUSSIAN ATTACK

① Austro-Russian forces attack the French right wing in overwhelming strength and force it back.

② Austro-Russian right wing holds French left wing.

KEY

(red arrow)	French	(blue arrow)	Austro-Russians
(red loop)			

NAPOLEON'S COUNTERATTACK

① French center storms the high ground, splitting the larger Austro-Russian Army in two.

② French center advances farther south to trap enemy left wing.

③ French troops push eastward through gap in enemy center.

④ French left advances against Austro-Russian right wing.

⑤ Austro-Russian forces are routed and in full retreat.

⑥ French reinforcements arrive to complete destruction of the Austro-Russian left wing.

Left: The Battle of Austerlitz, 1805, displayed Napoleon's tactical genius. Allowing the allies to press his right wing, Napoleon then unleashed Marshal Nicolas Soult's (1769–1851) corps to split the enemy center. Soult then encircled the allied left and, assisted by Davout, defeated it. The allied right was then enveloped by Marshal Jean Baptiste Bernadotte (1763–1844), and by nightfall the allied army had ceased to exist. Austerlitz stands as a tactical masterpiece to rank alongside Arbela and Cannae.

Davout (1770–1823), were fighting a battle against the main body of the Prussian Army, 50,000 men-strong.

Davout held his position and eventually forced the superior Prussian force to retreat. By early November Prussia was under French control. Napoleon could have made peace, but decided to wage war against Russia. He moved his forces into Poland and East Prussia, ready to do battle with the Russians. On February 8, 1807, the two sides fought the Battle of Eylau in the middle of a heavy snowstorm. The cavalry, led by Marshal Joachim Murat (1767–1815), saved the French from defeat. Casualties were heavy, and both sides were content to retire to winter quarters and reorganize.

Napoleon regained the initiative when campaigning resumed in the early summer of 1807. At Friedland on June 14, Napoleon quickly exploited the poor deployment of the Russians under Count Bennigsen. The czar asked for peace terms, and in July Napoleon signed the Treaty of Tilsit with Russia and Prussia.

After a brief campaign in the Iberian peninsula, Napoleon was caught off guard by Austria's declaration of war in 1809. Napoleon suffered his first defeat at the Battle of Aspern-Essling, fought east of Vienna on May 21–22. A few weeks later the French avenged their setback by comprehensively defeating the Austrians during the vast, two-day-long Battle of Wagram (July 5–6). The Austrians suffered about 40,000 casualties; the French around 35,000. Austria was forced to accept Napoleon's peace terms and surrender more territory to

THE IMPERIAL GUARD

The Imperial Guard originated as a small personal escort for Napoleon when he was a young general, but after his coronation it expanded from 12,000 men in 1805 to over 100,000 in 1814. The Guard contained infantry, cavalry, and artillery, replicating most units found in the rest of the army. Over the course of time, it was subdivided into young, middle, and old, with the most experienced soldiers assigned to the Old Guard. Its soldiers were paid much more than troops in ordinary line regiments, and they invariably received better rations and equipment. It was a great honor to be selected; men usually had to have five years' service and to have fought bravely in several battles before being eligible to join.

The infantry of the Old Guard usually formed Napoleon's tactical reserve, for use as a last resort. Such was its prestige that when the Guard's attack failed at the Battle of Waterloo, it was obvious that the battle was lost.

the French. Napoleon was master of most of Europe, but the British remained undefeated. However, by 1809 many of his best men were either killed or wounded, while the veterans were becoming exhausted by years of constant warfare.

Napoleonic Naval Warfare

Failed invasion attempts and defeat at the Battle of Trafalgar in 1805 meant the French attack on British power had to be waged by other means. Thus in 1806 Napoleon introduced the Continental System, targeting trade with Britain so as to undermine her economically. But with the Royal Navy supreme on the seas, Napoleon was unable to make his all-out economic blockade of British goods effective.

Ship design had changed little since the mid-18th century, with large sail-powered ships-of-the-line dominating naval strategy. Ships were always subject to the wind and weather, and required good seamanship if they were to be effective in battle. Life at sea was always dangerous, and far more ships were sunk as a result of bad weather or navigational errors than were lost through enemy action.

Throughout the wars with France, Britain's strategy was based on blockade, whereby British fleets patrolled close to enemy ports, keeping enemy trading vessels and warships imprisoned in their home ports. Such duties were never popular with the fleets, but they provided sailors and their officers with an excellent opportunity to improve and develop their seamanship. The French, by contrast, suffered from insufficient opportunities to exercise their maritime skills, which were anyway in short supply following the excesses of the revolution, when many officers had been executed on the guillotine or had gone into exile.

During the first years of the war the Netherlands and Spain had been Britain's allies, but French victories on land caused them to adopt a pro-French policy. By 1796,

British resources were stretched so thin that the Royal Navy pulled its fleet out of the Mediterranean, abandoning its allies and trading interests throughout the region. Late in 1796 the French tried to invade British-controlled Ireland, but the expedition failed because of severe weather that dispersed the French invasion fleet.

A further crisis for the British followed in April 1797, when sailors of most of the home-based fleet mutinied. The rebellious crews refused to obey orders in protest at poor food, late pay, and over-harsh discipline. Although the mutinies were suppressed, some of the mutineers' demands were met and the overall morale and discipline of the home fleet was generally improved.

The Royal Navy Regains the Initiative

Away from home waters the British fleets were not affected, mainly because their commanders took better care of the men serving under them. The Royal Navy began to regain the initiative in the naval war when Admiral John Jervis defeated a Spanish fleet during the Battle of Cape St. Vincent, fought off southwest Portugal on February 14, 1797.

Right: The Royal Navy bombards Copenhagen in September 1807. The action was designed to prevent Denmark and Russia from joining a European alliance with France. The plan worked: the Danish fleet surrendered.

In October, the British home fleet again proved reliable when it destroyed the Dutch at the Battle of Camperdown on the North Sea. The next year, Jervis sent part of his force back into the Mediterranean. Led by Admiral Horatio Nelson (1758–1805), this squadron went on to annihilate the French Mediterranean fleet at the Battle of the Nile on August 1, 1798.

When war between Britain and France resumed in 1803 after the brief Treaty of Amiens, Britain's enemies (in naval terms, France and Spain) had managed to rebuild their fleets and were ready to try once again to wrest control of the seas from the Royal Navy. Napoleon assembled his "Army of England" along the northern coast of France. He reasoned that if the British Navy could be kept from interfering while he transported his army across the narrow waters of the English Channel, then he could easily go on to conquer the whole of Britain.

Napoleon ordered the French fleet under Admiral Pierre de Villeneuve, along with various Spanish detachments, to a rendezvous in the Caribbean region. The French plan was to draw the Royal Navy away from the English Channel, thereby allowing the invasion army assembled by France to land without hindrance.

Nelson followed Villeneuve across the Atlantic but was unable to catch him. When he realized the nature of the French plan, Nelson returned to join the British fleet in the English Channel. On the way, Nelson learned that Villeneuve had

sailed back to the southern Spanish port of Cadiz. An impatient Napoleon then ordered Villeneuve to sail out from Cadiz, but by then Nelson's force was ready and waiting for him.

Villeneuve had 18 French and 15 Spanish ships. Nelson, with only 27 vessels, was outnumbered but he was so confident of the superior seamanship of his men that he steered his ships – in a formation of two columns – into the enemy line. Nelson himself was killed in the Battle of Trafalgar that followed on October 21, but 18 of the enemy ships were captured or sunk for no losses among the British ships (although 1,500 British sailors were killed or wounded), and any hope that Napoleon held of invading Britain was dashed for good.

There were no large-scale naval battles after Trafalgar, a confirmation of Britain's dominance at sea. The British blockade against France continued, confining the French to a land-based war. The importance of British naval strategy can be seen in the fact that the war in the Iberian peninsula and the war against Russia in 1812 were both consequences of European nations flouting Napoleon's ban and continuing to trade with Britain. And both these wars would eventually prove fatal to Napoleon's ambitions of a Europe united under his rule.

Right: The French flagship in flames during the Battle of the Nile, August 1, 1798. It was a catastrophic defeat for the French at the hands of Admiral Horatio Nelson.

The Peninsular War

The war in Spain and Portugal was important in several respects. Napoleon dismissively considered it a sideshow, but the Spanish in particular demonstrated how effective guerrilla resistance could be against an occupying army, offering an heroic example to other nationalities suffering under the French. The British, for their part, were able to show support for an ally and inflict defeats on the French Army in open battle.

With Spanish permission, Napoleon despatched a small army across Spain and into Portugal toward the end of 1807. The emperor, however, also made the decision to depose the Spanish monarch and replace him with someone he could trust to apply the Continental System more effectively. The new Spanish king was to be Napoleon's own brother, Joseph, and so it was that another French force was sent into Spain to install the new Bonapartist king on the throne in Madrid. The Spanish people immediately rose up in rebellion against the French in May 1808. A French force of 20,000 troops was even surrounded and forced to surrender at Baylen in July.

These events gave Britain an opportunity to intervene, and an expeditionary force was sent to aid the Portuguese. A young British general called Arthur Wellesley (1769–1852) defeated the French at the Battle of Vimeiro in August 1808, and the French commander, Junot, agreed to leave Portugal. This humiliation infuriated Napoleon, and he led a substantial army into the Iberian peninsula to solve the problem himself.

By the end of October 1808 Napoleon had 200,000 men massed in northern Spain, and in a whirlwind six-week campaign he smashed the second-rate Spanish armies opposing him and captured Madrid, the capital. He planned to complete the campaign by launching offensives into southern Spain and Portugal, but he was unable to do so because British troops commanded by General Sir John Moore had attacked his line of communications to the north.

Napoleon therefore ordered a powerful force to advance against Moore's forces. Moore made a desperate retreat and his men were evacuated by sea from La Coruña in December. They had succeeded in preventing Napoleon from carrying out his original plan, and he was forced to leave Spain at the end of the year in order to control the new threat from Austria. His generals were left to bring the Iberian campaign to a swift and successful conclusion, but this proved a far harder task than their emperor anticipated. The Spanish bravely continued to fight on, and the British built up their base in Portugal to lend them assistance.

Right: The Battle of Vitoria, fought on June 21, 1813, was the decisive battle of the Peninsula War. The French lost 7,000 men and 143 guns, forcing them back over the Pyrenees into France itself. Here, red-coated British infantry launch their final attack.

lack of food while Wellington's men were well supplied by provisions brought in by British ships.

The British forces were stronger by 1812, while the French could expect fewer reinforcements due to the campaign in Russia. Wellington defeated a French force at the Battle of Salamanca on July 12, 1812, but was forced to retreat later in the year after an over-ambitious offensive failed.

Wellington made no such mistake in 1813, when Napoleon's brother's army was virtually destroyed at the Battle of Vitoria on June 21. The remaining French forces had no option but to pull out of Spain entirely, and by early 1814 Wellington was advancing through southern France. The British captured the city of Toulouse on April 10, and two days later they learned that Napoleon had abdicated his throne.

Napoleon always thought that Spain was a minor theater of war, but it turned into a relentless drain on France's resources. The Peninsular War proved to the rest of Europe that Britain would help its allies and that French armies could be defeated in battle.

Napoleon never realized the problems faced by his commanders in Spain. Transport was exceedingly difficult, food was in short supply, and the Spanish people violently opposed the French occupiers. Relations between Spaniards and French were made worse by the occupiers' practice of living off the land, which caused the impoverished peasantry great hardship. Unable to defeat the French in open battle, the Spanish turned to waging a savage guerrilla war against the invaders, which in turn diverted tens of thousands of French troops away from military operations to guard lines of communication.

The fighting in Spain can be divided into two phases. Between 1809 and 1811 the French were the stronger, aiming to expel the British from Portugal. From 1812 until the end of the war in the spring of 1814, the British were in the ascendant, defeating French armies in central and northern Spain before advancing into southern France itself.

Throughout both periods the British were inspired by the careful but effective leadership of Wellesley, whose victories gained him the title Duke of Wellington. Wellington sometimes had to retreat, but he never lost a battle in either phase of the war. In the earlier period he attacked the French whenever he could, but knew he would usually have to fall back to Portugal if the French concentrated their forces against him.

Wellington ensured, however, that his base around Lisbon was effectively fortified by defensive positions known as the Lines of Torres Vedras. In 1810, when Wellington was forced to retire behind the Lines, the French Army that followed him withered away through

WELLINGTON'S WAY OF WAR

Arthur Wellesley, the Duke of Wellington, was the British commander-in-chief in Spain from the summer of 1809 until the invasion of southern France in 1814. He then went on to lead the British forces in the final decisive victory over Napoleon at Waterloo in 1815.

While Napoleon's French forces relied on swift maneuver on the battlefield and aggressive action, Wellington's victories were, for the most part, based on the defensive firepower of his infantry. Wellington generally allowed the enemy to initiate offensive action, while he kept the bulk of his forces hidden behind the crest of a hill, which protected them from the French artillery and skirmish fire. As the French advanced, they became disordered as a result of accurate fire from British artillery and light infantry. At the critical moment, Wellington ordered his infantry onto the crest of the slope, where they blasted the enemy with volleys of devastating close-range musket fire.

The 1812 Russia Campaign

Napoleon's advance eastward into the forbidding vastness of Russia, the product of his insatiable lust for power and glory, was to cost his army dearly, particularly in terms of experienced manpower. The French logistical system simply could not cope with the distances involved, and all the while bitter weather and an implacable foe combined to make the campaign a turning point in Napoleon's fortunes.

During 1811 relations between Russia and France became strained, because the Russians refused to act as part of Napoleon's Continental System. Eventually, Napoleon decided to resolve the matter by war. He mobilized a vast force, of about 600,000 men in total, which comprised troops from most of his European allies, although the core of the army remained French. Some 450,000 of these troops would advance into Russia under Napoleon's direct control, the remainder would protect the main army's flanks. Napoleon also ordered special preparations to be made for the unusual conditions that his troops would encounter in Russia – Napoleon's men could not expect to be able to live off the land to the extent that they had done in Germany or Italy.

The army would be required to march over 500 miles (800 km) to Moscow from the French-controlled state of the Duchy of Warsaw, which acted as Napoleon's forward base. The bulk of his supplies and replacements would have to come from France, several hundred miles farther west of the duchy.

Napoleon devoted much energy in attempting to resolve the problem of supplying his army while in Russia. He gave orders for huge quantities of rations and other supplies to be assembled, along with carts and pack animals needed to transport them while on campaign. In the event, however, the French logistical system was never capable of supplying such a large body of men over such great distances.

Napoleon ordered his army to cross the Niemen River into Russian territory late on June 23, 1812. As usual, he planned to fight a decisive battle as soon as possible and then dictate peace terms. Instead, the Russians retreated, having first destroyed any useful supplies the French might wish to capture. By mid-August Napoleon had advanced as far as Smolensk, and, despite his best efforts, he had still failed to bring the Russians to battle.

The main strike force of Napoleon's army had been about 250,000 strong when it crossed into Russia, but was now down to less than 160,000 because of disease, starvation, and general exhaustion. Napoleon halted for a week to rest and assess the situation, which was not going the way he had originally envisaged. On August 24 he ordered his troops to advance once again, still convinced that winning a "decisive" battle would bring the czar to the peace table.

The Russian emperor now appointed a new commander-in-chief: General Mikhail Kutuzov, who, while nearly 70 years old, was still a tough and cunning opponent. Kutuzov favored a strategy of attrition, although he eventually decided to offer battle to the French – but only on ground of his own choosing. Early in September, he ordered his men to prepare defensive positions near a village called Borodino, about 70 miles (112 km) west of Moscow.

The two sides deployed about 130,000 men each, although the Russians had slightly more artillery. Kutuzov's position was protected by a river, a number of ravines, and woods on one flank. The Russian artillery and part of their infantry were dug in on the crest of a series of hills. In the face of the well-prepared Russian defenses, some of Napoleon's senior officers suggested an outflanking maneuver. Napoleon, however, said this would only give Kutuzov another chance to slip away and avoid battle. Napoleon needed a decisive victory, and decided upon a frontal assault.

The battle was fought on September 7, and degenerated into a brutal slogging match. The French pushed slowly forward with fierce charges and counter-charges for the key positions, while mass artillery

Left: A key factor in Napoleon's defeat in Russia was the breakdown of his logistical system, a combination of poor roads, the devastation of the country, and partisans.

at Krasnoi on November 16–17. The French managed to cut through the Russian lines but suffered heavy casualties. At the end of November the French found that their retreat was blocked by the Berezina River. A few bridges were thrown across the icy waterway, but Russian artillery fire caused panic, and discipline was lost as men crowded across the only escape routes available to them.

When the French destroyed the bridges, thousands of their own soldiers were left trapped on the Russian side of the Berezina. After the battle the Russians claim to have counted 13,000 frozen corpses. Of the 600,000 French troops who started out only about 20,000 men finally escaped from Russia, ragged, starving, and frostbitten.

Napoleon left his troops to recuperate in Poland and hurried back to France. He swiftly put the catastrophe of the Russian campaign behind him and set to work organizing new armies for the battles that he knew were soon to come.

bombardments caused huge losses to both sides. By nightfall the French had captured most of the Russian defenses, but both sides were too exhausted to fight further. French casualties were over 30,000 men; the Russians suffered about 40,000 casualties.

Kutuzov retreated the next day, leaving the way open to Moscow. But it was not the victory that Napoleon wanted, for once again the Russians refused to come to terms. On September 14 the French marched into Moscow, only to find it virtually deserted. Over the next few days much of the wooden-built city burned to the ground in huge fires started on Russian orders. There would be little shelter and less food in Moscow for Napoleon's army, with the Russian winter fast approaching.

While in Moscow, Napoleon waited for a month in the hope that the war could be brought to a satisfactory conclusion. Eventually he realized that the Russians would not give up, and the retreat from Moscow began on October 19. Napoleon's army had now been reduced to 95,000 men.

Napoleon still hoped to inflict a crushing defeat on the Russians as he fell back from Moscow. He led the *Grande Armée* south from the capital and came up against Kutuzov's army at Maloyaroslavets on October 24. The French were unable to get the better of the Russians in this inconclusive battle, which made Napoleon decide to head north toward Borodino and then retreat westward following the same route he had used just a few months before, during his advance on Moscow.

By November 12 the French were back in Smolensk, where what was left of their logistical system broke down completely. Their numbers were down to 50,000 men as a consequence of repeated Russian raids, exhaustion, and lack of food. Horses were slaughtered for their flesh and there were incidents of cannibalism. The cold and snows of winter had also arrived.

The Russians were snapping at the heels of the disintegrating *Grande Armée*. Part of Kutuzov's army got behind the French and blocked their line of retreat

COSSACKS

Cossacks were originally bands of displaced men who lived outside the law on the Russian and Ukrainian steppes (the name "cossack" is derived from the Turkish word for vagabond). Later, mounted Cossack bands operated as mercenaries, fighting both for and against the Russian state. During the Napoleonic Wars they made up a large part of the light cavalry force of the Russian Army. Cossack troops were not usually very effective fighters in battle, but they excelled at harassing the enemy in skirmishes or launching hit-and-run raids. They were also able to cope better with the snow and extreme cold of the Russian winter than their enemies from farther west.

During the 1812 campaign the Cossacks played a vital role in wearing down the French. They captured their messengers, killed stragglers, and blocked supply convoys. During the retreat from Moscow, Napoleon himself was nearly captured by a Cossack band. Throughout the French withdrawal, Cossacks were always close at hand, helping to create the atmosphere of fear that eventually turned much of the retreating *Grande Armée* into a demoralized rabble.

Napoleon's Final Campaigns

By the spring of 1813, the French had been forced to retreat west of the Elbe River and were reorganizing for the coming offensive. For the first time in 20 years of war there were four major nations confronting France simultaneously – Russia, Prussia, Austria, and Britain – but even though the bulk of his army consisted of raw conscripts, Napoleon decided to attack before the enemy had further reinforcements.

At Lützen in eastern Germany on May 2, the French Army was caught by surprise by a larger force of Russians and Prussians. The French won but suffered many casualties. The armies fought again at Bautzen on May 20–21, but Napoleon's hoped-for decisive victory again failed to materialize and another tactical victory was achieved at the cost of further heavy casualties (the Russians had suffered almost as badly as the French in the fighting of 1812, and as they marched westward they had become extended and vulnerable to an attack). Both sides were now tired and disorganized, and agreed to a temporary cessation of hostilities.

This truce worked to the advantage of the allies, who had greater resources to call upon. The turning point came on August 12, 1813, when Austria declared war on France and fighting resumed immediately. The allies, now four nations strong, adopted a new strategy consisting of attacking parts of the French Army, but whenever Napoleon himself arrived with his reserves they would pull back. The French – and Napoleon – would eventually be worn down by this strategy. The decisive battle Napoleon craved finally came at Leipzig on October 16–19, 1813.

The largest single battle of the Napoleonic Wars, Leipzig pitted several allied armies totalling about 365,000 men against Napoleon's 190,000 troops holding the city. It was popularly dubbed as the "Battle of the Nations." Although the French fought with great determination, as the battle progressed superior allied numbers eventually began to tell, and the French were pushed back. When the Saxon corps deserted him, Napoleon's only option was an orderly withdrawal across the Elster River. The bridge, however, was blown prematurely and the French Army, having lost 60,000 men, withdrew toward the Rhine. Napoleon had managed to build up his forces to about 450,000 men for the 1813 campaign, but now he had only 70,000 left, plus stragglers and various garrisons cut off in Germany.

In 1814 Napoleon managed to assemble 100,000 troops to protect France from invasion, but his actual field army consisted of little more than 40,000 men. They faced three advancing allied forces of well over 300,000 troops in all. Napoleon, however, was not daunted and went on the offensive. Despite his worsening health, he showed some of his old brilliance and frequently outmaneuvered his enemies. The French won a series of battles in northeast France in early 1814. The allied leaders almost panicked, but eventually recovered their nerve and their armies closed in on Paris. At the end of March the allies reached Paris and Napoleon's generals urged him to step down. French politicians invited a member of the pre-1789 royal family to rule as Louis XVIII. On April 11, 1814, Napoleon abdicated and was sent into exile on Elba, a small island off Italy.

Little under a year later, Napoleon sailed back to France with just the 1,000 men of his personal guard. His march through France quickly became a triumph, however, as thousands of veterans flocked to the cause. The French royal family fled, and on March 20, 1815, Napoleon entered Paris as emperor once more. After he had allocated troops to France's borders, Napoleon had about 125,000 men left to use in his planned offensive against the British and Prussians in the Low Countries.

The odds against him were formidable. Napoleon realized that he lacked the fighting power to defeat the British and Prussian armies if they fought together, and so his strategy was to drive the two forces apart and then defeat each in turn. He marched his army through northern France toward Brussels. His first moves on June 15 were unexpected. The Duke of Wellington had ordered his army to concentrate in the wrong location, too far west of his Prussian allies under Field Marshal von Blücher (1742–1819). Blücher set about assembling his forces, but many of them would not arrive in time.

Two separate battles were fought on June 16. Wellington's advance guard was initially outnumbered at Quatre-Bras, but the French dithered and were slow to attack, so that each time the French seemed about to break through, sufficient British reinforcements were on hand to hold the position. By the end of the day Quatre-Bras was still in British hands, and Wellington had reorganized his forces.

Blücher, however, had been defeated. His 83,000 Prussians fought 77,000 French under Napoleon's personal command at the Battle of Ligny (known in France as the Battle of Fleurus). There was fierce fighting into the evening, after which the Prussians fell back in good order. Napoleon thought that Blücher's men had retreated eastward, losing touch with the British. In fact they had gone north, with Blücher still determined to support Wellington if he could. Unaware of this, Napoleon turned on the British.

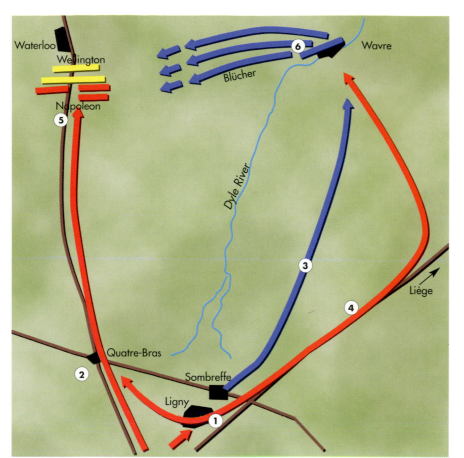

Left: The Waterloo campaign is an illustration of one of Napoleon's military principles: the placement of his army between two hostile armies to defeat each in turn.

DECISIVE MOVES

(1) Prussians defeated by French at Ligny on June 16.

(2) British mauled by French at Quatre-Bras and fall back to Waterloo.

(3) Prussians retreat north to Wavre.

(4) Part of French Army pursues Prussians but moves slowly.

(5) Napoleon attacks British at Waterloo throughout June 18.

(6) While French are held up at Wavre, the bulk of the Prussian Army moves westward. Its timely arrival completes the defeat of the main French Army at Waterloo.

KEY

🟥	French Army
🟥→	French movements
🟦	Prussian Army
🟦→	Prussian movements
🟨	British

Wellington retreated from Quatre-Bras, but, anticipating Blücher's support, he decided to make a stand along a ridge near Waterloo. Wellington had about 68,000 men and Napoleon about 72,000. The remainder of Napoleon's army, about 30,000 troops under Marshal de Grouchy, was sent to harry Blücher's Prussians. Grouchy not only set off in the wrong direction, but his pursuit was so leisurely that his troops would play no part in the coming battle. Blücher, meanwhile, was marching toward the French right flank at Waterloo.

Napoleon still had time to win the battle before any Prussians arrived, but instead his senior commanders made a series of poor attacks, which were blocked by Wellington. As June 18 progressed, increasing numbers of French troops were drawn into the battle on the right wing to hold the Prussians. Even so, by the evening Wellington's army was wavering and Napoleon called on the Imperial Guard to make the decisive breakthrough.

The Guard, however, was stopped in its tracks by well-directed British infantry fire, and was forced to retire. This was the signal for the exhausted French to begin a general retreat, which then disintegrated into a rout. Although Napoleon managed to escape from the field, his defeat at Waterloo marked the end of his attempt to regain his empire. Shortly afterwards, he surrendered to the British and went into permanent exile.

Left: The French cavalry at Waterloo succeeded in getting among the allied infantry battalions and forcing them into square formation. If Napoleon's commanders had brought their artillery forward to break open the squares, the battle might have ended in a French victory.

The War of 1812

By restricting US trade as part of its ongoing naval war with France during the Napoleonic Wars, Britain angered the United States. British warships had also seized sailors from US vessels, claiming that the men concerned were British subjects or had deserted from the Royal Navy. The right of US ships to sail the North Atlantic unhindered was thus the official reason for the US declaration of war on June 19, 1812.

The real motive of the politicians who most wanted war (a group known as the "War Hawks") was, however, to gain territory for the United States at the expense of Canada to the north. The boundary between the two countries had been in dispute since the conclusion of the American Revolutionary War in 1783. A further cause of US resentment was the support of Britain and Canada for the Shawnee chief Tecumseh in his struggle against US settlers in the Indiana and Ohio areas. The Shawnees had been defeated at the Battle of Tippecanoe in 1811, but Tecumseh would support the British in the coming war.

The US Army instigated hostilities with a three-pronged assault directed against Canada. All three ended in dismal failure, however. In the west, during August 1812, the British and their Native American allies captured Fort Dearborn (the site of present-day Chicago) and Detroit. On the central front, near Lakes Erie and Ontario, a force of over 3,000 US troops

suffered 1,000 casualties in the Battle of Queenston Heights, while the British lost just 14 killed. In the east, near Lake Champlain, US forces pulled back in November without even engaging the enemy. Undeterred, US secretary of war John Armstrong planned another invasion of central Canada in 1813, but again success proved elusive. An American force briefly occupied York (now Toronto) early in the year, but in the fall an advance toward Montreal ended in disaster. The year's fighting concluded with the British capturing Fort Niagara and burning Buffalo in upstate New York.

There was better news from the west, however. US troops commanded by General William Henry Harrison recaptured Detroit on September 29, 1813, then routed a British and Native American force at the Battle of the Thames River, an engagement in which Tecumseh was killed. Harrison's advance was made possible by the US naval victory at the Battle of Lake Erie on September 10. Both sides used the Great Lakes to transport their

Right: The War of 1812 came about through a combination of rising anti-British sentiment in the United States, and an American determination to annex Canada. Tension was increased by both French and British attacks on American shipping.

Left: The Battle of New Orleans was fought on January 8, 1815, shortly before news of the Treaty of Ghent reached America. A British force of 7,500 experienced veterans attempted to capture New Orleans, but were repulsed with heavy losses by an American force led by General Andrew Jackson (1767–1845). A number of pointless naval engagements were also fought before the arrival of the peace terms finally ended the War of 1812.

supplies and men, and each had built up squadrons of warships and gunboats to do so. The US commander on Lake Erie was Captain Oliver Hazard Perry, whose aggressive leadership tipped the balance in favor of the Americans. All six British ships surrendered to the nine US vessels, enabling Perry to grandly signal his superiors: "We have met the enemy and they are ours."

Despite this setback, the British went on the offensive in 1814. The temporary end of the war against Napoleon in Europe allowed the British to ship some of their veteran soldiers across the Atlantic to reinforce their troops in Canada, enabling the British to expand their area of action to include operations in the Chesapeake Bay area and later against New Orleans.

In Canada, two battles were fought on the Niagara front in July 1814, at Chippewa and Lundy's Lane, which was followed by more fighting around Fort Erie in September – neither side gained a decisive advantage.

A British advance along Lake Champlain with 10,000 troops was more threatening, for there were less than 5,000 US troops to oppose them. Both sides were supported by a squadron of ships on the lake, and control of the water was a prerequisite for any British advance. Although the two naval forces were evenly matched – with 12 gunboats and four larger ships – the Americans were more experienced. In a two-hour battle fought at point-blank range, the US force prevailed and the battered British vessels were forced to surrender. The US victory on September 11 was decisive – the British gave up their invasion attempts.

The British had more success in their landings in Chesapeake Bay. Some 5,000 troops went ashore from the Patuxent River on August 19, and then began the 40-mile (64-km) advance to Washington. They won the Battle of Bladensburg on the outskirts of Washington on the 24th, entered the capital and burned public buildings before withdrawing. They attacked Baltimore between September 12 and 14, but were forced to retreat.

Neither side was now really likely to achieve a decisive victory. The British were disappointed by the failure of their main advance down Lake Champlain, while the American economy was suffering and the US government was virtually bankrupt. Both sides wanted peace, and negotiations were begun to conclude the war.

The reasons for the economic problems faced by the United States lay in events at sea. Britain possessed 1,000 warships while the US Navy had just 14 at the outbreak of the war. The US Navy did far better than this ratio might suggest, however, because its ships were very well designed for solo raiding operations against British trade. The American ships were also individually more powerful than most of the escort vessels the British used for trade protection.

US ships captured more than 800 British merchant vessels in the course of the war. The two sides fought 16 minor naval engagements – most won by American ships – in locations as far apart as the southern Pacific Ocean, the Mediterranean, and the English Channel. Despite these embarrassments, the British maintained a complete blockade of US ports, cutting off almost all trade. The United States may have won the individual ship-to-ship naval engagements but Britain, with its larger navy, won the sea war.

The Treaty of Ghent was signed on December 24, 1814, which re-established the status quo between the two countries: the British were to respect American shipping rights, while the US government was to refrain from sending military expeditions against Canada.

US Expansionist Wars

The American Revolutionary War with Britain left the newly formed United States with possession of only a fraction of the continent – vast areas were still colonies of other European powers in 1800. The new nation thus began both to project its influence across the seas to other parts of the globe, and much closer to home there was much territory still to acquire, as well as the indigenous peoples to deal with.

In 1809 the governor of the Northwest Territory, William Henry Harrison, bought large areas of land in Indiana and Illinois from groups of Native Americans. Other Native Americans opposed the sale, claiming that land was indivisible, and that no one had any right to sell it. Those most against it were led by twin brothers from the Shawnee people, Tecumseh and Tenskwatawa. In 1811 Tenskwatawa fought a battle at Tippecanoe against US troops under Harrison. The battle was indecisive but Harrison's troops destroyed the main Indian settlement (Prophetstown) shortly afterward.

Tecumseh sided with the British in the War of 1812, and hoped to unite with the Creek people of Georgia and Alabama, who had also supported the British. Tecumseh, however, was killed at the Battle of the Thames River in October 1813, and the 900 warriors of the main Creek force were almost completely wiped out in the Battle of Horseshoe Bend in what is now eastern Alabama, on March 27, 1814. After this defeat the Creeks lost their best land and the future looked bleak.

Even before the naval successes of the War of 1812, the United States had been sending its military forces to other parts of the world. French interference with US trading ships had led to conflict with France between 1798 and 1800. Ships of the new US Navy (established in 1794) fought several successful engagements in the Caribbean before the dispute was resolved.

The Tripolitan War (from 1801 to 1805) was more serious. For centuries the Barbary States of North Africa – Algiers, Tripoli, Tunis, and Morocco – had practiced piracy. Foreign ships were regularly attacked, and crews and passengers enslaved. Buying off the local rulers was the normal method of dealing with the problem, but in 1801 President Thomas Jefferson decided to send a naval expedition to punish Tripoli. The US force did not achieve anything until Commodore Edward Preble took command in 1803 and adopted an aggressive policy of sinking Barbary ships whenever he encountered them. One of his officers, Stephen Decatur, even raided the harbor of Tripoli to burn a US ship, the *Philadelphia*, that had been captured after running aground on a reef a little distance outside the port. The fighting ended in 1805, with the United States confirming its refusal to pay tribute to Tripoli. Decatur returned to the region to command US forces in 1815, and forced the bey of Algiers to cease all attacks on American ships.

Right: A scene from the Tripolitan War fought between the United States and a number of North African states: Lieutenant Stephen Decatur leads American naval forces against a pirate ship in Tripoli harbor on August 3, 1804.

Left: Mexican troops break into the Alamo on March 6, 1836. The defense of the deserted mission gave the Texan leader Sam Houston time to raise and train an army, which defeated Santa Anna's army at the Battle of San Jacinto. All the defenders of the Alamo were killed.

At home, the relentless expansion of settlers continued to cause conflict with the Native American peoples. The Seminoles of Florida resisted the expropriation of their lands, and open warfare with the US government broke out three times: in 1818, between 1835 and 1843, and again from 1856 to 1858. The Seminoles proved masters of guerrilla warfare and used their swamplands to good effect. But, as elsewhere, superior US numbers and technology destroyed the opposition, the survivors being deported to camps in the "Indian Territory" of what later became Oklahoma.

Vast areas of what are now the western and southern United States were still European colonies in 1800. Much of the Mississippi River basin was bought from France in the Louisiana Purchase of 1803; Napoleon, desperate for money, willingly acceded to the sale. The US also acquired Florida and the Pacific Northwest from Spain as a result of the Adams-Onís Treaty of 1819. When Mexico declared its independence from Spain in 1821, its territory included the province of Texas.

Many US citizens had settled in Texas from the 1820s onward. In June 1835 they rebelled against the government of President López de Santa Anna. The Americans wanted to secede, and intended that Texas should become part of the United States. The Texans did not have an army, but some settlers volunteered to fight for independence, along with a number of men from existing US states. This force, never more than 1,000 strong, also included deserters from the regular army.

Santa Anna marched against the rebels early in 1836, but his advance was delayed by resistance at the Alamo, a deserted mission station just outside San Antonio. The siege lasted for 13 days, until the defenders were overwhelmed on March 6. The garrison of 188 men, all killed in the final assault, had inflicted 1,500 casualties, and their heroism gave heart to the Texan cause.

In the meantime, the Texans had declared an independent Republic of Texas on March 2, 1836. Sam Houston, a former governor of Tennessee, took command of the new Texan Army, which was training and gathering supplies while the Alamo garrison was buying them time. His 750 men encountered Santa Anna's force at San Jacinto on April 21.

The Texans charged straight at the Mexicans and the battle lasted just 18 minutes. When it was over, some 800 Mexicans lay dead out of an original force of 1,700 troops. The Texan Army, which caught the Mexicans by surprise, had gone into action shouting "Remember the Alamo" in memory of their fallen comrades.

Santa Anna himself was captured at San Jacinto, and he agreed to pull his forces out of the new Texas Republic. Houston became the first president of Texas, which remained independent until 1845, when it was voluntarily incorporated into the United States.

South America's War of Liberation

During the European colonization of the Americas, Portugal and Spain had distributed the territory of South America between them. It took three centuries for an anticolonial struggle to break out, and when it did the irony was that the popular resistance to French occupation of the Iberian peninsula provided the model of inspiration for those elites seeking to rule themselves without reference to the colonial power.

The movement for independence in Latin America (Brazil was controlled by Portugal, and most of the rest of Central and South America by Spain) was essentially engineered by the local aristocratic elites who wanted to transfer power from the mother country to themselves, although the ideals of the Enlightenment provided an ideological justification for their revolt and the transition to home rule.

The opportunity for rebellion came with Napoleon's invasion of Spain and Portugal and the ongoing, bloody war in the Iberian peninsula (1808–14), a period that tied up the attention and resources of the governments of the home countries, Spain and Portugal. The first colonial uprising came in Argentine in 1810, followed by a rebellion in Venezuela the following year. Although tacitly supported by Britain and the United States, the leaders of the rebellion – who included Simón Bolívar (1783–1830) and José de San Martín (1776–1850) – faced stiff opposition from the Spanish.

Initially, the Spanish retained the upper hand in Venezuela, especially with the release of Spanish troops from Spain after the allied victory there against the French in 1814. Despite suffering several defeats, however, Bolívar continued to fight for liberation. In 1819 he attacked the Spanish forces around Bogotá, and on August 7 Bolívar's men captured most of the Spanish Army at Boyacá. The Battle of Boyacá made the liberation of northernmost South America almost certain, although the Spaniards continued to fight against the insurgents. Entering Bogotá in triumph, Bolívar was proclaimed president of the new Republic of Colombia. One of Bolívar's commanders, Antonio José de Sucre, went on to liberate what is now Ecuador after his victory at the Battle of Pichincha in 1822.

Both sides were organized, equipped, and uniformed along European lines, and they fought in the European manner, often trying to imitate the approach and style of Napoleon himself. Forces were relatively small – rarely could a side field more than 10,000 men – but the distances were immense, the conditions difficult, and communications poor.

At the end of the Napoleonic Wars, large numbers of Europeans (and some North Americans) enlisted to fight for the rebel cause, drawn to the wars for a variety of motives: adventure, idealism, and loot. Among these

Right: Simón Bolívar (mounted on the white horse) enters Caracas, the capital of Venezuela, in 1821 following his victory at Carabobo. His wars of liberation also freed Colombia, Ecuador, and Peru from Spanish control.

Left: The independence movements throughout South America were ignited by the American Revolution and further stimulated by the French Revolution, bringing to an end to Spanish and Portuguese control of the region.

A key moment in the unfolding events in South America came in December 1824 when Bolívar's forces, under the command of Sucre, won a decisive victory at the Battle of Ayacucho in Peru. Sucre's force of 7,000 men comprehensively defeated the 10,000-strong Spanish Army. Sixteen Spanish generals and over 2,500 of their men were captured and 1,400 killed. In January 1826, the port of Callao, the last Spanish stronghold in Peru, surrendered.

The loss of Peru – hitherto the center of Spanish military strength in South America – turned the tide of war irrevocably in the rebels' favor. Farther north, in Mexico, the Spanish were more successful in suppressing early revolts, but even there a republic was proclaimed in 1824. The Spanish government finally accepted the inevitable, and in 1829 it relinquished any attempt to reconquer its former colonies in the New World. Spain's sole remaining possessions in the region were now the islands of Cuba and Puerto Rico.

foreign adventurers was a unit composed of Peninsular War veterans who were known as Bolívar's British Legion, and they played a major role in securing the rebel victory at Boyacá.

In the south, San Martín led his army from Argentina on an epic march across the Andes Mountains into Chile in January 1817. He defeated the Spanish at Chacabuco on February 12, and a further rebel victory took place at the Battle of the Maipo in April 1818, which forced the Spanish to retreat from Chile toward Peru.

A maverick British naval officer, Thomas Cochrane, then took command of San Martín's small navy. He won superiority at sea, and in September 1820 transported San Martín's army along the Pacific coast to mount a seaborne invasion of Peru. The fortunes of the consequent fighting in Peru swayed back and forth until July 1821 when the capital, Lima, was taken by the insurgents. San Martín then advanced northward to cooperate with Bolívar. The two liberators met at Guayaquil, Equador, in July 1822, and although no details of the meeting are known, San Martín abruptly handed over the leadership of the whole liberation movement to Bolívar. San Martín then retired from all revolutionary activity and left for Europe.

In the meantime, Brazil had also replaced its colonial master, Portugal, but with a very different (and largely peaceful) form of rebellion. Brazil was ruled by one of the sons of Portugal's King John VI, Dom Pedro. In 1822 Dom Pedro declared independence from his father and became Emperor Pedro I. Cochrane moved to take command of Pedro's navy and guaranteed Brazil's independence by eliminating any Portuguese naval opposition. In 1825, Portugal formally recognized the independence of its former South American colony. Brazil itself remained an empire until a slave revolt led to an uprising by plantation owners, who overthrew imperial rule and replaced it with a federal republic the following year.

Bolívar had hoped to create a united South America, but local disputes prevented any such vision becoming a reality, and local areas or regions set themselves up as independent states. Throughout much of the 19th century, South America was racked by local conflicts between the newly independent countries, and by revolution and civil strife from within. Latin American governments developed into dictatorships, which relied almost exclusively on the army for their support.

The US–Mexican War

Allowing Texas to be incorporated as a state was controversial within the United States, for powerful forces were opposed to the inclusion of another slave state into the Union. President James Polk had won the 1844 election on the basis of his expansionist policies, thus in 1845 Texas joined the United States. But vast areas of what is now the southwest USA still belonged to Mexico at the beginning of Polk's term.

Mexico had been in a state of upheaval since the loss of Texas in 1836, but at the end of 1845 a new president prepared to take a firm line with the United States. Polk countered this by ordering a strong US force to move close to the Texas border with Mexico, and this force was attacked near Matamoros on April 25, 1846. If Polk deliberately wanted to provoke war with Mexico, the bellicose Mexicans played right into his hands.

Steadily, more intense border skirmishes were fought along the Rio Grande. Some 6,000 Mexican soldiers were opposed by 3,500 US troops commanded by General Zachary Taylor (1784–1850), a veteran with experience of fighting Native Americans. Taylor and his men won two battles in the first days of May, at Palo Alto and Resaca de la Palma.

A lull in the fighting followed. Taylor built up his forces, but in Mexico rebellions broke out which only ended with the return of exiled General Santa Anna. By August 1846 Taylor's force of 6,000 was ready to advance from Camp Texas (now Brownsville) against his target of Monterrey, 160 miles (256 km) away. The Mexican garrison was about 10,000 strong and the attack began on September 20. After four days of fierce fighting the Mexicans agreed to give up the town, but were allowed to keep their weapons when they left.

Polk did not approve of the deal that Taylor had made, and ordered him to resume hostilities. Taylor advanced another 50 miles (80 km) to Saltillo, where he was reinforced by 3,000 troops who had made a difficult 600-mile (960-km) march from San Antonio in Texas.

Right: The US–Mexican War of 1846–48 resulted in the Mexicans giving up huge amounts of territory to the United States following military defeat. US forces had advantages in training, equipment, and leadership, and inflicted numerous defeats upon their numerically superior Mexican opponents.

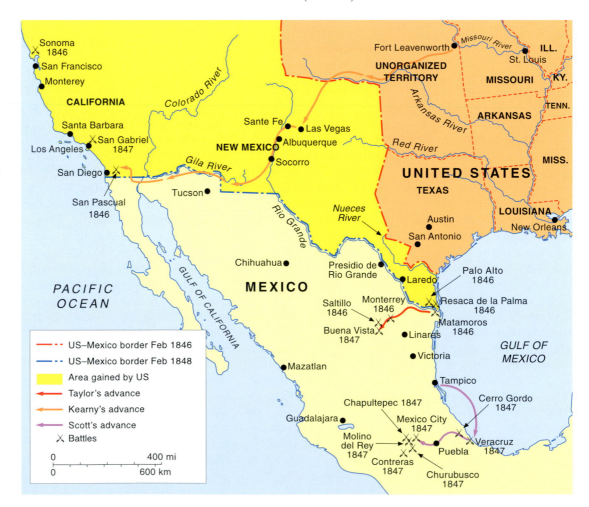

indecisive Battle of San Pascual near San Diego on December 6, 1846, and then joined up with the US Navy forces to win the decisive Battle of San Gabriel in January 1847. This ended the fighting in California.

The main US offensive was ready to start. General Winfield Scott (1786–1866) moved south from Tampico in February 1847 to begin landings near Veracruz on March 9. He surrounded the town, which surrendered on March 27 after a five-day bombardment.

The US leaders now developed a new strategy. They decided that desert terrain would make it impossible for Taylor to advance further into Mexico. Instead, the main assault would be made by sea to the port of Veracruz, and from there inland to Mexico City. Taylor's force was cut and men were transferred to the new expedition.

Santa Anna thought this gave him the chance to defeat Taylor before the Veracruz operation could begin. On February 22, 1847, the Mexicans attacked, but although heavily outnumbered Taylor's men had been forewarned and had taken up good defensive positions. As the fighting raged on, the advantage slowly passed to the Americans. Eventually the Mexicans retreated with about 1,600 casualties; the US force lost about 750 men dead, wounded, or missing.

Even before the main US invasion, American settlers had been disputing Mexican rule. In June 1846, settlers in the Sacramento Valley captured the town of Sonoma and declared a new republic, usually called the Bear Flag Republic after the symbol used on its flag. Captain John C. Frémont, coincidentally leading a small US exploratory expedition in California, was named as the republic's president. Subsequently, a US Navy force captured Monterey and claimed California for the United States. Also that June, General Stephen Watts Kearny had set off along the Santa Fe Trail from Fort Leavenworth with 1,700 Missouri volunteers. His orders were to occupy New Mexico and California. Kearny's small force reached Santa Fe without a fight in August.

Kearny then split his force into three. One group remained to control New Mexico, gaining the upper hand early in 1847. A second force marched south into Chihuahua province, where they eventually joined up with Taylor's army in northern Mexico. Kearny himself led the third and smallest group into California. When Kearny arrived in California he found that the Mexican population had regained control of much of the state from US forces. Kearny and his men fought the

Scott then led his 10,000 troops inland. Santa Anna stood ready with a force of 12,000 men at Cerro Gordo, 50 miles (80 km) from the coast. Some of Scott's officers scouted a little-known mountain road and were able to outflank and surround part of the Mexican force. Fought on April 18, the battle was another Mexican defeat.

By mid-May, Scott's advance had reached Puebla, about 80 miles (128 km) from Mexico City, but could go no farther. Many of his men had fallen sick and others had to be allowed to return home. By August Scott's effective force was up to about 11,000 men and he decided to leave the 3,000 sick men in Puebla, along with a small garrison, while he led the main army onward.

Santa Anna had about 30,000 troops left under his command, but did not resist Scott's advance strongly until it reached Contreras on August 19, about 10 miles (16 km) south of Mexico City. There was more fighting there and at Churubusco nearby the next day. For the first time in the campaign, US losses were heavy, at over 1,000 killed and wounded, but the Mexicans suffered worse: 4,500 killed and wounded and over 2,500 taken prisoner. In a telling sign that the war was going with the Americans, many Mexican troops also began to desert.

Scott agreed to a two-week truce to allow peace negotiations to get underway. When negotiations failed, he resumed fighting. Two further battles, at Molino del Rey on September 8 and at Chapultepec on September 13, confirmed the US military supremacy. Mexico City fell on September 14.

The war was effectively over with the capture of Mexico City, although the Treaty of Guadalupe Hidalgo was not signed by both governments until February 1848. For the Mexicans it was a humiliating defeat. Mexico recognized the Rio Grande as the southern boundary of Texas and gave up the whole of California and New Mexico (including the modern states of Nevada, Utah, Arizona, and parts of Colorado and Wyoming) to the United States.

The American Civil War
1861–65

The Civil War remains the key event in American history, as the outcome of the conflict laid the foundations for the political direction, military might, and economic prosperity of the modern United States. Victory for US president Abraham Lincoln (1809–65) ensured that the United States of America would emerge as a federal and indivisible union of states, and not the loose confederacy envisaged by the South. The Union victory also ensured the economic dominance of the industrial North and the end of slavery in the South.

Militarily, the Civil War witnessed a transformation in the conduct of war. Above all, it was an industrial conflict in which modern industrial processes, such as mass production, harnessed to relatively new technologies, including the railroad and telegraphy, decided the outcome of the war as much as the skill and bravery of both soldiers and generals. The Civil War was the first modern "total war," a conflict in which both sides used all of their principal resources, both human and economic, in the hope of achieving complete victory.

If the railroad and telegraphy were key factors influencing strategy – permitting rapid movement of men and information over vast distances – the war was also notable for a whole range of technical and tactical innovations that came together for the first time, and which included aerial observation by balloons, breech-loading rifles, machine guns, and rifled artillery.

Arguably, the single most important factor operating on the battlefield was the dominance of the rifle. Whether muzzle- or breech-loaded, the rifles used by infantrymen were able to deliver accurate fire at long distances with a rapidity that would normally reduce any enemy attack in the open to a broken standstill.

This simple yet profound fact was little understood in the early years of the war, as troops maneuvered in massed formations and officers led ostentatiously from

Right: Union and Confederate troops engage in combat at Franklin, Tennessee, in November 1864. At Franklin the Confederates, under the leadership of General John Hood, lost many veteran officers.

the front as if in a Napoleonic battle. As a consequence, casualties were invariably heavy. Toward the end of the war, armies increasingly began to dig in, building elaborate trench systems, foreshadowing those that would be used in western Europe during World War I.

Added to the strategic and tactical changes was the scale of the conflict, fought by millions of men over a main theater of war stretching well over a thousand miles. The Northern states of the Union drew upon the services of three million men; the Southern states of the Confederacy enlisted nearly one million. The determination of both sides to prosecute the war to the utmost led to four years of bloody conflict, and a combined casualty list of 714,245 killed and wounded before the Union's material resources brought the Confederacy to defeat and ruin.

The Conflict Over Slavery

The causes of the war were many and various, but centered on the vexed question of slavery, and whether this "peculiar institution" should be permitted in the western territories.

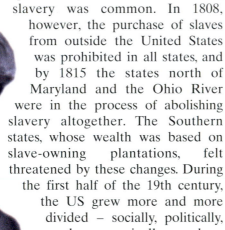

When the colonies declared their independence from Britain in 1776, slavery was common. In 1808, however, the purchase of slaves from outside the United States was prohibited in all states, and by 1815 the states north of Maryland and the Ohio River were in the process of abolishing slavery altogether. The Southern states, whose wealth was based on slave-owning plantations, felt threatened by these changes. During the first half of the 19th century, the US grew more and more divided – socially, politically, and economically – along North–South lines.

Antislavery groups grew increasingly vocal in the North, demanding an end to slavery throughout the US. The threat posed by the abolitionists could, however, be countered by the powerful block of Southern states that were able to thwart any antislavery legislation. The problem for

EUROPEAN VIEWS

Europe's need for Southern cotton resulted in foreign aid for the Confederacy's blockade-running effort. This was especially the case with regard to England, which allowed several blockade-runners to be built in her ports. Confederate leaders such as Davis and Lee always believed that France and Britain could be induced to recognize the Confederacy if the latter achieved a decisive military victory over the North. However, it is extremely unlikely that either country would have recognized a slave-owning state, especially as Great Britain had abolished slavery earlier in the century and took an active role in mounting antislavery operations using the Royal Navy. Economic expediency prompted both Britain and France to trade with the South, but after the Union blockade began to bite both states turned to India and Egypt to make up for the lack of imports from the Confederacy.

the Southern states lay in the opening of the West and the incorporation of new states into the Union. If these states became abolitionist, then the slave states would become outnumbered and isolated.

In those territories in the West edging toward statehood, there were violent clashes between pro- and antislavery groups. During the settlement of Kansas, for example, the violence between the factions was so intense that the territory was called "Bleeding Kansas." Southern attempts to force slavery on Kansas came to nothing, when in 1858 the state voted against slavery.

The political tension between North and South came to a head in the presidential election of 1860. To the dismay of the Southern states the Republican candidate, Abraham Lincoln, won a clear majority. A few weeks later, on December 20, 1860, a proslavery convention meeting in South Carolina voted to leave the Union. By the time Lincoln was inaugurated as president, on March 4, 1861, South Carolina had been joined by Georgia, Florida, Alabama, Mississippi, Louisiana, and Texas. These seven proslavery states formed the Confederate States of America, and elected Jefferson Davis (1808–89) from Mississippi as their president.

Most US forts and naval dockyards that had seceded from the Union surrendered to the Confederates. Four forts held out, however, including Fort Sumter in Charleston Harbor, South Carolina. Lincoln still hoped to avoid war, but he insisted that any attempt by a state government to seize US property was to be seen as an

Left: Jefferson Davis, a former US senator from Mississippi, was elected president of the Confederacy in early 1861 – a position he held for the duration of the Civil War. After the war, he served only two years in prison and died at his home in Mississippi in 1889.

act of insurrection. If such an event took place, Lincoln threatened that he would then use the army to invade the seceded states and restore Federal authority.

Lincoln's pronouncements failed to dissuade the Confederates, who besieged Fort Sumter. Attempts were made by the Union to reinforce the garrison, but in the face of heavy artillery bombardment the fort surrendered on April 14, 1861. When Lincoln heard the news, he called for 75,000 militiamen to serve for three months to suppress the rebellion. Later, when it became clear that the war would not be over quickly, he asked for three-year enlistments.

Lincoln's prime aim was to preserve the Union and, if this meant going to war, he would do so. In response to Lincoln's action, the states of Virginia, North Carolina, Tennessee, and Arkansas joined the Confederacy, although some individuals from Virginia and Tennessee fought instead for the North.

The distribution of major resources suggested that the North would have little difficulty in beating the South. The Union had better industry, railroads, and gold reserves. The North also had a far larger population, with 22 million people, compared to the South's five million whites. Over three million African Americans living in the South would take little part in the coming war, although some 200,000 would eventually fight for the North. The bulk of the US Navy and much of the regular army remained loyal to the Union.

The South did, however, have some advantages. At the start of the war, about one-third of the regular US Army's officers resigned to fight for the South, and provided a corps of professional soldiers to build the new Confederate Army. They included some of the finest commanders on either side, such as Robert E. Lee (1807–70) and Thomas "Stonewall" Jackson (1824–63), men who would make a major contribution to the Confederate war effort. The South also had the advantage of being able to fight on interior lines, while the North had to transport men and equipment over vast distances on exterior lines. And while the South's troops were outnumbered overall by the Union, they could often gain a local battlefield advantage through skillful use of the railroad system.

Facing the greater numbers of the North, Jefferson Davis hoped that a swift military success against the Union would lead to the recognition of the Confederacy by powerful foreign countries, especially Britain and France, eager to gain access to the South's raw materials, such as cotton. He also hoped that Northern politicians would grudgingly accept a peace settlement favorable to the South if the Union forces were defeated in battle, or if Washington, DC was menaced or even captured by Confederate troops. Unfortunately for Davis, Europe remained neutral and the North's resolve to see the war through to the end remained just firm enough, mainly thanks to Lincoln's leadership.

Left: This map shows the major battles of the Civil War, as well as the Union naval blockade that helped to isolate, and eventually defeat, the South.

The Opening Battles

In April 1861, President Lincoln called for 75,000 volunteers to serve for three months in the US Army in order to end the rebellion in the South. At the same time he allowed the Confederate states 20 days to return to the Union. This period was due to expire on May 5, 1861; on May 6, the Confederate leader Jefferson Davis signed a declaration of war on the United States.

At the beginning of the Civil War, the strategic initiative lay with the Union commanders, who decided on a three-pronged plan of action. This included a primary offensive designed to advance southward from the area around Washington, DC toward the Confederate capital Richmond, a little more than 100 miles (160 km) away in Virginia. A secondary offensive in the West was intended to secure the entire length of the Mississippi River. And finally, the US Navy would enforce a complete blockade of the Confederate coastline. The idea was that the Union naval blockade and control of the vital Mississippi River would starve the Southern economy, split the seceding states in two, and force an early surrender. The popular press in the North called the strategy the "Anaconda Plan," designed to crush the Confederates as surely as the giant snake squeezed its prey to death.

The First Bull Run

As part of the North's primary offensive, US General Irvin McDowell (1818–85) presented to Lincoln a plan to attack the Confederates around Manassas Junction in Virginia. The Confederates deployed around Manassas were also preparing to launch an attack on Washington, DC. If the Northern forces defeated the Southern troops at Manassas, the vital railroad junction linking Richmond with the Shenandoah Valley (an important grain-producing area) would be denied to the South.

THE FIRST VOLUNTEERS

Until 1861 the United States relied on voluntary units of ordinary citizens organized by their home states to provide much of its military force. Militia officers were elected and their part-timers assembled on weekends or holidays. At the start of the Civil War both the Confederacy and the Union called for volunteers. In each case the peacetime militia units provided the bulk of these volunteers. While enthusiastic, the volunteers were not trained soldiers and as a result were difficult to command and suffered heavy casualties in battle.

Both the North and South realized that they would need more manpower organized along professional lines. The South moved first, when, in April 1862, the Confederate government passed a law proclaiming that all able-bodied white males between the ages of 18–35 were liable for active military service. The North followed along similar lines on July 17 of the same year. Laws making military service compulsory were not popular, and there were riots against them, for example, in both Baltimore and New York. But in a war that was to be fought to the bitter end, both sides needed well-trained, long-serving, dependable soldiers.

And Richmond itself would then become vulnerable to a further Union advance.

McDowell's army marched southward on July 16, mustering 38,000 men (although only around 2,000 were regulars). Two days later McDowell found Confederate troops, again mostly militia, commanded by General P.G.T. Beauregard (1818–93) defending the Bull Run River. McDowell decided to outflank Beauregard by sending most of his

Left: A handful of Union troops (left) attempt to protect the retreat of General Irvin McDowell's defeated Northern forces as they flee from the First Battle of Bull Run.

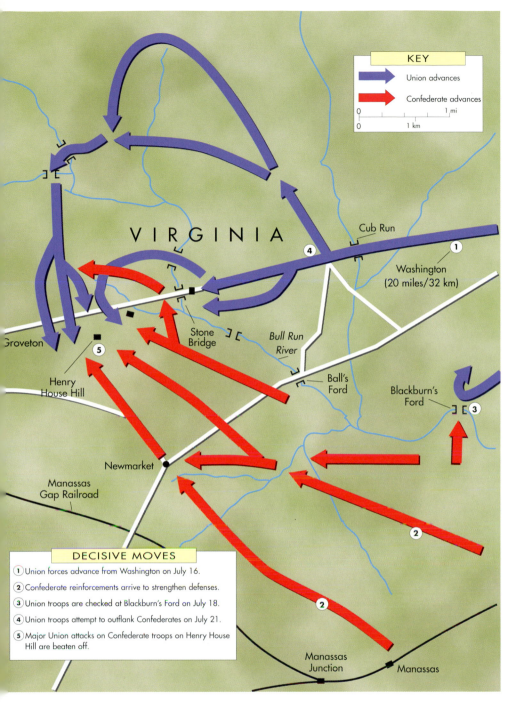

KEY

→ Union advances

→ Confederate advances

0   1 mi

0   1 km

VIRGINIA

Cub Run

Washington
(20 miles/32 km)

④

①

Stone
Bridge

Bull Run
River

Groveton

⑤

Ball's
Ford

Blackburn's
Ford

③

Henry
House Hill

Newmarket

②

Manassas
Gap Railroad

②

②

Manassas
Junction

Manassas

DECISIVE MOVES

① Union forces advance from Washington on July 16.

② Confederate reinforcements arrive to strengthen defenses.

③ Union troops are checked at Blackburn's Ford on July 18.

④ Union troops attempt to outflank Confederates on July 21.

⑤ Major Union attacks on Confederate troops on Henry House Hill are beaten off.

Left: In the opening major battle of the Civil War at Bull Run in Virginia, the Union troops initially caught the Rebels off guard, but the Confederates were able to hold off the Northern attack until reinforcements saved the day.

commanded by General Thomas Jackson provided a rallying point on Henry House Hill, the weakest part of the Confederate line. One Southern officer described Jackson's men as standing like a "stone wall" in the face of the Union attacks, thereby providing Jackson with his famous nickname.

McDowell gathered his troops for one more assault, but Confederate reinforcements now outflanked the Union line, and the whole Northern force began to retreat. When a wagon overturned at Cub Run Bridge, blocking the Union troops' line of retreat, the undisciplined soldiers threw down their weapons and fled the battlefield.

Other Early Battles

In Missouri, US General Nathaniel Lyon (1818–61) advanced his Union troops southwestward from Jefferson City to the town of Springfield with a force of about 7,000 men. At the beginning of August, he decided to attack a larger Confederate force of about 10,000 at Wilson's Creek, also in Missouri.

The Confederates at Wilson's Creek were commanded by Generals Sterling Price (1809–67) and Ben McCulloch (1811–62), whose troops, despite being badly equipped, were eager to fight. The battle, fought on August 10, ended in a narrow Confederate victory with both sides losing around 1,200 men. But the Southerners were too exhausted to capitalize on their victory, and Missouri remained in Union hands.

The only success for the North in the first summer of the war came in what was to become the state of West Virginia. General George B. McClellan (1826–85) won a minor victory at Rich Mountain on July 11. Partly as a result of this success, he was appointed McDowell's replacement on July 22. McClellan realized that he would have to train his new force, the Army of the Potomac, to fight as well as any regular army. A Union defeat, at Ball's Bluff, near Leesburg in Virginia, on October 21, reinforced this view. The war would be a conflict that could only be won by well-trained troops.

forces sweeping around the Confederate position. McDowell believed Beauregard commanded just 20,000 men, and was unaware that 12,000 troops commanded by General Joseph E. Johnston (1807–91) were rushing to Manassas to support Beauregard.

The battle, known as First Bull Run (or First Manassas), took place on July 21, 1861. The Union attack caught the Confederates by surprise, although the inexperience of the Union troops prevented them from striking a decisive blow against the Southerners. This gave time for Rebel reinforcements to rush from other parts of the Confederate line, and for others to arrive from the Shenandoah Valley. A brigade of Virginians

Defending Richmond

The Confederates were not strong enough to attack Washington, DC after their victory at Bull Run in July 1861. Nor was the new leader of the Army of the Potomac, General McClellan, willing to attack the South until his own troops had improved their battlefield skills. A rainy fall and hard winter kept both sides away from the battlefield. By spring, however, McClellan was aiming for an attack on Richmond.

In the spring of 1862 the war resumed in earnest. The Union troops led by McClellan had planned to maneuver the Confederate forces, now commanded by General Joseph E. Johnston, away from Manassas Junction. Johnston, however, had retired from his defenses around Manassas at the request of Jefferson Davis, who wanted the main Confederate Army in Virginia deployed nearer the capital to counter any Union threat from the sea.

McClellan reached Johnston's abandoned positions in Virginia and drew up a new campaign plan. He would ship a large force across Chesapeake Bay to Fort

BATTLEFIELD TACTICS

Civil War rifled muskets were much more effective than their smoothbore counterparts, while artillery could be murderous against dense formations of infantry on the battlefield. The result of this increased lethality was to change tactics, though at the beginning of the war linear battlefield formations still predominated in both armies.

It soon became apparent to commanders on both sides that neither infantry nor cavalry could attack frontally in the face of the combined firepower of artillery and small arms (Pickett's charge at Gettysburg was a prime example; only 150 men out of the 15,000 who took part broke through the Union line on Seminary Ridge).

Tactics changed in four ways: battlefield formations began to become more spread out and flexible; maneuvre replaced frontal assaults; there was a growth in field fortifications and trench warfare as troops under fire dug in; and cavalry shock action on the battlefield all but disappeared, with mounted operations focusing on screening and reconnaissance missions. Commanders still launched frontal assaults throughout the war, but the resultant casualty lists – Grant suffered 7,000 casualties in one hour at Cold Harbor – confirmed the tactical transition that had taken place. The lesson was not learned by European generals, who would repeat the mistakes made by early Civil War generals, with more tragic consequences.

Monroe, near Norfolk, Virginia, and then approach Richmond from the southeast. It was exactly the plan that the Confederate president had feared.

In the meantime, McClellan placed a force of about 10,000 soldiers, commanded by Brigadier James Shields (1810–79), at Winchester, Virginia, to protect the railroad line running west from Washington, DC to the Ohio River. The Confederates deployed about 5,000 troops, led by General Thomas "Stonewall" Jackson, to guard the Shenandoah Valley.

Jackson and his army of 4,500 made an attempt to attack Shields's troops, at Kernstown, Virginia, on March 23, but the Confederate general lacked enough troops to break through the strong Union defenses. Although he was forced to retreat at Kernstown, and lost some 450 men, Jackson's attack had a major impact on McClellan's campaign to strike Richmond.

McClellan's Union troops were already marching to the coast and embarking on ships that would ferry them south to Fort Monroe, when Lincoln ordered McClellan to leave behind 30,000 troops to guard Washington, DC against a possible attack by Jackson. Lincoln's orders, although disruptive, were not wholly impulsive since he had insisted early on that McClellan's plans to invade Richmond could go ahead only if the US capital was well guarded beforehand.

The loss to Washington of 30,000 troops might not have been strategically important, except that McClellan believed that he faced a much larger Confederate Army than was actually the case. While there were about 15,000 Confederate troops between the Union forces and Richmond, McClellan guessed at double that number.

McClellan cautiously made the 20-mile (32-km) march between Fort Monroe and Yorktown. The Confederate garrison at Yorktown remained in place to buy time for the main Confederate force in Virginia to place itself between McClellan's troops and Richmond. Once Yorktown was reached, McClellan instigated full-scale siege operations. On May 3 and 4, the Confederate defenders of Yorktown under General John Magruder (1807–71) retired back toward the Confederate capital. McClellan had lost valuable time, although Jefferson Davis and General Johnston remained concerned that Richmond would have to be abandoned if the Union armies advanced simultaneously.

The Union had powerful forces at its disposal. One army was deployed in West Virginia, commanded by General John C. Frémont (1813–90), while General Nathaniel Banks (1816–94) had 30,000 Union soldiers in the Shenandoah Valley. About 75,000 Union troops around Washington, DC and near Fredericksburg were under the direction of US secretary of war Edwin M. Stanton (1814–69) and President Lincoln. McClellan had about 100,000 soldiers of the Army of the Potomac around Yorktown and Fort Monroe.

Jackson's Shenandoah Valley Campaign

Johnston, Davis, and Davis's military adviser, General Robert E. Lee, ordered Jackson to attack Banks, and, if he felt he had time, Frémont as well. The fighting that followed, known as Jackson's Shenandoah Valley Campaign (May 1–June 9), was one of the most outstanding Confederate operations of the whole war.

On May 8, after having marched his troops over 90 miles (145 km) in four days in diversionary moves across Virginia, Jackson struck at part of Frémont's army under the command of Brigadier Robert C. Schenck (1809–90) in the south of the Shenandoah Valley at McDowell. The fighting lasted only four hours before the Union troops retreated to the Allegheny Mountains.

Jackson then turned his attention northward to engage General Banks's Union troops. On May 23 Jackson surprised some of Banks's men at Front Royal. The Confederates forced Banks's men to retreat and the whole of his Union force relocated to Winchester. Jackson remained close to Banks's heels, capturing several supply wagons the next day.

Left: By May 1862 General George McClellan was preparing his Army of the Potomac to march on Richmond with vast amounts of heavy artillery. Pictured is the Union supply depot at Yorktown with cannon balls, mortars, and cannons being made ready for McClellan's attempted siege.

On May 25, after having marched his troops all day and all night, Jackson finally caught up with Banks at Winchester. Despite Jackson's heavy artillery being outgunned by Union cannonfire, the Confederate's brigade broke the Union line sending Banks's troops running toward the Potomac River.

Lincoln and Stanton, fearing that Jackson was about to attack Washington, DC, ordered General Irvin McDowell to send troops under Shields to the Shenandoah Valley. They also ordered Frémont to advance northeastward back toward the US capital. Jackson, they hoped, would be caught between these two Union forces.

Jackson, however, used his position between the two Union forces to his advantage. On the morning of June 7, Jackson's Brigadier Richard S. Ewell (1817–72) set up good defensive positions at Cross Keys and was reinforced on the following day by Jackson's own troops at nearby Port Republic. Ewell's forces battled Frémont's all day until capturing the Union position that evening. The next day Jackson turned his attention to Shields's troops, who were trying to take the bridge at Port Republic. Although there was heavy fighting from both sides Shields eventually withdrew, thus ending Jackson's long engagement throughout the Shenandoah Valley.

During the month-long campaign Jackson had marched his men over 300 miles (480 km), won battles against three different Union armies, and immobilized some 60,000 Union troops. The campaign also made Jackson a Confederate hero.

WOMEN AT WAR

Women carried out many useful roles for both sides during the war. Some worked in war-related industries, such as uniform making, or took over government jobs usually held by men. Others joined drives to raise war funds, or were part of informal circles of friends who sent food parcels or warm clothing to soldiers in the front line. A few, however, took a much more direct involvement, particularly in the fields of nursing care and spying.

In the North, Dorothea Dix (1802–87), a social campaigner before the war, was appointed superintendent of the Union's corps of nurses and did much to improve the chances of men surviving their wounds. Clara Barton (1821–1912) became known as the "angel of the battlefield" for the nursing care she showed to soldiers during the war, and was later instrumental in founding the National Society of the Red Cross in America (1881).

Some women in both the North and South also became spies, the most famous of whom was Belle Boyd (1843–1900). Boyd, a Confederate spy, obtained military secrets from Union officers, was imprisoned twice, and even delivered diplomatic secrets to England on behalf of Jefferson Davis. Although popular, her behavior was not approved of by the more genteel women of the South.

Seven Days' Campaign

While Jackson's troops were busy routing the Union armies in the Shenandoah Valley, General Johnston's forces began battling McClellan's forces at the Battle of Seven Pines (also known as the Battle of Fair Oaks) outside Richmond on May 31. The battle was indecisive but bloody, with both sides losing around 5,000 men. The Confederate commander Johnston was himself badly wounded.

Before the battle was over Lee had been sent in to take Johnston's place as head of the main Southern force, named the Army of Northern Virginia. The battle finally ended on June 1 when Lee ordered a withdrawal of the Southern forces to their original positions. McClellan,

Left: General "Stonewall" Jackson's Shenandoah Valley Campaign lasted 30 days and was executed with great strategic and tactical skill. It also prevented Union forces from concentrating their firepower on Richmond.

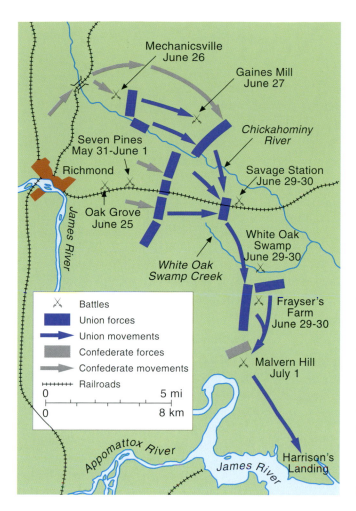

Battles
Union forces
Union movements
Confederate forces
Confederate movements
Railroads

0   5 mi
0   8 km

Mechanicsville June 26
Gaines Mill June 27
Chickahominy River
Seven Pines May 31-June 1
Richmond
Savage Station June 29-30
Oak Grove June 25
James River
White Oak Swamp June 29-30
White Oak Swamp Creek
Frayser's Farm June 29-30
Malvern Hill July 1
Appomattox River
James River
Harrison's Landing

Left: From Oak Grove to Malvern Hill, the Seven Days' Campaign in 1862 saw the South suffer heavy casualties. Nevertheless, they were able to keep the Union soldiers away from the Confederate capital of Richmond, at least for another two years.

Confederate victories, but McClellan's troops were forced to withdraw southward toward the James River.

The last battle of the campaign, fought at Malvern Hill, a little way to the north of the James River, on July 1, was, in fact, a Union victory. Lee launched his soldiers against the Union defenses on the hill's slopes and suffered over 5,000 casualties in just two hours, a telling example of the potency of defensive firepower. This Confederate defeat allowed the Union forces to retreat to Harrison's Landing, where they were protected by Union warships. McClellan sailed for Washington, DC where he blamed the politicians for his defeat. It would be two years before the Union Army had another chance to capture the Confederate capital.

Lee, on the other hand, learned from his defeats during the recent campaign. He restructured the Army of Northern Virginia to make it more efficient, and within two weeks of Malvern Hill was on the march to the north.

however, had been badly shaken by the large number of casualties and called a temporary halt to the Union's offensive campaign, choosing instead to wait for more heavy artillery to arrive in order to blast the Rebels away from Richmond.

While McClellan's Army of the Potomac waited, Lee's Army of Northern Virginia – which was joined by Jackson's victorious but exhausted troops – strengthened the military defenses around Richmond. On June 25, after weeks of anticipation, a Union reconnaissance force ran into a group of Rebel defenders at Oak Grove and the groups engaged in bitter fighting. By nightfall both sides had lost around 50 men each with several hundred wounded, but the action was enough to convince Lee that on the next day he should seize the initiative.

From Oak Grove on June 25 until the very bloody Malvern Hill on July 1, a series of battles known as the Seven Days' Campaign were waged, wherein Lee succeeded in forcing the Union Army to retreat. Many of the battles, including Mechanicsville (June 26) and Gaines Mill (June 27), did not result in clear-cut

Right: General Robert E. Lee took charge of the Army of Northern Virginia at the end of the Battle of Seven Pines. His command was a major turning point in the Civil War and his leadership and military skills earned him the respect of many – even the North.

Lee Invades the North

The successful defense of Richmond in June 1862 allowed the Confederate leadership to plan a major invasion of the North. This military campaign was to be led by Lee and his Army of Northern Virginia. Lee believed that by moving quickly he could defeat the larger Union armies one by one, before they had the chance to unite against him. His plan relied heavily on the support of generals like Jackson.

While the South was encouraged by the performance of its forces in the defense of Richmond, the Union command found itself in disarray. President Lincoln decided that the Union command structure needed reorganizing. He brought back to Washington two commanders who had recently won battles. General Henry Halleck (1815–72), who had been successful in Missouri, was appointed general-in-chief of all Union forces – this included being McClellan's superior – while General John Pope (1822–92), who had won in an area along the Mississippi River, was appointed commander of the Union troops remaining in the Shenandoah Valley.

Pope was an aggressive and abrasive commander, who did little to endear himself to the soldiers under his new command, comparing them unfavorably with his former troops. He instigated offensive operations and advanced toward an important railroad junction at Gordonsville, Virginia. Halleck, meanwhile, ordered McClellan and his troops to return to Washington.

Lee correctly interpreted the Union strategy and decided that his best plan was to engage Pope before reinforcements could be sent to him from the North. Lee's soldiers began marching toward Gordonsville on August 13, 1862.

The Second Bull Run

Jackson and his troops had already been sent back toward the Shenandoah Valley, and had narrowly defeated a Union force at Cedar Mountain, Virginia. This engagement marked the beginning of the Second Battle of Bull Run Campaign. Jackson's victory left the way clear for Lee to attack Pope. Unfortunately for the Union general, he was denied sufficient room for maneuver when Halleck ordered him to hold his position and await fresh reinforcements from McClellan, which, as usual, was slow in coming. Lee almost trapped Pope's army on August 19, but Pope understood the danger and retreated from the Rapidan River to the Rappahannock River.

During August Pope attempted to hold his own against Lee and Jackson, and on August 29 the Union and Confederate armies met on the old Bull Run battlefield. Pope was outmaneuvered by the two Confederate commanders, and the beaten and disorganized Union troops retreated.

After his victory at Second Bull Run, Lee believed that the Confederacy had a genuine chance to win the war and decided to press northward into Union territory.

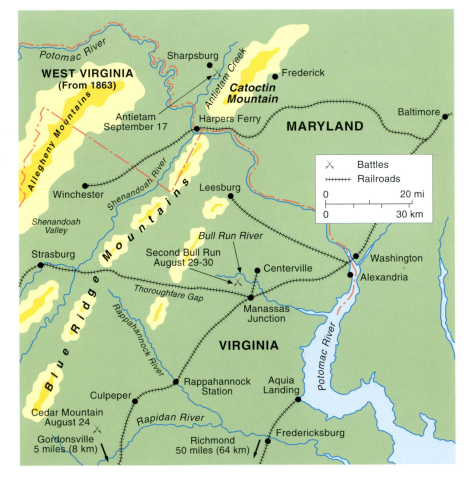

Left: In the late summer of 1862 Lee came close to invading Maryland. This map shows the major battles that led up to and included Antietam, fought on September 17.

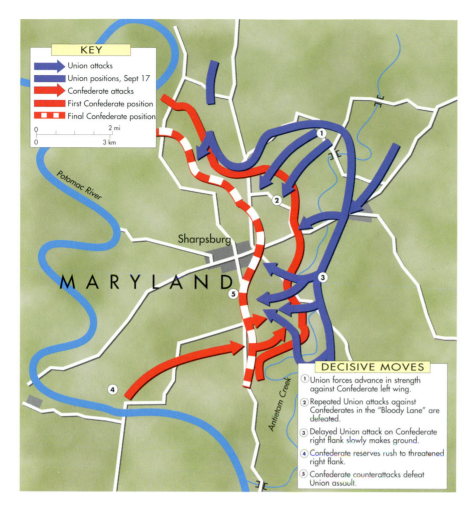

KEY
Union attacks
Union positions, Sept 17
Confederate attacks
First Confederate position
Final Confederate position
0   2 mi
0   3 km

Potomac River

Sharpsburg

M A R Y L A N D

Antietam Creek

DECISIVE MOVES
① Union forces advance in strength against Confederate left wing.
② Repeated Union attacks against Confederates in the "Bloody Lane" are defeated.
③ Delayed Union attack on Confederate right flank slowly makes ground.
④ Confederate reserves rush to threatened right flank.
⑤ Confederate counterattacks defeat Union assault.

Left: Although Lee was halted at Antietam, his troops, who were greatly outnumbered, made sure it was a close battle, with both sides losing thousands of soldiers.

There were elections to Congress due in the fall, and a Confederate victory in Maryland or Pennsylvania – close to Washington – might influence the sizeable group of antiwar Northern politicians to apply pressure on Lincoln to negotiate a political settlement.

As Lee advanced into Maryland, Lincoln recalled McClellan to lead troops to intercept the Confederate invasion. The Union Army – some 90,000 strong – caught up with Lee on September 15 along Antietam Creek, near Sharpsburg, Maryland. Lee prepared his 50,000 troops to face the Union.

Bloody Antietam

But McClellan waited two days before initiating the battle, giving Lee time to prepare defensive positions. The Union attacks were poorly coordinated and the outnumbered Confederates were able to hold their line. McClellan gave up the assault after the arrival of Confederate reinforcements, led by "Stonewall" Jackson, threatened the Union left flank. The fighting began at dawn and did not end until dusk. When it was over, it had claimed more American lives in a single day's fighting than any other battle of the war, with 26,000 casualties in total. Many had died fighting over a sunken road, which became known as "Bloody Lane."

After Antietam, Lee realized that he lacked sufficient forces to press further into Maryland and retired from the battlefield undisturbed by Union forces. McClellan, although outfought by Lee, could – and did – claim a victory of sorts, but Lincoln believed, rightly, that McClellan's slowness in following-up Lee's withdrawal had cost the Union a true victory.

In November, McClellan was removed from his command. Lincoln, however, did use the "victory" at Antietam to make clear his intention to issue his Emancipation Proclamation. On September 22, 1862, four days after Antietam, Lincoln published a preliminary proclamation stating that he would free slaves in the Confederacy on January 1, 1863, unless the Confederates returned to the Union. Although it would take several years for the emancipation to become a reality, the very fact of issuing the proclamation warned the Confederacy that Lincoln would not negotiate with them, only accept their surrender.

THE SHARPS CARBINE

In 1861, at the start of the Civil War, loading a standard rifle-musket, which had spiral grooves cut into the barrel, was a difficult and time-consuming task since the musket ball had to be loaded through the muzzle and the black powder packed around the ball with a rod. It was the same system that had been in use since the 16th century.

Gun designers long realized that to load the musket ball from the breech would allow easier reloading and more rapid shooting, but it was only after the development of precision machine tooling around the 1830s that military breech-loading weapons became practical.

The gunsmith Christian Sharps came up with an ingenious breech-loading system. To fire the carbine, the hammer pulled back and a lever opened the breech like a trapdoor. The black powder cartridge was then inserted into the breech, which was then pushed shut allowing the trigger to be pressed. The Sharps carbine was expensive and lacked the range of a rifle, but it did have a higher rate of fire and proved popular with cavalry units.

Grant's First Campaigns

By the spring of 1862 the Union was desperately in need of some good news. The war was going badly and the Confederate generals in Virginia had inflicted several major defeats on the Army of the Potomac. Although the eastern theater of operations was considered by both sides to be the key battleground, it was along the Mississippi that the Union began to turn the tide, partly due to the victories of Ulysses S. Grant.

At the start of the Civil War the state of Kentucky, although leaning in sympathy toward the Confederates, had hoped to remain neutral, but it soon found itself a battleground between the North and the South. It was the Confederates who first ignored the Kentuckians' wishes.

In September 1861 Southern soldiers occupied the town of Columbus, Kentucky, and placed heavy artillery on the high ground overlooking the Mississippi River. Union ships attempting to sail south down the Mississippi could be bombarded and sunk by these well-sited batteries.

In response, the Union commander at Cairo, Illinois, General Ulysses S. Grant (1822–85), occupied the town of Paducah, Kentucky, a position that directly threatened Columbus. Grant was already preparing to extend the campaign into Tennessee when the Confederate commander, General Albert Sydney Johnston (1803–62), realized the danger.

At the end of January 1862 a US naval officer, Andrew Foote (1806–63), took a force of soldiers and gunboats to attack the Confederate-held Fort Henry on the Tennessee River. On February 6, Foote surrounded the fort and bombarded it into surrender.

On the neighboring Cumberland River, Johnston sent substantial reinforcements to the Confederate post of Fort Donelson. With these new troops Fort Donelson was now defended by 15,000 soldiers. Undaunted, Foote sailed his gunboats back up the Tennessee to the Ohio River, and then down the Cumberland. Meanwhile, Grant marched overland toward Fort Donelson.

Grant and Foote reached Donelson, Tennessee, on February 12. Grant's troops surrounded the Confederate fort. Union gunboats prepared to attack from the Cumberland River. On the next day, Union troops attacked the fort, and on February 14, the Union vessels opened fire. The boats sailed close to the shore and several were damaged by Confederate guns.

The three Confederate generals in Fort Donelson – John Floyd, Gideon Pillow, and Simon Bolivar Buckner – decided to attempt to break out of the Union trap. They attacked one part of the Northern Army just before dawn on February 15. Grant was away conferring with Foote, and the Union defenses were still undergoing construction. Nevertheless, the Confederates were unable to make much impact, and while Floyd and Pillow escaped with some of their men on that night, Buckner and the rest of the garrison prepared to lay down their arms.

When the Confederates had asked for surrender terms, Grant replied that "no terms except an unconditional and immediate surrender can be accepted." Some 16,500 Confederate soldiers surrendered. The North had a much-needed victory and General U.S. Grant won a nickname: "Unconditional Surrender" Grant.

Left: During 1862 Union successes occurred along the Mississippi River and its tributaries. These famous battles, mostly due to Grant's leadership, included Fort Henry, Fort Donelson, and Shiloh.

A week later Johnston removed his Confederates from Nashville, Tennessee. He had been forced out of Kentucky by Grant's advance on Fort Henry, and now he had lost northwest Tennessee as well. Another Union force, the Army of the Ohio, marched through Bowling Green, Kentucky, to Nashville. Union troops occupied the Tennessee state capital on February 24, 1862.

The future also looked bleak for the Confederates elsewhere in the western theater. On March 8 their last attempt to take control of Missouri failed at the Battle of Pea Ridge in northwestern Arkansas. But the overall Union commander of the Mississippi area, General Henry Halleck, with three dispersed armies under his control, was slow to make use of his advantages.

The key to Union success was Grant's army, advancing along the Tennessee River toward Corinth, Mississippi, an important road and rail junction. On Grant's left was the Army of the Ohio commanded by General Don Carlos Buell (1818–98); on his right, an army commanded by General John Pope advancing down the Mississippi. Johnston realized that by beating Grant, it might be possible then to turn on Buell and Pope. All available Confederate soldiers in the area were assembled at Corinth. In early April they marched the 30 miles (48 km) toward Grant's army at Shiloh Church in Tennessee.

The Battle of Shiloh

On April 6, the Confederates caught Grant's troops completely by surprise, and Johnston seemed to have won the day, but Grant's forces held in two important places. General William Tecumseh Sherman (1820–91)

WAR IN THE WEST

In early 1862, the Confederate commander, General Henry Hopkins Sibley (1816–86), set out along the Rio Grande from Fort Bliss, Texas, with the aim of invading California. In February, he defeated a Union force at Valverde, New Mexico, before capturing Albuquerque and Santa Fe. Sibley ran short of supplies, however, and was forced to retreat. Union troops followed the Confederates down the Rio Grande, and by May 1862 had driven them back to Fort Bliss.

In early 1864 the Union prepared to invade Texas from Louisiana along the Red River. General Nathaniel Banks led the campaign and was supported by a fleet of river boats under Commander David Porter (1813–91). Porter was able to get a dozen of his gunboats past the rapids at Alexandria, Louisiana, and make for Shreveport. Banks headed overland to Shreveport by way of Grand Ecore. On April 8, Banks was attacked at Sabine Crossroads and forced to retreat to Alexandria. In the face of pressure from local Texan forces, Porter also had to retreat, and Alexandria was abandoned in May.

The last major action in the western theater took place in late 1864, when a Rebel force was defeated at the Westport, Missouri. The Confederates withdrew to Texas where they continued to resist until the end of the war.

resisted stoutly on Grant's left, while in the center, the "Hornet's Nest" was held by troops commanded by General Benjamin Prentiss (1819–1901).

The fight for the Hornet's Nest gave Grant time to construct a new defensive line about 3 miles (5 km) back from the original front with almost all the army's artillery on its left. When the Confederates reached this position, night was falling. Earlier in the day Johnston had been badly wounded twice and eventually bled to death. He was succeeded by General P.G.T. Beauregard. The delay in changing command was crucial to the outcome of Shiloh. Beauregard decided to reorganize the army and attack the next morning.

The Confederate leaders did not realize that Union reinforcements were arriving on the battlefield. Sherman met Grant that night. "We've had the devil's own day," he said. "Yes," Grant replied, "We'll lick 'em tomorrow, though."

The Union troops did exactly that. They surprised the Confederates beginning at 7:30 the next morning, and when Beauregard saw that he was outnumbered, he ordered his army to retreat back to Corinth, Mississippi. Shiloh was a Union victory although a costly one; while the South suffered 10,500 casualties, Grant lost about 13,000 men. Nevertheless, Grant's victory at Shiloh sealed the fate of the Confederacy along the Mississippi.

The same day that Beauregard retreated from the Shiloh battlefield, an important Confederate stronghold on the Mississippi River, known as Island Number Ten and held by Brigadier General William W. MacKall (1817–91), surrendered to Pope's army and a Union flotilla under the command of Foote. Three weeks later,

on the night of April 24–25, a Union fleet led by Admiral David Farragut (1801–70) defeated the Confederate Navy at New Orleans. Within the week of Farragut's naval victory, the city was occupied by Union troops.

Struggling to Reach Vicksburg

During May 1862, Halleck, who had assumed overall command of both Grant's and Buell's armies, marched on Corinth. (Beauregard, who had abandoned the city on May 29, was removed from command of the main Confederate Army, based then at Tupelo, Mississippi.) Memphis, Tennessee, fell to Union forces on June 6, so that the only remaining Confederate-controlled city between New Orleans and Memphis was Vicksburg. It seemed that victory for the Union in the western theater of operations was near, and that the South was in danger of being split in two.

The Union commanders, however, failed to take full advantage of the situation. Buell tried to take Chattanooga, Tennessee, but moved so slowly that the Confederate general at Tupelo in northern Mississippi, Braxton Bragg (1817–76), was able to transport 30,000 of his soldiers there first using the railroad – an early example of strategic movement by this new form of transport. Bragg then marched north to Kentucky and Buell was forced to retreat to protect his lines of supply. On October 8, at Perryville, the two armies fought a drawn battle, but Bragg retreated since he was far from his base at Chattanooga.

During the summer of 1862 Grant's forces were largely inactive, although they repelled an attack at Iuka, Mississippi, by Confederate soldiers from

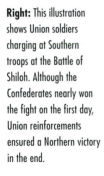

Right: This illustration shows Union soldiers charging at Southern troops at the Battle of Shiloh. Although the Confederates nearly won the fight on the first day, Union reinforcements ensured a Northern victory in the end.

Arkansas. These Confederates later assaulted Corinth, Mississippi, on October 3, where they were beaten off by troops under the command of General William S. Rosecrans (1819–98).

Rosecrans's success earned him promotion, replacing Buell as commander of the Army of the Cumberland. Grant, meanwhile, had to wait until November before he could resume his offensive. He moved against Vicksburg but was soon halted by his own commander, Halleck, who wanted to reinforce Grant with a combined army–navy expedition that would travel down the Mississippi from Memphis. After a delay of a month, Grant resumed his advance, with Sherman moving down the west bank of the Mississippi in support.

The delay allowed two large Confederate cavalry columns, one of 2,000 led by General Nathan Bedford Forrest (1821–77) and a second of 3,500 led by General Earl Van Dorn (1820–63), to get behind Grant's army. They destroyed railroad tracks and telegraph lines, and threatened the Union troop's lines of communication. Grant had to abandon his attack on Vicksburg to chase off the Confederate marauders and repair the damage they had done.

The Battle of Murfreesboro
As Grant paused, Rosecrans acted. Bragg and the Army of Tennessee were at Murfreesboro, Tennessee; Rosecrans was at nearby Nashville. Lincoln demanded action but Rosecrans waited until he had sufficient supplies before advancing. On December 26, Rosecrans marched toward the enemy, but after Confederate scouts spotted the Union forces approaching, Bragg decided to seize the initiative and attack first. Near Murfreesboro, on December 30, Bragg readied his troops for battle, launching his assault at dawn on New Year's Eve. Bragg believed that Rosecrans would retreat, but the Union troops held their ground despite repeated Confederate attacks of great ferocity. Casualties at Murfreesboro were equal, about 12,000 per side, but it was considered a Union victory since Bragg had to retreat.

As 1863 began the Union was able to look on the previous year with some hope, due mostly to Grant's victories. Although the Confederates had fought bravely and had shown the Union that the Southern troops could not be dealt with complacently, the North had secured the upper hand along the Mississippi. The only obstacle left to overcome was Vicksburg.

The War at Sea
Despite an uncertainty on land, the Union took more solace in their performance at sea. Although at the start of the Civil War many US naval officers sided with the Confederacy, the vast bulk of America's merchant shipping and navy lay in the North. And central to Union strategy was the economic strangulation of the South through maritime blockade.

Cotton was vital to the Southern economy, and while the North concentrated on securing the blockade, Southern naval commanders devoted their energies to breaking it. The Confederacy used privateers, such as the CSS *Alabama*, to roam the high seas attacking Union merchant shipping. These privateers had some success, but the North's resources were too great to allow them to affect the overall strategic balance. Over time, the Union blockade slowly drained the economic lifeblood out of the Confederacy.

Perhaps the best example of Southern ingenuity in conducting naval operations with limited resources was demonstrated at the Battle of Hampton Roads. The Confederate steamship *Merrimack* (CSS *Virginia*) was converted into an "ironclad" – its wooden hull was covered with an iron shell – and used to attack Union shipping in Hampton Roads off the coast of Virginia on March 8, 1862. First two wooden Union warships fell victim to the Confederate ironclad, then on the following day the Union deployed its own ironclad, the USS *Monitor*. The two ships battled it out with inconclusive results, although the *Monitor* prevented the *Merrimack* from sinking any more Union vessels.

NAVAL WARFARE

The influence of naval warfare on the events of the American Civil War was limited. Despite the actions fought throughout the war, the naval aspect was a sideshow compared to the war on land. The primary function of the Union Navy was to blockade Southern ports, and in this it was successful. Conversely, the main role of the Confederate vessels was the disruption of Union merchant and blockade traffic, plus the defense of major ports and fortifications. Though the Confederates did achieve remarkable results given the state of their maritime arm at the beginning of the war – they had no navy whatsoever – they failed to prevent the North erecting a virtual wall around the South's coastline.

The war did advance naval science, with ironclads (wooden ships modified as armor-plated vessels) being built and used by both sides. Another innovation was the submersible, which the South was particularly interested in for use against the North's blockade. In 1863, for example, Horace L. Hunley developed a submersible craft that was powered by eight crewmen. Though it sank during a test, killing its inventor, it was refloated and christened the CSS *HL Hunley*. On February 17, 1863, it attacked and sank the USS *Housatonic*, giving it the distinction of being the first submersible to sink its target. Unfortunately, the *Hunley* went down with its victim.

From Fredericksburg to Gettysburg

By mid-1863 Lee felt that he had a reasonable chance of ending the war if he could lay siege to Washington. Although he was outnumbered, the Confederate commander devised a bold plan whereby his army would defeat his opponents by first invading Pennsylvania and then heading south for the US capital. In early July the first part of Lee's scheme was realized when his troops met Union forces at Gettysburg.

President Lincoln's replacement for General George McClellan as commander of the Army of the Potomac, General Ambrose Burnside (1824–81), did not want the job. Burnside only agreed to accept the appointment in November 1862 because he would otherwise have had to serve under General Joseph Hooker (1814–79), whom he disliked intensely. Burnside, at least, seemed to have the military knowledge and experience needed to fill the post, and he had scored minor victories in landings along the North Carolina coast; troops under his command had captured the Confederate bases at Roanoke Island, New Berne, and Beaufort during February and March 1862.

Burnside's career as commander of the Army of the Potomac began well enough when he surprised Lee by reaching the area across the Rappahannock River from the town of Fredericksburg with a speed not seen under McClellan's command. Burnside viewed Fredericksburg

as a staging post for an advance on Richmond, but having gained a march on Lee, Burnside was then kept waiting for pontoon bridges to allow him to build bridges across the river. By the time the pontoons arrived, so had Lee's army, which occupied the hills above the town.

Lee's position at Fredericksburg was too strong for Burnside to be able to attack successfully. Burnside, however, stuck to his plan, and on December 13 the Army of the Potomac attacked the Confederate lines, only to be repulsed with heavy losses. The virtual slaughter of Union forces lasted for two days before Burnside finally retreated. Out of 100,000 Union soldiers at Fredericksburg, 15,000 were killed or wounded, to which Lincoln lamented: "the country cannot endure such losses."

When Burnside attempted to resume his campaign to capture Richmond in January 1863 he suffered another

Left: Union troops are fired upon while attempting to cross the Rappahannock River to reach Fredericksburg. General Burnside believed that by taking the town he could then mount an assault on the Confederate capital, Richmond.

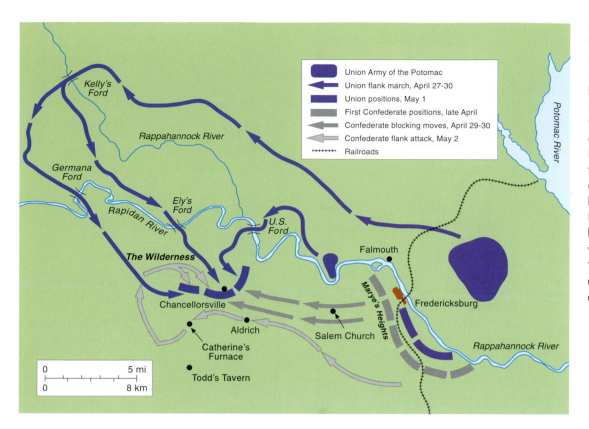

Union Army of the Potomac
Union flank march, April 27-30
Union positions, May 1
First Confederate positions, late April
Confederate blocking moves, April 29-30
Confederate flank attack, May 2
Railroads

Left: Many military historians believe that the Battle of Chancellorsville, 1863, was Lee's most brilliant performance. Heavily outnumbered and forced to leave nearly half of his troops back at Fredericksburg, he forced the Union Army to retreat after several days of heavy fighting. However, Lee's victory was bittersweet since his most valued general, "Stonewall" Jackson, was accidentally killed by his own men.

setback. After a month of dry weather, just as he began to move heavy rain turned the roads to mud, bringing the offensive to a halt.

This was the moment for recriminations within the Union military leadership to surface. Burnside's officers had complained to Lincoln about their superior's leadership, while Burnside went to the president with a list of generals he wanted removed. In the event, Lincoln got rid of Burnside, replacing him with the hard-drinking Hooker.

Throughout the spring of 1863 both Hooker's and Lee's armies remained inactive. The heavy rains continued, making it hard to move. Both armies, however, were also in no shape to attack. The Union Army suffered from poor morale, which Hooker helped raise through improving supplies and encouraging better military discipline. Lee's troops, by comparison, were very confident because of their recent run of victories, but they lacked food and equipment.

Hooker's troops numbered about 120,000, twice the number of soldiers that Lee had under his command. But Lee still held the strong defensive positions at Fredericksburg, where he had beaten Burnside. Hooker knew he was unlikely to defeat Lee by a frontal assault, so he decided to force him out of his defenses by outflanking the Confederates.

At the end of April 1863, Hooker led some 75,000 soldiers west along the Rappahannock, and crossed the river at United States Ford. He then entered an area of dense forest called the Virginia Wilderness. Meanwhile, Hooker left about 47,000 troops near Fredericksburg.

Lee had just over 50,000 in total, and faced a difficult military dilemma. If he attacked the Union forces left at Fredericksburg, Hooker, with the main army, would strike at the Confederate rear. If, on the other hand, he attacked Hooker's main army, the Union soldiers left at Fredericksburg would take the town and then be in a position to strike at his new rear. Hooker believed that Lee was trapped between the two Union forces.

Hooker's plan needed the larger Union force, in the Wilderness, to move rapidly. On April 30, he halted his forces at the edge of the Wilderness near a village called Chancellorsville. His generals expected him to continue advancing into more open country where the larger size of the Army of the Potomac would give them a greater advantage in battle. But Hooker refused to advance any farther, overcome by insecurity after realizing that Lee would not retreat and was prepared to fight.

Like Hooker, Lee also divided his army. He left 10,000 men at Fredericksburg, commanded by General Jubal Early (1816–94), and took the rest to the Wilderness. When Lee learned that Hooker had halted, he ordered an offensive. On May 2, "Stonewall" Jackson led 28,000 men around Hooker's right wing. When Jackson attacked, the Union soldiers, who were eating their evening meal, were caught off guard. The Confederate assault destroyed the corps commanded by General Oliver Otis Howard (1830–1909).

Jackson went forward to reconnoiter a ford across the Rappahannock, to prevent Hooker's army from retreating to Washington, but was accidentally shot by one of his own men while returning in the dusk. Jackson died a short while later after complications set in following the amputation of his left arm. With the loss of this skilled general, Lee was obliged to regroup.

On May 3, the Confederates resumed their assault. Hooker was wounded in the fighting, and was now more concerned with protecting his line of retreat through United States Ford than in attacking. By this stage the Union troops at Fredericksburg under General John Sedgwick (1813–64) had begun to move forward. Lee once again divided his army and halted Sedgwick's

advance at Salem Church on May 4. The following day, Hooker withdrew across the Rappahannock. Lee then decided to use the advantage he had gained at Chancellorsville to invade the North once again.

Lee Invades the North

During the first week of June 1863, Lee began marching from Fredericksburg into Pennsylvania. On the way, his troops seized free African Americans and sent them back to Virginia as slaves. In contrast, Lincoln had

Right: The Battle of Gettysburg, 1863, which lasted three days, is seen as the turning point of the war in the east. After it was over and the Confederates began moving back to Virginia, tens of thousands of soldiers had been killed or badly wounded.

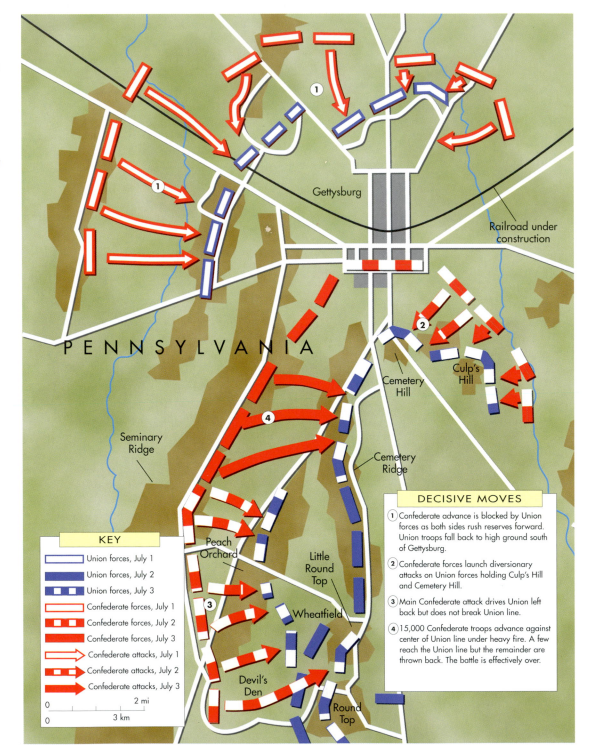

Gettysburg

Railroad under construction

PENNSYLVANIA

Culp's Hill

Cemetery Hill

Seminary Ridge

Cemetery Ridge

Peach Orchard

Little Round Top

Wheatfield

Devil's Den

Round Top

KEY

▭	Union forces, July 1
▬	Union forces, July 2
▭▬▭	Union forces, July 3
▭	Confederate forces, July 1
▬▭▬	Confederate forces, July 2
▬	Confederate forces, July 3
⇨	Confederate attacks, July 1
⇨	Confederate attacks, July 2
➡	Confederate attacks, July 3

0   2 mi
0   3 km

DECISIVE MOVES

1 Confederate advance is blocked by Union forces as both sides rush reserves forward. Union troops fall back to high ground south of Gettysburg.

2 Confederate forces launch diversionary attacks on Union forces holding Culp's Hill and Cemetery Hill.

3 Main Confederate attack drives Union left back but does not break Union line.

4 15,000 Confederate troops advance against center of Union line under heavy fire. A few reach the Union line but the remainder are thrown back. The battle is effectively over.

recently given freed slaves assurances that they were to be permitted to serve in the army.

Lincoln, instead of being alarmed by Lee's northward advance, was hopeful that if Lee was defeated deep in Union territory and many miles from his home bases, then his army might be destroyed. A Pennsylvanian, General George Gordon Meade (1815–72), replaced Hooker on June 28 as head of the Army of the Potomac. Hooker had resigned because a plan of his to trap Lee's army had been overruled by his superiors. Meade wanted to fight, and so did Lee. Their armies collided at Gettysburg, Pennsylvania, where, on July 1, Confederate soldiers approaching the town in search of shoes came under fire from Union cavalry.

Neither Lee nor Meade had actually prepared for the battle, but it gradually absorbed more and more of the two armies. When Lee arrived during the afternoon of the July 1, he decided that he could at least defeat a part of the Union Army. He ordered a general advance against the Union troops who were formed in a rough semicircle around the town of Gettysburg.

The fighting raged on into the evening. The constant pressure of Southern troops arriving on the battlefield caused part of the Union lines to collapse. General Oliver Howard's troops, who were mostly German-Americans, broke at a critical moment. The Union soldiers retreated through Gettysburg to the high ground southeast of the town, taking up positions on Cemetery Hill and Culp's Hill.

The battle resumed the next day, July 2. Lee sent word to General James Longstreet (1821–1904) for him to attack Meade's left flank. The key to the Union line was a hill at the southern end called Little Round Top. It was supposed to be defended by troops led by General Daniel Sickles (1819–1914), but he believed that he would find it easier to defend the ground to his front and during the morning he occupied positions known as the Peach Orchard, the Wheatfield, and the Devil's Den (an area strewn with large boulders). But the new positions exposed both his flanks to attack. By the time Sickles realized the danger he saw Longstreet's Confederates advancing toward him.

Longstreet, however, was slow in coming to battle. He did not launch his assault until the late afternoon. His men fought hard for the Wheatfield, the Peach Orchard, and Devil's Den, and the Confederates gradually pushed their way to Little Round Top. It looked as if the Union Army would be outflanked, until Meade's chief of engineers, General Gouverneur Warren (1830–82), dispatched troops to Little Round Top to prevent its capture by Longstreet's men.

On July 3, Lee sent his sole fresh division, commanded by General George Pickett (1825–75), together with two other divisions, to attack the center of Cemetery Ridge. The assault by some 15,000 of Lee's best troops followed the biggest artillery bombardment yet seen in American history. About 150 of Pickett's men broke into the Union position, but many more had been killed or wounded. The survivors retreated back to Confederate lines. The Battle of Gettysburg was over.

During the three days of desperate fighting, Meade had lost 23,000 men, either killed, wounded, or missing; Lee some 28,000 men. On July 4, a thunderstorm prevented Meade from following the Confederates, and Lee began the slow and painful retreat back to Virginia. Gettysburg was a turning point in the war. It had torn the fighting heart out of the Army of Northern Virginia, and, henceforth, Lee would abandon any hopes of defeating the Union by taking the offensive in favor of fighting battles to defend the Confederacy.

Grant Takes Vicksburg

Despite their best efforts, at the end of December 1862 all attempts by General Grant and his officers to reach Vicksburg had been unsuccessful. One of the worst setbacks for the Union had taken place in the previous July, when Admiral Farragut's fleet failed to destroy a Confederate ironclad, the *Arkansas*, near Vicksburg. As a result, the Union fleet was forced to retreat back down the Mississippi toward New Orleans.

The terrain around Vicksburg favored the Confederate defenders: swamps blocked the way to the city from the north, and the width of the Mississippi made all river crossings a difficult and hazardous operation, especially as Confederate artillery dominated the river banks around the city.

Since the bulk of Grant's army was at Milliken's Bend northwest of Vicksburg, there was no way to move it east of Vicksburg except by heading north and crossing near Memphis, Tennessee, or by going south. To cross the Mississippi south of Vicksburg required gunboats and transport for the troops. But vessels could not easily sail past Vicksburg to connect with the Union troops that would march overland. Grant had already tried to get east of Vicksburg by marching from the north, but found that such a move exposed his supply lines to attacks by Confederate cavalry.

The Union general decided that somehow he would have to approach Vicksburg from the south. Grant gave orders for a canal to be dug that would allow his troops to bypass the Confederate positions around Vicksburg, but the severe wet weather of early 1863 and swampy conditions forced Grant to abandon this approach. An attempt in March to cross the Yazoo River, just north of Vicksburg, was made by Grant, but also ended in failure. General John Pemberton (1814–81), the Confederate commander in Vicksburg, was able to take some satisfaction in Grant's frustrations, believing he had gained the edge over his Union opponent.

But on the night of April 16–17, Union Commander David Porter succeeded in running 12 ships down the Mississippi past the Confederate guns at Vicksburg. Grant now marched his army south to meet Porter's fleet. On April 30, 1863, the Union Army was transported across the Mississippi River at Bruinsburg, 30 miles (48 km) south of Vicksburg.

Grant was taking a great risk. His force was now south of Vicksburg, and there was no easy way for it to

Right: As this shows, Grant's plans to take Vicksburg depended on crossing the Mississippi south of the city, marching east to Jackson, and therefore securing their rear, then carrying on westward to Vicksburg.

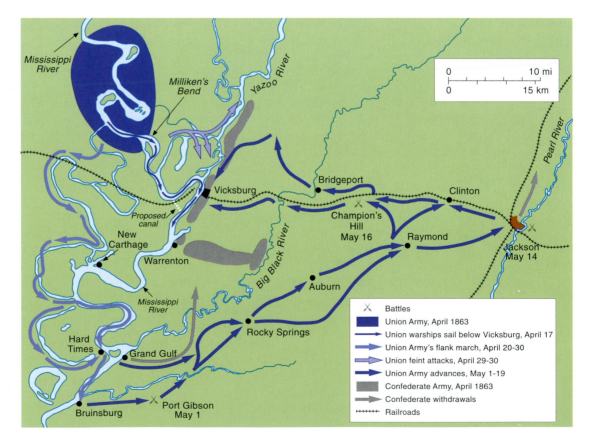

Left: Once the Union soldiers arrived on the eastern side of Vicksburg they were able to entrench themselves for a six-week-long bombardment until the city surrendered.

On July 3, knowing he had no hope of relief, Pemberton asked Grant for terms of surrender. Grant initially demanded an unconditional surrender, but changed his mind when reminded of the logistical problems of handling the prisoners – to transport nearly 29,000 prisoners would take most of the riverboats he needed to keep his army supplied. Consequently, Grant paroled the Confederates, permitting them to return home on strict condition that they would not take up arms again.

The next day city of Vicksburg surrendered and Union control of the Mississippi River inevitably split the Confederacy in two. Back east, Lee had lost at Gettysburg the day before. Now, the future of the Confederacy appeared doomed.

get supplies from its base at Memphis. Grant, however, ordered his troops to live off the land, drawing food from the farms and plantations of Mississippi as they marched to attack Vicksburg from the east. On May 1, Union Generals John McClernand (1812–90) and James B. McPherson (1828–64) defeated a Confederate force at Port Gibson, freeing its batteries at Grand Gulf for Grant's use as a base. Grant's next target was the Mississippi state capital, Jackson. If Union troops could capture the state capital, their rear would be secure while they advanced on Vicksburg.

On May 7, Grant began his northeastward march. His troops faced the possibility of being caught between two Confederate armies: General Johnston was moving from Tennessee toward Jackson, while Pemberton came out of Vicksburg. Grant's troops reached Jackson, Mississippi, in a week, finding that Johnston had arrived the day before, but Johnston had only 6,000 soldiers under his command. The Union forces, outnumbering the Confederates by four to one, overwhelmed the enemy entrenchments around the city, sending Johnston and his troops retreating eastward on May 14.

Quickly turning his army westward, Grant defeated Pemberton at the Battle of Champion's Hill on May 16. Two days later, the Union troops arrived outside Vicksburg itself. Grant hoped that a quick assault might capture the city and avoid a long siege. On May 19, therefore, Sherman's corps attacked the northern side of the city, but was driven off with the loss of 1,000 men. On May 22, the whole army went onto the offensive and once again suffered heavy losses.

Grant now recognized that he would have to besiege Vicksburg. He brought up guns and barges with mortars, and for six weeks the city was pounded. The gunfire was so heavy that it drove the people of Vicksburg into caves. The Confederate defenders maintained a determined defense, but as Pemberton watched his food supplies shrink so his men slowly began to starve.

PRISONERS OF WAR

During the opening phases of the Civil War, neither the Union nor Confederate armies had invested much thought in how to deal with prisoners of war. If soldiers were captured, commanders in the area would often work out an agreement to exchange them on a local, ad hoc basis.

But the number of prisoners captured by both sides increased rapidly during 1862, when strongholds such as Fort Donelson surrendered and overwhelmed the resources of commanders on the spot. In July 1862 both sides agreed to a formal system of exchanging prisoners. The arrangement held until the Confederates began capturing African-American soldiers fighting for the Union. These soldiers were either shot, sold into slavery, or imprisoned without hope of exchange. In response, the Union stopped all prisoner exchanges.

From then on captured soldiers were held in camps, which ranged from old forts to little more than wooden stockades surrounding an open field. Inside, the prisoners had the most limited of facilities. The camp with the worst reputation was the Confederate-run Andersonville. The treatment of its inmates was poor, and many of the tens of thousands of Union soldiers died there through disease, starvation, and general neglect. Such was the outcry against the conditions encountered at Andersonville, that its commander, Swiss-born Heinrich Wirz, was hanged after the war.

Tennessee Falls to the Union

General William Rosecrans's Army of the Cumberland had won an important victory at the Battle of Murfreesboro, in Tennessee. But the battle, which had lasted from late December 1862 to January 1863, claimed the lives of many Union soldiers and resulted in thousands of casualties. So damaging was the effect that Rosecran's army spent the entire spring of 1863 reorganizing itself.

By the beginning of June Rosecrans was finally ready to continue his campaign through Tennessee. But the long spring had also given the Confederate commander, General Braxton Bragg, time to gather most of the harvest from the farms of central Tennessee. These crops provided some desperately needed wheat for the hungry Confederate soldiers.

Bragg's troops held many of the passes through the rugged terrain of the Cumberland Mountains. But Rosecrans simply outflanked these defenses and marched to Murfreesboro again; the Confederates abandoned western Tennessee and retreated to Chattanooga. Lincoln urged Rosecrans to press the Confederates harder but Rosecrans remained at Murfreesboro for another six weeks. He used the time to gather supplies for his advance on his next target, Chattanooga, Tennessee. Rosecrans's army began to move in the middle of August.

Confederate president Jefferson Davis in Richmond recognized the danger posed by Rosecrans. He decided to reinforce Bragg, taking troops from Virginia, to be commanded by General James Longstreet, and sending

them by railroad to Tennessee. Bragg waited until these units arrived before starting offensive operations.

Rosecrans occupied Chattanooga on September 6 and then pushed south, heading toward Atlanta, Georgia. The various corps of the Union Army were too widely dispersed, however, unable to provide mutual support if attacked. The largest corps, commanded by General George Thomas (1816–70), was in position at Chickamauga Creek, near the Georgia town of La Fayette. Bragg thought he could strike at the flank and front of this corps with a good chance of success.

Unfortunately for Bragg, his subordinate corps commanders opposed the plan of attack, believing it to be too risky. Bragg tried again on the September 11, and once again his corps commanders objected to the plan. Thomas's exposed units now realized the danger and withdrew. Bragg wanted to attack another Union corps, that of General Thomas Crittenden (1819–93), on September 13, but once again his commanders objected and no assault took place.

The frustrated Bragg now waited six days before a plan was finally agreed upon, by which time many of

Right: This illustration shows the moment when the Union troops overwhelmed the Confederate soldiers holding Missionary Ridge outside Chattanooga. The ridge was a crucial site and when it fell to Grant, it was only a matter of time before the whole of Tennessee followed suit.

Left: Union troops advance to victory during the storming of Confederate defenses on Lookout Mountain outside Chattanooga on November 24, 1863.

Longstreet's reinforcements had arrived in camp. Bragg's bad luck continued, however. Thomas reorganized his defenses the night before the attack, shifting his position so that Bragg's troops would hit part of his front, instead of his flank.

On the September 19, the Southern troops battered the Union left at Chickamauga, where Thomas's troops were stationed. They gained very little ground, as the terrain was heavily wooded, making coordinated attacks almost impossible. That night Longstreet arrived with the remainder of his corps. The attack resumed the next day, with the Confederates again repeatedly attacking the Union positions for limited gains. Then Bragg received some compensation for his earlier bad fortune.

Rosecrans's staff had been reinforcing Thomas with troops from the right flank, but in the process lost track of their position. They ordered one division to move closer to Thomas's formation, not realizing that there was already a division there. The divisional commander, ordered to move, had to march around his neighbor, creating a wide gap in the line. Longstreet, coincidentally, launched his attack at just this point.

Most of the disorganized Union frontline collapsed as Longstreet's men attacked. The whole Union right fled back to Chattanooga, but Thomas hung on until dusk, beating off every Southern assault before retiring in good order to Chattanooga. For stemming the Confederate's advance, Thomas was nicknamed the "Rock of Chickamauga." Bragg had won a victory but with heavy losses; one-third of his 54,000 soldiers had been killed or wounded. He nevertheless followed Rosecrans and laid siege to Chattanooga.

By the middle of October, Rosecrans's army was in difficulty and Lincoln ordered two corps from the Army of the Potomac to march to his aid. Command of this force was given to General Joseph Hooker. At the same time, General Sherman, with four divisions, was sent from Mississippi. And as part of a major reorganization of the Union command structure, Grant was given command of all Union forces between the Appalachian Mountains and the Mississippi River. Grant replaced Rosecrans with Thomas, although he agreed to Rosecrans's plan to open a supply line from west of Chattanooga. This was accomplished on October 23.

On November 23, Grant ordered his troops forward to begin the Battle of Chattanooga. Hooker's troops climbed Lookout Mountain, a key position that overlooked Chattanooga and which was held by the Confederates. The next day Hooker's troops swept the three Confederate brigades off the summit. Meanwhile, Sherman launched an attack on Bragg's right, but achieved only limited success. The Confederate positions there were stronger than expected, and Sherman's troops were still tired from having marched to Chattanooga.

On November 25, Grant asked Thomas to lead his Army of the Cumberland out of Chattanooga against Bragg's center at Missionary Ridge. Sherman would resume his attack on the Confederate left at the same time. After a bitter struggle Thomas's men ejected the Confederates from Missionary Ridge, and soon the whole Southern Army was in retreat. The Army of the Cumberland had avenged its defeat at Chickamauga, and Tennessee was clear of Confederate troops.

Grant's War of Attrition

After his defeat at Gettysburg in July 1863, Lee shepherded the bulk of the Confederate Army of Northern Virginia back across the Potomac River into the somewhat safer confines of Virginia. Meanwhile, Lincoln was furious with his generals in the eastern theater for not chasing after Lee. In March 1864, Grant replaced Henry Halleck as the general-in-chief of the armies of the United States.

One of Grant's first commands in his new role was to order Meade, who remained at the head of the Army of the Potomac, to pursue the Army of Northern Virginia, explaining that: "Lee's army will be your objective point. Wherever Lee goes, there you will go also." Grant planned to fight Lee's army to a standstill.

On May 4, Grant took personal charge of the new campaign and, along with Meade, marched the Army of the Potomac south. The army crossed the Rapidan River – near the ford Hooker had used on his way to defeat at Chancellorsville in May 1863 – and advanced into the area of rough ground known as the Wilderness. The savage, confused battle began on May 5 and lasted for two days. On May 7, Grant resumed the offensive and attempted to get around Lee's right flank.

Although Lee was able to avoid Grant's outflanking maneuver, he was surprised by the determination of Union forces, who seemed willing to advance regardless of casualties. Battle was resumed at Spotsylvania Courthouse on May 9, another bloody engagement that cost both sides heavy casualties. Grant's attacks slowly pushed Lee back.

After a week in which both sides brought reinforcements from their rival capitals, Grant marched southeast. In June, he attacked Lee at Cold Harbor, 10 miles (16 km) east of Richmond, where the Confederate troops waited behind earthen fortifications. Many Union soldiers were convinced the attack would fail, and hundreds fatalistically wrote their names on pieces of paper, and pinned them to their uniforms to allow their bodies to be easily identified and returned home for burial. As it happened, many did die on June 3 in a failed attack on Lee's center.

Grant had lost over 50,000 soldiers in a month of almost continuous fighting. It was the highest casualty rate in the war. Lee had lost about half that many, but Grant had started with an army of 120,000 men while Lee had 64,000. The Union general-in-chief, without gaining a significant win, brutally demonstrated to Lee that he would endure whatever it took in terms of casualties to secure ultimate victory.

When Grant led Meade's Army of the Potomac into the Wilderness in May 1864, it was only one of three Union offensives that sought to drive the Confederate forces out of Virginia. The other two offensives consisted of a drive down the Shenandoah Valley and an assault along the James River north to Richmond. The Shenandoah offensive was designed to capture the city of Staunton but only got as far as the town of New Market, where it was defeated on May 15.

More hope was placed in the advance up the James River, comprising 30,000 men under General Benjamin Butler (1818–93). When he arrived at Bermuda Hundred, the Union base between the James and Appomattox rivers, there were just 10,000 Confederate soldiers deployed there, and only a few were between Butler's army and the Southern capital. If Butler had moved swiftly up the banks of the James, he might have captured the elusive goal of so much Union effort.

Butler's slowness gave the Southern commander, General Beauregard, time to gather reinforcements. At the Battle of Drewry's Bluff on May 16, Beauregard's soldiers attacked and forced Butler back to Bermuda Hundred. Although Butler was secure from attack behind his line of trenches, he was unable to use his army to help Grant. Despite his failure, Butler had at least placed an army near Richmond.

New Three-Pronged Plan

Now, Grant decided on a three-pronged plan of attack. The Union troops in the Shenandoah would try once again to advance south. At the same time the Army of the Potomac's cavalry, commanded by General Sheridan, would ride west to the Shenandoah. Sheridan's force would destroy the railroad as it went, and when it met up with the Union troops from Shenandoah, together they would act to stop food and other supplies from reaching Lee.

Grant would take Meade's army across the James River close to Butler's army and capture Petersburg. The Army of the Potomac began marching on June 12. One of the longest pontoon bridges in history was built across the James River, and on June 14 the bulk of the Union troops had crossed. On June 15, Grant's leading corps neared Petersburg. It numbered about 15,000 soldiers; only 2,000 Confederates, commanded by Beauregard, defended the Virginian city.

The Union commanders' inactivity in front of Petersburg allowed the Confederates time to rush troops to the threatened city. By the time Grant arrived with the bulk of the army – 65,000 Union soldiers – Lee had brought up his reinforcements.

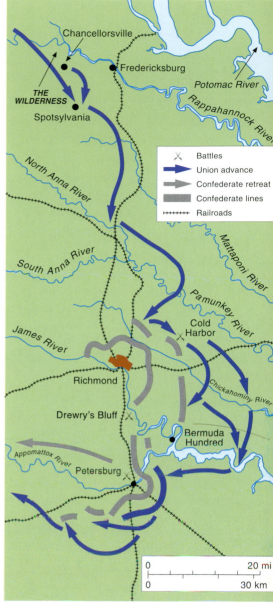

Grant ordered an assault on June 18 with the whole of this army. They found that Lee and Beauregard had moved their troops out of their trench lines and fallen back closer to the city, and instead of pushing forward, the Union soldiers halted. Once again, the chance of a quick decision was gone, and Meade and Grant accepted that they would have to besiege Petersburg.

For eight months the Union and Confederate armies sparred along the trench lines of Petersburg. Unable to take the city by storm, Grant attempted to cut the roads and railroads leading into Petersburg in the hope that Lee would retreat or surrender.

In October 1864, the Union finally gained total control of the Shenandoah Valley. Although the Confederate forces commanded by General Jubal Early had some initial success, which caused a temporary panic in the North that a Confederate raiding force might drive onto Washington, the weight of Northern material

Above left: General-in-Chief Grant, shown here outside his tent, took charge of the final bloody push to defeat Lee's Army of Northern Virginia.

Above right: Grant's campaign to capture Richmond involved great sweeping movements to the east and south of the Confederate capital, and a long siege of Petersburg.

superiority proved too great. Sheridan defeated Early at Cedar Creek on October 19, and with the Shenandoah in Union hands, Lee lost his main source of food.

Through the winter months of 1864–65, Lee's army shrunk, as his previously loyal soldiers now began to desert in large numbers. Lee did not have enough troops to hold the 35 miles (56 km) of trenches protecting Petersburg. Finally, in January 1865, bad weather cut Petersburg off from Richmond, and those left in Petersburg began to starve. At the end of March 1865, Lee decided that he must punch a hole through part of Grant's lines around Petersburg, and then retreat westward with what was left of his army.

Atlanta, Franklin, and Nashville

By the summer of 1864 the Civil War was moving into its final phase. It was not a question of if the South would surrender, but when. The Union had the men, the weapons, and the equipment to overwhelm the South. Still, the Confederates fought on. General Sherman planned to march through Georgia, destroying everything of value in his path. This campaign, known as the March to the Sea, was brutal but decisive.

While both Grant and Lee battered away at each other in the close confines of Virginia, in the west, the armies of General William Sherman (promoted to command all Union armies in the West in March 1864) and Confederate General Joseph Johnston had much greater room for maneuver.

Sherman's 1864 campaign got under way on May 5. He moved south from Chattanooga, Tennessee, and found Johnston and his army in front of Dalton, Georgia. Rather than launch a frontal attack, Sherman attempted to outflank Johnston by dispatching 30,000 men under General James McPherson to capture the town of Resaca to the rear of the main Confederate position. But McPherson's caution in the face of light Confederate resistance allowed Johnston to escape this trap and adopt new positions to the south of Resaca.

On May 13 Sherman began a three-day assault on Johnston's army at Resaca. After intense fighting in which the Union troops suffered heavy casualties, Johnston withdrew his army to Cassville, thwarting Sherman's efforts to bring him to a decisive battle. This process was repeated at Allatoona (May 25) and Kennesaw Mountain (June 23), in which the Confederates again inflicted heavy casualties on Union troops before retiring to new defensive positions.

Although Johnston had slowed Sherman's advance, by the end of June Union troops were closing in on Atlanta. The city was vital to the Confederacy: it was a center of trade, the hub of a key transportation system, and a major supplier of weapons to the Southern armies. For the South, the city had to be defended at all cost.

Jefferson Davis cared little for Johnston and on July 17 replaced him with General John Hood (1831–79). Within two days of taking command, Hood attacked Sherman's army at Peachtree Creek. The assault initially made good progress until the Confederate troops became entangled in a series of ravines. Union regiments came up to the edges of the ravines and fired down into the masses of Confederate infantry, and the advance came to a halt. Hood lost nearly 5,000 soldiers for no gain, yet he resumed offensive operations at Decatur 5 miles (8 km) east of Atlanta on July 22 and at Ezra Church, southwest of Atlanta, on July 28. Both assaults failed to stop Sherman from closing in on the city.

Sherman besieged Atlanta, bombarding it with his field artillery and severing the last railroad line into the city. Hood decided to retreat from Atlanta after losing a battle at Jonesboro below the city on August 31. With the way finally cleared, Union soldiers marched into Atlanta on September 2.

Sherman decided that in order to force the South to surrender, it was necessary to undermine both its political will and economic means to continue the fight. On November 15, he burned Atlanta to the ground, then led his army on a march to the key Southern port of Savannah, Georgia. In an orgy of destruction, Sherman's soldiers burned anything they could not plunder along a 40-mile-wide (64-km) strip of Georgia between Atlanta and Savannah, reaching the port on December 21, 1864.

The loss of Atlanta and Savannah was a mortal body blow to the South. For the Confederacy any hope of victory was long past, but its generals continued to fight hoping that

Right: Although Southern troops slowed Sherman's steady march toward Atlanta, they could not prevent the Union forces from capturing the important Confederate city.

by staving off total defeat they might win better peace terms if the North wearied of war.

Although Hood abandoned Atlanta on September 1, he still had 40,000 soldiers under his command, which he used to disrupt the railroad line between Chattanooga, Tennessee, and Atlanta. Sherman relied on this railroad to keep his troops supplied, and accordingly dispatched troops to force Hood back to Alabama. Sherman's march through Georgia to Savannah was only possible because he had left half of his army in Tennessee, under the command of General George Thomas, to contain any threat from Hood.

Nathan Bedford Forrest's (1821–77) Confederate cavalry raided into Tennessee to sever Northern supply lines. After Forrest returned from his hit-and-run campaign, Hood began marching north into Tennessee in the middle of November. Hood's plan was to recapture the state, then march over the Appalachian Mountains to link up with Lee's forces in Virginia. The scheme was far too ambitious, however, and had no chance of success.

Hood crossed over the Tennessee River in Alabama and marched north into Tennessee. He first tried to defeat the Union force commanded by General John Schofield (1831–1906) on November 14. Schofield was under orders from Thomas to delay Hood's march on Nashville. Hood attempted to outflank Schofield but the Union commander withdrew to defensive positions around Franklin, 15 miles (24 km) south of Nashville.

Hood pressed Schofield hard, determined to bring the Union forces to battle. On November 30, 1864, Hood unwisely ordered his troops to attack the well-defended Union force across open ground. Almost 7,000 of the 27,000 Confederate troops who attacked at Franklin were killed or wounded. Among the Confederate dead were six generals and many other senior officers. In contrast, Schofield had 2,300 men killed or wounded out of his force of 32,000.

Left: Together, the battles of Franklin and Nashville in late 1864 ended the hopes of Southern leaders of recapturing Tennessee.

Map labels:
KENTUCKY
Fort Donelson
Fort Henry
Cumberland River
Nashville December 15-16
Franklin November 30
Spring Hill November 29
Murfreesboro
Tennessee River
Columbia
TENNESSEE
Shiloh
Pulaski
MISS.
ALABAMA

X Battles
┼┼┼┼┼ Railroads
0   30 mi
0   50 km

Schofield withdrew his troops from Franklin to Nashville, where they linked up with Thomas, their combined force numbering 60,000 men. Hood had little more than 20,000 soldiers left as he headed for Nashville, which he reached on December 2. The defenses surrounding Nashville were exceptionally strong, and even Hood accepted that any attack would be doomed to failure. But now the net was closing in on the Confederate forces, as Thomas advanced remorselessly toward Nashville.

When Thomas did go onto the offensive, on December 15, the outnumbered Southern troops managed to repel the Union offensive. But this was only a temporary respite, as on the following day Union troops attacked again and broke through the Confederate lines. The Southern army was broken as a coherent fighting force, and Hood was relieved of his command in January 1865.

After the destruction of Hood's army at the Battle of Nashville, the only impediment to a swift and final Union victory was Lee and what remained of the Army of Northern Virginia. Lee's command, although short of all types of supplies, was willing to fight but it faced enormous odds. Union armies were closing in on the Army of Northern Virginia from all directions.

Left: This painting depicts the Battle of Jonesboro on August 31, 1864, the last Southern attempt to stop Sherman's forces from taking Atlanta.

The Union Preserved

Despite being tired and hungry, Confederate soldiers fought on during the spring of 1865, and in fact there were some pockets of very determined resistance by the Southern troops. Nevertheless, the war was nearing its end and even Confederate generals were resigning themselves to the inevitable. In Washington, Northern politicians were beginning to debate about how best to deal with the South after the war.

In February 1865, Jefferson Davis appointed Lee general-in-chief of all Confederate armies. It was to be a short-lived command. At the end of March 1865 Lee realized he could no longer remain in Petersburg, and that the Union siege was close to success. Although withdrawing from the city would mean that Richmond was almost certain to fall, it was a sacrifice that the Confederate commander was prepared to make in order to save what was left of the Army of Northern Virginia.

On February 22, Lee reappointed General Joseph Johnston to command the forces attempting to hold Sherman, who was now advancing through South Carolina. Sherman, however, had occupied Columbia, South Carolina's capital, on February 17, 1865. That night the city was destroyed by fire. Sherman pressed on into North Carolina, aiming to capture the town of Goldsboro. On March 19, at Bentonville, Johnston succeeded in halting the Union advance, but the Confederates could not break the Union line and two days later Johnston was forced to retreat.

Lee's attempt to escape from Petersburg opened with an attack on Fort Stedman, intended to draw away Union troops from the main breakout point. The attempt, however, failed with heavy Confederate losses. Grant, who had over 120,000 men to hand compared to Lee's less than 60,000, was preparing to take the fight directly to the Confederate general-in-chief. The Union commander sent a strong force of two cavalry divisions and an infantry corps, led by General Philip Sheridan, to march to the southwest of Petersburg and block Lee's intended route to the Carolinas.

On April 2, Grant ordered a general assault on Petersburg. All along the line the Union infantrymen clambered out of their trenches and charged toward the Southern defenses. Lee's frontline soldiers fought hard to gain time for an evacuation. The next day the Confederate forces finally abandoned Petersburg, and within hours Union troops entered Richmond. The Confederate capital, which had suffered a great fire while city officials and defenders fled, formally surrendered on April 3, 1865.

Lee's Last Stand

The remnants of the Army of Northern Virginia headed west, and met with the garrison from Richmond at the village of Amelia Springs. On April 5, the Confederates began a race against Sheridan's troops, who were attempting to contain Lee until the arrival of the main Union force. On April 9 near a railroad station called Appomattox Court House, Lee found two Union infantry corps in front of him and two more advancing from the rear. He was trapped. Knowing that further resistance was useless, the Confederate general-in-chief chose to surrender.

Right: In December 1864, outside Fort Fisher, Union and Confederate cavalrymen came to blows. The Confederates were able to hold off the Union troops for a few more weeks but by January 15, 1865, the key fort had fallen.

Later that same day Grant met Lee in a house at Appomattox owned by Wilmer McLean. Ironically, at the start of the war McLean lived near Manassas Junction but his house was damaged during the First Battle of Bull Run, so he moved his family to Appomattox thinking it would be safer.

In McLean's front parlor Grant and Lee set at separate tables and worked out the surrender terms for the Confederate Army of Northern Virginia. Farther south, Sherman accepted Johnston's surrender on April 26, and on May 26, 1865, the last Confederate army to lay down its arms was led by General Edmund Kirby Smith (1824–93).

The great architect of Northern victory, Abraham Lincoln, did not live to see the complete surrender of his Southern foe. On April 14, 1865, while attending a play in Washington, DC, Lincoln was assassinated by a pro-Confederate actor named John Wilkes Booth. Lincoln's opposite number, Jefferson Davis, was captured near Irwinville, Georgia, on May 10 and imprisoned until an early release in 1867.

Troubled Reconstruction

The death of Lincoln was, ironically, a blow to the South in the postwar period. Unlike many of his fellow Northern politicians, Lincoln had hoped to adopt a policy of reconciliation with the former Confederate states. But in 1867–68, Southern intransigence over giving former slaves full legal rights allowed the Northern Republicans to pass the Reconstruction Acts. These acts carved the South into five districts, each of which came under the control of a Union general who had authority over local state legislatures. In 1866 and 1875, the Civil Rights Acts were passed in an attempt to guarantee the freedoms of African-American citizens, especially their right to vote in all elections.

AFRICAN AMERICANS

Although the South did not seriously consider using its African-American slaves as soldiers, they did contribute to the war effort. Without slaves the plantations and farms would not have been able to feed the Confederate armies or provide capital for the purchase of weapons and equipment. African Americans worked with armies in the field fulfilling laboring duties, and they also built the fortifications that protected many of the South's major ports.

The North made use of freed or escaped slaves; about 200,000 "contrabands" (escaped slaves) worked as teamsters, cooks, and laborers with the Northern armies. More significantly, African Americans in the North took part in combat when the Militia Act of July 1862 allowed Lincoln to recruit soldiers from "persons of African descent."

The first African-American soldiers to fight belonged to a Kansas regiment, which was engaged in a skirmish in Missouri in October 1862. But that troop was overshadowed at the time by the two regiments raised by the abolitionist governor of Massachusetts, John Andrew.

One of these regiments, the 54th Massachusetts, led by Robert G. Shaw (1837–63), a young white officer from Boston, gained lasting fame for its attack on Fort Wagner, South Carolina, in July 1863. Many soldiers of the regiment were killed, including Shaw, in a brave but unsuccessful attack, and one of the survivors became the first African American to win the Congressional Medal of Honor. The determination of the 54th Massachusetts did much to convince those in the North that African-American soldiers were fit for more than just garrison duties. African-American units played a part in such key battles as Vicksburg and Nashville. In total, 186,000 African Americans fought in the Union Army during the Civil War, while probably another 20,000 served with the US Navy; about 100 were commissioned officers.

Deeply resentful of the military occupation of their lands, the Southern whites derided the Northern administration as "carpetbaggers" – unscrupulous opportunists who moved to the South with little more than a carpet bag. Southern bitterness was often directed toward former slaves, who were terrorized and prevented from voting and buying property. The Civil War and the Reconstruction era left a lasting legacy of bitterness among many Americans.

The Changing Face of War
1853–1913

The 19th century was an extraordinary and excessively bloody transition period for warfare. In the span of a hundred years, from the Battle of Waterloo in 1815 to the outbreak of World War I, the engagement of military conflicts evolved more quickly and dramatically than during any previous century. As new technological advances became widespread and the Industrial Revolution took hold, changes in artillery, transportation, communication, and shipbuilding completely altered the face of war around the world.

On the whole, the 19th century was a time of colonial expansion by, and increased tension between, the more powerful European nations. Wars raged around the globe, from the Franco-Prussian War in central Europe and the Native American battles on the plains of North America to the Boer Wars in South Africa and the Russo-Japanese War in the north Pacific. Each of these engagements held their own unique mixture of old and new aspects of warfare.

To cope with the increasingly changing face of war, military leaders had to adopt new and innovative strategies and approaches. The most famous and influential proponent of prewar planning was made by a Prussian, Karl von Clausewitz (1780–1831), a veteran of the Napoleonic Wars. In his book, *On War* (1819), he analyzed his own military experiences and attempted to create a methodical approach to warfare in general.

Alfred Thayer Mahan (1840–1914), an American, did for naval warfare what Clausewitz did for land battles. His book *The Influence of Seapower Upon History, 1660–1783*, was used as the basis for discussing the role of navies in the modern world.

The emphasis on strategy, combined with advances in weaponry – from breech-loading rifles to machine guns, and ironclads to submarines – made warfare a more precise and far deadlier affair than ever before.

Right: Perhaps no other single military event sums up 19th-century warfare better than the tragically futile charge of the British Light Brigade during the Crimean War. The enemy's superior weaponry and position along with the arrogant naivete of the British commander resulted in the senseless slaughter of hundreds of courageous cavalrymen.

The Crimean War

The Crimean War was the first substantial conflict between major European powers since 1815. Britain and France put aside their mutual mistrust and took up arms against Russia, who was attempting to spread its influence over the remnants of the Ottoman Empire, especially within Turkey. The war is best remembered for the poor quality of leadership on all sides and for the harsh, disease-ridden conditions of the wounded.

The ostensible origins of the Crimean War (1853–56) lay in Russia's eagerness to extend its influence in the territory surrounding the Black Sea, and in the claims of Czar Nicholas I (1796–1855) to have exclusive rights of protection for Orthodox Christians and Christian holy sites within the Muslim Ottoman Empire, especially those found in Jerusalem. At the same time, the Russians controlled the Black Sea from their base at Sevastopol in the Crimea and wished to secure the Dardanelles, the only sea route from the Black Sea to the Mediterranean.

France and Britain were fearful of this Russian plan of expansion into the Balkans and Mediterranean and supported the Turks, especially after Russian troops marched into the Ottoman-ruled Romanian provinces of Wallachia and Moldavia. Turkey, the seat of the Ottoman Empire, declared war on Russia in October 1853, while Britain and France dispatched naval forces to protect Constantinople, the capital of the Ottoman Empire, and the Dardanelles.

The land battle at Oltenitza, fought on November 4, 1853, went in favor of the Turks, but was followed by the important Russian naval victory at Sinop a few weeks later; in which the Russian fleet smashed the Turks.

The Russians seized the initiative and invaded Ottoman-ruled Bulgaria, laying siege to Silistria. Both

Britain and France declared war on Russia in March 1854, sending a joint army to Varna in Bulgaria. Other European states also felt threatened by Russia's invasion of Bulgaria, and the Austrians sent troops into the Danube River area in readiness to fight the Russians should they continue their advance into the Balkans. In the face of this pressure from the Austrians, the Russians abandoned their siege of Silistria and withdrew completely from Bulgaria in early August.

The Second Phase of the War

Following the Russian withdrawal, the allies – Britain, France, Prussia, and Austria – sent peace proposals to the Russians, which included a guarantee that the Russians would leave the Ottomans alone. The Russians rejected the proposals and the war continued, widening in scope. From then on, the strategy adopted by the French and British centered on the need to destroy Russia's power in the Black Sea, which involved the capture of the port of Sevastopol in the Crimea.

On September 7, 1854, an expedition was sent to the Crimea. It was commanded jointly by the British Lord Fitzroy Raglan (1788–1855), a 66-year-old veteran of the Napoleonic Wars, and the French Armand de Saint-Arnaud (1796–1854), who was seriously ill with cholera at the time.

Right: In this painting, lines of British troops advance against the Russians during the Battle of Alma River on September 20, 1854. After a hard-fought battle, the Russians were finally forced to retreat at the end of the day.

Left: This map indicates the main battle sites of the Crimean War, which had begun, in part, because the Russians wanted to gain control of the Dardanelles, the only access to the Mediterranean from the Black Sea.

from the worst of the winter storms. Two sites were chosen, one at Kamiesch for the French and the other at Balaklava for the British.

Both Kamiesch and Balaklava were to the south of Sevastopol, and to reach the sites the allies had to first march around the port, abandoning their line of retreat to their original landing beaches. Meanwhile, Menshikov marched his new army in pursuit of the allies.

The Siege of Sevastopol

The defenses of Sevastopol, particularly those facing Kamiesch and Balaklava, were far from complete when the siege began in early October 1854. Nevertheless, the allies failed to exploit the advantage and allowed the commander of the engineers building the Russian defenses, Colonel Franz Todleben, time to strengthen his position. The allied siege was also delayed by the death of Saint-Arnaud (September 29), as well as by a lack of necessary engineers and equipment to begin such an operation. Saint-Arnaud's replacement was General François Canrobert (1809–95).

The bombardment of Sevastopol began on October 17, but the allies faced a more pressing task: Menshikov, who had arrived in the area, was attempting to drive a wedge between the allied troops besieging Sevastopol and their main base at Balaklava.

The Battle of Balaklava (October 25) was, in fact, several battles in one. The Russians were able to capture a number of hilltop fortifications held by the Turks but their follow-up cavalry attacks were repulsed by a brilliant charge by the outnumbered British Heavy Brigade and the fire of the 93rd Highlanders, the famous "Thin Red Line."

The next phase of the battle – the charge of the Light Brigade – proved a disaster for the allies. Possibly due to a poorly worded written order, the foolishness of a young officer who identified the wrong Russian position to attack, or the pigheadedness of their commander, Lord James Cardigan (1797–1868), the British Light Brigade advanced up the wrong valley and ended up charging the main Russian Army.

The Russians were arrayed on three sides of the narrow valley through which the brigade charged. As the British cavalrymen advanced, they were first blasted by cannon and then at closer range by rifle fire.

The French and British forces left Varna in a convoy of over 150 warships and landed on the Crimean peninsula at Calamita Bay during the middle of September. Sevastopol lay 30 miles (48 km) from the landing beach and the allies – then comprising 50,000 British, French, and Turkish infantrymen, 128 cannon, and 1,000 British cavalrymen – began their advance toward the city on September 19. At the same time, the Russian commander, Prince Alexander Menshikov (1789–1869), who was also a veteran of the Napoleonic Wars, led his 37,000 troops to oppose the allied army.

The two armies first met along the Alma River on September 20. Menshikov placed his troops along the river bank and on the high ground beyond. When the fighting began the allies were able to cross the river without much difficulty, but the British infantry had to fight hard to push the Russians off the high ground. Despite hard fighting on both sides, the Russians eventually withdrew northward to join up later with reinforcements. In the battle the allies had suffered 3,000 casualties, while the Russians had lost 6,000 men.

With Menshikov out of the way temporarily, the allies were in clear sight of Sevastopol, but seizing the well-fortified city was not going to be straightforward. The Russians had blocked the harbor channel into the port with sunken ships, making allied naval cooperation in an assault on the city impossible.

Before they begin their attack on the city the allies would first need a secure naval base nearby where their heavy artillery could be brought ashore, to provide shelter for their troops, and to act as a safe anchorage

Left: This illustration shows the site of the British artillery used to bombard the Russian defenses surrounding Sevastopol. The siege lasted for nearly a year, from October 1854 until September 1855.

Remarkably the British cavalrymen reached the Russian artillery about a mile away from their start position, but they were then counterattacked by fresh Russian cavalry and forced to retreat back through the same valley and Russian artillery.

Brigade losses were heavy: 673 British officers and men had begun the charge; 247 men did not return, and of those that did many were wounded. In addition, nearly 500 horses were lost. Cardigan himself escaped without a scratch. Only a superb charge by units of French cavalry prevented losses from being even greater during the Light Brigade's retreat. At a stroke the allies had lost one of their finest cavalry formations. As one French general remarked of the charge: "It is magnificent, but it is not war."

Despite the failed charge, the Battle of Balaklava ended in stalemate and the allies held on to Balaklava, but the Russians had captured high ground to the north of the port. Menshikov decided to try for Balaklava again on November 5.

The ensuing Battle of Inkerman was badly directed by generals on both sides who failed to exercise much control. The fighting, mainly between British and Russian infantrymen, lasted most of the day. When the slogging match ended in a narrow allied victory, thanks to the timely arrival of French reinforcements, the British had sustained around 3,000 casualties; the Russians, however, had lost over 10,000 men.

The Impact of Public Opinion

Both sides settled down to ride out the worst of the harsh winter of 1854–55. It was a terrible time for the allies, especially the British. Their supply system was already badly organized and a fierce storm added to their problems by destroying 30 cargo vessels on November 14. The Russians also controlled the only decent road from Balaklava to the siege lines around Sevastopol, so that the allied soldiers there suffered from severe food shortages as their armies had to drag supplies over difficult muddy ground. Most of the allied troops lacked shelter or winter clothing, and to make matters worse, medical facilities were severely limited, so that disease, hunger, and cold killed many soldiers.

Public anger back in Britain, the consequence of reading newspaper reports in *The Times* of the soldiers' suffering, helped remedy matters. The supply system was gradually organized on a more sound footing, and thanks to the outstanding work of Florence Nightingale (1820–1910) and her nurses in the main hospital at Scutari, near Constantinople, medical facilities improved dramatically.

While reinforcements from Sardinia were arriving to support the allies, the first battle of the new year took place on February 17, 1855. The new Russian commander in the Crimea, Prince Michael Gorchakov (1795–1861), ordered his field army to advance against a road and railroad the allies were building from Balaklava to their troops outside Sevastopol. The Battle of Eupatoria was a halfhearted affair, however, and a Turkish force stopped the Russian attack in its tracks.

The allies took heart from this victory and intensified their siege operations. A massive bombardment between April 8–18 smashed much of Sevastopol's defenses. The Russians expected a full-blooded allied assault, but it failed to materialize, a consequence of squabbling between the allied commanders and their governments – an early example of the problems that could arise from telegraphic communication. Canrobert, furious at the failure to prosecute the attack on Sevastopol, resigned, to be replaced by General Aimable Pélissier (1794–1864).

The allies did gain a major advantage on May 24, when a successful operation against Kerch on the eastern seaboard of the peninsula ended the flow of Russian supplies to the Crimea across the Sea of Azov. Around Sevastopol itself the allies resolved their differences and launched a successful attack on the port's outer defenses on June 7.

The allies next turned their attention to attacking two of the key forts protecting Sevastopol: the French attacked the Malakoff and the British assaulted the Redan. At first, the twin operations, conducted on the night of June 17–18, were a complete failure. The French troops launched an uncoordinated assault and were shot to pieces by Russian rifle fire; the British columns were smashed in a deadly crossfire from over 100 Russian cannon. The allies suffered 4,000 casualties; the Russians slightly fewer. The aged British commander, Lord Raglan, died a few days later, and was replaced by General James Simpson.

After the disaster of the night attack, the allies settled down to bombard Sevastopol into submission, in the knowledge that the port was now isolated. The Russian garrison's losses reached over 300 troops a day, and it became obvious that the port would fall if a relief force could not break through. Gorchakov launched part of his field army against 35,000 allied troops holding high ground overlooking a small river on August 16. The fight, known as the Battle of the Traktir Bridge, lasted five hours; Gorchakov was forced to retreat, and the noose tightened around Sevastopol.

The allies planned a second attack on the Malakoff fortress, to commence on September 8. This was preceded by a massive three-day bombardment. At noon on September 8, the French swarmed out of their trenches, less than 30 yards (29 m) from the Malakoff, and captured the fort after some stiff hand-to-hand combat. The British attack on the Redan fortress was, however, halted by the Russians. The French, in the Malakoff, turned the guns on the Redan and the Russian troops defending there fell back. Without the protection provided by the outlying

Malakoff and the Redan forts, Sevastopol could not survive. Gorchakov ordered the port's garrison to be evacuated and its fortifications destroyed.

The war was effectively ended by the fall of Sevastopol, but minor operations dragged on until February 1856, followed by the signing of a peace treaty in March. The cost had been heavy on both sides. Although the total casualties numbered around 250,000, only 70,000 of the allied casualties came from the battlefield. The rest of the soldiers died from disease, hunger, and cold, while half the Russian casualties died from similar causes.

The Treaty of Paris (1856) ratified the peace terms, which guaranteed the integrity of the Ottoman Empire; the self-governing status of Moldavia and Wallachia was accepted; and Russia relinquished its self-styled role as protector of Orthodox Christians within Turkish domains. In effect, little changed as a result of the war. The Crimea did, however, mark a turning point in one respect. Henceforth, European armies paid closer attention to the well-being of their soldiers. The provision of food, clothing, shelter, and medical aid became central to war planning.

Right: *The Russian troops (left) attempt to defend the Malakoff fortress protecting Sevastopol against the French (right). This early use of trench warfare proved victorious for the French.*

The Indian Mutiny

By the mid-1800s the British had ruled India for a century, yet their position was more tenuous than they admitted. Up until then they had allowed parts of India to be governed by rival kings in order to prevent a united Indian force. They had also built up an army with seven times as many Indian as European troops. But in 1857, an incident at an army garrison sparked an uprising that almost ended British rule.

Disquiet between Indians and the British within the garrison of Meerut had been simmering for some time. British officers often treated their sepoys (local Indian soldiers) poorly, and, to make matters worse, a rumor developed among the sepoys that the British had introduced a new paper rifle cartridge, called a Minié, which was covered in grease made from either cow or pig fat to protect it from moisture. Before the paper cartridge could be used it had to be bitten open. But cows were sacred to Hindus and pigs were considered "unclean" by Muslims.

On May 10, 1857, more than 80 of the Meerut sepoys refused to use the Minié cartridges, and were imprisoned for disobeying orders. Outraged at their treatment, fellow sepoys released the 80 soldiers, and then together they attacked their British officers and wives while they were attending Sunday prayers. In this, the first of many atrocities committed by both sides, most of the Europeans were killed before the sepoys headed for Delhi, some 25 miles (40 km) away.

The Indian troops in Delhi and many local civilians joined the Meerut sepoys, declaring the Mughal ruler Bahadur Shah (1775–1862) as their leader. Many Europeans in Delhi were killed, but a few found sanctuary in the British compound outside the city, before fleeing to Meerut and Umballa. The news of the uprising spread across India and similar revolts occurred from Delhi in the north to Calcutta in the east, roughly the area around the whole of the Ganges River.

The British responded by sending a force of about 3,000 men toward Delhi, but their numbers were too few to have any immediate hope of recapturing the city. Although the mutiny never had real chance of eradicating the British from India, the fighting spread and other British garrisons were besieged by the rebels. At Lucknow, Sir Henry Lawrence (1806–57) had just 1,720 men, including 712 loyal sepoys, to protect the town and over 1,200 noncombatants. Sir Hugh Wheeler at Cawnpore had only a handful of troops to protect his 200 civilians.

Cawnpore was besieged by the rebels for three weeks and Wheeler, seeing no hope of relief, agreed to surrender terms in late June. On June 27 his garrison and the noncombatants, mostly British women and children, marched out with a promise of safe passage to Allahabad. They never reached safety, however. While the refugees were embarking on boats, the rebels opened fire, killing many of the Europeans. The women survivors and their children were imprisoned but then murdered on July 15, their bodies thrown down a well.

Left: The Indian Mutiny lasted from 1857 until 1858 and came close to ending British rule in India. This map shows the sites of the major battles during rebellion.

Left: British forces raze the Kashmir Gate leading into Delhi, which had been held by the mutineers since May 1857. The British siege to reclaim the city began on September 14, 1857, and lasted a further six days before they were finally able to defeat the Indian mutineers.

Sir Henry Havelock (1795–1857) at the head of 2,500 troops marched to the relief of Lucknow in early July. In nine days (July 7–16) Havelock traveled 125 miles (200 km) and defeated the rebels in three engagements. The last of these saw the British retake Cawnpore. Inside the city they found the butchered remains of the European prisoners at the bottom of the well. The British vented their fury, slaughtering many Indians, rebels or not. Havelock waited for reinforcements to arrive at Cawnpore before resuming his march on Lucknow on September 20.

End of Mughal Hopes

The British won a notable victory at Delhi on the same day. The initial force of 3,000 men attacking the city had captured some key high ground on June 8, but had to wait for heavy artillery and infantry reinforcements before attacking Delhi's great walls. Some 4,000 British troops stormed the walls on September 14, although it took a week to clear the city. Bahadur Shah was captured and executed. The fall of Delhi was a major blow to the rebels, but the fighting continued.

Attention now focused on Lucknow. On September 25, Havelock managed to cut a path through the 60,000 Indian besiegers to the city but in the process lost a quarter of his men. Havelock and the garrison lacked sufficient numbers to defeat the rebels, and the siege dragged on. During the fall of 1857 many of the garrison began to die from hunger, disease, and exhaustion. A second British relief force from Cawnpore under Sir Colin Campbell (1792–1863) arrived outside Lucknow on November 14, but had been forced back to Cawnpore the following week.

The British at Cawnpore under Campbell spent months waiting for reinforcements before mounting an expedition to drive the rebels out of Lucknow. The main addition to Campbell's command were 10,000 Gurkha soldiers from Nepal, highly professional mercenaries who fought for the British. After a week of bitter fighting, Campbell's forces recaptured Lucknow on March 16, 1858.

The first three months of 1858 also saw British forces under Sir Hugh Rose (1801–85) regain control of central India. Rose inflicted two defeats on the mutineers in February and March. He then advanced on the city of Jhansi, a center of rebellion, and placed it under siege. Rose defeated a rebel force of 20,000 on April 1 and captured the city two days later.

Rebel forces were defeated by Rose on several other occasions but his decisive victory came at Gwalior on June 19. Of the two rebel leaders present, one, the female Rani of Jhansi, was killed and the other, Tantia Topi (1810–59), fled. Topi was captured and executed on April 18, 1859, but by then the Indian Mutiny was already over. This ensured that British rule in India would continue into the next century.

Italy's Wars of Unification

By the mid-19th century, the Italian peninsula consisted of a number of independent states and kingdoms ruled in name by monarchs but actually controlled by the Austro-Hungarian Empire. Some Italians, however, wanted to end the Austro-Hungarian domination and replace the separate states with a strong, unified, and independent country. The movement for a united Italy was known as the Risorgimento.

In 1831 Giuseppe Mazzini (1805–72) formed a group called Young Italy, which aspired to educating and inspiring Italians to rise up against the reactionary rule of many local monarchs and the foreign domination of the Austro-Hungarian Empire. These ideals were later embodied in the Risorgimento (literally, "rise again") movement, and for the next two decades there were a few minor skirmishes, most of which were silenced quickly by the Austrians. Despite the defeats, the feeling of Italian nationalism had grown, and in 1848 the movement united behind the leadership of King Charles Albert (1798–1849) of Sardinia. The king's main possession on the peninsula was Piedmont, bordering France and northern Italy, which became the geographical focus of the unification movement. The enthusiasm demonstrated by the Italian nationalists initially caught the Austrians by surprise, and they were forced to withdraw into the "quadrilateral" of fortresses in northern Italy, which were found at Mantua, Verona, Peschiera, and Legnago.

However, the Austrians recovered quickly and under the command of Field Marshal Joseph Radetsky (1766–1858), who had been called out of retirement, they defeated an Italian army at the Battle of Custoza on July 23–25, 1848. The Italian city states that had supported the Risorgimento began to slip away soon after as Radetsky's army marched through northern Italy. The final blow to the uprising came with the defeat of the main Piedmontese Army at Novarra on March 23, 1849. The loss forced the abdication of Charles Albert in favor of his son, Victor Emmanuel II (1820–78), who was made to accept harsh Austrian peace terms.

Although the Italian uprising of 1848–49 had achieved little, it had drawn the French into the region. Under the adventurist leadership of Louis Napoleon (1808–73) – Napoleon III from 1852 onward – the French were keen to increase their influence in Italy, especially at the expense of their Austrian rivals. During the fighting, a French force had landed to secure the Papal States (centered around Rome) under the pretext of protecting the pope specifically and Catholic interests in general. Although the French were forced to withdraw at the conclusion of hostilities, they remained determined to gain a greater influence in Italian affairs.

In March 1859, Piedmont allied with France to try again to expel Austria from northern Italy. The plan was that Piedmont would become the dominant power in Italy, while France would receive the border territories of Savoy and Nice. The war that followed was best remembered for the battles of Magenta (June 4) and Solferino (June 24) in northern Italy. As a consequence of indifferent leadership, both sides suffered heavy casualties, although the French eventually prevailed. At Solferino, one civilian observer, the Swiss Jean Henri Dunant (1828–1910), was so horrified by the suffering of the wounded that he later founded the Red Cross.

Right: The French adventurer Emperor Napoleon III watches his troops as they advance on the Austro-Hungarian forces at Solferino, 1859. The French won the day-long battle, but in so doing nearly 40,000 soldiers from both sides were either killed or wounded.

After the defeat of the Austrians at Solferino, the French became fearful of a united Italy and suddenly backtracked from the original plan. While assigning the Lombardy region to Piedmont, the ensuing Peace of Zurich allowed Austria to retain Venetia, the area around Venice. This move outraged many Italian patriots, who were determined to carry on the war.

On May 11, 1860, a group of Italian nationalists, the "Thousand Redshirts" – so called because of their distinctive red shirts – led by one of Mazzini's followers, Giuseppe Garibaldi (1807–82), landed on the island of Sicily, part of the independent Kingdom of Naples. Garibaldi had the tacit backing of Victor Emmanuel II and Piedmont's premier, Camillo di Cavour (1810–61). The Redshirts routed the Neapolitan troops on the island, and using Sicily as a secure base, Garibaldi sailed to the Italian mainland on August 22.

The Redshirts captured Naples on September 7. Piedmont then invaded the Papal States. Garibaldi laid siege to the Neapolitan port of Gaeta, which fell on February 13, 1860, after which the Kingdom of Naples surrendered. A united Italy was proclaimed on March 17, 1861. The Papal States, however, were once again occupied by the French, and Venetia remained in Austrian hands. Garibaldi tried to incorporate the Papal States into Italy, but the new government was fearful of upsetting the French, who were determined that the pope should wield authority over his traditional domain. Consequently, Italian forces loyal to the government attacked and defeated Garibaldi in August 1862.

Above: On May 6, 1860, Garibaldi's Italian nationalists, numbering around 1,000, embarked on boats at the northern Italian port of Genoa to begin their journey to Sicily. Garibaldi went on to take the island in what was the first stage of his unification campaign.

Garibaldi made another attempt to bring the Papal States under Italian control in 1866, after a temporary French withdrawal from Rome. He did not have the backing of the Italian government, however, and his attempt failed. Refusing to be discouraged, Garibaldi tried again in 1867, but was severely defeated by the French at the Battle of Mentana on November 3 and captured (although freed soon after). This last defeat brought Garibaldi's campaigns in Italy to a close.

The Austrians relinquished Venetia in 1866, as a consequence of their defeat by the Prussians in the Seven Weeks War. Italy had prudently allied itself with Prussia, and although Italian forces had been defeated by the Austrians on land at the Battle of Custoza (June 24), and at sea at the Battle of Lissa (July 20), Italy received Venetia as a consequence of the Treaty of Vienna, which concluded the war.

Rome did eventually become part of an independent Italy in 1870, when the French withdrew their garrison as a result of the French declaration of war against Prussia. A 60,000-strong Italian army took the city on September 20. Less than two weeks later Rome was formerly incorporated into Italy, becoming its capital. The wars of unification were finally over, and Italy was no longer, as one wit had put it, merely a "geographical expression," but a new nation-state.

Prussia's Rise to Power

By the mid-19th century Prussia was the most ambitious of all the German states, and was at odds with many of them, including the Austro-Hungarian Empire. Before going to war with Austria, Prussia decided to gain of control over the German–Danish province of Schleswig-Holstein. In 1848 it had failed to take the province, but in 1864 Prussia was better prepared, quickly capturing and annexing the province.

The following year the Prussian political leader, Count Otto von Bismarck (1815–98), provoked a crisis with Austria, which had objected to the occupation of Schleswig-Holstein. Several other German states, fearing Prussia's growing power, supported Austria.

In June 1866, Prussia declared war on Austria and its allies in Germany, primarily Bavaria, Hanover, and Saxony. Italy, in an alliance with Prussia, also declared war on Austria. Although the Italians were defeated on land and at sea, they succeeded in tying down many Austrian troops south of the Alps.

What followed, the Austro-Prussian War, also known as the Seven Weeks War, was a Prussian triumph. It seemed to justify Bismarck's political maneuverings and his faith in General Helmuth Karl von Moltke (1800–91), chief of the Prussian General Staff.

Three Prussian armies marched through Silesia and Saxony to attack Austrian troops, while a smaller Prussian force of 50,000 men, under General Ernst Vogel von Falkenstein (1797–1885), defeated the Hanoverian Army at Langensalza (June 27–29).

In southeast Germany, Moltke used the railroad and telegraph to coordinate the movement of his three main armies. The Prussian Army of the Elbe and the First Army linked up and cut through advance elements of the main Austrian force at Münchengrätz on June 27 and Gitschin on June 29. The Second Prussian Army also won a victory at Nachod on June 27 and then pushed on toward Gitschin.

The combined Prussian armies of 220,000 men now sought to bring the main Austrian force to battle at Königgrätz. The battle was fought on July 3, but did not run smoothly for the Prussians in the opening stages. Their attacks were met by a ferocious Austrian response. Confusion over the deployment of the Army of the Elbe and the First Army was eventually resolved, however, and Moltke ordered the Second Army to advance to their aid. The Second Army attacked the northern section of the Austrian line in the early afternoon. The Prussians then pounded the center of the Austrian position, forcing them to withdraw. The Austrians had 45,000 casualties; the Prussians 10,000.

Königgrätz ensured an overall Prussian victory, and the Treaty of Prague, signed on August 23, 1866, made Prussia the head of a new North German Confederation containing all the German states north of the Main River. Austria, on the other hand, was forbidden from meddling in German affairs.

The Franco-Prussian War

In early 1870 Emperor Napoleon III (1808–73) and the French government became alarmed when Bismarck

---

INFANTRY FIREPOWER

The 19th century was dominated by the increase in infantry firepower. In the second quarter of the century, infantry weapons were improved first by the replacement of the flintlock by the more reliable percussion system; second by rifling, which increased both range and accuracy.

The Minié rifle fired a conical bullet whose hollow base expanded after firing to grip the rifling in the barrel. It was the dominant infantry weapon in the 1850s and 1860s. The breech-loader was a further improvement: the Dreyse needle-gun used a firing pin to strike a primer at the base of the bullet. This weapon could be fired twice as fast as the Minié – about seven rounds per minute.

The introduction of metallic cartridges in the 1880s further increased infantry firepower, as they made possible the production of magazine-fed, bolt-action rifles, such as the German Mauser, French Lebel, and British Lee-Metford. The result was an average rate of fire of 10–15 rounds per minute on the battlefield.

Left: Helmuth Karl von Moltke completely overhauled Prussia's military structure, including transforming the General Staff so that military campaigns would be planned and organized down to the smallest detail long before the fighting ever began.

tried to place a member of the Prussian (Hohenzollern) royal family on the Spanish throne. The French believed that with Hohenzollerns on both the Spanish and Prussian thrones they could face a war on two fronts in the near future. On July 15, 1870, France declared war on Prussia. Several German states – Baden, Bavaria, and Württemberg – sided with Prussia a day later.

Moltke had been preparing for war against France for some time. The Prussian mobilization plans, which involved the movement of hundreds of thousands of troops by railroad to the border with France, ran smoothly. The French mobilization, by contrast, was haphazard, slow, and incomplete. The Prussians had also been able to discover the complete order of battle of the French armed forces, a vital advantage in the deployment of the Prussian armies.

During the last week of July, three Prussian armies totalling close to 400,000 men amassed on the French border. The First Army, 60,000-strong, was deployed between Trier and Saarbrücken; 175,000 troops of the Second Army were concentrated around Bingen and Mannheim; and the Third Army (145,000 men) was stationed between Landau and Germersheim.

At the start only 220,000 French troops, commanded by the emperor and his war minister, Marshal Edmond Leboeuf (1809–88), were available for action. These were divided into eight army corps strung along the frontier and at fortresses near the border.

The first battle took place at Saarbrücken on August 2. It was a minor affair but led to the reorganization of the French command. The eight army corps were consolidated into two bigger commands: the Army of Alsace led by Marshal Marie MacMahon (1808–93) and the Army of Lorraine under Marshal Achille Bazaine (1811–88), although neither army possessed a regular staff to oversee operations.

While these changes were taking place, the Prussian Third Army surprised part of MacMahon's forces at the Battle of Weissenburg on August 4. The French were outnumbered and after losing 1,500 men pulled back to a better defensive position. The Prussians did not allow MacMahon to build up his strength, however. On August 6, the Prussian Third Army attacked at Fröschwiller. The French, numbering just 45,000 men, fought stubbornly. Heroic charges by MacMahon's cavalry held up the Prussians, but by nightfall the French were in retreat, heading for Châlons-sur-Marne, which they reached on the 14th. French casualties amounted to 17,000, while the Prussians lost about 10,000 men.

Meanwhile, the Prussian First and Second armies had been ordered to attack Bazaine's Army of Lorraine. The Army of Lorraine was dispersed among three widely separated groups, unable to provide mutual aid if attacked. The first French forces to be attacked were the 30,000 men under General Charles Frossard holding the high ground at Spicheren. On August 6, the Prussians tried to surround the French as increasing numbers of Prussian troops arrived on the battlefield. Bazaine was unwilling to support Frossard and, to avoid encirclement, the French withdrew.

Moltke was generally pleased with the way the campaign was developing; his armies had won several battles and the French were

Left: In the Seven Weeks War, 1866, of which the sites of battles are shown on this map, the Prussian military machine was far superior to that of its old rival, Austria.

THE CHASSEPOT RIFLE

The French Army in the Franco-Prussian War was equipped with the breech-loading Chassepot rifle, named after the French official responsible for its development. The weapon was the most advanced of its day, and outclassed the older Dreyse rifle carried by the Prussians.

The Chassepot had a better firing mechanism than the Dreyse, which allowed French troops to fire more rapidly than their Prussian counterparts. It also fired a lighter bullet, so French troops could carry more rounds into action.

Despite these advantages, the Chassepot did suffer from a number of problems. The barrel rapidly became fouled with gunpowder and had to be frequently cleaned; its ammunition deteriorated quickly, especially in damp conditions; and the vicious recoil made accurate fire difficult. But perhaps the greatest problem for the French lay in the fact that many French troops had little experience of the weapon before the war began, and standards of marksmanship were often poor.

in retreat along the entire front. Moltke then ordered his three armies to push deeper into France. The Third Army chased after MacMahon. While the First and Second armies pursued Bazaine, their main aim was to prevent Bazaine's and MacMahon's armies from linking up with each other.

The Prussian Second Army caught up with Bazaine on the 16th at Mars-la-Tour. Without waiting for the bulk of his forces to reach the battlefield, the army commander, Prince Friedrich Karl (1828–85), attacked the French in the knowledge that the rest of the army would hear the fighting and rush to his aid. The cavalry of both sides launched a series of ferocious assaults against each other in the afternoon. Friedrich Karl's other units gradually reached the battlefield and he felt able to order an all-out onslaught against the French. By nightfall both sides had suffered around 17,000 casualties, and both camped on the battlefield.

Bazaine did not expect help to arrive, and, fearful of resuming the battle, he withdrew his 115,000 men toward the fortress at Metz. This maneuver, however, cut off Bazaine from Paris. In effect, the Prussians had surrounded the Army of Lorraine, and Moltke now ordered that Bazaine's troops be forced from the high ground they were occupying between the villages of Gravelotte and St. Privat to the west of Metz before being sealed up inside the city. The two villages became the focus of some of the most bitter fighting of the war.

On August 18, Moltke ordered the attack on Bazaine's forces between Gravelotte and St. Privat. The Prussian Second Army on the left began the assault. The

village of St. Privat was the focal point of the first round of combat. The Prussians launched over 10,000 men against the French garrison from early morning to nightfall. The French were finally forced to retreat from St. Privat in the face of this Prussian onslaught.

While the fight for St. Privat was raging, a second battle was being fought for Gravelotte on the Prussian right. The Prussian attack got bogged down in a ravine and came close to collapse in the face of determined French resistance. Had Bazaine ordered a counterattack it is possible that the Prussians would have retired, but the French commander did nothing, giving the Prussians time to reorganize their forces. The loss of St. Privat, and the subsequent exploitation by the Prussian Guard and Saxon corps, made the French position untenable. Bazaine retired behind the fortifications of Metz, then the Prussians laid siege to the city.

With Bazaine bottled up in Metz, the Prussians moved to deal with MacMahon's forces. MacMahon had been at Châlons since August 14 and was ordered to march to Bazaine's aid on the 21st. His army, accompanied by Napoleon III, moved north, hoping to swing east toward Metz. This maneuver left him wide open to attack. Moltke ordered the First and part of the Second armies to keep up the pressure on Metz, while sending the Third Army and the rest of the Second, known as the Army of the Meuse, to engage MacMahon.

The Army of the Meuse fought two battles against MacMahon's forces, at Nouart on August 29 and at Beaumont a day later. These battles forced MacMahon farther away from Metz. A third battle, at Bazeilles on the 31st, saw the French forces pushed into a wide bend in the Meuse River at Sedan. Once again, the Prussians had been able to cut off a large French army from Paris.

The Battle of Sedan, fought on September 1, 1870, was a catastrophe for the French. MacMahon, who had been wounded at Bazeilles, was replaced by General Auguste Ducrot. The new commander was in an almost impossible situation: his army had the Meuse at its back and was facing over 200,000 Prussian troops advancing from the north, west, and south. The French had to break out of the ensuing trap.

Ducrot launched his cavalrymen against the Prussians but they were shattered by rifle fire. Prussian artillery, consisting of over 400 field pieces, pounded Sedan from the high ground circling the city. German cavalry was thrown back by fire from the newly developed Mitrailleuse machine guns, but time was running out for the French. By late afternoon the French had retreated into Sedan.

The battle was over but Ducrot's replacement, Emmanuel de Wimpffen, tried to persuade Napoleon to lead one last attack. Napoleon, believing such an action to be pointless, refused, and left the walls of Sedan under a white flag to surrender personally to Wilhelm I (1797–1888), the Prussian king. Wimpffen followed, leading 83,000 French soldiers into captivity. Over

15,000 Frenchmen were killed, wounded, or missing; the Prussians lost 9,000 men.

With one half of the French Army defeated at Sedan and the other half under siege at Metz, the way was open to Paris, the war seemingly over. But in Paris, a popular uprising overthrew the Napoleon's government and replaced it with the Third Republic. The republic's president, General Jules Trochu, was determined to defend the French capital. He hastily mobilized what was left of France's armed forces. Some 120,000 ex-soldiers were gathered together, along with 80,000 *gardes mobiles* (young recruits) and 300,000 *gardes nationales* (older reserves). Although they were no match for the Prussians in battle, in manning Paris's extensive fortifications they were a powerful force.

Moltke had no intention of launching costly assaults against the Parisian defenses and ordered his forces to lay siege to the capital. The Prussians were, however, stretched dangerously thin. They were engaged in two large sieges (Metz and Paris), their lines of communication with Prussia were under attack from bands of French *francs-tireurs* (guerrillas), and the Third Republic government, based in the city of Tours, was raising new field armies in the French provinces.

To the relief of the Prussians, Metz fell on October 27. Bazaine and more than 170,000 French troops surrendered after enduring a siege lasting 54 days. After securing Metz, Prussian troops marched into the valleys of the Loire River and its tributaries to take on the new French Army of the Loire, which was preparing to march to Paris. Operations were inconclusive, however, and dragged on throughout the winter.

On November 9 the French won the Battle of Coulmiers, which forced the Prussians to withdraw from the city of Orléans, although the Prussians responded by retaking Orléans on December 4. In northern France a French army led by General Louis Faidherbe (1818–89) also caused problems for the Prussian invaders. Faidherbe fought a drawn battle with the Prussians at Halluin on December 23 and at the two-day Battle of Bapaume on January 2–3, 1871. Although he was defeated at St. Quentin on the 19th, his army was able to escape to fight another day.

Another French army heading for Belfort arrived outside the fortress in mid-February. Although the French troops consisted of 150,000 men, they were inexperienced and defeated by the 60,000-strong force of Prussians on January 15–17. The Prussians rushed a relief army to Belfort and forced the French south toward Switzerland, leaving the garrison isolated. Pinned against the border, the French commander crossed into Switzerland with 83,000 men, who were then interned by the Swiss.

On January 26, 1871, the Paris garrison made a final attack to smash through the Prussian siege lines. This failed and Trochu agreed to an armistice with the Prussians. Paris surrendered to the Prussians on January 28. The regular French troops and *gardes mobiles* in the capital were made prisoner and the city's forts were turned over to the Prussians.

Only Belfort continued to resist. In a superb instance of defensive warfare, the garrison commander, Colonel Pierre Denfert-Rochereau, held out until February 15, when he was finally ordered to surrender by the French authorities. The siege had lasted for over 100 days, one of the few bright spots in a war that had gone disastrously wrong for the French.

The Treaty of Frankfurt that formally ended the war was harsh on France, which was forced to surrender its border provinces of Alsace and Lorraine, and to pay massive reparations. The Germans maintained an army of occupation in France until the money was paid, and did not complete their evacuation until September 1883.

Left: The Franco-Prussian War witnessed vast battles and some of the greatest loss of life since the Napoleonic Wars – in fact, it was the most important European war between 1815 and 1914. The war, which spread from the Rhine to west of Paris, forced the end of France's Second Empire and left Prussia as the strongest military power in Europe.

Naval Warfare Transformed

Although following the Battle of Trafalgar, in 1805, there were no major battles between fleets, naval warfare underwent drastic changes in the 1800s. New construction materials, various types of mechanical power, and devastating new weapons heralded the end of the wooden warships. And smaller warships were being introduced, which by the turn of the century threatened the role of the large battleships.

Gradually throughout the 1800s, and even more so during the last half of the century, the old wooden, sail-powered warships began to be replaced with iron – later steel – steam-driven battleships.

At first, the old wooden ships-of-the-line were simply clad in iron sheeting for greater protection, while keeping their sails as the sole means of propulsion. The next stage of development saw the emergence of ships with all-iron hulls and steam engines, although sails were still used for auxiliary purposes.

Sails were eventually abandoned as engines became more reliable. The first true ironclad warship was the French frigate *Gloire* (1859), which was followed by the Royal Navy's battleship *Warrior*, launched in Britain in 1860. The first battleship to dispense with sail power altogether was the British *Devastation*, designed in 1869.

Warships were also transformed by developments in weaponry. The old wooden ships had cannon arranged in broadsides on either side, as did many of the first ironclad vessels. The true revolution in naval artillery came with the revolving turret, which was first used in action by the USS *Monitor* at the Battle of Hampton Roads, in 1862,

during the American Civil War. The enclosed and deck-mounted turret could revolve, allowing the battleship's guns to fire in virtually any direction.

The muzzle-loading, smooth-bored cannons were replaced by new breech-loading rifled guns. Gunpowder was superseded by the more reliable and more powerful cordite charge (a smokeless explosive made from cellulose nitrate and nitroglycerine). Cannon balls proved useless against thick iron or steel sheets and were rejected in favor of the conical high-explosive shell, designed to penetrate most armored ship plates.

Although the newer battleships had far fewer guns than the old ships-of-the-line, they were more accurate and had a far longer range. As a consequence, naval battles no longer took place at ranges of a few hundred yards (or meters), but could be fought out over much greater distances, which by the end of the 19th century were measured in thousands of yards.

The late 1800s also saw the gradual introduction of a new and devastating weapon, the underwater torpedo. The best of a number of torpedo designers was an Englishman, Robert Whitehead (1823–1905), whose first

Left: The Battle of Lissa, depicted here, which took place in the Adriatic in 1866, saw the Austrian fleet defeat a superior Italian navy. Although both sides had ironclads, the Italians had more modern guns attached to theirs. The reason the Austrians won is that they rammed the Italian ships. As a result, navies equipped with ironclads continued to use ramming, as they had for centuries with wooden warships, until naval guns increased in accuracy, preventing such close contact between enemy vessels.

design was built in 1866. These early torpedoes were fired from surface vessels, and were responsible for the development of a new type of warship, the torpedo boat.

Torpedo boats were made to be speedy vessels and carried a number of torpedo tubes. They were considered such a threat to the bigger wooden and ironclad battleships that a new warship was developed to counter them. This vessel was the destroyer (originally the torpedo-boat destroyer), and it was a fast, gun- and torpedo-armed warship. The first such destroyer, Britain's *Havock*, was launched in 1893.

The torpedo proved most effective, however, when combined with a new type of vessel, the submarine, which could travel underwater. The first successful submarines were designed by an American, J. P. Holland (1840–1914), and these "Holland" boats were used by the US and British navies. Key technical innovations at the end of the 1800s made the modern submarine possible. First was the development of an internal-combustion engine small enough to be fitted into a submarine and used to power it on the surface. Second was the electric motor, powered by batteries, which, because it did not require a supply of air, allowed the submarine to travel underwater for longer distances.

The transition from sail to steam power dictated that a warship's range was restricted to how much coal (and later oil) it could carry at one time. Consequently, the major powers with large navies acquired refueling stations at strategic points around the world. Britain, the leading sea power in the 19th century, struck deals with local rulers or established major naval bases in British colonies, from Singapore to the Falkland Islands, where warships could take on coal.

In the 1890s the backbone of a modern fleet was the battleship (12,000–15,000 tons), relatively slow but heavily armored and equipped with heavy guns. Below the battleship was the cruiser (7,000–12,000 tons), a ship capable of independent action, faster than a battleship but less heavily armored and equipped with lighter guns. The light cruiser (2,000–4,000 tons) was used as a reconnaissance vessel, while the destroyer (300–600 tons) became a workhorse vessel capable of carrying out a variety of tasks.

Nearing the turn of century, as the industrial nations became wealthier and more efficient at shipbuilding, their rivalry among each other in terms of fleet size and strength intensified. In 1883 Britain had 41 battleships compared to 33 for France, Russia, and Prussia combined. By 1897, however, the margin had narrowed greatly, and by the early 1900s Britain's naval supremacy was under real threat, especially from Germany, which was capable of building ships faster than Britain.

Yet in 1906 Britain regained the high ground by launching *Dreadnought*, which became the model of the modern battleship. *Dreadnought* was turbine-driven, making it as fast as cruisers, more heavily armored than any other vessel at that time, and armed with 10 large guns mounted in five turrets.

Germany quickly began production of their own Dreadnoughts, planning to build 16 between 1908 and 1911. In the years leading up to 1914, Britain and Germany were locked in an aggressive naval race where each side was building stronger and faster ships, so that at the start of World War I between them Germany and Britain had 33 Dreadnoughts in service and a further 19 under construction, transforming naval warfare forever.

Native American Wars

From the end of the Civil War until the 1890s, there were almost continuous clashes between several Native American tribes and the US Army. The conflict stemmed from the ever-increasing numbers of white settlers colonizing tribal lands and hunting grounds in the West. The ensuing battles usually consisted of hit-and-run raids by the tribes involved, who were in turn pursued by US cavalry.

The US Army became embroiled in a campaign in Wyoming and southern Montana in 1866–67. The Sioux, Cheyenne, and Arapaho tribes opposed the building of new forts along the Bozeman Trail, which ran through the Rocky Mountains and passed through lands that had been reserved for the Native Americans by treaty. The fighting became known as Red Cloud's War, after a Sioux chief. Red Cloud (1822–1909) besieged forts Reno, Phil Kearny, and C. F. Smith, and then annihilated a cavalry force led by Captain William Fetterman (1833–66) on December 21, 1866. On August 2, 1867, a Sioux war party led by Red Cloud attacked woodcutters near Fort Phil Kearny and was driven off by soldiers armed with repeating firearms.

Red Cloud's War ended with the Treaty of Fort Laramie, signed in April 1868. Red Cloud promised to relinquish all warlike activity, while the US authorities abandoned their forts and restricted the movement of white settlers. But this was only a temporary setback in the white settlers' relentless drive westward.

NATIVE AMERICANS IN BATTLE

The traditional weapons carried by most Native Americans were the bow and arrow, long lance, club, tomahawk, and knife. Steel-bladed tomahawks and knives were often bartered from Europeans in exchange for animal hides. Some Native Americans also used shields for protection.

As the Native Americans came into contact with white traders, they began to acquire a range of firearms. Initially these were often old weapons, but eventually they fought with shotguns, hunting rifles, revolvers, and military carbines. Some weapons were taken from the dead after a battle or skirmish, while others were actually given to Native Americans by the US government for hunting.

Most Native Americans in the Midwest, Rockies, and Southwest fought on horseback, although they did sometimes fight on foot. Native American warriors were highly skilled in horsemanship and the use of their weapons, but they were no match for the superior numbers, discipline, organization, and technology of the US Army.

During the mid-1870s, the Sioux and Cheyenne together declared war on white settlers who had moved into the Black Hills, a sacred area to both tribes. The uprising was led by Crazy Horse (1842–77) and Sitting Bull (1831–90), both Sioux chiefs.

In early 1876, the US sent General George Crook (1829–90) to orchestrate a campaign against the uprising. On March 17, at the head of 800 cavalry, Crook surprised Crazy Horse at Slim Buttes, his winter camp, on the Powder River. After a good start, Crook was eventually forced to retreat.

Crook was then relieved of overall command, although he remained involved in the campaign. General Alfred Terry was brought in to take charge, and he sent two columns of soldiers into the Black Hills to link up with Crook. On June 17, Crook's men stumbled into Crazy Horse and about 5,000 warriors. Crook was outnumbered by five-to-one but the outcome of the Battle of the Rosebud, a creek flowing into the Yellowstone River, was undecided.

Crazy Horse withdrew to avoid being trapped, while Crook fell back to reorganize his battered command. Terry, however, knew nothing of Crook's battle and sent Lieutenant-Colonel George Custer and his 600-strong cavalry south to place themselves behind the Sioux.

Custer caught up with Crazy Horse along the Little Bighorn River. He should have waited for the rest of Terry's forces to catch up with him, but the publicity-seeking Custer attacked on June 25. He made a fateful error by dividing his small command into three groups in the face of a much larger enemy. Custer led 212 of his men into the center of Crazy Horse's warriors and was wiped out, while the two other columns had to fight alone for two days until Terry arrived. The Battle of the Little Bighorn was the greatest disaster suffered by the US Army during the Native American Wars.

Flight of the Nez Percé
In 1877, the US authorities also had to deal with the Nez Percé under Chief Joseph (1840–1904), probably the finest Native American military leader. The Nez Percé were ordered to leave their homeland in Oregon for a reservation near Lapwai (now Lewiston), Idaho. Chief Joseph eventually agreed to the move, but some white settlers were killed by a group of Nez Percé warriors and a cavalry detachment was sent by General Oliver

Left: This map indicates the sites of the major battles and confrontations between US troops and Native Americans in the second part of the 19th century.

The Elusive Geronimo

In the 1880s the US Army launched a campaign against the Apache in Arizona and New Mexico. The key Apache leader was Geronimo (1829–1909), who saw that his outnumbered forces could not hope to defeat the US through conventional means. Geronimo resorted to guerrilla warfare using hit-and-run tactics to strike at places where the army was weakest and avoid large detachments of troops.

Geronimo raided in Arizona and New Mexico, although he was forced to surrender to Crook on two occasions, but Geronimo managed to escape both times. After the second escape in March 1886, the army sent Miles to eliminate the uprising. Geronimo had a small band of warriors to protect more than 100 women and children. Miles, by comparison, had some 5,000 troops and 500 Native American scouts under his command.

Despite the odds, Geronimo eluded every attempt by Miles to capture him. For over five months, he crisscrossed Arizona and New Mexico, always one step ahead of the US Army. Geronimo was never defeated in the field but chose to surrender on September 4, 1886.

Howard (1830–1909) to round up the whole tribe. Chief Joseph and his warriors fought back with great skill, virtually destroying the cavalry detachment at the Battle of White Bird Canyon on June 17.

Pursued by US troopers, Chief Joseph led his tribe (just 700 people, including 300 warriors) on a great trek of nearly 2,000 miles (3,200 km) that took them through Oregon, Idaho, Wyoming, and Montana, with the aim of crossing the border into Canada. During the four-month flight, Chief Joseph defeated Howard at the Battle of the Clearwater (July 11–12) in Idaho and then won victories at the battles of Big Hole River (August 9–10) and Canyon Creek (September 13), both in Montana.

The Nez Percé were just 30 miles (48 km) from Canada, at Bear's Paw Mountain, when they were caught by General Nelson Miles (1839–1925) on September 30. Joseph fought for four days, despite being outnumbered, but was eventually forced to surrender and the tribe was then sent to Oklahoma.

Massacre at Wounded Knee

By 1890, the US had gained the upper hand against the tribes in the West, but there was one last, tragic act to play out. On December 15, Sitting Bull was killed in a battle in South Dakota, and the leadership of the Sioux now passed to a chief named Big Foot.

The army sent Colonel James Forsyth to return Big Foot and his followers to their reservation. Forsyth caught up with Big Foot at Wounded Knee, South Dakota, killing Big Foot and an estimated 200 of his followers, including women and children. During the skirmish, the cavalry suffered 25 killed and 39 wounded.

This "battle" at Wounded Knee was the last major incident of the long, destructive wars that had seen the Native American tribes of the United States surrender their tribal homelands. In the process they lost much of their traditional ways of life and culture, in the face of the steady westward expansion of white settlers.

The Zulu War

On December 11, 1878, the British colonial authorities in southern Africa issued a series of impossible demands to the Zulu king Cetewayo (1827–84), which, in effect, would have forced the Zulus to surrender their land and their independence. Cetewayo refused outright; while he had no desire to go to war with the British, he was determined to protect his people from invasion.

Under Lord Frederick Chelmsford (1827–1905), the British assembled an invasion force of 5,000 British regular troops and local Europeans, and more than 8,000 local native conscripts. Although Chelmsford was short of cavalry and wagons to carry his supplies, he decided to invade Zululand at three points. Like many of his contemporaries, he was convinced that a modern British army well equipped with artillery and rifles would be more than a match for any tribal opponent.

The Zulus were, in fact, formidable warriors. Armed with thrusting and throwing spears, shields, and wooden clubs, they were skilled fighters at close range. The Zulus were also highly organized: Cetewayo had an army of 40,000 men divided into a number of regiments (or *impi*). These could cover many miles a day on foot and had a well-tried and successful battle plan. A Zulu army on sighting an enemy formed up in four parts. The center block of the army attacked the enemy head-on to pin it down, while the two blocks on the wings would fan out and encircle the enemy. The final block was held in reserve, ready to finish off the enemy if required.

The British invasion began on January 11, 1879, but was soon in trouble. The central column, with Chelmsford at its head, pushed into Zululand. It consisted of around 1,800 European soldiers and 1,000 local native conscripts. After a few days, Chelmsford and part of the column pushed on ahead while the remainder (1,700 men) was ordered to set up camp below a hill known as Isandhlwana. A victim of inflated confidence, the officer in charge failed to build a fortified camp. Early on the morning of January 22, 20,000 Zulus launched their attack.

The British grabbed their weapons and positioned themselves a short distance from the camp and its supply wagons. At first their rifle fire killed many Zulus, but they soon began to run out of ammunition and the British frontline was overwhelmed. The Zulus raced into the camp, killing most of those present; less than 60 Europeans and 400 native conscripts escaped.

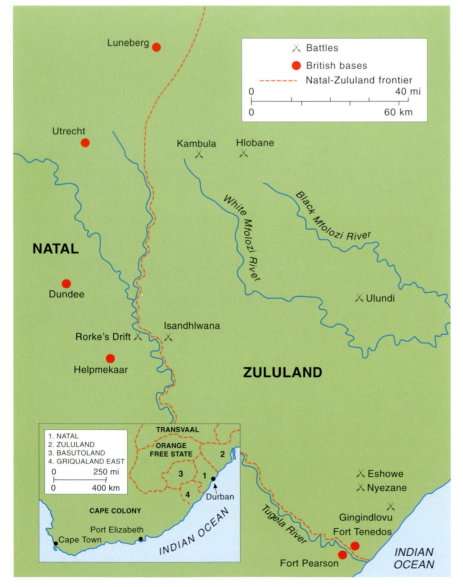

Left: The Zulu War, 1879, was instigated by the British who wanted to expand their territories in southern Africa. Major battles and sieges during the war are sited on this map, as well as an insert showing the areas surrounding Zululand.

THE ZULU ARMY

The Zulus had a well-organized military system. The basic military unit, the *impi*, was roughly equivalent to a regiment, and could vary in strength from around 500 men to more than 5,000, although the average *impi* contained about 1,500 warriors. The military units were made up of warriors of the same age, and each regiment had a distinctive ceremonial uniform and carried an oval shield made from cowhide. Younger warriors tended to have mainly black shields, while older men had white or reddish shields.

The main Zulu weapons included a thrusting spear with a long, broad blade and a lighter spear for throwing. Some Zulus did have firearms, although these were generally outdated weapons by 1879. However, the Zulus did capture a large number of modern rifles after crushing a British force at the Battle of Isandhlwana.

Zulu forces were famed for the speed of their movement. The warriors generally averaged 20 miles (32 km) in a day, although distances of up to 40 miles (64 km) were not unknown. By comparison, a British unit would have been lucky to march more than 10 miles (16 km) a day while on campaign. The Zulus traveled light, while the British needed huge numbers of oxen and wagons to move their supplies and ammunition.

The Zulus then attacked a British supply post at Rorke's Drift. The post was defended by 139 soldiers, 35 of whom were sick, while the Zulus had about 3,500 warriors. Rorke's Drift was well fortified, and in a battle lasting from the afternoon of January 22 to the morning of the 23rd, the British fought off the siege.

This British victory was, however, followed by more setbacks. The Zulus defeated a British force at Hlobane on March 28. The southernmost British column, after a victory at Nyezane, built a camp at Eshowe but was besieged. The siege lasted from the end of January until early April, when a relief column overcame a Zulu force at Gingindlovu.

Hlobane marked a turning point in the Zulu War, being the last Zulu triumph. A day later a British force showed how devastating modern weaponry could be. On March 29, 1879, at Kambula, 2,700 British troops took on a Zulu army of 20,000 warriors. The British fought from inside trenches and behind wagons on high ground. The attacking Zulus were shot to pieces, and at least 1,000 warriors were killed.

Right: This illustration depicts a Zulu warrior in ceremonial costume with shield and spear common in the 19th century. During the war against the British, however, such a Zulu warrior would have worn much simpler, lighter clothing when actually going into battle.

The British spent most of April and May of 1879 gathering troops for a second invasion of Zululand. On this occasion nothing was left to chance, and, having learned from their mistakes, the troops were under strict orders to build secure fortifications when they stopped for the night. By the end of May, Chelmsford was ready to invade Zululand again.

Heavy Artillery of the Second Invasion

The second British invasion was far less complex than the first. Only one column was used, comprising 4,500 European troops and 1,000 native conscripts. Chelmsford planned to head directly for the Zulu capital, Ulundi, thereby forcing the Zulus to engage him on ground of his own choosing.

On July 4, the British troops advanced on Ulundi in a square formation, with artillery and machine guns sited at each corner. The Zulus took the bait and 20,000 warriors launched themselves at the British positions. None reached the British line, however, such was the hail of bullets and high explosives. As the Zulus wavered, British lancers charged out from the square and routed their enemy. The Zulus had at least 1,500 warriors killed, while the British suffered just 100 casualties. The Battle of Ulundi broke the back of Zulu power. Cetewayo was captured on August 28, 1879, and his lands were incorporated into the British Empire.

Britain's Wars in Egypt

In an attempt to modernize Egypt, the Egyptian government in the mid-1800s, with help from the French, financed the building of the Suez Canal. The canal, although an engineering triumph, proved too much of a financial burden for the country and Egypt sold its shares in the project to the British. These moves and the territorial ambitions of its leader, Ismail Pasha (1830–95), made the government very unpopular.

In 1881 unrest in Egypt escalated into a full-scale rebellion led by Ahmet Arabi (1839–1911), which threatened both France's and Britain's economic and strategic interests in the region. Both states feared that their warships and merchant fleet might be refused access to the Suez Canal. An Anglo-French expedition was sent to Egypt in 1882, and on July 11 warships bombarded the Egyptian port of Alexandria, where during the previous month several Europeans had been killed by Arabi's supporters.

The bombardment was followed by the landing of 25,000 British troops. The British now sought out Arabi's main army. During an engagement at Tel el-Kebir, fought on the morning of September 13, 1882, Arabi's troops were defeated. The British now took a dominant position in Egyptian affairs.

While Britain was effectively taking over Egypt, the Egyptian-controlled province to the south, the Sudan, was being swept by a religious-inspired rebellion led by Mohammed Ibn Ahmed el-Sayyid Abdullah (1848–85), known as the Mahdi, or "Guided One of the Prophet." The followers of the Mahdi, or Mahdists, were a strict Muslim sect and led a simple life of poverty. They were forbidden to drink, use foul language, dance, or take part in festivals.

On a military level, the Mahdists were organized into units akin to regiments that were combined into larger corps. Part of the army was mounted on either camels or horses, but most were foot soldiers. Their weapons consisted of spears, swords, and shields, although rifles were acquired through trade or, more importantly, taken from the dead of those defeated in battle. The Mahdists also captured artillery and a few machine guns, but these were used to defend settlements along the Nile River rather than by the main army in the field. The chief Mahdist tactic involved creeping up on an enemy and then launching a charge at close range, a surprisingly effective tactic against inexperienced troops.

In November 1883, near El Obeid, Mahdists wiped out an Egyptian military expedition of 7,000 men led by British officers. One of the Mahdi's generals, Osman Digna (1840–1926), crushed a second expedition near

Trinkatat in the eastern Sudan. The British, who had relatively few troops in Egypt and the Sudan, ordered the evacuation of the Sudan until they could amass a force large enough to defeat the Mahdist.

A British officer, Charles Gordon (1833–85), was ordered to oversee the evacuation of the Sudan and established his base in the Sudanese capital of Khartoum, located at the point where the Blue and

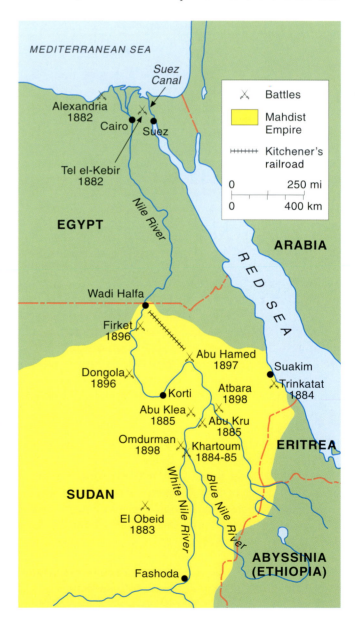

Right: For nearly 20 years the British were involved in battles in both Egypt and the Sudan. This map shows the sites of the main battles during the British campaign to take control of region, of which the fervent and cunning Mahdists were the major obstacle.

White Nile rivers meet. Gordon arrived in January 1884, but before he could effect an orderly withdrawal of Anglo-Egyptian forces, the Mahdi's troops placed the city under siege. Gordon had few military resources, and as the siege dragged on shortages of food and ammunition made his position much worse.

After considerable delay, the British government finally accepted the necessity of sending a relief expedition, but troops would have to travel long distances across hostile desert terrain from Cairo to Khartoum, a journey of over 1,000 miles (1600 km). The only really practical route to Khartoum was along the Nile River, even though the upper reaches were blocked to heavy river traffic by a series of rapids. The relief expedition set off for Khartoum in October 1884 but progress was painfully slow.

When the expeditionary force was at Korti, about 200 miles (320 km) from Khartoum, it was decided to send a fast-moving column of troops overland to Khartoum. This force, known as the Desert Column, began its march in January 1885. The Desert Column beat off two attacks by the Mahdists, at Abu Klea on the 17th and at Abu Kru two days later.

On January 21, river steamers that had escaped from Khartoum reached the Desert Column, clear proof that Gordon was still holding out. After what was to prove a fatal delay, some of the steamers, packed with soldiers, headed back up river. They arrived at Khartoum on the 28th, but the city had fallen just two days before, after a siege lasting over 300 days. Gordon had been killed in the final attack, and the British completed their withdrawal of the Sudan. In June 1885 the Mahdi died and the empire he had created was left in the hands of one of the Mahdi's generals, Khalifa Abdullah (1846–99).

After a long period during which the British consolidated affairs in Egypt, they launched another expedition to reconquer the Sudan. Commanded by General Herbert Kitchener (1850–1916), the expedition got underway in 1896. His army of 25,000 troops included British, Egyptian, and Sudanese units.

Kitchener planned the campaign in great detail. He ordered a railroad to be built to transport troops in northern Sudan and constructed a number of shallow-draught river steamers that could travel through the Nile rapids. Kitchener made slow but steady progress in 1896. The advance up the Nile continued in 1897, with his forces winning a victory at Abu Hamed in August.

During the first half of 1898 the British expedition advanced deep into Sudan. By August, Kitchener was ready to move against the main Mahdist army, which was in position around Omdurman, a short distance from Khartoum. Kitchener deployed his troops in a horseshoe formation, with the Nile at their back and a protective thorn barricade (*zareba*) to the front. The army was supported by machine guns (Maxims, which fired 600 rounds per minute) and artillery, and could count on fire support from the river steamers. Kitchener waited for the Mahdists to attack.

On September 2, the Mahdist forces, some 40,000 men, advanced toward Kitchener's army. They charged the British lines but were swept away in a storm of rifle, machine-gun, and artillery fire. Mahdist losses at Omdurman were very heavy: 10,000 killed, an equal number wounded, and 5,000 captured. Kitchener's casualties were less than 500, and his troops occupied Omdurman after the battle. The Mahdists had been defeated and Britain was free to take complete control of Egypt and the Sudan.

The Spanish–American War

The Spanish–American War was the largest overseas operation launched by the US armed forces up to that point. The US had been angered by the way the Spanish Cuban civilians were evicted from their homes and placed in camps, where many died. Then, on February 15, 1898, the USS *Maine* was mysteriously sunk while anchored in Havana Harbor. Spain was blamed and war became inevitable.

Certain sections of the American press, particularly the newspapers owned by media mogul William Randolph Hearst, whipped up anti-Spanish feelings and called for war in order to avenge the deaths of the 250 crewmen who lost their lives aboard the USS *Maine*. At the same time, powerful figures in the government and business were eager to protect or extend US interests overseas, especially in Cuba's sugar fields. Although there were voices in Washington, DC, that opposed taking direct military action, the United States nevertheless declared war on Spain on April 25, 1898.

The war had two areas of operations, the Spanish colonies of the Philippines and Cuba. Although the United States had declared war, its undersized army was far from ready to fight. Some 200,000 men volunteered for action but they had to be equipped and trained for battle. In the meantime, however, the US Navy was dispatched to fight the Spanish.

Fighting in the Philippines

The first action of the war took place in the Philippines. When war was declared, Commodore George Dewey (1837–1917), commander of the US Asiatic squadron, was refueling in the harbor at Hong Kong. He ordered his warships, which included five cruisers and two smaller gunboats, to head directly for the Philippine capital of Manila despite the threat of Spanish marine mines. Dewey's objective in Manila was to destroy the small Spanish fleet that was guarding the port. The American flotilla arrived off Manila during the night of April 30, 1898, and took his squadron into the confined waters of Manila Bay the next day.

The Spanish naval squadron of four cruisers, three gunboats, and a number of older ships, under the command of Admiral Patricio Montojo, lay at anchor off Cavite, under the protection of its coastal artillery batteries. The battle began early in the morning and ended in the early afternoon. The Spanish squadron, which was inadequately armed, was totally destroyed, as were the Cavite coastal defense guns. When the battle was finished some 380 Spanish troops lay dead or wounded, while no Americans were killed and only eight wounded. Dewey had Manila at his mercy but had to wait for the arrival of US Army units to complete the occupation of the city.

Some 10,000 American troops led by General Wesley Merritt arrived off Manila on June 30 and disembarked at Cavite. Once these troops were ashore, they quickly placed Manila under siege, aided by Filipino guerrillas commanded by Emilio Aguinaldo (1869–1964), a

Left: This painting shows one of the charges made by US troops when they were attempting to capture the strategically important San Juan Hill outside Santiago, Cuba. The US forces came under heavy fire, but despite great losses they took the ridge on July 1, 1898.

Right: The Spanish–American War, 1898, had two main theaters of operation, the Philippines (main map) and Cuba (inset). The Americans won in both areas, and their victory propelled them to being a major force on the world stage.

leading figure in the 1896 rebellion against the Spanish. There was no hope for the Spanish garrison in Manila, which was too far from home to expect reinforcements. The US forces attacked on August 13 and the city surrendered.

Shifting to Cuba

With the Spanish defeated in the Philippines, the focus of the war switched to Cuba, where the Spanish had built up the island's defenses. On April 29, 1898, Spanish Admiral Pascual Cervera (1839–1909) had sailed for Cuba from the Cape Verde Islands, at the head of four cruisers and three destroyers. Cervera was able to avoid the US naval blockade around Cuba, and his fleet anchored off Santiago on the south coast of the island on May 19. Although surprised by Cervera's arrival, the commander of the nearby US squadron, Rear Admiral William Sampson (1840–1902), reacted quickly. He sailed for Santiago and bottled up the Spanish, ensuring that they could not prevent the landing of US ground forces on Cuba.

US General William Shafter (1835–1906) was chosen to lead the invasion force. He was given command of 17,000 troops, and these began landing at Daiquirí to the east of Santiago on June 22. The landings took three days, but went smoothly. The Spanish garrison on Cuba did not interfere. Most of the US troops were regulars but there were units of volunteers present, including the First Volunteer Cavalry, better known as the "Rough Riders." Shafter had to cope with many problems, however: his cavalry units were short of horses, some vital equipment was lacking, and many of his men fell prey to various tropical diseases.

Shafter moved his forces to besiege Santiago. The Spanish had 35,000 troops in the area but only 13,000 were deployed to defend the city. Before Shafter could close on Santiago, however, he had to deal with the 1,200 Spanish soldiers holding San Juan, a ridge running across the road to Santiago. The Spanish fought fiercely and the Americans suffered heavy casualties before they gained the summit of San Juan. The capture of the ridge, accomplished by the evening of July 1, 1898, virtually decided the fate of Santiago.

If the fall of San Juan was a major blow to the Spanish, what followed was a disaster of equal size. On July 3 Cervera decided to lead his squadron out of Santiago Bay to prevent it from falling into US hands. The US Atlantic Fleet, however, was waiting for him. Sampson was away from the fleet so command rested with Commodore Winfield Schley (1839–1909). Seeing the advance of the Spanish fleet, Schley ordered his own warships to steam straight for the enemy.

In the running fight that followed, the US warships fired 8,000 shells at the Spanish. Less than 200 hit their targets, but they were sufficient to destroy the Spanish fleet. All six of the Spanish vessels were forced to run aground as a result of the heavy US fire. The Spanish lost about 500 sailors either killed or wounded, and nearly 1,800 men were taken prisoner. US casualties were minimal: one man killed, one man wounded.

The Battle of Santiago Bay effectively ended the Spanish–American War. Santiago surrendered on July 17, and the Spanish West Indian island of Puerto Rico followed suit on August 25. The end of the war was confirmed by the Treaty of Paris, which was signed on December 10, 1898. As a result of the treaty, Spain was forced to give Cuba its independence and cede the Philippines, Puerto Rico, and the Pacific island of Guam to the United States for $20 million. The United States had gained great prestige from the war and became a major power in the Pacific. Spain, on the other hand, one of the first colonial powers, had lost its last colonies in the Pacific and Latin America.

The Anglo-Boer Wars

The First Anglo-Boer War was prompted by a British takeover of the Transvaal in April 1877, but fighting did not begin until the Boers formed their own republic at the end of December 1880. The Boers attacked British troops and laid siege to British garrisons, but the main action took place around Laing's Nek, a pass through the Drakensberg Mountains that separated the Boer Republic from British-held areas.

The Boers, farmers of Dutch origin, did not have a trained army, but all Boer males were expected to fight. They were highly mobile and usually fought from mountain tops, or in trenches. Meanwhile, the British, who advanced in close ranks and wore red uniforms, made easy targets.

Between January and February 1881, the British failed first trying to take Laing's Nek, then attempting to capture the Majuba Mountain. In the latter battle, 100 soldiers out of a force of 500 were killed, with a further 180 either wounded or captured. The British defeat at Majuba led to a peace treaty, signed on April 5, 1881, that recognized the right of the Boer Republic to exist in southern Africa.

Despite the defeat and the treaty, Britain remained determined to take control of Boer lands. In 1899, the president of the Boer Republic, Paul Kruger

(1825–1904), demanded the withdrawal of British forces massing in Natal for a possible invasion. The British refused; the Orange Free State sided with the Boer Republic and war broke out in October.

The Boers, who attacked quickly before the British could rush reinforcements to southern Africa, fought in local units, known as commandos, which typically had a strength of a few hundred men. They did not have trained officers as such, their military leaders were elected by their men. They were all mounted and could move at great speed. Most were farmers and excellent marksmen who had sharpened their skills hunting. They also knew the geography of southern Africa much more clearly than the British.

The Boers opened their offensive with mounted columns attacking three British garrisons. Boers from the Transvaal under Piet Cronjé (1835–1911) laid siege to Mafeking, while Boers from the Orange Free State surrounded Kimberley. The largest Boer force, commanded by Petrus Joubert (1834–1900), won four battles in October – Laing's Nek, Talana Hill, Elandslaagte, and Nicholson's Nek – and took the garrison at Ladysmith.

Despite having few soldiers immediately available, the British decided to relieve all three towns at the same time. A force of 10,000 commanded by General Lord Paul Methuen (1845–1932) struck out for Kimberley. Some 7,000 Boers led jointly by Cronjé and Jacobus De la Rey (1847–1914) rushed south to stop Methuen.

The Boer commanders' plan was to occupy hilltop positions in front of the British and then cut them down with rifle fire as they advanced across the open plains beneath them. Methuen launched a frontal attack on the Boers, who

Left: This map depicts the main battles and sieges that took place during the Boer Wars. For most of the fighting the Boers outwitted and outmaneuvered the British troops.

Left: At the beginning of the Second Boer War (1899–1902) the British cavalry, seen here moving out of their camp to engage the Boers, were grossly understaffed, enabling the mounted Boers to move around the conflict zones of southern Africa at will.

The British now struck into the Boer heartland, capturing the key cities of Johannesburg (May 31) and Pretoria (June 5). The war seemed over, but some Boers, known as "bitter-enders," were determined to continue fighting. They waged a guerrilla campaign, launching raids on British outposts, ambushing small columns of troops, and destroying railroad lines.

The British responded in three ways. First, they used fast-moving columns of cavalry and mounted infantry to chase the Boers. Second, they built a network of small forts connected by barbed wire, to deny the Boers freedom of movement. Third, most controversially of all, they began destroying Boer farms and herding women and children into camps, thereby denying the Boer fighters the local support they needed to survive.

The war finally ended when a peace treaty was signed at Vereeniging in May 1902. As a result, the Boer republics were incorporated into the British Empire, but, from 1907, given self-government. Militarily, the war exposed many shortcomings in the organization and tactics adopted by the British forces. Over the following decade the British began to dramatically improve their shooting skills, a painful lesson learned from the Boer Wars that would stand them in good stead in 1914.

were in position along the banks of the Modder River, on November 28. It was a failure. On December 10–11, Methuen threw his forces against the Boers at Magersfontein and lost 1,000 men for no result.

While Methuen's troops were being mauled by the Boers, General Sir Redvers Buller (1839–1908) led over 20,000 British troops to Ladysmith. He, too, met with defeat. At the Battle of Colenso the Boers did not dig in on the hilltops, but at their foot. While the British advanced across the open plain in front of the Boers, their artillery fired at the nonexistent Boer positions on the hilltops. The British suffered nearly 1,000 casualties while the Boers reported only 50 men killed or wounded. British newspapers christened the series of December defeats "Black Week," and a rattled British government stepped in to replace Buller.

Turning the Tide

In January 1900, overall command of the British forces was given to Field Marshal Sir Frederick Roberts (1832–1914), who realized that the Boers' chief asset was their mobility. He decided to increase the proportion of cavalry in his own forces, and made extensive use of Canadian and Australian mounted troops. While this build-up was taking place, however, the British suffered further defeats. Buller, still trying to reach Ladysmith, was halted by the Boers at Spion Kop (January 23) and Vaal Kranz (February 5).

At the end of January Roberts embarked on a campaign to drive the Boers out of Kimberley. Within weeks part of his army advanced against Boer troops blocking the most direct route to the town, while he led the remainder around the Boers' flank, forcing them to retreat. Kimberley was relieved on February 15.

On February 18, the British caught up with the Boers at Paardeberg. The British settled down to a siege of the Boer camp and forced Cronjé with some 5,000 Boers to surrender on the 27th. A day later, at the third attempt, Buller finally reached the garrison at Ladysmith. Mafeking was reclaimed on May 17–18, ending seven months of siege by the Boers.

CONCENTRATION CAMPS

A controversial aspect of British military strategy in the final phase of the Boer Wars was the forced use of concentration camps. These were filled with old men, women, and children who had aided the Boer troops, or were suspected of doing so. Before they were herded into the camps, the farms of these civilians were destroyed.

The camps were unhealthy places. Sanitation was at best inadequate, much-needed water was often in short supply or tainted, and what food was provided was of poor quality. Little medical aid was available. Some 120,000 people were kept in the camps and an estimated 20,000 of them died through malnutrition or illness.

A few Britons attempted to improve conditions in the concentration camps. The most important of these was Emily Hobhouse, who visited many of the camps and began a public campaign in Britain to improve conditions. An all-woman group, the Fawcett Commission, went to southern Africa and published a damning report on the camps in December 1901. As a result of the ensuing outcry, the conditions in the camps improved and death rates at the camps declined dramatically.

The Boxer Rebellion

By the late 1800s there was growing resentment among many Chinese at the increasing involvement of various foreign powers, including Britain, Germany, Japan, and Russia, in the domestic affairs of China. This resentment was manifest in a secret society known as the Boxers, and in the summer of 1900, beginning in Beijing, the group began attacking and murdering Chinese Christian converts and foreigners.

By the early summer of 1900 power in China lay in the hands of the Dowager Empress Tzu Hsi (1834–1908), who had recently deposed her young nephew, Emperor Kuang-hsu (1871–1908). At the beginning of the uprising Tzu Hsi told the foreign powers that she was trying to eliminate the Boxer menace, while in actual fact members of her inner circle at the imperial court were covertly helping the Boxers. Senior court officials objected to the unfair trading rights that had been forced on the Chinese, and were sympathetic to many of the Boxer movement's aims.

Boxer attacks on foreigners intensified on June 9, 1900, when part of Beijing's racecourse was burned down. Two days later the Japanese ambassador was murdered. These events caused the various foreign legation staffs to fortify their embassies, yet on the 19th, the German ambassador was murdered. In the late afternoon of the following day the legations came under Chinese fire for the first time.

A multinational relief force of 2,000 troops, chiefly British, German, Russian, and American soldiers led by a British admiral, Sir Edward Seymour (1840–1929), was already advancing to the aid of the legations. Seymour's troops, who had left their base near the Taku Forts on the same day that the Beijing racecourse was set alight, were heading toward Tientsin along the Pei-Ho River. From Tientsin they hoped to travel by rail to Beijing, some 100 miles (160 km) to the north.

However, Seymour never reached Beijing. A combination of Boxer attacks, destroyed railroad tracks, and a lack of supplies halted his advance some 30 miles (48 km) from the capital, at the village of An Ting. The relief column, fighting off Boxer attacks supported by units of the Chinese Regular Army, fell back to Tientsin, reaching the outer suburbs of the city on June 26. By this time, however, the Boxers were in control of parts of the city, and as a result, Seymour took up a defensive position just outside Tientsin.

Meanwhile, other multinational forces were arriving off the mouth of the Pei-Ho. The commanders decided to attack the Taku Forts, which were guarding the river gate to Tientsin, and then advance to the city. The dried-mud forts were captured on June 17, and part of the multinational force rushed to Tientsin. The European quarter of the city was under attack, but the Boxers and Chinese Army soldiers were being held back in no small part due to the defenses prepared by a young engineer, Herbert Hoover (1874–1964), who years later would become president of the United States.

After hard fighting and heavy losses on both sides, Tientsin was finally cleared of Chinese forces by July 23. Plans were then made to move on Beijing, and by this time the multinational force consisted of 20,000 troops, including some 10,000 Japanese, 4,000 Russians, 3,000 British, 2,000 Americans, 800 French, 200 Germans, 58 Austrians, and 53 Italians.

The advance north was extremely difficult for the relief force: high temperatures, bad roads, and Boxer attacks made progress slow. But by August 12, the city of Tungchow, 12 miles (18 km) from Beijing, had been occupied by the multinationals, and it was decided to

THE BOXER MOVEMENT

The Boxers, also known as the Righteous Harmonious Fists, were members of a Chinese secret society. By the late 19th century, they had gained many sympathizers in the Chinese court who, like the Boxers, resented the presence of foreigners on Chinese soil. There were two main areas of conflict. First, foreign missionaries were having increasing success in converting Chinese to Christianity. Second, foreign powers had colonized key ports on the Chinese coast, from which they monopolized China's trade for their own benefit.

In the last decades of the century, against a background of flood and famine, the Boxers began to whip up unrest among the ordinary Chinese, blaming their poverty on the foreigners' ruthless exploitation of China's resources.

The Boxers began to attack foreigners and Chinese Christians. They used traditional weapons, such as swords, spears, and shields, and believed that they could not be harmed by bullets. The Boxers were not equipped to take on the modern forces fielded by the foreign powers and suffered heavy losses. When the war ended in Chinese defeat in 1901, part of the peace settlement demanded the disbanding of the Boxers and made attacks on foreigners a crime punishable by death.

storm the Chinese capital two days later, even though it was not known at the time if the embassies had fallen to the Chinese because there had been no communication.

Inside Beijing

The embassies, defended by about 400 regular troops and various armed civilians, were holding on, but suffering greatly from shortages of food and water. On June 23, the Boxers had set fire to market buildings hoping that the flames would spread to the embassies, and on July 13 they had exploded a mine under the French embassy. Sniper and artillery fire added to the dangers endured by the embassies' defenders and the Europeans and Chinese Christians sheltering behind their walls and barricades.

The final battle to relieve the embassies began on August 14. Although the various foreign forces outside Beijing had been given precise timetables and objectives, the assault degenerated into a race; each foreign force wanted the glory of reaching its own embassy quarter first. The race was barely won by the British, but the scramble to reach the embassies clearly showed that the multinational alliance was falling apart as the various nationalities put their own interests first.

Over the following days the rest of Beijing was captured, and the allies then spread out from the Chinese capital to crush the remaining pockets of Boxer resistance. In late October the operations were brought to an end. Apart from looting and destroying many works of Chinese art, the international force imposed a harsh peace treaty on the Chinese that included heavy fines and the disbanding of the Boxer society.

The impact of the Boxer Rebellion eventually led to the downfall of the Manchu dynasty in 1912. It was the first time that the world's leading powers had acted together for their mutual benefit. And yet, the solidarity they showed in dealing with the Boxer Rebellion was not destined to last. Within five years of the rebellion, Japanese and Russians would be at war, and within 14 years virtually all of those who had contributed troops to the relief of the embassies in Beijing would be fighting each other in World War I.

Above: In order to reach Beijing and rescue the besieged embassies there, the multinational force first had to defeat the Boxers who had fortified themselves along the Pei-Ho River. This map shows the major engagements on the route to Beijing in 1900.

Left: This photograph, taken on August 14, 1900, shows American soldiers firing on the walls of Beijing during the final battle to relieve the city under Boxer attack. Up until this point the multinational rescue force had no news of the condition or fate of the Chinese Christians and foreign nationals under siege within the city.

The Russo-Japanese War

At the start of the 20th century Japan held an increasingly dominant position in the northern Pacific. But to gain further control of the region Japan would first have to diminish Russia's influence in the area. Japan decided to go to war with Russia in 1904 with three aims in mind: capture Port Arthur, the main Russian naval base in the region; destroy the Russian Far East fleet; and crush the Russian Army in Manchuria.

The Japanese did not issue a formal declaration of war but launched a surprise attack with torpedo boats on the Russian fleet as it lay at anchor in Port Arthur's harbor on February 8, 1904. Considerable damage was caused, after which the Japanese blockaded the port. War was declared two days later.

On paper Russia, with a standing army of 4,500,000, should have been an intimidating enemy for the Japanese, who had a standing army of only 280,000, plus 400,000 reserves. But the Japanese knew that Russia had less than 150,000 men within reach of Port Arthur and that it would have been far too difficult for Russia to transport the bulk of its army along the Trans-Siberian Railway, which ran 5,500 miles (9,300 km) from Moscow to Port Arthur with a 100 mile (160 km) break at Lake Baikal. Quick action gave the Japanese the advantage.

Following the surprise attack in early February, the Japanese still held the initiative and followed up the Port Arthur attack by landing at Chemulpo on the Korean peninsula on February 17, 1904. They then advanced north to the Yalu River, Korea's border with Russian-controlled province of Manchuria.

The blockade of Port Arthur continued but the arrival of a dynamic Russian naval officer, Admiral Stepan Makarov (1849–1904), threatened to break the stalemate. Makarov launched a series of sorties, taking care to avoid full-scale battle with the main Japanese fleet under Vice-Admiral Heihachiro Togo (1847–1934). These Russian attacks were successful until Makarov's flagship, the *Petropavlovsk*, hit a mine on April 13. The entire crew including Makarov were killed. The death of Makarov had a devastating effect on morale in Port Arthur, and the Japanese blockade stayed in place.

The Russians, aware of the threat to Port Arthur and of the Japanese landings in Korea, tried to gather their forces to repel the invasion. The Russian military commander, General Alexei Kuropatkin (1848–1925), knew he was outnumbered and wanted time to build up his troops, but Kuropatkin's superior, Admiral Evegeni Alekseev, disagreed and demanded immediate action. The folly of this plan became clear in late April when the Japanese over-whelmed a small Russian force along the Yalu River.

The Japanese kept up the pressure on the Russians during May by landing troops 40 miles (64 km) northeast of Port Arthur and began to advance on the base. Another Japanese ground force then landed to the west of the Yalu.

On May 25, Japanese troops moved toward the Russians holding Hashan Hill, part of Port Arthur's outer defenses. Outnumbering the 3,000-strong Russian force 10 times, the Japanese launched repeated

Left: The Russo-Japanese War was a major success for Japan, both on land and sea. This map shows the sites of the most important engagements during the conflict.

Left: On February 8, 1904, in a surprise attack before war had been formally declared, Japanese warships opened fire on the Russian defenses protecting Port Arthur, as illustrated here. At the same time, the Japanese torpedoed the Russian warships anchored in the port's harbor.

frontal assaults. Japanese casualties were heavy (4,500 men) but the hill was captured, which also allowed the Japanese to use a nearby port as a naval base for the concentration of another large contingent. The siege of Port Arthur began in earnest in June 1904.

The Russian ships at Port Arthur were eventually ordered to flee, but the attempt ended in disaster at the Battle of the Yellow River on August 10. Admiral Vilgelm Vitgeft's 19 warships were caught by the Japanese under Togo. The Russian flotilla was pounded for 90 minutes: one was sunk and the surviving ships, many damaged, sought sanctuary in neutral ports or scurried back to Port Arthur.

The Japanese began their land attacks against Port Arthur in early August but suffered heavy casualties for no appreciable gain. Even the arrival of heavy siege artillery in October failed to break Russian resistance. But slowly the balance of force turned against the defenders. The fighting centered on a Russian position known as 203 Meter Hill. If it fell, Port Arthur and the remains of the Russian fleet would be at the mercy of the Japanese. The final battle for the hill lasted from November 27 to December 5, when the Japanese took the position. Port Arthur could not survive and the Russians surrendered on January 2, 1905.

While the siege was progressing, Russian troops tried to eject the Japanese forces in Manchuria. Their early attacks in 1904 were repulsed and the Russians were forced to retreat. The Japanese followed the Russians and fought an inconclusive battle at Liaoyang (September 3). The Russians began to fall back on

Mukden, their center of operations, as each side jockeyed for position in preparation for the engagement that would decide the land war. The Battle of Mukden involved more than 300,000 troops on each side, spread out and entrenched over a distance of 40 miles (64 km). The fighting began on February 21, 1905, and lasted until March 10. The Japanese narrowly won the battle, forcing the Russians to accept overall Japanese victory.

The fighting on land was over, but the Russians suffered one more disaster at sea. The Battle of Tsushima, fought on May 27–28 between the Russian Baltic fleet led by Admiral Zinovi Rozhdestvenski and a Japanese fleet commanded by Togo, remains one of the most tactically decisive naval engagements of all time. The Russian Baltic fleet had sailed half way around the world only to be annihilated in the straits between Korea and Japan. Togo's warships outgunned and outmaneuvered the Russians. The Russian fleet of eight battleships, eight cruisers, nine destroyers, and a number of smaller craft was smashed by long-range gunnery and torpedo attacks in the two-day battle. Only one cruiser and five destroyers escaped.

After such catastrophic defeats on land and sea, the Russians accepted the terms of the Treaty of Portsmouth, which was arranged by US president Theodore Roosevelt, on September 6, 1905. Japan took over Port Arthur and other nearby territories; the Russians had to withdraw from Manchuria; and Korea was recognized as being firmly within the Japanese sphere of influence. At a stroke, the Japanese had become the most dominant force in the northern Pacific.

War in the Balkans

In 1911 Italy, who wanted to carve out its own empire in North Africa, declared war on the Ottoman Empire, which had been declining steadily for well over a century, in order to seize Turkish-held Libya. At the same time, former Turkish domains Bulgaria, Greece, and Serbia, encouraged by Russia, formed the Balkan League with a view to wresting Montenegro from the Turks and forcing them out of Europe.

The Balkan League, in alliance with the small state of Montenegro, declared war on Turkey on October 8, 1912. Together the League and Montenegro could muster about 350,000 troops, while the Turks had fewer than 250,000 men available to them in Europe. Toward the end of October forces from each of the Balkan countries marched into Turkey's European territories.

The Greeks under Crown Prince Constantine (1868–1923) advanced into Turkish-held Macedonia from the south and defeated an Ottoman force at Elasson on October 23. Despite the initial success, Constantine soon ran into trouble first at Venije Vardar and later at

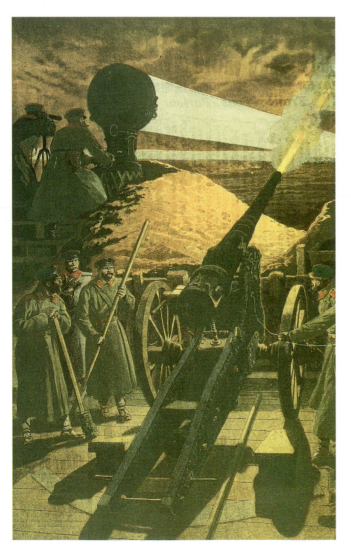

Kastoria and Banitsa. By November 5, however, the Greeks had overcome their adversaries and claimed an important victory at Venije. The Greek Army then pressed eastward to Salonika. Both the Greeks and the Bulgarians coveted this vital port, the possession of which would allow its owner domination of the Aegean.

Meanwhile, the Serbs, led by General Radomir Putnik (1847–1917) advanced into Macedonia from the north, defeated the Turks at Kumanovo on October 24, and forced them to retreat to Monastir. The Battle of Monastir, held on November 5, was a hard-fought contest with both Serbs and Turks showing great bravery. An impetuous Serb assault on a Turkish position was thrown back by the Turks with heavy Serb casualties. But this attack weakened the Turkish center, and allowed the Serbs to launch a frontal attack, which made inroads into the Turkish position. Threatened by a Greek force advancing from the south, the Turks retreated, having lost 20,000 men in the battle. The Greeks then captured the fortress of Salonika four days later and placed a number of other Turkish garrisons, including Scutari, under siege.

The Turks fared no better in Thrace, where they faced the Bulgarians. Three small Bulgarian armies advanced on a broad front and defeated the Turks at Seliolu and Kirk Kilissa at the end of October. The Turks fell back toward Constantinople (modern Istanbul) to hold a 35-mile (56-km) long defensive line between Lülé Burgas and Bunar Hisar. Two of the Bulgarian armies pressed eastward after the Turks, while the third placed the city of Adrianople under siege.

The Bulgarian attacks on the Turkish defensive line at Lülé Burgas on October 28–29 were successful and the Turks pulled back toward Constantinople. They took up a position along the Chatalja Line, their last defensive barrier before the Turkish capital. The Bulgarians tried to smash through the line during November, but all their efforts proved unsuccessful and Constantinople was safe from the Bulgarians. As a result of intervention by the major European powers, however, peace talks began in December and an armistice brought the war to a halt temporarily.

Left: Although the First Balkan War was nearly at an end in December 1912, the new government in Turkey refused to give up. This illustration shows Bulgarian troops taking aim at Turkish targets in Adrianople with the aid of searchlight in February 1913.

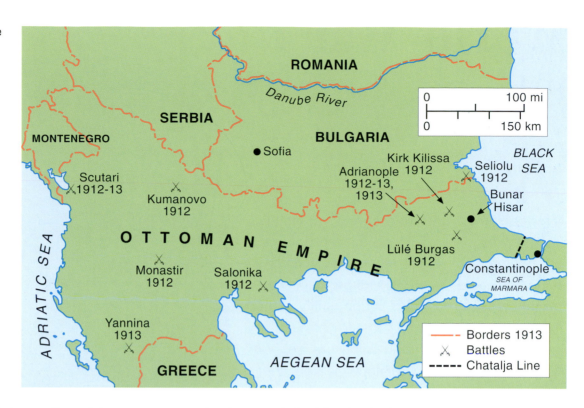

Right: The two wars in the Balkans not only ended the Ottoman Empire's foothold in Europe but created new states. It also brought to the surface many regional hostilities. This map shows the scope of the conflicts from the Adriatic to the Black Sea.

Peace negotiations collapsed, however, as a result of the incompatible demands of the various states. Turkey was required to surrender most of its European possessions, and a new state of Albania was to be created on the Adriatic, although this latter move was bitterly opposed by Serbia and Montenegro. But the chief cause of dispute lay in Bulgaria's well-grounded fear that Greece and Serbia were conspiring to divide Macedonia among themselves at the expense of Bulgaria. The Balkan League might have been united in their determination to defeat the Turks, but their own regional ambitions would prove their undoing.

Complicating matters further, the Turkish government was overthrown in January 1913 and replaced by a fiercely nationalist group known as the "Young Turks," led by Enver Bey (1881–1922). The new Turkish government was determined to carry on the war in the hope of gaining better peace terms for Turkey. Despite their best efforts, the Turkish armies suffered further defeats in 1913. The Turkish cities of Yannina (March 3), Adrianople (March 26), and Scutari (April 22) all fell to the Balkan League, forcing the Turks to sue for peace. The ensuing Treaty of London saw Turkey lose virtually all of its possessions in the Balkans.

The Second Balkan War

The Balkan League did not survive its victory in the First Balkan War, and national rivalries soon tore the alliance apart. Hoping to get a larger slice of Macedonia and, above all, the port of Salonika, Bulgaria attacked the Serbs on May 30, 1913, before declaring war on both Serbia and Greece. Bulgaria severely underestimated the strength of its former allies, and by June 30 its forces

were halted by the Serbo-Greek coalition. On July 2 Serb forces under Putnik drove back the Bulgarians, and despite a failed counteroffensive, the Bulgarians were virtually defeated.

Then an already desperate situation faced by Bulgaria worsened when, on July 15, Romania sided with Serbia and Greece against Bulgaria. With great speed the Romanian troops advanced on the Bulgarian capital of Sofia. At the same time, taking advantage of Bulgaria's troubles with Serbia, Greece, and Romania, the Turks recaptured Adrianople.

The Bulgarians were quickly forced to the peace table and on August 10, 1913, the Treaty of Bucharest brought the war to a close. Bulgaria was forced to give up most of the land it had gained during the war against Turkey, as well as losing some of its northern territories to Romania. Greece, on the other hand, was given Crete and southern Macedonia, and Serbia gained Kosovo and northern Macedonia, although Austria forced them to relinquish their gains in the newly formed Albania.

The peace in the Balkans did not last long, however, and the region remained unsettled as the competing ambitions of the Balkan states were supplemented by the larger ambitions of the rival great powers, Russia and Austria-Hungary. Bulgaria remained resentful as a result of the losses it had incurred at the end of the Second Balkan War, while Turkey licked its wounds and with the help of Germany set about modernizing its armed forces. Within the space of a year, in Sarajevo, Bosnia, the assassination of Archduke Ferdinand, heir to the Austro-Hungarian throne, by a Serb nationalist would throw the Balkans into chaos and spark the outbreak of World War I.

World War I
1914–18

World War I was the first great conflict to fully harness the powers of the Industrial Revolution. Huge forces battled on land, at sea, and, for the first time in military history, in the air. Technology and industrial output became keys to success on the battlefield. Victory no longer depended on soldiers alone, but also on the ability of the civilians and industries at home to provide armed forces with the vast numbers of weapons and supplies needed to continue the fight.

The immediate origins of World War I lay in hostilities between the Austro-Hungarian Empire and the neighboring state of Serbia over control of Bosnia, a mainly Slav state under Austrian jurisdiction.

On June 28, 1914, a young Serbian nationalist, Gavrilo Princip (1894–1918), assassinated the Archduke Franz Ferdinand (1863–1914), who was conducting an official visit in the Bosnian capital of Sarajevo. The archduke was heir to the Austro-Hungarian throne and his murder sparked a diplomatic explosion. Despite Serbian apologies for the incident, Austria threatened Serbia with war. Serbia was, however, protected by its fellow Slav nation Russia, and the Austrian threats were a first step toward a general European war.

The wider origins of World War I owed much to the nationalist rivalries that had developed in Europe during the 19th century. Competition between the European great powers was conducted at the economic and political level, as each fought to gain greater power at the expense of the other. The fight for colonies and economic markets made international rivalries more intense, which in turn led to the alliance system – which was also a factor encouraging the drift toward war.

Germany and Austria banded together as the Central Powers, and were opposed by Russia and France. The other remaining European great power, Britain, was hostile toward Germany, and, while it had an informal arrangement with France, it remained outside the formal alliance system. Italy, on the other hand, was formally

Right: Trench warfare, although not a new defensive tactic in battle, became the indelible symbol of World War I, especially along the Western Front. Here, French soldiers are dug in at Verdun, a battle that lasted nearly the whole of 1916 and claimed a million casualties.

Right: In August 1914, German troops marched into Belgium, as seen here entering Brussels. Although they progressed steadily at first, within a few months they became entrenched in a defensive line stretching from the English Channel in the north to Switzerland in the south. Both sides remained along this line, known as the Western Front, for the remainder of the war.

allied with the Central Powers in 1914 but remained neutral until 1915 when it officially entered the war on the side of France and Britain.

The European alliances were initially intended to be essentially defensive in nature, but a series of international incidents – Morocco (1905), Bosnia (1908–09), and Agadir (1911) – increased tensions so much that the European powers became polarized into two armed camps. The army general staffs began to draw up plans for the probability of outright conflict.

The strategic situation was geographically determined: Germany and Austria-Hungary held the center, "surrounded" by France and Russia, while Britain occupied a peripheral position. By 1912–13, Germany had become increasingly concerned by the rising economic might of Russia, its millions of miles of railroads – and therefore capability of transporting millions of soldiers relatively quickly – and the German General Staff began to advocate war before the Russian Army could take advantage of the relative decline in German industrial and military power.

While the Central Powers had the advantage of operating on interior lines, Germany faced the prospect of a war along two fronts – and her strategic plans reflected this dilemma. The chief of the German General Staff during the key years of 1890–1905 was Count Alfred von Schlieffen (1833–1913). During that time and in part until his death, Schlieffen worked on a strategy that entailed first striking a swift and decisive blow against France, then turning eastward to deal with Russia, whose powerful and cumbersome army would, he believed, be slow to mobilize.

BRITISH EXPEDITIONARY FORCE

In terms of military organization, Britain was the exception among the European countries in 1914. Other states gave most of their young soldiers some rudimentary military training and planned to recall them for service in huge "citizen armies" in time of war. Britain, instead, relied on a smaller force of professional, regular troops. British soldiers were well trained and of higher quality than their European counterparts, but many of them became casualties in the first few months of World War I.

By the end of 1914 Britain's generals realized that the war would last more than a few months, and that it would be necessary to expand their army. However, the casualties and the small original size of the force ensured that it took nearly two years for the British to assemble a large and efficient army ready for frontline service.

Britain's army in France was known as the British Expeditionary Force (BEF), and was initially commanded by General Sir John French (1852–1925) until his replacement by General Sir Douglas Haig (1861–1926) at the end of 1915. During 1915–16, the BEF expanded in size, so that by June 1916 there were 58 British divisions on the Western Front. From the middle of 1916 onward, the British were able to play a broadly equal role alongside the fully committed French Army.

Schlieffen's plan was a gambler's throw, dependent on the speed of German mobilization over Russia's and the completeness of the victory over France. These variables were problematic enough for the German High Command, but the plan achieved infamy because of its grotesque inflexibility: no matter from where the threat of danger to the Central Powers originated, Germany must immediately invade France.

At the end of July 1914, doubts were cast as to the advisability of attacking in the west, as the source of the conflict lay in the Balkans, but the German General Staff crushed all dissent by insisting that to change the rail schedules would throw the German Army into complete disarray, and so make it vulnerable to its enemies. Once committed, there was no going back.

This was the first great act of madness of World War I: strategy had been subordinated to the demands of the railroad timetable. In addition, although of little interest to Schlieffen and his fellow planners, the invasion of France also involved the violation of Belgian and Dutch neutrality. Prussia had been a cosignatory to the foundation of an independent and neutral Belgium – and so had Britain.

Sure in the knowledge of German support, Austria-Hungary overrode Serbia's diplomatic attempts to prevent conflict and declared war on the Balkan kingdom on July 29, 1914. Russia then mobilized its frontier forces. On August 1, Germany declared war against Russia, and two days later issued a declaration of war against France. On August 3, German troops invaded Belgium, and on the following day – in order to fulfill its guarantee toward Belgian neutrality – Britain declared war on Germany.

Weapons of the Great War

Throughout most of the war fighting on the Western Front was characterized by the combination of trenches, barbed wire, and machine guns, all of which favored a defensive operation, making infantry advances over open ground against well-prepared positions all but impossible. Generals on both sides, desperate to sustain offensive maneuvers, struggled against a unique combination of military circumstances.

Artillery seemed to hold the best hope of overcoming strong defensive positions by destroying enemy positions and, through the provision of a creeping barrage, protect attacking troops. If sufficient numbers of guns were employed, and the gunners were suitably trained, artillery could

smash holes through the enemy defenses. But, as it turned out, the infantry on both sides remained too slow and vulnerable to be able to exploit any such opportunities at a strategic level.

As a consequence, commanders looked toward new technology to resolve the trench stalemate. Chemical weapons were one way forward, with the Germans pioneering the use of poison gas at the Second Battle of Ypres in 1915. Although gas inspired terror when first used, frontline soldiers eventually became used to it, and especially after the introduction of gas masks, it did not prove a war winner.

Armored vehicles were the next major development intended to transform the strategic outlook in favor of mobility. Utilizing armor plate, the internal combustion engine, and caterpillar tracks, the first such vehicles – called tanks – made their debut in 1916 at the Battle of the Somme. Although the tank achieved some tactical successes between 1916 and the end of the war, it lacked the speed and reliability to be a truly decisive weapon.

The internal combustion engine also made aircraft possible. The first aircraft flew in 1903, and by 1914 the armies of the great powers had their own aviation branches to act as airborne reconnaissance troops. As the war developed so too did aviation technology, which greatly expanded the range and quality of military aircraft. By 1918, the reconnaissance aircraft had been joined by fighters, bombers, and ground-attack aircraft.

At sea, battleships remained the chief weapons; nevertheless the indecisive Battle of Jutland in 1916 was the only major encounter between main battle fleets. A relatively new weapon, the submarine, also began to play a key role in warfare. Submarines were used to sink enemy warships and, more importantly, to attack enemy supply ships. The war at sea also saw the beginnings of naval aviation.

Contrary to myth, military leaders placed great hope in technology, but, despite having much potential, the military hardware they received was generally insufficient. In the end, victory went to the side that had the will and the material means to endure the longest. And even though the German troops were generally superior in training, tactics, and leadership to those of its enemies, the Allies had the material means and the numbers of soldiers to win a war of attrition.

Left: Count Alfred von Schlieffen, the chief of the German General Staff at the turn of the century, devised the strategy for Germany's two-part attack on first France and then Russia.

The Western Front 1914–15

France's strategy at the outbreak of World War I was based upon Plan XVII, which aimed to avenge the humiliating defeat of 1870–71 and recover the former French territories of Alsace and Lorraine through a frontal assault across the Franco-German border. Initially, France deployed over a million troops in five armies, and the plan was to dispatch three of these armies into Alsace and Lorraine.

The French commander-in-chief, General Joseph Joffre (1852–1931), realized that Germany might try to outflank his forces by advancing into France through Belgium, and so he held his other two armies in reserve to guard against this. The French, however, underestimated the size of the German forces deployed against them, which totalled almost 1.5 million soldiers.

The German Schlieffen Plan was to be executed by General Helmuth von Moltke (1848–1916), Schlieffen's successor as chief-of-staff and nephew of the great Helmuth Karl von Moltke who had built up the Prussian and German armies in the 19th century. Schlieffen's idea had been to concentrate the bulk of the German Army on the right wing, which would march through Belgium, swiftly overrun northern France, capture Paris, and then swing around to attack the main French forces advancing on the Alsace and Lorraine territories.

The German invasion began with an advance into neutral Belgium on August 3, 1914. The Germans easily pushed aside the small Belgian Army, using super-heavy guns to smash the Belgian border fortress at Liège. Brussels was captured on the 20th. The newly arrived British Expeditionary Force and the two reserve French armies tried to hold the German advance along the border between Belgium and France. The Germans came off best in these engagements and the Allies were forced to retreat into France.

In the meantime, the bulk of the French Army had been trying to carry out Plan XVII, but French attacks in Alsace and Lorraine failed miserably. The clumsy and badly handled French offensive was easily repulsed, and the French were forced to retreat back over the border having suffered heavy casualties.

Although in retreat, Joffre kept calm and maintained control over his forces, whereas Moltke was beginning to show signs of strain. By the start of September, the Allies had retreated from northern France almost as far as Paris, but the German right flank had became increasingly exposed as the Germans advanced over the Marne River. The French had assembled reserve forces and Joffre exploited the situation skillfully. In the Battle of the Marne, fought between September 5 and 10, French and British troops held the Germans, and a nervous Moltke ordered a general retreat.

The Allied resistance in the Battle of the Marne confirmed the failure of the Schlieffen Plan. Instead of knocking France out of the war in a matter of weeks, the German generals would have to face their nightmare of a war on two fronts. Moltke was then replaced by General Erich von Falkenhayn (1861–1922).

Although Marne had been a strategic defeat for the Germans, the fighting continued. The German and Allied armies were now concentrated in eastern France, north of Paris, but there were few troops between these positions and the English Channel to the north. Both sides tried to maneuver around the northern end of their respective lines, aiming to outflank their opponent.

From late September through November, vicious but indecisive battles were fought along the Aisne River, and then in the Artois and Picardy regions of northern France, before finally moving into Belgium around Ypres. These increasingly desperate attempts to find the enemy's open flank became known as the "Race to the Sea." Neither

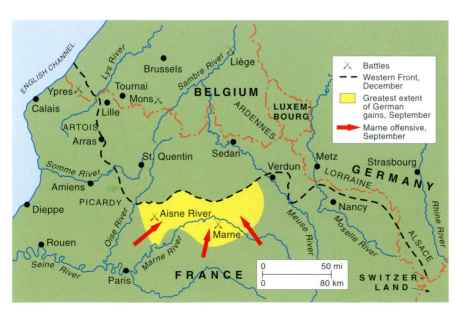

Left: In 1914 the Germans had swept through eastern France, but were halted at Marne. By December both sides had dug the trenches that would set the tone of the war.

trenches; the Allies needed heavy guns firing high-explosive shells, and both were in short supply in 1915.

The Allied offensives of 1915 took place in three distinct phases: from the start of the year into the early spring; during the early summer; and again in the fall. The attacks were launched in two areas: in the Champagne region northeast of Paris, and in Artois nearer the northern end of the Western Front. Weeks of fighting would end in the capture of a mile or two of territory, but only at the cost of huge casualties. The French suffered 1.3 million men killed and wounded and the British lost another 280,000 soldiers. British failure at the Battle of Loos in September led to the appointment of a new commander along the Western Front at the end of 1915, General Sir Douglas Haig.

The Germans largely remained on the defensive in the West during 1915, although they launched a limited offensive around Ypres in April that became notorious for the early use of poison gas as a weapon of war.

side won the race, and 1914 came to an end with the exhausted armies digging in along a continuous 400-mile (640-km) front that stretched from the English Channel in the northwest to the Swiss border in the southeast.

The generals of both sides, who had not expected the war to last more than a few months, were forced to take stock of the situation. Their armies were exhausted, they were short of winter clothing and supplies, and there seemed no obvious and quick way of winning the war before the spring of 1915.

In August 1914 soldiers on both sides had hoped that the war would be "over by Christmas." Many had fought with enthusiasm, seeing the war as both just and patriotic, and as a means to escape dull civilian life. By the end of the year such optimism was buried in the freezing mud of the trenches and the massive casualties of four terrible months of modern war. Almost a million men had been killed or wounded on each side.

Battling in the Trenches

Throughout the whole of the war, the French fielded the majority of the troops on the Allied side along the Western Front, and their generals wanted to recapture the parts of France that the Germans had taken in 1914. The problem was to break through the increasingly powerful German defenses.

Defensive positions usually consisted of lines of trenches defended by barbed wire. Infantry attacking the trenches would be held up by the wire and killed by machine-gun and artillery fire. Attackers needed to find a way of blasting gaps in the barbed wire, smashing the enemy trenches, and knocking out their machine guns and artillery. Attackers also needed to stop counterattacks and, most important of all, coordinate their artillery fire with their own troop movements.

One answer was to use an artillery bombardment, but, as the French and British discovered, they did not have enough guns and shells to do the job. Their guns mostly fired shrapnel shells that were ineffective against

GAS ATTACK

On April 22, 1915, British and French troops defending their lines north of the Belgian town of Ypres saw a greenish cloud spreading out from the German trenches and being blown slowly toward them by the wind. The first soldiers it reached began gasping for breath and choking; others, rightly terrified, ran for their lives. The greenish cloud was made up of poisonous chlorine gas, and represented the first large-scale use of a chemical weapon in modern warfare.

The Germans had not realized just how effective the gas would be in this instance, and did not have enough troops on hand to exploit the gap it made in the opposing lines. Although the results were often not fatal, the effects of gas were often debilitating for long periods, as well as being very frightening for inexperienced troops.

Equipment to counter the effects of gas was quickly developed, the most effective being individual respirators that gave soldiers reasonable protection from the gas. Unfortunately, these masks were cumbersome to use and not always completely effective, especially against the new types of gas introduced later in the war.

War in the East 1914–15

Not long into the war, the Austro-Hungarian armies found themselves dueling with both the Russian and Serb forces. The many battles, especially those with the Russians, that collectively would be known as the Eastern Front, took place sometimes hundreds of miles apart. Even though casualties were in the millions within the first two years in the east, trench warfare was not as much of a feature as it was in the west.

In 1914 the Austro-Hungarian chief-of-staff, General Franz Conrad von Hötzendorf (1852–1925), developed grandiose plans for simultaneous offensives against the Serbs and the Russians – and was overwhelmed by both. The outnumbered Serbs fought the Austrians to a standstill in August and September 1914, while the Russians overran much of the Austro-Hungarian province of Galicia. At the outbreak of the war Austrian soldiers were unsuited for modern warfare, and many of the subject peoples of the empire were hostile to Austro-Hungarian war aims.

The Russians, in an attempt to help their French ally, invaded the German province of East Prussia in August 1914. The invasion of East Prussia was assigned to Army Group Jilinsky, consisting of the First Army, under the command of General Pavel Rennenkampf (1854–1918), which would attack from the east, and the Second Army, led by General Aleksandr Samsonov (1859–1914), which would attack East Prussia from the south. On August 20, the First Army scored a minor tactical victory at Gumbinen, which threw the German commander, General Max von Prittwitz (1848–1917), into a temporary panic. As a consequence of his suggestion to abandon East Prussia, Prittwitz was replaced as commander by Colonel General Paul von Hindenburg (1847–1934), with Major General Erich Ludendorff (1865–1937) as his chief-of-staff.

Although outnumbered, the Germans had several advantages. The two Russian armies opposing them were operating in virtual isolation from each other, and their radio transmissions were never coded, allowing the Germans to gain a fairly accurate idea of the Russians' positions and future movements.

Utilizing their strategic railways, the Germans adopted the proposal of a staff officer, Colonel Max Hoffman, and concentrated their forces against Samsonov in the south. The Germans caught the Russians scattered around the village of Tannenberg on August 20, and in a four-day battle of encirclement utterly destroyed the Second Army. While the remnants of the Second Army fled back to Russian-controlled Poland, Samsonov committed suicide.

Immediately following the battle the Germans, employing their railways again, turned eastward and pushed Rennenkampf out of East Prussia during the first week of September in a series of engagements known as the Battle of the Masurian Lakes.

Despite the recent heavy casualties, the Russians renewed the offensive by striking farther south into the German territory of Silesia. The attack, however, was halted by a German advance around Lódz in November. Throughout the autumn of 1914 battle succeeded battle as each side temporarily gained the advantage without being able to secure a permanent strategic result.

In 1915, the stalemate along the Western Front and the plight of the Austro-Hungarian armies, forced the German chief-of-staff, General von Falkenhayn, to adopt a new strategy that centered on a major offensive against Russia. After bitter winter fighting in the

Right: Within the first two years of the war along the vast Eastern Front, the Central Powers had inflicted over two million casualties on the Russians, while also driving the Serbs into Albania. But it had been a bloody start to the war for the Central Powers as well.

Carpathian Mountains, the Germans prepared to deliver the knockout blow against Russia in Galicia.

A newly formed German Eleventh Army, commanded by General August von Mackensen (1849–1945), was secretly brought up to the Gorlice–Tarnow sector where the main offensive would be launched. After a short, intense bombardment on May 2, the German infantry advanced toward the devastated Russian lines. The German breakthrough, which was rapidly followed by a carefully planned exploitation, caught the Russian troops completely by surprise.

In just two weeks the Germans advanced over 80 miles (130 km) and by the end of May the Eleventh Army alone had taken over 150,000 prisoners. The Russians began to fall back along their entire front and Warsaw fell on August 4, and three weeks later Brest-Litovsk was in German hands. The German-led advance continued until September, when it petered out as the Russians eventually established a new frontline that was able to stem the German offensive.

The Austro-German forces had made massive gains. Not only had they advanced nearly 300 miles (500 km) but they had inflicted an estimated two million casualties on the Russians. To almost any other nation such a defeat would have been a mortal blow, but Russia not only survived but increased the expansion of its war industries, and by 1916 was even contemplating offensive operations.

In the south, Serbia remained a thorn in the flank of the Central Powers throughout 1915 and when they signed a treaty with Bulgaria in September, plans were drawn up to eliminate the Serbian irritant for good. Field Marshal August von Mackensen (1849–1945) was sent to direct the combined Austro-German-Bulgarian forces against Serbia. In October, the Austro-German armies invaded Serbia from the north while two

Bulgarian armies struck in the east. Outnumbered and outflanked, the Serbs – soldiers and civilians – were forced to retreat through the mountains of Albania.

British and French forces landed at Salonika in Greece, but their advance was barred by the Bulgarians. Anglo-French troopships were sent to pick up the survivors of the grueling march through the Albanian mountains, but this was the only help the Western powers could offer their Balkan ally, and 1915 witnessed the temporary demise of "plucky little Serbia."

RAILROADS IN WAR

Germany was the first of the great nations to recognize the importance of railroads to the conduct of warfare. As early as 1842, a scheme was put forward in Prussia for the construction of a network of strategic railroads that would allow simultaneous operations against France and Russia.

On the outbreak of World War I, the strategic railroads that Germany had constructed in the West allowed her to concentrate forces for the invasion of France. In this way Germany was able to rush troops through Belgium and on toward Paris.

France also used her railroads effectively: her general mobilization began on August 2, 1914, and the shipping of troops from depots to the front began at midday on the 5th and was completed on the 19th. Between these two dates, some 4,500 military trains ran on the French railroad network, which also transported the British Expeditionary Forces to the front.

It can be seen that railroads had become a crucial element in the strategy of waging war.

The War against Turkey

The Ottoman Empire, based in Turkey, formerly allied with the Central Powers in October 1914. This proved a huge problem for the Russians since the Turks prevented any British or French ships from sailing through the Dardanelles and into the Black Sea in order to supply Russia with much needed guns and munitions. For the Western Allies gaining control of the Dardanelles became a primary objective.

At the beginning of 1915, an Anglo-French fleet was dispatched to bombard Turkish forts on either side of the Dardanelles. This operation seemed to go well and on March 18, a full-scale naval attack got underway. However, at a critical moment in the engagement, four Allied battleships suddenly struck mines and sank, and the Allied fleet withdrew.

Next the Allies decided to conduct an amphibious landing on the Gallipoli peninsula, on the northwestern side of the Dardanelles, and advance overland to the Turkish capital, Constantinople. Unfortunately for the Allies, it took weeks to prepare the invasion force, and the Turks used the time to rush troops to the area and construct a formidable array of defenses. When the Allies began landing on April 25, the Turks had managed to assemble sufficient troops to bring the assault to a standstill on the beaches.

The Allied force, which included a substantial contingent from Australia and New Zealand, soon found that what had been planned as a deft strategic maneuver turned into another version of the Western Front, with few alternatives to frontal attacks against well-defended enemy positions placed on hills overlooking the Allied trenches. Despite their best efforts, the Allies could not break out of their beachhead around Sedd El Bahr.

The Allies tried to restart their advance by making landings on a new series of beaches around Suvla Bay in August. The Turks were initially caught by surprise, but weak British leadership and poor organization destroyed any chance of success.

Finally, toward the end of 1915 a new Allied plan was devised that involved the evacuation of the landing forces. Pulling out under the noses of the Turks was a complex and dangerous operation but it was brilliantly planned and executed. No Allied lives were lost throughout the two-stage withdrawal in December 1915 and January 1916. During the earlier fighting, however, each side had suffered about 250,000 casualties.

The Dardanelles campaign had been a humiliating defeat for the Allies, who had underestimated the fighting strength of the Turkish forces. The Allies would meet with similar determination when fighting the Turks in the other theaters of war.

Battle of the Empires

As the war progressed Britain became Turkey's main opponent, if for no other reason than that British colonial possessions butted up against the boundaries of the Ottoman Empire. The British had occupied Egypt to ensure the protection of the Suez Canal, a vital link in the route between Britain and British Empire territories in India, Australia, and New Zealand. The Suez Canal was vulnerable to attack from Turkish Palestine and in January 1915, 20,000 Turkish soldiers crossed the 100 miles (160 km) of the Sinai Desert from Palestine to

Left: The Allied campaign to capture the Gallipoli peninsula was the most poorly executed campaign by the British during the whole of war. Inept leadership forced British soldiers to endure the kind of trench warfare similar to that being fought along the Western Front.

Egypt. The Turkish force was too small to be effective, however, and when it attacked the British lines on February 2, the Allies easily defeated it, forcing the Turks to retreat back to Palestine.

Because of their commitments in other areas, neither side did much on this front until the summer of 1916, when the British began an advance across the Sinai Desert. The advance was slow as the troops had to build a water pipeline and a railroad to carry their supplies. The only battle of note occurred at Romani in August 1916, when a Turkish attack on the Allied advance was repulsed. By early 1917 the British had nearly advanced to Gaza in Palestine.

In June 1916 the Arabs living in what is now Saudi Arabia rose up against their Turkish overlords. They captured the holy city of Mecca and began to attack Turkish outposts. The British sent guns and advisers to help the Arabs, notably T. E. Lawrence (1888–1935), later known as "Lawrence of Arabia." Lawrence and the principal Arab leader, Faisal ibn Husayn, led the Arab forces in a daring and successful attack on the port of Aqaba in July 1917. From this new base the Arabs continued their guerrilla attacks on isolated Turkish garrisons and their long lines of communication that extended through Arabia and southern Palestine.

The British too had their problems from indigenous groups. Beginning in late 1915, British forces in Egypt faced a new enemy, the Senussi, a Muslim people based in Libya. In December 1915 the Senussi invaded Egypt from the west. The British used cavalry and armored cars fitted with machine guns to counteract the Senussi's desert mobility, defeating them in February 1916. The Senussi went on to conduct a guerrilla campaign, launching hit-and-run raids and ambushes but avoiding large-scale battles. The Senussi tied down over 100,000 Allied troops before making peace in April 1917.

By March 1917 the British troops, commanded by General Sir Archibald Murray (1860–1945), believed they were ready to invade Palestine. They attacked along the coast near Gaza on March 26. Initially, the attack went well: the Turkish forces were surrounded and on the verge of retreat when, as the result of a signals failure, the British commander withdrew some

WAR IN AFRICA

Aside from the war against the Ottoman Empire, the Allies found themselves involved in a series of campaigns in Africa against the Germans. The war in Africa involved European soldiers and local troops, many of them black Africans, supported by large numbers of civilians and noncombatants who acted in a logistical role.

The German colonies of Togo and the Cameroons were too small and isolated to put up much resistance. German Southwest Africa (modern Namibia) was invaded by a South African force, along with some British troops. The South Africans quickly captured the few railroad lines in the country and took the capital, Windhoek, in May 1915. The Germans surrendered soon after.

German East Africa, now mostly part of Tanzania, was the most important of Germany's African colonies and proved to be the hardest to capture. The German commander, Colonel Paul von Lettow-Vorbeck (1870–1964), was a master of guerrilla warfare. He never had more than 16,000 men, (only about a quarter of them European) under his command, but at one time or another over 130,000 Allied troops were employed in an attempt to track him down. Yet by November 1918 he was still fighting, and only surrendered after the German defeat in Europe.

units from the battle. The Turks recovered and threw the British back to their start line. A second British attack was similarly repulsed during the following month. The British government fired Murray and sent out General Edmund Allenby (1861–1936), with orders to capture Jerusalem by Christmas.

Allenby built up his forces over the summer and planned a daring attack for October. Instead of moving along the coast once again, he decided to strike inland near Beersheba, southwest of Jerusalem. It was a risky plan because the Turks held all the best water sources in this desert area; the British would have to capture them in the first hours of the battle to ensure an adequate supply of water for their mounted units.

Allenby's careful planning paid off: the British captured Beersheba on October 31, and the Turkish troops were forced to retreat northward. Allenby and his men

Left: Toward the end of the war, British heavy artillery in Mesopotamia, pictured here, became an integral part of the successful campaign to defeat the Ottoman Empire.

Left: Turkish soldiers, some of whom are seen here at the start of the war, were ill equipped compared to their Allied enemies, yet they maintained stiff resistance throughout.

1913 Britain had made a deal with Persia that gave the British access to its biggest oil field. This oil field was vulnerable to attack from Turkish-controlled Mesopotamia, so when war broke out Britain sent troops to protect British interests in Persia. Russia also had oil interests in the region, around Baku on the Caspian Sea, and as British forces began to occupy southern Persia in 1914, so the Russians began to move into northern Persia.

Britain sent troops from India to the Persian Gulf with the first objective to protect the Shatt al-Arab waterway along which oil supplies from Persia reached the Persian Gulf. A British warship bombarded a Turkish fort near the entrance to the Shatt al-Arab on November 6; riverboats and land forces then captured Basra on November 23. The initial defensive force had been massively reinforced during the fall and winter of 1914, and the British decided to invade Mesopotamia and advance on Baghdad. But neither the troops nor their commanders realized the difficulty of the terrain and weather conditions they would encounter.

entered Jerusalem on December 8, meeting his deadline with a couple of weeks to spare. The British advance through Palestine came to a temporary halt through a shortage of manpower, as units were withdrawn to Europe to stem the German spring offensive of 1918.

By the late summer of 1918 the arrival of Indian reinforcements allowed Allenby to advance once again. The result was a victory at Megiddo on September 19. Allenby made good use of his mounted forces, as well as the small number of aircraft at his disposal. The Turks were routed and their army began to disintegrate. The victorious Allied army reached the Syrian capital of Damascus on October 1, 1918, entering the city at almost the same time as Lawrence and the Arab guerrilla forces.

By the last week of the month the Allied advance had reached Aleppo in northern Syria, and on October 30 Turkey surrendered. In little more than a month Allenby had advanced 360 miles (576 km), capturing 75,000 Turks at a cost of just 5,600 casualties, an indication of the extent of the Turkish collapse.

Mesopotamian Conflict

The other important theater of war in which British and Turkish troops were involved lay further to the east in Mesopotamia. Britain's navy required large amounts of oil, and in

Right: The Middle East, which was controlled mostly by the Ottoman Empire, was the location of many fierce battles during the war, including Aqaba, Beersheba, and Megiddo.

Right: After the British troops surrendered at Kut, the Allies turned the tide in Mesopotamia (modern Iraq), finally defeating the armies of the Ottoman Empire in 1918.

The British commander, Major General Charles Townshend (1861–1924), began the advance up the Tigris River in May 1915. By September Townshend's men had scored victories at both Al-Qurna and Kut-al-Amara. The Turks pulled back to Ctesiphon, some 20 miles (32 km) south of Baghdad. Townshend's troops attacked them there in November.

The Turks had about 18,000 troops and Townshend about 11,000. Despite the imbalance of numbers, Townshend's assault nearly broke through on the first day of the battle. The Turks managed to hold out, however, and by the fourth day Townshend's army had suffered some 4,000 casualties. Turkish losses were heavier, but the British and Indian troops were exhausted. The British had advanced some 400 miles (640 km) from the sea and were short of supplies, and consequently fell back to Kut-al-Amara, only to be surrounded by the Turks. A long and desperate siege ensued, and although the British tried to relieve the garrison, Townshend's men were forced to surrender on April 29, 1916.

During the second half of 1916, the British assembled new forces, and by December 1916 they were ready to advance up the Tigris from their base around Basra. The new commander, Sir Frederick Maude (1864–1917), was a better general than his overconfident predecessor, and his army had been greatly reinforced. Maude's troops beat the Turks under Khalil Pasha in two battles, at Kut-al-Amara in February 1917 and near Baghdad in early March. After these successes the British captured Baghdad itself on March 11.

Maude sensibly halted his forces at this point to avoid campaigning in the fearful summer heat. The British made important advances in early fall, but Maude, who had done much to regain the British losses following Kut, died of cholera in November. With Baghdad well secure, the British decided to halt their advance in Mesopotamia for most of 1918.

Following Russia's disasters on the Eastern Front in November 1917, Russian forces in Persia and the Caucasus region were gravely weakened. The British were concerned that the Turks (and later the Germans) might attempt to seize the oil fields of northern Persia and the Caspian Sea region. The British advance into Mesopotamia took a back seat during the first half of 1918, as a force under General Lionel Dunsterville was sent from Baghdad north and east into Persia and toward Baku on the Caspian.

After the Allied victories in Palestine in September 1918, it was obvious to the British that the Ottoman Empire was on the verge of collapse. In October, British forces in Mesopotamia were ordered to join in the general Allied advance. Once again the objective was a group of oil fields, this time around Mosul in northern Mesopotamia. The Turkish Sixth Army was swiftly beaten in a few days of fighting and surrendered on October 30, the same day the Turks agreed to a general armistice. The British then pushed on farther to the north and occupied Mosul two weeks later, a victory that marked the end of the fighting in Mesopotamia.

The War at Sea

At the start, both the British and German navies were equipped with the most sophisticated battleships, and the only time the enemy fleets clashed at sea – the Battle of Jutland – proved indecisive. Otherwise, the Germans, with their U-boats, concentrated on disrupting British shipping in the north Atlantic. Yet the most infamous U-boat attack was on the passenger liner *Lusitania*, which prompted US entry into the war.

In the 100 years before the outbreak of World War I, Britain possessed the world's strongest navy and the largest merchant fleet. Maritime trade was vital to Britain's prosperity and to the very survival of the British people. During the 1890s, however, Germany began to build its own strong navy that directly threatened Britain's superior position. Germany's aggressive naval shipbuilding program led to an arms race, and encouraged Britain into an anti-German alliance with France.

The introduction of a new type of battleship – the dreadnought – gave the British an advantage in the race to have the most powerful navy, although Germany soon began to catch up. When war began in 1914, the British Royal Navy had 29 dreadnoughts in service, compared to Germany's 18. Along with its powerful steam turbine engines, the importance of the dreadnought battleship lay in the arrangement of its main armament, which consisted of heavy guns, each of the same calibre, mounted in turrets along the ship's center line. As a consequence, all the dreadnought's heavy guns could fire equally well to both port and starboard.

Britain's strategy for the naval war was based on blockade. The blockade would protect Britain's trade, mainly by keeping Germany's warships imprisoned in their home ports, and was intended to be an effective means of preventing trade by German merchant ships.

The Germans had several fast warships – called commerce raiders – that did some damage to British merchant shipping at the start of the war, but the Royal Navy eventually sunk or rounded up these vessels. At the same time, German maritime trade came to a virtual halt, preventing strategically important goods – such as rubber and some pharmaceuticals products – from reaching Germany.

The Only Major Sea Battle

The Germans gave their main naval force the title of the High Seas Fleet, but it spent the majority of its time in port. Britain's geographical position effectively blocked German access to the oceans: only narrow channels led out of the North Sea to the Atlantic Ocean, and these were guarded by Britain's naval forces or protected by minefields. To reach the high seas, Germany would first have to defeat the Royal Navy's Grand Fleet.

Germany realized that if the Grand Fleet was defeated then Britain would starve and therefore lose the war. At the same time, Britain too recognized its own

Right: The original HMS *Dreadnought*, pictured here not long after its launch in 1906. By 1914 both the British and German navies had copied and improved on its design, making it the model for the modern battleship.

dependence on the Grand Fleet. This placed a huge responsibility on the Grand Fleet's commander, Admiral John Jellicoe (1859–1935), a competent seaman who made few mistakes during the tenure of his command.

The German naval leaders were very cautious, and only on one occasion – May 31, 1916 – did the High Seas Fleet sail out into the North Sea with the intention of committing itself to a full-scale encounter with the British. The resulting Battle of Jutland, which took place about 50 miles (80 km) west of the coast of Denmark, began in the afternoon and lasted into the early night.

The Germans came off best in the early stages, but the British, with 37 dreadnoughts against the German's 21 (both sides had accelerated their already-massive naval building program since 1914), soon gained the advantage. Jellicoe almost trapped the Germans and their commander, Admiral Reinhard Scheer (1863–1928), was forced to organize a retreat. By then it was a dull, hazy evening, with visibility made worse by the smoke from the guns and funnels of the 250 ships involved in the battle. The Germans slipped away into the gloom and escaped before the next morning.

After Jutland the British blockade remained as effective as before, while the German High Seas Fleet was kept bottled up in port for the rest of the war, contributing nothing to the German war effort.

Taking the War below the Sea

If Germany's fleet of surface warships failed to accomplish much, its U-boat arm proved a highly potent weapon. World War I was the first conflict in which submarines were employed in large numbers, and throughout the war, both sides' submarines took every chance they could to sink enemy warships. Then in February 1915, Germany decided to use U-boats to impose its own blockade, sinking British and neutral merchant shipping around Britain's coastal waters. This

first period of unrestricted submarine warfare lasted until September 1915, when the Germans called a halt in the face of bitter protests from the United States and other neutral countries. A particular factor influencing American public opinion was the sinking of the passenger liner *Lusitania* on May 5, 1915, in which 1,198 people, including 128 Americans, lost their lives. The Germans renewed their all-out attacks for a brief period in 1916 but again stopped them after US objections.

At the start of 1917 the Germans decided that the danger of drawing the United States into the war was an acceptable risk if the Allies were to be defeated. They calculated that they could sink enough ships to starve Britain into submission, and even if this meant an American declaration of war, Germany believed the war would be won before the United States was ready to fight effectively on the Allied side.

The German strategy came very close to fruition. The U-boats sank over 1,000 British ships in 1917, and the Royal Navy had failed to come up with an effective method of defeating the underwater menace. By May 1917, the British government calculated that there was only six weeks' supply of food in the country. As a last resort, the British instituted a merchant convoy system that, to the relief of the British government, seemed to work. Progress in antisubmarine technology – depth charges, improved mines, hydrophones – also blunted the U-boat campaign.

British shipping losses in 1918 were at half the rate of those in 1917. The German submarines had failed to starve Britain into submission. Even worse for the Germans, the last unrestricted submarine warfare campaign was the main reason behind the United States' long-expected declaration of war on Germany in April 1917. In addition to failing in their war against British trade and food supplies, the U-boats were unable to halt the transportation of US troops across the Atlantic to France in 1917–18.

Verdun and the Somme

At the beginning of 1916 both the Allies and the Central Powers desperately wanted to take the offensive in the war and weaken the enemy's army. Germany struck first by attacking the fortresses surrounding Verdun, then in June 1916 an Anglo-French offensive hit at German lines near the Somme River. Together these battles witnessed the heaviest artillery fire up until that point and the highest numbers of casualties.

In 1916 the German chief-of-staff, General von Falkenhayn, decided to strike a mortal blow against the French Army, which had already been weakened by almost two million casualties since the outbreak of war. Falkenhayn planned to "bleed France to death" by attacking a section of the line the French felt compelled to defend, regardless of casualties.

The salient around the fortress of Verdun was chosen as the killing ground since it allowed the Germans to bring the maximum amount of artillery to bear on the defenders. Artillery would act as the cornerstone of the German plan, while limited attacks by infantry would seize key points in order to force in French reserves for the "grinding mill" of the German guns.

The German Fifth Army, under the command of Crown Prince Wilhelm (1882–1951), was assigned to attack Verdun and comprised six assault divisions with a further three in reserve. On February 21, 1916, the 1,200 guns (over half of heavy calibre) of the German Fifth Army opened their bombardment, the most devastating yet experienced in warfare. Later in the day, groups of German infantry advanced into the shattered French trenches. Despite the ferocity of the bombardment, the Germans were surprised to find pockets of French

troops still holding on. Determined German pressure eventually wore down the French resistance, and the Germans advanced remorselessly, capturing the key stronghold of Fort Douaumont on February 25.

On the same day General Henri Philippe Pétain (1856–1951) was appointed to command the Second Army defending Verdun. Pétain was an excellent tactician, and, with a reputation for caring about his men, he immediately set about organizing the supply, reinforcement, and relief of his hard-pressed troops. The only route into Verdun was under constant artillery fire, but 300 trucks a day brought the men and munitions to defend Verdun along what became known as *La Voie Sacrée* ("the Sacred Road").

German casualties at Verdun mounted steadily in the face of the Second Army's increasing artillery fire and determined counterattacks. Throughout the spring the battle raged and to the consternation of the Germans, they too found that their troops were going through the "grinding mill." Prince Wilhelm extend the width of the assault, and during April and May the Germans waged bitter battles for possession of the hills and ridges of the east bank of the Meuse River.

The French began to waver in June, but Joffre urged his commanders to hang on for a little longer, knowing that the imminent Anglo-French offensive on the Somme and a Russian offensive on the Eastern Front would take pressure off the exhausted defenders. Thus Pétain's request of June 23 to evacuate his forces to the left bank of the Meuse was refused. The battle raged on, and the French managed to hold their ground.

On July 1, 1916, the Allied offensive on the Somme forced the Germans to close down their operations at Verdun, while, at the end of the month, the French went on the offensive and by December had won back most of the territory lost to the Germans earlier in the year. Total casualties claimed by the long battle were over 300,000 men on each side, and while the battered French Army hung on to Verdun, the instigator of the German plan, General Falkenhayn, was sacked and replaced by the command team from the Eastern Front, Generals von Hindenburg and Ludendorff.

Left: The Battle of Verdun resulted from a German offensive that began in February 1916 with some of the heaviest shelling in history. The long and bloody battle did not end until December 1916, with no territorial gains on either side.

Right: The Anglo-French offensive along the Somme lasted from July to November 1916. When it was all over the Allies had advanced only 10 miles (16 km), yet they'd lost 600,000 soldiers and inflicted casualties of between 400,000–600,000 on the Germans.

During the summer of 1916, while the Battle of Verdun was still raging, the Allies planned to finally execute an offensive that Joffre had devised much earlier but had been postponed due to Verdun. The offensive would focus on a line near the Somme River and the British were to take the leading role, with 12 French divisions in support. The main attack would come from the British Fourth Army, commanded by General Sir Henry Rawlinson. Some 14 British divisions were assigned to the initial attack, along with five French divisions south of the Somme River.

The British relied heavily on their expanded artillery arm, which included just over 2,000 artillery pieces, and substantial supplies of ammunition. In an eight-day preliminary bombardment, over 1.7 million shells were fired, sufficient, the British High Command thought, to destroy the German defenses. But the British did not have reliable heavy calibre guns, nearly a third of the shells fired were defective, and the German dugouts proved more shell-proof than anticipated.

Confident that the guns had done their work, however, the British infantry went "over the top" in perfect order on the morning of July 1, 1916, only to be cut down by well-directed German artillery and machine-gun fire. Out of an attacking force of about 100,000 men, over 57,000 became casualties in the first day's fighting, with nearly 20,000 men killed outright. The British attack was stopped in its tracks.

During the evening of July 1, several German officers, sickened by the slaughter, allowed temporary truces so that some of the badly wounded could be recovered. Other British casualties crawled in under cover of darkness, but many lay undiscovered until after they had died of their wounds; it was the highest daily casualty figure for any army in the history of warfare.

The French, whose attack was supported by plentiful heavy artillery, took the Germans by surprise and made considerable gains at a relatively small cost. The contrast between their flexible infantry tactics and the straight, rigid lines of their ally's advance was a factor in the heavy losses suffered by the British. More important, however, was the failure of the British artillery to overwhelm the defenders.

Although a terrible setback for the British, July 1 was only the first day of the great summer offensive, which was to continue until November. Lessons were learned and more flexible approaches adopted. A successful dawn attack on July 14 marked a vast improvement in British staff work. But every attack soon became bogged down in desperate trench warfare, especially as the Germans operated a policy of vigorous counterattacks; the commander of the German Second Army, General Fritz von Below (1853–1918), instructed his men, "to

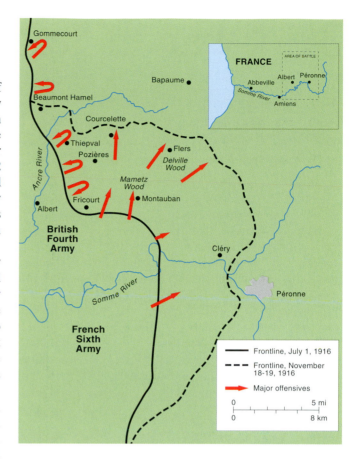

hold our present positions at any cost. The enemy should have to carve his way over heaps of corpses." This order accounted for the 330 German attacks or counterattacks that punctuated the Allied advance on the Somme.

On September 15 the British sent in their Mark I tanks, marking the first use of tanks in battle. Although never considered war winners in 1916, they did manage to catch the Germans by surprise. Local gains, however, were dashed since they were too slow and unreliable for the strains of warfare on the Western Front.

The last phase of the battle ended with the capture of Beaumont Hamel on November 13, when cold rain had turned the battlefield into a sea of freezing mud, making effective operations impossible. The five-month offensive had produced 415,000 British, over 200,000 French, and between 400,000–600,000 German losses.

For great loss of life and scant territorial gains, Verdun and the Somme personified the horror of trench warfare on the Western Front. Although the Germans had held the line on the Somme, the casualties they suffered represented, in the words of one German officer, "the muddy grave of the German field army." The British, while also suffering enormous casualties, had emerged as a fully professional force able to take its place on the Western Front alongside its French ally with full equality. The French Army, however, had suffered grievously in more than two years of sustained bloodletting, and after Verdun and the Somme its powers of resistance were beginning to wane.

The War in Italy

When war broke out in 1914 Italy was allied with the Central Powers, although it remained militarily neutral. There were, however, many Italian-speaking people living in areas along the Austro-Hungarian–Italian border, and some Italian politicians wanted to annex these places to Italy. This became the primary reason for Italy joining the Allies against the Austro-Hungarian Empire and the other Central Powers.

As the Austro-Hungarian forces were already heavily committed to the war against Russia and Serbia, they remained on the defensive on the Italian front after Italy declared war in May 1915. The strategic initiative lay in Italian hands, and their forces launched a series of attacks along the disputed border region with Austria-Hungary.

The fighting took place in two regions: in the Trentino district – north of Lake Garda and in the Dolomite Mountains – and along the Isonzo River, close to where it flows into the Adriatic Sea. The inhospitable terrain of both regions made offensive action difficult, although the high mountains of the Trentino were a particularly hard barrier to cross and became the preserve of mountain troops.

The Italian chief-of-staff, General Luigi Cadorna (1850–1928), decided to concentrate on the Isonzo sector, while his specialist mountain troops were deployed in the Trentino. No battlefield soldier, Cadorna planned elaborate battles on paper that took little or no account of the problems his men actually faced on the ground.

The only part of the Isonzo front capable of military operations was about 20 miles (32 km) wide and, whatever Cadorna planned, his attacks ended up battering against well-prepared Austro-Hungarian positions. During 1915, Cadorna fought four battles along the Isonzo; the Italians lost about 180,000 casualties to 120,000 Austro-Hungarians, and gained almost no ground at all.

The Fifth Battle of the Isonzo (March 1916) was a similar failure, after which the Austro-Hungarians began planning an attack of their own. The Austro-Hungarians had been able to build up their forces in the region, receiving reinforcements freed by the defeat of Serbia at the end of 1915. The Austro-Hungarian chief-of-staff,

Right: The campaign in Italy was one of he most difficult of the whole war. The terrain was largely mountainous, which added to the dangers endured by the troops. Supplying armies became a nightmare, especially during the winter months.

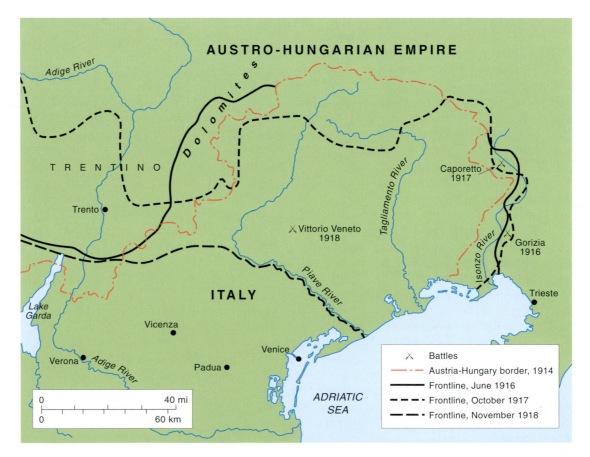

General Conrad von Hötzendorf, was as badly out of touch with the realities of fighting in such terrain as Cadorna. He ordered an offensive in the Trentino region, but failed to ascertain if such an attack was feasible over the high Alpine passes.

The Austro-Hungarians concentrated 160,000 men against 100,000 Italians in this sector, and made substantial gains when their offensive was launched on May 14, 1916. However, bad weather and the mountainous terrain prevented the Austro-Hungarians from maintaining momentum, and by the end of the month the attack had ground to a halt. Soon afterward, any remaining Austro-Hungarian reserves were called away to hold a Russian offensive on the Eastern Front.

More Fruitless Battles

The Italians resumed the offensive in the Isonzo region, as battle followed battle without any tangible result, except a mounting casualty list. The Sixth Battle of the Isonzo (August) was followed by the Seventh (September), the Eighth (October), the Ninth (November), and then, after a pause for winter, the Tenth Battle (May 1917). Despite outnumbering the Austro-Hungarian defenders between two and three to one, the total Italian advance in the first 10 Isonzo battles was only about 12 miles (18 km). Only one attack, the Sixth Battle, which captured the town of Gorizia on the Austro-Hungarian side of the river, could remotely be called successful.

Despite these failures, Cadorna was not ready to give up. In August 1917, he assembled his strongest attack force yet and launched the Eleventh Battle of the Isonzo. This time the Italians did better, pushing forward six miles (9 km) in one sector. Fearing an enemy breakthrough, the Austro-Hungarians called for help from their German allies, and the arrival of German reinforcements on the Isonzo Front forced Cadorna to abandon his offensive.

The arrival of high-grade German troops on the Italian front altered the balance of forces in favor of the Central Powers, who decided to go onto the offensive. The Italian forces still slightly outnumbered their enemies, but the German and Austro-Hungarian troops were concentrated within crucial sectors, trained in new battle tactics, and equipped with a new type of poison gas. When they attacked on October 24, they smashed the Italian front wide open. This Battle of Caporetto was a disaster for the Italians, who were forced to retreat over 70 miles (112 km) to the Piave River. The advance by the Central Powers was only halted when French and British reinforcements arrived to help the Italians.

In June 1918, the Austro-Hungarians attacked once again, but their generals had underestimated how well the Italians had recovered from the Caporetto disaster. Although the Austro-Hungarian force made some early progress, Italian resistance increased and a surprise Italian counterattack forced the Austro-Hungarians to retreat. By October 1918, with the Germans and their allies retreating on every other front, the new Italian chief-of-staff, General Armando Diaz (1861–1928), decided that the moment had come for a new Italian offensive.

Assisted by substantial British and French forces, the Allies attacked across the Piave River and in the Trentino on October 23, 1918. The exhausted and wavering Austro-Hungarian forces, now showing little enthusiasm for a war they could not win, collapsed. Over 300,000 Austro-Hungarians were taken prisoner in this final Allied offensive, known as the Battle of Vittorio Veneto. It was the largest Italian victory of the war, and the most decisive. The day after the battle ended, October 28, the Austro-Hungarians asked the Allied powers for an armistice, which duly came into effect on November 4, 1918.

The fighting in Italy had been terribly costly in terms of lives lost, and the futile slaughter certainly bears comparison with the losses suffered in Flanders.

Right: Two Italian soldiers equipped with gas masks on sentry duty at the front in the Isonzo sector of the Italian Front. Extensive trench lines made offensives costly in terms of casualties, especially as the terrain tended to funnel attacks into small areas.

War in the Air

Though hot-air balloons and lighter-than-air airships did participate in World War I, the future of military aviation lay with the heavier-than-air aircraft driven by one or more engines. Used in limited numbers in 1914, by the end of the war these aircraft were playing an important role in supporting ground operations, as well as flying long-range bombing missions.

In August 1914, France's *Aéronautique Militaire* was probably the most powerful and efficient of the fledgling air arms, with approximately 130 frontline aircraft. By 1918, airpower had become a vital component of every battle plan and, by way of comparison, at the end of the war Britain's Royal Air Force possessed over 22,000 aircraft. Although aircraft played a part in every theater of the war, both sides sent their strongest air forces to the Western Front. The air battle over the trenches became as fierce and deadly as the fighting on the ground.

The aircraft used by all sides in 1914 were flimsy and underpowered. They carried no weapons; their sole military role was that of reconnaissance. As the ears and eyes of the army, aircraft were far more effective than cavalry, although their capabilities were limited in many other respects. Pilots had no means of signaling the information they discovered to friendly troops unless they flew back to their own territory to drop a message, or landed and delivered one personally.

The Pace of Development

The Farman MF-7 – used by France and Britain – was fairly typical of the aircraft available in 1914. It was an unarmed "pusher" biplane (with the engine and propeller mounted behind the fuselage) with a top speed of about 60 mph (96 km/h). Within the space of four years, the pace of technological change was such that a Spad S-XIII fighter – in service with France and the United States – was twice as fast as the Farman and carried two machine guns as armament.

By the end of the war it was not only the aircraft that had changed beyond recognition, but also the range of tasks they performed. Reconnaissance remained the most important air role throughout the war, but the reconnaissance aircraft were soon joined in the air by fighters and bombers.

Within a few months of the war's start, the capabilities of reconnaissance aircraft were transformed by the introduction of aerial photography, which made possible the assembly of extremely detailed maps of enemy positions. Another reconnaissance mission was artillery spotting, observing the fall of shells, and making corrections where necessary. At first, reconnaissance aircraft employed flags and colored flares to signal to observers on the ground, but simple radios were gradually introduced, which made communication far more effective.

For all types of mission, reconnaissance aircraft had to fly over a particular area on a straight and level course. This made them vulnerable to fighter aircraft, which had been developed as a countermeasure to aerial reconnaissance, as well as ground fire – aircraft were nothing more than wood and canvas frames.

Initially fighter pilots used pistols and other hand-held weapons to attempt to shoot down their enemies, but it was obvious that machine guns were much more effective. A necessary requirement for an effective fighter aircraft was a front-mounted machine gun. Front-mounted machine guns worked well with "pusher" type aircraft, but designers soon discovered

STRATEGIC BOMBING

Most aerial bombing in World War I was carried out against military positions and installations at or near the front, but by 1918 aircraft began to attack targets deep behind enemy lines. Such raids, typically aimed at munitions factories or transportation centers, were the first examples of strategic bombing.

A German aircraft dropped bombs on Paris during the first month of the war, while the first long-range raid by the Allies was carried out by the British later in 1914, its target being Zeppelin sheds in Düsseldorf.

German Zeppelins carried out strategic bombing raids up to 1917, when they were replaced by faster Gotha aircraft. The German raids against London caused consternation, especially when civilian targets, such as schools, were bombed. The Gothas and their British equivalents, the Handley Page 0/100 and 0/400, proved vulnerable to the enemy fighters and antiaircraft artillery, but without sophisticated detection tools, such as radar, they were difficult to locate.

These early air raids caused little physical damage and relatively few casualties, but they were a terrifying reminder that the war could reach and destroy civilian targets.

that these had a limited performance. "Tractor" type aircraft, with the engine and propeller at the front, could usually fly faster and higher, which was an obvious advantage for a fighter, but the arc of the propeller prevented the machine gun firing forward.

The problem was solved by Anton Fokker, a Dutch engineer working in Germany. He designed a synchronizing device, or interrupter gear, which stopped the machine gun firing during the instant that one of the propeller blades was in front of the muzzle. This device was first used in the summer of 1915 and gave the Germans complete air superiority until the spring of 1916, by which time the Allies had devised their own versions of the interrupter gear.

Sky Heroes

The best pilots became famous as air aces. Newspapers and government propaganda sources boasted of their exploits and described them as modern-day knights, jousting chivalrously with their enemies above the clouds, though they seldom commented on the short life expectancy of airmen. Pilots like Eddie Rickenbacker, the top American ace with 26 "kills," and Canada's Billy Bishop with a score of 72 aircraft shot down, became household names. But for most pilots the prospects of survival were at least as grim as for the ordinary soldier in the trenches, perhaps more so since parachutes only came into service towards the end of the war. Germany's

top ace, Baron Manfred von Richthofen – the Red Baron – shot down at least 80 enemy aircraft, more than any other pilot, but even he was killed in 1918.

Bomber aircraft also underwent a dramatic transformation. It did not take long for grenades dropped by hand by a crewman to be replaced by larger bombs carried on a bomb rack. By 1918, bombers included large two- and four-engined types designed for long-range strategic bombing against the enemy homeland, and smaller designs for use over the battlefield, the latter the forerunner of the ground-attack aircraft. Some even carried armor plating to protect their pilots and crucial components from enemy fire during low-level missions. Aside from the power to hit towns and cities, bombers also gave commanders the ability to strike at enemy reserve formations.

The balance of power in the air over the Western Front swung first to one side and then the other, as new aircraft designs came into service and briefly held the advantage over the enemy in terms of armament, speed, maneuverability, or rate of climb. The Germans had two periods when they were on top in this way: from the summer of 1915 into the spring of 1916, and from the fall of 1916 through to the spring of 1917. The odds were more even at most other times during the war, although by the middle of 1918 the Allies had built up a huge material superiority that the Germans could never hope to match.

Stalemate in the West

Both sides had grand plans to end the war on the Western Front in 1917. General Robert Nivelle (1856–1924), fresh from his successes in the final stages of the Battle of Verdun, was promoted to command the whole French Army. His massive offensive would begin in the spring, while the British also planned a major assault in 1917. Both ended in terrible slaughter.

The terrible casualties the German Army had suffered during the Battle of the Somme and at Verdun in 1916, for little or no territorial gain, convinced General Ludendorff – the military brains of the German Army – to adopt a new strategy for 1917. Outright battles of attrition were a two-edged sword for the army, Ludendorff decided, which in the long run would benefit the Allies, who had more men and resources than Imperial Germany.

Ludendorff ordered that the German Army should drop its old policy of automatically counterattacking every Allied advance. He even voluntarily retreated from a large area of captured French territory to the so-called Hindenburg Line. He knew that the French and British would continue with offensive operations, and he hoped that by adopting a defensive strategy he would suffer less casualties and exhaust the Allies.

The German withdrawal to the Hindenburg Line forced General Nivelle to modify his plan of attack at the last minute, although he was still confident that his French soldiers could break through the German lines and win the war. Unfortunately for the French, the Germans were well prepared and had secured good information of Nivelle's intended plans.

Nivelle's offensive, officially known as the Second Battle of the Aisne, began on April 16, 1917. It was soon obvious that it was not going to result in a decisive victory, and within four days the French had scaled down their efforts after suffering about 120,000 casualties. Limited attacks continued into the second week of May, but with nothing like the gains that Nivelle had promised.

By the standards of some earlier battles the results were not all that bad, but the high expectations that Nivelle had raised caused deep disappointment, and recriminations abounded throughout the army and government. In the trenches, the ordinary French soldiers felt betrayed. In addition to the constant drain of casualties, they had to put

Left: The Battle of Passchendaele was the British Army's major offensive in 1917. A combination of wet weather and enemy resistance turned it into a slaughter for little gain — the British suffered 300,000 casualties.

Left: The Battle of Cambrai in November 1917 was an indication of what tanks could achieve, notwithstanding that most broke down or were destroyed on the first day. It was a taste of future war.

infantry advance started on July 31. The Germans held a strong position, made even more redoubtable by skilfully linked concrete pillboxes armed with machine guns.

Although the British had more guns and air superiority, the marshy ground conditions and the weather favored the defense. When the battle began so did the torrential rain, while at the same time artillery shells smashed the land drainage system to pieces. The result was that the battlefield became a swamp. The British maintained the offensive until the middle of November. At this point they had sustained about 300,000 casualties and won just five miles (8 km) of ground. The Germans had suffered heavily, too, so much so that the German High Command began to have doubts as to how long its army could survive repeated batterings of this nature.

up with poor food, almost no leave, and the most rudimentary medical services. Toward the end of April, thousands of troops began to mutiny, most refusing to resume offensive operations against the Germans, and some refusing to obey all orders from their officers.

Nivelle was relieved of his command on May 15, to be replaced by Pétain. The new commander gained the trust of the men and the mutinies fizzled out, but they had come as a profound shock to the Allies, and it would take months for the French Army to recover. As a consequence, the brunt of the fighting on the Western Front would pass from the French to the British Army.

Field Marshal Douglas Haig and the other British generals had never shown much faith in Nivelle's plan, even though they had agreed to support it with a limited advance of their own in April. Haig's preference was for an offensive at the northern end of the Western Front, around Ypres. The first stage of the offensive was a clear-cut success for the British. On June 6, they attacked an important German position south of Ypres at Messines. Over the previous months the British had dug 19 vast mines under the German frontlines, and had packed them with huge amounts of explosives. At zero hour, shortly before the attack, they were detonated and blasted a series of huge gaps in the German lines, and the British and Canadian infantry secured Messines Ridge with relatively few casualties. But the victory at Messines was only a prelude to the main offensive around Ypres.

The Third Battle of Ypres, or, as it became popularly known, the Battle of Passchendaele, was launched in July. After a long preliminary bombardment, the

The Battle of Cambrai

The Battle of Cambrai, which began on November 20, concluded offensive operations on the Western Front in 1917. Although little more than an extended raid, it achieved fame for being the world's first tank-led battle. Some 320 British tanks smashed a gap in the German lines, but the British lacked reserves to push forward and exploit the gap. During the first day's fighting, over half the British tanks were either knocked out or broke down, and the remainder soon suffered a similar fate over the next couple of days. Resolute and well-handled German counterattacks pushed the British back in most areas, and captured new ground elsewhere.

The year 1917 therefore ended with all the armies on the Western Front having suffered terrible casualties with little apparent gain. The Allies, however, had a trump card that they would be able to play in the following year's fighting: the arrival of the United States Army. The German advocacy of unrestricted submarine warfare had turned American public opinion against Germany, while during the course of the war a close economic partnership between the Allies and the United States had developed. The final straw for the United States had been the discovery of German diplomatic interference in American–Mexican affairs. On April 6, 1917, the United States declared war on Germany. For Germany, hopes of achieving victory were fast diminishing.

Collapse in the East

By 1917 Russia was a creaking edifice ready to collapse. The massive casualties suffered during three years of war, combined with social upheavals at home, resulted in the collapse of the Russian war effort in 1917. As the Russian Army fell apart, the Eastern Front became a quiet sector for the German High Command, who switched troops to the Western Front in France.

During 1916, however, the imminent collapse of Russian military power had not yet become clear. The Brusilov Offensive – named after its Russian commander General Alexei Brusilov (1853–1926) – was aimed against Austria-Hungary, and, lasting from June to October, was Russia's most successful military operation of the war. Brusilov's success even persuaded a previously neutral country, Romania, to join the war on the Allied side. But the Russian triumph was to prove short-lived and ultimately illusory.

By virtually knocking the Austro-Hungarian Army out of the war, the Russians ensured that Germany would take complete control of operations on the Eastern Front. One of Germany's major war aims was to dominate the whole of eastern Europe and exploit the region's economy. Romania was the first country to experience just how ruthless this policy could be.

Romania joined the war hoping to grab land from Austria-Hungary, but it turned out to a foolish and short-sighted decision. In a three-week campaign in November and December 1916, a German army overran almost the whole of Romania. For the rest of the war, grain and oil seized from Romania would help feed and fuel the German war effort.

Catastrophic Russian losses

The fall of Romania led to an extension of the Russian frontline down to the Black Sea and acted as a further drain on the country's reserves of manpower. By the end of 1916, Russia's total casualties were estimated to be around five million. Shortages of foodstuffs in the bitter winter of 1916–17 led to riots in the major cities, and a growing mood of disquiet among the Russian population. In March 1917, against a background of mass demonstrations and the breakdown of discipline in the army and the police, Czar Nicholas II was deposed and a provisional government installed in his place.

The new government, essentially liberal in character, was committed to the continuation of the war, and, to the delight of Russia's Western allies, seemed set to expand the war effort. The Provisional Government's authority was, however, increasingly undermined by the activities of left-wing political groups, whose insistent demands for "peace and bread" met with a positive response from Russia's war-weary and long-suffering peasants and soldiers.

Despite the growing dissatisfaction within the Russian Army, the minister for war, A.F. Kerensky, decided to renew offensive action to encourage his forces and the Russian people. Known as the Kerensky Offensive, the operation got underway on July 1, 1917. Some progress was made in the initial stages, but a devastating German counterattack brought the Russian advance to a dead halt. The Russian soldiers had had enough, and began to retreat regardless of their officers's orders. In Lenin's famous phrase, "they voted with their feet." From August onward the army began to fall apart, as desertions and mutinies became ever more common among units.

New Tactics

In September, the Germans exploited their defeat of the Kerensky Offensive with a limited offensive of their own, the attack and capture of the Baltic port of Riga by General von Hutier's (1857–1934) Eighth Army. The attack was notable for the what was probably the first instance of "predicted shooting," in which the German artillery fired on their targets without using ranging shots prior to the attack. Predicted shooting restored the advantages of surprise to an attack, and would be widely used on the Western Front in 1918.

Within Russia itself, the weakness of the Provisional Government enabled the Bolshevik faction of the Social Democrats to seize power in November 1917 (the famous "October" Revolution – so called because of Russia's adherence to the old Julian calendar some 13 days behind the international system). Under the determined leadership of V.I. Lenin (1870–1924) and Leon Trotsky (1879–1940), the Bolsheviks had little trouble ousting the government, and once in power immediately set out to gain peace terms from Germany.

In December 1917, the Bolshevik leaders began negotiations with the Germans. An armistice was agreed on the 15th, as negotiations for a permanent treaty got underway. Over the next two months of talks, Germany demanded huge tracts of territory, which the Bolsheviks were reluctant to concede. The Germans forced the issue and sent their troops advancing deep into Russia. The Bolsheviks, having limited military means, were forced to give way. By the Treaty of Brest-Litovsk, signed on March 3, 1918, Germany took control of well over 25 percent of the Russian people, 75 percent of Russia's coal and iron resources, and a vast swathe of territory covering what are now the independent states of Estonia, Latvia, Lithuania, Belarus, and the Ukraine.

German forces moved into all these areas to exploit them for Germany's benefit. With the end of fighting against Russia, many of the German formations, until now committed to the Eastern Front, were redeployed to France, where Germany's leaders planned new offensives for 1918. The outcome of these battles would also determine whether Germany would be able to defeat the Allies in the west and keep its new empire in eastern Europe. The offensive in the West was to be Germany's last chance to avoid defeat.

Though Russia had lost much territory, under the direction of Trotsky her fledgling Red Army would become a powerful force, albeit one still essentially peasant in nature. Trotsky was a tireless administrator and organizer who basically transformed the Bolshevik armed forces from a ragged militia into an effective, highly motivated fighting force. His methods involved employing czarist officers as commanders in the Red Army, while he ensured that the rank and file received supplies and rewards for their services. He used Russia's railroad system extensively, switching forces from one sector to the other during the Civil War against the so-called Whites (a loose collection of royalists, anti-Bolsheviks, and nationalists). In this way he helped to preserve the young Communist state. He also did not hesitate to mete out harsh punishments if the circumstances warranted such action. Strangely, this also helped to improve morale, as soldiers could see that incompetence would not be tolerated, especially among the high command. The reverse had been true in the czar's armies, which had led to so many deaths.

Left: Lenin addresses a crowd outside a railway station in St. Petersburg in April 1917. He ended Russia's participation in World War I.

Germany's Last Gamble

At first glance Germany was in an excellent position to win the war in 1918. Having brought the war in the East to a successful conclusion, her military dictatorship of Hindenburg and Ludendorff could concentrate on the Western Front. But time was running out for Germany, especially with the imminent arrival of hundreds of thousands of American troops.

American troops would not arrive in great numbers before the summer, however, and Ludendorff and other senior German officers believed this gave them a brief window of opportunity for an all-or-nothing spring offensive. The Germans had defended successfully on the Western Front throughout 1916 and 1917, even though they had been outnumbered. Now, with Russia out of the war, they could switch troops from the Eastern Front and obtain a numerical superiority over the Allies – at least until the Americans arrived in strength.

The German planners decided to focus their attack at or near the juncture of the French and British armies, with the aim of exploiting different national priorities: the French would feel compelled to block a German advance toward Paris, while the British would be more concerned to defend northern France and the ports on the English Channel.

The road and rail communications between these northern areas and the rest of France passed through the city of Amiens. Ludendorff planned to attack Amiens and drive the British north and the French south. Once he had captured Amiens, he surmised, the British and French would be unable to support each other, and he could then defeat each army separately.

The German attack began on March 21, 1918, with a five-hour bombardment by almost 10,000 guns and mortars. Three reinforced German armies faced two British armies (one understrength) along a 45-mile (72-km) front south of the town of Arras. Much of the British frontline was smashed by the German barrage, but the damage done to the British command centers and artillery positions was more important. Only some of these were knocked out, but most were made useless by having their communications cut and their men prevented from moving by a hail of poison-gas shells.

By the end of the first day of the battle, the British were in retreat and already had over 20,000 men taken prisoner. By March 25, the Germans had advanced about 25 miles (40 km), farther and faster than in any Western Front battle since 1914. It seemed as if Ludendorff's grand strategy was working, too, for Pétain, the French commander-in-chief, was refusing to send any significant help to the British.

The gravity of the situation did, in fact, force greater Anglo-French cooperation. On March 26, the British and French governments appointed General Ferdinand Foch (1851–1929) to coordinate their operations on the Western Front and supervise their national commanders, Haig and Pétain. From that point onward the Allies worked together much more effectively. Although the German attacks were still gaining ground, their advance was being held in the most vital sector near Amiens.

By early April, Ludendorff reluctantly accepted that his efforts to push the British out of Amiens had failed, and he halted the offensive on the 5th. Both sides had suffered about 250,000 casualties, but these were casualties that the Germans, in particular, could ill afford. Ludendorff moved operations farther north and launched a new assault, this time around the city of Ypres. The renewed offensive began on April 9, with the Germans employing the same infiltration tactics. Some parts of the Allied frontline were breached, but once again desperate Allied defense halted the German advance within a few days.

Ludendorff was not yet finished, however. He had decided that the British were his chief opponents, but he

STORM TROOPERS

During the 1918 spring offensive, the German Army employed new infantry and artillery tactics. Artillery bombardments were short but intense, and concentrated on specific targets, the aim being to create gaps in the chain of defensive strong points and confuse the enemy commanders and artillery batteries. Gas was extensively used to create disorder in the rear areas.

Specially trained elite infantry known as storm troopers then took up the attack. The first wave made no attempt to capture frontline enemy strong points, but was instructed to slip past them and cut them off from their own rear areas; follow-up troops would capture them later.

The main aim of these German infiltration tactics was to advance swiftly through the opposing frontline, disrupting the enemy as much as possible. If all went to plan, a large gap would be opened up in the enemy's lines, and its command and control centers would be overwhelmed and be unable to direct reinforcements to plug the gap.

believed that he could not achieve a breakthrough until he had drawn the bulk of the Allied reserves away to the south. He switched his artillery and his remaining reserves of storm troopers south to the Chemin des Dames area of the Aisne River sector. The hurricane bombardment crashed out once again on May 27. The local French commander made a mess of his defensive plans, and the Allies were thrown back along a 25-mile (40-km) front.

By the end of May, the German offensive had gained another 30 miles (48 km) of ground. They had reached the Marne River at Château-Thierry and seemed poised to drive on toward Paris. It was not to be, however, for their troops were exhausted and Allied reserves were in position to counterattack.

Enter the Americans

For the first time in the war, US troops played a significant part in the fighting. General John Pershing (1860–1948) was placed in command of the troops earmarked for Europe, the American Expeditionary Force (AEF). The first Americans had arrived in Europe in June 1917, and Pershing planned to have one million troops ready for action by May 1918.

Pershing's US troops first fought battles at Cantigny, Château-Thierry, and Belleau Wood during late May and June 1918. At Cantigny, the US 1st Division captured the German-held village and then held off desperate German counterattacks. At Château-Thierry, the US 3rd Division halted the German advance across the Marne and then repulsed the enemy. The US 2nd Division, mainly composed of US Marines, suffered over 50 percent casualties but helped halt the Germans and then drove them back in the Battle of Belleau Wood in early June. Ludendorff halted the German assault on June 4.

Ludendorff decided that he had to keep attacking to keep the advantage, but many of his highly trained storm troopers had been killed in his earlier offensives. Their replacements were inexperienced

and less aggressive in battle, and most German infantry units were now badly understrength. But unable to think of other options, Ludendorff ordered two more offensive actions. Each of these attacks suffered the same fate, winning ground for the first two or three days before being halted by the Allies. Most ominous for the Germans was the fact that the Allies were able to halt these attacks without committing all their reserves. The balance of power had turned irrevocably in favor of the Allies on the Western Front, and Foch now planned a series of offensives to drive the Germans back to their homeland and ultimate defeat.

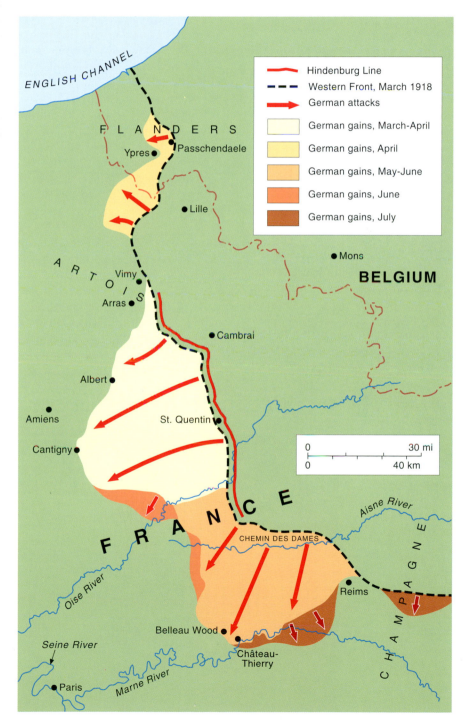

Right: The German offensive on the Western Front in 1918 was designed to defeat Britain and France before US troops arrived. It started promisingly, but then ran out of steam.

The Collapse of the Central Powers

The German offensive in the West had failed by July 1918, and now it was the turn of the Allies to hit back. Reinforced by the Americans, Allied armies began to counterattack all along the front. The German Army, its reserves spent and its morale cracking, fell back. Its great gamble had failed, and it now faced certain defeat in the face of overwhelming material and numerical supremacy.

Ludendorff's last, desperate offensive of 1918 gave the Allies their cue to take the initiative. The German operation, known as the Second Battle of the Marne, began on July 15. Ludendorff planned to advance on two fronts, east and west of the city of Reims, but good Allied intelligence and clever defensive tactics ensured that the attack east of the city was halted before it could get going. West of the city, the Germans did somewhat better and managed to push a large force across the Marne River. Within two days, however, they had been fought to a standstill by the French, with American assistance.

Ludendorff now realized that his men were exposed and vulnerable in the great salient they had carved into the Allied line. Unfortunately for the Germans, the Allied commanders had spotted this weakness too, and were themselves ready to attack before the Germans could pull back from the salient. The Allied advance began on July 18, and the assault smashed into the German right flank. Most of the attacking troops were from the French Tenth and Sixth armies, but these formations included American, British, and even some Italian units.

The offensive was supported by 2,000 guns, 1,200 aircraft, and over 500 tanks. These weapons helped the advance gain almost eight miles (13 km) of ground on the first day. By the time the Allied generals halted their drive to reorganize their forces at the start of August, all the territory the Germans had captured in the Aisne and Marne sectors in May and June had been retaken.

In the meantime, other Allied forces were ready to increase the pressure on the Germans. After the mainly French victories of July, the British were ready to take over the lead in August. The British Fourth Army was secretly reinforced and conducted a crushing attack along the Somme sector on August 8 (the Battle of Amiens). In keeping with the majority of Allied attacks from then on, it relied on a combination of infantry, artillery, tanks, and aircraft to break through the enemy lines. The Germans were taken by surprise and pushed back as much as eight miles (13 km) along the 20-mile (32-km) attack front on the first day.

Right: US forces approaching the front prior to the opening of their offensive against the Germans in the Second Battle of the Marne in July 1918. US troops were arriving in France at the rate of 300,000 per month.

Right: The US-led offensive at St. Mihiel was a joint attack by US and French forces. The aim was to smash through a bulge in the German frontline. At the cost of 7,000 US casualties, the attack succeeded.

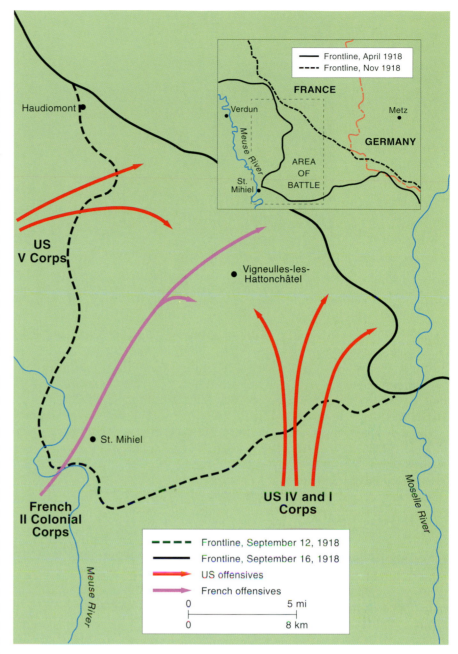

The German commanders were dismayed to learn that some of their frontline forces had panicked or surrendered after putting up only minimal opposition. Ludendorff went so far as to call August 8, the "black day of the German Army." The British kept their advance going for almost a week, but day by day their progress began to slow. The tanks had played a big part in the initial success, but only six of the 414 used on the first day were still fit for action by August 12. Many had been knocked out by German artillery fire, but more had simply broken down or become stuck in difficult ground.

Both sides had now devised tactics that made it possible to break through a tough enemy defense line. The Germans used hurricane artillery bombardments and infantry infiltration tactics, while the Allies had added tanks and strong air forces to their broadly similar infantry and artillery techniques. However, the Allies were now discovering what the Germans had found earlier in 1918, that breaking through was one thing, but taking advantage of a success was another. Neither side had the mechanized forces capable of bursting through the initial gap torn in enemy lines to convert a tactical advance into a strategic victory.

During 1916 and 1917, the Allied generals had been criticized for stubbornly continuing with offensives for months, long after any momentum had been lost. Now they tried a different and more effective strategy. On August 15, they decided to halt their advance east of Amiens and switch their efforts farther north.

The British Third Army attacked successfully in this area between August 21–29, and then the First Army took over the lead farther north still at the end of August. By constantly switching the point of their attacks in this way, the Allies could prevent the Germans from holding reserves at critical points in the line, while maintaining the momentum of their own advance.

By early September the Germans had decided that the bulge in their lines around the town of St. Mihiel on the Meuse River was likely to be attacked by the Allies. The Germans chose to pull out, but the withdrawal orders came too late. On September 12, the US First Army, led by General Pershing, attacked with some 300,000 men. By September 16, when the battle ended, the whole of the bulge in the German line had been captured along with 15,000 German prisoners, at a cost of fewer than 7,000 American casualties.

By mid-September, the Allied advance along the entire front had regained all the ground the Germans had won in the first half of the year, and more in areas such as St. Mihiel. The Germans had fallen back to the Hindenburg Line.

The Allied attacks resumed on September 27, and it was the British forces that struck the decisive blow. Ludendorff hoped to hold out there long enough to

Right: African-American troops move up to the front in the Argonne Forest in November 1918, the month World War I ended.

convince the Allies to agree to a peace treaty favorable to Germany. He was shocked when carefully planned British attacks smashed through the much vaunted Hindenburg Line in three days.

Farther south, the French and Americans opened a new offensive in the Argonne. The AEF had to be transferred northward to its start position with the utmost rapidity, a maneuver that proved too much for the US staff organization. Once the battle got underway, the American soldiers showed a forceful resolution in attacking German positions, but their progress slowed due to logistic shortcomings. Nonetheless they refused to give up the advance, which continued throughout 47 days of almost constant fighting. Once supplies to the forward troops were put on a sound footing (with the help of French and British staff officers), the Americans steadily forced the Germans back.

From then until the end of the war in November, there were few spectacular big battles, but rather a continuous series of smaller advances by the Allied forces. German machine-gun troops often put up a tough fight and caused many casualties, but many more German troops began to give up the fight and either surrendered to the Allies or deserted from their army.

Germany and its allies had now lost the war. Bulgaria gave up fighting at the end of September, Turkey ceased hostilities at the end of October, and by early November the Austro-Hungarian Empire was falling apart. Peace negotiations between Germany and the Allies actually started in late September but dragged on into October, as the Germans still tried to insist on a deal that allowed them to hold on to captured territory in eastern Europe.

The reality was that Germany had no choice but to accept the Allied terms. Without allies, and with strikes and antiwar protests at home turning into revolution,

the outlook for Germany was grim. But the main reason for Germany's problem in coming to the peace table lay with the German Army: it had been defeated in battle but its military leaders still refused to admit this humiliating fact. .

The German Army's plans had been instrumental in starting the war in 1914. Germany's generals had virtually ruled the country for most of the war, and had insisted on achieving outright military victory, whatever it might cost – ignoring opportunities for a negotiated peace that might have benefited the German people. This strategy had failed and the Allies were poised to overrun Germany, if not in late 1918 then certainly in the spring of 1919.

A new civilian government took over in Germany in early October. Ludendorff was forced to resign from his post as Germany's chief military planner on October 27, clearing the way for the German government to finally agree with the Allies on an end to the fighting. The armistice came into effect at 11.00 a.m. on November 11, 1918. People in all countries hoped that the conflict would be the "war to end all wars."

The costs of a war that had lasted four years and had dragged in almost every European state had been massive. The estimated military battle deaths in the belligerent nations were as follows: France, 1,357,800; British Empire, 908,370; Russia, 1,700,000 (plus a staggering 2,000,000 civilian dead); Italy, 462,390; United States, 50,585; Belgium, 13,715; Serbia, 45,000; Montenegro, 3,000, Romania, 335, 700; Greece, 5,000; Portugal, 7,222; Japan, 300; Germany, 1,808,546, Austria-Hungary, 922,500; Turkey, 325,000; Bulgaria, 75,844. This gives a grand total of just over eight million men killed on the battlefields alone. The total number of wounded exceeded 22,000,000, and civilian deaths are estimated to have been 6,642,000. The sheer scale of the casualties somewhat deaden the senses, yet they were proof, if proof was needed, that the machine gun and artillery piece made frontal infantry attacks near suicidal. And yet, both the French and German armies entered the war with tactical doctrines that stressed the importance of seizing and maintaining the initiative.

As the war progressed several important developments took place. Motor transport in theory gave commanders the means to exploit breaches of an opponent's front before enemy reserves could be committed. In the event, this would only become apparent in World War II. Similarly, the development of aircraft added another dimension to warfare. By 1918 aircraft were major factors in both land and air warfare. Again, this would become apparent in World War II, when aerial superiority became crucial to the success of both Axis and Allied land offensives.

In the light of the massive national effort made by the Allies to secure victory, it was hardly surprising that they should seek to impose harsh peace terms on the Central Powers, especially Germany. According to the terms of the Treaty of Versailles, Alsace and Lorraine were returned to France, and Germany lost further territories in the east, notably to the new state of Poland. In addition to the imposition of heavy reparations, Germany's armed forces were severely curtailed: the air force was abolished, the navy was denied U-boats and capital ships, while the army, which became known as the *Reichswehr,* was limited to 100,000 men.

The old empire of Austria-Hungary was completely dismantled, bringing into existence the new states of Yugoslavia, Czechoslovakia, and Poland. Bolshevik Russia was ostracized by the Western powers, while Finland and the Baltic States achieved full independence at the expense of Russia. Turkey lost its Arabian empire to become a republic based in its heartland of Asia Minor.

By the early 1920s, Europe had achieved some sort of political order, but the Versailles Treaty was not the guarantor of a permanent peace settlement. Germany had been humiliated, and the Nazi rise to power in the 1930s signaled the resumption of the great power struggle for national dominance in Europe. Tragically, World War I had failed to resolve this issue – it was the first round in a conflict that would erupt again in open warfare in 1939.

Right: Some of the prisoners taken by the Allies in the late summer of 1918. Ironically, the morale of German soldiers began to fall when they came across well-stocked Allied dumps behind the lines – their own supplies were limited.

World War II
1939–45

World War II remains the most violent and destructive conflict in human history. What began as an essentially regional dispute in 1939 was transformed into a global war that culminated in the dropping of the atomic bomb on Japan six years later. Over 50 million people were killed in the war, two-thirds of them civilians. In addition, the ideological conflict between the Axis and the Allies helped give the conflict its particularly violent character.

The scale of the casualties in World War II reflected not only the length and nature of the war, but also the weapons used. Land warfare involved few weapons that had not been used in World War I, but they had become much more deadly in the subsequent world war. The power and reliability of the internal combustion engine was greatly improved, making possible the introduction of swift and well-armed and armored tanks. Artillery, as the war progressed, also became much more mobile. By the end of the war, infantry had their own mechanized troop-carriers, which provided them with a degree of protection on the battlefield and greatly improved their mobility. In stark contrast to the mud-bound battlefields of 1914–18, World War II witnessed a re-emergence of movement on the battlefield. And movement combined with firepower became the cornerstone of military success.

At sea, the battleship, though still important, gave way to two vessels whose mode of operation took place above and below the surface: the aircraft carrier and the submarine. The age of warships slugging it out within view of each other was at an end. Naval battles were conducted without the rival fleets meeting head-to-head, as aircraft were able to attack surface targets miles from their home bases. Submarines were used to great effect by both Axis and Allies to destroy merchant shipping, and those countries which relied on maritime trade, such as Britain and Japan, suffered heavily.

The greatest transformation in the conduct of warfare came in the air. Rapid technological advance was crucial in the development of highly effective

Right: US Marines fighting on the island of Tarawa in November 1943. Five days of battle cost the Marines 985 dead, while only 100 of the 4,700 Japanese garrison survived.

Right: Nazi Brownshirts putting up leaflets urging Germans to boycott Jewish-owned shops in the 1930s. Hitler had written in *Mein Kampf*: "Thus did I now believe that I must act in the sense of the Almighty Creator: by defending myself against the Jews I am doing the Lord's work." Once in power the Nazis began a systematic persecution of Jews by introducing laws that prevented them from taking part in everyday life, such as being excluded from the civil service and other professions.

fighter, bomber, and transport aircraft. As a consequence, whole cities were raised to the ground by vast aerial armadas, and by 1945 jet aircraft had become a reality. Ground troops could be flown into battle for the first time, either in gliders or dropped by parachute.

One of the greatest changes in warfare, due largely to radio communication, was the effective coordination of land, sea, and air forces in amphibious landings. The war in the Pacific, for example, was won by the United States through the intelligent application of amphibious warfare techniques, and the Normandy landings of 1944 remain as the largest combined air–sea–land operation of all time.

Technological progress ensured that frontline soldiers required more equipment, which in turn meant that increasingly large numbers of serving men and women did not fight directly. Their job was to get soldiers into battle and keep them fighting. Estimates suggest that for every man in action four or five others were required to support him with food, clothing, weapons, ammunition, and medical services.

World War II also transformed the political landscape of the globe: the decline of Europe was mirrored by the emergence of the United States and the Soviet Union as superpowers of the Nuclear Age who would dominate the world stage for half a century. Of the two, the United States was vastly superior both militarily and economically. Industrial expansion in the United States between 1940 and 1944 rose by over 15 percent a year, with no adverse affect on the civilian sector of the economy. At the war's end only the United States, with its surplus of production and materials, could revitalize the world economy, which came about with the Marshall Plan and the distribution of $13 billion worth of economic aid to European states.

But the Communist Soviet Union rejected American hegemony, and set about creating its own sphere of influence. This competition resulted in the Cold War: the creation of two blocs in Europe, the escalation of rivalry from Europe to the rest of the world, an increasing arms race, and the creation of Soviet and Western alliances across the globe. The creation of the United Nations, though incapable of bringing about world peace, helped to prevent all-out war between the two.

The Causes of World War II

The Treaty of Versailles, which followed Germany's defeat in World War I, caused deep resentment within Germany. As well as being deprived of overseas colonies, Germany lost border territories (mainly to France and Poland) and was forced to pay the Allies heavy war reparations. This mood of national bitterness was cleverly exploited by the right-wing demagogue Adolf Hitler (1889–1945) to further the aims of his National Socialist (Nazi) Party. In the political turmoil of postwar Germany, Hitler emerged as a skilled orator, delivering speeches to discontented ex-soldiers and workers. By 1923 he had gained control of the fledgling Nazi Party, which grew in strength during the 1920s.

Hitler's rise to power in Germany was preceded by Mussolini's in Italy. Benito Mussolini (1883–1945) was another fascist dictator who had come to power in 1922. His regime had achieved some notable successes, such as road building, balancing the budget, and agricultural reform, and he also built up his army, navy, and air force. He glorified war and talked of the Mediterranean as being *Mare Nostrum* – "Our Sea."

In the Far East, a militaristic Japan annexed Korea and overran the whole of Manchuria, which was renamed

Manchukuo. In 1936 it signed the anticommunist Anti-Comintern Pact (to counter the subversive activities of the "Comintern," the Soviet-controlled system of international communist parties) with Germany and Italy, thus becoming part of the Rome–Berlin–Tokyo Axis.

The economic hardship caused by the Great Depression of the early 1930s and the fear of mass unemployment played into the hands of the Nazis. Hitler promised the German people that he would overturn the Versailles Treaty, solve the country's economic woes, and return Germany to a dominant position in Europe. After making substantial gains in the elections to the German Reichstag (parliament), Hitler was appointed Chancellor in January 1933. Almost immediately, the Nazis set about undermining the institutions of the German state and consolidating their own power. The communists and other left-wing parties were brutally suppressed, trade unions were banned, and the persecution of the Jews began in earnest. In August 1934, Hitler felt sufficiently confident of his position to dispense with the German parliament and declare himself Führer (Leader). Germany was becoming a totalitarian state.

In breach of the Versailles Treaty, Germany began to rearm, concentrating on aggressive instruments of war such as tanks, bomber aircraft, and U-boats. The growing strength of Germany's armed forces led Hitler to adopt an increasingly belligerent foreign policy. He was aided by the refusal or inability of other major powers to discourage his territorial ambitions. The Soviet Union and the United States were not members of the League of Nations, and both states adopted a policy of non-intervention in world affairs. Britain and France were the two major powers within the League, but, weakened by their efforts in World War I, neither country had the will to put a brake on Hitler's demands. In fact, the Western democracies lacked the will to meet German and Japanese expansionism, compounded by the fact that in both Britain and France there was a belief that the Treaty of Versailles had been harsh on Germany and that some of Hitler's demands were indeed "just."

German Territorial Conquests

In 1936, Germany reoccupied the Rhineland, without opposition from France and Britain. German troops were also sent to Spain to aid General Franco's forces fighting against the Spanish government. The Spanish Civil War (1936–39) would provide the German Army and Air Force with valuable lessons in the conduct of modern warfare. In March 1938, German troops marched into Austria, which now became an integral part of the German Reich. Later in 1938, Hitler put pressure on Czechoslovakia to cede those of its territories in the Sudetenland region that contained large numbers of ethnic Germans. An international conference took place in Munich in September 1938 that sanctioned the dismemberment of Czechoslovakia. The French Army and Navy had been partially mobilized

during the Sudenten crisis, but the country was in favor of a peaceful settlement, and French premier Edouard Daladier received a hero's reception after the Munich Agreement.

Hitler's success in forcing concessions from France and Britain encouraged him further. Formerly, his demands had been to restore lands inhabited by German-speaking majorities to the German Reich. But in March 1939 he crossed this line when he annexed the remains of Czechoslovakia (inhabited by Czech-speaking Slavs). This alerted Britain and France to his real intentions, and when, in the summer of 1939, he demanded the return of the Danzig Corridor from Poland, the governments of Britain and France signed a treaty with Poland to come to its aid in the event of a German invasion.

Prelude to War

Hitler was undeterred by the new resolve of the Western Allies, especially as he had signed a secret non-aggression pact with the Soviet Union. Hitler considered the communist Soviet Union to be his natural enemy, and the pact was little more than a temporary expedient that would enable Germany to avoid the possibility of a two-front war. Under the terms of the treaty, Germany would be given a free hand in Poland; in exchange the Soviet Union would receive territory in eastern Poland and influence in the Baltic States. Between June and August 1939, there were a number of border incidents between Germany and Poland which heightened international tension and led to repeated warnings from both France and Great Britain. On September 1, 1939, German forces invaded Poland; two days later Britain and France declared war on Germany. World War II had begun.

Above: The key players at Munich (left to right): Neville Chamberlain, Edouard Daladier, Adolf Hitler, and Benito Mussolini.

Victory of the Blitzkrieg

In 1939 the German Army was far ahead of its rivals with regard to mechanized warfare. The Blitzkrieg (Lightning War) doctrine, with its tactics of speed and shock, was a new approach to war, and when it was unleashed the results were spectacular. Poland was conquered in 27 days, Denmark in 24 hours, Norway in 23 days, Holland in five, Belgium in 18, and France in just over five weeks.

The key to German successes during the early stages of World War II lay in the skillful combination of powerful armored and aviation units, coordinated by radio communications. This was the cornerstone of the Blitzkrieg philosophy. The soldier who did most to promote armored warfare in Germany was a former signals officer, Heinz Guderian (1888–1953). His belief in aggressive offensive action, spearheaded by tanks, won him both enemies and supporters in the German Army. Fortunately for Guderian, he gained the favour of Hitler, who invariably encouraged bold solutions to problems, whether military or political. In 1937 Guderian was appointed commander of a corps that contained three panzer divisions — the largest such formation in existence at the time.

Blitzkrieg was put into practice as German troops crossed into Poland. The Germans deployed 1,500,000 troops in five armies; the Poles were able to mobilize just under a million men when the Germans struck. In the first phase of the German offensive, the Luftwaffe (German Air Force) attacked Polish air bases and was so successful that in a matter of days the Polish Air Force ceased to exist as an effective fighting force. Thereafter, the Luftwaffe acted in support of ground operations and bombed Polish towns and cities at will.

The German Army's assault was spearheaded by nine mechanized divisions that easily ripped through the Polish frontier defenses. The Polish Army had been deployed too far forward along their borders, allowing the mobile German forces to encircle isolated Polish formations. Lacking good radio communications and effective mechanical transport, the slow, unwieldy units of the Polish Army were destroyed in detail by the Germans.

After penetrating the frontier defenses, German tanks pressed deep into Poland, so that by September 7, lead units were only 25 miles (40 km) from Warsaw. The bulk of the Polish Army found itself encircled. An attempt by the Poles to break out on the River Bzura was held and then crushed by the Germans on September 17. On the same day, Soviet forces invaded Poland from the east. The Soviet action made the situation hopeless for the Poles.

On September 18, the Polish government fled to Romania (and then on to France and Britain, where it established a government-in-exile). Small pockets of Polish troops continued to resist, but the campaign was effectively over with the capture of Warsaw on September 27.

After the fall of Poland, the attention of Germany and the Allies began to focus on Scandinavia. Germany relied heavily on imports of iron ore from Sweden, which were shipped to Germany via the Norwegian port of Narvik. The British and French began to consider ideas to intercept these shipments, even though they took

Left: One of Germany's Panzer IV tanks. Well armed and highly mobile, the panzers were the Blitzkrieg's spearhead.

THE GERMAN BLITZKRIEG

At the heart of the Blitzkrieg concept was the panzer (armored) division. The cutting edge was provided by a powerful complement of tanks, although each division had its own supporting infantry, engineer, antitank, artillery, and antiaircraft units.

The panzer forces were not generally employed to attack an enemy's strongest point, but instead concentrated on areas of weakness in order to drive deep behind enemy lines to cause maximum confusion and prevent the enemy regaining the initiative. Major enemy defenses or large bodies of troops were avoided. The potency of the panzer assault was greatly helped by the close support provided by the Luftwaffe. Dive-bombers attacked enemy troop concentrations, headquarters, and key communication points, such as bridges, to act as a form of "aerial artillery."

place in Norwegian territorial waters. Hitler became aware of possible Allied interference and, sympathetic to the German Navy's demand to have access to Norwegian ports, he decided to invade Norway.

Norway had a small fascist party led by Vidkun Quisling, which could be relied to support any German invasion. The invasion duly came on April 9, 1940, and involved a daring plan using air, naval, and ground units to simultaneously seize key positions in Oslo, Kristiansand, Stavanger, Bergen, Trondheim, and Narvik. Although caught by surprise at the speed of the German operation, Britain and France dispatched troops to Norway.

The conquest of Norway

The Germans relied on gaining maritime supremacy in the waters around Norway, but suffered heavy losses from local forces and the British Royal Navy. During the two naval battles of Narvik (April 10 and 13) 10 German destroyers were sunk, while further south, the cruiser *Blücher* was sunk and the pocket battleship *Lützow* damaged. Meanwhile, German airborne units seized airfields in Norway. This allowed them to reinforce the invasion and redeploy fighter and bomber aircraft to be used against Royal Navy warships patrolling off the Norwegian coast.

Although the Norwegians fought resolutely against this unprovoked attack, they lacked strategic control and suitable weapons and equipment. The Germans had captured many Norwegian military depots, leaving hastily summoned reservists without even the most basic of weapons. Franco-British forces (supported by Polish troops recently escaped from Poland) landed at Narvik (April 14) and Trondheim (April 18), but they lacked

adequate equipment, while a confused chain of command acted against decisive action.

The Allies' attempt to secure Trondheim ended in failure and their troops were either forced to surrender or be evacuated on May 3. In the northern port of Narvik, the Allies did better and eventually wrested the town from German hands on May 28. By then, however, the German invasion of France and the Low Countries had transformed the Allies' strategic priorities. Narvik was abandoned on June 8, and Norway came under German control.

Norway and Denmark remained under German occupation for the remainder of the war, and Quisling was eventually installed as a puppet ruler of Norway. The German campaign in Norway was a triumph of planning and decisive execution, in marked contrast to the blundering half-measures adopted by the Allies. Yet, Hitler's triumph was less than complete. The Germans had suffered heavy naval losses that prevented the German Navy from providing sufficient forces to mount a credible invasion plan of Britain later in the year. And while German sources of iron ore were secured, vast numbers of German troops were tied up in Norway for the duration of the war.

Triumph in the West

Despite its success, the campaign in Norway was always a sideshow. Hitler's attention was firmly fixed on the destruction of the Allied armies in the West in France. The German plan called for Army Group B (General Bock) to launch a powerful but limited offensive through the Low Countries, to knock out Holland and Belgium (two countries that wanted to stay neutral, and in which there were no Allied forces) and to draw in French and British troops. Meanwhile, the main blow – spearheaded by élite panzer divisions – would be struck farther south by Army Group A (General Rundstedt) in the hilly Ardennes region. The imaginative German plan was largely the work of General Erich Manstein (1887–1973), a brilliant soldier who was then acting as chief-of-staff to Army Group A. Although both sides were evenly matched in numbers and firepower, the Germans had a telling superiority in organization, training, and leadership.

On May 10, 1940, German troops of Army Group B swept into Holland and Belgium. Unprepared for mobile warfare, the Dutch were quickly overwhelmed and forced to accept surrender terms on May 15. The Belgians fell back to defensive positions and awaited the arrival of French and British reinforcements. The Belgian Army placed great reliance on an extensive line of fortifications, which included the fortress of Eben Emael that many considered impregnable. But in a daring raid led by gliderborne paratroops, the fortress was captured, allowing the Germans to advance deeper into Belgium and engage and pin down advancing Allied formations.

Meanwhile, the panzer divisions of Army Group A threaded their way through the wooded defiles of the Ardennes, emerging on May 13 to smash through the flimsy French defenses on the River Meuse. Meeting little opposition, the German panzers raced toward the English Channel. The stunned Allied High Command made feeble attempts to stem the flood of German armor, but it was always a case of too little too late.

On May 17, Colonel Charles de Gaulle (1890–1970) attacked the Germans at Montcornet, but his small force of tanks could make little impression on the advancing German columns. On May 21, a British counterattack at Arras caused initial consternation to the German High Command, but the situation was restored by the energetic action of the commander of the 7th Panzer Division, Major-General Erwin Rommel (1891–1944). Just 10 days after the opening of the offensive, tanks of Guderian's XIX Panzer Corps reached the coast at Abbeville, establishing the "Panzer Corridor" that now cut the Allied armies in two.

Outflanked and facing disaster, the British Expeditionary Force (BEF) fell back toward the port of Dunkirk to prepare for evacuation. Although this left the French in an increasingly desperate position, the British situation was also proving untenable, especially when the Belgians surrendered on May 28. Altogether some 338,000 men (a third of them French) were evacuated from Dunkirk, but the BEF left behind all its artillery, vehicles, and supplies. The operation was hailed as a triumph in some quarters, and while it preserved the nucleus of the British Army, in reality it merely confirmed German mastery of the battlefield.

Now that the Netherlands, Belgium, and Britain were out of the running, the Germans turned south to deal with the remainder of the French Army, which was attempting to establish a new line to protect Paris and the interior. On June 5, with panzers to the fore, the Germans sliced through the French defenses: Paris fell on the 14th; advance units captured Lyons on the 20th; and on the 22nd, Marshal Philippe Pétain (1856–1951), the newly installed French prime minister, signed an armistice with the Germans. Hitler insisted that the French surrender should take place

Right: The German attack in the West in May 1940, the key to which was an armored thrust through the Ardennes.

at Compiègne, in the same railway carriage that had been used for the 1918 Armistice.

Within the space of six weeks Hitler had totally defeated France, his major opponent, and had forced the British Army to scuttle back across the Channel. The Germans directly occupied northern and western France, but allowed Pétain to form a puppet administration in the south of France, named Vichy after the city where it was based. Mussolini, convinced that France was defeated, launched an invasion of southern France on June 10, only to see his 32 divisions thrown back by six French divisions in the Alpes Maritimes. It was a foretaste of military humiliations to come.

The French Army was disbanded (save for a small self-defense force), although the powerful French Fleet remained in being. As the new French government was no longer an ally, the British were extremely concerned that these ships might be used against them. On July 3, 1940, British warships were dispatched to the main French base of Mers-el-Kébir in Algeria, demanding that the ships be surrendered, or at least immobilized. While the French had no intention of permitting a German takeover, they refused the British demands. In reply the British opened fire, sinking or damaging

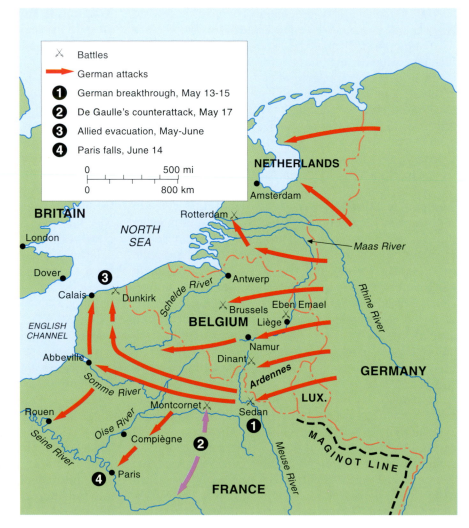

✕	Battles
→	German attacks
❶	German breakthrough, May 13-15
❷	De Gaulle's counterattack, May 17
❸	Allied evacuation, May-June
❹	Paris falls, June 14

several ships and killing 1,297 French sailors. Understandably, the incident caused great French ill-will toward Britain, but it showed to the world — the Americans in particular — that Britain would be ruthless in continuing the fight against Hitler.

In a brief campaign the Germans had conquered all of Western Europe. Only Britain and its far-flung empire remained to oppose Hitler's armed forces. Steeled by the speeches of the new prime minister, Winston Churchill (1874–1965), the people of Britain prepared for the impending German invasion. Hitler had ordered a plan of invasion to be drawn up (Operation Sealion) but before the German Navy could transport the panzers across the Channel, the Luftwaffe had to win control of the skies over southern England. To mount an invasion the navy also had to secure the English Channel against the Royal Navy, which would be impossible without German aerial superiority.

The Battle of Britain

The struggle for air superiority, known as the Battle of Britain, was a close-fought event, and was the first campaign to be fought solely between rival aircraft. Throughout the summer of 1940 the Luftwaffe squadrons, flying mainly from bases in northern France, attacked Royal Air Force (RAF) airfields dotted across southern England. RAF Fighter Command had the significant advantage of an extensive early-warning radar system and a highly capable leader, Sir Hugh Dowding (1882–1970). Dowding made the most of his limited forces to repel the attackers, although during

Above: RAF pilots race to their Hurricane fighters during the Battle of Britain. In total the RAF lost 915 aircraft, while Luftwaffe losses were 1,733 aircraft shot down.

August and early September the RAF was losing more pilots than it could replace and its airfields were being pounded to destruction by the German bombers. During this period over 450 British fighters were destroyed, while 103 of the RAF's pilots were killed and a further 128 wounded.

The turning point in the battle came when Hermann Göring, commander-in-chief of the Luftwaffe, switched his forces from attacks on the RAF's fighters and their airfields to the bombing of London. The British capital was beyond the range of the best German fighters, leaving their bombers unprotected. Heavy losses forced the Germans to turn to night bombing raids. The people of London and other major British cities endured great suffering during the "Blitz," but these attacks gave the RAF time to regroup. Unable to defeat the RAF in battle, on October 12 Hitler postponed Operation Sealion indefinitely.

Hitler believed that an invasion of Britain was relatively unimportant. By the autumn of 1940 his main focus of interest had turned toward the invasion of the Soviet Union. Hitler had always planned to conquer the Soviet Union, a country he detested and whose people he wanted to enslave. However, there is no doubt that the Battle of Britain was one of the crucial victories of the war, if only in so much that it ensured that Britain could become a launch pad for any future invasion of Nazi-occupied Europe.

Hitler Turns East

Operation Barbarossa, the German attack on the Soviet Union in June 1941, was the largest land invasion in history. Its initial successes were colossal, as whole Soviet armies were surrounded and destroyed in vast battles of encirclement. But the Germans failed to take Moscow and destroy the Red Army in 1941, and their 1942 offensive ended in disaster at Stalingrad, marking the turning point of the war.

Hitler's belief that he could crush the Soviet Union with impunity proved to be his costliest blunder. By invading the Soviet Union, without first defeating Britain, he was forced to fight on two fronts for the rest of the war. Germany could not take on the might of the Soviet Union and the Western Allies at the same time, particularly after the United States entered the war in 1941 and Soviet forces had been fully mobilized.

The German plan to invade the Soviet Union was codenamed Barbarossa (after a medieval German emperor, Frederick Barbarossa – "Red Beard") and was scheduled to last no more than four months. At the time this appeared to be a conservative estimate. On the Allied side most observers were in agreement that the German invasion would succeed. The chief of the British Imperial General Staff, for example, gave the Soviet Union's Red Army a mere six weeks to hold out. Some British intelligence sources thought the Soviet Union would surrender in just 10 days. Such fears were perhaps justified as a consequence of the massive purges of senior officers carried out in the late 1930s by the Soviet leader Josef Stalin (1879–1953). To add to the chronic shortage of trained and capable officers, the Red Army was poorly equipped and largely under the control of Communist political officials (commissars) with very limited military skills.

The German plan called for an attack along a 2,000-mile (3,200-km) front by Army Groups North, Center, and South. The German aim was to capture Moscow and Leningrad and annihilate the Red Army west of the Dvina/Dnieper line (Hitler did not want to pursue a fleeing enemy army into the Russian interior) in a series of huge battles of encirclement that would take the German Army to the banks of the River Volga, 300 miles (480 km) east of Moscow. Hitler believed this could be achieved in four months. Each army group consisted of a number of infantry armies and a panzer army, and was well supported by the Luftwaffe. Ground units were drawn from across German-occupied Europe, but with hindsight it is clear that they were not sufficiently well equipped for the task ahead. For the invasion to succeed, the Germans would need a vast supply of robust motor vehicles, yet they had too few, and many of those available were unlikely to function in extreme weather conditions. Such was the confidence of the German planners, however, that they did not expect to have to fight through the winter.

The number of German armored divisions was doubled, mainly by stripping the existing ones of half their tanks and allocating them to the new formations. Although the more powerful Mark III and IV tanks had now largely replaced the light and inadequate Mark Is

Left: German troops edge forward behind a Czech-built tank during the first few weeks of Operation Barbarossa. In this period German gains were massive, as Hitler's armies took Minsk and Smolensk, netting 290,000 and 100,000 prisoners respectively. A greater victory occurred when Kiev was taken on September 19, 1941, with 665,000 Soviet troops being captured. But Red Army reserves seemed inexhaustible.

Left: Two German Panzer III tanks advance through a Soviet village during the attempt to take Moscow in late 1941. By this time most panzer units had been reduced to 50 percent of their original combat strength, and infantry units were in a similar condition. In early December the Soviet counteroffensive began, reinforced by 100 fresh divisions. The German Army was thrown back as the offensive continued into 1942.

and IIs, Germany still lacked sufficient numbers of armored vehicles to take on the Red Army. Russia's rail network, which might have been used to speed supplies to German forward units as they pushed deeper into the Soviet Union, ran on a different gauge from that of Germany, and all goods had to be transshipped from one gauge to the next.

Fighting in the Balkans, which diverted large German forces into southern Europe between April and May 1941, delayed the start of Barbarossa for a crucial five-week period as the Wehrmacht conquered Yugoslavia, Greece, and the island of Crete in a whirlwind campaign. Although, in fact, there were some advantages to the revised June 22 start, not least the favorable weather and long summer days.

Barbarossa – the Attack

At dawn on the 22nd, from the Arctic Circle to the Black Sea, an army of over three million men advanced into the Soviet Union. The Luftwaffe devastated the great lines of Soviet aircraft that it caught on the ground, and German armored units forged ahead as they had in France. Army Group North (Field Marshal Leeb) raced forward along the Baltic region, and by July 14 forward units were closing in on Leningrad, the Soviet Union's second city, which was promptly besieged. Army Group Center (Field Marshal Bock) had the bulk of Germany's panzer forces and its target was Moscow. Initial progress was swift, the German tank units fighting vast encirclement battles against the surprised Soviets. The capture of Minsk on June 29 trapped over 300,000 Soviet soldiers. Army Group South (Field Marshal Rundstedt) advanced into the Ukraine, but short of mechanized forces and faced by vast distances, it made less striking progress.

The tank was the decisive weapon in the war on the Eastern Front, yet the German armored units found themselves facing a considerable enemy in the Russian KV-1 and T-34 tanks. They were well-armored and were more than a match for the German tanks facing them in battle. Only the Germans' vastly superior tactical handling of their armored forces tipped the scales in the invaders' favor.

The Racial and Political War

The war on the Eastern Front was the most ferocious in the history of warfare. Not only were vast numbers of troops involved in fighting over an enormous area stretching from the Baltic to the Black Sea, but the nature of the fighting was pitiless. Hitler believed this to be a war of extermination, and the German armed forces were instructed to behave accordingly. Jews, Communists, and government officials were to be killed on the spot, while prisoners were treated so badly that the vast majority of the six million Soviet troops captured on the Eastern Front died of starvation and disease. For their part, German soldiers knew that if they were captured they would be killed or treated as slave labor.

Despite the speed of their advance, the Germans also found it necessary to commit large numbers of troops — men they could ill-afford to spare — to contain Soviet partisans in conquered areas. Although they had suffered a series of calamitous defeats, Red Army soldiers continued to fight on. In the wide spaces of German-occupied Russia and the Ukraine, Soviet soldiers overtaken by the German advance waged a brutal guerrilla war against the invaders.

By mid-July the Red Army had undergone considerable organizational changes. Commanders were given more independence to make their own decisions, and the senior officers held in Stalin's prisons since the 1930s were released. Although it would take time for these improvements to take effect, it was a promising pointer to the future for the Red Army.

Throughout July and August, the German armies pressed the Red Army backwards. On July 19, Army

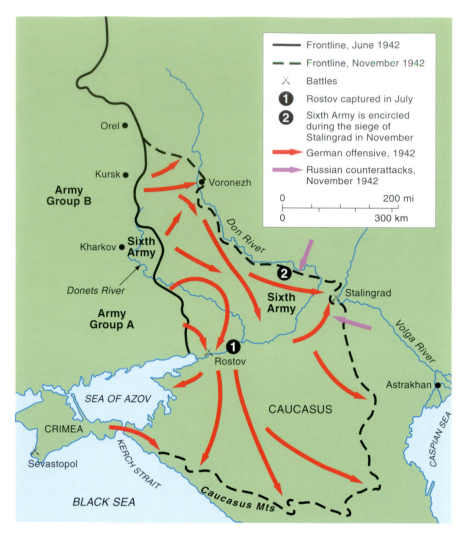

Soviet spy operating in Japan, had discovered that the Japanese had no intention of attacking the Soviet Union, so the Siberian troops could be moved eastward to face the Germans. By the end of 1941 the immediate threat to Moscow had been lifted. The Red Army's heavy counterattacks continued throughout January and February of 1942 but were held by the Germans, who had set up formidable defensive positions. The situation settled into a stalemate during the spring thaws, which made the movement of men or machines almost impossible.

On May 8, 1942, the Germans renewed their onslaught to eliminate the gains achieved by the Red Army during its winter offensive. Hitler decided to move the point of attack away from Moscow to the mineral-rich regions of southern Ukraine and the Caucasus. Substantial advances were made in the Crimea. Sevastopol, a key Soviet port, was captured by early July and some 100,000 Red Army troops were eliminated. The German spring offensive was swiftly followed by the opening of their summer attack on June 28, codenamed Blue. This was aimed at Rostov, the gateway to the Caucasus and its oil fields, and at Stalingrad, farther north on the River Volga. By deciding to attack both targets simultaneously, Hitler divided and weakened his overstretched forces, as well as opening up a dangerous gap between the two army groups involved.

Group Center's advance on Moscow was slowed when Hitler insisted, against his generals' advice, on diverting key armored forces to help Army Group South's encirclement of Kiev. Although the maneuver, completed in September, netted 600,000 Soviet prisoners, progress was delayed in securing the key objective of the campaign: Moscow.

As winter approached, the race to Moscow, codenamed Operation Typhoon, intensified, but the Germans were too late. Rain set in and vast seas of mud literally stopped the panzers in their tracks. Following the rains, temperatures began to fall, catching the Germans unprepared. Few had been equipped with warm clothes, and severe cold added to their growing casualty list. By November over 750,000 Germans had been killed, wounded, or taken prisoner.

The German Army was exhausted and its ability to wage offensive operations was severely diminished; Hitler was reluctantly forced to accept a halt to operations on December 8. During the same week the Red Army launched a massive counterattack. Many of these troops had been dispatched from Siberia, where they had been placed to halt any possible Japanese attack on the Soviet Union. However, Richard Sorge, a

The Drive to Stalingrad

The drive eastward began on July 13. German troops of Army Group A quickly captured Rostov, but the advance on Stalingrad by Army Group B was slowed by the diversion of more forces to the south. Then, angered by the slow advance on Stalingrad, Hitler withdrew units from those forces earmarked to support the attack on Rostov and sent the units back to Stalingrad. The advance of Army Group A in the south, hampered by inadequate resources, ground to a virtual halt in the foothills of the Caucasus Mountains, as German attention was switched to the attempt to take Stalingrad.

Throughout the fall of 1942, the German Sixth Army, commanded by General Friedrich Paulus (1890–1957), fought for Stalingrad, in what the German soldiers

PRISONERS OF WAR

During the initial German drive into the Soviet Union hundreds of thousands of Red Army soldiers were captured. The Geneva Convention, a series of regulations governing the treatment of prisoners, was recognized by most countries, but the contempt in which the Eastern European peoples were held by Hitler ensured that many of them were murdered outright or worked to death. German soldiers taken by the Soviets, in their turn, could expect savage reprisals if captured. Few Germans who went into Soviet prisoner of war camps returned to their homeland, most dying of disease, starvation, and overwork.

Other Allied prisoners fared better at the hands of the Germans. Most were sent to German prisoner of war camps, where they were usually treated according to the Geneva Convention. Conditions were far from luxurious, but at least the prisoners were dealt with reasonably fairly. The Red Cross was allowed to send them parcels with food and other everyday items. A few prisoners of war in Germany managed to escape (often with the help of European resistance movements), but the vast majority accepted their fate and waited for liberation.

referred to as the "Rattenkrieg," or "war of the rats." The bitter fighting in the ruins of the city was a nightmare. Every yard of the city was contested. The Soviet defenders deliberately waged a war of attrition, weakening and exhausting the German forces. General Vasili Chuikov (1900–82), the Soviet commander in Stalingrad, was provided with just enough resources to hold his position. Paulus initially received generous reinforcements, but they were unable to make headway in the rubble of the city. Eventually, the Germans began to run out of men and munitions, and the pendulum of battle swung in favor of the Red Army.

The Soviet Trap Closes at Stalingrad

During September and October, as ever greater numbers of German troops were committed to the grinding mill, the flank defenses on either side of Stalingrad were assigned to inexperienced low-quality troops (mainly Romanians and Hungarians). Meanwhile, the Soviet forces around Stalingrad were being steadily reinforced for a counterattack. On November 19, as winter began to close in, the Red Army struck on either side of the city. Four days later the pincer movement met up, leaving the German Sixth Army and much of the Fourth Panzer Army trapped in and around Stalingrad.

Although the Germans made attempts to break through to Stalingrad in December, and Field Marshal Erich Manstein did manage to penetrate to within 35 miles (56 km) of the city on December 19, the Red Army encirclement held firm. Army Group A had been unable to break through into the oil-rich region around Baku (on the Caspian Sea) and it now faced being cut off by Soviet forces advancing toward Rostov. Under the cool leadership of Manstein, the troops of Army Group A were extricated from the Caucasus region, but the men of the Sixth Army in Stalingrad were doomed. Under increasing Soviet pressure, the Stalingrad pocket became ever smaller, and on January 31, 1943, Paulus (who had just been appointed field marshal by Hitler) surrendered. Over 100,000 Germans marched into captivity, from which few would return, and 1,000 panzers had been destroyed. Stalingrad was the turning point in the war on the Eastern Front, and one of the most decisive battles of the whole conflict.

Left: German soldiers in the ruins of Stalingrad. The battle for the city annihilated the Wehrmacht's Sixth Army.

War at Sea

As well as land engagements, some of the most important battles of World War II were fought at sea, particularly over the control of sea lanes, such as those across the north Atlantic that supplied Britain.

As a result of the Washington Conference (1921–22) naval expansion was limited among the major maritime powers, as part of an attempt to prevent the arms race that had helped lead to the outbreak of war in 1914. In the 1930s, however, Germany and Japan ignored the restrictions and began to build powerful modern navies. The United States and Britain felt compelled to follow suit.

The German Navy, particularly its fleet of submarines, would soon wage a deadly war to halt the flow of Allied supplies across the north Atlantic from North America to Britain, and also from Britain to the Soviet Union. The German U-boat service, commanded by Admiral Karl Dönitz (1891–1980), considered itself an élite; its crews were highly trained and ready for action.

The battle for control of the sea lanes across the Atlantic was the longest and most crucial naval campaign of the war. Writing in his postwar memoirs, Churchill stated, "the Battle of the Atlantic was the only thing which really worried me during the war." The German naval commanders tried with every means at their disposal to destroy enough merchant shipping to starve Britain out of the war, and by the spring of 1943 they seemed dangerously close to victory.

And yet the greatest threat in the early months of the war came from Germany's surface raiders, which included the pocket battleship *Graf Spee* and the battleships *Gneisenau* and *Scharnhorst*. The *Graf Spee* achieved early fame in 1939 during a cruise of the south Atlantic, but on December 13 the German raider was caught and damaged in a running battle with Royal Navy ships off the River Plate, and was forced to retire to the Uruguayan port of Montevideo. Trapped by the arrival of further British vessels, the *Graf Spee* was scuttled by her captain, who then committed suicide.

Scharnhorst and *Gneisenau* slipped into the Atlantic on three raiding cruises: November 1939, February 1940, and January–March 1941. Although these missions did not sink many Allied merchant vessels, they were effective in dispersing the efforts of the Royal Navy over a wide area, making the poorly protected convoys all the more vulnerable to the prowling U-boat packs.

The U-boat Threat

The fall of Norway and France in 1940 transformed the strategic situation, enabling German vessels to operate from Norwegian and western French ports. The number of merchant ships sunk increased steadily. Although convoy protection improved, losses remained high and the U-boats proved elusive to Allied countermeasures. During 1941–42, the British began to have some success, with improvements in sonar detection, better depth charges, and the introduction of long-range aircraft fitted with new types of radar that could detect submarines on the surface. Perhaps even more crucial was the cracking of the supposedly invincible Enigma codes, used by the German naval commanders to communicate with their U-boats at sea. The Allies were able to re-route their convoys away from known concentrations of U-boats, and were able to send escort vessels to attack the enemy submarines.

The entry of the United States into the war provided desperately needed reinforcements, although in the short term the U-boats had initial success attacking unescorted vessels sailing along America's eastern seaboard. Early 1943 proved to be the crucial phase in

THE U-BOAT ACES

Germany's top submarine commanders were afforded the same kind of adulation that was heaped on top fighter pilots. They were much praised at home, and feared abroad. The three most famous, Günther Prien, Otto Kretschmer, and Joachim Schepke, were all awarded the Knight's Cross with Oakleaves, one of Nazi Germany's highest decorations.

Prien earned his medal for a daring attack on a Royal Navy battleship at anchor on October 14, 1939. Steering *U-47* through the supposedly impassable antisubmarine defenses stretching across the harbor at Scapa Flow, Prien torpedoed HMS *Royal Oak*, before extricating his submarine to return to a hero's welcome in Germany. Kretschmer and Schepke, commanding *U-99* and *U-100* respectively, were credited with the largest numbers of enemy shipping sunk in the first 18 months of the war. But the U-boat aces had to pay a high price for their daring. In March 1941, Prien and Schepke were killed at sea and Kretschmer was taken prisoner. Although U-boats continued to sink Allied vessels, the loss of these and other aces was the first of a number of body blows that wore down the German submarine force.

the Battle of the Atlantic, as increased numbers of U-boats took their toll. In March, 82 merchant ships were sunk, and Britain's food stocks stood perilously low. With over 200 submarines in the north Atlantic, the German U-boat service threw everything into a last effort to break the convoy system. In a series of hard-fought battles, the increased numbers of Allied vessels and the improvements in antisubmarine warfare made themselves felt. In May, 41 U-boats were sunk for the loss of just 34 merchant ships. Dönitz was forced to call off the battle – the convoys had gained the upper hand.

Germany's surface ships caused the British some alarm, but only temporarily. The German battleship *Bismarck* was sunk in May 1941 after a long chase in the north Atlantic, which saw the sinking of the British battlecruiser *Hood*. *Bismarck*'s sister ship *Tirpitz* was based in Norway and along with the *Scharnhorst* posed a constant threat to Allied convoys sailing through the Arctic Ocean to Murmansk in Russia. The *Tirpitz* was crippled by X-craft mini-submarines in September 1943 (and later sunk by Lancasters of Bomber Command) and the *Scharnhorst* was sunk in December 1943 at the Battle of North Cape.

The Naval War in the Mediterranean

In 1940 the British maintained a large naval force in the Mediterranean, dedicated to protecting Malta, Gibraltar, and British bases in Egypt, and to maintain the vital sea routes through the Mediterranean to the Far East via the Suez Canal. When France surrendered and Italy declared war against the Allies in June 1940, the British found themselves in a very difficult position.

Although the Italians had a powerful fleet, they were always short of fuel, which restricted their ability to wage offensive operations, and, significantly, they had no aircraft carriers. In November 1940 the British used a handful of carrier-based torpedo-bombers to sink an Italian warship and badly damage two others at anchor in Taranto harbor. It was a lesson in the power of naval aviation, and one that directly influenced the Japanese attack against Pearl Harbor in December 1941.

THE CONVOY SYSTEM

The idea of using convoys had been developed during World War I, and involved the grouping together of merchant ships and their protection by naval escort vessels. Reintroduced after some delay during World War II, convoys were found to be a generally effective means of reducing shipping losses. The key to the system was the role of the escorts, which consisted of corvettes and more heavily armed destroyers, their role being to shepherd the slow merchant ships into some sort of order and to counterattack any U-boats they encountered.

During the early stages of the Battle of the Atlantic there were insufficient escorts to provide proper cover for most convoys, allowing German U-boats easy pickings. But as the war progressed so more escort vessels came onto service, and with the introduction of better technology for submarine detection, notably sonar and later radar, the convoys became progressively safer. While the smaller and slower escorts stayed close by the merchantmen, independent groups of destroyers worked with aircraft in a hunter-killer role. By the summer of 1943, the now adequately protected convoys proved a match for the U-boat.

The need to support British forces in North Africa seriously overstretched the now outnumbered Royal Navy, which was vulnerable to Axis aircraft flying from land bases in the Mediterranean. When Luftwaffe units began operating from Sicily in early 1941, British losses soared. Malta in particular was subject to repeated attacks by Axis bombers. The island was a vital halfway point between the western and eastern Mediterranean, and the British also deployed Malta-based submarines against German and Italian shipping supplying Axis forces in North Africa. At the same time, the Germans redeployed Atlantic U-boats against the British. The combination of Axis attacks from the air and underwater had seriously weakened the Royal Navy's position in the Mediterranean by early 1942. Throughout that year, the Luftwaffe continued to savage British convoys and Malta.

When the tide of the conflict in the land war in North Africa turned in favor of the Allies in late 1942, the German and Italian warships were denied the use of forward bases from which to operate. This was, perhaps, the decisive aspect of the struggle in this region, and by the end of 1943 Allied naval supremacy was re-established over most of the Mediterranean.

Left: A German U-boat under attack in the Atlantic Ocean during a German hunt for Allied merchant ships transporting supplies to Great Britain.

The North African Campaign

The entry of Italy into the conflict following Mussolini's declaration of war on France and Britain in June 1940 made North Africa a crucial theater of the war, as Italian offensives were launched from Libya to capture the strategically vital Suez Canal. Though they were halted, Hitler sent Erwin Rommel to bolster his ally and the North African campaign would last for three years before Axis forces were finally defeated.

In early September 1940, a little over 35,000 British troops in Egypt faced over 200,000 Italians stationed in Libya. General Sir Archibald Wavell (1883–1950), the British commander in the Middle East, was fortunate that his opposite number, Marshal Graziani, was not a man for bold moves. He refused to launch an offensive until Mussolini threatened to dismiss him.

On September 13, five Italian divisions crossed into Egypt from Cyrenaica. The Italians cautiously advanced to Sidi Barrani, where they constructed a series of fortified camps. Despite his numerical inferiority Wavell was confident that a counterattack would succeed in throwing the Italians out of Egypt. The British counterattacked on December 9, driving across the North African desert in a series of spectacular advances led by the field force commander, General Richard O'Connor. The Italians were defeated time and again. On January 22, 1941, the key Italian port of Tobruk fell to the British. As a result of an audacious move by O'Connor, the British drove across the rough desert of Cyrenaica to cut off the Italians at Beda Fomm. Altogether approximately 130,000 Italians were captured in the two-month offensive.

Hitler had already decided that he could not permit the Italians to be crushed in North Africa, and so the first German units began to arrive in the Libyan capital of Tripoli early in February 1941. The charismatic panzer commander General Erwin Rommel was sent to command the improvised German desert army, which was soon called the Afrika Korps. Despite the small size of his forces, Rommel wasted no time in preparing an offensive against the British, whose vulnerable supply lines stretched from the River Nile westward to Beda Fomm. When the attack came on March 31, 1941, the British bases at El Agheila, Agedabia, and Benghazi fell quickly to the audacious German thrust.

Although forced to retreat back toward Egypt, the British were determined to prevent Tobruk from falling into German hands. The port was surrounded, and on April 10 the first attacks were launched. Tobruk was defended by 15,000 men (many of them Australians). The Allied troops repulsed repeated assaults and survived intense artillery and air bombardment. Most spent their time underground in bomb-proof shelters during the bombing. Despite his best efforts, Rommel failed to capture Tobruk.

Gazala and the Fall of Tobruk

The campaign ebbed and flowed across the North African coastal strip for the next year as attacks were met by counterattacks. After a period spent building up reinforcements, the British launched a major offensive in 1941 (Operation Crusader) which, after much hard fighting at Sidi Rezegh, wore down Rommel's armored strength, forcing him to retreat back to his original starting point. In February 1942, Rommel again advanced from his sally port of El Agheila and drove the dispersed forces back to the Gazala Line. Following a short pause the Axis forces struck with the greatest vigor at the end of May 1942, inflicting a massive defeat on the British Eighth Army at Gazala. Tobruk was captured with little resistance on 21 June following a well-

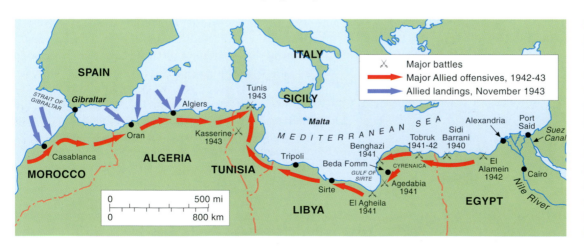

Left: The fighting in North Africa between 1940 and 1943 was concentrated along the narrow coastal strip, and possession of ports such as Tripoli and Tobruk. As the war progressed, Axis forces under Rommel were hampered by increasing Allied air and sea superiority in the Mediterranean, which sunk his supply ships.

coordinated ground and air assault, and the British were flung back deep inside Egypt.

The British commander, General Sir Claude Auchinleck (1884–1981), decided to make a stand at El Alamein, barely 55 miles (88 km) west of Alexandria and the Suez Canal. His troops dug in along a position defended to the south by the Qattara Depression. This low, impassable desert area forced Rommel to make a frontal attack along the coastal strip. By July 7, Rommel's now tired forces – short of petrol – were halted.

Dissatisfied by Auchinleck's tenure of command in the Western Desert, Churchill had him replaced. General Bernard Montgomery (1887–1976) took over direct command of the Eighth Army on August 13. Rommel attacked Montgomery in the first week of September at Alam Halfa, but the well-prepared British were able to repulse the German offensive with little difficulty. Rommel went to Germany on sick leave, ill and exhausted by his efforts to achieve final victory in North Africa.

On October 23, 1942, Montgomery began the second and strategically decisive Battle of El Alamein. A huge artillery barrage pounded the German lines, prior to the advance of infantry through the enemy minefields. The fighting was locked in stalemate until November 3, when Rommel (who had returned on October 23) ordered the withdrawal of his battered forces. Hitler demanded that Rommel halt the retreat on November 5. However, British pressure and Rommel's need to find a defensible line forced the retreat to continue.

Above: Some of the 38,000 Italian prisoners taken by the British during General Sir Archibald Wavell's counteroffensive in Libya in December 1940.

The final blow against the Germans and Italians was struck on November 8, 1942 in Operation Torch, when over 100,000 US and British troops commanded by General Dwight D. Eisenhower (1890–1969) landed in Algeria and Morocco. It was the first major involvement of US ground forces in the war against Hitler. Algeria and Morocco were French colonies and under the authority of the German-controlled Vichy government in France, but the Allies were spared serious action when the Vichy troops surrendered, after putting up only limited resistance.

Although reinforced by Hitler, the Axis troops in Tunisia were forced to adopt a defensive position. The Allies advanced slowly, hampered by the mountainous terrain and poor winter weather. Rommel inflicted a sharp defeat against inexperienced US forces at Kasserine in February 1943, but he was unable to exploit his success through lack of resources. Eisenhower rallied his troops, and supported by Montgomery, began to advance against the Axis line in April. Hitler replaced Rommel with General Jürgen Arnim, but the new commander was in a hopeless position. Tunis fell on May 7, and by the 14th the remaining German and Italian forces in North Africa were in captivity. The victory in North Africa was the first Allied victory in an entire theater of the war. Total Axis losses in North Africa were estimated at 620,000 men, while the Allies lost an estimated 258,000.

Japan's Pacific Blitzkrieg

During the 1930s Japan developed into a fiercely nationalistic state. Unable to gain direct access to vital raw materials (the US had imposed an oil and steel embargo on Japan in the 1930s), the Japanese planned to destroy American might in the Pacific, while conquests in the Dutch East Indies, Malaya, and the Philippines would create the "Greater East Asia Co-Prosperity Sphere" and thus economic self-sufficiency.

The air attack on the US naval base of Pearl Harbor in the Hawaiian Islands began early in the morning of Sunday, December 7, 1941, a day chosen because it was estimated that a large part of the US Pacific Fleet would be in port. The first wave consisted of 183 dive- and torpedo-bombers, with fighters providing protection; they flew off six carriers that had sailed to within 250 miles (400 km) of the Hawaiian Islands. Although the Japanese aircraft were eventually detected by radar operators, they were mistaken for a squadron of US bombers flying in the vicinity. Japanese surprise was total.

While part of the Japanese force attacked US fighter aircraft that were parked at various airfields, the torpedo-bombers made runs across the anchorage toward the battleships lying off Ford Island in Pearl Harbor. Six of the battleships were soon sunk, sinking, or very badly damaged. A second wave of 167 aircraft attacked fuel stores and airfields. The Japanese believed that by sinking the battleships they had crippled the US fleet. However, the carriers *Enterprise*, *Lexington*, and *Saratoga* were not at Pearl Harbor, and subsequent events were to show that carriers and not battleships would be the key vessels in the Pacific theater of war.

The Japanese attack on Pearl Harbor immediately brought the United States into the war. The Axis powers came to the support of Japan, in turn declaring war on the United States. World War II had now become a truly global conflict.

Pearl Harbor was only part of an audacious Japanese war of conquest. Heavy air attacks were launched against the Philippines, and a naval task force dispatched to invade British Hong Kong and the British colony of Malaya. Singapore, which lay at the southern tip of Malaya and was Britain's main base in Southeast Asia, was quickly overrun by the Japanese, the British garrison surrendering on February 15, 1942. The loss of Singapore was Britain's greatest military defeat.

The speed of Japan's advance caught the complacent Western powers off-guard. Japanese amphibious landings in the oil-rich Dutch East Indies took place between January and March 1942, and soon overwhelmed the badly organized defenders. In the Philippines, the large American-backed Filipino armed forces, under the command of General Douglas MacArthur (1880–1964), also proved vulnerable to the Japanese onslaught. Although a desperate rearguard action in the Bataan peninsula and on the island of Corregidor held up the Japanese advance, resistance was over by May 6, 1942. The British suffered further humiliations as the Japanese crossed from Thailand into Burma, forcing a British retreat to the border with India.

Attempts were made by the Western Allies to organize their naval forces to intercept the Japanese invasion fleets, but these too ended in failure. The British Force Z, comprising the battleship *Prince of Wales* and the battlecruiser *Repulse*, was destroyed off Malaya on December 10, 1941, both ships being sunk by Japanese aircraft. An Anglo-Dutch flotilla attempting to defend the East Indies was repulsed with heavy losses in the Battle of the Java Sea on February 27, 1942.

Beginning in January, units of the Japanese Fourth Fleet seized Rabaul in the Solomon Islands, which

Right: The Japanese surprise attack on Pearl Harbor left 2,280 military dead and 1,109 wounded.

Left: Between December 1941 and the summer of 1942, the Japanese launched a series of offensives in the Pacific. These attacks had two specific aims. First, to establish a series of island bases to protect the territories they had captured. Second, to secure areas that produced vital raw materials, especially oil.

became the principal Japanese naval and airbase in the southwest Pacific. Amphibious landings then seized Salamaua and Lae in Papua and footholds on Bougainville in March. By the middle of 1942, the Japanese armed forces had gained all their territorial objectives. To secure its conquests, the Japanese High Command began to look at ways to extend their perimeter to form an effective defensive barrier around their new-won possessions. This desire was confirmed by the Doolittle Raid of April 18, 1942, when a carrier-launched US bomber force was able to reach and bomb Tokyo. The Japanese decided to push northward to the Aleutian Islands, east toward Midway Island, and south into New Guinea.

The decision to attack Port Moresby on the southern coast of New Guinea brought the Japanese invasion fleet into conflict with an American force in what became known as the Battle of the Coral Sea – the first engagement in naval history in which the ships of the opposing fleets fought each other without visual contact, the entire action being conducted by carrier aircraft. It was also a Japanese strategic defeat.

Between May and June, Japanese forces continued to attempt to push their defensive perimeter to the southeast, and to develop an airfield on Guadalcanal, an island in the Solomon chain. Once that was achieved, the Japanese planned to attack Port Moresby again. And despite the Japanese failure in the Coral Sea battle, Admiral Isoroku Yamamoto (1884–1943), commander of the Japanese Combined Fleet, thought he could destroy the US Pacific Fleet under Admiral Chester W. Nimitz (1885–1966) in one decisive action on the high seas.

Having broken Japanese codes, the Americans refused to be drawn toward the Japanese offensive in the Aleutian Islands, concentrating their forces instead in the decisive central theater of operations: the Japanese attack to secure the isolated island of Midway.

Unaware of the strength of the waiting US carrier fleet, the Japanese sailed toward Midway and the engagement began on June 4. Three Japanese carriers – *Kaga*, *Akagi*, and *Soryu* – were sunk and a fourth crippled (*Hiryu*, later to sink). The now battered Japanese Navy was forced onto the defensive, transferring the strategic initiative to the ever-expanding US Navy.

Encouraged by the victory at Midway, MacArthur and Nimitz began planning for the first American offensive of the war. Codenamed Operation Watchtower, it aimed to secure communications with Australia, take the Solomon Islands and New Guinea, and capture the Japanese base at Rabaul on the island of New Britain. Until the end of 1943, fighting in the Pacific theater concentrated in this area at the southeastern edge of the Japanese defensive perimeter.

Guadalcanal lies in a key strategic position in the Solomon Islands. If captured by the Japanese, it could have been used to cut the sea routes between the United States and Australia. On August 7, 1942, a US Marine division landed unopposed on Guadalcanal and captured the airfield the following afternoon. As the airfield, named Henderson Field by the Marines, became operational on August 20, Japanese reinforcements were landing at a point 20 miles (32 km) east. An attack by the Japanese was repulsed and the force almost destroyed. On September 12, another assault was driven back at the Battle of Bloody Ridge, located on the southern edge of the airfield's defensive perimeter. Control of Guadalcanal was bitterly contested by both sides until February 1943 when the Japanese finally abandoned the island.

The Fight for Italy

Following the end of the war in North Africa, the Allies decided to continue the war in the Mediterranean by invading Sicily and Italy. It was hoped that this would knock the war-weary Italians out of the war – which it did in mid-1943 – but the Germans responded quickly and took over the Italian mainland and thereafter conducted a skillful defense in the face of Allied numerical and aerial superiority.

At the Casablanca Conference in January 1943, the strategy of the Western Allies in Europe was shaped. The decision was taken that victory in the war would only come with the unconditional surrender of Germany, Italy, and Japan. Where next to commit Allied ground forces was initially a problem. The Americans wanted an immediate cross-Channel invasion to open the "second front," while the British argued for an invasion of Sicily to reopen Allied sea lanes to the eastern Mediterranean and provide a base for further offensives against Italy. The fact that there were masses of Allied men and material in North Africa made Sicily a logical option.

On July 10, 1943, some 180,000 men of the US Seventh Army and British Eighth Army landed on the shores of Sicily, the first step to clear the way for the invasion of the Italian mainland. Complete air cover was assured by 4,000 Allied aircraft. Montgomery's Eighth Army met with little opposition at its landing ground just south of Syracuse. Resistance at the Gulf of Gela, disembarkation point for the US forces, was stiffer but overcome with relatively light casualties. Syracuse fell on July 12, although Montgomery's push to Messina on Sicily's northeastern coast slowed in the face of determined German resistance.

The advance of the US forces, commanded by General George S. Patton (1885–1945), was hampered by mountainous terrain, and he chose instead to make a looping attack around the northern coast, taking Palermo on July 22. Patton's troops reached Messina on August 22, shortly after the German evacuation across the Straits of Messina to the mainland.

On July 23, Italian dictator Benito Mussolini was placed under house arrest by members of his own government, and intelligence reports indicated to Allied leaders that the Italians wanted to end the war and would leave the Axis. But when the Italian government asked for an armistice in September, the Germans reacted with surprising speed and took over the country, rescuing Mussolini and setting him up as leader of a puppet state in northern Italy. German reinforcements poured into Italy. The Allies had lost the initiative, and it would cost them dearly.

Across the Straits of Messina

The Allied commanders began to draw up plans for the invasion of Italy. On September 3, the British crossed the Straits of Messina and landed in Calabria. The landings were virtually unopposed. In contrast, the amphibious assault on Salerno by combined US and British forces had a much harder time. The German defenders were able to predict the landing sites and the troops under General Mark Clark (1896–1984) fought desperately to establish a beachhead. The British plan was to drive through Calabria and link up with Clark, trapping the Germans in the process. The skill with which the defenders held their positions forced the Allies to rethink their plans, and the Germans escaped the pincer movement.

Superiority of numbers and command of the skies proved the Allies' greatest asset as they slowly advanced northward up the "boot" of the Italian peninsula. The key port of Naples fell on October 1, and the air bases around Foggia were secured five days later. These were the two prime Allied objectives of

Left: A British officer (with peaked cap) talks with men of the US 82nd Airborne Division during the battle for Sicily.

the early phase of the invasion, especially as the latter brought Romania's oil fields (a major supplier of fuel to the German war effort) within striking range of Allied bombers.

Field Marshal Albert Kesselring (1885–1960), the German commander in Italy, set up a series of complex defensive lines across the peninsula. With hopes of an early victory dashed, the Allied commanders pressed on slowly toward Rome, their next major territorial objective. The Gustav Line stood directly in their path, which persuaded the Allies to embark on an amphibious assault at Anzio, in the hope of outflanking the German defensive line. Codenamed Operation Shingle, the assault was little short of a disaster. Although an attack

on the Gustav Line at Monte Cassino, a key hilltop position, diverted some of Kesselring's forces, the Allies failed to push inland from the Anzio bridgehead after an almost unopposed landing on January 22, 1944. For the next four months the Allies were pinned down in the Anzio bridgehead, and unable to break through the Gustav Line.

On the Gustav Line, a renewed Allied offensive in May 1944 was exploited by Polish forces who stormed Monte Cassino. The monastery on Monte Cassino had been virtually destroyed by Allied bombing before the assault. The breakthrough against the Gustav Line allowed General Clark to advance on Rome, which fell on June 4, just two days before the D-Day landings in Normandy. The Germans fell back in good order to take up another defensive position along the Gothic Line, although large numbers of their reserves were diverted to northern France to oppose the Normandy landings.

The final offensive
During the winter of 1944–45, there was a lull in operations caused by renewed bad weather and the change of focus of both Allied and German strategy caused by the fighting in France. In the spring of 1945, US and British divisions launched a final attack on the Gothic Line. Massive aerial bombardment of German forward positions had weakened the German defenses, which began to crumble in the face of the Allied advance. Bologna was liberated on April 21 as Allied forces broke through into the Po Valley. Allied aircraft systematically destroyed bridges and passes in northern Italy, denying the Germans the possibility of a retreat in good order over the Alps, in a superb tactical operation.

The German surrender on May 2, 1945, brought to an end the bitterly contested and costly Italian campaign. Benito Mussolini and his mistress were captured by Italian partisans and executed, their bodies strung up for public display in a square in Milan. One of the original leaders of the Axis alliance was no more.

Left: Italy's mountainous terrain favored the defense, and was made full use of by the Germans in 1943–45.

The Eastern Front, 1943–44

The German defeat at Stalingrad had dealt a massive blow to Hitler's territorial ambitions in the East, and by the beginning of 1943 the Red Army, receiving massive quantities of manpower and hardware, was was threatening the entire southern wing of the German Army. Manstein's masterful generalship gave the Wehrmacht a breathing space, but then Hitler threw away any chances of German victory at Kursk.

The annihilation of the German Sixth Army at Stalingrad stunned Germany. After a run of brilliant victories, the German armed forces were shown to be fallible. Soviet armies were also threatening Field Marshal Manstein's northern flank around Kharkov, a vital rail depot and major industrial city. Hitler ordered the city to be held and was furious when the forces deployed to hold Kharkov abandoned it on February 15 on Manstein's orders.

Hitler immediately ordered Manstein to recapture the city. Given the fact that his army group had been forced to retreat hastily from the Caucasus, it is remarkable that Manstein could even consider fighting back. The Germans attacked on February 20. The Soviet forces, low on fuel and supplies, were rapidly driven back. The Soviet commander, General Vatutin, tried to halt the retreat, but the German momentum was too great. Kharkov fell on March 15, and the Red Army suffered over 72,000 casualties and had 600 tanks destroyed. Manstein had inflicted a resounding defeat on his Soviet opponent, and had been given time to restore some semblance of order to German frontline positions.

The lull in fighting during spring 1943 came at a vital time for the Germans, who desperately needed time to rest and re-equip. The spring thaw had, as expected, turned the landscape into a swamp, conditions in which the German tanks could not operate. This gave the field workshops time to catch up with their backlog of repairs.

The Battle of Kursk

In order to straighten their line, the Germans planned a major offensive against the Kursk salient. Delays in the start of the offensive, however, allowed the Soviet forces under General Georgi Zhukov (1896–1974) time to prepare defensive works around Kursk. To the Germans, the attack on Kursk seemed an opportunity to destroy substantial Soviet forces, despite the fears of some German generals that the operation was far too ambitious. Indeed, over the passage of time the original plan for a limited assault expanded into a major offensive involving two armies.

The German attack, Operation Citadel, was planned for July 5, 1943, with the Ninth Army, under the command of General Walther Model (1891–1945), driving south from Orel in a two-pronged attack. On the southern flank of the Kursk position, the Fourth Panzer Army planned to drive northeast to cut off the Soviet retreat. The Soviet commanders were fully aware of the German plans, having been given information by a Soviet spy in Britain (who had access to decoded

Left: Soviet offensives in southern Russia in early 1943 were defeated by Manstein at Kharkov, but German failure at Kursk dealt a mortal blow to the Wehrmacht in the East.

Left: German troops move through a village during Manstein's masterful counterattack in February 1943. By abandoning Kharkov and waiting for the Red Army to outrun its supplies lines and grind to an exhausted halt, he was able to use his panzer divisions to surround and then annihilate enemy forces west of the city. Kharkov was then recaptured in March 1943 and the southern sector of the Eastern Front had been stabilized.

Enigma material) and from the "Lucy" spy-ring based in Switzerland. As a consequence, the Red Army had constructed formidable defenses, utilizing minefields and antitank guns to funnel the German armor into prepared killing grounds.

The German advance rapidly bogged down among densely sown minefields. In the north, the offensive was stopped dead in its tracks only 12 miles (19 km) from its starting point, and Model had lost half of his tanks by July 12. In the south, the larger number of German tanks allotted to the Fourth Panzer Army seemed an advantage, but the Red Army's antitank gunners were just too strong. The Germans were unable to make any headway until July 8. Two days later the German forces managed to break through the Soviet frontline to the village of Prokhorovka. There, on July 12, the Red Army launched a counterattack with over 850 tanks. The 700 German tanks opposing them were compressed into a small area, and any advantage the Germans had previously possessed through superior skill in maneuver was largely lost. The Soviet tank crews, many women among them, fought with tenacity and heroism. Manstein's forces were thrown back in some disorder, losing 10,000 men and 350 tanks in the process.

In July, the Soviet High Command instigated a general offensive. In the north, Soviet forces attacked toward Orel, while in the south they opened a 40-mile (64-km) gap in the German defensive line. Red Army units then poured through this gap and headed for Kharkov. On August 20, Hitler made a rare decision: to sanction a general retreat. In the following week, Soviet forces crossed the upper reaches of the Donets River, while other troops drove far enough westward to threaten to crush German forces in the south. The

German defeat at Kursk marked the last major German attack on the Eastern Front. The strategic initiative passed over to the Red Army, which had begun its steamroller advance to Berlin.

The Hagen Line, a German defensive position near Kursk, was attacked on August 29. Weakly defended by 300 or so tanks, the Germans were driven back, at some points over 150 miles (240 km). In the south, German troops were forced to retreat as far as the Dnieper River, where engineers set to work constructing elaborate defensive works on the river's western banks. Yet, on September 24, the Red Army established small toeholds on the west bank of the river. Thousands of Soviet troops then poured across the river, followed by armored support once pontoon bridges had been erected in several places. By mid-October, the Germans had been pushed back along a 440-mile (708-km) front. On November 3, Soviet forces assaulted Kiev, but encountered strong resistance from the German defenders, who held the city until the 12th. In the Crimea, the German Seventeenth Army had been cut off, and faced the prospect of annihilation unless it could be evacuated in time.

In January 1944, the Soviets finally lifted the siege of Leningrad, while in the south, at the Battle of Korsun, Konev's Second Ukrainian Front trapped two German corps and inflicted 100,000 casualties on the enemy. The Red Army then continued its advance across the rivers Bug and Dniester as Manstein tried desperately to stabilize the front. But the strategic iniative was with the Soviets, as the Red Army steeled itself for the final onslaught that would drive the invaders from the Soviet Union. Defeat for the Germans on the Eastern Front was now only a matter of time.

The Struggle for the Skies

World War II was the first war in which air power was decisive. Aerial superiority was essential to early German victories, while air power aided Allied victories against Axis forces in North Africa and Europe.

The interwar years had been a time of fierce debate on the future role of aircraft. Some theorists believed that the key to military success lay almost exclusively in aircraft that could deliver heavy bomb loads over long distances, effectively destroying an enemy's ability to fight. Others spoke for the deployment of fast medium bombers and dive-bombers, operating in a tactical role in supporting ground forces. The Germans favored this latter role, while the British and Americans encouraged the use of long-rang heavy bombers.

Of all the European nations that entered the war in 1939, Germany was the best prepared to fight a large-scale air war. Though forbidden to do so under conditions of the Treaty of Versailles, the Luftwaffe had built up its strength during the mid-1930s and possessed the most powerful fleet of aircraft in the world by 1939.

Between the wars, the British Royal Air Force's (RAF's) senior command clung to the belief that strategic bombing would form the key to any future air war and so the production of heavy bombers was given priority; other vital areas of military aviation were largely ignored, especially naval aviation. It was largely due to the energies of a few people, notably Sir Hugh Dowding, chief of RAF Fighter Command, and minister for production Max Beaverbrook, that the RAF's fighter strength was at a level that could withstand the might of the Luftwaffe when the test finally came in the summer of 1940.

In America, the United States Army Air Force (USAAF) underwent a crash program after the outbreak of war in Europe to build up its strength and train an adequate number of pilots. By December 1941, it had 25,000 personnel and 4,000 aircraft, including the B-17, the only four-engined strategic bomber in the world at the time. These long-range bombers, operating from airfields in eastern England, would play an important role in the outcome of the war by launching mass daylight raids on German-occupied Europe from 1943 onward.

World War II saw the introduction of high-speed monoplane fighters, which included Britain's Spitfire, Germany's Messerschmitt Bf 109, America's P-51 Mustang, and Japan's Mitsubishi A6M Zero. The RAF Spitfire and Hurricane were the first such fighters to see service, although the Luftwaffe responded quickly with the Bf 109. At the start of the war the main role for fighters was either to attack or defend bombers. Later on in the conflict, fighters increasingly began to be used in a ground-attack role.

RADAR

Although research and development work was carried out in the interwar years by many countries, including Britain, Germany, Japan, the United States, and the Soviet Union, it was the British who led the field in aerial radar on the outbreak of war. As far back as 1937, construction had started on a land-based early warning system around the eastern and southern coast of England. During the Battle of Britain this system gave the British a vital advantage by enabling them to predict the strength, direction, and height of attacking German aircraft. In 1940 a crude form of airborne radar became available, and was used with increasing success by night-fighter units to locate enemy bombers.

A vital breakthrough in the Battle of the Atlantic came when Allied maritime patrol aircraft were fitted with radar in their hunts for surfaced U-boats. Capital ships on both sides also used radar to detect other enemy vessels, which enabled naval battles to be fought at night with considerable success.

The Air War in Europe

The use of long-range fighter escorts, such as the P-51 Mustang and P-47 Thunderbolt, to protect USAAF bombers operating over Europe was a significant development in the air war. Previously Allied bombers had to attack targets deep in Europe without fighter protection, because the range of their escorts was so limited. The development of wing-mounted drop-tanks transformed the capability of US fighter aircraft, enabling them to fly alongside the bombers to the target and back. Before this change, Allied losses to German fighters were huge, but with the deployment of escorts, losses fell dramatically.

Germany tried to counter the growing Allied superiority in fighters and bombers with increasingly sophisticated aircraft such as the Messerschmitt Me 262 jet fighter, but the production lines could not meet demand in the face of incessant bombing. More to the point, the destruction of Germany's sources of oil meant that many of the Luftwaffe's aircraft were grounded for lack of fuel. In the last months of the war, Allied forces enjoyed almost complete air superiority over Germany and roamed the skies at will.

The USAAF was farsighted in its purchase of the B-17 Flying Fortress bomber in the late 1930s. Although the RAF had concentrated on strategic bombing during the interwar years, it could field only 350 bombers in 1939. But by 1944 – the height of the offensive against the Axis powers – the USAAF and RAF had around 10,000 bombers in service.

Early bombing operations, particularly by the British, were carried out during daylight hours. Experience quickly showed the RAF that such tactics, without fighter escorts, were suicidal. Losses grew to dangerously high levels, and the British switched to night raids on enemy targets, believing that the cover of darkness would reduce losses to acceptable levels.

Allied Bombing Tactics

All air forces had entered the war with a policy of attacking military targets only, although in the face of military reality this policy was soon abandoned. The inability of the RAF to accurately bomb individual targets at night with any degree of accuracy led to the chief of Bomber Command, Sir Arthur Harris, to adopt "area bombing," which involved the wholescale destruction of civilian neighborhoods.

When the massive bomber resources of the United States became available for use in Europe, a joint Allied bombing program was instigated. From 1943 onward night offensives were conducted against the industrial cities of the Ruhr, Hamburg, and Berlin by the RAF, while US bombers, protected (from 1944 onward) by long-range fighters, continued mass daylight raids.

Germany did not develop a long-range bomber force, and apart from the "Blitz" raids on British cities during 1940–41, never launched a strategic bomber offensive. However, during 1944–45 Germany used the world's first long-range rockets, codenamed V-1 and V-2, to hit London and other civilian targets in Western Europe. They did not influence the outcome of the war, but frightened civilians and showed the potential of such rockets in modern warfare.

WOMEN AT WAR

With the exception of the Soviet Union, where women fought in both ground and air units, the rival countries in World War II did not use females in combat roles. However, women did serve near the front as nurses in field hospitals or in administrative positions with most armies. British women volunteered to serve in organizations such as the Wrens (Women's Royal Naval Service). Women's jobs were vital because they freed men for combat roles and provided the backup that allowed commanders to use their troops to the best advantage.

Women also worked in factories, making weapons and ammunition, as well as armored vehicles and aircraft. Others were or became pilots, and flew aircraft from aviation factories to frontline airfields. In the United States, Women's Airforce Service Pilots (WASPs) transported all types of military aircraft over a total of 60 million miles (96 million km) in support of the USAAF.

Contrary to popular belief, German women also worked, whether in administrative positions or in factories. German propaganda made much of the Nazi ideal that women should be confined to the home, bringing up children, but in reality millions of German women worked directly in support of the German war effort.

Japan was subjected to very heavy Allied strategic bombing raids from late 1944, after American forces had captured islands within bombing range of the Japanese heartland. Attacks devastated many of the major Japanese cities, which contained large numbers of wooden buildings and structures, but the enormous destruction and loss of life did not force the Japanese to surrender or end their will to fight on. It was only the dropping of the first atomic bombs on the Japanese cities of Hiroshima and Nagasaki in August 1945 that ended the war in the Pacific.

Left: A flight of P-51 Mustang fighters of the United States Army Air Force over Europe in 1944. Aside from the Mustang's firepower, one of its advantages was its range, which allowed it to escort US bombers on their missions over Germany and Japan.

The Pacific Tide Turns

By the beginning of 1943 the Allies were on the offensive in the Pacific, and won a series of important victories that virtually destroyed Japanese maritime aviation. On land, US forces won a series of hard-fought victories in the Gilbert and Marshall Islands, and also landed in the Philippines. In Burma, meanwhile, the British fought a series of savage actions against the Japanese to retake the country.

Throughout the fall of 1942, Japanese supply convoys – nicknamed by American troops the "Tokyo Express" – continued to reinforce their positions on the Solomon Islands, with the primary purpose of attacking the American air base at Henderson Field on Guadalcanal. In the seas surrounding Guadalcanal and others of the Solomon Islands, the US and Japanese navies fought seven battles to secure control of the waters off the islands. The Japanese did well at first but in the end the balance of success began to weigh in favor of the Americans.

On land, the Japanese forces were crippled by supply problems and were forced to retreat to the northern tip of Guadalcanal by US offensives. Due to their mounting losses, the Japanese began to withdraw from Guadalcanal on December 31, 1942, and by February 9, 1943, the island was firmly in American hands. The final capture of Guadalcanal brought telling advantages to the Allies: Australia and New Zealand were safe from Japanese attack, and Allied forces now stood ready to launch further counterattacks in the southwest Pacific.

New Allied Strategic Objectives

On Papua, Australian troops made contact with Japanese units advancing across the island's Owen Stanley Mountains toward Port Moresby in August 1942. A month of savage combat raged along the narrow Kokoda Trail, the only practical route through the mountains; the Japanese were repulsed and forced to take up defensive positions. These were captured in January 1943, but only after some of the bitterest combat of the war. Fierce fighting continued elsewhere through the spring.

In March, a large Japanese convoy taking troops to New Guinea was successfully attacked by US aircraft in the Battle of the Bismarck Sea. This action effectively cut off the Japanese forces on New Guinea and led the Allies to develop further strategic aims. They planned a two-pronged attack, codenamed Operation Cartwheel. Admiral Halsey's US Third Fleet moved through the Solomons in July, with the aim of capturing the main Japanese base of Rabaul on New Britain, while General MacArthur concentrated on operations in New Guinea.

Landings on the New Georgia island group in the eastern Solomons were coordinated with assaults on New Guinea to the west by a predominantly Australian force under MacArthur. The rapid advance of MacArthur's troops along the coast of New Guinea was achieved by a series of leapfrogging amphibious assaults, ending in the capture of the vital port of Finschhafen on October 2. On Christmas Day 1943, the battle-weary troops who had fought so hard to secure the northeastern parts of New Guinea witnessed a magnificent demonstration of their success, a huge American invasion fleet passing them to invade New Britain, MacArthur's next target.

Halsey's forces were equally successful. Battling through the central Solomons during the summer of 1943, they forced the Japanese to withdraw to Bougainville, the most northerly island of the Solomons group. An assault by US Marines began on November 1, which allowed the Americans to launch sustained air attacks against Rabaul on New Britain, effectively neutralizing it as a base for enemy operations.

The Conquest of Makin and Tarawa

In the central Pacific, an ambitious assault prepared by Admiral Nimitz got underway the late summer of 1943. With the return of Halsey's fleet to his command after its successes in the Solomons, Nimitz amassed an impressive armada with which to attack the key sections of the Japanese perimeter, driving westward across the Pacific. On November 20, 1943, US amphibious forces landed on Makin and Tarawa in the Gilbert Islands. Both were captured after a few days of hard fighting.

With the battles for the southwest and central Pacific islands won, the US planners began to focus on the next phase of their offensive. While Admiral Ernest J. King (1878–1956), commander-in-chief of the US Fleet and chief of Naval Operations, favored a direct assault on Formosa (Taiwan), MacArthur argued for an attack on Luzon, the main island of the Philippines. MacArthur was successful, although Nimitz was charged with preparation for an offensive against Iwo Jima and Okinawa, islands that would provide a jumping-off point for an invasion of Japan itself.

Under threat from the converging US drives from the southwest and central Pacific, the Japanese fleet sailed to challenge Nimitz's forces around the Mariana Islands, and suffered a decisive defeat at the Battle of the Philippine Sea in June 1944. The "Great Marianas Turkey Shoot" cost the Japanese three carriers and over 400 aircraft, losses they could ill-afford.

Right: By mid-1944, the British and Americans had breached the Japanese defensive perimeter in the Pacific. US resources were making themselves felt, particularly at sea, where Japan lost a series of crucial carrier battles.

The Battle of the Philippine Sea brought an end to any real hope the Japanese had of stemming the American advance through the Pacific. With powerful naval units covering the amphibious landings, the US assault on Guam, one of the main Mariana Islands, was launched on July 21, 1944. The fighting on Guam and the nearby islands of Saipan and Tinian was over by mid-August. The capture of the Marianas was vital to the American bombing offensive, the islands being within flying range of the Japanese homelands.

The Philippine campaign opened on October 22, 1944, when General Walter Krueger's Sixth Army landed on Leyte, but this successful action was largely overshadowed by the naval battle for Leyte Gulf. The Japanese were fully aware that the establishment of American air bases on Leyte, just 300 miles (480 km) to the southeast of Luzon, would make their position on the Philippines untenable – and without the Philippines not only would their access to the resource-rich south be cut off, but their defensive perimeter protecting the home islands would be fatally breached.

The Japanese had already planned a last-ditch operation, codenamed Sho-Go, just in case the Americans made any attempt to recapture the Philippines. As part of this operation the Japanese planned to draw Halsey's Third Fleet into a naval action, crush it, and thereby hope to save the Philippines. The plan called for the use of every remaining major Japanese warship. These were split between two strike forces, while a third force, consisting of Japan's four remaining large carriers, was to be used as bait to draw the US fleet into a trap.

A series of battles was fought in the waters around the Philippines between October 23–25. By the time the Japanese retreated their navy had virtually ceased to exist as a fighting force. Four aircraft carriers, three battleships, and 22 other warships had been sent to the bottom. Some 500 Japanese aircraft had been destroyed and 10,500 sailors and airmen killed. US losses were comparatively light: three small carriers, three destroyers, and 200 aircraft, along with some 2,800 men killed and 1,000 wounded. In desperation, the Japanese began to form Kamikaze ("Divine Wind") units to halt the advance of the US juggernaut, but they could not halt the landings on Luzon, however, which began on January 9, 1945.

After their successful invasion of the Malay peninsula in 1942, the Japanese had moved against Burma. Rangoon had fallen to them on March 7; by April 29 Lashio, a key town on the Burma Road (a twisting supply route through Burma over the mountains to China), was in Japanese hands.

A limited British offensive on Burma's northwest Arakan coast was launched in December 1942 but was thrown back with heavy losses. In March 1944 the Japanese finally launched their much-heralded invasion of India by striking at the towns of Kohima and Imphal. The British, under General Sir William Slim (1891–1970), forced the Japanese to retreat. By November 1944 the British had crossed the Chindwin River and were near Mandalay. The capture of Wanting by the Chinese in January 1945 permitted the reopening of the Burma Road. Rangoon fell to the British in May. As Slim prepared for the liberation of Malaya the Japanese surrendered.

The Defeat of Nazi Germany

D-Day, the largest amphibious invasion in history, opened the Second Front against the Germans in Europe. As massive amounts of Allied men and hardware poured into northwest Europe, the Red Army burst into Poland and the Balkans. In the face of certain defeat, however, the Wehrmacht continued to conduct a skillful defense, while overhead Allied bomber fleets reduced German cities to rubble.

Both the Allied campaigns in North Africa in 1942 and Italy in 1943–44 delayed the opening of the invasion of northwest Europe. Throughout 1943, Stalin had been demanding that the Western Allies open a "second front" to take some of the pressure off the Red Army, which was tying down the vast bulk of the German Army. But the Allied planners would not be rushed, aware that for any amphibious expedition to succeed the balance of forces would have to be greatly in their favor, and that failure would be disastrous.

While the Allies steadily built up their own forces in Britain during 1943–44, Hitler set about constructing coastal defenses – the Atlantic Wall – to repel any invasion. Both sides knew that if Germany was forced to fight simultaneously on the Eastern Front and in Western Europe, then it would lose the war.

The decision to invade Europe through Normandy was accepted among the Allies by the end of 1943, and planning for Operation Overlord passed to General Montgomery, commander of the invasion. Overall control was vested in the newly appointed Supreme Allied Commander, General Eisenhower.

Elaborate deception plans were put in place, which depended largely on the messages of double-agents and radio. Fake radio transmissions were sent to suggest that the US First Army Group – a formation that existed only on paper – was to invade across the narrowest part of the English Channel, from Dover to Calais. In reality, the massive invasion force was gathering in southern England for a projected assault on five beaches in Normandy, well away from Calais and its defenses. The force, consisting of nearly three million men, was to be supported by a massive air and sea bombardment. Control of the air was a vital part of the Allied plan and attacks on Luftwaffe bases were given priority status. In addition, an interdiction bombing campaign was targeted on northern France, with the aim of disrupting road and rail communications to isolate the Normandy beaches from swift German reinforcement.

The Allied deception plan proved highly effective, with almost all the German commanders believing that the attack would be made in the Calais area. The German generals were not in agreement, however, over the right tactics to be adopted to repel the invasion force. The commander of German forces in Western Europe, Field Marshal Rundstedt, believed there was little hope of containing the Allies on the beaches and favored maintaining a strong reserve to launch counterattacks. Field Marshal Rommel, now commander of Army Group B, insisted that Allied air power would destroy German reserve units before they could engage the invaders, and he backed a plan to fight on the beaches. Rommel was the only senior German commander who had experienced Allied air power at first hand, and his fears were largely justified. Hitler imposed a compromise plan that satisfied neither general.

Left: US forces pour ashore on D-Day, the Allied invasion of Normandy. By the end of June 6, the bridgehead was secure and five Allied divisions were ashore.

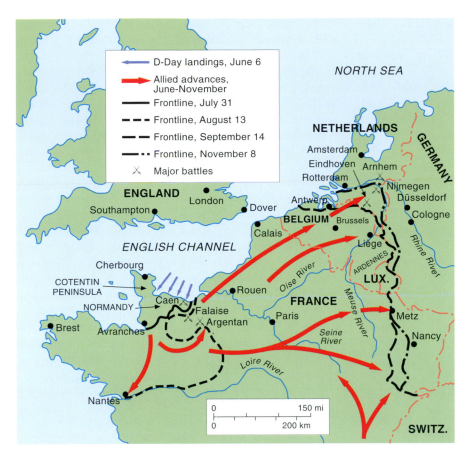

Left: The Allies reached the German border at the end of 1944, but by then their supply lines were stretched and the advance had run out of momentum.

the German forces in the combat zone. The US First Army, led by General Omar Bradley (1893–1981), made a vital breakout to Avranches on July 31, while the battle at Caen drew in German reserves that might have stopped Bradley's advance. Finally, the sweeping advance of US mechanized formations, commanded by General Patton, forced the Germans to retreat. Many, however, did not escape in time, and trapped by the British advancing south from Caen and the Americans swinging round to the northeast, some 50,000 Germans were forced to surrender in the Falaise–Argentan gap in mid-August.

The military situation facing the German High Command was made worse by the Allied amphibious landing in southern France on August 15. The US Seventh Army spearheaded an advance northward up the Rhone valley, linking up with elements of Patton's forces on September 11.

The 2nd Free French Armored Division and the US 4th Infantry Division had liberated Paris on August 25. Optimism that the war might soon be over was high in the Allied camp, but lack of supplies slowed the Allies and gave the Germans time to prepare their defenses. General Eisenhower continued with the plan of advance along a broad front, provoking arguments between his field commanders, Montgomery and Patton, who were both eager to see a concentration of effort behind their own respective lines of attack.

Eisenhower did, however, support Montgomery's plan for a large-scale Anglo-American airborne assault on the Netherlands. Montgomery argued that by capturing the main bridges over the Rhine, the Allies would have an easy passage into Germany itself. The attack began on September 17, and while some of the bridges were captured intact, the main bridge at Arnhem remained in German hands. The defeat at Arnhem showed that, although the Germans were retreating they were far from beaten. As the weary Allies settled down for the winter of 1944–45, the Germans were planning a last-gasp counterattack through the Ardennes, the scene of their great breakthrough in 1940.

At the close of 1944, Hitler still had 65 divisions with which to defend Germany's western border. But very few were adequately equipped frontline formations, and many were filled with old men and youngsters.

Covered by an air umbrella of over 10,000 aircraft, the Allied amphibious force steamed across the English Channel, set to land on the Normandy beaches at D-Day: June 6, 1944. British and Canadian troops stormed ashore on their allotted beaches, Gold, Juno, and Sword. These landings met with some resistance, but on all three beaches the troops overcame the German sea defenses and advanced inland.

Farther west, the American landing on Omaha beach was hindered by heavy surf, steep cliffs, and much more stubborn German resistance. Losses were heavy, but at the close of the first day of fighting a small, tenuous foothold had been gained. At Utah, the other American landing beach, troops met less resistance. By the evening of June 6, the Allied landing troops were ashore and beachheads had been established.

Hitler was slow to react to news of the invasion; still believing the Normandy landings to be a diversion, he delayed moving troops from the Calais region, and refused to commit the panzer reserves to the fighting until too late. Allied air attacks hampered German divisions moving toward Normandy during the weeks after the landings, allowing the Allies to push farther inland. German resistance was always determined, and storms in the Channel destroyed one of the artificial concrete Mulberry harbors erected to facilitate the unloading of troops and supplies at the beaches.

American forces captured the port of Cherbourg on June 26, and by July 1 the Allies had achieved parity with

Armaments and fuel were in short supply. Despite the military reality that defeat was staring him in the face, Hitler decided on this last offensive to retrieve Germany's fortunes.

British and Canadian troops had fought a hard battle during October and November to clear German-occupied islands at the mouth of the Scheldt Estuary, which led to the important port of Antwerp. The first supplies reached the port on November 28, and from then on the Allied supply position began to improve. Accordingly, the recapture of the port became a German priority.

For his Ardennes attack Hitler scraped together 24 divisions, 10 of them armored, organized into the Fifth Panzer and Sixth SS Panzer Armies, with the Seventh Army in support. The Allied High Command considered an attack through the heavily wooded Ardennes was unlikely in the depths of winter. That sector of the Allied line was considered "quiet" and the units stationed there were thinly spread. Hitler aimed to punch through the line, split the British and American forces, and then swing northward toward Antwerp.

The attack came on December 16, and the Germans achieved complete surprise. They overran the US forces facing them on a 60-mile (96-km) sector of the front. The defenders were troubled by low cloud that grounded almost all aircraft, but US units to the north and south of the bulge held firm. Allied reinforcements were rushed into the battle and fought determinedly to defend the vital road junctions at St. Vith and Bastogne.

An acute shortage of fuel hampered the German assault. Although panzer units came close to capturing the massive fuel dump south of Spa, they were eventually driven back. German vehicles began to run out of fuel, and the advance petered out, while Allied reinforcements, supported by ground-attack aircraft, began to compress the German bulge. The besieged town of Bastogne was relieved on December 26. By the end of January 1945 all the early German gains had been lost. Hitler's last gamble in the West had failed.

The Allies now continued their advance toward the Rhine, the last great physical barrier between them and the German heartland. Hitler typically refused to sanction any withdrawals behind the river, condemning

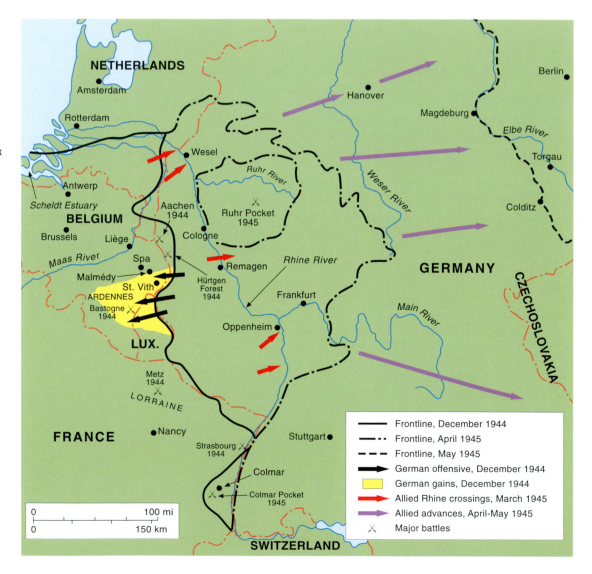

Right: The German Ardennes Offensive was a gamble that failed, and cost Hitler 120,000 men killed, wounded, or missing. Material losses included 600 tanks, 1,600 aircraft, and 6,000 vehicles. Though the attack delayed Allied operations in the West for six weeks, it used up Germany's slim reserves that might otherwise have been used on the Eastern Front. With the renewal of the Allied advance in the West, the Germans were able to offer only token resistance.

Legend:
— Frontline, December 1944
—·—· Frontline, April 1945
---- Frontline, May 1945
➤ German offensive, December 1944
▮ German gains, December 1944
➤ Allied Rhine crossings, March 1945
➤ Allied advances, April–May 1945
✕ Major battles

many of his remaining troops to prisoner of war camps. Trapped enemy units at Colmar had surrendered by February 9. On March 7, the Allies had a stroke of luck when a US infantry patrol captured the bridge over the Rhine at Remagen intact, enabling US troops to pour into Germany without significant opposition. The Rhine was breached again on the 22nd when Patton bridged the river at Oppenheim. The British under Montgomery crossed the Rhine at Wesel on the 23rd. Effective German resistance began to collapse. As the Soviet armies drove toward Berlin, the Ruhr – center of German industry – was overrun during April, along with 300,000 German troops. By the beginning of May, American units had reached the Elbe River, meeting up with Soviet forces advancing from the east.

Advances of the Red Army

On the Eastern Front, after the lull of late 1943, Soviet forces launched a series of offensives along the whole length of the frontline early in 1944, intending to expel the German invaders from all Soviet land. The Red Army entered Romanian territory – the site of Hitler's vital oil fields – on March 26. The German and Romanian troops trapped in the Crimea were overwhelmed, the remnants fleeing west across the Black Sea. Sevastopol was captured on May 12.

When the Soviet command launched the summer offensive of 1944, there could be little doubt about its outcome. Two huge Soviet thrusts pierced the line held by the German Army Group Centre. Codenamed Operation Bagration, this offensive was designed to clear German forces from Byelorussia on the western border of the Soviet Union and place the Red Army within striking distance of Warsaw. The attack began on June 22, punching toward Minsk (captured on July 3), and German forces in the sector crumpled under the hammer blows delivered by the Red Army.

The Soviet advance crossed the Soviet–Polish border and halted just to the east of Warsaw on August 7. A few days previously, the underground Polish Home Army had risen up against the German garrison in Warsaw. It is not certain why the Red Army refused to cross the Vistula to help the Poles, but after an epic struggle the Polish rising was crushed by the Germans at the end of September.

Right: On the Eastern Front, the German Army was overwhelmed by the numerical superiority of the Red Army.

The focus of the offensive now switched to the south as Soviet forces drove deep into Romania and Hungary, both nations suing for peace in early September. Bulgaria changed sides on September 8 when Soviet forces crossed the Danube. In Yugoslavia, the communist-backed Partisans harried the retreating Germans from the country, taking the capital Belgrade on October 20. By the end of October, the Soviet First Baltic Front drove through to the Baltic and entered East Prussia. With winter approaching, however, Soviet offensive operations were halted.

The final Soviet offensive of the war was launched on January 12, 1945. Overwhelmed by the sheer weight of men and armor, the Germans fell back. Marshal Zhukov reached the Oder River on January 31. A last-ditch German counterattack was launched, but crushed. Crossing the Austrian frontier, Soviet forces took Vienna on April 15. Berlin was the next objective. Three Soviet armies opened the final attack against Berlin on April 16. The Red Army encircled the city on April 25, the same day that US forces met up with Soviet troops at Torgau on the Elbe River. The Battle for Berlin was savage, the Red Army driving toward the last bastion of Nazi power: the bunker beneath the Chancellery that held Adolf Hitler, who committed suicide on April 30. The remnants of German forces accepted the Allies' unconditional surrender terms, which were signed on May 7, 1945. The war in Europe was over.

The Defeat of Japan

By the beginning of 1945, it was clear that Japan was facing defeat in the Pacific. American industry was churning out vast numbers of ships and aircraft, which were sinking her warships and merchant fleet, while US aircraft were reducing Japan's cities to rubble. However, the Japanese continued to fight, and only the use of atomic bombs saved the Allies a costly invasion of Japan itself.

Early in 1945, with the Philippines virtually secure, the American planners in the Pacific moved on to the next phase of the war: two major amphibious assaults against Iwo Jima and Okinawa — the latter part of Japan itself.

Iwo Jima was the first target for assault on February 19, 1945. The Japanese had constructed a complex series of fortifications, most of them underground, and proof against the heaviest American bombardments. The US invasion fleet moved V Amphibious Corps into position on the night of February 18. The landings were preceded by a mass naval bombardment. However, the US Marines were met with heavy fire as they came ashore, taking 2,420 casualties on the first day alone. Once ashore, the Marines turned south to attack the prominent feature of Mount Suribachi, which was taken

on the 23rd. The remainder of the 23,000-strong Japanese force held out until March 20.

By the end of March, airfields on Iwo Jima were in operational use against Japan, allowing fighters to escort heavy bombers to targets throughout Japan. The capture of the island was an important step in the strategic bombing campaign, but the price in American casualties had been high: over 6,800 US Marines had been killed and more than 18,000 had been wounded. Only 216 Japanese prisoners were taken. Admiral Nimitz summed up the Marines' performance at Iwo Jima with the words, "uncommon valor was a common virtue."

As the battle for Iwo Jima ended, so the Americans prepared to attack Okinawa. The assault was the largest and most ambitious of the entire Pacific campaign. A sustained naval bombardment of Okinawa began on March 23, and was matched by a huge air campaign. The actual invasion began on April 1, 1945. One Marine corps and one army corps provided the strike force for the landings, which, unlike at Iwo Jima, met little immediate opposition. Most of Okinawa's 130,000-strong garrison had withdrawn to strong defensive positions in the interior, especially in the south of the island.

US troops had secured the north of Okinawa by mid-April, before turning to the prepared defenses of the Shuri Line in the south. On May 3, the Japanese launched an all-out but ultimately unsuccessful counterattack, while in the seas around Okinawa, Kamikaze suicide aircraft attacks were launched against the American fleet. In all, 21 vessels were sunk and another 43 were put out of action by the Kamikaze pilots.

On Okinawa itself, US ground troops launched an assault on May 11 in dreadful weather conditions.

Left: US Marines under fire on the beach during the fighting on the island of Iwo Jima.

They drove the Japanese back to the hilly ground at the southern tip of the island. Reaching the hills on June 1, the Americans made a final attack that eventually overcame the enemy, who had virtually fought to the last man. Many Japanese civilians preferred to commit suicide by jumping off steep cliffs rather than surrender, despite American pledges to treat them fairly. Desultory fighting carried on until June 21, but by then Japanese casualties had exceeded 100,000 dead; US casualties totalled over 12,000 killed and nearly 37,000 wounded.

The battles for both Iwo Jima and Okinawa were extraordinarily bloody for the United States, the two most costly in terms of the number of soldiers killed of the whole Pacific campaign. The heavy losses incurred on Okinawa, in particular, persuaded many in the American High Command that the use of the newly developed atomic bomb was the only way to end the conflict quickly.

With the capture of Okinawa, the final phase of the US bomber offensive against Japan began. During February and March 1945, bombers had already been attacking Japanese industrial cities; on March 9–10, a raid on Tokyo left much of the city in ruins. At the same time, the US naval blockade of Japan by both surface vessels and submarines began to make itself felt, so much so, that by the summer of 1945 Japan had been destroyed as an economic entity, its people on the verge of starvation.

Despite this, Japan's military will to continue the war seemed undiminished, and a plan of invasion was brought forward: a first assault in November and the second in March 1946. However, events elsewhere were to make such plans unnecessary. On July 16, 1945, the world's first atomic bomb was detonated at Alamogordo, New Mexico. On August 6, an atomic bomb was exploded over Hiroshima. This was followed by the Soviet declaration of war against Japan and the invasion of Manchuria by the Red Army on August 8, which totally shattered Japanese forces located there. A second atomic bomb was dropped on Nagasaki on August 9. Six days later the Japanese emperor announced his decision to surrender; the terms were signed on board the USS *Missouri* on September 2, bringing World War II to an end.

HIROSHIMA AND NAGASAKI

On August 6, 1945, the US Air Force B-29 Superfortress *Enola Gay* unleashed the most powerful and destructive weapon ever seen on the Japanese city of Hiroshima, the atomic bomb. The Germans, British, and Americans had been developing atomic weapons for a number of years, but the Americans were the first to use an atomic bomb. The bomb dropped on Hiroshima was nicknamed "Fat Man." It was produced by Robert Oppenheimer and the team working on the secret Los Alamos project.

Nearly 80,000 people died as an immediate result of the explosion and 75 percent of the mainly wooden buildings in the city were destroyed by blast or fire. In subsequent weeks and months a further 70,000 succumbed to the effects of radiation sickness and burns.

Three days after the Hiroshima explosion, "Little Boy" was exploded in the sky above the Japanese industrial center of Nagasaki. Forty thousand people died and nearly half the city was destroyed. Japan offered to surrender on the following day. What the Japanese did not know was that the Americans at the time did not have any more atomic bombs to drop on them.

Warfare in the Modern World

The end of World War II in 1945 did not herald the beginning of an age of peace. The various Allies who had beaten Germany and Japan soon split along political lines: one group was dominated by the United States; the other by the Soviet Union. The United States and the Soviet Union instigated the undeclared conflict known as the Cold War, which lasted until the 1980s. Thereafter ethnocentric and nationalist conflicts have plagued the international arena.

Warfare since 1945 has been dominated by rapid advances in military technology. Weapons of all types have become more powerful, flexible, and capable of inflicting huge casualties. Aircraft, for example, can fly farther, faster, carry a greater variety of weapons, and hit a target with greater accuracy than ever before. The introduction of smart technology is in the process of revolutionizing military weapons, and will continue to do so. However, modern equipment is hugely expensive and prone to mechanical failure; few countries can finance fully modern armies, and those that do spend great sums keeping their weapons in serviceable order.

The most distinctive form of warfare that developed post-1945 were the wars of national liberation. They were usually Third World conflicts – notably in Africa and Asia – where nations fought to free themselves of their former European colonial masters. The speed of change was often remarkable. In Africa in 1945, for example, the vast majority of states were ruled or administered by Europeans; within the space of a few decades the Europeans had departed for good. As a consequence of the Cold War, many of these conflicts took on a wider political character, with many essentially national struggles being seen as a wars of Communism versus the West. The Soviet Union (and to a degree China) actively supported nationalist groups in Africa and Asia, simply as means to cause discomfiture to the United States and the West.

Right: The outbreak of small-scale ethnic conflicts toward the end of the 20th century required the deployment of peacekeeping forces drawn from the world's armies. These are British troops deployed to Bosnia. Such deployments are fraught with political problems.

Revolutionary China

If the United States and the Soviet Union were the world's two undisputed superpowers in 1945, another contender emerged in the shape of the former "sleeping dragon," China. During the 19th and 20th centuries, China was the victim of repeated interventions from outside powers, and it was only after the Communist victory in 1949 that the country began to develop as a major military power on the world stage.

The history of modern China dates back to 1911, when a revolution overthrew the long-standing Manchu dynasty and the country became a republic. The revolution, however, failed to provide China with the strong government that it needed to end years of political unrest. Most of China was controlled by warlords, who acted as local dictators in their own spheres of influence. In 1926 the main political party in the Chinese republic, the nationalist Kuomintang, launched a military campaign against the warlords.

The Kuomintang armies were commanded by General Chiang Kai-shek (1893–1975). They had the support of the Chinese Communist Party, which had been founded in 1921 and had allied itself with the Kuomintang. Chiang Kai-shek's campaign against the warlords was highly successful, and by 1927 he had gained control of most of China. Feeling in a strong position, he then turned against his Communist allies, whom he mistrusted. He banned the Communist Party and killed many thousands of Communists, as well as crushing uprisings in cities such as Canton and Shanghai.

Those Communists who survived Chiang Kai-shek's repression fled to the countryside. In 1928 Chiang set up a Nationalist government in Nanking and he was soon widely recognized as the country's legitimate ruler. The Communists continued to resist him, however, and set up their own government in Jiangxi province in 1931. Mao Zhedong (1893–1976), the son of a peasant farmer, seized the leadership of the Chinese Communist Party. Traditionally, Marxism had taught that city-based factory workers would be the spearhead of revolution, but Mao argued that Chinese peasants could provide the basis for a revolution achieved through waging war in the countryside.

At first, however, it seemed the Communists might be wiped out in China, and they were forced to flee from Jiangxi to escape extermination by Chiang's forces in 1934. After the hardships of the Long March, as the Communists's escape from Jiangxi became known, they reached the remote Shaanxi province in 1935. There they began to build up support among the peasants and prepared to attack the Kuomintang.

The support of the peasants was the key to the Communists' eventual victory. Whereas the Kuomintang (or Nationalists) stole food from the peasants, the Communists usually paid. The Communists also freed peasants from the burden of debts and high rents by banishing or killing local officials who had collected money from the peasants. The Kuomintang were identified with the landlords, who were hated by the peasants,

Left: This map shows the main battles of the Chinese Civil War in the 1930s and 1940s, including the epic Long March, which has entered Chinese Communist folklore.

offensive to retake Manchuria. His troops were able to occupy the Manchurian cities, but were then encircled by rural-based Communist forces, so that the Nationalists suffered a string of defeats. The Communist forces, known since 1946 as the People's Liberation Army (PLA), were strengthened with large quantities of captured equipment and deserting Nationalist troops, who enrolled in the PLA in their tens of thousands.

By 1948 the PLA was in full control of Manchuria. The Communist forces then pushed southward. They inflicted a catastrophic defeat on Chiang's armies in a battle around Jin Xian in October, in which about 500,000 Nationalist troops were either killed, wounded, or taken prisoner. By this time, the economies in Nationalist areas were collapsing; soldiers's pay was worthless, removing the only reason for fighting. The Kuomintang armies began to fall apart.

In April 1949, the PLA crossed the Yangtze River and began to occupy southern China. By the last months of the year almost all of mainland China was under Communist control, and in October 1949, in Peking (Beijing), Mao Zhedong proclaimed the People's Republic of China. Chiang and his followers, who had fled to the island of Formosa, now Taiwan, continued to claim to be the legitimate Chinese government. They remained safe from Communist assault because of the protection offered by the United States, which until 1972 recognized the Nationalist leadership in Taiwan as the legitimate government of all China.

while Mao's troops killed thousands of landlords and other so-called "oppressors."

In 1937 the political situation was transformed by the Japanese invasion of China. The well-armed and disciplined Japanese made huge inroads into China, forcing Mao and Chiang to declare a truce in order to better resist the invader – creating the Anti-Japanese United Front. Despite this alliance, Japanese forces soon occupied most of northern and eastern China. Although fighting occasionally flared up between the Nationalists and Communists, the truce basically held until the expulsion of the Japanese from China in 1945.

The Communists fought a guerrilla war of hit-and-run raids and ambushes against the Japanese in occupied areas of rural China. This allowed them to spread their influence over wider areas of the countryside, and in the process convinced large sections of Chinese rural society to believe that the Communists were the true champions of Chinese independence. Chiang, for his part, was widely blamed for failing to prevent the Japanese occupation in the first place. In 1945, war between the Nationalists and the Communists broke out once more.

On paper the Nationalists had stronger forces. They also enjoyed the support of the United States, although this did not extend to the deployment of US troops in China. The Kuomintang leadership had, however, become corrupt and unpopular; the rank and file suffered from poor morale, and desertion was commonplace. In contrast, the Communists were able to recruit hundreds of thousands of fresh troops from the ranks of the peasantry.

The Soviet Union, which had occupied the Chinese province of Manchuria at the end of World War II, allowed Mao's forces to establish themselves there in 1945–46. Chiang Kai-shek ill-advisedly launched an

MAO'S REVOLUTIONARY WARFARE

Between 1927 and 1949, Mao Zhedong developed a theory of "people's war," based on his experience of the fighting in China and on his reading of ancient Chinese military writers. He believed that a revolutionary war had to start in the countryside. His Communist forces survived among the peasants, as Mao said, "like fish in the sea."

Although militarily weaker than their enemies, the revolutionaries had a stronger will to fight. Refusing to stand their ground against superior enemy forces, the revolutionary guerrillas would only give battle when they had a sufficient local advantage in numbers and weapons to ensure victory.

The eventual aim of Maoist warfare was to progressively weaken and demoralize the enemy, and when the time was right, the revolutionaries would relinquish guerrilla activities in rural areas to launch a conventional military offensive to take over the cities and win power.

War In Indochina

In the second half of the 19th century, the present-day states of Vietnam, Laos, and Cambodia were part of the French Empire. French defeat at the hands of the Germans in 1940 weakened the credibility of French rule in the area, which was exploited by the revolutionary Ho Chi Minh, the founder of the Indochinese Communist Party. The French responded militarily, but would lose socially and politically.

In 1941, the anti-French Vietnamese created a nationalist movement in the northernmost part of Vietnam, Tonkin. Normally known as the Viet Minh, this Communist-dominated movement also attracted support from other groups hostile to the French and Japanese. Ho's leading military deputy, Vo Nguyen Giap (1912–), began a guerrilla campaign against the Japanese and, after World War II, the French.

Initially, the Viet Minh was a small organization with almost no military power, and operations against the Japanese did not start in earnest until 1944. However, the Viet Minh was well placed to take advantage of the confused events of early 1945. Those French forces that had continued to keep order in Indochina during the Japanese occupation were suddenly imprisoned or confined to a particular area by the Japanese, allowing the Viet Minh to extend their influence without resistance.

Immediately after the Japanese surrender in 1945, Ho Chi Minh (1890–1969) occupied the city of Hanoi in the north and declared himself president of an independent Democratic Republic of Vietnam with Hanoi as its capital. In the south – where the Viet Minh was weaker and the British moved troops in to supervise the Japanese surrender – French colonial power was restored. In the north, however, the Viet Minh remained in control. On March 6, 1946, France formally recognized the Democratic Republic of Vietnam as a self-governing part of the French Empire. Lulled by this compromise measure, Ho allowed French forces to enter Hanoi and Haiphong, the chief port.

In November 1946, however, clashes between Ho's supporters and the French increased in Haiphong. The city was bombarded by the French fleet, and 6,000 people were killed. The following month, the Viet Minh withdrew from Hanoi to the north's isolated interior and resumed the guerrilla war. The Viet Minh, now stronger and better armed than before, harassed the French with ambushes and skirmishes. The guerrillas slowly extended their hold over much of the rural north, terrorizing village elders and killing government officers who remained loyal to the French. These attacks marked the start of the French–Indochina War, which lasted until the French defeat in 1954.

Neighboring China fell to the Communists in 1949, which opened up supply routes and safe havens for the Viet Minh in China. French outposts near the Chinese border were now vulnerable to attack. During 1950 a fierce struggle was fought over a key highway, the only link between Hanoi and Cao Bang, a vital town near the Chinese border. Eventually the Viet Minh won the struggle for Dong Khe, the key to the route, and a great number of Cao Bang's French garrison were killed.

Emboldened by this success, in 1951 Giap decided to launch an offensive to seize the vital Red River delta and possibly end the war. But the French were now commanded by General Jean de Lattre de Tassigny, who had built fortifications to defend the delta. The Viet Minh assaults were beaten off with heavy casualties.

Right: The brilliant revolutionary leader Vo Nguyen Giap, head of the Viet Minh's military wing (left), lectures recruits during the fight against Japan during World War II.

Giap recovered swiftly from his mistake, and reverted to guerrilla tactics, to which the French had no real answer. The roads on which those French forces defending key towns and villages largely depended for supply and reinforcement were hopelessly vulnerable to ambush and sabotage. Nor could the French prevent terrorist attacks in urban areas, which undermined morale. Giap was waging a classic revolutionary campaign.

Dien Bien Phu

In May 1953, General Henri Navarre was put in charge of saving the French position, which was deteriorating rapidly. Navarre gambled on a decisive battle at Dien Bien Phu, some 200 miles (320 km) west of Hanoi, his aim to draw the Viet Minh into open battle. French troops, the first of 15,000, parachuted into Dien Bien Phu in November 1953. The base Navarre constructed at Dien Bien Phu was intended as a lure: it was to be the killing field on which he would destroy the Viet Minh. Giap, whose forces had grown both in size and experience, eagerly took up the challenge. It would indeed be a killing field – for the French. Navarre totally underestimated the capabilities of his opponent.

The key to the Viet Minh victory at Dien Bien Phu was logistics. By March 1954, in almost impassable terrain (or so the French thought), General Giap had assembled and supplied an army of about 40,000 men around the French base, complete with heavy artillery supplied by the pro-Viet Minh Chinese government. The airstrip at the base, on which the French depended for resupply, was smashed by shelling almost as soon as the Viet Minh onslaught began. Although the French parachuted in some supplies and reinforcements, they were inadequate to defend the position.

The Viet Minh's artillery was positioned on the reverse slopes of the hills that ringed the base. Out of range of French artillery, the guns bombarded the besieged troops. The French defenders fought with a bitter determination, but without relief they knew they

were doomed. In vain, the French appealed to the United States to use its air power – even the atom bomb – to prevent a Viet Minh victory. The US government refused, and Dien Bien Phu was overrun on May 7.

The defeat at Dien Bien Phu came as a profound shock to the French, who began to look for ways to end the fighting. The French agreed to independence for Laos, Cambodia, and Vietnam, although the latter state was temporarily divided in two at the 17th Parallel pending nationwide elections. The elections were never held, however. North Vietnam became a Communist state under Ho Chi Minh, and South Vietnam was run by the US-backed regime of Vietnamese politician Ngo Dinh Diem. The seeds of the later Vietnam War were sown in this compromise peace.

The Fight for Korea

Following the defeat of Japan in 1945, Korea was divided into a northern Soviet-occupied zone and a US zone in the south. The former became the Communist Democratic People's Republic of Korea, ruled by Kim Il Sung, while the US zone became the Republic of Korea under Syngman Rhee. Ideological rivalry and territorial ambitions made conflict inevitable. It erupted in June 1950.

From 1949 onward tension between North and South Korea grew and there were frequent clashes between their forces along the 38th Parallel, the border between the two states. On June 25, 1950, Kim Il Sung launched a massive invasion of the South. Committed to resisting the spread of Communism around the globe, the United States wanted to intervene militarily in defense of South Korea, and the Americans called on the United Nations (UN) to authorize armed intervention. By chance, the Soviet representative to the UN, who could have voted against any UN action, had temporarily withdrawn from the organization in protest over another matter. So the UN ordered a force to South Korea.

Although many other countries, including Britain, France, Canada, Australia, and New Zealand, aided the UN effort, about 300,000 out of the 345,000-strong UN force that fought in Korea were from the United States. The UN forces were placed under General Douglas MacArthur (1880–1964) with orders to repel the North Korean invaders.

The initial 1950 North Korean onslaught, by massed infantry assaults, swept through the South Korean defenses, and the South Korean capital Seoul fell into Communist hands. Both South Korean and American troops were forced back into a position around the port of Pusan in the south, defending an area that became known as the Pusan Perimeter. After reinforcing the Perimeter, MacArthur counterattacked with a bold amphibious landing at Inchon, a port behind the North Korean frontline to the west of Seoul, on September 15. The over-extended North Korean forces were caught completely off guard. By the end of the month UN forces had recaptured Seoul and the North Koreans were in full retreat.

Left: The Korean War sucked the West and China into a conflict that had reached a stalemate after one year of fighting. The next two years of bloodshed achieved nothing.

Left: A US soldier searches a Chinese captive while a South Korean keeps watch. Sheer weight of numbers initially gave Chinese forces sizeable territorial gains in the war.

Short of food, ammunition, and reinforcements, they came to a halt about 45 miles (72 km) south of Seoul. On January 25, 1951, the UN launched a counterattack. This time the UN forces used their massive firepower, both artillery and air strikes, to overwhelming effect. The UN "meatgrinder," as this massive use of firepower became known, inflicted more casualties than even the Chinese could sustain. From January to March 1951, the UN troops ground their way back to the 38th Parallel, recapturing Seoul on March 14.

Totally committed to victory, MacArthur now wanted to raise the stakes again. He not only intended a renewed invasion of North Korea, but wanted to blockade mainland China, attack Chinese bases and industries in Manchuria, and use Nationalist Chinese troops from Formosa (Taiwan) against the Communists. He even contemplated the use of the atom bomb to force the Chinese to quit the war. But MacArthur's political masters in Washington had had enough of his challenges to the president's Constitutional authority. On April 11 he was replaced as commander by General Matthew Ridgway.

By the end of May 1951, the war had reached a stalemate. A Communist counteroffensive at the end of April had failed after heroic resistance by the British 29th Brigade, and especially the British Gloucestershire Regiment, at the Imjin River. A last Chinese offensive in May failed to penetrate beyond the 38th Parallel. The front stabilized roughly along the line of the prewar border between North and South Korea. Both sides made raids and conducted artillery bombardments, but there were no full-scale battles. Peace negotiations were opened in July.

It took two years for negotiators to agree to an armistice, which was signed on July 27, 1953. Many thousands had died during the discussions. The situation in Korea returned to almost exactly what it had been before the war broke out, with Korea divided between a Communist North and a pro-American South. The Korean War cost the lives of about 84,000 UN and South Korean troops. The cost in North Korean and Chinese casualties cannot be accurately counted, but was probably between one and two million killed and wounded. Tensions in the region did not end with the 1953 armistice, and both North and South Korea continued to view each other with suspicion, a sentiment that is only now abating.

The Communist government of China gave clear warning that it would intervene in the conflict if the UN forces invaded North Korea. But MacArthur had no intention of halting his advance north from Seoul at the North Korean border. He told the US government: "Unless and until the enemy capitulates, I regard all of Korea open to our military operations." By the last week in October, UN forces had advanced northward to within 65 miles (104 km) of the Yalu River, the border between North Korea and the Chinese province of Manchuria.

The Chinese Communists had prepared their response. In October 1950 China entered the war on the side of North Korea. At first only relatively small Chinese forces were sent into Korea, but as the UN advance continued, Chinese troops (the "People's Volunteers") had already begun secretly crossing the Yalu River. By November 25, an army of about 300,000 troops had assumed positions that surrounded the vanguard of the UN advance. With no tanks or air support, the Chinese relied on mass attacks; their infantrymen were ordered to advance on the UN troops regardless of casualties. MacArthur's men were overwhelmed by surprise and the enemy's skill in night fighting – and their great numbers. In another swift about turn, demoralized UN troops were soon beating a hasty retreat southward.

Some UN units fought back with distinction. The US 1st Marine Division, led by General Oliver Smith, was surrounded by eight Chinese divisions in the Chosin Reservoir area. Smith and his troops carried out an epic fighting retreat in the face of repeated attacks and bitterly cold winter weather between November 27 and December 9.

Eventually, the Chinese advance ran out of steam as their supply lines began to stretch to breaking point.

Wars of Liberation

In the 30 years between 1945 and 1975, the European powers gave up all but a few remnants of their empires. In some cases, this retreat from empire was a reasonably dignified transfer to designated successors, but in others it happened only after nationalist groups had fought bitter campaigns against the colonial authorities. These campaigns forced European armies to develop counterinsurgency tactics.

The French fought two major colonial wars against nationalist insurgents. The first was in Indochina, the second in Algeria. The war in Algeria began in 1954, just as the Indochina War was drawing to a close. A massive territory in North Africa, Algeria was technically not a colony, but a part of France. It was dominated by about a million European settlers, known as *pieds noirs*. The other 90 percent of the population were either Arab or Berber Muslims.

When a few hundred members of the Algerian nationalist *Front de Libération Nationale* (FLN – National Liberation Front), formed by a group of radical Muslims, began a campaign in Algeria on November 1, 1954, it seemed to pose little threat to French authority. In 1956 France granted independence to Algeria's nearest neighbors, Tunisia, and Morocco, but felt it could hold on to Algeria itself. FLN fighters were later able to use Tunisia as a safe haven, forcing the French to build a barrier, the Morice Line, to stop them from crossing between the two countries.

The FLN rapidly built up support among the Muslim population, who, not unnaturally, were resentful of being treated as second-class citizens in their own country. There were brutal massacres and countermassacres, as the FLN attacked *pied noir* families, and the *pieds noirs* and the French Army retaliated with random attacks against Muslims. The FLN became secretly established in the Muslim *casbah* (old market) area of the Algerian capital, Algiers, and from its warren of narrow streets and small houses carried out terrorist attacks in the European part of the city.

In January 1957, paratroop commander General Jacques Massu was ordered to clear Algiers of FLN terrorists. Massu carried out a campaign that was, on the face of it, highly successful. In the so-called Battle of Algiers, he saturated the *casbah* with troops, who carried out house-to-house searches for FLN fighters and weapons, and set up checkpoints at key points. The intelligence gained from these measures was supported by the interrogation of FLN suspects, often involving the use of torture. Massu was able to build up a detailed picture of the FLN network in Algiers, and then move in to destroy it. But the brutality of Massu's methods, especially the use of torture, provoked widespread criticism in France and began to undermine France's political will to resist the Algerian nationalists.

There appeared to be no doubt about France's military ability to take on and defeat the FLN. Guerrillas operating inside Algeria were subject to an intense counterinsurgency offensive. One of the first measures taken was the mass relocation of Muslims from areas under guerrilla influence; as many as two million people may have been shifted to regions under the control of the French Army. The French then launched a series of large-scale search-and-destroy operations, sweeping through guerrilla strongholds.

By 1960 the FLN's military wing, the *Armée de Libération Nationale* (ALN – National Liberation Army) was only able to survive in remote mountain regions. With about 500,000 heavily armed French troops deployed in Algeria, along with some 150,000 anti-ALN militiamen, the authorities had the military situation well in hand. But the political situation had slid

MERCENARIES IN AFRICA

Bands of white mercenaries became an important force in Africa during and after the withdrawal of the colonial powers. Local military forces were often so weak that a few well-armed mercenary troops led by bold officers could have a decisive impact on conflicts.

Mercenaries first appeared in the former Belgian Congo in the 1960s, where independence was followed by a series of confused civil conflicts. British, French, and Belgian officers recruited men, mostly from Rhodesia and South Africa, on behalf of various parties in the Congolese wars. At one point, in 1967, some mercenaries even planned to take over the Congo themselves, but the attempt was a complete failure.

Mercenaries were later recruited to fight in the Nigerian Civil War of 1967–70, and in Angola in 1976. The Angolan adventure ended disastrously for the mercenaries, who soon broke up when faced with properly armed and trained Cuban forces. After the Angolan fiasco – which saw the arrest, imprisonment, and even execution of some of the mercenaries – mercenary activity in Africa has been minimal.

Right: British-equipped Kenyan militia head out on patrol. The insurgency against the Mau Mau guerrillas lasted from 1952 to 1956 and cost 12,000 lives.

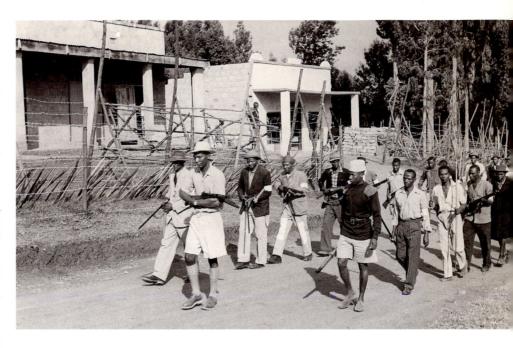

into a disastrous confrontation between French Army officers and *pieds noirs* on one side, and the French government on the other.

French political leaders wished to end the conflict in Algeria. The cost in men and money was more than the French people would willingly bear, and the manner in which this war of torture and massacre was being waged also caused much unfavorable reaction in France. But the French Army leaders in Algeria and the *pieds noirs* were totally committed to keeping Algeria French.

In May 1958, with the cooperation of some French army officers, the *pieds noirs* seized control of Algerian cities. They demanded a French government committed to French Algeria. The army officers even considered flying troops to Paris to take power and install a military government. Under this pressure, the government of the French Fourth Republic collapsed. Former French soldier Charles de Gaulle (1890–1970), a hero of World War II, was appointed president of a new government.

Once in power, de Gaulle began to favor the idea of self-government for Algeria. He vigorously suppressed attempted army revolts in Algeria in 1960 and 1961. Despite a terrorist campaign by the *Organisation Armée Secrète* (OAS – Secret Army Organization), a group dedicated to keeping Algeria French, de Gaulle negotiated with the FLN and reached an agreement on Algerian independence in March 1962.

Britain's Victory

The British in their Southeast Asian colony of Malaya showed how a counterinsurgency campaign could be fought and won. The Malayan Emergency, as the campaign came to be known, lasted from 1948 to 1960. The Malayan Communist Party (MCP) launched a major guerrilla campaign in 1948. The Communists had some support among the colony's ethnic Chinese living in Malaya, a large minority who made up about 40 percent of the country's total population. Malays, on the other hand, were almost wholly united in their opposition to the guerrilla uprising. So the MCP could, at best, count on some support from only a minority of the Malayan population.

The MCP's guerrilla forces, known as the Malayan Races' Liberation Army, first tried to establish bases in populated areas, but these proved too vulnerable to counterattack by the British colonial forces. The guerrillas soon withdrew to bases in remote jungle areas, where they easily evaded sweeps by large-scale British army formations. The jungle was a difficult environment for the guerrillas, however. They only survived through support from Chinese "squatters." These were Chinese who, during the hardships of the Great Depression of the 1930s and the Japanese occupation of Malaya in 1941–45, had taken refuge in unoccupied land on the fringes of the jungle. Their villages were almost completely out of government control, and were a source of food, medicine, and recruits for the guerrillas.

The Communists carried out a sustained campaign of terrorist attacks and sabotage that especially targeted members of the local police forces and European managers of rubber plantations and tin mines. By 1950, the security situation was deteriorating and new policies were clearly required. General Sir Harold Briggs was appointed director of operations, and under his guidance coordinated action by the police, the army, and the civilian authorities replaced a purely military effort against the guerrillas. There was an emphasis on intelligence-gathering and small army units were sent out to hit identified guerrilla targets. The British authorities also began relocating the Chinese squatters, who numbered over 400,000, in protected villages where they would be under the control of the authorities.

After General Sir Gerald Templer was appointed High Commissioner of Malaya and commander-in-chief in 1952, these military policies were intensified. But much of Britain's positive result was owed to the idea that, in Templer's words, the answer to guerrilla activity lay "not in pouring more troops into the jungle, but in the hearts and minds of the people." The British also pursued a political solution along with their counterinsurgency effort, which ended with the granting of independence to Malaya in 1957. It had been a textbook example of how to fight insurgents.

Arab and Israeli Wars

By 1947 Britain, who had controlled Palestine since World War I, decided that it could no longer govern the region in the face of increasing Jewish and Arab terrorism. The United Nations (UN) intervened to end the violence, and urged that Palestine should be divided into two separate states, one Jewish, one Arab. The Arabs rejected this solution. The scene was set for a series of short but intense wars.

On May 14, 1948, Jewish leaders declared their part of Palestine independent and named the new state Israel. In the process, many Arabs were displaced from their homes and lands, and tension developed into outright hostility. Israel was then invaded by the Arab states of Egypt, Syria, Iraq, Lebanon, and Transjordan (now Jordan).

On the face of it, this first war between the Jews and their Arab neighbors was an unequal struggle that the Israelis should have lost. But the Israeli Defense Forces (IDF) had the advantage of defending a small area with good internal communications, and many Israelis had acquired military training before and during World War II. Since the Arab attacks were largely uncoordinated, the Israelis were able to switch their forces between the different fronts to meet each threat as it arose. The Israelis also began to receive considerable quantities of modern military equipment from Europe and, especially, the United States.

During the first month of fighting, the Israelis won control of the northern part of the Jordan River, driving off the Syrians and Lebanese advancing from the north and the Iraqis in the west. On June 11, the United Nations arranged a truce, but this was broken a month later when the Egyptians attacked on the southern front. The IDF successfully held off the Egyptians in some of the heaviest fighting of the war, while at the same time launching its own offensives against the Syrians in Galilee and the Jordanians around the city of Jerusalem.

By mid-July, when a second truce came into effect, the Israelis had thoroughly taken the strategic lead. They used the break in the fighting to further build up their arms and to organize a decisive attack. On October 28, the IDF went on the offensive in Galilee, on the Lebanon border, clearing the area of Arab forces in three days. The Israelis were then able to concentrate all

their forces against the Egyptians. They seized control of the Negev Desert and invaded Egyptian territory at Abu Aweigila on December 27.

International pressure forced the Israelis to pull back from invading Egypt itself, but they had clearly won the war. Divided and demoralized, the Arab states agreed to armistices with Israel between February 24 and July 20, 1949. The armistice lines became, in effect, the borders of the new state. Israel now consisted of the part of Palestine originally allotted to the Jews under the UN's 1947 partition plan, plus half of Jerusalem and areas on the Lebanese border to the north and the Egyptian border in the south. Jordan remained in occupation of the West Bank of the Jordan River and the eastern section of Jerusalem, and Egypt held the Gaza Strip.

The first Arab–Israeli conflict left an unstable situation in the area. None of the Arab states recognized Israel's right to exist, and continued to see the Israeli state as an illegal occupant of Arab territory. Hundreds of thousands of Palestinian Arabs had fled from their homes in what was now Israel, and lived as stateless refugees in camps around Israel's borders. The Israelis, for their part, saw their territory as difficult to defend, and looked for a chance to expand Israel's borders to more defensible lines.

In 1952, a group of military officers led by Gamal Abdel Nasser (1918–70) seized power in Egypt. In July

Right: Israeli armored forces advance through Lebanon in US armored personnel carriers during Operation Peace for Galilee in June 1982.

November 7. The French, British, and Israeli forces were withdrawn from Egypt under the supervision of UN monitors.

For the next 10 years Arabs and Israelis lived side by side in an uneasy peace. It was a time of important changes in the region, however. The major anti-Israel Arab states, Egypt and Syria, won the backing of the Soviet Union, while the United States became gradually drawn into supporting Israel. The Israeli economy flourished and the country grew in population and in military strength. Many Palestinian Arabs ceased to believe that the Arab states would ever defeat Israel through conventional military action. In response, a Palestinian businessman and militant, Yassir Arafat (1929–), created the guerrilla movement *Al Fatah* to carry out armed raids on Israel. In 1964, the Arab states themselves created the Palestinian Liberation Organization (PLO), which became the coordinating body for anti-Israeli Arab commando groups.

In 1967, guerrilla raids on Israel and Israeli counterstrikes against guerrilla bases in neighboring Arab countries increased, and both sides began to feel that a new military showdown was approaching. Egypt took the initiative. In May, Nasser sent his troops into Sinai, ordered UN observers to quit the border with Israel, and declared the closing of the Strait of Tiran to Israeli shipping. Israel considered this was sufficient cause for war, and decided to launch a preemptive assault.

In the early hours of June 5, 1967, the Israeli Air Force (IAF) attacked Egyptian air bases to devastating effect. Almost the entire Egyptian Air Force was knocked out in two hours. The IAF then turned its attention to Egypt's allies, Jordan and Syria, inflicting similar damage on their aircraft. With complete command of the air, the Israelis crushed the Egyptian Army in the Sinai peninsula, winning a series of desert tank battles against numerically superior armored forces. By June 9, the Israelis were in control of the east bank of the Suez Canal.

Meanwhile, the Jordanians had launched an offensive on June 5 in support of the Egyptians. After some hard fighting the Israelis drove the Jordanians back and, on the 7th, took control of the whole of the West Bank and Jerusalem. The IDF was now free to turn its attention to the Syrians, who were occupying fortified positions on the Golan Heights, the hilly region of northern Israel, dominating Galilee. On June 9, a combined assault by Israeli infantry, tanks, and aircraft captured the Golan Heights and drove the Syrians back in disarray.

By June 10, 1967, the Six-Day War, as it became known, was over. It left Israel in occupation of the West Bank, the Golan Heights, the Gaza Strip, and Sinai.

1956, Nasser announced the Egyptian takeover of the Suez Canal, which was then under the control of Britain and France. Believing that the nationalization of the canal threatened their strategic interests, the British and French governments responded by making a secret agreement with Israel to attack Egypt.

On October 29, 1956, the IDF invaded Sinai and advanced on the Suez Canal. This was the prearranged excuse for Britain and France to attack Egypt and seize control of the canal, allegedly to protect the international waterway from the fighting. By November 5, the Israelis had complete control of the Sinai peninsula. British and French paratroopers were dropped into the Port Said area and, the following day, the French and British forces made landings at the Mediterranean end of the canal.

But France and Britain had failed to take into account the global balance of power. Their action was condemned by both the Soviet Union and the United States as an example of outdated colonialism and a clear violation of Egyptian independence. International pressure forced them to accept a cease-fire on

THE BAR-LEV LINE

In March 1969 the Israeli forces occupying the Sinai peninsula completed the construction of a defensive fortification along the east bank of the Suez Canal. Stretching 100 miles (160 km) from the Mediterranean Sea to the Gulf of Suez, it was known as the Bar-Lev Line after the Israeli chief of staff, General Chaim Bar-Lev.

The line was a complex arrangement of bunkers, trenches, and strongpoints, designed to be manned by lightly armed infantry. Behind the line, two north–south roads were built to allow self-propelled artillery and armored vehicles to arrive rapidly in support of any point in the line that came under attack by the Egyptians.

When the Egyptians launched their Yom Kippur offensive across the Suez Canal in 1973, the Bar-Lev Line was undermanned and did not prove much of an obstacle. It has also been argued that the existence of the Bar-Lev Line contributed to Israeli overconfidence, making them less prepared for the serious battles they would encounter in 1973.

Military victory was not followed by political or diplomatic successes, however. The Arab states were left more embittered than ever, and the large Palestinian populations in the West Bank and Gaza presented a potentially serious security threat for the Israelis. The UN condemned the continuing Israeli occupation of these areas and Sinai, increasing Israel's isolation.

The Six-Day War was not followed by peace. Egypt, reinforced with new equipment from the Soviet Union, engaged in a campaign of attrition against Israel across the Suez Canal in 1969–70, which led to serious clashes in the air and on the ground. It was not outright war, but a series of air and artillery attacks, and small-scale clashes between troops. The Israelis built a number of fortifications, the Bar-Lev Line, to defend the east bank of the Suez Canal. Meanwhile, Arafat's *Al Fatah* group became the dominant force in the PLO, and Palestinians began resorting to international terrorist attacks to publicize their cause.

In 1973, open war flared once more. On the Jewish holy day of Yom Kippur, October 6, Egypt and Syria attacked Israeli forces in Sinai on the Suez Canal and the Golan Heights respectively. The Egyptians quickly broke through the Bar-Lev Line, which was only lightly defended. Armed with the latest Soviet antitank and ground-to-air missiles, the Egyptian forces inflicted heavy losses on Israeli armor and aircraft, which counterattacked haphazardly.

Meanwhile, similar fierce battles developed on the Golan Heights, where an early Syrian breakthrough was driven back by the Israelis, but once again at the cost of heavy casualties. The turning point of the Yom Kippur War came on October 14, when the Egyptians attempted an over-ambitious advance into the heart of Sinai. The Israelis countered with devastating speed and power. They destroyed much Egyptian armor and, on October 15, established a foothold on the west bank of the Suez Canal. This cut off the Egyptian Third Army on the east bank of the canal and left Cairo virtually at Israel's mercy. At the same time, the IDF fought its way forward into Syria, threatening the Syrian capital Damascus.

With the United States and the Soviet Union thoroughly committed to opposing sides in the war, it became essential to bring about a cease-fire to avoid the risk of a global war between the two superpowers. The Arab oil states had also begun to stop shipments of oil to western Europe and North America. A cease-fire was agreed by both sides on October 22. Although Israel had once more ended the victor, the Yom Kippur War was a severe blow to Israeli morale. Israeli losses of 1,854 dead were high by their standards. The initial response to the war had revealed disturbing levels of complacency. The Arab states, on the other hand, had gained prestige.

After the Yom Kippur War, much skillful diplomatic work brought peace at last between Egypt and Israel in the Camp David accords of 1978. This agreement was arranged by US president Jimmy Carter between Israel's prime minister Menachim Begin and Egypt's president Anwar Sadat. The agreement was finalized at Camp David, the US president's retreat in Maryland, and signed in Washington, DC, on March 26, 1979. But the key issue of the Palestinian Arabs, who were still demanding a homeland, remained unresolved.

The Invasion of Lebanon

Antagonism between rival Christian and Muslim political groups in Lebanon, and the presence of large numbers of armed PLO fighters, helped reduce Lebanon to a state of civil war from 1975. In March 1978, the Israelis carried out a sudden invasion of southern Lebanon in an attempt to destroy Palestinian guerrilla bases. However, the Palestinians withdrew farther north. The following month the Israelis withdrew, leaving a pro-Israeli militia behind to patrol a zone in southern Lebanon, where UN peacekeepers also took up position.

In June 1982, the Israelis embarked on a second, larger-scale invasion of Lebanon – Operation Peace for Galilee. They advanced on three fronts, overwhelming Palestinian resistance. In eastern Lebanon, the IDF encountered Syrian forces that had been in Lebanon since 1976. The result was a devastating display of the superiority of the Israelis' latest US-supplied technology to the Syrians' Soviet-supplied hardware. Using highly developed electronic warfare equipment to identify Syrian targets and confuse their radar, Israel destroyed most of the Syrian Air Force and Syria's antiaircraft surface-to-air-missile (SAM) systems at hardly any cost to its own air force.

From mid-June, the IDF laid siege to the western part of Beirut, the headquarters of the PLO, which was defended by a mixture of Palestinians, Syrians, and Lebanese Muslims. The siege lasted for more than two months, during which the Israelis subjected the city to artillery and air bombardment. Eventually, an agreement was reached for the Palestinian fighters to evacuate Beirut under the supervision of a Multi-National Force (MNF). The evacuation was completed in August and the MNF withdrew on September 10, and four days later the Israelis moved into the western section of Beirut. Israel's Lebanese Christian militia allies carried out a notorious massacre of defenseless Palestinian civilians in the refugee camps of Sabra and Chatila. The militia had been allowed into the camp by the Israelis to search for Palestinian terrorists, who may have played a part in the recent assassination of Lebanon's newly elected president.

The MNF was hurriedly redeployed on September 20, but its presence only contributed further to the savage chaos into which Lebanon descended over the following years. On October 23, 1983, 297 members of the US and French MNF units were killed in Lebanese terrorist suicide attacks on their barracks. The MNF withdrew the following year. Israel also effected a slow, step-by-step withdrawal, although attempting to keep its control of a part of southern Lebanon along the border with Israel.

Through the 1980s it became increasingly clear that Israeli military superiority in the Middle East could not guarantee peace and security for Israel. In 1987, widespread disturbances began among the Palestinian population of the occupied territories of the West Bank and Gaza. This unrest, known as the *Intifada*, presented a new kind of challenge to Israeli soldiers, trying to maintain order and uphold authority in the face of stone-throwing youths and chanting demonstrators.

Faced with the prospect of endless civil disturbances and

terrorist attacks, in 1993 the Israeli government of Prime Minister Yitzhak Rabin at last gambled on peace. Rabin and Arafat signed a peace agreement that gave the Palestinians self-government in the West Bank and Gaza. In return, the PLO accepted Israel's right to exist.

Arafat was elected leader of the new Palestinian Authority in January 1996. However, the control of Jerusalem and the issue of an independent Palestinian state remained unresolved.

Right: The wars that Israel fought in 1967–73 were highly successful territorially, although possession of Gaza and the West Bank would create long-term problems.

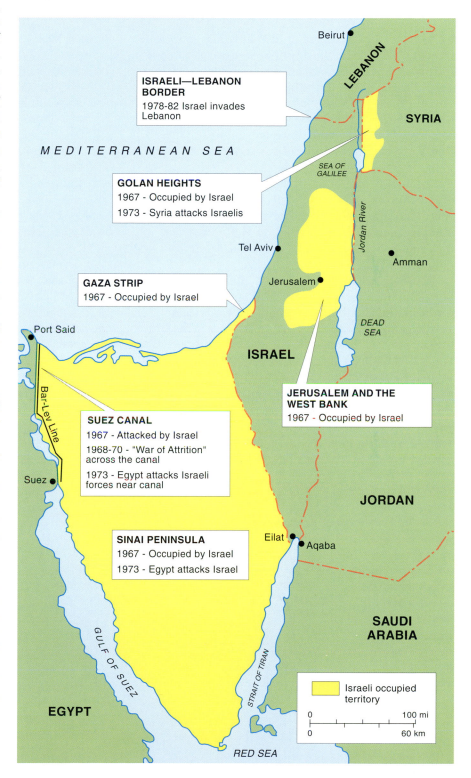

287

The Cold War

The United States and the Soviet Union had been allies during World War II, but their political differences quickly came to the surface once the fighting ended. In March 1946, speaking in Fulton, Missouri, the former British prime minister Winston Churchill summed up the political division of Europe, talking of an "iron curtain" that had descended across Europe, dividing into Communist East and capitalist West.

The creation of Communist governments, which controlled the countries of Soviet-occupied eastern Europe, between 1945 and 1947 – actually single-party states based on the unrestrained power of their secret police forces – deeply offended Western opinion. In March 1947, President Harry S. Truman (1884–1972) committed the United States to preventing the spread of Communism. The first test of US commitment came in 1948, when the Soviet Union blocked access to West Berlin, which had been occupied by US, British, and French forces since 1945, but lay within the Soviet-controlled East Germany. The Americans and British mounted an airlift that kept West Berlin supplied with food and fuel under difficult conditions from June 1948 until September 1949.

The Soviet Union dropped its attempt to force the Western allies out of West Berlin in 1949, but the confrontation between East and West intensified. The North Atlantic Treaty Organization (NATO) was formed, linking the countries of western Europe and the United States and Canada in a military alliance directed against the Soviet Union. The Soviet Union formed a similar alliance with the countries of eastern Europe, the

Warsaw Pact, in 1955. The news that the Soviet Union had tested its first atomic bomb in 1949 was followed by the fall of mainland China to the Communists. These events raised American fears about Communism to a new degree of anxiety.

The following year the Korean War broke out, pitching the Western allies, under the UN banner, into open war against Communism. The US government held back from using atomic weapons, and took measures to stop the war spreading. The Soviet Union supported both the North Koreans and their Chinese Communist backers in the fighting, but did not openly commit its own forces. Thus the pattern was set for the Cold War: the United States and the Soviet Union would push their rivalry in every way possible, short of directly fighting one another. Both also equipped and trained the armed forces of friendly or client states.

In the 1950s the two superpowers embarked on a nuclear arms race that was to last until 1987. At first, the two rivals concentrated on producing more powerful bombs to be delivered to a target by long-range aircraft. The first hydrogen bomb, tested by the Americans in 1952, was soon matched by the Soviet Union. By 1962

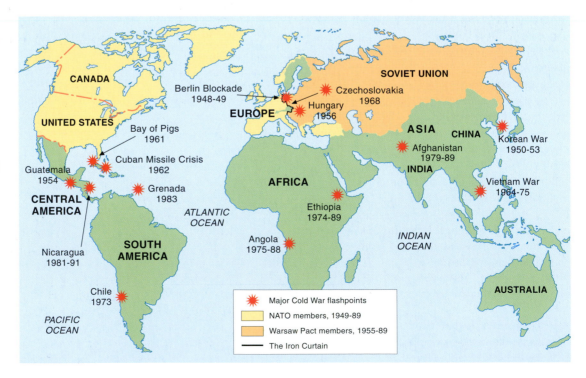

Right: Denied the chance to fight each other directly – the risk of global destruction was too great – the United States and the Soviet Union used conflicts in the Third World to further their aims and strike at their superpower rival. Soviet arms killed US soldiers in Vietnam, while Western weapons killed Soviet soldiers in Afghanistan. Hundreds of thousands of locals also died in these Cold War flashpoints.

Left: The end of World War II saw Europe divided up into two politically and militarily divided zones. The divide ended in the late 1980s when the Soviet Union collapsed.

NATO members, 1949–89

Warsaw Pact members, 1955-89

States belonging to neither military alliance

The Iron Curtain

the Soviet Union exploded the largest bomb ever, delivering 58 megatons (a megaton is an explosive force equivalent to that of one million tons of the explosive TNT), which was equal to 3,000 World War II atom bombs.

The focus of the arms race had by then long shifted to the development of intercontinental ballistic missiles (ICBMs), generally delivering a smaller atomic bomb, but in far greater numbers and with a greater likelihood of getting through the enemy's defenses. The first effective ICBM, the American Atlas-D, entered service in 1958. The following year the United States began deployment of submarine-launched Polaris ballistic missiles, each missile armed with several nuclear warheads. The Soviet Union proved it could match American developments, although mostly a step behind.

Strategic thinking developed alongside the introduction of the new weapons. By the mid-1960s, both the United States and the Soviet Union planned to launch their own counterstrike before the enemy missiles arrived. This created nuclear deterrence known as MAD, or Mutually Assured Destruction. In a MAD world, each side knew it could not afford to start a war, because it would itself be destroyed.

The nearest the superpowers came to nuclear war was the Cuban missile crisis of 1962, when the Soviet Union planned to place medium-range Soviet nuclear missiles in Cuba. In the subsequent stand-off nuclear war came perilously close.

In the 1980s, new measures destabilized the nuclear balance. These included the siting of US Cruise missiles with nuclear warheads in Europe and the "Star Wars" or Strategic Defense Initiative (SDI). SDI planned to give the United States the ability to defend itself from nuclear attack through space-based defense systems, and thus end the mutually assured destruction on which deterrence was based.

The sudden collapse of Soviet power, and then of the Soviet Union itself, between 1987 and 1991 brought the 40-year-old Cold War to an end because one of the two superpowers, the Soviet Union, lost both the political will to sustain a battle for world supremacy and the financial ability to compete with the much richer United States.

THE TRUMAN DOCTRINE

During the winter of 1946–47, President Harry S. Truman had to decide whether to resume America's traditional policy of isolationism. Truman could have reduced America's armed forces and halted America's direct involvement in overseas events, but he was hostile to Communism and suspicious of the plans of the Soviet leader Joseph Stalin. When Britain declared itself no longer able to maintain the role of resisting Communist pressure on Greece and Turkey, countries vital to the security of the West, Truman agreed that the US would take on the responsibility.

On March 12, 1947, President Truman announced: "I believe it must be the policy of the United States to support free peoples who are resisting attempted subjugation by armed minorities or outside pressures." This "Truman Doctrine," committing the United States to resist the spread of Communism worldwide, whether occurring through an internal revolt or through pressure from Communist forces, governed American foreign policy for the next 40 years.

THE ENCYCLOPEDIA OF WARFARE

Threat of Terrorism

Western democracies have traditionally been the target of terrorist groups, be they Arab extremists, left-wing organizations (often backed by Communist regimes), or violent nationalists. In their efforts to achieve often fanciful ends, such groups have resorted to kidnapping, hijacking, and assassination, often with horrendous results. The response was the formation of elite units to combat terrorist groups.

One of the bloodiest terrorist campaigns of the period immediately after World War II was that waged by the Jews in Palestine against the British government, which controlled the territory, and the local Palestinian Arabs. The Jewish community was trying to create an independent state, but was opposed by the local Arab population, while the British attempted to maintain order.

The Jewish resorted to terror tactics to force the British to leave Palestine. One notable incident was the bombing of the British administrative headquarters in Jerusalem, the King David Hotel, by the Jewish terrorist group *Irgun* in July 1946. The bomb killed 91 people, many of them civilians. The *Irgun* had, in fact, telephoned a warning about the bomb, but it was ignored by British officials at the hotel. The British also faced other terrorist campaigns by groups seeking independence, notably on the island of Cyprus (1955–58) and in Aden (1963–67).

A Global Problem

It was only in the late 1960s, however, that terrorism became an international activity and a threat to world stability. The rise of international terrorism was largely the result of two simultaneous developments: the growth of Palestinian Arab groups dedicated to the overthrow of the Jewish state of Israel, and the spread of extreme left-wing ideas among certain groups in Europe.

Al Fatah, the Palestinian group led by Yassir Arafat, began raids on Israel in 1964. However, it was the Popular Front for the Liberation of Palestine (PFLP) that from 1968 began to attack targets outside Israel to publicize the Palestinian cause. The attacks were aimed chiefly at El Al, the Israeli airline, but soon spread more widely. The PFLP saw the struggle as part of a worldwide revolution, and targeted the moderate Arab states, the United States, and other Western nations.

The classic terrorist tactic was the "skyjack." In the absence of strict security measures at airports, terrorists found it easy to board aircraft while carrying arms and hijack them, forcing the pilot to fly to a "safe" airport. Once there they would hold the aircraft and passengers hostage, making demands – usually for the release of other terrorists captured in earlier operations.

The climax of the PFLP's campaign came in a spectacular flurry of air hijacks in September 1970.

Palestinians seized no less than four airliners – two American, one British, and one Swiss – and just failed to seize an Israeli jet in the Netherlands. Three of the airliners were flown to Dawson's Field in Jordan, where they were eventually blown up in front of the world's television cameras. The immediate response to the hijacking was an attack on armed Palestinian groups by Jordan's King Hussein's armed forces, which drove the Palestinians out of the country, forcing them to relocate in Lebanon and Syria.

The PFLP's view that the Palestinian struggle was part of a world revolutionary struggle made it natural for them to establish links with left-wing terrorist groups that were forming in Europe at the end of the 1960s. These groups were of two distinct kinds. One type consisted of students or middle-class intellectuals, such as the notorious "Carlos the Jackal" (Ilich Ramirez Sanchez), who had become disillusioned with peaceful politics after the failure of the students' and workers' movements that had rocked western Europe in 1968. They decided to turn to an armed struggle. The most notable examples were the Red Army Faction in West Germany, also known as the Baader-Meinhof gang, and the Red Brigades in Italy.

The other type of European terrorist movement was essentially nationalist, such as the Irish Republican Army (IRA, at the time known as the Provisional IRA) in Northern Ireland, and the Basque separatist movement in Spain. Both engaged in terrorist campaigns on a considerable scale in the 1970s.

Palestinian Terrorists

It was a terrorist group from Asia, however, that first revealed to the world the extent of Palestinian international contacts. On May 30, 1972, three members of the Japanese Red Army were among passengers who disembarked from an airliner at Lod airport near Tel Aviv, Israel. Firing indiscriminately and throwing hand grenades inside the airport building, they killed 26 people and injured a further 76.

It was not the PFLP but another Palestinian group under Arafat's direction, Black September, that was responsible for the most notorious incident of the whole period, the attack on Israeli athletes during the 1972 Olympic Games in Munich. Eight terrorists entered the Olympic village and broke into the building where the

because many of the passengers on board were Jewish.

The success at Entebbe, in which most of the hostages were rescued, showed that the world was becoming a less easy place for terrorists. Governments across the world had been ill-prepared to meet the upsurge of international terrorism, but from the early 1970s, they began to organize antiterrorist squads, coordinate intelligence, and put up resistance to terrorists. Specialist units such as Britain's SAS (Special Air Service), the German *Grenzschutzgruppe* (GSG 9 – Border Action Group 9), and the US Delta Force were trained in antiterrorism.

The turning point in the fight against international terrorism came in October 1977. Baader-Meinhof took hostage a West German businessman, Hanns-Martin Schleyer, and demanded the release of all their members held in German prisons, including most of the movement's leadership. At the same time, a Lufthansa airliner was hijacked by Palestinian terrorists to support the Red Army Faction's demand.

GSG 9, aided by two SAS troopers, pursued the hijacked airliner to Mogadishu, Somalia. There they stormed the aircraft and freed the hostages, killing or capturing all the terrorists.

The IRA and Basque movements were far more durable because they had deep roots in minorities hostile to the government: Catholics in Northern Ireland and Basques in Spain. The IRA sustained a terrorist campaign against the British both in Northern Ireland and on the British mainland for 27 years, from 1970 to 1997, with a few cease-fires. The Basques began their campaign against the Spanish government and authorities in 1967; to date they are still fighting.

Right-wing terrorism is also ultraviolent. In Italy, extreme right-wing terrorists took far more lives than the Red Brigades did, killing 80 people, for example, in a single bombing at Bologna railway station in 1980. In the United States, the bombing of the Alfred P. Murrah building in Oklahoma City in April 1995, in which 168 people died, was the work of right-wing extremists.

The list of terrorist outrages is unlikely to end. Prominent incidents included the blowing up of a Pan American Jumbo jet over Lockerbie, Scotland, in December 1988, killing 270 people. Despite the use of massive resources to counter terrorism, it still remains a threat to peace and stability.

Israelis were housed, killing two, and taking nine hostages. German negotiators agreed to provide an airliner to fly the terrorists and their hostages to Tunisia. At the airport, however, police marksmen attempted to kill the terrorists. After a firefight, all the hostages were killed before the last terrorists were captured.

By 1973 the Palestinian cause had been brought to the attention of the world. The main Palestinian leaders, including Arafat, decided to end the international terror campaign, but there were plenty of smaller Palestinian groups prepared to carry on the terrorist tradition.

The government of Iraq backed terror chief Abu Nidal, who masterminded a string of attacks, especially on Palestinians who favored some agreement with Israel. The Libyan leader Muammar Gadhafi set up his own terrorist movement, National Arab Youth for the Liberation of Palestine (NAYLP). The PFLP's international network was inherited by Wadi Haddad, head of the movement's overseas operations, who continued his campaign independently.

Haddad's terror campaign from 1973 to 1978 depended heavily on his links with the German Red Army Faction and with the Venezuelan Carlos the Jackal, who masterminded European operations. Baader-Meinhof terrorists took part in the Carlos-led kidnapping of the world's leading oil ministers in Vienna, Austria, in December 1975, an operation intended to "punish" wealthy pro-Western Middle East states for their failure to back the Palestinians. German terrorists also took part in the Entebbe, Uganda, hijacking in 1976, which was ended by an Israeli anti-terrorist squad. The Israelis had become involved

The War in Vietnam

US backing for the corrupt South Vietnamese regime of Ngo Dinh Diem as a bulwark against the spread of Communism in the region gradually sucked in United States military resources. In the early 1960s there were a few hundred military advisors in South Vietnam; by 1969 over 600,000 military personnel were engaged in trying to defeat the Viet Cong and their North Vietnamese supporters.

In 1959 South Vietnamese Communist guerrillas of the National Liberation Front (NLF), popularly known as the Viet Cong, began a campaign to overthrow Diem. Backed by North Vietnam, the NLF uprising rapidly spread through much of rural South Vietnam. Many of the Viet Cong's weapons and supplies were transported along the Ho Chi Minh Trail, which stretched from North Vietnam, through Laos and Cambodia, into South Vietnam. In 1961 the United States, which was already training the South Vietnamese army (ARVN – Army of the Republic of Vietnam), started sending military advisers and helicopter pilots into action.

The US government was deeply worried about the situation in Southeast Asia. Laos, another of the countries of former French Indochina, was in the grip of a complex civil war and could be an easy target for a Communist takeover. Basing their policies on the "domino theory" – that the fall of one pro-American regime in Southeast Asia might lead to the fall of others – US administrations were sucked into stopping the spread of Communist power in South Vietnam at almost any cost.

In 1963 the US backed a South Vietnamese coup against Diem, because they thought he was too ineffectual and unpopular to defeat the Communists. Diem was killed in the coup, which installed a new government. But this only plunged South Vietnam into further political instability and bound the US ever closer to that country. Meanwhile, the Communist guerrilla movement continued to advance, outmatching the government forces in commitment, popular support, and fighting skills. By 1964 it seemed only a matter of time before the South Vietnamese capital, Saigon, fell to the NLF.

US secretary of defense Robert McNamara, along with other US

Left: The US was involved in the Vietnam War from 1965 to 1975, during which time it never defeated the Viet Cong guerrillas. The cost was 50,000 American dead.

political and military leaders, felt that the key to the military situation lay in North Vietnam. However, the desire to keep the conflict limited and avoid a war with one of the major Communist powers (Russia or China) ruled out an invasion of the North. The Americans decided to increase pressure on North Vietnam in order to persuade its leaders to call off the war in the South.

In August 1964, US harassment of North Vietnam led to the Gulf of Tonkin incident, when a US destroyer, USS *Maddox*, sailing just off the North Vietnamese coast, was attacked by North Vietnamese vessels. A similar incident was reported but unconfirmed two days later. Whatever the truth of this shadowy incident, it provided a pretext for US bombing raids on North Vietnam and for the passage of a resolution by Congress that effectively gave the president, Lyndon B. Johnson, a free hand to increase US involvement in Vietnam.

Escalation in US Involvement

In February 1965, the United States began the systematic bombing of North Vietnam, a campaign known as Operation Rolling Thunder. In the same month US Marines landed at Da Nang in South Vietnam, the first US ground combat units committed to the war. By the end of the year, 181,000 US troops were operating in South Vietnam. Commanded by General William C. Westmoreland (1914–), they took over most of the responsibility for fighting the Viet Cong from the poorly functioning South Vietnamese Army.

The American soldiers' task was a difficult one. The Viet Cong, supported by increasing numbers of North Vietnamese Army (NVA) troops, effectively controlled about 70 percent of South Vietnam, including areas within 15 miles (24 km) of Saigon. Although lightly equipped, they were skilled in the guerrilla arts of concealment, ambush, and the use of booby traps.

Westmoreland chose to use what he saw as his two great advantages over the Viet Cong: mobility and firepower. The use of fleets of helicopters would allow the American troops to move swiftly into the heart of Viet Cong territory and search out the enemy. When contact was established, American commanders would call in the massive destructive capacity of US air power, artillery located at firebases, and naval guns to destroy guerrilla formations. The measure of success came to mean the "body count" – the figures for numbers of Communists killed that were regularly published by the Americans.

As the US poured ever-larger numbers of troops into South Vietnam, rising to over 480,000 by the end of 1967, they undoubtedly succeeded in stemming the tide of the guerrilla campaign. Major operations, such as Cedar Falls in January 1967 and Junction City in February through May of the same year, at least temporarily won back areas of the country long held by the Viet Cong.

But the problem for the Americans was that, whatever military successes they scored, they seemed no nearer a decisive victory. The bombing of North Vietnam

FIREBASES

Fire support bases were an essential element in American plans for fighting the Vietnam War. Placed in areas where contact with guerrillas was expected, they were intended to provide artillery cover to infantry patrols and to contribute to the "body count" by inflicting heavy losses on enemy units drawn into attacking them.

At the heart of the average firebase was a helicopter landing zone. A circle of mines and barbed wire formed the boundary of the base. Inside this, a ring of foxholes commanded a clear field of fire. The battery of artillery in a firebase normally consisted of about half a dozen 105-mm or 155-mm howitzers.

If the firebase came under attack, its commander could call in an astonishing array of aircraft to provide support, including helicopter gunships, cargo planes fitted out as fixed-wing gun platforms, ground-attack aircraft, and even B-52 bombers. Very few US firebases were ever overrun during the Vietnam War.

only strengthened the resolution of the North Vietnamese to fight on. The supply route from North Vietnam to the fighters in the South, the Ho Chi Minh Trail, continued to function, despite large-scale US air attacks on both the route and convoys traveling down it.

Meanwhile, the scale of American losses in the war was beginning to trouble the US public; 9,378 Americans died in Vietnam in 1967. A growing minority in the United States was troubled by the war itself. It was difficult to distinguish between guerrillas and peasants in South Vietnam, and US forces did not always trouble to make the distinction. American military action led to the destruction of villages, the destruction of crops, and the incidental killing or maiming of civilians. Critics pointed out that these things were being done to the South Vietnamese, the very people the Americans had been sent to protect.

The critical moment of the American war in Vietnam came in early 1968. On January 31, Viet Cong guerrillas and North Vietnamese troops attacked more than 100 cities and towns throughout South Vietnam. This Tet Offensive (named after the Vietnamese holiday on which it started) was a clear military failure. Counterattacks by American and ARVN forces won back all the towns or districts that had been seized in the initial attacks, inflicting heavy losses from which the Viet Cong never fully recovered.

However, the Tet Offensive delivered a profound shock to the American public, who were astonished to see guerrillas attempting to take over the US Embassy in Saigon after three years of efforts to suppress them. It

Right: US infantry slug it out with "Charlie" (the Viet Cong) in Vietnam. The guerrillas were elusive foes, and thought nothing of abandoning ground if under threat of being defeated. These tactics were frustrating for US soldiers on the ground.

made both the American public and US leaders doubt that the war in Vietnam could be won.

In March 1968, President Johnson turned down General Westmoreland's request for yet more troops to fight in Vietnam, and to extend operations into Laos and Cambodia. Instead, the president scaled down the bombing of North Vietnam as a first move toward negotiations with the Communists. Peace talks began in Paris in May, but the war continued.

Between the spring of 1968 and the autumn of 1969, as the war in South Vietnam continued with unabated ferocity, American firepower gradually had an impact. The fighting was increasingly concentrated in more remote regions of the country, away from Saigon and the other coastal cities. Meanwhile, the Phoenix Program run by the US Central Intelligence Agency (CIA) targeted the Communists' underground network operating in government-controlled areas, identifying and then eliminating leading Communists and sympathizers.

But the Americans' will to fight had been fatally weakened. In June 1968 Westmoreland was replaced as US commander by General Creighton W. Abrams. Abrams (1914–74), who vigorously pursued a policy of Vietnamization, making the ARVN gradually replace US troops in the frontline of the war. Against a background of mounting antiwar protests and adverse media coverage of the war, Richard M. Nixon was elected president in November 1968. Although strongly anti-Communist, Nixon was committed to bringing the US troops in Vietnam home. The US public would no

longer stand for the huge numbers of American casualties. Also, by 1969 the US Army in Vietnam was becoming demoralized, with a high level of drug abuse and antiwar sentiment increasing in the ranks.

While instigating US troop withdrawals in 1969, Nixon also widened the war to attack North Vietnamese bases in Cambodia. He authorized bombing attacks on Cambodia and ground raids into both Cambodia and Laos. The Americans also backed the overthrow of Cambodia's ruler, Prince Noradom Sihanouk, by an army officer, Marshal Lon Nol. The upshot of these actions was to make the government of Cambodia unstable and to cause an increase in activity by the Cambodian Communist guerrilla movement, the Khmer Rouge.

In March 1972, the nature of the fighting in Vietnam fundamentally altered. With American ground troops rapidly shipping home and no longer directly engaged in a ground combat role, the North Vietnamese leadership decided to invade South Vietnam. The attacks by the NVA were soon halted due to a combination of US air power and unexpectedly stiff resistance from the ARVN, but a cease-fire in October left the North Vietnamese in control of key border areas in the north and west of South Vietnam.

After a final display of American power in the second half of December 1972, when B-52 bombers devastated targets in the Northern cities of Haiphong and Hanoi, the US signed a peace agreement with the North Vietnamese and the NLF on January 23, 1973. By the time of the peace treaty, over 46,000 US troops had died in action in Vietnam.

WAR AND THE MEDIA

The Vietnam War has been called "the first television war." Daily TV news reports brought the war into American homes with a vividness unmatched by earlier media. Although briefed and directed by military press officers, TV and print journalists were mostly able to cover the war freely. They often filed stories that painted a gloomy view of the military situation, especially during the Tet Offensive of 1968. Journalists also highlighted the suffering of civilians in the war, thus promoting antiwar sentiment (the most notable case was the massacre of South Vietnamese civilians by US troops at the village of My Lai in March 1968).

Some US military leaders felt that, in effect, the press lost the war in Vietnam by undermining morale at home, when the army was on the point of winning in the field. Since Vietnam, US armed forces have been determined to control news coverage in time of war. However, it seems clear that it was in fact the nature of the Vietnam War, its heavy casualties and lack of decisive victories or clearly understood aims, which undermined public support in the United States.

Where the NVA and the ARVN confronted one another, occasional small-scale fighting continued throughout 1973 and 1974. The North Vietnamese methodically built up their supplies and equipment for a renewed offensive. Meanwhile, South Vietnam was still almost totally dependent on the United States for money, supplies, and equipment; when Congress cut off military aid in 1974, South Vietnam was doomed.

The end came with startling speed. A series of NVA advances began in December 1974, and by March of the following year it had become clear that the ARVN was falling apart. The United States refused to intervene to save its former ally. On April 30, amid chaotic scenes in Saigon, as Americans and favored South Vietnamese officials fled by helicopter, North Vietnamese tanks rolled into the former capital. While South Vietnam was overrun by the Communists, so too were neighboring Laos and Cambodia.

The Cost of the War

The war had had a devastating effect on Vietnam, which was officially united in June 1976. Millions of peasants had been killed, wounded, or driven from their homes. A third of the land in the South was poisoned with chemical sprays or had been laid waste by bombs and artillery shells.

The Communist takeovers did not bring an end to suffering, or an end to the fighting. The Khmer Rouge regime, installed in the Cambodian capital, Phnom Penh, in 1975, immediately proved itself more extreme and brutal than anyone had believed possible, driving the population of the city into the country to become slave laborers. In Vietnam itself life was hard, both through the effects of the war and poor management of the economy.

In December 1978, the Vietnamese invaded Cambodia in force and drove out the Khmer Rouge government. China, which backed the Khmer Rouge, invaded Vietnam in a brief border war the following year. The Khmer Rouge continued to fight a brutal guerrilla war against the Vietnamese until Vietnam withdrew its troops in 1989. The occasional outbreaks of fighting and the complex political conflicts continued in Cambodia throughout the 1990s.

Left: The collapse of the South. North Vietnamese troops race through Saigon's Tan Son Nhut airbase in 1975. The South's collapse was sudden and total.

Gulf Wars

The Persian Gulf is an area of great economic and strategic significance, especially to the West, which is dependant upon its oil. In the 1980s the West supported the Iraqi leader, Saddam Hussein, in his eight-year war against the radical Iranian Muslim regime of Ayatollah Khomeini. But the West was forced to take action against Saddam himself when he occupied Kuwait in August 1990.

After increasing border clashes, Saddam Hussein (1931–) ordered a major invasion of southern Iran on September 22, 1980. During the following month the Iraqis captured the city of Khorramshahr, but they failed to seize the crucial port and refinery city of Abadan. Iraq's armed forces were superior in tanks, artillery, and aircraft to the Iranians, but the Iranians were inspired by religious and patriotic zeal and fought back with an almost total disregard for the human cost. The Iranian Revolutionary Guards, consisting of those Iranians most loyal to Khomeini, led human-wave attacks on Iraqi positions, driving Iraqi forces back across the border.

The conflict quickly became deadlocked, with neither side able to win a decisive victory. And neither side showed much imagination or flexibility, the Iraqis using their firepower to inflict heavy losses on the Iranians, while the Iranians relied on sheer weight of numbers. Losses, particularly Iranian, were very heavy. Iraq extended the war into the Persian Gulf itself by attacking Iranian shipping. Both sides carried out long-range missile attacks on one another's cities, but with very limited effect.

By 1988, as Iran seemed to be getting the upper hand on the battlefield, Saddam took the decision to use chemical weapons, but to little effect. It was the last act of a conflict that neither seemed able to win. A cease-fire was agreed on in August, ending a war that had killed at least a million people.

During the Iraq–Iran conflict, the Western powers and Arab states, such as Saudi Arabia, had backed Iraq, fearing that Iran's Islamic revolution would spread. But Saddam soon revealed himself as an even greater threat to peace and stability in the Middle East than the religious leaders in Iran. The war with Iran had left Iraq saddled with huge debts. Its ability to pay off these debts was threatened by falling oil prices, caused in part by the failure of other Arab countries,

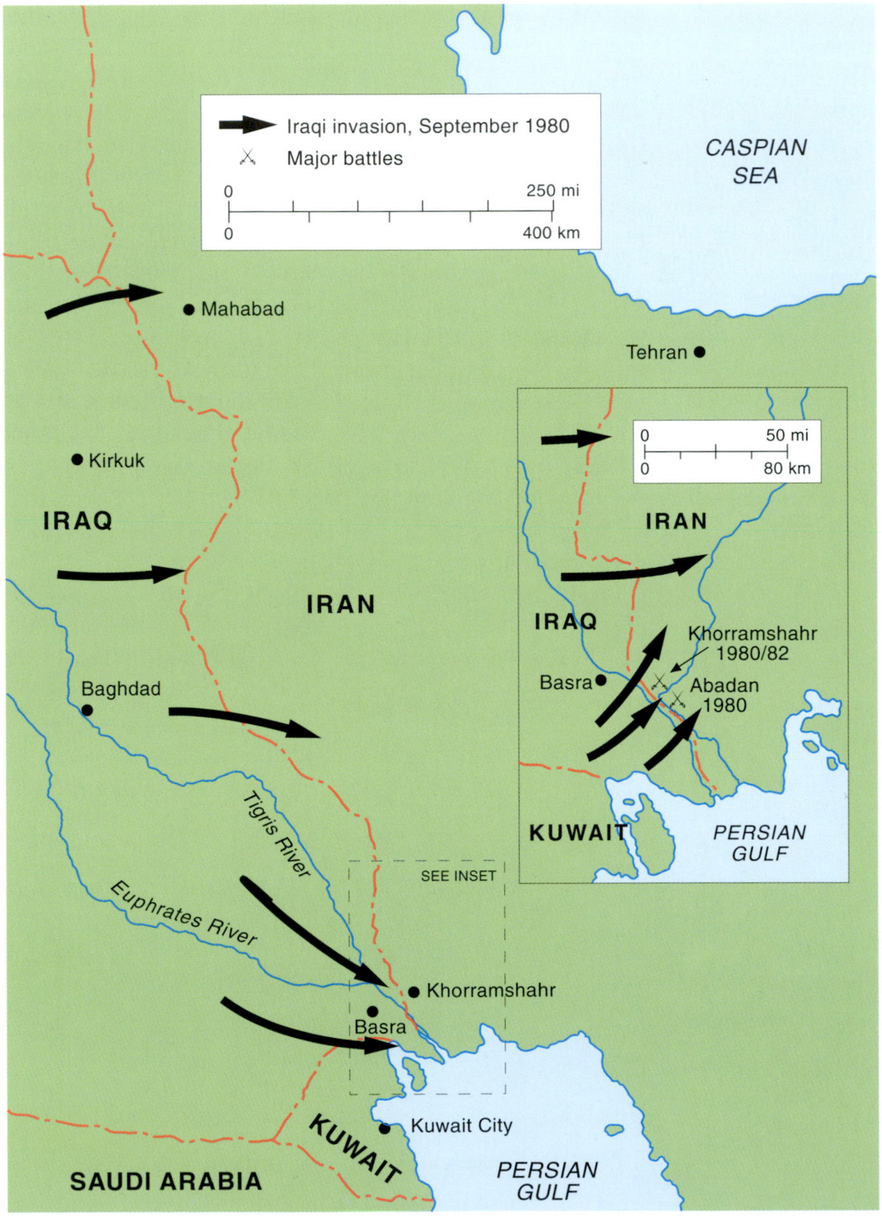

Left: The Iran–Iraq War lasted from September 1980 until August 1988. It soon became characterized by deep trench lines and fortifications – and great slaughter.

Map legend:
- Iraqi invasion, September 1980
- ✕ Major battles
- 0 — 250 mi
- 0 — 400 km

CASPIAN SEA

Mahabad

Tehran ●

Kirkuk

IRAQ

IRAN

Baghdad

Tigris River

Euphrates River

SEE INSET

Khorramshahr

Basra

Kuwait City

SAUDI ARABIA

KUWAIT

PERSIAN GULF

Inset map:
- 0 — 50 mi
- 0 — 80 km

IRAN

IRAQ

Basra ●

Khorramshahr 1980/82

Abadan 1980

KUWAIT

PERSIAN GULF

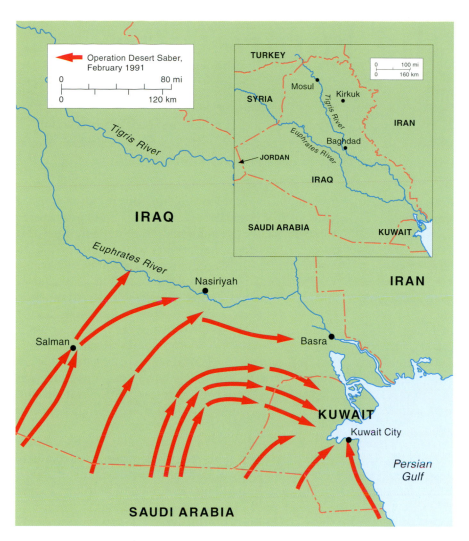

Left: Operation Desert Saber was the ground offensive that was launched against Iraqi forces in Kuwait on February 23, 1991. The Iraqis were smashed in four days.

including Kuwait, one of the leading oil-producing countries in the Middle East, to stick to agreed production quotas. In July 1990, Iraq began to increase its pressure on Kuwait by reopening an old and largely specious territorial dispute.

Iraqi armored columns invaded Kuwait on August 2 – in less than 24 hours the country was under Iraqi control. The UN responded by imposing tough economic sanctions on Iraq, which prevented Iraq and other countries from trading with each other. The United States, Britain, and other states sent forces to Saudi Arabia.

The initial deployment of the forces to block Saddam, called Operation Desert Shield, was designed to defend Saudi Arabia and its vast oil reserves from a possible Iraqi attack. In November, however, the United States decided on a major addition to its forces in the region, increasing its troop levels in Saudi Arabia from 200,000 to 500,000 men. Britain and France also increased their commitment, and Egypt and Syria contributed troops – which, altogether, would be called the Coalition forces.

With almost 2,000 aircraft, General Norman Schwarzkopf (1934–), the US commander of the Coalition forces in the Gulf, opened the campaign with an air assault. Operation Desert Storm, the air offensive against Iraq, was launched on the night of January 16–17, 1991. Over the weeks that followed, aircraft and missiles systematically destroyed Iraq's military command and communications systems. Iraq retaliated with medium-range missile attacks on Israel and Saudi Arabia, but fears that the Iraqis might use their chemical warheads proved unfounded.

After more than a month of "softening up," Operation Desert Saber, the ground offensive to liberate Kuwait, was launched on February 23. It became clear that the Iraqis had been utterly demoralized by the long bombardment they had suffered from air and land. On February 27, Kuwait City was taken by Coalition troops. The United States ordered a cease-fire on the morning of February 28 – exactly 100 hours after Operation Desert Saber had begun. Coalition casualties were 192 killed; Iraqi military losses were probably around 50,000 dead.

STEALTH WARFARE

Stealth – the term used to describe the various technologies that make it difficult for an enemy to identify an aircraft on radar – has become a vital element of modern warfare. The United States was the first country to develop and deploy stealth aircraft: the F-117 Blackhawk and the B-2 bomber. The Blackhawk first saw service in the invasion of Panama in December 1989, but was deployed in much greater numbers during the 1991 Persian Gulf War.

Much of stealth technology remains top secret, but two of its components have been documented. First, the angular shape of the F-117 ensures that radar waves bounce off it at odd angles, and most are not reflected back to enemy radar stations. Second, the aircraft is coated in a radar-absorbing material, which again reduces the intensity of radar waves being bounced back. Consequently, it is very difficult for enemy radar to get a fix on a stealth aircraft.

Conflict in the Future

It was believed that the ending of the Cold War would usher in a period of world peace. This somewhat naive view was shattered in the 1990s, as a number of vicious racial and nationalist conflicts erupted in various parts of the globe – a result of long-nurtured grievances and territorial disputes. In addition, the proliferation of nuclear and chemical weapons only added to general worldwide instability.

Although both the US and the Soviet Union have made dramatic cuts in their numbers and types of nuclear weapons since the end of the Cold War, other countries have been trying to develop similar weapons of mass destruction. Although they refuse to confirm ownership of nuclear weapons, Israel and South Africa almost certainly have them at their disposal. The United Nations inspectors investigating Iraq's weapons program after the 1991 Persian Gulf War found a large schedule for developing nuclear missiles and warheads. Both India and Pakistan conducted a number of tests of nuclear devices in 1998, and North Korea has tested missiles able to carry nuclear weapons. These incidents suggest that the number of members within the "Nuclear Club" will increase in the future.

Although it is unlikely that the new or emerging nuclear countries would use them against the world's leading powers, it is quite possible that they could be used in localized, regional conflicts. Pakistan and India,

for example, have a long-running dispute over areas of Kashmir that both claim as their own, and have been to war twice in previous decades (as both states are now nuclear powers, the stakes have been raised considerably – ironically over land that is largely uninhabitable). Also, there have been persistent rumors that the material for the manufacture of nuclear weapons has been spirited away from the former Soviet Union, most likely to countries eager to develop their own weapons.

Conflict in the immediate future seems most likely to occur between neighboring states that have long and deep-seated rivalries, or within a single state where ethnic/religious groups are in conflict over economic or political power.

The most obvious example of ethnic and religious warfare in recent times occurred in the former federal state of Yugoslavia during the 1990s. There, Serbs, Croats, and Bosnians (Christian and Muslim) fought

Right: During the ethnic war in the former Yugoslavia in the 1990s, Croatian troops fire on Serbian opponents in the town of Vukovar. The conflict in this former federal state contained many of the factors that have sprung up the post-Cold War world: ethnic strife, extreme nationalism, and violent religious divisions.

Left: A US Army soldier stands guard over local villagers in Somalia, East Africa, in December 1992. The problems US forces had in the area, including how to use non-violent force in the face of severe provocation from the locals, brought home the difficulties of employing military personnel in peacekeeping operations.

THE UNITED NATIONS

Dedicated to the "maintenance of international peace and security," the plan to found the United Nations (UN) was agreed upon between Britain, China, the Soviet Union, and the United States at the Dumbarton Oaks conference, held in Washington, DC, in October 1944. The body itself came into force on October 24, 1945. The UN originally contained just 51 countries, but today contains over 180.

All members of the UN's General Assembly, the UN's debating chamber, are allowed up to five delegates and all have a single vote on any issue brought before the Assembly. The UN also has the Security Council, which consists of five permanent members – Britain, China, France, Russia, and the United States – and 10 other member countries drawn from the wider UN membership who serve terms of two years. The Security Council is considered the main body for keeping international peace and security.

If war breaks out between members of the UN, the Security Council and, occasionally, the General Assembly can offer to negotiate between the warring sides, arrange a cease-fire, and provide forces to oversee it. UN peacekeeping forces, identified by their blue helmets, are allowed to fight only in self-defense and must be withdrawn if the host country makes such a request. The only time UN forces have actually been called upon to fight other than in self-defense was during the Korean War (1950–53). UN forces also provide humanitarian relief. The overall scale of UN operations increased massively in the 1990s.

each other to either create their own independent homelands or purge areas of other ethnic groups. The conflict gave the world a new phrase – "ethnic cleansing" – meaning, in effect, the murder, torture, and forced expulsion of other ethnic groups, who had previously lived together for decades. After the end of hostilities, conflict broke out again farther south in the former Yugoslav republic of Kosovo, as Serb and Albanian forces sought for control of the province.

The world's leading powers have always been willing to intervene directly in other countries, if the conditions are right. Sometimes the intervention might be for humanitarian reasons, such as to assist civilians caught up in the fighting, as was the case during the war in Yugoslavia, and during the civil war between rival warlords in Somalia, East Africa, in the early 1990s. Sometimes, however, powerful nations use military power for more complex reasons. The United States invaded the Caribbean island of Grenada in October 1983. The pretext given was to protect US civilians and restore order after the murder of the island's leader, but the US was also concerned to prevent Grenada extending links with Cuba's Fidel Castro.

Wars will continue for the foreseeable future, and they are likely to be highly destructive – on a local scale at least. There seems less likelihood of a global confrontation, or a war that involves the use of nuclear weapons. It is to be hoped that agencies such as the United Nations will be able to prevent warfare in the future, but as history shows, this has rarely been the case. It is likely that wars and terrorism will continue to inflict suffering on many peoples throughout the globe. In addition, the greater availability of materials to create nuclear weapons, and the willingness of some states to sell them to the highest bidder, does nothing to make the world a safer place. We are entering an uncertain era in the history of mankind.

antitank gun A type of artillery designed specifically to destroy armored vehicles, such as tanks. Such guns fired shells that could pierce armor plate. The guns were either towed or fitted to the modified chassis of a tank.

armored division A fighting formation comprising tanks, mechanized infantry, artillery batteries, antitank gunners, and reconnaissance units.

arquebus A type of hand-held gunpowder weapon. Developed in the 16th century, it was produced in standardized lengths and calibers.

barrage A usually long-lasting artillery bombardment, which often heralds an offensive.

blockade A form of naval strategy by troops or warships. Its aim is not chiefly to destroy an enemy's fleet but keep it in harbor, and prevent an enemy's merchant fleet from sailing.

breech-loader A rifle or artillery piece loaded at the rear of the barrel rather than down the muzzle.

cartridge A charge of gunpowder and a musket ball wrapped in paper.

column A type of military formation in which the depth of the unit (number of ranks of men) is greater than its width.

colunela A word of Spanish origin first used in the late 15th century and early 16th century to describe a unit of infantry commanded by a cabo de colunela (chief of column).

conventional warfare A conflict in which those taking part use all the means at their disposal to win outright victory but stop short of using nuclear weapons.

corps A large force of soldiers of between 20,000 and 30,000 men. In the 19th century, corps could consist of just cavalry or infantry, but they more usually contained both cavalry and infantry, as well as artillery.

defense in depth A term referring to line upon line of trenches or other fortifications.

division The basic building block of a corps, a division consists of two or three brigades, amounting to approximately 10,000 soldiers.

dreadnought A fast, heavily armed, heavily armored battleship. The first was launched by the British in 1906.

exterior lines Communication lines that splay outward from the front. They are often very long, which can threaten movement and supply.

forward slope An exposed tactical position on a hillside facing toward the enemy.

galleass A type of large galley powered by sails and oars used by several Mediterranean countries in the 16th and 17th centuries.

ground-attack aircraft A specialized type of aircraft. Their role, as a type of "flying artillery," is to hit enemy ground targets threatening to stop an advance by friendly forces.

guerrilla warfare A type of warfare usually fought by outnumbered forces against large armies. The guerrillas launch hit-and-run raids on the enemy, carry out ambushes, and strike at an enemy's weak points.

gunpowder An explosive made by combining quantities of saltpeter, sulfur, and charcoal. It was probably developed by the Chinese in the ninth century, but was first used regularly in warfare in Europe from the mid-14th century.

handgun In warfare, an early type of short-range firearm consisting of a heavy barrel mounted on a wooden stock. Not very accurate.

hoplite Heavy infantry troops, chiefly found in Greece. They wore armor and carried a large shield. Their chief weapons were a sword and spear.

horse-archers Mounted troops whose chief weapon was the bow. They were rarely armored and used their speed to avoid an enemy force.

ironclad A 19th-century armored warship. Built of wood and powered by steam, the wooden part of the ship above water was covered in a shell of protective iron.

investment A tight containment of a garrison by a military force.

limes The lines of fortifications that protected the boundaries of the Roman Empire.

limited wars Conflicts in which one or both sides go into battle with a particular objective. The 1991 Persian Gulf War was a limited war in that the aim was to evict Iraqi troops from Kuwait, not to invade and conquer Iraq.

logistics The supply of all an army might need to fight effectively. This includes food, clothing, weapons, and so on. Also the handling of details involved in a military operation.

longboat A Viking warship powered by oars and a single sail. These wooden vessels were extremely seaworthy and could sail in inshore waters because of their shallow draft.

man-at-arms A professional medieval soldier who was usually retained by a lord or knight.

militia Civilians who have undergone a degree of military training. Called into action in time of national or local emergency.

monitor A type of warship fitted with one or more revolving turrets that each contain one or more guns.

mortar A type of light, short-range cannon consisting of a circular metal tube and a two-legged support. Shells are dropped into the tube and flung out in a plunging arc. Several shells a minute can be fired, and mortars are particularly useful for firing over obstacles, such as a hill.

parallel A siege trench, usually dug "parallel" to the walls of an enemy fortification, from which the artillery could attack.

paratrooper A highly trained soldier who is dropped into a war zone by parachute or landed in a glider. Paratroopers are used to seize vital targets by surprise in advance of the main army. They are usually lightly equipped. All US paratroopers volunteer as members of such units.

peltast A type of light infantryman equipped with a sling, bow, or javelin.

phalanx A dense block of spearmen developed by the Greeks and copied by other ancient states.

pillbox A small low fortification, usually concrete or steel. Houses a machine gun to halt enemy attack.

regiment A military unit of between 500 and 1,000 men, which evolved in the 17th century.

reserves Troops held back from the opening of an attack. They are usually thrown into a battle to exploit any advantage won in the first stages of an offensive or to block any enemy successes.

reservists Men (now also women) who have had military training and returned to civilian life. They return to their units during times of war.

rifling A technique used on both rifle and artillery barrels that allowed weapons to fire farther and with greater accuracy.

sapper A type of military engineer. The term comes from the term "sap," the narrow, zigzag trench a sapper would dig toward an enemy fortress.

self-propelled gun A type of mobile artillery that can be moved under its own power rather than being pulled by another vehicle.

shrapnel A type of explosive cannon ball developed by Englishman Henry Shrapnel in 1784. His cannon ball consisted of an iron shell filled with musket balls and an explosive charge, which burst in the air after firing at a target.

skirmishers Infantrymen trained to fight in open order rather than the closed ranks of ordinary soldiers. Used to prepare the way for a main attack or disorganize a counterattack by sniping at the enemy.

smart weapons A term used by the military to identify weapons, such as bombs and missiles, that have a high chance of hitting a target. Some, usually missiles, have an onboard computer that can be programmed to guide the weapon to its target once fired. Others include bombs, which can home in on a target that has been "illuminated" (identified) by a laser beam.

special forces Air, ground, and naval forces that, because of their special training, weapons, and equipment, are used to carry out difficult and dangerous operations generally thought to be beyond the abilities of ordinary soldiers. Such units may operate in small groups behind enemy lines or be trained in antiterrorist methods.

square A defensive formation adopted by foot soldiers when threatened by cavalry. The soldiers fixed bayonets, faced outward, and fired at the cavalrymen as they charged. Cavalry charges were rarely able to break into a square, but the formation was vulnerable to artillery fire because it made a large, usually stationary target.

staff A group of highly trained officers, usually specialists in a particular aspect of warfare, such as supply and troop movement.

strategic bombing The use of long-range bombers to smash an enemy's ability to wage war by destroying its industries and transportation systems. In World War II, the Allies carried out such a policy of round-the-clock bombing against Germany from 1943.

torpedo A weapon for destroying ships. Unlike modern self-propelled torpedoes, those used in the Civil War consisted of an explosive device fitted to a long wooden spar. The spar was attached to a small vessel, which was sailed at a target. The device detonated on contact.

trench A deep, narrow, often zigzagging defensive position dug into the earth and protected by piled earth and barbed wire. Trenches also had shell-proof shelters where troops could take cover from artillery fire.

trireme An ancient wooden warship powered by sails and three banks of man-powered oars.

unconventional warfare Conflicts in which there are no large battles but frequent patrols, ambushes, and hit-and-run raids, usually against stronger enemy forces. The aim is to wear the enemy down, undermining morale until it gives up the struggle.

volunteer An individual who becomes a soldier of his or her own free will.

war of attrition A military strategy based on the idea of gradually wearing down an enemy's armies and war industries until they are no longer able to continue to fight. For both sides, a war of attrition usually involves heavy casualties and large-scale destruction.

Addington, Larry. *America's War in Vietnam*. Indiana University Press, 2000.

Bartusis, Mark C. *The Late Byzantine Army: Arms and Society, 1204–1453*. University of Pennsylvania Press, 1997.

Berlin, Ira, Field, Barbara J., Miller, Steven F., Reidy, Joseph P., and Rowland, Leslie, S. (editors). *Free at Last: A Documentary History of Slavery, Freedom, and the Civil War*. The New Press, 1992.

Blanning, T.C.W. *The French Revolutionary Wars, 1787–1802*. St. Martin's Press, Inc., 1996.

Burn, Alfred H. *The Agincourt War*. Wordsworth Editions Ltd, 1999.

Carman, John, and Harding, Anthony. *Ancient Warfare*. Sutton Publishing, 1999.

Chandler, David. *The Art of Warfare in the Age of Marlborough*. Spellmount Publishers, 1990.

Commager, Henry Steele. *The Story of the Second World War*. Brassey's, Inc., 1998.

Connolly, Peter. *Greece and Rome at War*. Stackpole Books, 1998.

Creveld, Martin van. *The Art of War*. Cassell Military, 2000.

Damon, Duane. *When This Cruel War Is Over: The Civil War on the Home Front*. Lerner Publishing, 1996.

Davis, Paul K. *Encyclopedia of Invasions and Conquests*. ABC Clio (Reference Books), 1997.

DeVries, Kelly. *Infantry Warfare in the Early Fourteenth Century*. Boydell and Brewer, Inc., 1998.

Duffy, Christopher. *The Army of Frederick the Great*. Emperor's Press, 1996.

Duffy, Christopher. *Fire and Stone: The Science of Fortress Warfare, 1660–1860*. Stackpole Books, 1996.

Dupuy, Trevor N. *The Military Life of Julius Caesar: Imperator*. Barnes and Noble, 1996.

Esdaile, Charles J. *The Wars of Napoleon*. Longman, 1996.

Forty, George. *At War in Korea*. Sterling Publishing Co., Inc., 1997.

Fuller, J.F.C. *The Generalship of Alexander the Great*. Da Capo Press, 1989.

Gaunt, Peter. *The British Wars, 1637–1651*. Routledge, 1997.

Greene, Jack P., and Pole, J.R. *The Blackwell Encyclopedia of the American Revolution*. Blackwell Publishers, 1994.

Hall, Bert S. *Weapons and Warfare in Renaissance Europe*. Johns Hopkins University Press, 1997.

Halpern, Paul G. *A Naval History of World War I*. United States Naval Institute, 1994.

Harris, Meirion, and Harris, Susie. *Last Days of Innocence: America at War, 1917–1918*. Franklin Watts, 1992.

Howard, Michael. *The Franco–Prussian War: The German Invasion of France, 1870–71*. Routledge, 1998.

Hughes, Matthew. *Allenby and British Strategy in the Middle East, 1917–1919*. Frank Cass Publishers, 1999.

Joll, James. *The Origins of the First World War*. Addison Wesley Longman, 1998.

Kagan, Donald. *The Outbreak of the Peloponnesian War*. Cornell University Press, 1994.

Keegan, John, and Wheatcroft, Andrew. *Who's Who in Military History: 1453 to the Present Day*. Routledge, 1998.

Keenan, Jerry. *Encyclopedia of American Indian Wars, 1492–1890*. ABC Clio (Reference Books), 1998.

Keppie, Lawrence. *The Making of the Roman Army: From Republic to Empire*. Barnes and Noble, 1994.

Knecht, R.J. *The French Wars of Religion, 1559–1598*. Longman, New York, 1996.

Knight, Ian. *Great Zulu Battles, 1838–1906*. Sterling Publishing Co., Inc., 1998.

Lucas, James. *War on the Eastern Front: The German Soldier in Russia, 1941–1945*. Stackpole Books, 1998.

McCauley, Martin. *The Origins of the Cold War, 1941–1949*. Longman, New York, 1998.

Macdonald, Lyn. *1914–1918: Voices and Images of the Great War*. Penguin Books USA, Inc., 1991.

Nofi, Albert A. *Spanish–American War, 1898*. Combined Publishing, 1996.

Parker, Geoffrey (editor). *The Thirty Years' War*. Routledge, 1997.

Parkman, Francis. *Montcalm and Wolfe: The French and Indian War*. Da Capo Press, 1995.

Rawding, F.W. *The Rebellion in India, 1857*. Cambridge University Press, 1977.

Rodgers, W.L. *Naval Warfare Under Oars: 4th to 16th Centuries*. Naval Institute, 1990.

Ross, Stewart. *Arab–Israeli Conflict*. Steck-Vaughn Company, 1996.

Sawyer, Peter (editor). *The Oxford Illustrated History of the Vikings*. Oxford University Press, Inc., 1997.

Schulzinger, Robert D. *A Time For War: The United States and Vietnam, 1941–1975*. Oxford University Press, Inc., 1997.

Sire, H.J.A. *The Knights of Malta*. Yale University Press, 1996.

Smith, Gene. *Until the Last Trumpet Sounds: The Life of General of the Armies John J. Pershing*. John Wiley & Sons, Inc., 1998.

Spiers, Edward M. *Sudan: The Reconquest Reconsidered*. Frank Cass Publishers, 1998.

Strickland, M.J. *Anglo-Norman Warfare*. The Boydell Press, 1992.

Trudeau, Noah. *Like Men of War: Black Troops in the Civil War, 1862–65*. Little, Brown and Company, 1998.

Verbruggen, J.F. *The Art of Warfare in Western Europe During the Middle Ages*. Boydell and Brewer, Inc., 1997.

Wawro, Geoffrey. *The Austro-Prussian War*. Cambridge University Press, 1997.

White, Colin. *The Nelson Companion*. Annapolis Naval Institute, 1997.

William, Noel St. John. *Redcoats Along the Hudson: The Struggle for North America, 1754–63*. Brassey's, Inc., 1997.

Young, John W. *Cold War Europe, 1945–1991: A Political History*. St. Martin's Press, Inc., 1996.

5/02